D0014430

SOLDIERS

SOLDIERS

A Global History of the Fighting Man, 1800–1945

JOHN A. HAYMOND

STACKPOLE
BOOKS

Guilford, Connecticut

Stackpole Books
An imprint of The Rowman & Littlefield Publishing Group, Inc.
4501 Forbes Blvd., Ste. 200
Lanham, MD 20706
www.rowman.com

Distributed by NATIONAL BOOK NETWORK

Copyright © 2019 by John A. Haymond

All rights reserved. No part of this book may be reproduced in any form or by any electronic or mechanical means, including information storage and retrieval systems, without written permission from the publisher, except by a reviewer who may quote passages in a review.

British Library Cataloguing in Publication Information available

Library of Congress Cataloging-in-Publication Data available

ISBN 978-0-8117-3795-1 (hardcover)
ISBN 978-0-8117-6794-1 (e-book)

∞™ The paper used in this publication meets the minimum requirements of American National Standard for Information Sciences—Permanence of Paper for Printed Library Materials, ANSI/NISO Z39.48-1992.

Printed in the United States of America

Contents

Preface vii
Chapter One: "Following the Drum" 1
Chapter Two: Drill and Training. 33
Chapter Three: Officers, NCOs, and "Other Ranks". 60
Chapter Four: Identity and Belonging 89
Chapter Five: Marching and Manual Labor 106
Chapter Six: Tools of the Trade 126
Chapter Seven: Bully Beef, Salt Horse, and Hardtack . . .155
Chapter Eight: Water, Rum, and Whiskey. 190
Chapter Nine: "Hell with the Lid Off" 203
Chapter Ten: Boredom, Fear, and Courage 231
Chapter Eleven: Misery and Mud 261
Chapter Twelve: The Fog of War 297
Chapter Thirteen: Enemies and Allies. 313
Chapter Fourteen: Discipline and Punishment. 356
Chapter Fifteen: Garrison Life. 376
Chapter Sixteen: After the Army 396

Acknowledgments 415
Notes. 417
Bibliography 442
Index 460

PREFACE

This book is not really about war, although war is the setting for much of what fills the pages ahead. This book is about soldiers—how they were recruited and trained, how they went from being civilians to soldiers, and how, if they lived long enough and survived the hazards of their profession, the day eventually came when they went back to being civilians again, forever altered by the years they spent in uniform. This is an examination of how they lived, worked, fought, and how many of them died. This book is about the ordinary soldier, the man standing in the ranks in the years between 1800 and 1945, and that span of 145 years is what is meant by "this period" in the pages ahead. By whatever name the common soldier was known to his generation, his comrades, and his enemies—whether they called him doughboy, dogface, Tommy, GI Joe, Ivan Ivanovitch, Abdul, Johnny Turk, leatherneck, *poilu, landser,* or grunt—he was the man at the sharp end of it all.

Books beyond numbering have been written about these men and their wars, many of them penned by soldiers themselves, so right here at the outset it is fair to ask, "What makes *this* book different from all those others?" A couple of very important details, as I trust will quickly become apparent in the pages ahead.

For one thing, this is an international history. It is not just about the American soldier or his British counterpart, though they figure most prominently in these pages. It is about them, yes, but it is also about their German, French, Russian, Canadian, Australian, Italian, Japanese, Chinese, Turkish, Polish, and Spanish opposite numbers. I have thrown the net wide to try and draw in as many voices as possible from the ranks of armies all over the world, enemies and allies alike. Second, this is a comparative study, exploring the idea that men who fought against each other often had such similar experiences despite the differences in their languages, uniforms, and allegiances that they sometimes had more in common with their enemies than they did with their own civilian countrymen back home.

I hesitate to use the term *universal* to describe the experiences of the soldiers whose accounts appear in this book, because that would probably be going one adjective too far. It *is* safe to say, however, there were common experiences that transcended national identities. Certain experiences and perspectives appear over and over in the personal stories of soldiers throughout this period, which is why each chapter that follows focuses on a particular aspect of army life. For instance, most soldiers in their personal accounts made no claim to being brave and courageous, although many of them wrote of having witnessed such behavior demonstrated by other men. On the other hand, almost every soldier admitted to feeling boredom, apprehension, and fear. Most soldiers' narratives (certainly the honest ones unhobbled by literary pretensions) contain descriptions of misery, exhaustion, frustration, anger, and sorrow. And it may surprise some readers, though probably not any who were ever soldiers themselves, that many of those recollections of army life also contain a wry humor and a genuine satisfaction at having once been a part of it all, no matter how grim or terrible it sometimes was.

In researching this book, I have deliberately concentrated on the narratives and perspectives of soldiers at the sharp end, as they described their lives in their own words. The voices here are those of privates, noncommissioned officers, and junior officers. This book ignores questions of strategy and issues relevant to the "art of war"; it also disregards the perspective of the upper command echelons. This is not a "big picture" account—this is a small picture point of view, the perspective of men who usually saw no more of their wars than what was to their immediate front and the men on their left and right. These were the men whom one Confederate soldier described as "the fellows who did the shooting and killing, the fortifying and ditching, the sweeping of the streets, the drilling, the standing guard, picket and videt, and who drew (or were to draw) eleven dollars per month and rations, and also drew the ramrod and tore the cartridge."[1] These men are the focus of this book.

The fact that the bulk of sources in this text are accounts written or dictated by soldiers themselves explains why this study only begins in

1800. Before that point in history, narratives from the common soldier were relatively rare. Part of that is because of high rates of illiteracy in those eras, but it is also because the rank-and-file view of soldiering was not what people of that day were usually interested in reading. This dearth of common soldier narratives was what another soldier of the American Civil War referred to when he wrote, "In studying the history of the Revolutionary War, I have often wished I could read the diary of a private soldier of that time, that I might form an impression of the life of the soldier in the ranks during that war."[2] These literary and social factors began to change around the time of the Napoleonic Wars.

This book closes at the end of the Second World War in 1945 for several reasons, not least of which is the fact that if we come much farther forward into the twentieth century, the bulk of material frankly gets to be overwhelming for an international study. But my main reason for ending this text before the Cold War era (with its decidedly hot conflicts of Korea, Malaya, Vietnam, etc.) is that maintaining a distance from the evidence of the past might allow it to better stand on its own—soldiers today have more in common with men in centuries gone by than they might suspect, and I hope that keeping this study firmly rooted in the past will make that commonality stand out all the clearer to modern readers.

In relying so heavily on soldiers' own narratives and personal memoirs, I have accepted a certain risk as a researcher. Many of these accounts—most of them, in fact—were written or recorded years or even decades after the events that the narrators described. Memory is a tricky thing and not always reliable, as we all know. Very few soldiers writing at the time of their experience knew the broader details of the war in which they were serving, and those men who wrote long afterward often did not have the overall context of the history of which their individual narratives were smaller pieces. It is not at all uncommon to find that some soldiers' recollections can be accurate in the personal details, but at the same time demonstrably at odds with the established history as soon as they start talking about things beyond what they themselves saw, heard, or did. I would suggest there is really no reason why we should expect anything else of them. Most of these men were not professional historians, after all, and few of them claimed to be authorities on the epic events in which they participated.

The value of these first-person narratives is that their accounts give us small but powerful insights into the past that professional, third-person history never can. It is just that we must be careful to set these individual vignettes into the supporting context of the history of which they were a part, in order to get the most accurate impression of the event. The eminent British historian John Fortescue, in his introduction to an essay he wrote about the memoirs of one nineteenth-century soldier, said, "Experience has taught me to be suspicious of such documents. The writer is almost invariably inspired by literary ambition, to which he sacrifices the homely veracity which we desire of him. . . . Quite half if not more of the book (it contains 1,200 pages) is inflated rubbish; another quarter is insufferably dull. But there is yet a remnant which gives us a glimpse of the natural man and of those about him."[3] That is an accurate summation of both the pitfall and the prize inherent in this sort of history.

The "glimpse of the natural man" that Fortescue mentions is precisely what I have tried to capture here. Ordinary soldiers often knew surprisingly little about where they were most of the time, or what was going on at the brigade or division level, or what part of the overall strategy their contribution represented. For the most part, they could not have cared less about those things. Even in their old age when the army was far behind them, what most veterans wanted to talk about was why they joined up in the first place, how they felt when they were under fire, how far they had to walk, all the times they were hungry or wet or tired or all three at the same time, who their friends were, and whether or not their sergeant was a draconian bastard or their lieutenant was an officious idiot. Those were the things they cared about, and those are the things I have focused on here.

This is a study of soldiers' lives in peace and war. Four conflicts in particular provide the bulk of the narratives here: the Napoleonic Wars, the American Civil War, and the two world wars. But there was no shortage of conflict and strife during the years between those major wars, and all of those disparate conflicts—whether they were large, small, famous, or all-but-forgotten—are the setting for the chapters ahead. The Consular War of 1800, the War of 1812, the Seminole War, the Sikh War, the Mexican-American War, the Crimean War, the Franco-Prussian War, the Indian Wars of the United States, the Boxer Rebellion, the Spanish-American War, the Philippine-American War, the Russo-Japanese War, the Sino-Japanese War, the Russian and Chinese Civil Wars—these conflicts and others provide the background for the soldiers' experiences that fill this book.

There is also a dark side to this history, as anyone familiar with military history already knows, and it should at least be acknowledged. The grim truth is that almost every army in the world, at some point in its existence, has been a force of unjust oppression or something even worse. During the period covered in this book, European armies carried colonial rule into Africa, Asia, and the Americas. The British were foremost among them as an imperial power, though they were certainly not the worst offenders—that distinction, I would argue, belongs to the Belgians in the Congo. The U.S. Army was the military arm of a nation that pushed indigenous peoples off their traditional lands and then went on to enforce American imperialism in the Philippines. The army of the Ottoman Turks perpetrated massacres in Greece and the Balkans in the nineteenth century and was an agent of genocide against the Armenians beginning in 1915; the German military exceeded them in genocide on an even more appalling scale after 1939. In 1945 the Soviet Army perpetrated mass rape across Eastern Europe and Germany on a scale unequaled in modern conflict. In terms of sheer scale of savage brutality, the Japanese Army's conduct in China in the 1930s is almost without equal in modern warfare. At first glance, armies might appear to be monolithic masses, but they are made up of individual men, and as individuals some of those men are good and some are bad; some are ethical, and some are criminal. Some of the men who made this history never did a thing to stain their souls, but others of them committed some of the most horrible acts of massacre, rape, and savage inhumanity in all the bloody history of the world, and sometimes they did not even bother trying to excuse their conduct by saying that they were ordered to do such things. My focus in this book is not on those grim vignettes of history, but I think it is necessary to at least recognize that those things happened, even if we do not delve into them too deeply here.

On a different point, a preemptive apology might be in order. As a former soldier myself, I know very well that armies are comprised of so much more than just the combat arms of the infantry, cavalry, artillery, and sappers. There is a reason why the support services—those concerned with "beans and bullets," to use an American expression—make up the majority of a modern army's end-strength. The combat arms carry battle to the enemy and do the actual fighting, and it is still the individual infantryman with a rifle who holds the ground on which he stands. But unless those soldiers in the combat units are transported, supplied and resupplied, evacuated and treated when wounded, and supported with communications, intelligence, and maintenance services, they will not and *cannot* fight for long. In fact, it could be argued that an army that lacks support assets in sufficient quantity is well on its way to being beaten before the first shot is ever fired.

In my own career as an infantry NCO, during which I served in airborne and light infantry regiments, I recognized early on that while my fellow infantrymen and I were very good at breaking things, we frankly didn't know the first damn thing about *fixing* anything. The support services of transport, communications, food, maintenance, medical aid, and all the other necessities of military life are an absolutely crucial part of every army. The personnel of the support services are soldiers every bit as much as are their counterparts in the combat arms. Just as an alligator is more tail than teeth, so is an army. But as vital as those soldiers are in the military scheme of operations, this book is not about them.

This book is about the other part of the army, that part where the job is not to supply, but to fight, and to often go without adequate food or water while doing it; where the job is not to heal, but to kill and maim and wreak unholy havoc on other people; where the mission is sometimes to build, but more frequently to destroy. It is that part of the army, after all, where the men in the ranks are often called upon to hazard their very lives and sometimes die, in greater numbers than is ever expected of their comrades in the support services. This book is about the men at the toothy end of the army's alligator, the men in the combat arms: the infantry footsoldier, the artillery gunner, the cavalry trooper, and the engineer sapper.

Finally, one last mea culpa. I realize that the term *soldier* is properly reserved for army personnel, and that the marines of the world are altogether separate military entities who take a justifiable pride in their distinct identities. The personal experiences of marines in this period, whether they were the men of the U.S. Marine Corps, the British Royal Marines, or the Japanese Imperial Marines, and so on, are an important part of this history, and so their narratives appear in these pages along with those of their army counterparts. To simplify the text, I use the words *soldiers* and *army* to describe all these men collectively, even those remarkable sailors of the British Royal Naval Division who fought as infantrymen at Gallipoli and Arras, and the German *Fallschirmjaegers* who were actually members of the Luftwaffe rather than the Wehrmacht. I mean no disrespect by referring to them all as "soldiers," and I hope that all their collective shades (and their modern descendants) will forgive my presumption.

I am a historian now, but I was a soldier for more than twenty years, and I am more than a little biased on behalf of the rank-and-file soldier no matter where we encounter him. I hope, in the pages that follow, you will see something of the ordinary soldier as he was, with all his flaws, faults, and failings clearly displayed along with his often-remarkable strength and resilience and his coarse but somehow endearing good humor. Soldiers are always poor candidates for sainthood, and the intention here is not to canonize them or sanitize their reputations. The soldiers whose experiences fill this book were ordinary men who quite often endured incredible hardships and faced terrible dangers, and most of them did it very well, and they often received very little thanks for it. That alone, I would suggest, is worth a measure of enduring respect.

Rudyard Kipling was never a soldier himself, though you would not know it to read his realistic depictions of the British soldier. Kipling was unabashedly pro-soldier in his outlook, and he championed the common soldier in a way that few writers of his era did. If you want an unvarnished description of the British Army of the Victorian period, Kipling's poetry and stories say it as well as anyone ever has: "The red-coats, the pipe-clayed belts and the pill-box hats, the beer, the fights, the floggings, hangings and crucifixions, the bugle-calls, the smell of oats and horse-piss, the bellowing sergeants with foot-long moustaches, the bloody skirmishes, invariably mishandled, the crowded troop-ships, the cholera-stricken camps, the 'native' concubines, the ultimate death in the work-house."[4] There were more than just these factors to the army, of course, but there was still considerable truth in Kipling's scathing depiction of the common soldier's life.

So then, what was life like in armies around the world in the years between 1800 and 1945? If it was as bad as all that, why did men ever choose to enlist when the choice was theirs to make? Why did many of them choose to remain soldiers, if the life was so hard and the treatment so bad and the living conditions so wretched? In part, it was because life in most armies was more than just hardship and sorrow, and many of those men genuinely wanted to be soldiers. Beyond that, the answers to those questions are as varied as the men themselves, and that is what this book is about.

CHAPTER ONE

"Following the Drum"

Enlistment

Oh why did I join the Infantree when I joined the bloody army?
Because, because, because, because, BECAUSE I was bloody well barmy.
—BRITISH MARCHING SONG OF THE FIRST WORLD WAR

WHY DID ANY MAN, OF HIS OWN VOLITION, join the army? After all, the army during this period never seemed to have had quite the same sort of romantic allure that the seafaring life of the navy offered, at least not for American or British men. By the beginning of the nineteenth century, conventional armies no longer practiced the moneymaking customs of freebooting and holding prisoners for ransom, so even though prize money was still shared out in some European armies, very few men went off to join the army with any serious hope of making their fortunes in a monetary sense.

Nonetheless, there were always men who were willing, if not exactly eager, to leave it all behind and join the army. "Joining up," "following the drum," "joining the colors," "taking the sovereign's shilling"—by whatever term it was known, there were always new recruits for the army's ranks. The reasons for enlistment were as varied as the soldiers themselves, but there were common themes that transcended eras and nationalities.

For much of the nineteenth century, two reasons predominated the motivations of men who enlisted in the U.S. Army: economic necessity and the siren song of adventure. At the same time, a persistent barrier to their decision to enlist was the fact that the American public for much of this period regarded its own army either as a threat to liberty and a drain on the treasury or as the last refuge of scoundrels and miscreants. As one historian observed in 1908, "In time of peace the American people will never tolerate the maintenance of a large standing army; its presence being considered, justly or unjustly, a menace to republican institutions."[1] Forty years earlier, a sergeant serving in the 18th U.S. Infantry on the western frontier wrote to his mother back in Ireland to say, "A soldier here is put down as a loafer, you may [think] a soldier bad at home but here he is thought less than a dog if I may say it."[2] He was not exaggerating about the low opinion that many civilians had of soldiers. Around the same year, a correspondent to a New York newspaper declared, "The Regular Army is composed of bummers, loafers and foreign paupers."[3] It was a view shared by far too many citizens in the decades both before and after (but not during) the American Civil War.

British men contemplating the army faced much the same sort of anti-army prejudice from their civilian population, at least in the early years of this period. There are two pieces of contemporary art that illustrate very well the British perspective of military recruiting at different points in the nineteenth century. The first, titled *Listed for the Connaught Rangers*, is a rural scene painted by Lady Elizabeth Butler. It shows a recruiting party of a sergeant and drummer boys, along with two new recruits, walking along a rather lonely-looking country road in Ireland. One of the newly enlisted men looks back over his shoulder, as if trying to catch a last glimpse of a home he may never see again, but the other man walks along with his head up and his eyes on the horizon; whatever lies behind him, the painting suggests, he is leaving in the past.

The other piece is an 1882 illustration from the *Illustrated London News*. It is an urban scene, and in it there is just a single recruiting sergeant without the drummers, but now the group of new recruits is larger. A quick study of the picture tells you almost everything you need to know about the different men who have made the decision to join the army, in particular their markedly different personal situations. Several of the men are obviously working-class types, most wearing workmen's clothes and one in a laborer's smock. Two of their new companions, however, are clearly of slightly higher social status. One of these chaps strolls along smoking his pipe, his hat tipped back and his walking stick on his shoulder, looking for all the world as if he hasn't a care in the world. The other well-dressed fellow, however, has his hands jammed in his pockets as he trudges along with his eyes on the ground—whatever compelled him to enlist, one senses that it was not a choice he really wanted to make. The first well-to-do man looks as if he has nothing to lose by joining the army; the other one looks as if he is joining because he has lost everything.

There is one other detail that makes this picture interesting. On the right side of the scene are a woman and her young son. The boy is turned half around, staring with obvious interest at the tall figure of the recruiting sergeant with his gleaming boots and his befrogged uniform jacket. His mother is looking at the recruiter also, but with an expression that indicates horror rather than admiration as she pulls her little boy down the street.

These are representative images of army enlistment in Britain for much of this period, certainly at least until the late 1800s. For them as well as their American counterparts, regular surges of patriotic adventurism in times of war that caught the British national interest swelled the ranks of the army, which were almost always quickly reduced to skeleton strength as soon as peace broke out again. It was not the same in the armies of the various German states, or Russia, or France, where mandatory conscription continued to pull men into the army during times of peace as well as war, whether or not they had any desire to be soldiers. For men of those countries and others like them, individual choice perhaps played a smaller part in the matter.

The culture of the society in question was always part of the dynamic at work in an individual's decision to enlist in his country's army. For instance, part of the problem in creating a professional Chinese army during these years was the long-standing and deeply entrenched cultural bias that held that a soldier was, by definition, a man deficient in just about every desirable trait. "It is better to have no son than one who is a soldier" was a common maxim in nineteenth-century China. It was not until after World War II that Chinese cultural attitudes toward soldiering finally shifted away from the old proverb that for centuries had declared, "One does not use good iron to make nails, and good men do not become soldiers."

An entirely different cultural perception existed in Japan at the same time. Japanese society viewed military service as an essential aspect of duty and fidelity to one's overlord and, ultimately, to the semideific person of the emperor. Like the Chinese, the Japanese of the Meiji Restoration had a proverb to express their culture's prevailing view of the soldier, but it was one that conveyed a markedly different opinion on the subject. "Among flowers, the best is the cherry blossom," the Japanese said; "among men, the best is the soldier."

In the United States and Great Britain, more than a few men during this period enlisted out of simple desperation. For them the soldier's pittance was the best of a lot of bad options, and sometimes it was the *only* option apart from crime or starvation. This is a familiar theme in the history of the both the British and American armies, all the way from the beginning of this period to its end. One Danish immigrant who arrived in the United States in 1873 was typical of many men of that era. He enlisted in the army, he later said, because "it was either the soup house, starve, or the recruiting depot."[4] Sixty-seven years later, very similar circumstances impelled a young New Yorker named William Wills into the ranks. "I joined the Army in 1940," he recalled decades later. "I volunteered. What made me decide? Well, it was during the Depression and there were no jobs. I was 21 and for three years I'd been bouncing around, doing temporary work and it was a good way to get a job so I joined the Army."[5]

Henry Windolph left Germany in 1870 to avoid being conscripted into the Prussian Army, so it was more than a little ironic that he wound up in the U.S. Army shortly after arriving in America. "A good many German boys like myself had run away from the compulsory military service and the Franco-Prussian War," he said, "but about the only job there was for us over here was to enlist in the United States Army. Always struck me as being funny; here we'd run away from Germany to escape military service, and now, because most of us couldn't get a job anywhere else, we were forced to go into the army here." Windolph enlisted for the 7th U.S. Cavalry; twenty years later he retired from the army as a first sergeant.

Another veteran of the 7th Cavalry was William Slaper, who enlisted from his home state of Ohio. Slaper's experience was a fairly common one for men who found their way into the U.S. Army in the years after the American Civil War. "Early in September 1875," he wrote, "I found myself out of a job, and while walking along the street, wondering what I had better try next in the work line, I observed the sign, 'Men Wanted,' in front of the United States Army Recruiting Station. Although I had passed that sign numberless times before, it never held any attraction for me until that morning." Slaper had no prospects for employment and no reason to think that any might materialize, and that paucity of opportunities led him to consider a choice he might not otherwise have. "I stopped and read it. Then I wondered if they would take me as a soldier. Half-heartedly I went upstairs to the office, almost hoping I would be rejected."

He was not rejected. "There and then," he recalled, "I took an oath to serve Uncle Sam to the best of my ability, for the regal sum of $13 a month." Less than a year later, in his first combat action as a trooper in M Troop of the 7th Cavalry, Slaper fought at the Battle of the Little Bighorn, where Lt. Col. Custer and 267 men were killed in the worst defeat the U.S. Army ever endured at Indian hands.[6]

Simple desperation appears as a motivation in the narratives of many British soldiers, as well. Samuel Hutton was orphaned at a young age in England in the early 1800s and found that when he reached his maturity, all doors but one were closed to him. "My being willing to work, and unable to get employment," he said, "was not taken into consideration. I was frequently in absolute want of food. . . . There was but one asylum before me—the army." Even then his troubles were not over; he was so malnourished and underweight that he was unable to pass even the rudimentary enlistment examination of that era. "I offered myself to a recruiting sergeant," Hutton said; "I was too short. To another—I was below the standard." Eventually he found a captain in the 12th Regiment of Foot who was willing to take a gamble on him. "He ventured to take me in the hope that I might grow," Hutton remembered, and so at last he was in the army, where at least he would not starve.[7]

For men of military age who possessed no trade skills, the army was sometimes their only option. One anonymous Englishman who used the pseudonym "Kent Soldier" when he wrote his memoirs in the late nineteenth century said, "The reasons that led me to take this step were briefly, inability to obtain employment. . . . At an early age I found myself face to face with life & in no way ready to grapple with its problems." The army was often seen as the last resort of desperate men, and by his own admission Kent Soldier fit that description. Another contributing factor in his case, as he remembered it, was that he was "very young & with little capacity for judgment or discrimination." Years after leaving the army, he was adamant that the combination of economic necessity and personal immaturity were what had driven him to enlist.[8]

Until at least the latter half of the 1800s, as one historian notes, "the army was, in a real sense, the only welfare service provided by the British state."[9] Even when the army was the only option left to a man, however, it was still not necessarily a good option. At least, that was how many people in polite society saw it. Even after Waterloo, when the British public had good reason to be grateful for its army, the individual soldier's lot was still hardly better than miserable. The great lexicographer and famous wit Samuel Johnson once cynically quipped that no man would enlist in the army who could get himself into prison instead: "A man in a jail has more room, better food, and commonly better company."[10] Well on into the nineteenth century, his remark still held true on at least the first two points.

Refuting the third point, British Army regulations as early as 1812 admonished recruiters that "no suspicious characters, nor those who cannot give a proper account of themselves, are to be enlisted," but the reality in almost every army was often very different.[11] Characters who were more than a little suspicious, and who were often downright unsavory, were sometimes enlisted with not even a token nod to the official line. When an army's need for men overrode the regulatory standards, the guidelines were often observed in the breach. Here again similar situations prevailed in the U.S. Army during those years—official regulations always spelled out the standards of enlistment, but those guidelines were frequently ignored if the recruiting officers were so inclined.

Even when the army desperately needed men, so that the individual soldier was at least *notionally* a valued commodity, the common soldier's lot was not a particularly attractive one. Well into the 1840s, living conditions for British soldiers were simply wretched. The food was substandard in both quality and quantity; the barracks were overcrowded, unhygienic, and unhealthy. The army had an abysmal reputation in polite society as being a refuge for scoundrels, drunkards, gamblers, and syphilitic degenerates. It was no wonder, then, that in Britain for much of the nineteenth century, "the right sort of young men had no desire to join the Army."[12] To some degree the same negative social perceptions were at work in the United States during that era. As William Slaper remembered, "At that time, any young man wearing the uniform of a United States soldier was looked upon as an idler—too lazy to work. Being in my own town, and well known, I felt somewhat ashamed of being seen in my uniform."[13]

Throughout much of the nineteenth century, a common soldier's life was hard, discipline was excessively harsh, and the pay was often little better than a pauper's pittance, but at least there was pay of some kind. In an era when abject poverty was a common plight and regular wages could be hard to come by, army pay offered a steadier income than many men could find in the civilian world. "Soldiers," it has been noted, "and by extension their wives, were induced to tolerate the squalor of the barrack-room and the discomforts of the campaign by the prospect of steady pay." Even the very word *soldier* has its antecedents in the concept of pay: the English word comes from the French *soude,* or "pay," and the Latin *soldati,* which means "paid men."[14]

This economic incentive was not unique to Western armies. All professional armies were distinguished by the fact that their soldiers served for pay of some sort, and this was true of the Chinese and Japanese armies of the period just as it was true of those in Europe or the United States. This did not automatically mean, however, that a paid soldier was therefore a well-trained or effective soldier.

Provincial warlords dominated China during the final decades of the Qing Dynasty, through the latter half of the nineteenth century and into the early years of the twentieth, and service in the local warlord's army was often the only paying work a poor man could find. The Chinese soldier, as historian Jock Haswell puts it, most often "became a soldier in name since he had been hired to fight, but he remained largely ignorant of soldiering."[15] This lack of professional training marred the performance of Chinese armies for generations, from the Opium Wars through the

Boxer Rebellion. Even the imperial Manchu bannermen, the notionally professional soldiers of the late Qing Dynasty, were long on hereditary privilege and short on martial skill. One European observer noted in the late 1800s that "their pay is given them because of their fathers' prowess, and not at all from any hopes of their efficiency as soldiers," a fact that was demonstrated with disastrous consequences whenever they came up against European armies.

For men who had nothing, even the miserly dole of a soldier's pay was better than the hand-to-mouth living that was their existence outside the army. It was even enough, on occasion, to bring a man *back* to the army after he had left it. Englishman John Shipp earned an ensign's commission while serving in India in the first decade of the 1800s, but found himself wracked with mounting debts when he returned to England. To pay off his creditors he was forced to sell off his commission and leave the army. Within six months of resuming civilian life, he wrote, "I found myself without a shilling, without a home, and without a friend. Thus circumstanced, my fondness of the profession induced me to turn my thoughts to the army again."[16] Against all probability, he worked his way up through the ranks a second time and won another commission for gallantry in the field, perhaps the only man in the history of the British Army to have climbed that ladder twice.

Money, then, played an obvious role in many men's motivation to enlist, but it was never much money. I have referred to the soldier's wage of the nineteenth century as a "pittance," and it was never much better than that, at least not until the First World War. In the British Army for most of the years between Waterloo and the Crimean War, a private's pay was set at a mere seven shillings a week. Even this was a notional amount, though, for as one historian notes, "all except 2 ¾ d (1p) a day was taken from him in charges for messing, laundry and maintenance."[17] William Holbrook joined the Royal Fusiliers in 1909 as an underage recruit, which entitled him only to partial pay until he was of full age. "I only got a shilling a week, boy's pay," he remembered.[18]

By 1914 the financial situation for the rank and file of the British Army had changed for the better, not least of all because the army finally reduced the drain caused by semiofficial stoppages for everything from food to equipment to laundry. Charles Carrington, who enlisted in the British Army as soon as he could after the start of the First World War, remembered with satisfaction that he had finally managed to become "a soldier, drawing pay at the rate of one shilling, with subsistence allowance at the rate of two and ninepence per day." To the modern reader that might not seem like much, but in context of the times, it was not at all bad. "Twenty-seven and sixpence a week," Carrington wrote, "was a good wage for a working man in those days."[19]

The U.S. Army, by comparison, paid its men marginally better than other countries paid their soldiers through this period, but a man was no more going to get rich wearing American blue than he would wearing British red. "One important feature in the life of a soldier was the matter of his pay," Leander Stillwell wrote in his memoir of his Civil War service. "When I enlisted in January 1862, the monthly pay of the enlisted men of a regiment of infantry was as follows: First sergeant, $20; duty sergeants, $17; corporals and privates, $13. By act of Congress of May 1st, 1864, the monthly pay of the enlisted men was increased, and from that date was as follows: First sergeant, $24; duty sergeants, $20; corporals, $18; privates, $16."[20] Most soldiers were all too aware of how low their pay actually was, when one stopped to think about what was required of them to earn it. Another Union Army infantryman, James Dargan, copied a short poem in his diary that expressed the enlisted man's perspective quite clearly:

Thirteen dollars a month to be shot at
Is all the poor fellows' pay
Whilst those that send them out to fight
Have eighteen dollars a day.[21]

Soldiers in the Confederate Army were paid at about the same rate, at least in theory. The economic reality was that as the war went badly for the South, Confederate currency became increasingly worthless and most of the men in grey soldiered on for almost no meaningful monetary recompense at all.

In the U.S. Army during the era of the Indian Wars, a private soldier's pay continued to hover at around $13 a month, hardly ever rising above the Civil War rate of pay. (In fact, the parsimonious U.S. Congress at one point in that era actually reduced soldiers' already pitifully low wage.) Beyond the problems of low pay, American soldiers in those years also had to contend with the fact that paydays came around rather infrequently. Service in the remote outposts of the American frontier meant that troops often went months without a visit from the army paymaster. This was such a common occurrence that soldiers had a rhyming witticism about it: "They say some disaster / Befell the paymaster." To make matters even worse for the rank and file, the Federal government occasionally seemed to regard military funding as an inconvenient afterthought. "Once, in 1878," as one historian notes, "Congress nonchalantly failed to appropriate and let the Army go an entire year without pay."[22]

It is an old literary trope that men who sought a place in the French Foreign Legion were often driven to enlist in its ranks by sheer desperation, whether that desperation was of the economical, criminal, or lovestruck sort. Those who were so destitute that they enlisted to escape starvation would indeed be fed in the Legion, but there was not much more recompense than that—they were some of the lowest paid soldiers in any nineteenth-century European army. Legionnaires of that era drew five centimes a day in pay—the pathetic sum of only one and a half francs a month. On the other side of the world, as late as the Second World War, a private in the Japanese Imperial Army received little more than the equivalent of two dollars a month.

Monetary bonuses were sometimes offered for enlisting, which enticed more than one young man to try a soldier's life. The United States offered enlistment bonuses, or bounties, throughout much of the Civil War, and thereby created an illicit industry for men who would enlist, receive their bonus, and then desert at the first opportunity so as to enlist again into another regiment for another bonus. In the British Army during the Napoleonic Wars, this same practice was called "pear making." Enlistment bonuses were sometimes also offered during times of peace, though in smaller sums. When Edwin Rundle enlisted with the British 17th Regiment of Foot in 1857, he received a cash bonus, though he apparently went through it quickly—Rundle recorded that he spent most of it at the regimental canteen, buying extra food to offset the limited rations that were served in the mess.

———

The contract of service when a man enlisted (and a contract it most certainly was), differed greatly depending on the era, the army, and whether or not there was a war on at the time. Men who enlisted in the state volunteer regiments of the U.S. Army at the outset of the American Civil War were initially enrolled for only three months, as noted earlier, and that was a case of an overoptimistic expectation of a war's duration if ever one was. Men who enlisted in the U.S. Army during the Indian Wars, 1866–1890, signed on for five years. When Needham N. Freeman joined the army a year before the Spanish-American War, he was enlisted "for a service of three years, unless discharged before the expiration of that time." Soldiers in the U.S. Army during both world wars were most commonly enlisted (whether they volunteered or were drafted) for the duration of the conflict, as were their British counterparts in the same eras.

At the beginning of the period, enlistment in the British Army was essentially for life, or at least until one was no longer able to soldier on because of age, injury, or infirmity. Henry Franks, a cavalryman who fought with the British Army in the Crimean War as a troop sergeant major in the Heavy Brigade, enlisted in 1845 for "unlimited service," a term that meant "that a man had to serve as long as he was able to do any duty at all, and every man, previous to his discharge, had to pass a Board of Medical Officers, who certified that he was unfit for further service."

A few years later the British Army changed the lengths of service to twenty-four years for cavalry enlistments and twenty-one for the infantry and artillery. In the context of the times, however, "this was part of its appeal; it meant at the very least twenty-one years of regular food and shelter." Sometime later the lengths of enlistment were reduced even further. Edwin Rundle, who spent a long career in the British Army (and who was somewhat remarkable for apparently never hearing a shot fired in anger even though he served more than twenty years in the Victorian-era army), recalled that the question put to him at the point of enlistment was "Are you free, willing, able to serve . . . for ten years, not exceeding twelve, if Her Majesty so long requires your services?"

For men of other countries who entered the military because they were forced into the ranks by conscription, rather than by choice, the lengths of service differed widely from army to army, as we will soon see.

Despite the profusion of anecdotes describing desperation as a strong motivation for enlistment, it would be wrong to assume that the grim specter of starvation was the only thing that led men into the ranks. The prospect of steady pay, attractive though it was, was not always the primary drawing factor. A desire for a life more adventurous than that of a farm laborer or millworker motivated many a young man to try a soldier's life, just as that siren song has always attracted men to the army. This was especially true if the army in question already had a well-established reputation for great victories and grand adventures, as was the case with the international Grande Armee that Napoleon gathered for his invasion of Russia in 1812. One young Frenchman who set out on that doomed expedition later recalled his reasons for rallying to the imperial eagles. "I would have my chance to distinguish myself," he wrote. "There I would be able to obtain decorations and promotion of which I would be proud and which I could hold up to the world!"[23] In the event, he was lucky to get through it alive—most of the men who marched into Russia with that army died there.

Other men left respectable, if somewhat lackluster, civilian employment not because they needed work, but because they did not like the work they already had. Needham N. Freeman enlisted in the U.S. Army in 1898. He had found farmwork to be "too commonplace and not fulfilling desire nor expectations," and he went on to a succession of other respectable but thoroughly uninspiring jobs: first working for the Santa Fe Railroad, then at a Dallas cotton mill, and finally as a motorman with a streetcar company. None of those satisfied his urge for something more exciting. "One night," he wrote later, "while with several friends, the subject of enlisting in the army was discussed; this strongly appealed to me, and studying the matter further, I became enthused over the idea." The money was not what attracted him—he was making forty-five dollars a month with the streetcar company, and the army paid only one-third that amount. Freeman didn't care: "This made little difference to me," he said. "I was anxious to be a soldier and live the life of one." He enlisted in the 14th Infantry Regiment and wound up fighting in the Philippine-American War.[24]

John Douglas, who left a memoir of his service in Wellington's army during the Peninsular War, was another man who had a good job but wanted a more exciting one. "I being apprenticed to a trade against my inclination," Douglas wrote, "served five years faithfully, with credit to myself and gain to my master, at the expiration of which my friends came forward most handsomely with their purses, to set me up in business on my own account." A steady career as a tradesman was his for the taking, but Douglas had other ideas. He left it all and set off for Belfast, where, as he recounted, "the first Regiment that offered, I took the shilling to serve his Majesty in the 1st or Royal Scots."[25]

Edwin Mole was a journeyman builder in England in 1862 when he joined the army. He had long considered the military, and in fact had run away from home to join the Royal Navy when he was younger, but was sent home to his parents when it was discovered that he had lied about being an orphan. A couple of years later, he was working in Charing Cross, a locale frequented by numerous recruiting sergeants of various regiments. One fateful day in June 1863, he had an argument with his employer, walked off the job, and bumped into a recruiting sergeant with whom he had previously struck up an acquaintance. That led to a pub, and then to the sergeant's quarters, where the talk inevitably turned to enlistment.

Despite his admitted interest in the army, Mole was reluctant to take that last irrevocable step. He was making decent money in his job, he told the recruiter, and would feel better if he could enlist with a friend. "Why, lad, you've only to 'list, and once your chum claps eyes on you in the Hussar uniform there's nothing'll stop him from coming after you," the sergeant said. "As for your earning good money, see the mucking work you have to do for it. And you'll never want money in the 14th Hussars." There were other side benefits as well, the recruiter promised: "You'll get your fun and plenty to drink free gratis; for the girls will fight for you and you'll always find a Christian ready to stand treat. The Fourteenth get the pick of the girls wherever they go."

Mole still hesitated. Another recruiting sergeant, whom he knew a bit better than the recruiter from the 14th Hussars, happened along, and Mole put the question to him. "Tell me, Sergeant; do you really like the service?" he asked. The sergeant replied, "I have only one wish, and that is that I had entered it four years sooner; and a man can't say more than that, can he?" "I took his reply at the moment as being the highest compliment he could pay to the charms of a soldier's life," Mole remembered, "and was satisfied accordingly." Writing his memoirs decades later, however, a different meaning in the recruiter's reply suggested itself to him. "But, as Sergeant Hudson had seventeen years' service, and four more would have completed his time," he mused, "there were two ways of interpreting his reply." At the age of seventeen, however, that possible ambiguity in the sergeant's answer did not occur to Mole, and after a night's drinking with the two recruiters, he woke up in the morning to find that he had taken the Queen's shilling and enlisted. Twenty-five years later he retired from the army as a troop sergeant major, after a career as a cavalryman in the 14th Hussars and having seen active service in India and South Africa.

Erwin Rosen left Germany and moved to Texas in the 1890s, but even a stint as a newspaper correspondent during the Spanish-American War was not enough to fill his appetite for adventure. In 1905, he took ship to France and enlisted in the Foreign Legion. After passing the very cursory physical examination, he was presented with the enlistment papers. "It was a formal contract for five years' service in the Foreign Legion between the Republic of France and the man who was foolish enough to sign it," Rosen wrote. "There were a great many paragraphs and great stress was laid on the fact that the 'enlisting party' had no right upon indemnification in case of sickness or disability, and no claim upon pension until after fifteen years of service."[26] Rosen was unconcerned with what lay fifteen years in the future—his only concern was for the immediate present, and he signed up.

The life of a soldier always offered certain attractions to footloose young men. Or, it might be more accurate to say, the soldier's life as it was portrayed by recruiting sergeants appealed to many of them, but that was a version that did not always turn out to be true to life. George Farquhar's fictional army recruiter, the eloquent Sergeant Kite, posted notices that read: "If any gentleman soldiers, or others, have a mind to serve Her Majesty and pull down the French king; if any prentices have severe masters, any children have unnatural parents; if any servants have too little wages, or any husband too much wife; let them repair to the noble Sergeant Kite."[27] As Sergeant Kite presented it, joining the army was as much about escaping the odious burden of one's domestic responsibilities as it was about serving king and country.

John Shipp remembered that when he was a young boy, he heard a British recruiting sergeant give an inspiring pitch: "It was all about 'gentlemen soldiers,' 'merry life,' 'muskets rattling,' 'colours flying,' 'regiments charging,' and shouts of 'Victory! Victory!'"[28] The sergeant's idealized picture of army life stayed with Shipp, and he enlisted as soon as he was of age.

Another Englishman who heard a similar siren call was Timothy Gowing, who joined the British Army in 1854. "I was now fast approaching my twentieth year—a dangerous age to many unsettled in mind," he wrote in his memoir; "and the thrilling accounts that were constantly coming home from the East, worked me up to try my luck as others had done before me." Gowing enlisted in the Royal Fusiliers, a regiment he chose precisely because he was entranced by its history of "noble deeds of valour." It was a choice that over the next twenty years would take him to battlefields in the Crimean War, the Indian Mutiny, and Afghanistan.[29]

Patriotic fervor is often cynically discounted by many sources, not least of all by soldiers themselves (who as a group seem to be inclined to sentimentality or cynicism, often in equal parts), but it has always played an undeniable part in inducing some men to enlist, particularly in times of war. The American Civil War saw a surge of voluntary enlistments in both the Union and Confederate Armies, especially in the first year of the war. Leander Stillwell enlisted in the Union Army at the onset of the conflict, and his reasons were simple enough: "When they began organizing a regiment in our vicinity, and which would contain a fair proportion of my neighbor boys and acquaintances," he recalled, "I intended then to volunteer. It was simply intolerable to think that I could stay at home, among the girls, and be pointed at by the soldier boys as a stay-at-home coward."[30] Eighty years later the same sentiment was pushing young American men into the ranks during the Second World War. "I volunteered for the Army," George Tompkins said of his enlistment in 1942, "because everybody my age did not really want to be seen on the streets of Lynchburg if they were physically able to be in the service."[31]

This was the same sort of thinking that motivated a young Minnesotan named John Bowe as the Spanish-American War loomed in 1898. "Hearing that we might possibly have a war with Spain," he wrote, "I went down to the Armory. . . . Got acquainted with Captain Diggles, of Company B, who declared that war was certain, and inquired why I did not enlist. Told him I would have no objection, provided the regiment went into active service, but would not care to enlist for garrison duty."[32] Bowe did enlist and got his wish for active service when he was sent to the Philippines, but he found that the regimentation of army life did not suit him at all.

E. P. F. Lynch, an Australian soldier who fought in France during the First World War, wrote in his journal of a conversation in which he and his messmates discussed their individual reasons for enlisting. "The argument turns to why we enlisted," he wrote. "We hear the old one about enlisting whilst drunk, but know that is all lies and rot, just so much camouflage to hide the real reason." What was the real reason? "Darky tells us he enlisted because he was impelled by love of country and pride and race to do so, and gets called a hero and is shouted down. Longun says, 'I enlisted because I was a bloomin' coward and too flamin' frightened to face the things they were saying about the coves who didn't enlist.' And he too is disbelieved." For Lynch, the truth lay somewhere between the two: "Many of us realize," he concluded, "that our own enlistments were brought about by a blending of the reasons given by Dark and Longun."[33]

Some sources from this period reveal other reasons for enlistment that are completely lacking in ambiguity or venal motivations. Some men enlisted for reasons that could actually be called "noble" without the slightest bit of cynicism. Samuel Cabble was a former slave who joined one of the newly formed black regiments of the Union Army during the

Civil War; his letter is quoted here with its original spelling and style intact. "Dear wife i have enlisted in the army," he wrote to his wife, who was still held as a slave in a southern state. "i look forward to a brighter day when i shall have the opertunity of seeing you in the full enjoyment of freedom. . . . i am a soldier endeavry to strike at the rebellion that so long has kept us in chains."[34] Cabble survived the war and was eventually reunited with his wife, both of them free at last. His service as a soldier was clearly motivated by a higher purpose than either adventure or fiduciary gain.

Beyond those reasons, the simple concept of duty compelled many men to enlist who would otherwise have avoided military service. Samuel Wing, who served in the Union Army during the Civil War, admitted in his memoirs, "I was not there because I thought myself brave, nor because I liked excitement. In fact I should have made a good Quaker." What spurred him to join the army, he said, was a sense of duty, plain and simple. "The rebellion must be put down . . . and then, if it must be put down, whose duty is it to go and help? Was it not every good citizen's and patriot? Then, why not mine? Was there any reason for me to be excused?" With that line of reasoning, he enlisted in 1861.[35]

The perception of war as an exciting adventure, at least to young men who had not yet had any experience of it, is such a recurring theme in the personal narratives of soldiers' enlistment decisions that it comes close to being a cliché. J. W. Vaughan, who served in the First World War with the Princess Patricia's Canadian Light Infantry, joined up with a friend. "We were young and we had the same idea that everybody did," he later wrote. "'Oh, the war will be over in about three months, so we'll get a nice trip home out of it and we'll soon be back'. Well, how wrong can you be?"[36] In the same war, on the other side of the world, an Australian soldier said, "They wanted Australia to send men—and I was one of the mugs. . . . We said it wouldn't last a week, or two at the most. What fun it would be. That's what we thought, actually. We were proved to be a lot of suckers."[37]

In time of war, men who were so young as to barely be men at all often rushed to enlist because they feared they would miss out on the adventure of it all if they waited to come of age. Edgar Platts, who enlisted in the

Royal Naval Division to fight in the First World War, lied about his age in order to join the Royal Naval Volunteer Reserve. He was fifteen years old when he enlisted; he was just seventeen years old and a lieutenant in the Royal Marines when he was killed at Gavrelle on April 28, 1917—he may have been the youngest British officer to die in the war.[38]

Cecil Withers also lied about his age to join the British Army in the First World War; he survived the war and died in 2005, just a few weeks shy of his 107th birthday. Withers ran away from home so that he could enlist in the East Surreys Regiment. "I was under age so I had to lie to the recruiting sergeant," he said, decades after the war. "I said I was eighteen years old and my name was Sydney Harrison. If I hadn't, my father would have got them to send me back home and that would have been humiliating." In time, though, Withers began to think that there might be some things worse than humiliation. He wanted to stay in the army, but he decided to do so under his real name. "I told the truth later, though. . . . If I'd been killed as Harrison, nobody would ever have known what had happened to me," he remembered. His conscience-clearing confession came at a slight price to his dignity. The first day after he told the army his real name, his sergeant called him out of formation in front of the entire company. "Harrison yesterday, Withers today," the sergeant shouted at him. "When was the bloody wedding, then?"[39]

American boys also lied about their age in order to get into uniform for a war they feared would be over if they waited. Joseph L. Argenzio was sixteen when the Japanese attack on Pearl Harbor propelled the United States in the Second World War. His father had served with the 1st Infantry Division during the First World War, and Argenzio was desperate to follow that example. Rather than wait until he was old enough, he took a more expedient method—he tried to alter his birth certificate. "I changed the date to show that I was 17 and went down to join the Marine Corps," he said. "I didn't do a very good job and they looked at it and threw me out. I went next door to the Navy and they did the same thing." Argenzio was undeterred. "I was determined. I was going to go," he said. "I changed my baptismal certificate and went down to the draft board and said I was 18, which I had to be to go in the Army in those days. They said 'Are you serious? You're 18?' I said 'Oh yeah, definitely.'

They said 'When would you like to leave?' I said 'Well, tomorrow is fine.' They said 'How about two weeks? You'll be taking the place of a married man.'" With that, Argenzio was in the army. He went on to make the landing on Omaha Beach as a rifleman and fought his way across Europe, ironically in the same battalion of the same infantry regiment in which his father had served, two decades before him.[40]

The Second World War was one of the first major conflicts in American history for which men could enlist not for a regiment, as in the Civil War, but for a specific branch of the service with a promise of training and assignment in a particular military job (those who waited to be conscripted, of course, were enlisted for the needs of the service and had little choice in the matter). Men who wanted specialized training, or who wanted to avoid being stuck in the infantry as riflemen, were eager to sign up for the Army Air Corps or noncombat jobs such as signal, maintenance, transportation, medical, and the like.

Edmond Sworsky joined the army from Minnesota and had no interest in the infantry—he wanted to be a gunner on a B-17 bomber. When he reported for induction, he put that down as his first choice. "They said, 'it's all filled up. Sorry about that,'" he recalled. "What the hell do you mean?" Sworsky demanded. "The war's just starting. How can it be filled up?" The admin NCO replied, "We see by your application that you ran a [Caterpillar]. . . . You'd make a very good armored man." Sworsky insisted that he wanted the Air Corps, not the armor branch, but the army was intractable. "So, I signed up and became a tanker," Sworsky said, but he did not remain one for long. After he arrived in England, he heard that the army was forming a 2nd Ranger Battalion, and he volunteered for that elite unit. That was how a man who wanted to be in the Army Air Corps reluctantly enlisted for the armored branch instead, but wound up fighting in Normandy as a ranger. Considering the terribly high casualty rates among bomber crews at the height of the war, he may have had good reason to feel that he got a better deal than the one he originally thought he wanted.[41]

Some men joined the army because soldiering seemed to be the one thing they were good at. Men who had fought on the losing side in one war often turned up in the ranks of another country's army a few years later. This was true in the aftermath of the American Civil War—the ranks of the frontier garrisons of the U.S. Army in the 1870s contained many men who had worn Confederate grey just a few years before. "Not a few of the former Confederates who entered the ranks of the postwar regulars," historian Don Rickey has noted, "had held commissions in the Southern army."[42] This also explained why there were so many Germans in the U.S. Army in the years after Germany's mid-nineteenth-century wars against Denmark, Austria, and France. Many of them were already experienced veterans. Englishmen were well-represented in the American army—William Parnell fought in the Crimean War as a British cavalryman and participated in the Charge of the Light Brigade at Balaclava, then emigrated to America, where he was awarded the Medal of Honor for valor during the Nez Perce War while serving as a lieutenant in the 1st U.S. Cavalry. Most famously, the ranks of the French Foreign Legion were regularly populated by men who had served under the flags of other nations, sometimes as former enemies of the Legion itself.

Some armies of this era also held the attraction of being quick paths to assimilation for new immigrants. This was always a particular characteristic of the American military, one that continues to this day. During the Civil War, some entire units, especially on the Federal side, were comprised of immigrants. The Union Army's Irish Brigade got its name from the national origins of its men; in a moment of almost poetic tragedy, it found itself fighting against the Irish Brigade of the Confederate Army in the carnage of Marye's Heights during the Battle of Fredericksburg in 1862. Union veteran John Billings, in his reminiscences of the Civil War, blamed the Union defeat at the Battle of Reams Station on the fact that one Massachusetts regiment had "about two hundred German recruits . . . not one of whom could understand the orders of their commanding officers."[43] That regiment was not alone in its international makeup; a sister regiment, the 13th Massachusetts, received a draft of replacements after Gettysburg that one commentator said included "Confederate deserters and a rich variety of New Brunswick plumbers, Scottish and English seamen,

Belgian shoemakers, Prussian machinists and Irish laborers. A more toothsome assemblage of foreigners and bounty-jumpers would be difficult to find anywhere."[44]

After the Civil War, the U.S. Army continued to draw immigrant recruits, even as its end strength was whittled away by a parsimonious Congress. More than a few men who served in the American West during the Indian Wars of the late 1800s were literally just off the boat. For military-aged men who had no personal contacts in their new country and who often could speak little or no English, the army offered place, purpose, and livelihood while they learned American ways.

This did not mean, however, that they left their attachments to the old countries behind them when they put on the uniforms of the U.S. Army. They retained their national pride along with the accents of their homelands, and that was the cause of some minor international conflicts in unlikely places. "In 1870," one account relates, "German musicians in several garrisons blared forth *Die Wacht am Rhein* to celebrate the victories of the Franco-Prussian War. Although French-born soldiers sang *Le Marseillaise* at the top of their lungs, they were drowned out, and fists and horns flew till the guard was turned out."[45]

A sense of just how many immigrants found a place in the U.S. Army in the latter years of the nineteenth century can be gained from looking at what is probably the most famous engagement of the U.S.-Indian Wars: The Battle of the Little Bighorn. Of the 839 troopers of the 7th Cavalry who fought there in June 1876, no fewer than 367 of them were foreign born. Three countries of origin dominated the regiment's muster rolls: 128 were Irish, 125 were from Germany, and 53 had emigrated from Great Britain.[46] The bugler who was probably the last surviving trooper to see Custer alive in that fight was Trooper John Martin, an Italian who had originally enlisted in the army under the name Giovanni Martini.

The reasons for enlisting were as varied as the men themselves, and those men were a wide array of human specimens, to put it mildly. When veteran soldiers described their impressions of new recruits, they were apt to be blunt in their evaluations. In 1879, Corporal Emil Bode of the 16th U.S. Infantry went to the train depot at Caddo, Texas, to take charge of a group of new recruits who were reporting for duty. His description of them was insightful:

Oh, what a variety of humanity, from a very intelligent society man, to Darwin's missing link of some backwoods—just fresh from the farm, with a frame and walk like a cart horse, back like a camel, with brains to match a monkey. Another was from the Puritan City in the Bay State, a real Yankee "by gosh." He read too many dime novels, poor boy, and wanted to go west to kill Injuns, and wished he'd never left home. There stood a young man, apparently from a better class and more intelligent than the general run. He had both hands in his pockets and a languid look... We found men without the least knowledge of the English language who had enlisted after unsuccessful attempts to obtain work. [One] said he wanted to join "soldier boys," a very dubious honor, another had to leave on account of a girl. We found men of intellect and stupidity, sons of congressmen and sons of farmers, rich and poor, men who are willing to work and cannot find it in civil life, men who are looking for work and hope that they never may find any: gamblers, thieves, cutthroats, drunkards, men who were formally commissioned officers. There was a combination and variety of stock which, under careful training, had produced some of the best soldiers on the frontier.[47]

Just a few years earlier, Bode himself had been one of those green recruits, as he noted in his journal; he had immigrated from Germany and found the army very much to his liking.

If patriotic altruism was not derided with outright cynical scorn as a motivation for enlisting, it was often viewed with suspicion by many soldiers of the period. Or at least that is the representation frequently put forward by later commentators. To some degree this was probably true, especially among those soldiers who found themselves embroiled in unpopular wars of doubtful outcome, but even allowing for this degree of cynicism, we cannot just completely write off the motivating power of patriotism. The fact remains that love of king and country, so to speak, compelled many men to enlist in their countries' armies. This was neither a constant nor a universal motivation, but there were always some men who joined up for no other reason than they believed it to be their duty. Both world wars were marked by surges of voluntary enlistments in answer to the nation's call for men—almost every belligerent country of the First World War saw this effect at work at one time or another. France, in particular, was swept by patriotic energy as men enlisted to fight back against the German invaders.

One view of the British experience in the First World War that has gained recent traction is the one that argues that as the war dragged on and the casualty lists mounted, enthusiasm for military service fell off to practically nothing, that after 1916 Britain had to conscript men en masse to fill the depleted ranks. This ignores the fact that as late as 1917, the British Army was still able to raise full replacement drafts of soldiers purely from voluntary enlistees. True, the British government had instituted conscription by that point, but thousands of men were still joining of their own volition, and there were still expressions of unaffected enthusiasm. Why this was so remains a matter of some conjecture and scholarly argument. Britain was not facing a threat of imminent invasion, after all, and after the losses on the Marne and the cataclysm of the Somme, few illusions remained about the reality of the war. Yet still, British men from all walks of life left their hearths and homes and enlisted. In many cases, their reasons for doing so were no more complicated than a sense of duty, that it was the thing to do.

Similar feeling propelled American men into that war, even before their own country formally entered the conflict. Kiffin Rockwell was one of numerous Americans who joined the French Foreign Legion not for adventure or martial glory, but because they felt a moral duty to fight against Germany and did not want to wait to see if America would declare itself in that cause. Wounded in the trenches in 1915, Rockwell wrote home to his mother in North Carolina and tried to explain his motives for involving himself in this particular war. "If I was killed I think that you ought to be proud in knowing that your son tried to be a man and wasn't afraid to die and that he gave his life for a greater cause than most people do—the cause of all humanity," he wrote. "To me that doesn't appear a bad death at all. Whereas otherwise I may never do anything worthwhile or any good to anyone after the war and may live to regret that I wasn't killed in it." If that was truly his hope, he got it—two years later Rockwell was killed in action, still fighting under the French flag.[48]

The popular American impression of the U.S. experience of the Second World War often describes that conflict as the "good war," a war in which American men rushed to join the military, eager to do their part to combat the clear threats of Nazism and Japanese militarism. For someone approaching the history from this perspective, it can be something of a revelation to discover that military service was far from a voluntary choice for many American GIs who served in that war. There certainly were surges of voluntary enlistment, particularly in the wake of the Japanese attack on Pearl Harbor in December 1941, but that did not translate into an enlistment pool that was sufficient to sustain America's military manpower needs through a war that had to be fought in two separate theaters simultaneously. Many American men joined up of their own choice, but many more were drafted into the military whether they wanted to serve or not.

Even then, the majority of American soldiers of that war seem to have had at least an ambiguous attitude toward the army. The sense of having a job to do, and that as soon as it was done they could get back to normal life, is prevalent in many of their personal narratives. A very common attitude, found among both voluntary enlistees and draftees alike, was that the war and the U.S. Army were interrupting their regular lives, but they were proud to serve in a cause that most of them regarded as worthwhile. "We'd all bitch and moan and groan about things but I think deep down, all of us felt it was something that we had to do and we're glad that we did it," one American soldier recalled. "When Uncle Sam called, we answered that call. That's all."[49]

This was true on the other side of that war, as well. A German soldier named Herbert Winckelmann was probably typical of many military-aged German men in the 1940s when he wrote, "I had not been enthusiastic about going to war but was determined to do my duty by defending my country. I had no ambition to become a general or a war hero."[50]

The opposite of patriotic fervor as motivation for enlistment is probably the one most frequently employed by governments throughout history—conscription, or, to use the American term, the draft. Most armies throughout this period had to rely on conscription at different times, resulting in soldiers of widely varying degrees of quality. During the Napoleonic Wars, France conscripted massive segments of the male citizenry to man its armies. When Robert Guillemard was called up in May 1805, he was not keen to serve, but the only option that could have saved him from the army was beyond his family's financial reach. "My father wished to purchase a substitute," he wrote, "but they were extremely [expensive] at that time, and the purchase would have made a considerable breach in his fortune at a critical moment, hence I would not hear of it, and prepared for my departure."[51] In the event, Guillemard served eighteen years in the army and fought in Italy, Spain, Germany, and Russia, among other places.

By 1814 French conscription had reached so deep into the population that military-aged men were resorting to ludicrous lengths to avoid the army's press-gang tactics. Robert Batty, serving in the British Army in the Peninsular War, recalled that when the British made their first entry into France in 1814, among the civilian refugees they encountered were "young men . . . disguised as women, to avoid being detained by the French authorities for the new conscription."[52] The French situation underscores one of the consistent realities about conscription—it is often very unpopular with those men who are subject to its demands. This is even more the case when they are being drafted into armies that are fighting unpopular wars or, even worse, wars that are clearly all but lost.

Even a war fought to defend one's country against foreign invasion did not always generate enthusiasm on the part of those forced into the army's ranks. The French invasion of Russia in 1812 produced a groundswell of pro-tsarist feelings and patriotism among many Russians, particularly those in the educated and aristocratic echelons of society, but the reaction among Russia's lower classes was decidedly mixed. Petty landowners, who were charged with contributing serfs to fulfill the government's conscription levy (an echo of the feudal system that had existed in the West a few centuries before), often tried to shirk the muster requirement or honored it in the breach by sending only their most worthless peasants to fill the army's ranks. For the serfs themselves, the motivation to serve as soldiers must have been low indeed, since they already lived in a state of de facto slavery and military service did nothing to raise them from their hereditary social condition.

On the eve of the Napoleonic Wars, the heavy hand of military conscription fell particularly hard on Russia's peasants, as it had throughout Russian history. Selected by lots of one for every hundred men, this involuntary enlistment was for life—men who were called up for the army might just as well have been sent into a foreign exile, so far as their homes and families were concerned. The terms of service were eventually reduced to twenty-five years, and by the time of the Crimean War in 1856, Russian conscripts were obligated to a dozen years of active duty with three subsequent years in the reserves, or the *opolchaniya*. Twenty-five years later this service obligation was changed yet again to five years of active service followed by thirteen in the *opolchaniya* for infantrymen and a requirement of five and fifteen years for cavalrymen and artillerymen, respectively. These reforms, however, do not seem to have made military service any more popular among the peasants who were subject to the conscription.

When the United States precipitated itself into its Civil War in 1861, both the United States in the north and the newly formed Confederacy of southern states put out calls for men. The Confederate Army began the Civil War flush with eager volunteers ready to fight for the Southern cause—the use of names such as "The War to End Yankee Aggression," "The War for Southern Independence," and "The Second American Revolution" all illustrated the Southern view of the Civil War. There were so many volunteers, in fact, that the Confederate War Department could not equip and arm all of them with any sort of military uniformity. On the other side, the Federal government was quickly able to raise volunteer regiments from the individual states to augment the small force of the Regular Army, but in a case of unfounded optimism, it enlisted many of them for only ninety days, a mistake that required painful rectification before the year was out. Enlistment terms were increased to one year's service, but even that proved inadequate to meet the army's needs in a war that was far tougher, costlier, and lasted much longer than anyone seemed to expect.

As the Civil War developed into a hard-fought, seemingly interminable struggle, the manpower situation changed for both sides. The Federal government, although the eventual (and probably inevitable) victor in that war, still found it necessary to institute conscription to fulfill the U.S. Army's manpower needs. Conscription was so virulently unpopular in some parts of the country that antidraft riots broke out; "a rich man's war and a poor man's fight," was the slogan of rioters in New York City in 1863. Ironically, the same phrase was used by angry Confederate soldiers when their government announced a policy that would allow any man who owned at least twenty slaves to leave the army and return home. The Confederate government, which had enjoyed an almost religious fervor of support from the Southern populace at the war's beginning, found that as the war went on, voluntary enlistments fell off sharply and desertions increased in huge numbers, particularly among those soldiers from North Carolina.

Conscription was instituted by all the belligerent nations in both world wars, but the relative efficacy of the conscription system and the populace's reactions to it varied widely from country to country. Of the European nations, Germany undoubtedly had the most effective and well-practiced conscription model in place, based on the system that had so convincingly proved its worth during the Franco-Prussian War of 1870. Every able-bodied German man had a military service obligation as a duty of his citizenship, and from that group the army every year called up a number of men for short-term active service. After completing an initial active-duty service of two or three years, these men were committed to another five years in the regular reserve, followed by another twelve years in the Landwehr, and then carried on the roster of the Landsturm until they were forty-five years of age. This meant that a huge manpower pool of trained soldiers was available to the army at any time. Unlike other European nations that also required long reserve service of their male citizens, the Germans maintained a system of effective reservist training under the guidance of a cadre of professional officers and NCOs, which meant that their reservists were actually able and ready to augment the army's regular ranks if called up.[53]

The French government, for its part, required active military service for three years of most men at twenty years of age. (Before 1914, this initial service requirement had stipulated a period of only two years in uniform.) Once discharged from this initial obligation, seven years in the Territorial Army and a further seven years in the Territorial Reserve followed. But whereas Germany saw its reserve manpower pool as front-line soldiers-in-waiting and trained them to that standard, the French never placed much confidence in the combat ability of their reservists and neglected to train them to be able to serve at the level of regular troops on short notice.

Russia might just as well have been trapped in a time warp when the First World War began in 1914, because her army was no better in a professional sense than it was when Napoleon invaded in 1812, and the manpower problem was handled with the same inept, counterproductive methods of a century before. To say that Russia had a manpower problem, however, does not mean that there was a shortage of men—on the contrary, Russia's human resources were so large as to dwarf those of every other belligerent nation in the war. But while Russia had vast quantities of men, they were of the worst quality in terms of soldiering. The Russian soldier could be unbelievably brave, and his capacity for enduring hardship was legendary, but that was about the extent of his martial qualities in 1914. The average Russian infantryman was illiterate, backward, provincial, and still very much the product of the feudal system of serfdom that had repressed the Russian peasantry for centuries.

Those factors alone, of course, did not mean that Russian soldiers could not have been trained to a respectable degree of military competence, but that would have required serious work by committed military professionals, and those professionals Russia also lacked. The Russian officer class (and it was very much a class system) was notoriously hidebound and intransigent. In terms of their professional skills, they were frequently incompetent or, at the very least, untrained; in terms of their personal commitment to the army, they were often characterized by systemic corruption and self-indulgence. The Russian soldier was very much the product of a military system that viewed him as an expendable asset, and not a very valued one at that. The common man's view of this was summed up in a phrase common whenever the conscription time came around: "The Tsar commands and God permits." In light of this, it was not at all surprising that the Bolsheviks found such fertile ground when they set out to foment unrest and mutiny in the imperial army's ranks in 1916–1917.

It was almost a case of poetic justice, then, that when the Bolsheviks began creating their own military force in the guise of the new Red Army, they encountered a host of problems that were largely of their own creation. The one man most responsible for the formation of the Red Army was Leon Trotsky, who "started with all sorts of splendid ideas about socialist freedom and democracy, the greatness of the cause being a substitute for discipline . . . only to find that you cannot run an army on Communist principles." True egalitarianism simply does not work in the vertical hierarchy necessary for military command and control, and proletariat committees are hinderances when decisive action is needed in the field.

Another problem the nascent Red Army encountered was that it quickly found it needed the former soldiers of the tsarist army, the very same men whom the Bolsheviks had subverted to cause the collapse of the Russian Army in 1917. These men were not eager to trade one system of military servitude for another: "They had discovered already that their new masters were no improvement on the old, and furthermore they had no wish, having got out of the army, to be pushed back into it again."[54] In the end, the change of political systems from monarchy to Communism had almost no impact on the men who were subject to Russian conscription. "Joining up was part of life, as traditional in Russian villages as wife beating and painted eggs," one historian notes. "The army had always taken men."[55]

Even in those nations that saw military service as a noble duty, authorities often found that as the wars dragged on, enthusiasm in the manpower pool waned. Germany encountered increasing resistance to its conscription efforts toward the disastrous ends of both of the world wars. John Morse, fighting for the Russians in Poland during the First World War, recorded his impression of some German prisoners he encountered. They were, he said, more deserters than prisoners. "Lots of them hated the military service, and had taken the earliest opportunity to run away from it—into the arms of their enemies," he wrote. "A soldier of the 54th regiment declared himself to be a Socialist, and said he did not like killing his fellow-men. Another declared that the only men he wished to kill were his officer and his sergeant-major, who had been cruel to him."[56]

Despite Germany's early victories in Poland and Western Europe in the early years of the Second World War, some military-aged German men still wanted no part in that war. The long arm of conscription drew them in, regardless of their preferences. From the impressions recorded by Allied soldiers who encountered them as prisoners of war, and from their own accounts, an appreciable number of German soldiers never became die-hard, ideologically committed National Socialists. They were just ordinary men, as were most of the British and American soldiers facing them, and all that most of them wanted to do was to survive the war and go home, assuming they had a home still standing in the rubble of Germany's bombed-out cities.

Another manifestation of Second World War conscription, as in earlier conflicts, was that men of conquered countries were sometimes forced into the armed forces of an occupying power. The Japanese Imperial Army conscripted Koreans, just as the ranks of the German Wehrmacht held more than a few reluctant Poles. One of those was Aloysius Damski, a Polish citizen who fought in Normandy as an artilleryman in the 352nd Artillery Regiment. "I was impressed into the German Army in February 1943," Damski said. "I was working in the office of a munitions factory in Blomberg when the manager called me in and said I could either go into the German forces or be declared 'politically undesirable,' which almost certainly meant a concentration camp." Damski was caught between two bad choices. "I was only twenty years old and I loved life," he recalled, "so I chose the army."[57]

For the most part, conscription prompted negative reactions in populations that were subject to it. The differences from country to country or between one army and another were more a matter of degree than anything else. Even when conscription was accepted as a hard necessity, the label of "conscript" still drew strong reactions, especially in countries that did not have militarized cultures. "Canada relied on voluntary enlistments until 1917; unable to replace its infantry losses solely through recruiting, it was forced to initiate conscription," historian Desmond Morton says. "The concept was widely unpopular, though, so much so that the use of the word 'conscript' was officially prohibited within the army."[58]

Men became soldiers throughout the period for many reasons, and some even joined enthusiastically of their own volition. Few men, though, seem to have welcomed the prospect of being forced into uniform against their will. Once they were in the army, some draftees went on to fight well, even heroically; others were committed malingerers, shirkers, and occasionally deserters—there were no universal truths to the matter when it came down to the individual experience.

By whatever means a man came into the army, whether it was the army of his own country or the army of another, it was just the first step in his transformation from civilian to soldier. Whether he was an eager volunteer or a reluctant conscript, life as he had known it was ended, and a new life of military regimen, strict discipline, and hard living was begun, and with it the hard and sometimes painful process of learning the rituals, skills, and customs expected of him in his new identity as a soldier. After the recruiting sergeant, the new soldier next encountered the drill instructor, that loud, intimidating, and perpetually ill-tempered human personification of military training. No one ever forgot that introduction, or the experiences that followed it.

Chapter Two

Drill and Training

Turning Recruits into Soldiers

ONCE ENLISTED, a man's life as a soldier was begun in earnest, and things usually began happening for him very quickly. Or, as more than one narrative indicates from the perspective of the disoriented and slightly stunned new recruit, things began to happen *to* him. Many men, even those who were initially enthusiastic about joining the army, found the transition from civilian to soldier to be a daunting process. Others found the process to be nothing less than a horrible experience from the first day, one that they recalled in vivid language decades after they left the army and returned to civilian life.

In the years immediately following the Civil War, the U.S. Army's new recruits went to Governors Island in New York, or Carlisle Barracks, Pennsylvania, if they were enlisted for the artillery or infantry. Cavalrymen went to St. Louis Barracks, Missouri, until 1878, when the cavalry depot was transferred a few miles away to Jefferson Barracks. The system was shuffled a bit in the 1880s when David's Island in New York and Columbus Barracks in Ohio were designated as recruit depots for infantrymen, which remained the arrangement until the depot system was finally done away with in 1894. On the whole, the depot system never managed to provide the American army with an efficient means of in-processing recruits, and right up to the day it was finally abolished, it was notorious for the inconsistent quality of the truncated training it provided to new soldiers.

Some of the experiences of recruits 200 years ago are instantly familiar to soldiers today. Even in 1800, the British Army employed that initiation remembered so ruefully by most veterans: the first official haircut. In the Standing Orders of the 51st Regiment of British Militia, haircuts were mandated for all new recruits: "The officer commanding the company [the recruit] is appointed to, will immediately give directions that his hair be regimentally cut."[1] John Shipp, who enlisted in 1800, remembered that on his first day after joining up, "I was taken to a barber's, and deprived of my curly brown locks. My hair curled beautifully, but in a minute my poor little head was nearly bald."[2] Another British recruit from 1853 recalled that he was still reeling from his first sight of the bedlam of his training barracks when "a huge Yorkshire fellow made his appearance, who had been installed as hair-cutter, or rather hair-shearer to the establishment; and who, *ex officio*, was armed with an enormous pair of scissors, which reminded me of the implement used by farmers for clipping hedges."[3] In short order the recruit was shorn of his hair. From that point on, as most new soldiers saw it, things got considerably worse before they got any better.

Hugh Knyvett, who enlisted with an Australian unit for the First World War, had a typical impression of his first days in the army:

For a man that has never previously had military training, the first few weeks in camp is the most humiliating and trying experience that could be inflicted on him. I am quite sure that were it a prison and a treadmill he could not hate it the more. Here was I, never been under orders since I was breeched . . . suddenly finding myself with every movement I was to make laid down in regulations, with about a score of men round me all day to see that I carried them out correctly. . . . In those first weeks I think I would have gladly murdered every sergeant. . . . It is not often realized what a purgatory the educated, independent man who enlists as a private has to go through before his spirit is tamed sufficiently to stand bossing, without resentment, by men socially and educationally inferior. . . . I have great sympathy with the soft-handed rookie, for in those three weeks it seemed to me that it was an easy thing to die for one's country, but to train to be a soldier was about the worst kind of penal servitude a man could undergo.[4]

The first military personage of note whom most soldiers encountered was their drill instructor. Different armies filled this crucial role in different ways, and the rank of the individual instructor varied, but the effect on the recruit seems to have been the same across the spectrum, no matter the era or the nationality. Few soldiers remembered their drill instructors fondly. Englishman Edwin Rundle, who enlisted with the 17th Regiment in 1858, was something of the exception to the rule when he recalled his drill sergeant as "an excellent, good-natured instructor, Color-Sergeant Summers, who had served in the Crimea," but on the whole, the men who were tasked with turning raw recruits into soldiers were remembered with much different language than Rundle's somewhat nostalgic description.[5]

Needham Freeman was initially enthusiastic about enlisting in the U.S. Army in 1898, but found the nature of his training NCOs to be an unpleasant surprise. "The manner of all the drill masters was very objectionable to me at first," he recalled. "I did not like the way they spoke to a soldier and gave commands. . . . The month I drilled as a recruit I was under Sergeant Robert Scott. . . . During that time I thought Sergeant Scott the most unkind man I had ever seen. He looked ugly and talked harshly. I thought he meant every word he said."[6] Freeman's perspective of the drill instructor, most soldiers would agree, is a much more common opinion than Rundle's before him.

Emil Geissler, a German soldier who enlisted in a Prussian regiment in 1895, described his recruit training in terms that might have made Freeman count himself lucky. "On the parade ground we were tamed, tortured and hit by the trainer," Geissler wrote. "He would stamp on our toes with his rifle—they felt like they had been completely crushed. . . . I had three types of basic training with the Pioneers. Drill, working on the land with cramp irons and shovels, and water duty: all three bestial torture, not to mention the coarse vulgarity of the sergeant and NCOs."[7]

A Japanese soldier who was drafted into the Imperial Army in early 1945 described his training NCO as "a tough 'devil' sergeant from hell. . . . I was exhausted from the time it took me every night to keep the machine gun in good working order. If we were lax in our care, the devil sergeant would slap our faces and scold us, saying, 'I can replace you draftees with a single red card, but I can't immediately replace a light machine gun.'"[8] A red card was the official draft notice that Japanese men received notifying them that they were being conscripted; the new solder's low value in the military system was thus made painfully clear to him from the very beginning.

The negative stereotypes about initial entry training existed in almost every military system and were so widespread that they were familiar even to people who had never, themselves, encountered a drill instructor. The narrator who used the pseudonym Kent Soldier, who enlisted in the British Army in 1891, said that when he got off the train to report to his regiment, he asked for directions to his training camp "from one of the railway officials. 'Oh,' said he with a sneering grin, 'I suppose you're a 'cruity;' well, I pity you,' at which I felt very indignant. . . . I was soon to find out that his pity was not altogether misplaced."[9]

Australian E. P. F. Lynch, who fought in France during the First World War, remembered that the training regimen in his battalion was decidedly unpleasant. "Morning is upon us with a blast of bugles," he wrote. "An hour's torture from a loud-mouthed physical instructor and we're ready for breakfast, ready for a far better one than we get. A whole morning's route march with full pack and then a whole afternoon of 'hop-overs' [trench assault drills]. We hop-over and charge trench after trench. For hours and hours we get insulted and abused and sworn at for not doing it better." On one particular occasion the trainees fell far short of their instructor's unyielding expectations, a failing that prompted the sergeant to unleash an especially memorable tirade of profane, outraged invective—"We hear a lot about ourselves that we never knew before," Lynch wrote in his journal.[10]

A hundred years before Lynch, an anonymous British soldier left a compelling record of his service with the 71st Regiment during the Peninsular War. Writing of his initial experiences as a recruit in 1807, he said, "Now I began to drink the cup of bitterness. How different was my situation from what it had been! Forced from bed at five o'clock each morning, to get all things ready for drill; then drilled for three hours with the most unfeeling rigour, and often beat by the sergeant for the faults of others."[11]

This narrative invokes the oft-repeated stereotype of the drill instructor as a type of sadistic tyrant, one that frequently appears in both factual and fictional accounts of army life. The stereotype had its exceptions, though, as stereotypes always do. There were undoubtedly some draconian bastards to be found among the world's drill sergeants, and NCOs in a few military systems such as the bushido-driven Imperial Japanese Army or the notoriously strict nineteenth-century Prussian Army were wont to knock recruits about with some frequency, but those methods were by no means applied to such a degree by all armies during the period. It is true that many armies at the beginning of this period applied a liberal amount of physical correction in their training regimens—instruction was often delivered at high volume and with an occasional blow from fist or stick for punctuating emphasis. All the same, though, a considerable amount of careful method was incorporated into most armies' approach to the training of new recruits.

In 1892 the Standing Orders of the British Army's Scots Guards, issued from Aldershot, stressed the importance of professional training as opposed to tyrannical bullying. Section No. 12, "The Recruit Establishment," made several important points:

110. It must be borne in mind that the first impression of a soldier's life received by a young man may go far either to make or mar him, therefore all such things as undue harshness on the part of the instructors at drill, bullying or extortion on the part of old soldiers, exorbitant charges for messing or necessaries, should be put down with a firm hand.
121. The colour-sergeants at the [training] Depot will be men most carefully selected by the Lieutenant-Colonel, after consultation with the Officers Commanding battalions. They should be pay-sergeants of some standing, and their qualifications should be not so much smartness on parade (though, of course, that is desirable) as known integrity of character, good judgment, and tact, and a kindly disposition.
125. They will watch the instruction of the recruits at drill by the drill instructors, and at once check any tendency to bullying, and they will carefully look after the barrack-room instruction by the old soldier, and prevent anything approaching to extortion.[12]

Most soldiers, looking back on their training days as new recruits, would probably not have used the words *tact* or *kindly* to describe the noncommissioned officers of their training units, but the fact that the army felt that these were important traits for its training supervisors to have is nonetheless worth noting. As for the drill instructors themselves, the 1892 Standing Orders had more to say on that score: "The drill-instructors should be good drills, and should be capable of imparting instruction. They should be intelligent, well educated, and of good temper; steady and sober men, who will themselves set a good example."[13]

Contrary to the prevailing negative stereotypes (many of which had more than a little bit of factual basis behind them), this enlightened sort of drill instruction sometimes actually *did* exist in practice. After Edwin Mole enlisted in the 14th Hussars in 1863, he was pleasantly surprised by his first day of dismounted drill. "From the tales I had heard about drill sergeants I dreaded them more than anything else," he wrote, "believing they took a delight in bullying, but I found the non-commissioned officer in charge of us patient, although strict, and the exercises not only easy but interesting."[14] That was one of several reasons why Mole found army life to be even more to his liking than he had dared hope.

The Imperial French Army of the Napoleonic period was largely a conscripted force, but the training philosophy applied to its new soldiers was rather enlightened for that day. Robert Guillemard, who was conscripted as an infantryman in 1806, wrote that the lieutenant and two sergeants who were in charge of his recruit detachment "treated us with great mildness, and endeavored to inspire us with predilection for military life." The reason for this restrained approach, as it was explained to him, was that it produced better soldiers. "Care was taken in those days to give the charge of young conscripts to none but those who had seen active service," he wrote. "For in the army, as in every other profession, he who has done nothing, displays his superiority only by arrogance and petty vexations, so that those who are under him detest not only the individual but the orders he issues."[15]

Japanese recruits of the period would probably have found the French and British practices absolutely alien in the light of their own experiences. Corporal punishment was the hallmark of Japanese military training; so inextricably linked were they that one Japanese solder spoke for many when he wrote, "My military life was filled with training and beatings. We were made to form a single line and stand at attention and then ordered to clench our teeth. Then they hit us with their fists. This was better than the occasions when they struck us with the leather straps of their swords or their leather indoor shoes." Looking back on his experience, this man was still bitter years after the fact. "This method of inflicting brutal punishment without any cause and destroying our power to think was a way of transforming us into men who would carry out our superiors' orders as a reflex action," he wrote. "The number of blows I received, which I vowed I would never forget, was 264."[16]

This was a perspective shared by many Japanese veterans of the 1930s and 1940s. It was customary in the Imperial Japanese Army for superiors to strike subordinates for the most minor of infractions. It was not uncommon for senior officers to slap junior officers, even in front of the men, and the privates at the bottom of the hierarchy were abused by nearly everyone above them in the rank structure. The senior privates were perhaps the most vicious of all, taking all their spleen out on the junior privates, who had no one below them to pass it on to. A former infantryman named Watanabe Katsumi wrote, "For forty-some years I've suffered from ringing in my ears. This is the aftereffect of severe beatings by higher-ranking privates when I was a draftee. It was the norm in the military that new recruits and draftees were beaten for no reason."[17]

In other military systems where outright physical abuse was not the norm, good drill instructors were composites of disciplinarians, philosophers, comics, psychologists, and teachers. "The best drill instructor," a British veteran of the First World War wrote, "is he who can deal with every lapse or negligence, however trivial, as though it were an unprecedented phenomenon, a demonstration deliberately planned to sap loyalty, to sow dissension in the ranks, to debauch the nation, to enhearten the enemy, and to bring the Empire crashing to the ground."[18] He recalled that his senior drill instructor was just such a man—an engaging, motivating instructor in the classroom, and an absolute terror on the drill field.

Observers who have no personal experience of military life have often questioned the necessity of this sort of intensive rote training, and armies' methods of transforming civilian recruits into soldiers have come in for frequent criticisms through the years. Some of the opprobrium is merited, but much of it is not. Brainwashing is a fairly modern pejorative that is sometimes used far too readily by critics of military training, but brainwashing it most certainly was *not*, at least not in most Western armies in this period. There might be more merit to the argument that brainwashing was exactly what was involved in the intense political indoctrination sessions undertaken by the Red Army during the Soviet period or the Chinese Communist forces during the years of the Chinese Civil War, but those methods were not widely applied elsewhere.

On the contrary, the reason for the intensity and repetition of initial military training owed everything to its ultimate purpose—to transform civilians with no military experience into trained, skilled, and capable soldiers. As one Union Army veteran of the Civil War put it when he described his early days in uniform, "What I didn't know about war, at that stage of the proceedings, was broad and comprehensive, and covered the whole field."[19] The only way to trade that ignorance for knowledge and skill was through hard, focused training, and it was on that premise that every professional army operated.

Aside from the occasionally ill-tempered, often-profane drill instructors who frightened the daylights out of many recruits, there was also the matter of having to adjust to a way of life and a culture the likes of which most men had never before encountered. A young man from a sheltered upbringing, or who was a particularly sensitive soul, could find the unvarnished realities of military society shocking. "I could not associate with the common soldiers," the anonymous soldier of the 71st Regiment remembered of his early days in the British Army. "Their habits made me shudder. I feared an oath—they never spoke without one; I could not drink—they loved liquor. Thus I was a solitary individual among hundreds."[20] He was not the only man to feel that by joining the army he had allowed himself to be flung in among savages, or at the very least, among men of markedly different character than he was used to. William Jett enlisted as a cavalryman in the U.S. Army in 1881; in his memoir years afterward, he recalled his initial impression of his fellow recruits in the training depot at Jefferson Barracks. "My new associates, with few exceptions, were of the lowest type," he wrote. "Many of the men had the most unclean diseases, and with these you had to eat and drink and occupy the same quarters, where the vilest conversation and profanity prevailed."[21]

Another British soldier, who joined the 43rd Light Infantry in 1803, recalled that his first night in the regiment's depot was utterly unlike anything he had ever experienced before:

> *The sleeping room of which I was an inmate was an oblong building of unusually large dimensions, and was occupied by three companies, of an hundred men each. They were chiefly volunteers, and, of course, young soldiers, many were Irish, many more were English, several Welshmen were intermingled, and a few Scotsmen came in to complete the whole. Most of these, and that was the only point of general resemblance, had indulged in excessive drinking. Some were uproariously merry; on others the effect was directly the reverse; and nothing less than a fight, it matter not with whom, would satisfy. Meantime, as they were unable to abuse each other in language mutually unintelligible, exclamations profoundly jocular or absurdly rancorous ran through the building. Never will the occurrence of that night be effaced from my mind. Surely, I thought, hell from beneath is moved to engulf us all.*[22]

When Joseph Donaldson enlisted in the 94th Regiment of Foot in 1838, he very quickly found that he had little in common with his new comrades-in-arms, not only in terms of their characters but in their intellectual pursuits as well. There were few enlisted men in his company, he wrote, who

> *had an idea beyond the situation they were in; those who had were afraid to show that they possessed any more knowledge than their comrades for fear of being laughed at by fellows that in any other circumstances they would have despised. . . . If [a soldier] did not join with his neighbors in their ribald obscenity and nonsense, he was a Methodist—if he did not curse and swear, he was a Quaker—and if he did not drink the most of his pay, he was a miser, a d–d mean scrub and the generality of his comrades would join in execrating him. In such a society it was a hard matter for a man of any superior education*

to keep his ground, for he had no one to converse with. . . . Thus many
men of ability and information were, I may say, forced from their
intellectual height which they had attained down to the level of those
with whom they had to associate; and everything conspired to sink
them to that point where they became best fitted for tractable beasts of
burden. *Blackguardism held sway, and gave tone to the whole. Even*
the youngest were led to scenes of drunkenness and debauchery by men
advanced in years. All, therefore, with few exceptions were drawn
into this overwhelming vortex of abject slavishness and dissipation.[23]

It is something of a cliché to assume that the common soldier of the
period—the rank-and-file infantryman, trooper, or gunner—had little
interest in intellectual pursuits or that he lacked sufficient intelligence
in that regard, but as Donaldson's experience indicated, it was probable
that many men felt it better to be circumspect about their intelligence
in order to just get along without attracting the wrong kind of notice.
Charles Willeford was an aspiring writer when he enlisted in the U.S.
Army in 1935; the first night after he arrived at his initial posting in the
Philippines, he recalled, he quickly learned "not to tell anyone else I was
a poet."[24]

At the same time, it bears noting that the enlisted men of the period
were not all rough, rude, and vile—if for no other reason than statistical
probability, there had to be exceptions to that overused stereotype. Some
observers, once the remove of a few years provided some perspective or the
chance for closer acquaintance presented itself, found that their uncouth
comrades were actually not so bad as all that. William Robertson, who
finished his career in the British Army as a field marshal but started it as
a private, wrote of his early service in 1877:

Regiments were, therefore, still composed mainly of old soldiers who,
although very admirable comrades in some respects and with a com-
mendable code of honour of their own, were in many cases, not in
all—addicted to rough behavior, heavy drinking, and hard swear-
ing. They could not well be blamed for this. Year in and year out they
went through the same routine, were treated like machines—of an

*inferior kind—and having little prospect of finding decent employ-
ment on the expiration of their twenty-one years' engagement, they
lived only for the present, the single bright spot in their existence being
the receipt of a few shillings—perhaps not more than one—on the
weekly pay-day.*[25]

The nature of military life was that every army throughout the period
was comprised of a varied assortment of characters. Inevitably there were
always some men in the group who were the military equivalent of the
local village idiot, and more than a few soldiers left personal narratives
in which they questioned whether their armies were not recruiting from
some residual group of modern-day Neanderthals, but those types were
not usually in the majority. They were, however, apparently a common
enough feature in the military service of every nation to be noted in most
men's accounts of their army experience.

Nearly every army had its share of knuckle-dragging oafs in the ranks.
In 1916 a French cavalry veteran using the nom de plume Ex-Trooper, in
a book comparing the armies of Britain and France, said, "There is as great
a percentage of stupid people in France as in any other country; a voluntary army is at liberty to reject fools as undesirable, but the nation with a
conscript system must train the fools as well as the wise ones."[26] British
and American veterans would probably have disagreed with his assumption that fools were apt to be rejected in armies manned by voluntary
enlistment—more than a few halfwits and imbeciles somehow inveigled
their way into the ranks of those armies, as well, in all eras of this period.
Or, it would probably be more accurate to say, unscrupulous recruiting
sergeants inveigled them in, in spite of regulations to the contrary.

There were always men who remembered some of their fellow soldiers in much the same way that Canadian soldier Harold Baldwin did.
"Most of my companions in France," he said, remembering his service
in the First World War, "were savages; common, common little people
who proved a far greater trial than the real horror."[27] This was a prevailing stereotype, both inside and outside the army's ranks, but there are
enough countering views to suggest that the presence of the "savages"
was balanced by solid men of good character. If not, it is unlikely that so

many men would have placed such great value on the friendships forged in their military service as they did when they later wrote of their experiences. Most soldiers, though, whatever the era in which they served, could probably identify with the words of the fictional soldier Lieutenant John J. Dunbar in *Dances with Wolves,* when he wrote in his diary, "Were it not for the vulgarity of my companion, I would be having the time of my life."

Almost every army had its educated men-turned-soldiers, those fellows who were fallen on hard times, trying to escape something in their past, or who just wanted to try their hand at soldiering; just as every army had men who came from their nation's sturdy, hardworking peasant stock or its social equivalent. It also was just as true that every army had its share of uniformed criminals, petty or felonious, along with the ubiquitous drunks and social misfits. By and large, though, most of the armies in question were manned by professional soldiers, men of good (though perhaps undistinguished and certainly untrained) intellects, men who could learn almost any skill required of them and who set themselves to accomplish the tasks before them no matter the cost, and who did it all with a rough humor and a pride in themselves and their fellows. The blowhards, bullies, and dim-witted oafs were always there, but perhaps not in the numbers that generalizing stereotypes might suggest.

Many of the soldiers who left records of their service during this period reported the same sense of initial dismay at meeting the apparently ill-bred, uncouth louts who were to be their comrades-in-arms, but there was another factor at work that many did not take into account, at least not at first, and that was the influence that the army itself would bring to bear on those men. George MacMullen, who joined the British Army just before the Crimean War in 1853, had this sort of reaction when he first encountered his fellow soldiers. "Hard fare I little care for, and it matters not to me how rough my bed might be; privations of this nature are inseparable from a soldier's lot," he wrote. "But the prospect of mingling for any lengthened period with some of the individuals I saw in the Receiving house was, I must acknowledge, excessively disheartening." The passage of time and the acquisition of experience gave him a different perspective. "I was not then aware," he admitted, "what a surprising alteration for the better in many respects, subjection to a strict and uniform discipline would affect them in a little time."[28]

The sudden, forced subordination of individuality to the group dynamic has always been a reality of military service, and it has always been a difficult process for some men, particularly for those from Western cultures. Some new recruits struggled to fit in; others tried to find some space apart for themselves away from the army's constant interference. The worst thing about Leander Stillwell's training camp in the U.S. Army in 1861, as he remembered it, was "the utter absence of privacy. Even when off duty, one couldn't get away by himself, and sit down in peace and quiet anywhere. And as for slipping off into some corner and trying to read, alone . . . the thing was impossible."[29] Fifty-odd years later Stillwell's complaint was echoed by Sidney Amatt of the Essex Regiment, serving in the First World War, who said, "That's one thing about the British Army—they never allowed you any time to yourself if they could find a job for you to do."[30] For soldiers in the lower ranks, their experience of army life during the Second World War was much the same— "List among other army complaints," an American soldier wrote in 1944, "always a private and never alone."[31]

<hr />

Most of a new soldier's time was taken up with training, or, in the parlance of the day, "drilling." A few soldiers found the repetitious monotony of drill to be enjoyable, but they were distinctly in the minority. John Shipp, whose experiences occurred at the beginning of this period, described his initial training by saying, "Our very lives were drilled out by brigade field-days, from three and four o'clock in the morning, until seven and eight o'clock at night."[32]

James Stone, of the U.S. Army's 21st Massachusetts Volunteer Infantry during the Civil War, described drill as being "the principle work of the day, at first in march, company drill, platoon drill, squad drill." As things progressed, he said, the training turned to exercises with their new weapons, although in his case, new was not the best word to describe the firearms issued to his regiment. "After a time we received muskets and then began the exercises in the manual of arms," he said. 'Those muskets were of the most horrible kind imaginable, but they answered to drill with. That, however, was all that they were good for excepting old junk."[33] At least Stone's regiment was able to drill with actual firearms, antiquated or not; other soldiers found themselves carrying wooden replicas of rifles until enough weapons were available for general issue.

The problem of insufficient equipment for a newly expanding army in a period of national emergency was not unique to the nineteenth century, and it always had an impact on training. In the first year of the First World War, the British suffered the same handicap, as did the U.S. Army in the years immediately before its entry into the Second World War. "Weeks went by," Charles Carrington wrote of his early days in the British Army in 1914, "when we had no uniforms, no arms, no apparatus for teaching the military techniques. Marching, squad drill, physical training, was all that we could do from dawn to dusk, and we were avid to become soldierly. When it rained someone lectured us on map-reading (without maps) or on musketry (without rifles), so that the rate of progress was limited."[34]

Aside from monotonous drill, the other most common training regimen that most recruits encountered was route marching. Jokingly or not, infantrymen have long described themselves as beasts of burden. Roman legionaries of the late Republican period wryly called themselves "Marius' Mules," after Gaius Marius, the general whose military reforms greatly improved the Roman Army and standardized the soldiers' considerable marching load. The sentiment has been frequently expressed in different languages ever since, and not always in complimentary terms.

The simplest way of toughening new soldiers to the requirement of marching long miles under the weight of pack and weapon has always been the simplest way—put them out there with their gear and send them down the road, usually with an NCO or two snapping at their heels like cattle dogs and harrying them along with a few well-chosen words of inspired profanity. Modern infantrymen today use route marches as a regular training technique, and it was a method employed by most armies throughout the nineteenthth century, especially in certain seasons. "The only drill during the winter," Edwin Rundle recalled of his training in the 1850s, "was route marching."[35] Route marching, and apparently the occasional lecture—which was the more monotonous undertaking, in the view of the soldiers, is not immediately clear.

When Needham N. Freeman enlisted in the U.S. Army, he joined his infantry battalion just before it was to leave on a 120-mile training march across the Texas backcountry. "Of course I wanted to go," he said, "thinking it would be a picnic." He found out very quickly that it was not in any way a picnic; the purpose, rather, was for the soldiers "to get a little hardened by this practice march." Freeman's company was out for fifteen days. He developed serious blisters the first day out and, to his chagrin, was ordered to ride in one of the ambulances for the rest of that day. He recalled that the march was an eye-opening experience. "Twenty miles a day through chaparral bushes and cactus is a good day's march for soldiers with all their equipage," he wrote.[36]

No matter the army, the uniform, or the era in which they served, infantry recruits usually found similar experiences awaiting them in the early days of their enlistment. Remembering his training in Egypt in the First World War, one Australian infantryman wrote, "And then, of course, we route-marched—in the desert. . . . We were not supposed to do more than fifteen miles a day, but on the desert there were no milestones, and the distance was 'estimated' by the officer in command. Some of these officers must have been city treasurers in private life, for their estimate of distance was like estimated annual expenditure, generally much under the mark. Mostly they would know when we had gone far enough, which for us was too far, and then we would get lost coming back."[37] A hundred years later, his experiences are still immediately familiar to modern infantrymen.

Soldiers of other arms also found their initial training to be a challenging experience. A recruit in the 6th U.S. Cavalry, out on his first bivouac in 1885, later wrote of it, "It was the first time in my life that I had slept out of doors, and what with the stomping and snorting of the horses, and the rattling of the chains on the wagon tongues—where the mules were tied—sleep was out of the question. Besides, the ride had made me so stiff that all the bones in my body ached."[38]

At the same time, there were always other soldier skills that needed to be learned, and most of them required more than just the methodical physical conditioning of route marching or the mindless repetition of parade-ground drilling. The fulfillment of the infantry's role at the sharp end of the army always came down to the individual soldier's skill in musketry—in other words, his ability to put rounds downrange, on target, and as rapidly as possible. Marksmanship training received less or more emphasis in different armies throughout the period, sometimes coming perilously close to being neglected altogether, but the truth throughout this period was that when the marching stopped and the fighting started, marksmanship was always the infantry's most important technical skill.

It was a skill often notable for its absence. In 1877, the *Army and Navy Journal* printed a letter by a U.S. Army officer in which the writer discussed the cavalry's performance in the campaign against the Nez Perce that had just concluded, and one of the things considered was the individual cavalryman's level of shooting expertise. "Our soldiers of all arms have had too little practice with their [weapons]," the writer declared. "The target practice and the firing with blank ammunition have been limited by a false idea of economy. It is now in better shape, but the necessity is the best limit in the expenditure of ammunition, for nobody but the post commander and those officers who are under him can tell beforehand how many times a man must fire to gain the requisite skill—some more and some less."[39]

It was a persistent problem. In the U.S. Army of the post–Civil War years, marksmanship training went through a period of systematic neglect. One veteran of the 18th U.S. Infantry said that his regiment conducted no small arms training at all for the entire year of 1866, "because of the short supply of ammunition." This particular unit was at that time actively campaigning against Sioux and Cheyenne Indians, and marksmanship was a crucial skill for them. Even when the army adopted an official policy requiring regular target practice in 1872, it was not widely enforced. It was not until the end of that decade that marksmanship finally came to be regarded by the U.S. Army as the preeminent and most necessary skill an infantry soldier should have.

Coincidentally, during the same decade, rifle marksmanship was in serious decline in the British Army as well, at least as far as the cavalry regiments were concerned. Field Marshal Sir William Robertson, the former cavalry private, was of the opinion that training standards were nearly obsolete when he was a young trooper. "Military training lagged far behind," he wrote, "notwithstanding the many lessons furnished by the Franco-German War of 1870, and was still mainly based on the system inherited from the Peninsula and Crimean campaigns. Pipe-clay, antiquated and useless forms of drill, blind obedience to orders, ramrod-like rigidity on parade, and similar time-honoured practices were the chief qualifications by which a regiment was judged."[40] When it came to marksmanship training, the situation was no better. Robertson said that when the old horse pistols were phased out and carbines were issued to cavalrymen, "for some years musketry was universally hated and deemed to be a degradation and a bore. In no case could it have been made of much value, since the annual allowance of ammunition was fixed at forty rounds a man, and thirty rounds of these were fired at distances between 500 and 800 yards."[41] Forty rounds of practice per year might have qualified a man to hit an elephant at close range, but just barely. At distances of 500 to 800 yards, targets might just as well have been on the far side of the moon.

In some armies, marksmanship training was neglected not because its importance was not recognized, but because limited resources simply did not permit it. This has always been the case with insurgent forces, or in guerilla armies that had to rely on battlefield capture to arm and outfit their units; it has also been the case with conventionally organized units in civil wars where the supply of arms and ammunition was limited by political or economic constraints. For the Communist Chinese fighting against the nationalist Kuomintang army before 1939, this was their hard reality—rifles and ammunition were so limited that the Communists could not train their soldiers in target practice, since those assets had to be reserved for actual fighting. This produced a beneficial result, at least in a Darwinistic sense. "Training by actual combat," as one commentator has observed, "is always expensive but, for those who survive, effective."

Realistic training in this period was often notable by its absence. Robert Blatchford, a British soldier of the mid-nineteenth century, was of the opinion that "men were not taught to shoot, that not one man in 500 could use a bayonet effectively against sword or bayonet. . . . There was no instruction in taking cover, that the men had no practice in making trenches. . . . Scouting was not known, that too much time was wasted on mere pageantry, marching past, manual exercise, and other nonsense."[42]

Even if Blatchford is dismissed as a solitary, disgruntled soldier who had no favorable impressions of the army in which he served, the majority of other soldiers' personal narratives give some credence to his assertions. For decades, effective tactical training in the British Army was neglected more often than not, and the same sort of lapse occurred in the U.S. Army at almost the same time.

It was perhaps ironic that this was so, because at the beginning of this period, the British Army fielded what were probably the best-trained infantry formations in the world, at least in terms of their battle drill in musketry. The British practice of forming double lines of infantry-men who fired in alternating volley gave them a huge advantage in the amount of firepower they could bring to bear across their linear front; to achieve this in battle, they drilled their infantry regiments with a single-minded intensity. What made this training so effective, especially when those infantrymen stood in their ranks and leveled their muskets at the oncoming enemy on fields from Salamanca to Inkerman, was the fact that the British infantry fired live ball ammunition in their musketry drills. Remarkably, few other armies of that time did, though that may have had something to do with economics: "A single round," as one historian notes, "cost at that time almost as much as food for a full day."[43] Other armies recognized the combat value of the British tactics, but could not hope to match them. The Prussians, recognized as outstanding soldiers in their own right, "pointed out that their own troops, even in three-deep lines, did not have the discipline, training and individual stability to hold such formations and didn't try to use them."[44]

In contrast with the British, the French during the Napoleonic Wars deployed their infantry in massed columns, bringing the physical force of the columns to bear on an enemy's static position, which could never be as deep, front to back. It was the principle of the battering ram against the wall, and it was a tactic that consistently worked in battle against European armies of conscripted soldiers. It did not work against the fearsome mus-ketry of the British infantry. In battle after battle in the Peninsular War, the British demonstrated that a wide front of highly trained, well-disci-plined infantrymen who would stand their ground and fire one crashing volley after another in quick succession almost always trumped the more visually intimidating bulk of a brigade in column. Forty years later, in the Crimea, the same principle of British arms triumphed again when the disciplined, well-trained volleys of musket fire of Sir Colin Campbell's Highlanders, immortalized in William Howard Russell's description of a "thin red streak tipped with steel,"[45] stopped a Russian cavalry charge at Balaclava without ever forming into square. This redoubtable skill makes it all the more ironic that the British Army then proceded to neglet its marksmanskip training so badly during the 1870s.

Recruits who joined cavalry or artillery regiments might have thought their lives would be easier than their compatriots in the infantry, since at the very least their job descriptions entailed less walking, but they were quickly disabused of any notions of easy living. Novice cavalrymen and artillerymen had even more to learn in their new professions than did infantry recruits. After all, their chosen arms of service had the added requirements of horsemanship and technical skills, neither of which came naturally or easily to some men.

Contrary to what modern observers might assume, not every man of this period knew how to ride a horse; many, in fact, had never ridden at all before they joined the army. The process of learning to ride was often a daunting challenge. Some men found it to be more than they had bargained for, especially since the officers and NCOs who were their instructors had little sympathy for the new recruits' injured feelings. William Jett, who served with the 4th U.S. Cavalry in the 1880s, recalled one day's riding practice at the recruit depot at Jefferson Barracks:

> *Upon another occasion when the officer, with a whip in his hand, had us going around in a circle on the walk, trot, gallop, and run, a recruit fell from his horse to the ground, rolled right in the path of the running horses, and was trampled by several steeds before he could crawl to one side. "Get up," said the officer, "you will never make a good soldier till you get killed two or three times." The recruit wished for no second killing and could not be found the next day nor any day thereafter. We supposed he went home to his mother.*[46]

Learning to ride was not an overnight process. French soldiers who chose cavalry or artillery regiments when they were conscripted in the years just before the First World War were enlisted for two years, and no one was under any illusion that this was enough time to turn them into skilled horsemen. "Except in the case of men who were skilled riders before they came up for training," a French veteran wrote, "the French cavalry conscript is not a complete soldier by the time he has finished his two years. . . . All that can be done to make him efficient is done, though."[47] One can infer from this that the unfortunate conscript cavalryman was at least able to stay in the saddle by the time his enlistment was up, but perhaps little more than that.

When Fred Lloyd tried to enlist in a British infantry regiment in 1916, he was disqualified for being an inch too short at 5'7". When he was told that he could qualify for the Royal Field Artillery, Lloyd jumped at the chance. "I said that would do me all right," he remembered, "cos I'd be able to ride horses, even though I'd never touched a horse before." He learned quickly enough, though he initially found the big artillery horses to be intimidating.

Ascan Gobert, a German soldier of the First World War, had at least learned to ride before he enlisted into an Uhlans regiment, but there were still many things about the cavalryman's life that were utterly new to him. The old regulars of his regiment, he said, "were accustomed to everything, while we had never lived with a horse. The horse was the main thing for the next forty or fifty months. I never had a bed until I think November 1915, because we had always to sleep with the horses in granges or elsewhere."[48]

Gobert's perception of life with horses was shared by cavalrymen on the other side of that war. A British soldier of the Bedfordshire Yeomanry expressed his complaints about the horse as an article of military issue:

He debars you from spending the night anywhere in the neighborhood of civilization, because he takes up such a lot of room. . . . He keeps you standing about two hours longer than you need after a long march, because he is unable to clean or feed himself, and will leave you altogether unless firmly secured. . . . He drags you miles, two or three times a day, through mud that he has churned up with his feet and then refuses to drink at the end of it; he wears a mass of impedimenta with an unlimited capacity for getting dirty and unserviceable; he will bite or kick you on the smallest provocation, and at night he will keep honest men from their beds, because, unless closely watched, he will either hang himself or savage his neighbor.[49]

The somewhat ambiguous relationship of the cavalryman to his horse was common to the mounted arm in most armies. One French trooper echoed the opinion of cavalrymen the world over when he wrote, "As in all armies, the French cavalryman considers himself as good as two infantrymen." The truth, however, was a bit more nuanced. "Certainly, he rides," this soldier went on to say, "and this fact he is always ready to impress on the infantryman; what he keeps quiet about is that he has to groom the horse he rides, and to attend to its needs when the infantryman, having finished his march at practically the same time as the cavalryman finished his, has his meal cooked and eaten before his fellow of the mounted unit has got away from stables."[50] This reality was apparent to cavalry recruits almost from their first morning with their new regiments.

Alexander Somerville enlisted in the Scots Greys in 1831. The Greys were one of the British Army's premier heavy cavalry regiments, which was part of their attraction for Somerville; the fact that he barely knew one end of a horse from the other did not seem to have factored into his decision much at all. His description of a cavalry recruit's morning tasks gives an idea of how much work went into caring for cavalry horses and how unfamiliar everything would have been to soldiers who had never before worked with horses:

At a quarter to five in the morning the recruits must dress, roll their bedding on the iron bedstead, fold the blankets, the two sheets and the rug so that the colours of the rug shall appear through the folds of the sheets like streaks of marble. They must take the point of a knife and lay the edges of the fold straight until they look artistical to the eye. At 5.15 the stable trumpet sounds, and all hasten down to the stables. The litter must be shaken out, and all that is dry tied up, the other cleaned away. . . . If the recruit has not been active in getting downstairs to have his turn on the limited space, others will be there before him [and] if he be not yet beyond the point of having tricks played on him, he may be seen laying out his plaited bands and fancy straw on the stones, horses on each side kicking their hindfeet within a yard of his head. . . . A man tickles one of them to make him prance and strike the stones, or to toss back his litter upon the recruit. As if in a rage, the man professes to command the horse to stand still, and ask if it means to knock Johnny Raw's brains out?[51]

During the American Civil War John Billings served in a U.S. Army artillery battery; he found a great deal of amusement in the spectacle of new recruits who had a hard time adjusting to life with horses:

It was fun in the artillery to see one of these dainty men, on his first arrival, put in charge of a pair of spare horses. . . . It was expected of him that he would groom, feed, and water them. As it often happened that such a man had no experience in the care of horses, he would naturally approach the subject with a good deal of awe. When the Watering Call blew, therefore, and the bridles and horses were pointed out to him by the sergeant, the fun began. Taking the bridle, he would look first at it, then at the horse, as if in doubt which end of him to put it on. In going to water, the drivers always bridled the horse on which they rode, and led the other by the halter. But our unfledged soldier seemed innocent of all proper information. For the first day or two he would lead his charge; then, as his courage grew with acquaintance, he would finally mount the near one, and, with his legs crooked up like a V, cling for dear life until he got his lesson learned in this direction. But all the time that he was getting initiated he was a ridiculous object to observers.[52]

Charles Willeford had also never been astride a horse in his life when he enlisted in the U.S. Cavalry in the 1930s. "If you have the time," he wrote, "and the cavalry has all the time in the world, there's no better way to learn to ride a horse than the cavalry way:

Horses are big, and they frighten men who don't know anything about them. The first thing a man has to overcome is his basic, if unadmitted, fear of horses. We were all assigned gentle horses, well-trained trooper's mounts, and most of them were at least twelve years old. Each horse had its own personality and peculiar ways, and these had to be learned. A man could get hurt very easily if he wasn't careful.[53]

Recruits who enlisted for cavalry and artillery regiments quickly came to suspect that the army valued their horses more than them; the four-footed beasts certainly seemed to warrant more care and attention than did their two-footed counterparts. One British trooper, R. G. Garrod, remembered how the army impressed upon him the fact that monetarily, horses were more valuable than men: "They could get a new man for [one shilling]—a day," he wrote, "but a horse cost [forty pounds]."[54] The military requirement of accounting for every bit of army-issued equipment extended to horses, as well. The French Army in the Crimean War marked its horses' hoofs with a stock number—dead horses had to be accounted for by turning in the severed hoof to the quartermaster. "Every horse's corpse had its hoof amputated . . . to justify its loss to the Commissariat," trooper Charles Mismer wrote, "because in the middle of all this disaster, routine was the most important thing." Violations of that routine, even when caused by the demands of war, were not accepted by the bean counters in the supply sections. "In rain or snow, at the risk of killing one's own horse, it had to be done," Mismer recalled. "I have to say that the dilemma 'hoof or death' more than once drove me to exasperation."[55] Seventy years later, Willeford encountered a similar attitude in the U.S. Cavalry. "We took very good care of the animals," he wrote. "After all, a horse cost $145, whereas a new man to take care of this expensive horse could be found under almost any railroad bridge in America."[56] That was not far off the mark, in those grim years when the country was in the grip of the Great Depression.

A regular witticism among infantrymen of the nineteenth-century U.S. Army, as historian Don Rickey recounts, was the early morning remark, "There go the sore-asses to chambermaid their horses" when cavalry troopers on a combined-arms post had to head off to stable call while the infantry soldiers were still laying abed.[57] The sheer amount of work necessary to keep a horse in military order was almost always something of a shock to new recruits. When that labor was extended to the bewildering tinker's load of tack, saddlery, and other assorted paraphernalia that the regiment expected to be maintained along with the horse, more than a few cavalry recruits probably wished they had opted for infantry regiments, instead. "It may be imagined that the way of the cavalryman is not an easy one," a French soldier wrote, "for he has far more to learn than the infantryman. . . . He has to groom his horse, clean his saddle, keep the stables in order, and do all the things that are absolute necessities where horses are concerned. Then, too, he has nearly twice as much personal kit to look after as the infantryman."[58] It was much the same routine for cavalrymen of all armies. As Willeford remembered, "We spent about four hours each morning with the horses, which included riding, grooming, and cleaning equipment." There was at least one upside to the daily grind, he thought: "Riding every day explained why there were so few fat men in the cavalry. . . . A man could eat all he wanted, but daily riding kept his weight down to trim."[59] Many infantrymen begrudged the fact that the cavalry rode everywhere rather than walked, but probably few foot soldiers truly understood how much extra work was involved in the mounted arm.

Artillerymen in the age of horse-drawn artillery were in much the same situation as their colleagues in the cavalry, as far as their equine workload was concerned. If anything, gunners may have had even more to contend with. All the infantry recruit had to maintain was himself, his equipment, weapon, and barracks room; the cavalryman had all that plus his horse, its equipment, and its stable; the artilleryman had everything the infantryman and cavalryman had *plus* an extra horse apiece and the gun itself to look after. No wonder, then, that an artilleryman's "remarks, on coming in on a wet day after two or three hours' parade with the guns, might cause a little consternation in what is known as polite society, for two muddy horses with their saddlery and fittings, all to be dried and cleaned for the battery officer's inspection within a given time, are not conducive to elegance of expression or restraint."[60] A horse, as more than one disgruntled trooper or gunner would have complained as he picked burrs out of a matted tail while keeping an eye out for the occasional random kick, was almost more trouble than it was worth.

Armies have always understood that for training to be effective, it must be as realistic as possible. "As early as 1879," one history of the U.S. Army during the Indian Wars observes, "Sixth Cavalry replacements were taken on what would later be termed practice marches and bivouacs, to teach them something of conditions on active duty in the Southwest." This training was designed to include "simulated skirmishes" in which the new soldiers were "instructed in the tactics and techniques employed against the hostiles."[61] The results of insufficient or poor-quality training were painfully manifested on the battlefield, if the unprepared recruits were ever unfortunate enough to find themselves actually facing an armed enemy.

Ironically, then as now, the reality of soldiering was that the efficacy of an army's training could only fully be assessed in the crucible of actual war—up to that point, no matter how realistic it tried to be, the training inevitably had to fall short of the final reality. "There have been soldiers," Charles Carrington wrote in his First World War memoir, *Soldier from the Wars Returning,* "who have spent their lives in barracks without smelling powder, but we cannot judge their quality. A sailor is judged by sailing, but a soldier by fighting. In time of peace his training has an element of make-believe and his worth is not known until he comes under fire."[62] Thus, there was always an element of the unknowable when it came to the efficacy of soldiers' training, an element of the unknown that lasted right up until the shooting started, when the catalog of strengths and weaknesses could finally be evaluated in the only test that mattered. Still, some things *could* be taken as truisms. "Well-trained troops can fight effectively, even when poorly armed and equipped," one commentator notes of the Italian Army of the Second World War. "In contrast, superb weapons are of little use in the hands of badly instructed soldiers."[63]

From a modern military perspective, armies before the First World War did not usually train their soldiers in a wide array of individual skills, particularly during periods of peacetime service. The problem was not that the value of hard training was not recognized then—professional soldiers have *always* understood how important it is. But in the eras before the soldier's repertoire of tasks expanded to include such skills as radio communications, operating and maintaining crew-served infantry weapons such as machine guns and mortars, basic medical first-aid proficiency, indirect-fire coordination of artillery, and land navigation, there was not then as wide or intensive a variety of essential training as there is today.

Tough, effective, and realistic training is one of the factors that has always set professional soldiers apart. It is usually a costly process, which is one of the reasons why maintaining a ready-to-fight professional army has always been a prohibitively expensive proposition for any national treasury. The process of transforming recruits from civilians to soldiers is an essential part of any military system, though, and throughout this period different methods were employed by different armies to bring this transformation about. The results varied widely, as one might expect. At any rate, once this initial training was complete, the next step in the process was for new soldiers to begin finding their way in this new life and to understand their place in it. They also began to understand the structure and complexities of the relationships that governed military society and confronted the fact that they now had a pantheon of demanding new demigods to placate and obey—the NCOs and officers who were the taskmasters of this uniformed world.

CHAPTER THREE

Officers, NCOs, and "Other Ranks"

Superiors and Subordinates

The generals risked their reputation, the private soldier his life.
— SAM WATKINS

IT IS (OR SHOULD BE) SELF-EVIDENT that the army is a strictly hierarchical society. Even people who have no personal experience of the military know at least *that* much about it, though they often err in their impressions of just how the hierarchy actually works in practice. In every army there are those who lead and those who are led, those who command and those who obey. By the beginning of this period, in 1800, that demarcation was clearly defined in most armies by codified regulations that stipulated three distinctly separate strata of soldiers: officers, noncommissioned officers, and enlisted men. The first two categories are easily identified, but the third is a bit more problematic in a comparative international history such as this, because the terms used to describe that bottom tier vary a bit from army to army and decade to decade.

The collective term *enlisted men* perhaps best suits our purposes here, but it brings with it its own seed of confusion: NCOs are themselves enlisted men (though during much of this period the most senior NCO ranks in the British, French, and German armies were often designated as warrant officer positions), but in this context, they are absolutely distinct from the enlisted men of lower ranks. The British Army has long used the term *other ranks*, or ORs, to distinguish between its NCOs and private soldiers. Historically, private soldiers is precisely what the lower ranks were traditionally called. In both the American and British armies, it was once also common to use the phrase "officers, NCOs, and men" when referring to a unit entire. With the modern inclusion of women into military positions that until recently were exclusively male, this descriptive phrase has largely been discarded, but it can still be applied in some cases.

When Needham N. Freeman enlisted in the U.S. Army in 1898, it was not a spontaneous decision—he thought about joining up for a long time before he finally took that step. Soldiering was tougher than he expected, but still he adapted quickly enough to the physical requirements of his new profession. What was harder for him to accept was the institutionalized hierarchy of rank that governed every aspect of military life. Writing after his discharge from the army at the completion of his term of service, Freeman wrote, "A private may think all or anything he pleases, but he does not have an opportunity to say very much about anything. He must obey the commands of his officers."[1] For a young man raised in the independence-minded society of the United States, where individualism was prized and subservience of any kind was an anathema, the army's culture of unquestioning obedience was truly foreign to many native-born recruits.

Some men adapted quickly, almost effortlessly, to military life, but others struggled to come to terms with it their entire time in uniform. In order to get by in the army, one American observer wrote, a man had to tell himself, "'be calm—be calm, indignant heart' almost every day of his life; must muzzle his tongue, quell his spirit." That was a very hard thing to do for men who resented a system in which they toiled at the bottom, even if it was their own decision to enlist that put them there in the first place. As the writer quoted above described the U.S. Army's chain of command, "the corporal 'sits down' upon the private; the sergeant upon the corporal; the lieutenant upon the sergeant; the captain upon the lieutenant; the major upon the captain; the lieutenant-colonel upon the major; the colonel upon the lieutenant-colonel; and the General upon the whole pile. Thus, the nethermost man gets pretty well flattened out, if the others are in bad humor." It was a social order that soldiers of every army were familiar with and resented in their individual ways.[2]

The subordination of self to the restrictive and very vertical structure of the military lifestyle was perhaps easier for men in some cultures than others. Young German men, from the famously militarized society that characterized Germany in the Bismarck years and afterward, entered the army with full expectation of the rigid command environment they encountered in the ranks—even if they did not like it, they were at least culturally prepared for it. This was also true of Japanese soldiers, particularly those who served in the Imperial Army in the years following the Meiji Restoration, when their civil society was increasingly dominated by the Japanese military.

This is not to say, however, that German and Japanese men were therefore always enthusiastic soldiers who gladly subjected themselves to the sometimes-brutal regimens of military discipline. The narratives of veterans from both of those armies often expressed their deep unhappiness at being pulled from their civilian lives and forced into uniform whether they wished it or not. Whether it was for reasons of culture or something else, though, the evidence in their own personal stories is that they were usually not surprised by the iron-handed leadership and harsh treatment they endured while they were in uniform—that seems to have simply been the army that they expected, and so it proved to be in fact.

No army of this period could be said to have been a truly democratic organization. Such a concept is completely at odds with the necessities of military life and the abiding reasons for armies' very existence. In 1918, as we have already seen, the Bolsheviks famously tried to run their first incarnation of the Red Army on egalitarian lines, and just as famously failed in the attempt. For the United States and Great Britain, the two countries most responsible for the development of modern democracy, there were always questions about the compatibility (or incompatibility) of an autocratic military system composed of men who had to relinquish many of their rights as citizens as soon as they enlisted. The irony of men being deprived of their individual liberties so that they could fight in defense of democratic ideals was an irony not lost on them or on numerous outside observers.

The First World War correspondent Philip Gibbs considered this question at length. British soldiers of that war, he wrote, "had been told that they were fighting for liberty. But their first lesson was the utter loss of individual liberty under a discipline which made the private soldier no more than a number. They were ordered about like galley-slaves, herded about like cattle, treated individually and in the mass with utter disregard of their comfort and well-being." A soldier's lot could be one of thankless servitude, at least when the military's treatment of them seemed to neglect their individual value as men. It was an insult to British soldiers as Englishmen, Gibbs wrote, that they "were bullied and bundled about, not like human beings, but like dumb beasts, and in thousands of ways injustice, petty tyranny, hard work, degrading punishments for trivial offenses . . . made the name of personal liberty a mockery."[3]

What Gibbs described in literary terms, private soldiers expressed for themselves from their own experiences. Bill Sugden enlisted in the British Army in answer to his country's call for men, but what he found once he was in uniform was an unpleasant shock. "Our sergeant major is an absolute pig," he wrote. "He swears and strikes the men. . . . It is a cowardly thing to do as he knows the men dare not strike back. . . . They seem to forget we have all given up our jobs to do our best for the country, and do not expect to be treated like a lot of rifraf [sic]."[4] American soldiers made similar complaints—if not in the particulars, then certainly in the sentiments.

In a discussion of this aspect of the soldier's life, it can be tempting to accept the plethora of national stereotypes that muddle this part of military service—that Germans were unquestioning followers of strong leadership, or that Americans and Australians were so undisciplined as to barely be soldiers at all, that British soldiers in the early nineteenth century were so truly "the scum of the earth" that brutal punishments like flogging were the only thing that kept them in line, or that Italians as a rule made poor soldiers. The overused generalities go on and on nearly ad infinitum. As Oliver Wendell Holmes once so wryly pointed out, "No generalization is worth a damn, including this one,"[5] and so it bears remembering there were exceptions to be found in every case, in every army, throughout this period.

Another stereotype (one that has perhaps a bit more truth at its foundation) is the old and somewhat tired maxim that senior commanders do not understand the trials and tribulations of the individual men who make up the human mass of the armies under their command. This criticism was certainly true of some, perhaps even most, of the generals of this period, but here again there were notable exceptions. Even in an age when the holding of high military rank was usually the exclusive preserve of the aristocratically born and politically well-connected, there were always some departures—the American army never really fit that mold, after all. As a representative example of what I mean, consider the case of Robert Hall. Hall's career in the U.S. Army was notable, but it was by no means singular or even very unique. A veteran of the "Old Army" of the pre–Civil War years, Hall had originally emigrated from Scotland and enlisted as an artilleryman in 1848. He rose through the NCO ranks and was a sergeant major when the Civil War began in 1861, at which point he accepted an officer's commission as a second lieutenant. Soldiering apparently suited him, because he stayed on in the Regular Army as an artillery officer after the war. Before he died on active duty in 1874, he had received brevet promotions all the way up to the rank of brigadier general of volunteers; his last brevet was awarded, in part, "for completeness as an officer during the time he held a command in the Army." He was by no means the only man to start low and finish high, and to do it all on the basis of his individual merit. Likewise, the postrevolutionary French Army under Napoleon was in notable cases led by men whose glittering imperial titles never completely obscured the fact that they came from decidedly unaristocratic origins.

The British Army of the Victorian era was very much a microcosm of the class-conscious society from which it was drawn, yet it also had its exceptions to this norm, even if there were far fewer such cases. William Robertson, whose career spanned the years 1877 to 1920, famously enlisted in the army as a private and retired as a field marshal, and even served as chief of the Imperial General Staff. Granted, he was the only man in British history to have made such a climb through the ranks, all the way from bottom to top, but he did it, and there were other officers of equally plebeian origins whose careers were equally impressive, even if they did not rise quite as high. In an age when most officers of the British Army advanced in rank based on their ability to purchase the next step in promotion, rather than being promoted based on any merit or ability, John Colborne was a notable exception. A protégé of General Sir John Moore and a veteran of the retreat to Corunna in 1804, Colborne entered the army as an ensign and retired as a field marshal without having purchased a single step of advancement along the way—his promotions were all awarded on the basis of his outstanding professional ability.[6]

Even when these exceptions to the rule are acknowledged, though, it still holds true that a gulf of separation existed between the foot soldier in the rifle company and the general who commanded the corps in which that man was just one soldier among thousands. It is not in the least bit spurious, I believe, to say that by and large the generals who commanded armies in this period had little empathy with the day-to-day existence of the soldiers beneath them. That does not mean they did not care, or that they were unable to remember from their own experience as junior officers what that life had been like, but the remove of years and the intervening levels of rank created what was often a complete disconnect. If nothing else, by the twentieth century the reality of war increasingly meant that the higher an officer's rank, the further to the rear of the lines his duties placed him, and that physical distance from the hazards and risks of battle translated into an emotional and mental distance from the lives of the soldiers who did the fighting and dying. At the same time, it is worth pointing out that in the First World War, at least seventy-eight British generals were killed in action or died in the course of serving in the lines. This would to some degree refute the persistent notion that tens of thousands of British soldiers died in that war because of the calloused incompetence of generals who issued their orders so far from the front that they had no concept of the reality of the ground—that idea is a mainstay of popular histories of the First World War, but it is not always accurate.

Reading through the narratives of ordinary soldiers, however, it is clear that the common soldier frequently believed his senior commanders had little regard for him as an individual or understood his problems. One French veteran of the First World War wrote, "So far as the rank and file of the French Army are concerned, no officer above the rank of colonel is of consequence, for the man in the ranks is not likely to come into contact with a general officer once in a twelvemonth."[7] Opinions such as that become more common, and even more negative, when the soldier at the sharp end felt that their leadership was of poor quality.

An American soldier serving in a Minnesota regiment during the Civil War, writing home after the bloody disaster of Fredericksburg in December 1862, expressed the ranker's opinions of who it was that suffered when incompetent generals were given command of the army.

"Gen. Burnside may say that he left nothing behind in his retreat," he wrote, "but the upturned faces of the dead give a silent but overwhelming contradiction."[8] A month later little had changed. "In feeling, the army is much demoralized," the same soldier wrote in January. "Confidence in the leaders and in the success of the cause being almost wholly wanting . . . nothing can dissipate the gloom but a change of commanders."[9]

Almost the exact same sentiments were expressed in different armies. During the savage fighting for the Wytschaete Ridge in 1917, British troops were thrown against stubborn German defenses in wave after wave of assaults. The British attacks were successful, but at terrible cost— whether the tactical value of the position was worth the lives lost to take it was a matter of bitter skepticism for the men in the ranks. The reasons for the horrifically bloody offensive, one observer wrote, were "only known by our generals and God."[10] Whatever those mysterious reasons were, the men in the ranks concluded, they had paid too high a price for an objective for which no one felt they deserved an explanation.

When soldiers resented their officers, particularly those at the senior echelons of command, they did not restrain their bitterness. "Our people treated us like dogs. They were cruel bastards compared with the Germans," one British infantryman of the First World War said. "I remember a major from the East Surreys. In any conditions, he used to get us out on parade, march us up and down. He was a rotten swine. Eventually we heard that somebody shot him. That sort of thing could happen."[11] On the other side of that war, an Austrian soldier wrote, "Our General Staff was in part very bad. . . . These gentlemen sat with their backs turned and gave their orders. Hardly ever did they see the men at the front or where the bullets whistled. During the war the troops learned to *hate* the General Staff." As was demonstrated time and again throughout this period, the enlisted men on both sides of a conflict often bore more animosity toward their own generals than they did their enemies.[12] French soldiers of the First World War had a saying that left no doubt as to the bitterness that lay behind it: "Generals die in bed."

Some of the most insightful and bitingly irreverent commentaries on overly officious, spit-and-polish officers come from soldiers who were keen observers and who also had a gift for expressive language. The senior commanders whose priorities often seemed utterly pointless to men who lived in the midst of death, misery, and fear drew the bitter resentment of the junior ranks in all armies. A. P. Herbert, who served with the Royal Naval Division (RND) in the hell that was Gallipoli, expressed the widespread frustration the men in the division felt with their new commander, Major General Cameron Shute. The RND was an anachronistic formation of sailors and marines that fought ashore as an infantry division but stubbornly clung to its naval traditions; Shute's strictly conventional military mind could not abide that, even though the RND proved itself a first-rate combat division. After one of Shute's critical inspections of the RND's trenches at Ancre, Herbert wrote a poem to commemorate the event:

> The General inspecting the trenches
> Exclaimed with a horrified shout
> 'I refuse to command a division
> Which leaves its excreta about.'
>
> But nobody took any notice
> No one was prepared to refute,
> That the presence of shit was congenial
> Compared to the presence of Shute.
>
> And certain responsible critics
> Made haste to reply to his words
> Observing that his staff advisors
> Consisted entirely of turds.
>
> For shit may be shot at odd corners
> And paper supplied there to suit,
> But a shit would be shot without mourners
> If somebody shot that shit Shute.

It was not polite, nor was it refined literature, but it was a feeling that soldiers the world over could appreciate.

COMMISSIONED OFFICERS

Contrary to what one might think, it is not necessarily true that soldiers' lives are ruled by the capricious whims of their officers. Officers themselves, after all, are also governed by military rule and regulation, and theirs is not an unlimited authority. Neither do the officers always enjoy lives of indolent luxury and gentrified ease, even if the enlisted men often accuse them of doing so. After all, during this period the officers at the company, battalion, and regimental levels of infantry, cavalry, and armor units lived and fought with their men, led them conspicuously from the front, and frequently died there. If officers of that day were accorded greater creature comforts and a better quality of life than were the men under their command, it was also true that those officers were expected to display greater bravery and a more nonchalant attitude toward personal risk than was perhaps expected of the common soldier.

Even so, the quality of leadership that men observed in their officers is one of the most commonly cited factors that influenced whether they remembered their time in the army as being a good experience or a bad one. Warren Olney, who fought in the American Civil War, wrote, "No one who has not been through the experience can realize the anxiety of the private soldier [concerning] the character and capacity of his commanding officer."[13] A conscientious, humane, and professional officer could make something of the most mediocre company; an officer who was a petty tyrant, or a martinet who insisted on living by the rule book, or who was just plain stupid, could ruin the best company. "It is a mistake to think that private soldiers are not, after a certain amount of experience, able to size up their commanders in a fairly correct way," another Civil War veteran wrote. "If there is a master mind at the head, they know it very quickly."[14]

That perspective is echoed in the accounts of enlisted men of all eras. "The enlisted men had the same gripe about the officers, I'm sure, that they've had ever since Hannibal," Robert Fair said of his time in the 1st U.S. Infantry Division in 1944. "The Army didn't know what they were doing, they were making mistakes, they were getting us in trouble, we're going to win despite our officers." Despite those grumbles, he went on to say, he and his fellow infantrymen had a much more positive outlook on their officers than that litany of complaint would suggest. "That was just normal," he said. "We didn't really feel that way. We had a lot of confidence in our leadership."[15] Another veteran of the same division said, "As far as the officers, they can't keep me off of KP now so I'll tell you this. We never had a bad officer the whole time. We had two or three different company commanders, platoon leaders. . . . We never had a bad officer."[16] Many American soldiers expressed that sort of view, when it was warranted, but confidence in the leadership ability of their platoon and company officers did not mean that other grievances were not simmering beneath the surface.

"Officers," Raymond Gantter wrote of his experience in the U.S. Army during the Second World War, "do not fully appreciate the small miseries that wear on enlisted men."[17] His observation was not just the complaint of an enlisted man who resented the privileges of his superiors—Gantter enlisted as a private and finished the war as a lieutenant, so he saw the matter from both sides of the issue. The disconnect that he described was particularly true during the eras when rigid social lines separated officers and enlisted men. Not only the inherent authority of an officer's rank, but also the dividing strata of social class, ornate uniforms, and such ritualized arcana as the officers' mess further served to emphasize the gulf that separated the leaders from the led in some armies.

When other features of officers' privilege during this period were added to the equation, such as separate latrine facilities for officers and the fact that officers were allowed to drink alcohol in situations when the enlisted men were forbidden to imbibe, a natural and understandable resentment quickly percolated up from the lower ranks. These institutionally imposed dividers between officers and enlisted men were rigidly in place at the beginning of the period and to varying degrees all throughout it. All European armies, certainly the British, applied this stricture. Even the rather more casual American military endorsed this rigid demarcation of privilege between officers and enlisted men at least until after 1945, a fact that was a sore point in the narratives of many U.S. Army enlisted soldiers during the period.

Of course, officers were not a monolithic entity, not in any army. There were bad ones, to be sure, but others who were excellent. "I got to know some good officers and I got to know some real jerks," one German soldier said of his time on the Eastern Front in the Second World War. "There were some who when they had the uniform on remained good soldiers, there were others who became self-important. That's probably true in all armies."[18] Most enlisted men of other armies would probably have agreed with that statement. As one American veteran of the Philippine-American War wrote, "The army is all right when its officers are all right. But many of them fall far short of the standard—officers who will not give a private justice as he should."[19]

If draconian, overly officious, or inept officers had the ability to crush a unit's spirit and destroy its cohesion, an officer who inspired respect by his personal example had exactly the opposite effect. Merritt Hinkel, who fought in the Philippines in 1944 as an airborne infantryman with the U.S. Army's 188th Glider Infantry Regiment, had the utmost respect for his platoon leader, Lieutenant Bush. "He was a man, a soldier's soldier," Hinkel wrote. "He always put us first. His family needs to know what happened. . . . On Nichols Field or near Fort McKinley when several of our guys were hit, the guys said, 'We'll go get them.' I think there were two men out there." Lieutenant Bush, Hinkel recalled, refused to let anyone else take the risk, saying, "'No, they are my men. Just cover me.' They were in a ditch or draw, and Bush went over the top to rescue the men. And this guy [a Japanese soldier] jumped up and before anybody could do anything, he shot and killed Bush."[20]

Howard Baxter, a USMC paratrooper who survived the maelstrom of Iwo Jima, watched his platoon's combat effectiveness crumble as one officer after another was killed. "We lost three platoon leaders. . . . We'd lost a lot of men, and our morale was low," Baxter said. "You reach a point and you'd say, 'The hell with this. I'm not going to get out of my foxhole.'" All of that changed with the arrival of the next replacement officer, Second Lieutenant Ira Goldberg. The new lieutenant, Baxter remembered, had no combat experience, but he was a natural, effective leader and he quickly turned things around. "He was a very quiet man, a learned man, well educated," Baxter said. "He never shouted or lost his temper. He was only with us four or five days. He instilled morale in the platoon the short time he was with us. Whenever we had to start advancing again, he didn't shout or yell at us. His coolness under fire, leadership, he was the kind of

Marine we wished we could have been. He led us by example." As was so often the case, it was an example that came at a high price. "A few days later, he got cut in half by a machine gun," Baxter said.[21]

German narratives give plenty of examples of soldiers' views of their leadership, both good and bad. One German infantry NCO who survived the savage fighting on the Somme in 1916 wrote of his experience when his company of the 66th Infantry Regiment held out under ferocious British assault for nine days, a performance that he directly attributed to the leadership of his battalion commander, Hauptmann Niemeyer:

> *How was it possible for the 4th Company to hold out from 5th to 14th September? Here the old catch phrase applied, 'Words teach, but deeds impress.' Our battalion commander, through his actions, gave his men an incomparable example of devotion to duty. Day and night he lay forward amongst us in shell holes, wherever the fight was hottest. He held on when all around him failed. The fact that the Schwaben Redoubt held out during those days was due to the devotion to duty of our battalion commander, Hauptmann Niemeyer. I well remember that there were times when only he and those closest to him held on forward in a shell hole, the remainder have fled. When the fire slackened, we used to lead forward the soldiers as unobtrusively as possible, so that he would not notice anything. He really put us to shame and in so doing earned the total loyalty of all his soldiers to their commander.[22]*

Soviet soldiers in the early days of the Second World War suffered from a lack of effective combat leadership as a direct consequence of their army's subordination to a rigid political system. As a Wehrmacht assessment of the Soviet Army noted, "Lower echelon Russian commanders revealed a certain lack of initiative in the execution of orders." That dry, official language understated what was the abiding handicap of Soviet tactical leadership—frontline officers, the ones actually in the fight, could not or would not alter the plans dictated to them from above, and thousands of enlisted men died as a result. "While the Russian soldier had the innate faculty of adapting himself easily to technological innovations and overcoming mechanical difficulties, the lower echelon commanders seemed incapable of coping with sudden changes in the situation and acting on their own initiative," the German report continued. "Fear of punishment in the event of failure may have motivated their reluctance to make independent decisions."[23] That was not an exaggeration. There were far too many examples of battalion and company commanders being summarily executed by the NKVD for anyone to doubt the accuracy of the assessment, and ordinary Soviet soldiers paid the price with their lives.

As already noted, enlisted men often assumed that the life of a commissioned officer in the army was one of privilege and deferment, having all the prerogatives and privileges of command with none of the labor, drudgery, and deprivation that fall to the lower ranks. Like most stereotypes, there is an element of truth buried somewhere in that perception, but the reality is usually rather different than that narrow view, and this was true of most of the armies we are considering in this text.

Military rank draws a clear line of separation between the leaders and the led, for reasons that often have little to do with archaic notions of social class or entitlement. This division between the officers and the men owes as much (or more) to the simple reality that the nature of military operations relies on obedience to orders, and there is truth in the old idea that familiarity breeds contempt. An officer could enjoy the respect and obedience, and even the affection, of his men, but he had to walk a fine line of professional propriety to not transgress too far into the realm of casual friendship. After all, the nature of the martial profession required that those officers must be willing, when the situation called for it, to order those same men out to their probable deaths. An officer needed to be humane and accessible, but also had to maintain a professional distance from the men he led.

Critics who inveigh against the privileges enjoyed by the army's officers too often overlook the counterweight to that privilege—the enormous burden of responsibility. The greater the rank, the greater the responsibility, and in most armies, that reality has always held true. Enlisted men were not completely off the mark when they complained that senior officers reaped all the glory from battles and wars that were actually won by the rank and file's fighting and dying, but the same criticism could not as fairly be made of officers at the sharp end. An officer

73

on the front lines could be strict but still personable, and good leadership inspired fierce loyalty. One British infantryman described his regimental commander, Colonel Crawshay, as "the best we ever had." The colonel was described as being "a stickler for discipline," a fact that did not prevent him from being almost revered by the enlisted men. That probably had everything to do with his style of leadership. This soldier wrote that when his regiment went into the trenches, "no matter what the conditions were, [Crawshay] was always visiting the front-line trenches and seeing things for himself. He had a cheery word for everyone and was as brave as they come."[24] Officers like that, most soldiers agreed, were worth following.

The nature of battle throughout this period meant that officers were expected to lead from the front, and so when the privates in the rifle line hunched their shoulders against the weight of their own mortality and walked forward into the enemy's fire, they did so with their company officers leading the way. One might argue that a greater courage was required of the young officer in a nineteenth-century infantry company or cavalry troop, because while the social conventions of that era would at least understand that an illiterate tradesman's son might be overcome by the natural fear of battle and make a break for the rear, a similar latitude was not extended to the much younger viscount's son who was supposed to be the personification of insouciant fearlessness and unperturbed courage.

At the beginning of this period and through much of the nineteenth century, many of the young men who held rank as company-grade officers were shockingly young. Some of them were still boys, literally. In the era when the British Army allowed officer's commissions to be purchased, and the U.S. Army appointed some of its officers on the basis of political appointment or popular election, the ensigns, cornets, lieutenants, and captains at the sharp end of the spear might well be callow youths, boys barely out of puberty.

Enlisted men held opinions of their officers that varied according to the officers in question, and those opinions were not always expressed with the deference that military customs and courtesies might have required. Soldiers in the lower ranks were not free to say whatever they felt in plain language in the hearing of their commanders (though they most assuredly expressed themselves freely when out of earshot, and usually in terms of astonishingly creative profanity), but they were masters of biting sarcasm whenever they thought they could get away with it. Carlton McCarthy, a Confederate infantryman, wrote of a favorite means of the common soldiers to express their feelings about their officers:

Occasionally, when the column extended for a mile or more, and the road was one dense moving mass of men, a cheer would be heard away ahead, increasing in volume as it approached, until there was one universal shout. Then some favorite general officer, dashing by, followed by his staff, would explain the cause. At other times, the same cheering and enthusiasm would result from the passage down the column of some obscure and despised officer, who knew it was all a joke, and looked mean and sheepish accordingly.[25]

If nothing else, there was a safe anonymity in numbers, and many enlisted men took full advantage of the faceless mass of the ranks to vent their feelings when they thought they could get away with it. Confederate soldiers had a particular reputation for doing this (much as Australian soldiers would some years later), and they held nothing back when it came to their dislike for the staff echelons. "The average staff officer and courier were always called 'yaller dogs,' and regarded as noncombatants and a nuisance, and the average private never let one pass without whistling and calling dogs," one infantryman remembered. "In fact, the general had to issue an army order threatening punishment for the ridicule hurled at staff officers and couriers. . . . They were looked upon as simply 'hangers on,' or in other words, as yellow sheep-killing dogs."[26]

Years after the fact, released from the constraints of military regulations, many enlisted men remembered the good officers they had known with praise and the bad ones with altogether different opinions. An American cavalryman named Ami Frank Mulford wrote in 1878, "Bad officers are sure to spoil good soldiers. . . . I believe the principal cause of desertion is the manner in which many of the harsh officers treat the enlisted men."[27] Many of his contemporaries in the U.S. Army of the Indian Wars era shared that perspective, but that was not to say that all officers were bad or that all enlisted men resented them. A group of enlisted men in the

25th U.S. Infantry, then serving in Fort Davis, Texas, wrote a memorial for their late company commander which was published in the *Army and Navy Journal* in 1873:

> *Whereas, Our Creator has been pleased to deprive us of our beloved company commander, Captain James H. Patterson, Twenty-fifth Infantry; therefore be it Resolved, That while we meekly bow in submission to the will of God, we realize that by his death the Army has been deprived of a faithful and honorable officer, and we of a just and kind commander, who ever listened to our slightest grievances, and who was never known to injure in the least degree any enlisted man; he was a father to our company; his loss is irreparable. Resolved. That to his noble wife and to his little boy Johnny, "our pet," we tender our heartfelt sympathy.*[28]

Officers were never all of a single type, of course, though certain characteristics were commonly found in certain armies of the period. The same individual differences that applied to the enlisted men were at work among the officers, as well—it was just that by dint of their positions and authority, officers had an outsized influence over the lives of the men under their authority. Those who thought their rank was the only thing that mattered were generally not well-regarded by their subordinates.

Joachim Pusch offered such an assessment more than sixty years after his time in the Wehrmacht had ended. He remembered one case where a young lieutenant, newly arrived in his company, ignored the warnings of the veteran NCOs that he should reverse his cap so the insignia would not draw the fire of Soviet snipers. The lieutenant scoffed at the warning, and a moment later a bullet creased his scalp. "See, this is what the ordinary soldiers and the NCOs didn't like," Pusch told his American interviewer. "This kind of an attitude of 'nothing can happen. . . . I'm a lieutenant.' You see. They won't take warnings or anything. They just knew better. I'm dead sure that this was encountered in your army the same way. I'm sure. I don't think in that respect armies are different."[29]

There was some truth to that. The story of bullheaded officers charging headlong toward disaster over the protestations of their experienced

NCOs is almost a fixture in armies around the world, a tale overtold and often exaggerated. Here again, though, this caricature of incompetent leadership has at least a few underpinnings of fact buried in all the fiction. One American infantryman's experience in France in 1944 provides a case in point. A new lieutenant in his unit ordered a three-man recon team to cross an open field toward a tree line that he suspected concealed a German position. There were indeed Germans hiding there, and when they opened fire, all three men of the recon were killed. "Undaunted still, the lieutenant proposed to lead the rest of the platoon over the same route," this soldier wrote. "Our noncoms saved a lot of lives that day; they flatly refused to obey his orders, and he gave way before their fierce insubordination."[30]

NONCOMMISSIONED OFFICERS

Kipling famously wrote that "the backbone of the Army is the non-commissioned man."[31] That this has long been true in the American, British, and German armies, is borne out by the fact that in those forces the NCOs are the link between officers and enlisted men and have functioned as the instructors, trainers, disciplinarians, counselors, and overseers of the armies in which they serve. They also serve as first-line combat leaders. It is the long-service NCOs, more than any other strata of the military hierarchy, who are the institutional memory of their armies.

The role of the noncommissioned officer, in his varied forms, was recognized all throughout this period even though not all armies placed equal weight of responsibility or authority on the position. In the earlier days most armies had only two ranks of noncommissioned officer—corporals and sergeants. As time went on and the administrative systems of nineteenth-century armies expanded, so too did the need for the professional skills and experience that career NCOs brought to the equation, and so the NCO ranks were expanded to meet those needs. Both the American and British armies designated the senior NCO in a regiment or battalion a sergeant major. (Instead of sergeants major, British cavalry regiments for a brief time had corporals-major, an archaic rank that sounds absolutely odd to the modern military ear.) At various times there were also quartermaster sergeants, colour sergeants, lance corporals, lance sergeants, staff sergeants, and others. Cavalry regiments had positions such as saddlers, farriers, and riding masters, which were all specialized positions held by NCOs. The U.S. Army of the nineteenth century added the position of first sergeants to their ranks, then master sergeants (which might or might not be the same pay grade, depending on the year in question), and over time the various rank titles of technical sergeants, specialists (fourth class up to eighth class), and platoon sergeants appeared and disappeared from the rosters.

The process by which soldiers were promoted from the ranks to fill these positions of responsibility was usually one into which armies put a good deal of careful thought. Proven experience was almost always a prerequisite, along with a demonstrated capacity for what the U.S. Army refers to as "technical and tactical proficiency." A combination of ambition, intelligence, demonstrated ability, and the regiment's need usually brought about promotion to NCO rank. The 1848 Standing Orders of the British Army's 90th Light Infantry stipulated that "Intelligence and Good Conduct alone will entitle the Non-Commissioned Officers to promotion; seniority will never be considered, unless accompanied by merit." In times when the army was rapidly expanded at the outbreak of war or widespread mobilization, however, it was all too common that men who were barely more than novices themselves were rapidly promoted to NCO rank, not knowing much more than the men whom they were placed in charge of.

Men of long service made up most of the NCOs in any given regiment, but not every man with years of soldiering to his credit aspired to an NCO's chevrons. In every army of the nineteenth century there were always some men who were career privates, never receiving or seeking promotion and never rising much above the rank at which they had first enlisted. Sometimes this was a result of a career checkered with disciplinary infractions; sometimes it was a case of a clear lack of intelligence or ability. Often enough, however, it was also the case that some men simply had no ambition for advancement, and had no desire to deal with the additional responsibilities that came with promotion.

In the U.S. Army, some soldiers worked for promotion and tried to climb the ladder, even to the point of applying for one of the officers' commissions that were available to enlisted men each year. Other men refused even the minor advancement to corporal and did everything they could to stay as far as possible from positions of responsibility (and the increased proximity to officers that such promotions entailed). When William Jett was informed that he was being promoted to corporal in his company of the 4th U.S. Cavalry, he tried to decline the stripes, he wrote, "because a non-commissioned officer is brought in such close contact with officers, and the less an enlisted man comes in contact with an officer the better off he is." Jett's troop commander overruled his protestations, and he reluctantly sewed on the two chevrons of his new rank. He was nothing if not determined, however, and he contrived to lose the unwanted promotion at the first opportunity so that he could revert to being a private, once again going about his business at a comfortable distance from the officers.[32] That reluctance to accept the responsibility that came with promotion was not limited to American soldiers. Martin Poppel, a German *fallschirmjaeger* of the Second World War, wrote that in his company the "*Hauptgefreite* and *Stabsgefriete* [privates first class and lance corporals, essentially] could really give their superiors a rough time. Moreover, they were always careful to commit some major or minor misdemeanor so they wouldn't get promoted. They were brave fellows but they just wanted to go their own way."[33]

Once a man sewed on the chevrons of a corporal or sergeant, the simple life he knew instantly changed. As the Standing Orders of one Scottish regiment instructed in 1812, "From the moment a private soldier is promoted to the rank of corporal, all intimacy between him and the men should cease."[34] Variations of the same admonishment appeared in British Standing Orders throughout the nineteenth century, such as the one that directed, "A Non-Commissioned Officer is on no account to drink or associate with the men; he must associate with those of his own rank."[35] Another issue of Standing Orders declared, "It is impossible for a Non-Commissioned Officer to preserve authority over the men if he ever associates with them on terms of familiarity; this is, therefore, most positively forbidden." These orders went on to say that NCOs were to "never, on any pretense whatever, walk in the streets with private soldiers."[36] The same proscriptions were in place in the U.S. Army at various times.

The responsibilities shouldered by NCOs were considerable, so much so that by 1897 the British Army's general Standing Orders stated, "The duties of a Non-Commissioned Officer are so numerous and various that it is hardly possible to enumerate them all."[37] Sergeants were the primary trainers of new recruits and young officers alike; they also were the subject matter experts in parade drill, marksmanship, horsemanship, gunnery, and the long list of other martial skills necessary for professional soldiering.

In both garrison and field environments, NCOs filled numerous roles in the running of their units, both with their own inherent tasks, and by default when the officers of their units were killed or wounded. The list of what could be described as "sergeants' business" was apparently limitless and ever-expanding, and carried with it considerable stress. Earnest Shepard was a company sergeant major serving in France during the First World War, and his description of his duties sounds familiar to any senior NCO. Even in the chaos of shell fire and combat actions, the army's obsession with paperwork never let up. "I get very little rest, as in addition to doing trench duties, care of stores and supervision of discipline, etc.," he noted in his diary, "I write out every report required by Bn HQ, i.e. situation reports at 3 a.m. and 3 p.m., ammunition and stores required report, Intelligence report 11 a.m., casualty report 12 noon, tactical progress 2 p.m., location of casualties 6 p.m." And so on it went, almost without end. The army's administration functions and bureaucratic processes continued despite the war being fought in the trenches. "Every few hours I get a message asking for names of men for course of Lewis gunnery, trench mortar, Stokes gun, physical training, cooking, signaling, etc.," Shepard wrote in his diary. "We are already under strength a good deal, and this constant demand for men to be trained as specialists causes less strength now, and later when these men have finished their courses they are likely to be called for to fill vacancies caused by casualties in the various specialist units. The whole idea is entirely wrong to my thinking."[38]

Sergeants were also the first strata of military authority in a soldier's world (and often the loudest and most profane voices of that authority) and were the nearly omniscient and apparently omnipresent figures of discipline. When they were good, they were father figures to their men; when they were bad, they were tyrants. In 1843, a British soldier offered his opinion on why so many men chose to desert the ranks from one particular station. "I have frequently heard it stated since by every class of soldiers, and my own experience leads me to be of the same opinion, that the generality of the non-commissioned staff at Chatham are morally the lowest and most contemptible of their grade in the service," he wrote. "It is a fact, of the truth of which I have myself been often a witness, that some of them are perfect adepts in every species of fraud, and the larger part are of the most depraved habits otherwise."[39] Field Marshal William Robertson, remembering his days as a private cavalry trooper when he was a young soldier, agreed with that view. "A troop sergeant-major occupies a position which enables him to exert, for good or for evil, great influence over his men," he wrote in his memoir. "It is said that the non-commissioned officer is the backbone of the army, but it is equally true that he can do much harm unless he is strictly impartial and identifies himself with the interests of his men."[40]

Enough soldiers encountered their share of bad superiors that it was practically a trope of enlisted men's narratives. As one American veteran of the Spanish-American War remembered, the men of his company of the 13th Minnesota Volunteer Infantry worked up a rhyme about it:

Now that we're here, we must obey
What "Shoulder Straps" and "Non-Coms" say
But such is life, so what can you do?
They know that they have the hulge on you
Just wait till we're free from the government's yoke
We can tell them to go where there's plenty of smoke
It's then we'll get even, and that's no joke
Their stripes will not bother us then.

When the NCOs in question took their tyrannical inclinations a step too far, it could result in even more extreme reactions from the men who felt themselves abused, especially in the chaos of battle. Julius Koettgen, a German soldier, referred to this in his memoir of his experiences in the First World War:

I conversed with a mate from my company and asked him for the loan
of his pocket knife; he drew from his pocket three cartridges besides

his knife. I was surprised to find him carrying cartridges in his trousers' pockets and asked him whether he had no room for them in his cartridge case. "There's room enough", he replied, "but those three are meant for a particular purpose; there's a name inscribed on each of them". Some time after—we had meanwhile become fast friends— I inquired again after the three bullets. He had one of them left. I reflected and remembered two sergeants who had treated us like brutes in times of peace, whom we had hated as one could only hate slave drivers. They had found their graves in French soil.[41]

This was an extreme case of the rank and file taking their own form of retaliation, and it was not necessarily a common event, but it shows up frequently enough in the international narratives to indicate that there were always a few soldiers in most armies who thought about getting a little payback, even if they did not actually carry it out.

Examples of this can be found in both American and British sources, as well, and it is by no means only a feature of more recent conflicts such as the Vietnam War. Soldiers of the nineteenth century were just as capable of criminal violence as men of any other era, and as soldiers they had ready access to the means of doing it. When noncommissioned officers exercised their authority by the excessive use of physical force, intimidation, and corporal punishment, it naturally drew the animosity of soldiers who felt themselves abused and mistreated. One night in December 1887, First Sergeant Emanuel Stance, the senior NCO of F Troop, 9th U.S. Cavalry, was shot dead at Fort Davis, Texas, by persons unknown. Suspicion quickly fell on two privates in his troop who had previously threatened him. There were no witnesses to the crime, however, and not enough evidence to prosecute anyone, so the murder went unsolved. The *Army and Navy Journal* printed an obituary of First Sergeant Stance, in which his eulogizer described him as being "a very strict disciplinarian"; the soldiers of his troop, on the other hand, said that he was "dirty mean." One suspects that theirs was perhaps the more honest assessment of the man.

It is an established part of military law today that the lowest ranking soldier still has certain personal rights under military law and that the authority of those over him is not unlimited or absolute. These are not modern concepts. Throughout most of this period, even when soldiers were still liable to corporal punishments such as flogging and other harsh treatments, most armies also had clearly stated regulations that insisted that the enlisted rank and file were entitled to certain protections and measures of due process. Most of these protections were expressed in the form of Standing Orders or other written instructions that governed the actions of officers and NCOs in their dealings with private soldiers.

The U.S. Army, almost from its inception, codified the common soldier's legal right to redress in the Articles of War. One British regiment's Standing Orders in 1848 mandated: "A Non-Commissioned Officer will *invariably* take any man he may have to complain of before the Officer of the Company, and he will never, on any account, make a report of a man behind his back; nor will an Officer ever award a punishment however trifling, without having enquired into the complaint in presence of the Soldier."[42] In America and Britain, then, the official policy was clearly one that was designed to insure that soldiers were not charged or punished without being fully apprised of the situation and afforded the opportunity to have their side of the story heard. Whether this policy was always faithfully followed in practice is impossible to say, but the fact that it was considered important enough to be made a matter of formal regulation is worth noting.

The chain of command, so much a part of hierarchical military life, existed then much as it does today, and it operated in almost exactly the same way. The right of an American or British soldier to present his grievances directly to his commanding officer, and to take his case to the next higher authority if still unsatisfied, existed at every point in this period just as it does in the present. However, the same requirements as to the exercise of this privilege also applied; soldiers wishing to speak to their commanders were required to put their case to their sergeants first. The Seaforth Highlanders' Standing Orders of 1857 are representative of most policies concerning soldier–officer appeals during the period. "A Soldier desirous of speaking to an Officer," the Orders stated, "must always be accompanied by a Non-Commissioned Officer; but this need not prevent his being allowed to speak privately to the Officer."[43]

A particularly important role of the noncommissioned officer, especially as this period passed into the twentieth century, was that of trainer and teacher to younger NCOs and newly commissioned officers. In the U.S. Army, many a newly minted infantry second lieutenant would be advised by his first company commander that he would do well to remember that his practical knowledge of soldiering was almost nil, and that he would be wise to heed the quiet advice of the senior NCO in his platoon. If the senior NCO in question was not a capable, experienced, and professional soldier, however, the outlook for the entire platoon was grim.

Officers in other armies often found this practice of drawing on their NCOs' experience to be valuable even when official policy did not suggest it. A newly commissioned Japanese lieutenant named Sakata Shintaro remembered the weeks he spent aboard a troopship in 1944:

> *It was aboard that ship that I received the best officer training in my six years' in military service. In the mixed unit that was formed in Sakai were gathered soldiers from all parts of the country. Among them were about ten noncommissioned officers who had seven to eight years of battlefield experience from the time of the China War. They lectured me persuasively and taught me some practicalities of the battlefront—nothing like what I had been taught as a young officer.*
>
> *For example: (1) Even if there should be a fierce battle, never give the order to 'Charge!' Soldiers die needlessly due to orders to charge rashly given by young officers. (2) Don't make a frontal assault on powerful enemy forces in tanks or in pillboxes. Avoid them rather than opposing them. It is all right to flee.*[44]

During both world wars, the German Army garnered a reputation for having an NCO corps of unparalleled professionalism and outstanding tactical ability. German sergeants at all levels were spoken of as tough, hard taskmasters of their soldiers, but they were also known for being excellent combat leaders. One Wehrmacht veteran of the ferocious fighting in Russia from 1942 to 1944 remembered the NCOs of his unit as being "irreplaceable. No officer could replace them. Absolutely none."[45]

ENLISTED MEN

There is a wide range of opinions when it comes to the soldiers who make up the enlisted portion of every army's manpower. Some commentators see the men at the bottom of the military ladder as being either the downtrodden servants of too many masters, or a uniformed rabble kept in their proper place only by the consistent application of firm discipline. Other perspectives argue that the enlisted men, who after all are the numerical majority of all armies, are in fact the strong base of the military pyramid without whom there is no foundation. The truth, as is often the case, lies somewhere between those diverging points of view and differs depending on the army in question.

Most of this book is concerned with the perspectives of the men at the bottom of the ladder—the privates, troopers, gunners, fusiliers, pioneers, sappers, riflemen, and other members of the rank-and-file mass whose voices are so often unheard in the great sweep of military history. As we have seen, more than one soldier during this period left an account of his personal dislike of the officers who ordered him about and whom he blamed for injustices both real and imagined. One of the most interesting perspective on officers, from an enlisted man's point of view, comes from the Civil War memoir of Sam Watkins, who served in the Confederate Army. "I always shot at privates," he wrote. "It was they that did the shooting and killing, and if I could kill or wound a private, why, my chances were so much the better. I always looked upon officers as harmless personages. . . . When we got down to close quarters I always tried to kill those that were trying to kill me."[46] There was a fine logic to his thinking.

We've considered the enlisted man's view of those above him in the hierarchy, but what were their views of him? What of the perspectives of officers and NCOs who had to deal with the men in the line? How does the normal soldier—the average Tommy, GI, *poilu*, and what have you—come off in the view of the men who found themselves responsible for him? More than a few officers went into the army with one perspective of the private soldier and then found that their views were altered by the experience of actually dealing with him. One British officer wrote very eloquently of this. "For the first time in my life I, a boy from a public school, was doing manual work beside men who were manual workers," he wrote. "In a flash of revelation, caused perhaps by a flash of a bursting shell outside, I saw that instead of my being superior to them they were superior to me."[47]

Good leaders, NCOs and officers alike, were able to maintain a multifaceted perspective on the men in their charge, keeping in mind their human failings, qualities, and individual peculiarities, as well as the factors that sometimes made the enlisted men's lives harder than their own. One British officer who fought at the Somme wrote in his diary, "Liquid mud lies at the bottom [of the trenches] in some places 2 feet deep. Several times this filthy slime has been well above my field boots and my legs and feet are, and have been for hours, completely wet and numbed with cold." Bad as it was, he still thought it was worse for his soldiers. "In my own misery, I feel intensely for the men who, with puttees only, are worse off than the officers," he wrote. "They are marvelous in their uncomplaining fortitude."[48]

Experienced leaders always kept in mind the fact that the soldiers they led were not mass-produced automatons. Each soldier was an individual, with his individual characteristics and personality, and the ability to get that mass of individuals to function as a cohesive unit was one of the things that distinguished good leaders. Donald Kyler was an American infantry sergeant during the First World War; he recalled one time when he was placed in charge of a detail of soldiers from different platoons for the despised nightly chore of carrying supplies into the forward trenches. "These men, I knew, were the most undesirable ones in their respective platoons," he wrote. "They were considered unreliable for one reason or another. Some were inept. Some were just ornery. All were older than I was. For those reasons it was with apprehension that I took command of the group." Despite that reluctance, Kyler found a leadership approach to his motley band of misfits that actually worked. "I soon learned to respect and trust them," he wrote. "Some of those men had been badly treated in their squads and platoons. I think it was mostly because of a lack of understanding by their leaders." He used a different method. "One cannot motivate all men the same way," he noted. "I found that by being generous with compliments when deserved, and spare with reprimands though deserved, that better results would be obtained. A light reprimand with an air of holding back more that might be added, may be more effective than a harangue would be."[49]

Every unit, or nearly all, had a soldier or two who was far from being a model specimen of military discipline and good behavior. Many of them were what NCOs in the U.S. Army today wryly describe as "leadership challenges." Every sergeant from this period who left a personal narrative seems to have had one or two of these characters in his squad, section, or platoon, at one time or another; most lieutenants and captains had a soldier or two whose names they got to know very well for the simple reason that those men always seemed to be getting into trouble and being brought up on charges.

Most NCOs would probably be able to identify with the feelings of Edwin Rundle, a British sergeant who served in the era just after the Crimean War. Rundle at one point had a problem soldier, a man whom he found himself dealing with more often than he would have liked. "About this time I had some trouble with a man in my company," Rundle wrote. "His general conduct was such as required watching; he was constantly being punished. He would desert and be brought back, tried by district court-martial, sentenced to be flogged and imprisoned for perhaps 112 days. One night I called the roll at tattoo and found him wanting." Rundle reported the man absent without leave, inventoried his equipment, and said with understandable sincerity, "I hoped he would not return."[50]

Sergeant Thomas Morris, who served as an infantryman in the British Army during the Napoleonic Wars and who fought the French on numerous battlefields including Waterloo, believed that the French Army was better than the British in some important ways, specifically the view from the bottom up. "History furnishes but few instances of such devotion and enthusiasm," he wrote, "as was exhibited by the French soldiers towards [Napoleon]; even the dreadful reverses to which they were subjected . . . were not sufficient to wean their affections from the Emperor; they were still willing to fight for him—to die for him."[51] The reasons for this amazing loyalty, Morris believed, owed everything to Napoleon's practice of promoting on merit and always identifying himself with his soldiers, as opposed to the British system of selling commissions and promoting its officers by their purchasing power instead of their military merit.

This aspect of the French Army was also remarked upon by French soldiers themselves. One veteran of the Napoleonic Wars, who had originally thought he might join the navy, declared himself greatly relieved to have wound up in the army instead after his regiment spent some time aboard a naval vessel and he saw the maritime culture for himself. The greatest difference, he felt, was in how officers interacted with enlisted men in the different services. "A midshipman of eighteen speaks in the most contemptuous terms to a grey-haired boatswain," he wrote. By contrast, "every post in the army is within the soldier's reach, because all the different ranks form but one chain, every link of which he may run through in succession; and an officer never forgets that nothing prevents the soldier whom he is addressing from one day becoming his equal."[52]

In this matter of the relationships between the leaders and the led—the officers, NCOs, and private soldiers of the world's armies—overly broad generalities will not serve. Examples abound of both good and bad at all levels of the rank structure. Resentment of their leaders was a commonly expressed sentiment of the men at the bottom of the heap, but the privates also voiced admiration and respect for the good leaders they encountered. All the same, it is probably safe to say that the negative impressions resonate louder through the narratives than do the positive ones. For readers who have personal military experience to draw on, other soldiers' grievances are easy to empathize with, even when they come from centuries past. One British soldier, nearly eighty years after his time in the trenches in France, had lost none of his dislike for the sergeant who made his life miserable back then. "He made me clean the metal washbasin with sand. The water was ice cold, and the sand got into my broken chilblains," he said. "Since 1919 I have been looking for that bastard. It's not too late yet to kill him."[53] That was a sentiment that many privates could understand, having nursed their own grievances and grudges through long hours of work details, KP, guard duty, and the infinite other vexations of military life at the bottom of the pile.

CHAPTER FOUR

Identity and Belonging

THERE IS A COMMONLY BELIEVED AND FREQUENTLY REPEATED perception of military culture that insists that wearing a uniform involves the systematic suppression (or the outright elimination) of everything that is individual about a person. It is a view most often expressed by people who themselves have little personal experience of the military, but the idea persists so stubbornly that it warrants some consideration. Is it true? Does being a soldier require the loss, or at least the subordination, of everything that makes a person unique and individualistic?

Well, sometimes it does and sometimes it doesn't. There is no simple, all-encompassing answer to that question. The variables that apply to it are innumerable; it depends on the army in question, and the era, and the culture of the population from which that army recruits, and that nation's predilection to militarism, and the methods of indoctrination and training used by that army, and so on, ad infinitum, ad nauseam. Some of the armies studied in this book absolutely sought to erase the individual's sense of self in the process of creating the soldier, but other armies accepted, with varying degrees of reluctance, the theory that recognition of recruits' individual personalities could sometimes make for better soldiers.

The issue of the individual's identity within the monolithic mass of the military system is probably a subject worthy of a book in its own right, but not this book. I am a conflict historian, not a sociologist, and that specific question might better be served by someone of the latter discipline. My concern here is with the matter of how soldiers identify themselves with the army and as part of the army, and with their fellow soldiers, and how the feelings of belonging or alienation are formed and experienced. To that end, I think it best to work from the top down: armies, regiments, platoons and squads, and finally the single soldiers.

Different armies have attached different values to this, and the reasons are as varied as the organizations themselves. Sometimes the organization itself is the primary source of identification: U.S. Marines identify themselves first and foremost as Marines, and there is no insult likely to piss a Marine off more than mistaking him or her for a soldier, in the sense of assuming that they are part of the army. They are not soldiers, as they are quick to point out; "once a Marine, always a Marine," is a favorite saying. I cannot recall that I have ever heard a similar expression used by a veteran of the U.S. Army. For most U.S. Marines, their identification as a member of the Marine Corps trumps all other associations or qualifications, even if the lengths to which they take that line strike everyone else as a bit ridiculous or tiresome.

Robert Guillemard, who was conscripted into the French Army in 1805, described his experience of the process of identifying with the military organization. He was initially very reluctant to serve in the army, and recalled that most of his fellow conscripts felt the same way. As time went on, though, he said that "the soldiers at last (to use their own language) looked to the eagle of their regiment as their village steeple, their company as their family, and sometimes their captain as their father." He began as an unhappy conscript, but Guillemard quickly evolved into a professional soldier and served eighteen years in the army, staying in the ranks long after his initial service obligation was completed.

In the British military, the regimental system for many years provided the primary element of identification for the individual soldier. Many British regiments had long histories before they were bureaucratically decimated by a series of amalgamations in the late twentieth century. These regiments had decades of association with particular cities, counties, depots, and postings; they were more often familiarly known by historically significant names rather than their numeric designations. Thus, we find regiments such as the Green Howards, the Sherwood Foresters, the Ox and Buffs, the Black Watch, and others. British men enlisted for specific regiments, and they usually spent their entire military careers within the familiar ranks of a single regiment that became the principal identifier of their time in the army.

The American military has never had a regimental system as extensive or strong as that of the British Army. Regimental affiliation in the

U.S. Army is a much more ephemeral concept, to borrow a line from English historian Richard Holmes. As an element of identification, the American regimental system was at its strongest during the nineteenth century when the army was still a very small organization. Henry Windolph, who fought with the 7th U.S. Cavalry at the Battle of the Little Bighorn in 1876, remembered feeling that he was "part of the finest regiment of cavalry in the world,"[1] and many men expressed similar sentiments about their own units. Going forward into the twentieth century, however, regimental identification in the U.S. Army was mostly restricted to the combat arms—infantry, armor, and cavalry units, in particular, but even in those cases the regimental nominator held no lasting attachment in a practical sense. As was the case in both world wars, American soldiers joined the army (or were drafted into it) and were then assigned to whatever unit the army needed them in, without their preference for a particular unit playing any part in the process. One exception to that was when soldiers took the additional step of volunteering for the paratroops, in which case they sought membership in an elite formation that required additional standards of qualification, usually as part of an arduous selection process.

In terms of morale and unit cohesion, a regiment with two hundred years of history behind it and a long list of battle honors to its credit often has a head start in the process of inculcating its new soldiers with a sense of pride and belonging. It should not automatically be assumed, however, that a newly created unit is therefore fatally disadvantaged because it lacks the renown enjoyed by more famous regiments. The hastily created battalions of the "New Army" that the British fielded after 1914 were often every bit as committed, motivated, and imbued with the martial spirit as were some of the traditional regiments that were centuries old. When the U.S. Army formed the 101st Airborne Division, its second paratroop division of the Second World War, neither the division nor the three infantry regiments that formed it had any prior combat history at all. General William Lee, its first commander, was well aware of this when he told his men, "The 101st has no history, but it has a rendezvous with destiny."[2] The paratroopers of the new division fought their way across Western Europe, and today the 101st Airborne Division (Air

Assault) is one of the premier combat divisions in the U.S. Army, with campaign credits from five wars.

Soldiers in combat tend to identify more closely with their immediate comrades—the men in their sections, squads, and platoons—than they do with the larger units whose insignia or distinguishing emblems they actually wear, proud though they may be of that larger identity. C. E. Montagu, just after the First World War, referred to this when he wrote, "Whatever its size a man's world was his section—at most, his platoon; all that mattered to him was the one little boatload of castaways with whom he was marooned on a desert island making shift to keep off the weather and any sudden attack by wild beasts."[3]

This feeling was what one British veteran of that war described when he remembered his Lewis gun crew:

We were part of the battalion, but at the same time we were a little crowd on our own. You could talk to your pals about anything and everything. I mean, these boys were with you night and day, you shared everything with them. We each knew where the others came from, what their lives had been and where they were. You were one of them—we belonged to each other. It's a difficult thing to describe, the comradeship between us. I never met any of their people or any of their parents, but I knew all about them, and they knew all about me and mine.[4]

The strength of this close-knit bond in a small group was that it motivated men in ways that official unit affiliations seldom could, and that was also its greatest weakness. The personal connections between men made the effects of combat losses strike home all the harder, as the same soldier experienced. He was wounded by a German artillery shell on September 21, 1917, but that was not the worst injury:

I didn't know what had happened to the others at first, but I was told later that I had lost three of my mates. . . . We were a little team together, and those men who were carrying the ammunition were blown to pieces. I reacted very badly. It was like losing a part of my life. It upset me more than anything. We had only been together four months, but with hell going on around us, it seemed like a lifetime.[5]

Official military policy makers have not always recognized how important this small-unit identification is to the individual soldier. In the Second World War, the U.S. Army handled its personnel replacement process in a manner that, in hindsight, seems highly insensitive, if not downright stupid. Unfortunately, that war was not an anomaly in the history of American military personnel policies. As Russell Weigley points out, historically the U.S. Army has not exactly distinguished itself with its troop replacement systems. "On the one hand," he writes, "Civil War regiments fought themselves almost out of existence; on the other hand, the . . . method of bringing men in and out of the war as solitary soldiers diminished unit pride and individual self-esteem."[6] The harsh reality of military life is that soldiers are small cogs in enormous martial machines, and any replacement systems that erode a soldier's sense of belonging can only work to the detriment of both the soldier and his army. "Thus," as historian Mitchell Reid says of the U.S. Army in the Second World War, "the army broke down the fundamental loyalty most soldiers felt—that to their platoon or company."[7]

Almost every American GI of that war expressed the feeling that his platoon was the most important identifier of his military life. "You see, your little platoon was your life," one rifleman of the 16th Infantry Regiment recalled. "Oh, you'd know the guys. Maybe you'd know them by their first name, last name, nickname, but some of the replacements you never got to know at all, but you'd recognize them as belonging to the company; but other than that, no. It wasn't like you'd go to chow and sit down with the whole company."[8] Beyond that fraternal brotherhood of the platoon, everyone else was just a name, if even that, and soldiers from echelons above that hardly mattered at all.

The American system was particularly counterproductive in the European Theater of Operations. Historian Stephen Ambrose said it was "one of the dumbest things the Army did,"[9] and soldiers in combat units certainly felt the same way. "The fellows don't want to leave when they're sick," one American GI wrote. "They're afraid to leave their own men—the men they know. They don't want to get put in a different outfit. Your own outfit—they are the men you have confidence in."[10] By that same token, the veterans of a combat-tested unit usually did not welcome replacement personnel with much enthusiasm. Having passed through the cauldron of battle, they knew all too well what the odds were for survival and so often chose to maintain an emotional distance from the newcomers, more as a measure of emotional self-protection than from any sort of arrogant hostility. "You accept them but you didn't want to be that good of friends," one paratrooper of the 507th Parachute Infantry Regiment (PIR) said. "Because most of them were going to die. And you didn't want to be that close to them."[11]

Joseph Argenzio was an American rifleman in the 16th Infantry who fought across Europe with the 1st Infantry Division, from the Normandy landings to Czechoslovakia. He joined his battalion just days before D-Day, and he knew what it was like to be a replacement soldier inserted into a unit of veterans, but in short order he, himself, was the veteran, and recalled what it was like when replacements arrived in his company. "You didn't want to get too friendly," he recalled. "Of course, right away, they wanted to tell you about their girlfriends, their wives, their mother and father and it was better you didn't hear all this. As much as you wanted to really get in and mix with them, I always tried to stay aloof. . . . I knew I was going to lose them or they'd lose me." Between June of 1944 and April of 1945, he said, "We must have turned over [personnel] 20 times."[12] Other veterans, who repeatedly saw new men join the unit only to disappear onto the casualty lists before their names were hardly learned, shared that view.

The dynamic of soldiers identifying with the small elements rather than the large is common to most armies. Even with the almost mythical aura surrounding the British regimental system, British soldiers felt more attachment to their squads than to their regiments, at least during periods of heavy fighting and high casualties. "We must not get too misty-eyed about the pulling power of the regiment," Richard Holmes argues. "In a sense the system had always worked best when it was needed least:

in peacetime or small wars." The traditional system was simply unable to cope with the high casualties and manpower demands of both world wars. "By 1944," Holmes says, the regimental system "was in tatters . . . scarce replacements arriving in theatre might be posted haphazardly to whichever regiment had the greatest need of them." The result was a breakdown of one of the most important aspects of soldiers' ability to identify with their units.[13]

The detrimental effect of this disruption of unit identification has had disastrous results for most armies in which it has occurred. The 1940–1941 campaign in Greece and Albania was an unmitigated catastrophe for the Italian Army—the Italians lost 39,000 dead, 51,000 wounded, and 64,000 incapacitated from injury or illness, compared with Greek losses of 13,800 dead and 42,000 wounded. There were many reasons attributable for the defeat, not least of which was Mussolini's absolutely inept mishandling of the army. The Italian dictator's "decision to demobilize one-third of the army for economic and political reasons three weeks before the invasion of Greece," one historian says, "was probably the greatest contributor to the disaster. . . . None of the reinforcing divisions hastily rushed to Albania after the Italian retreat had any unit cohesion."[14]

Unit cohesion directly affects combat performance, and this is most clearly demonstrated by its absence, when unit cohesion is lacking. It is not an earth-shattering revelation to any military leader to say that soldiers fight better when they feel a bond with the men to their left and right, although that familiar relationship comes with a price. "I can remember that one of my comrades got wounded," a British soldier in the Hertfordshire Regiment recalled of his First World War experience, "and this induced in me a sense of desolation which would normally only come if you lost a very close family. . . . There is that feeling of comradeship which can't be understood by anybody unless they were actually in the front line in the war."[15]

The feeling that someone could only truly understand the experiences of a soldier in the line if that person had shared the experience was expressed by soldiers of every nation in almost every war. Herbert Sulzbach was a German infantryman from Frankfurt who went home on leave in 1918 and found that he could not relate to civilians. "People were fed up with war," he wrote. "They wanted the war to be ended as soon as possible, victory or no victory. After a fortnight I went back to the front line, to my comrades, to my guns, and I felt at home amongst the mud, the dirt, and the lice."[16] In that sentiment he had something in common with his enemies on the other side of no-man's-land. A British soldier of the Warwickshire Regiment also wrote of the experience of going home on leave, saying, "One got annoyed by the attempts of well-meaning people to sympathize, which only reflected the fact that they didn't really understand at all. So there was almost a sense of relief when one went back into the man's world [of the trenches], which seemed the realest thing that could be imagined."[17]

The gulf of separation that existed between soldiers and their civilian populations could feel insurmountable to men whose world was bounded by the violence, deprivation, and miseries of war. "One thing I really noticed was that after being with the young fellows in the Army, we were a race apart from these civilians," a British corporal remembered. "You couldn't talk to the civilians about the war, you'd be wasting your time. They hadn't got the slightest conception of what the conditions were like and so forth. So after a time you didn't talk about it."[18] Theirs was a brotherhood of exclusive membership, with a price for belonging that many of them would rather have never paid, but once in that fraternity they struggled to relate to people who were still part of the world they had left behind them.

Hans Roth, the German *Panzerjaeger* who fought in Russia in the Second World War, expressed this feeling very clearly when he wrote in his journal, "Here on the front, we who proudly bear the name '*Frontschweine*' have become an inseparable brotherhood of men who have been hardened, who have been welded together by death and blood into a close community." Considering that the word *Frontschweine* can be translated as "pigs of the front," his meaning was clear. Another German veteran of the Eastern Front wrote, "Out here we really feel the force of the destiny which binds us together as Germans. Here a man looks at other Germans and sees his brother, his home. At home things are different—people walk straight past each other and only take any notice at marches or rallies." The men at the sharp end—enduring the danger and misery—took a grim pride in sharing an experience that no one who had not stood beside them could ever comprehend. It also tended to make them cynically unsympathetic to the lesser problems of civilians. In a later entry, Roth described his reactions to a letter that one of his comrades received from home. "In it, someone is complaining about working overtime, the shortage of beer and cigarettes, and other similar matters," he wrote. "How little does that idiot understand about the things that go on out here? Is that the voice of the homeland?"[19]

This sense of battle-tested brotherhood is one reason why soldiers of all nations value the visible insignias that identify them to each other as men who have spent time in harm's way and served at the sharp end of the spear. The American army adopted combat service stripes for the uniform during the First World War, each stripe on the lower sleeve declaring to all who saw it that the wearer was a man who had spent six months in a combat zone. When high casualty rates among American infantry threatened morale during the Second World War, the U.S. Army created the distinctive uniform items for infantrymen that every American soldier recognizes today—the blue discs backing the collar brass worn on the collar, the blue shoulder cord worn over the right arm, and, most importantly, the Combat Infantryman Badge. Wound stripes were awarded in the British Army to distinguish those men who carried the physical scars of their passage through the maelstrom. Probably no army in the world took this process of identification badges to a greater degree than the German Wehrmacht of the Second World War, which awarded a long list of badges to set the combat soldier apart from his fellows in the rear: Infantry Assault Badge; Close Combat Clasp; Tank Battle Badge; Anti-Partisan Guerilla Warfare Badge; Tank Destruction Badge; Arm Shields denoting particular campaigns; the Wound Badge in Black, Silver, and Gold; Cuff Titles; and so on.

Decorations for valor were prized, to be sure, but soldiers in every army grumbled that medals were not always awarded to those who most deserved them. Joachim Pusch, a German signalman who fought on the Eastern Front, remembered the badge he was proudest of. "The close combat badge, called a *Nahkampfspange,* was special to me because it reflected the appreciation the infantry had for my assistance to them," he said. "I preferred being with the infantry. Even though I was ordered many times to come back to my original unit, I said we have something to do out here and I'm going to stay another week or so."[20]

Enlisted men frequently nursed a bitter suspicion that officers got more than their share of medals. Combat-identifier badges and insignia, on the other hand, were usually awarded without regard to rank, so many soldiers valued those items as much or even more than medals. Cynics notwithstanding, the badges and baubles of military heraldry *do* play an important part in how soldiers identify themselves. The first official divisional insignia to be adopted by the modern U.S. Army, the "Big Red One" shoulder patch of the 1st Infantry Division, was created at the behest of the division's commander during the First World War when he wanted an emblem that would give his soldiers a distinguishing identification they could wear on their uniforms. Before that, Federal units in the American Civil War wore semiofficial emblems designed to identify particular brigades. Most soldiers placed a genuine pride in the insignia that set their unit apart from the rest of the army, for the understandable reason that the unit's individuality became in some measure a part of their own unique, individual identity. "It is characteristic of good soldiers to cherish any little peculiarity of uniform or equipment which differentiates their own Regiment or Corps from others," one British commander remarked in 1924, and that dynamic was just as true in most other armies.[21]

Elite units always engender a degree of personal pride in the men who serve in their ranks, pride that to a considerable measure is created by the rigorous selection and training processes required to become a member of those formations. Soldiers who felt that they had to endure a tougher training than their fellow soldiers, who were then held to a higher standard of physical fitness, tactical skill, or personal discipline, and whose combat missions were perceived to be more hazardous than the norm naturally felt themselves to be a special breed, head and shoulders above "ordinary" soldiers.

Getting into an elite unit was usually on a volunteer basis, which meant that almost anyone could apply; actually making it through the rigorous selection process was another matter altogether. Donald Frederick was an artilleryman in the U.S. Army when he volunteered for the

Ranger Battalion that was forming in 1943. The process of eliminating the applicants began almost immediately. Arriving by train in Scotland, where the Ranger training camp was located, Frederick remembered the first test. "Where's the camp?" he recalled asking. "Well, the camp is five miles away" was the answer; "you're going to run to it." The results were probably predictable: "That weeded out quite a few at that point," he recalled.[22]

Most American soldiers who volunteered as paratroopers in the early days of the war had enough experience in regular units to know why they were signing up for the airborne. Some of them spoke of a desire to get into a unit with better discipline or better quality of personnel; others were attracted by the certainty of frontline action rather than the monotonous grind of a rear-echelon formation. Some men specifically mentioned the additional jump pay as being an incentive; others admitted to being attracted by the paratroopers' distinctive uniform items of jump boots and silver parachutist's badge, and their reputation as an elite unit. Regardless of their individual motivations, many of them found the training to be tougher than they had perhaps expected.

John Hinchliff volunteered for the paratroops in 1942. "I remember we lost a lot of people from the training [in jump school]," he recalled. "They couldn't take it. . . . They'd run you until you couldn't run any more. And then if you didn't get up after they kicked you in the butt a little bit, they'd wash you out." It was almost more than Hinchliff was prepared for. "I was in darned good shape," he said. "But I found out I wasn't quite as good a shape as I thought I was." He made it through the course, but many of his fellow candidates did not. "I remember they only graduated sixteen of us out of that whole barracks [of thirty men]." Once through that initial qualification course, Hinchliff was assigned to the 507th PIR. From that point, the training only intensified. "We were making night jumps out into the swamps and one man would jump at a time," he said. "They'd give us azimuth readings to get our way out of there, which was kind of scary because there were snakes and alligators and everything else in the cotton-picking swamp. Then we had lots of heavy marches and, naturally, weapons training. Out on the range. A lot of critiques." As a former coast artilleryman, Hinchliff had absolutely no experience in infantry tactics, so everything he learned as a paratrooper was on-the-job training. The quality of the instruction he received at Fort Benning, he recalled, was "excellent training. Excellent!"[23]

Regardless of the type of unit they joined, new soldiers faced the challenge of fitting in to the very insular and often-closed society of their new squad, platoon, or troop. "The term 'recruit' in the mouth of a veteran," Civil War veteran John Billings recalled, "was a very reproachful one." Men who joined units that were already actively campaigning were often not fully accepted until they had their first experience with combat and the older soldiers could see how they handled themselves. A new man's lot could be a rough one, especially if he tried to cling to civilian notions of justice and fair play; most recruits, Billings said, "got their fine sentimental notions pretty well knocked out of them before they had been many weeks in camp."[24]

Settling in to a new unit could be a slow process. The timetable of the path to social acceptance was set by the older veterans, not by the newly arrived recruit. "When a new man joins an old regiment," one British soldier wrote, "there is a reserve about the others which is rather chilling. They wait to see whether he is going to fit in, before they make any attempt to fit him in."[25] The experience was essentially the same in the U.S. Army; there "the new soldier was subject to the sharp scrutiny and silent, sometimes unfavorable, judgement of the veterans."[26] The older men watched, judged, and were seldom silent about their conclusions. They commented at length on their negative assessments of the new soldiers, with their verdicts deliberately delivered so as to be overheard by their subjects. Bullying, hazing, and harassment were not officially standard practice in most armies, but were common in all—so common, in fact, that official policies were frequently written in effort to counter them. The Standing Orders of 1892, written in the era when administration in the British Army was already well-standardized, addressed bullying directly. "Bullying," Article 110 stated, "should be put down with a firm hand."[27] The official attitude toward bullying was clear, but that did not (and has never) completely put a stop to it.

How a man was received by his new unit often had a great deal to do with how he responded to what bullying or intimidation he *did* encounter. The anonymous British narrator from the 71st Regiment in the Peninsular War remembered that he was hounded unmercifully by the company bully until, having finally reached the limits of his forbearance, he knocked the other man down—after that day, he said, no one ever bullied him again. In Soviet Russia's conscript armies, bullying was practically institutionalized. Older soldiers nearing the end of their two-year mandatory service would beat the hell out of every new recruit in the barracks on a nearly nightly basis. Only those who fought back, or who showed a complete lack of intimidation, were accorded any respect. In many situations, soldiers noted that the bullies were themselves the dregs of the unit. "In fact," Billings wrote, "those who abused the recruits most were themselves, as a rule, the most unreliable in action."[28]

The process of measuring up in the eyes of one's comrades was a vital part of every recruit's transition from civilian to soldier. When men were found lacking in the final determination, the treatment at the hands of their peers could be very rough, indeed, but in such cases there was often a more deliberate purpose than mere bullying. During the Indian Wars era of the U.S. Army, those recruits "who did not measure up were treated harshly, and if several members of a troop or company strongly objected to their presence, they were sometimes driven to desert."[29] In the mutually dependent society of army life, where men had to live, work, fight, and even die together, men who were judged as unreliable were never trusted or completely accepted.

For all of this hard-handed initiation, though, there were always men in every unit who were willing to help the newcomer adapt and fit in. Even if the sergeants and corporals in a recruit's new and unfamiliar universe seemed to be loud, frightening figures of military authority, there were usually other soldiers in one's squad and platoon who would impart a few words of advice or encouragement. The British Army recognized the vital role of this peer mentorship early on; the 1812 Standing Orders of the 51st Edinburgh Regiment of British Militia directed the new recruit's commanding officer to "see that the non-commissioned officer of the squad [the recruit] is allotted to, gives him an old soldier for a comrade, who is best qualified to instruct him in the duties of a soldier."[30] Even though such a relationship was not command-directed in the nineteenth-century American army, it still almost always worked out that "recruits were likely to find men who recalled their own earlier experiences, and helped the newcomer to find his place in the unit."[31]

In the maelstrom of the First World War, it was most often the old professional core of sergeants who helped the new men become part of the army. The NCOs, as one commentator on the British Army of that war wrote, "were the best schoolmaster of the new boys, the best friends and guides of the new officers, stubborn in their courage, hard and ruthless in their discipline, foul-mouthed according to their own traditions, until they, too, fell in the shambles."[32]

In every army, innumerable touchstones of custom and tradition reminded the new recruit that he was inconsequential and insignificant compared to the veterans whom he stood beside in the ranks. Charles Willeford, who enlisted in the U.S. Army for the first time in 1935, remembered one such token that set the old soldiers apart from the new. "There was an unwritten rule in the Army, which I learned about later," he wrote, "that didn't allow men on their first enlistment to grow a mustache. So men on their second hitch . . . almost always wore a mustache. It distinguished them visibly, and as a rule they did not talk to the younger soldiers who were not yet drawing fogy [longevity] pay."[33] Veterans also marked their superior status by the service stripes that denoted their years in uniform, the medals that indicated service in past campaigns, and often by wearing tailored uniforms that were of better quality than the standard-issue clothing.

These manifestations of years in harness were one of the many reasons why the career NCOs in a unit were creatures of myth and lore to young recruits. As one American soldier remembered, "The old-time, regular sergeant was a person to be revered, respected, and avoided. Usually a veteran of some fifteen to twenty years service, he was oracle, boss, and tyrant." He went on to describe the monthly payday ritual of his company's three senior NCOs. "When Oberg, Bergmark, and Harrell (dressed in their tailor-made blue with a profusion of white [service] stripes) set off for the city two or three days after pay day," he wrote, "they marched abreast down the center of the walk, a sum total of eighteen and one-half feet of beef and brawn. Twenty-four hours later they made the return trip, just as straight, but a bit more careful in planting their feet, ready to take up the job of running the company until another pay day came around."

Sergeants were the demigods of the private soldier's world—they were almost forces of nature, so much so that many a man was temporarily at a loss when he himself made that elemental transition from the ranks of the privates to the noncommissioned officers. Suddenly, by the process of a promotion ceremony and the sewing on of a few chevrons, he was no longer part of "us"; he was now one of "them," and that shift could take a while to process.

Beyond the social connections of regiment, company, and squad, all armies were familiar with the existential, sibling-like rivalries that existed between soldiers of the different arms of service—especially the infantry, cavalry, and artillery. Members of each branch suspected that they carried more of the load than their brothers in the other arms; at the same time, they knew with absolute certainty that theirs was the best arm of the service, and they were perpetually annoyed that soldiers of the other branches seemed unable to recognize and accept that supposedly self-evident truth.

Infantrymen and cavalrymen (and soldiers of armored regiments, once they replaced the horse-mounted cavalry) have long enjoyed a spirited rivalry with each other. "The infantry seemed to know exactly what to say to torment cavalry and artillery, and generally said it," one Confederate artilleryman wrote of his experience in the American Civil War, and that was true in almost every army in every nation.[34] The infantry begrudged the cavalry for having their posteriors a little higher off the ground than themselves and for riding everywhere while the foot soldiers slogged along in the mud. Cavalrymen, as they curried their horses and cleaned their tack, resented the infantry's apparently carefree life. Once tanks and armored vehicles took the place of horses, armor crewmen expressed the same profane complaints about other soldiers' easier lives as they struggled to repair a broken track or tried to recover a tank mired to its belly in the mud. Artillerymen, for their part, usually stood apart from the internecine fray, congratulating themselves on having had the good sense to enlist for a more refined arm of the service while they happily shrugged off the nicknames like "gun bunnies" and "cannon-cockers" that resentful infantrymen hurled at them. The artillery, after all, was the "King of Battle," for the simple reason that the heavy guns were the great killers of the modern battlefield; the infantry by contrast was the "Queen of Battle," and very proud of it. Between themselves, infantrymen and artillerymen privately agreed that the cavalry/armor branch were at best a bunch of Jokers who were not much good to anyone once they were separated from their horses or tanks.

This is an old enmity, going back across long eras of military history. A Confederate artilleryman recounted one episode between a Southern gunner and a Federal cavalryman, a confrontation that has more a tone of sibling acrimony about it than outright warfare:

> *It happened that an artilleryman, who was separated from his gun, was making pretty good time on foot, getting to the rear, and had the appearance of a demoralized infantryman who had thrown away his musket. So one of these lively cavalrymen trotted up, and, waving his sabre, told the artilleryman to 'surrender!' But he didn't stop. He merely glanced over his shoulder, and kept on. Then the cavalryman became indignant and shouted, 'Halt, damn you; halt!' And still he would not. 'Halt,' said the cavalryman, 'halt, you damn son of a bitch; halt!' Then the artilleryman halted, and remarking that he didn't allow any man to speak to him that way, seized a huge stick, turned on the cavalryman, knocked him out of his saddle, and proceeded on his journey to the rear.*[35]

Men who had a well-founded sense of superiority, through either their professional experience, personal accomplishments, units of affiliation, or any other source of identity, were usually better soldiers in the clinch than their counterparts who lacked that moral underpinning. It was an abstract factor that could make good soldiers better, and give them the motivation to go far beyond their own perceived limitations. It was also one more commonality that occurred across all national lines, in all armies of the period.

CHAPTER FIVE

Marching and Manual Labor

*The poor devil in the Army marches tremendous distances; he's in the
mud; he's filthy dirty; he hasn't had a full meal . . . and he fights in a
place he's never seen before.*
—George C. Marshall

Imagine four different soldiers from four different points during
this period: a British fusilier in 1808, an infantryman of the U.S. Army
in 1863, a German *landser* in 1914, and a Japanese imperial guardsman
in 1942, all in the month of August in their respective years. Their uniforms, equipment, and weapons are different; so are their languages and
personal appearances. But even across that broad expanse of years, there
are still some things that each man's experience has in common with all
the others.

The summer heat is a factor for each of them: the fusilier in Spain, the
Union infantryman in Virginia, the *Landser* in France, and the guardsman in Burma. Each man is sweating profusely, no matter if his headgear
is a leather shako, a felt kepi, a *pickelhaube*, or a steel helmet. The straps
of their packs are too thin, or their packs are too heavy for the straps, or
the loads aren't adjusted properly. Whatever the reason, the weight is a
constant physical presence that alternates between a hot stabbing pain
in the shoulders and a crushing ache in the lower back. Their individual
weapons, whether a Land-Pattern Tower musket, or an M1861 Springfield rifle-musket, a Gewehr 98 Mauser, or a Type 38 Arisaka rifle, are all
muzzle-heavy and imbalanced and add just that much more weight to
their already-overladen shoulders.

Each of these men is tired, but that word does not even begin to
truly describe the level of their exhaustion. They are dehydrated to the

point that pounding headaches are hammering away behind their eyes, and they are feeling sick—either because they are just getting over a bout of dysenteric diarrhea or because they are coming down with one. They don't know if the cause of their illness is bad food, bad water, or both, and it wouldn't make any difference if they did, because there's nothing to be done about it. Their feet hurt, but that is just one ailment among many—knees, backs, and shoulders hurt, too, and which hurts the worst at any moment is a question with an ever-changing answer. Their shoes are poorly fitted, heavy and inflexible, if not literally falling apart. These men are chafed, blistered, filthy, sweaty, exhausted, and they smell bad—very, very bad, considering that none of them have bathed recently, perhaps not for months.

All of these things they have in common with each other, regardless of the decades that separate their experiences, because they are all infantrymen on the march, putting one weary foot in front of the other for mile after mile after seemingly endless mile, going from where they were to somewhere they are not yet, because that is what they were told to do. Probably every infantryman of almost every army in the world during this period would understand their situation exactly, because it was the same for almost all of them.

The word *marching* conjures up different images in civilian and military minds. For many civilians, the term evokes pictures of formations of soldiers moving in step—their pace, stride, and even the swing of their arms dictated by the precise cadence of military uniformity. That, indeed, is one form of marching; but for soldiers themselves, the word also refers to route marches, or road marches—the long, monotonous, exhausting experience of men in open tactical order or single file, walking for miles under the crushing weight of weapons and equipment. Even the word *walk* is perhaps too limited a term—sometimes the pace is an open, swinging stride, sometimes it is an exhausted shuffle, and sometimes it is a fast dogtrot that requires an incredible degree of physical conditioning to maintain over long distances. It is an experience that has added its own terminology to the military vocabulary of most armies—American soldiers of later wars called it "humping," and British soldiers called it "tabbing" or "yomping." Whatever men called it, it all was of a single purpose—to convey the infantryman to some distant place by the locomotion of his own two feet, often for reasons that no one bothered to fully explain to him.

Generals do not much figure into this book—they only matter here insomuch as the ways in which their decisions and actions affected the rank-and-file soldiers whom they commanded. Here we are only considering the actions of commanders in terms of how they were perceived and remarked upon by the men to whom questions of grand strategies and broad campaigns mattered much less than how far they had to march, how heavy were the loads they carried, and how long it had been since they last felt warm, clean, safe, and rested. "We, the private soldiers, did not know what was going on among the generals," Confederate infantryman Sam Watkins remembered in his memoir of the American Civil War. "All that we had to do was march, march, march. It mattered not how tired, hungry or thirsty we were. All that we had to do was march."[1] Soldiers the world over understood this perspective, and they expressed it in different languages, with varying degrees of vehement profanity to underscore their true feelings on the subject.

The notionally simple process of getting from one place to another presented armies with tremendous difficulties. Infantrymen in particular, as foot soldiers, have always had an intimate acquaintance with the physical rigors of long marches, and the increased motorization of armies toward the end of this period did not change that reality nearly as much as one might expect. Even today, the basic reality of the infantry arm remains unchanged—it is essentially a man on the ground carrying enough gear to cripple a donkey, trudging over miles of bad ground just to get to the place he is supposed to fight. The French Army during the Napoleonic Wars conducted such tough foot marches on a regular basis that a common saying among the French infantry was "Our Emperor makes war not with our arms but with our legs."

Today, the U.S. Army's official description of the infantry's role is "to close with and destroy the enemy by means of superior firepower and maneuver." That is all well and good, but infantrymen themselves have always understood that before they destroy anything, they first must get within range of their adversaries. Throughout history, the process of getting there has most often been accomplished by the simple, expedient method of having overburdened and exhausted soldiers put one foot in front of another for mile after aching mile. "Ten miles with an eighty-pound pack on your back, through heavy sand, is as much as a man can endure," Australian Hugh Knyvett wrote of his infantry training in the First World War; "after that he doesn't endure, he just carries on, and on, and on, and on."[2] The effort of carrying weapons and packs for miles required considerable physical fitness, mental toughness, and a capacity for endurance that most men did not even know they possessed until the circumstances demanded it of them. "A man wants to be strong in the back and weak in the head to make a good infantryman," one veteran of the First World War wryly observed.[3] When there was no apparent point to the marching, frustration compounded the physical weariness.

Randolph McKim, serving in the Confederate Army during the Civil War, recalled that when he rejoined his regiment after the battle of First Manassas, he proceeded to endure "two months of marching and countermarching, without any object that we could divine, under conditions of more acute discomfort than we had ever known before, enlivened by an occasional skirmish or artillery duel."[4] Even the dangers of a pitched battle, he thought, would have been preferable to the endless marching back and forth across miles and miles of countryside with no discernible purpose.

As many men did on both sides of the Civil War, Confederate infantryman Leon Louis kept a diary throughout the war. Many of his short, terse entries recorded nothing more than a sequence of foot marches in all weather and all conditions:

April 15—We got orders to march this evening. Went five miles through mud and water, and it raining like fury. I shall long remember this march…
May 8—We left here at 8 A.M., to return to Kinston, and got there at 3 P.M.—ten miles—awful road. Waded through mud, water and sand the whole way. My feet are cut up pretty badly.
May 21—left this morning, marched twenty-one miles, halted at 5:30. It is a very hilly country, warm and dusty.

May 23—Marched fifteen miles and halted. On our to-day's march we saw any amount of dead horses, which did not smell altogether like cologne.[5]

Louis fought at Gettysburg, and a week after that epic battle he wrote: "July 14—The roads are so bad that it is hard work to trudge along. We are now, thank God, on Confederate soil, but oh, how many of our dear comrades have we left behind. We can never forget this campaign. We had hard marching, hard fighting, suffered hunger and privation."[6] Another Confederate soldier, Charles Taylor, complained in a letter to his father, "A great many of the boys of the brigade are deserting and I don't blame them a bit for we are treated worse than negroes. Marched 20 miles without anything to eat and through the hot sun and some without water. . . . We was told we had only to 8 miles up the river but I found it to be a rather lengthy 8 miles. I got into camp about sun down as near broke down as I ever want to be again."[7]

Soldiers of other armies in other wars would have understood everything that these men were describing, even though they served under different flags in different parts of the world. Private Shiro Tokita, of the Japanese Army's 215th Infantry Regiment, recalled a forced march in Burma in 1942 that was, in his words, "the hardest I had ever experienced." Loaded down with weapons, ammunition, and the other detritus of the soldier's profession, Tokita's unit found it hard going. "Even though we infantrymen were accustomed to walking," he said, "the soles of our feet were covered in blisters. . . . We asked our medical corpsman to treat our feet during our short rest period, but finally he had to give up."[8] It was the same across the spectrum. "March, march, for hour after hour, without no halt," one British soldier wrote in the First World War; "we were now breaking into the fifth day of continuous marching with practically no sleep in between."[9] If this was not a universal view of the infantryman's life, it was very nearly so.

The French Foreign Legion for much of its history lived by the infamously harsh mantra of "march or die." In the desert wastelands of North Africa where many of the legionnaires served out their enlistments, to fall out of a route march very often had fatal consequences, and there was no compassion for men whose endurance failed this basic test. Special operations units such as the U.S. Army's Merrill's Marauders and the British Chindits, both of which served in Burma during the Second World War, lived and fought well beyond the supply lines of the conventional army, and the necessity of going on far past the perceived limitations of physical strength was the standard by which they lived and died. "When a man walks and walks and walks and the damned mountain gets no closer," one British soldier of the Royal Anglians told me years ago when we were suffering through a training course with the French Foreign Legion, "all he can do is try to think about sex, and keep walking." Sometimes, even that distraction was not enough.

After the Battle of Gaines' Mills in Virginia in June 1862, Union Army infantryman Samuel Tiebout described the route march his regiment was ordered to undertake. It was tough going, even for veterans. "The weather was very sultry, the roads very dry & dusty & as we each carried about 70 lbs. weight, our sufferings were terrible," he wrote in his diary. "In my own company (of some 70 or 80 men) 4 Serg'ts, 3 Corp'ls & 29 Privates fell out from exhaustion and were unable to rejoin the Regt until the following morning and some are even still missing."[10]

The reality for most soldiers, of every army and each of the combat arms, was that sooner or later they came up hard against what they had thought were the limits of their physical endurance. American infantrymen referred to this as "hitting the wall." Every man seemed to reach that point sooner or later, and most men discovered that they were capable of pushing on past it—exhausted, sore, and mentally drained, perhaps, but still they could keep trudging on under the crushing weight of their trade. Those who could not do so often appeared on the casualty lists. N. W. Bancroft, a British artilleryman who served in India in the mid-nineteenth century, learned this truth in his own career. "No man can estimate his own powers of endurance," he wrote, "until he is taught by experience what he can do in this way—or any other."[11]

That experience usually came through an excess of trial and tribulation, and many men were later never quite sure how they had gotten through it. "There were many days when I simply don't know what happened because I was so damned tired," a British gunner named J. W. Palmer wrote of his experience in France during the First World War. "The fatigue in the mud was something terrible. You reached a point where there was no beyond, you just couldn't go any further."[12] And yet, men did press on, far past the point of what they thought was their limit. A British infantryman with the Royal Fusiliers in 1918 described a situation familiar to combat soldiers everywhere. "I was wet and cold and they were shelling the blinking road out of Arras," he said. "I was carrying this bloody 48-lb. tripod, I mean it's heavy. I was wishing a bloody shell would drop on me. The only time in the war I hoped a shell would drop on me. But it didn't drop on me, so on I had to go."[13]

When men were required to carry on far past the point of normal exhaustion, the essence of military leadership often came down to officers and NCOs keeping them going long after they themselves were ready to fall out, keeping their men moving by the sheer force of their own self-discipline. Arthur Gibbs, a junior officer in the Welsh Guards during the fighting on the Somme in 1916, recalled the incredible effort it took to keep his company together one night when they finally came out of the lines. His men were so exhausted, he wrote, "it was just like driving animals along: I had had very little sleep for 4 days, and I certainly fell asleep at least once on the march. I also went to sleep standing up."[14] It was not at all an unusual thing for men to be so exhausted that they slept on their feet, even when marching—one encounters the same experience in the accounts of soldiers of nearly every nationality, and it is something I have experienced myself.

Infantrymen frequently remarked upon the degree to which physical exhaustion became a constant part of their lives. Men could be so tired that sleeping while walking was not uncommon. Paul Totten, an American infantryman who served in Russia in 1918 during the multinational expedition against the Bolsheviks, recorded one road march in his diary where his company set off at 3:00 a.m. and marched for eight hours. "On this trip I realized I had slept some on the march," he wrote. "I learned later that this phenomena, while not a frequent occurrence, did occur at times. But it happened to me—so help me. It was a baffling experience and one that is difficult to believe."[15] Exhausted men would fall asleep at the first opportunity. American infantrymen had a favorite saying: "Never stand when you can sit; never sit if you can lie down; and if you can lie down, then you might as well go to sleep." Soldiers of other armies expressed a similar idea in their own languages.

"If we were halted for one minute," Sam Watkins wrote of his Civil War experience, "every soldier would drop down, and resting on his knapsack, would go to sleep." Even when there was no tactical need to stay awake, exhausted men were not always allowed to rest undisturbed. "Sometimes the sleeping soldiers were made to get up to let some general and his staff pass by," Watkins remembered. "But whenever that was the case, the general always got a worse cursing than when Noah cursed his son Ham black and blue."[16]

Some armies acquired a particular fame (or notoriety) for hard marching. Stonewall Jackson's Confederate infantry were known as "Stonewall's Foot Cavalry" in the campaigns of the Shenandoah Valley during the Civil War, because of their repeatedly demonstrated ability to cover astonishing distances in a short time and arrive on the field still able to fight. In the British Army of the Napoleonic period, the Rifle Brigade moved at a faster marching pace than did the regular infantry regiments of the line. Japanese infantry were also known for their ability to cover considerable distance across tough terrain with surprising speed.

Paratroops are a relatively recent addition to the military structure, and the soldiers who wear their armies' airborne badges on their uniforms often wear them with an air of self-assumed superiority that their non-airborne qualified comrades find rather irritating. But paratroopers are legitimately an elite force, by nature of their selection and training, and their pride is well-earned even if their propensity for expressing it can be a bit tiresome to everyone around them. What is often overlooked, however, is that parachute drops are simply the means of getting those soldiers to the battlefield. For airborne infantry regiments, the reality is that once they are on the ground they have to walk everywhere, just like all other infantryman. This is one of the reasons why the parachute infantry units of the world's armies demand incredible levels of physical conditioning from their soldiers.

Martin Poppel, a German paratrooper who fought through the Second World War in Holland, Crete, Russia, and France as a *fallschirmjaeger,* recalled one training march his battalion did during the early months of the war. "We had a really murderous march exercise to Bayreuth," he wrote. "When I took off my boots in Bayreuth the pus and filth was running down my legs, blisters on top of blisters." The purpose of the route marches was clear, though, and Poppel knew it: "These weeks were exhausting us, but they hardened us," he recalled.[17]

Marching could be an arduous experience for a variety of reasons. Weather was a constant factor. Whether the conditions were rainy and wet, or hot and dusty, or freezing cold, the weather often compounded the physical hardships. Describing the German advance through Belgium in the summer of 1914, Julius Koettgen remembered marching "in the scorching midday sun; dust was covering our uniforms and skin."[18] Considering that the German uniform of the time was wool, even for summer campaigns, the physical discomfort would have been considerable.

Terrain was another obvious problem, with mountains presenting a particular challenge. Confederate infantryman Sam Watkins, remembering the Appalachian Mountains that his regiment marched through, said, "It seemed that mountain was piled upon mountain. No sooner would we arrive at a place that seemed to be the top than another view of a higher, and yet higher mountain would rise before us."[19] Eighty years later, on the other side of the world, another American soldier expressed the same impression of his service in Burma with Merrill's Marauders. "Toward the last," he wrote, "it became a matter of getting over one more hill and still another mountain over and over again with the certain knowledge that by no other means could we ever hope to terminate the torture."[20]

Even the relatively civilized landscape of central France held its own unique forms of torment for marching men. "The marching round this district is torture," Ernest Shephard of the Dorsets wrote in his First World War diary, "owing to the bad condition of the roads, which are paved with stone, very uneven, with about 2 inches of road refuse on top, with result that every pace taken you slip back or sideways a few inches."[21] It is worth noting that these two men, of different armies in different wars, both described hard marching as "torture," a word that appears in many memoirs in many languages.

The physical strain of long movements on foot while carrying a staggering amount of weight was a form of suffering that no infantryman ever forgot. Thomas Morris, a British sergeant, described the advance to Paris immediately after the Battle of Waterloo as almost a footrace: "It was important to reach Paris, before the scattered French troops could rally," he recalled. For the infantrymen of the line regiments, it was hard going. Morris remembered a daily average of thirty miles marching, a distance, he said, that was "tolerably good traveling, considering the heat of the weather and the weight we had to carry,—viz. musket, accoutrements, knapsack, canteen, camp-kettle, blankets, greatcoat, haversack, and provisions, and about 120 rounds of ball cartridge; making altogether about 60 lbs., which the infantry have each to carry." Morris had quite a bit of campaign experience to draw on by this point in his career, and the march to Paris stood out in his mind as being incredibly tough, even years after the event.[22]

One English veteran of the French Foreign Legion described in excruciating detail the tortuous route marches he endured during his initial training as a legionnaire in North Africa. A normal day's march was anything from twenty to forty-five miles, but as the training went on it was not unheard of to do sixty miles in a twenty-four-hour period. And the distance was compounded by the weight that had to be carried. "Our equipment was the standard desert-march pack," he wrote, "two changes of clothing, one blanket, shelter half, spare shoes, and overcoat. On the pack we carried a small bundle of firewood for our cooking fires. Each man also carried a kitchen utensil and two bottles full of water. One of these was to be used by the cooks, the other was for ourselves. The whole equipment including arms and ammunition weighed just about one hundred and five pounds a man. Strange as it may seem we needed the overcoats, for the Sahara Desert gets bitterly cold at night." Several years later, serving in Europe in the early days of the Second World War, he commented wryly, "The Legion did not waste any money on train fare when the men could march."[23]

Hard marching was one half of the infantryman's rough life; hard work was the other. Infantrymen found themselves engaged in drudgery more often than they felt was entirely fair. American infantryman John

Traub, who served during the Civil War, wrote, "It is always our luck to build breastworks and fortifications for others. . . . Our brigade has been to work every day except Sunday and sometimes Sunday, and night as well as day time. . . . Now [that] the most of the work and roughest of the work is done we are relieved." Relieved to move on to somewhere else and start digging all over again. Like rank-and-file infantrymen the world over, Traub felt himself much put upon by the workload. "They always ride a free horse to death," he grumbled.[24]

British troops in the Crimea in 1854 could have told Traub a thing or two about physical drudgery and its attendant miseries. Timothy Gowing, a sergeant in the Royal Fusiliers, described his regiment's trials in the siege of Sebastopol in language that gives a vivid depiction of his experience of the infantryman's lot in life:

Sometimes we would dig and guard in turn; we could keep ourselves warm, digging and making the trenches and batteries, although often up to our ankles in muddy water. All our approaches had to be done at night, and the darker the better for us. As for the covering party, it was killing work laying down for hours in the cold mud, returning to camp at daylight, wearied completely out with cold—sleepy and hungry; many a poor fellow suffering with ague or fever, to find nothing but a cold bleak mud tent, without fire, to rest their bones in; and often not even a piece of mouldy biscuit to eat, nothing served out yet. But often, as soon as we reached camp, the orderly would call out, "Is Sergeant G. in?" "Yes, what's up?" "You are for fatigue at once." Off to Balaclava, perhaps to bring up supplies, in the shape of salt beef, salt pork, biscuits, blankets, shot or shell. Return at night completely done up; down you go in the mud for a few hours' rest—that is, if there was not an alarm. And thus it continued, week in and week out, month in and month out. So much for honour and glory![25]

Infantrymen had their share of complaint, but the reality was that soldiers in the cavalry and artillery arms were never free from manual labor, either. Cavalrymen always had the added burden of their horses to contend with—more than one trooper expressed the futile hope that horse breeders would someday produce a horse that could look after itself. After a long day in the saddle, cavalrymen had to tend to their horses before they could see to their own needs. In American and British regiments, horse grooming was a twice-a-day chore, and a similar schedule was enforced in most other armies. In garrison, there were always stable duties to be done, mucking and scraping and cleaning and sweeping. And in the nineteenth century, the summer months were always filled with laying in fodder for the winter—sometimes the army contracted civilians to mow and rick the hay, but frequently those agrarian chores fell to the troopers themselves.

Artillerymen, especially during the era of horse-drawn artillery, had the cavalrymen's share of work and more besides. Where the individual cavalry trooper had one horse to keep, artillery drivers had two horses, and both of those horses had their assortment of tack: "Harness did not simply have to be cleaned but polished, with leather and brasswork shining," one historian notes. "Metalwork, like bits and chains, was unplated steel, and was burnished bright."[26]

For all of this, however, the infantry still felt they had it worse, so much so that it was almost part of their job description. Hard physical labor on the order of penal servitude was something with which most infantrymen were painfully familiar, and still are today. Of all the onerous chores demanded of them, digging and carrying were the two most common and most hated forms of work.

Digging was a frequent cause of complaint, particularly when a unit occupied a static, frontline position, and the process of improving the fortifications never seemed to end. One American infantryman serving in the Russian expedition of 1918 recorded his feelings on the subject in his diary:

Sunday, May 11, 1919 Worked all day gouging our trenches. Helped string barb wire at night. . . . We're exhausted. . . .
Monday, May 12, 1919 When do we rest? Another day of toil on fortification.
Tuesday, May 13, 1919 Up again long before the cock crows. Another day on the trenches. Nothing else of importance excepting some aching arms.

Wednesday, May 14, 1919 Another day of grind on the trenches. Started on Block houses. They are made from logs that we cut.
Saturday, May 24, 1919 Activity for today as listed below: work, work, work, dig, dig, dig. More work and more digging today—That's all!
Sunday, May 25, 1919 Worked on dug out in the morning. That blue clay getting tougher every day, or night, as the case may be.[27]

And so it went, until the day his company was ordered to leave that position and occupy another and started work on that one.

It might be assumed that digging trenches and constructing field fortifications would be the responsibility of the engineers (also known as sappers or pioneers), which every army has in its ranks. The reality, however, was that engineers were never numerous—even today, in the U.S. Army, there is only one combat engineer battalion to support an entire infantry or armored division. Engineers often provided the technical expertise for defensive works and sapping operations, but the manual labor was usually provided by unenthusiastic and resentful infantrymen. Resentful, that is, unless they were digging in under fire. In that case, self-preservation trumped all other considerations. "Did you ever see one of the steam shovels at work on the Panama Canal?" one veteran of the First World War wrote; "well, it would look like a hen scratching alongside of a Tommy 'digging in' while under fire, you couldn't see daylight through the clouds of dirt from his shovel."[28]

The trench warfare of the First World War was notorious for the demands it placed on combat soldiers, and those demands did not lessen when units came out of the lines for a rest period. It was usually anything but restful, as many men recalled it. Sergeant Major Shephard, writing home to his brother, wryly commented, "You say when we are at rest, that is *non est*, only rest we get is standing alternatively on right & left foot."[29] Another British soldier recalled one time when his battalion was rotated out of the line. "But it was not for a rest," he wrote; "for every night we had to go up digging and consolidating the trenches regained and digging communication trenches."[30] Staying below ground and thus out of sight of the enemy was a matter of survival in France—digging, improving, and repairing trenches were tasks that had no end.

As the fighting in France dragged on into 1916 and 1917, digging took on new and gruesome dimensions. One British soldier alluded to the problem when he referred to a German trench that his unit seized after a fierce fight. "We buried the nearest corpses, English and German," he wrote. "We set the men to work improving the trench, a hopeless task as every shovelful of mud thrown out slithered slowly back again."[31] The practice of burying the dead as quickly and expeditiously as possible (when it was possible to bury them at all) meant that bodies were interred very close to the trenches, and sometimes inside the trenches themselves. Inevitably, the decomposing corpses were frequently disinterred by shell-fire or the shovels of soldiers digging new positions.

"Our parapets," a British sergeant said, describing his unit's position in the battle of Ypres, "only consisted of a *single* thickness of sandbags, and shells bursting in the soft earth in front blasted them inwards." The only solution was to repair and improve the trench, but the previous occupants of the position were still there, in a macabre way. "All the time we were digging for material to fill sandbags," he remembered, "we were digging up dead bodies."[32] His experience was by no means unique.

"In the dug-outs we occupied on the 21st we found 3 dead Frenchmen," Sergeant Major Shephard wrote in his diary. "The back of trenches are full of them just covered over with earth, and in getting earth for our sandbags we strike into them."[33] Sometimes the process of digging up the dead was cause for a rather macabre humor. "In digging new trenches and new dugouts," Australian soldier E. P. F. Lynch wrote, "bodies and bits of bodies were unearthed, and put into sand-bags with the soil that was sent back down a line of men concealing their work from German eyes waiting for any new activity in our ditches. 'Bit of Bill,' said the leading man, putting in a leg. 'Another bit of Bill,' he said, unearthing a hand. 'Bill's ugly mug,' he said at a later stage in the operations, when a head was found."[34]

Even when digging did not involve the accidental uncovering of rotting corpses, it was still an unpleasant task, and soldiers in every army seemed to loathe it with equal intensity. "January also was a month of backbreaking work," a German soldier of the First World War wrote. "Each platoon began by removing the mud from the immediate vicinity of its dugout, by means of shovels, buckets and pumps."[35] American infantry doctrine held that one never actually stopped working on a fighting position—men just continued improving, strengthening, and working on it until they moved on to the next position. Thus, digging of one form or another was a perpetual activity that never really had an end.

~ ~

Digging was bad, as most men remembered it, but the sheer drudgery of carrying drew the greatest amount of profanity-laced complaint. "Carrying parties," the British called it—the back breaking work of conveying supplies forward by hand. Every infantryman had to do it; everyone hated it.

James Hall was an American who was visiting Britain when war broke out in 1914; almost on impulse, he enlisted in the British Army. Months later he was in the trenches in France, and the experience was beyond anything he had imagined. Describing his battalion's nightly routine in the lines, he wrote:

> *Like furtive inhabitants of an infamous underworld, we remained hidden in our lairs in the daytime, waiting for night when we could creep out of our holes and go about our business under cover of darkness. Sleep is a luxury indulged in but rarely in the first-line trenches. When not on sentry duty at night, the men were organized into working parties, and sent out in front of the trenches to mend the barbed-wire entanglements. . . . Ration fatigues of twenty or thirty men per company went back to meet the battalion transport wagons at some point several miles in rear of the firing-line. . . . The men who most bitterly resented the pick-and-shovel phase of army life were given a great deal of it to do for that very reason.*[36]

Hall served through some of the hardest conditions on the Western Front during the first two years of the war and published his account of his experiences in 1916. He was reported killed in action a year later, on June 28, 1917.

No matter the era, the army, or the war, the manual labor of hauling supplies had to be done and often in the worst weather and over the most difficult terrain. One American soldier who fought in Italy in 1943 remembered, "The mountain was so steep that a mule couldn't climb it, but we packed ammunition up in the mud and rain, sometimes 'till twelve o'clock at night."[37]

Cavalrymen and artillerymen at least had their saddlebags and caissons in which to carry some extra gear. Infantrymen, on the other hand, could carry only a much more limited amount of equipment, and this was particularly true before the advent of mechanized infantry units. Weapons and ammunition were items of first priority, with food and water next in order of necessity. Even those essentials, though, could not be carried in sufficient quantity to sustain one man for more than three days, on average. Once in combat, ammunition, food, and water had to be pushed forward to them in short order if they were to be able to continue fighting. Whether the mode of transport was horse-drawn wagon or motorized truck, the supply units could bring material only so far forward. A supply dump was usually established close behind the lines, and from there everything had to be carried forward by hand. Every box of rations, every crate of ammo, every can of water, every coil of razor wire—everything the infantryman needed to fight and live, he had to carry for some distance, and he had to carry it in rain and mud, over hills and mountains, through ditches and ravines, and often with the enemy adding a dose of hostile fire to his accumulated difficulties.

"Ammunition, boxes of rations, and five-gallon cans of water were brought up as close to us as possible," U.S. Marine Eugene Sledge wrote of his time on Okinawa. "But because of the mud along a shallow draw that ran to the rear . . . all the supplies were piled about fifty yards away in a supply dump on the other side of the draw." To get everything from the dump to where it was needed, men had to carry it. "We spent a great deal of time in combat carrying this heavy ammunition on our shoulders," Sledge said. "On Okinawa this was often done under enemy fire, in driving rain, and through knee-deep mud for hours on end."[38]

Carrying duty was universally loathed. Ancient armies might have used slave labor or hired porters to carry the paraphernalia of war, but in armies of this period, that task, inevitably, fell to the perpetually exhausted men of the infantry. The poet A. P. Herbert, who fought in the Royal Naval Division at Gallipoli, remembered, "There was no rest to be had in the camp during the day; and at night we marched out in long columns to dig in the whispering gullies, or unload ships on the beach. There were many of these parties, and we were much overworked, as all infantry units invariably are."[39]

The situation in France was much the same. "Working parties carrying stores were a normal nightly occupation when in support—one of the worst horrors of the war," a British soldier remembered; "endless toiling in the dark through mud, shell holes and old wire, carrying a heavy load of duckboards, rations or ammunition, always losing the man in front or being lost by the man behind, everyone hurrying, trying to pass some special danger point before the inevitable shell came."[40] Charles Carrington served as a private and then a junior officer in the First World War. "Carrying parties," he wrote, "loom up in the memory as the most persistent, fatiguing, hateful chore of the war in France and Flanders—everything by hand." What made it even worse, as he recalled, was the necessity of doing it under cover of darkness:

> The trench stores would have been a heavy burden for fresh men walking on good roads by daylight. In the dark, in the mud, it was so much worse with the added nightmare quality that came from the conformation of the trenches. A roll of barbed wire spitted on a stake and carried by two men is at any time an awkward burden. Now maneuver it along a deep muddy ditch in the dark. . . . It would be trouble enough to work your two-man load round corner after corner if you could see your way, but you slip in a shell-hole underfoot; your helmet is whipped off your head by a trailing wire; you catch your slung rifle on a projecting root; you tear your hand or your sleeve on the damnable wire-coil; you stumble and your mate swears at you... You've lost touch with the men in front and don't know where you're going until the sergeant's hoarse whisper makes it plain that the delay is all your fault.[41]

Moving at night while maintaining unit cohesion was difficult enough—most men remembered it as a particularly challenging, and often frightening, experience of war. Moving at night when burdened like a human pack mule was infinitely harder. "With those unhappy carrying-parties, where three-fourths of the men carried two heavy sacks of bread and tinned meat and other food, and the rest two petrol tins of water, or a jar of rum, or rifle oil, or whale oil, besides a rifle, and a bandolier, and two respirators, and a great-coat," Herbert wrote, "you must move with exquisite slowness, or you will lose your whole party in a hundred yards." Even that sort of careful movement was easily disrupted, often by the most innocuous things. "Half-way down the line a man halts to ease his load, or shift his rifle, or scratch his nose; when he goes on he can see no one ahead of him, and the cry 'Not in touch' comes sullenly up to the front."[42]

American infantrymen referred to this as a "break in contact," but the results were the same for them as for the British. The whole group ahead of the break had to halt and hold their position while the officer or sergeant in charge of the detail went back along the line of movement to try and locate the lost sheep, a very nerve-racking and dangerous proposition if they happened to be in an exposed position at the moment. When the rear group was found, it was almost always instantly apparent who the guilty party was—the first man in line among the stragglers was usually the man who had lost touch with the man to his immediate front. Anyone who thinks that savage fury and physical threat must be rendered at high volume in order to be effective has never heard the absolute viciousness that an angry, stressed, and weary sergeant can infuse into whispered profanity when he finally locates a lost group of soldiers who broke contact in the dark.

Night after night, in different armies, different eras, and different wars, men struggled through hostile darkness, overburdened and exhausted, carrying things that were both necessary and not, depending on whose perspective was being considered. Rank-and-file soldiers in every army have always been keen discerners of make-work, those chores assigned to them just to keep them busy. For the most part, these carrying parties that made the arduous treks between rear supply dumps and the forward lines were not that type of undertaking. Their tasks were absolutely necessary. A unit in the lines for two weeks would literally cease to exist as a fighting force if food, water, and ammunition were not regularly brought forward to them. So even though the infantry dreaded their inevitable turn at carrying, they all understood its necessity. That did not, however, make soldiers hate it any less, just as most of them never regarded digging as anything other than a necessary evil.

CHAPTER SIX

Tools of the Trade

The soldier cannot be a fighter and a pack animal at one the same time, any more than a field piece can be a gun and a supply vehicle combined. The idea is wrong at the start. Yet it is always being repeated."
—GENERAL J. F. C. FULLER

THE INDIVIDUAL COMBAT ARMS SOLDIER, whether an infantryman, cavalry or armor trooper, sapper, or artilleryman, is the ultimate factor in war. His ability to fight, to endure, and to accept the innumerable risks, dangers, and deprivation of the life is often what proves to be the difference between battles lost and battles won. On the eve of the Battle of Waterloo, Wellington supposedly pointed to a British infantryman who was passing by and said, "There; there, it all depends upon that article whether we do the business or not. Give me enough of it and I am sure." In that instance, as in so many others, the combat qualities of the British infantry were enough to carry the day.

Beyond the human factor of the individual soldier, the variables multiply exponentially. There are always the issues of the weapons with which soldiers are armed and with which they are expected to fight, the uniforms they wear, the loads they carry, and all the bewildering mass of army-issued gear and equipment and assorted detritus that weighs them down. Beyond the infinitely diverse human spectrum of the soldier himself, there is all this *other*: the tools of his martial trade.

The question of how the individual soldier should be equipped, and what items of gear are absolutely essential to his combat capability, is the holy grail of operational planning—armies devote incredible amounts of time and effort to puzzling this one out and trying to get it right, yet seldom do they ever get it just right. In part, this is because tactical situations change so frequently that no one solution can fit all bills. As a result, mission planners and military bureaucracies have usually erred on the side of caution and loaded the infantrymen down with a donkey's load of supplies and equipment, all on the premise that some of it *might* be needed.

As a result, the line infantry of most well-equipped armies are usually terribly overequipped, and that was true in almost every era throughout this period. In the Napoleonic Wars era, French infantrymen carried about fifty-five pounds of gear; their British adversaries were loaded with nearly seventy pounds on average. In the Crimean War, the British soldier was still carrying nearly the same weight, and his French counterpart's load had increased to almost the same amount. The American soldier of the Civil War carried a basic load of about fifty pounds, but during the Indian Wars of the following three decades the standard equipment of the infantry amounted to as much as sixty pounds per man, a considerable load for troops that were expected to be mobile and fast-marching. Japanese soldiers of the Second World War carried around sixty pounds each, more than half the body weight of an average Japanese man. For most of these men, these burdens were not just their marching loads, but also the weight they were expected to carry while fighting. In contrast with this, some troops, such as Soviet soldiers of the Second World War, were renowned for carrying only the bare essentials of weapons and ammunition and hardly anything in the way of personal gear or rations.

Surveying the infantryman's load across recorded history, it is apparent that most armies from ancient times to the present day have equipped their soldiers to about the same degree of weight—about fifty pounds per man, or something close to a third of the average man's body weight. Pile on a load heavier than that for sustained operations, and serious degradations in speed, mobility, and efficacy quickly begin to appear. From a soldier's perspective, this is self-apparent. One of the greatest misnomers in the modern military lexicon is the phrase *light infantry*, because a soldier's load in those types of units is anything *but* light. All the term means in modern warfare is that those troops do not have armor, heavy equipment, or much in the way of vehicular assets. Everything a light infantryman needs he carries on his person, and the long and heavy list of what his commanders think he needs sometimes approaches the absurd.

No matter the era or the army, for infantrymen, in particular, two factors were always a concern—the weight of their individual equipment and the condition of their feet, which for most men had much to do with the quality of their shoes. Throughout this period, the individual soldier's loadbearing equipment changed from leather straps to canvas or cotton webbing, but the basic effect was nearly always the same—too much weight, imperfectly loaded.

All armies experimented with different configurations of load-bearing systems, and those experiments met with varying receptions by the soldiers who actually had to use that gear. It was always a process of trial and error. Shortly after the U.S. Army adopted a new pattern of individual loadbearing equipment in 1875, a medical officer in the 13th U.S. Infantry wrote:

> *I am unable to state whether the accoutrements have any effect on the health of the wearers—not having seen the new equipments used in the field. The present plan of carrying the pack which throws most of the weight on the shoulders is a decided improvement upon the old, but the material is too heavy especially the straps and I am of the opinion that the knapsack with Blanket & overcoat attached if carried day after day on long marches, will develop in men not decidedly robust, diseases of the Heart and Lungs, that would permanently disable them for active service.*[1]

The irony is that the 1875 Pattern equipment actually *did* represent some improvement over previous systems, even if it wasn't perfect. The American soldier might have had reason to grumble about his load, but at least he was not wearing the high leather stock collars of his British predecessors during the Napoleonic Wars, the constrictive cross belts of the Crimean War era, nor any of the other officially mandated impediments with which armies all over the world hampered their soldiers during the period. Bad as it was, it could be worse—in many eras, it really was worse.

Even armies that were renowned for their organization and efficiency did not get it right consistently. Gas warfare marked the First World War, and the memory of that experience meant that almost every belligerent European nation went into the Second World War prepared to counter gas. In fact, gas was almost never used in that war. The results of equipping soldiers with a piece of equipment that they soon determined to be useless were nothing if not predictable. Wehrmacht soldier Joachim Pusch said, "One of the things we did that was against the rules was to throw away our gas masks. They were in big tubes. We put food in there instead. Food is one thing that sustains you." American and British soldiers did exactly the same thing. As George Bernard Shaw wrote in *Arms and the Man*, "You can always tell an old soldier by the inside of his holsters and cartridge boxes. The young ones carry pistols and cartridges; the old ones, grub." Shaw was no particular admirer of the military, but he certainly got that detail right—when I was an infantryman I always kept one extra ammunition pouch on my harness just for cigars and pogey bait.

UNIFORMS

Armies, as more than one commentator has observed, are just a short step away from being an armed rabble, mobs in all but name. Discipline is usually cited as the one thing that prevents the former from disintegrating into the latter, but uniformity also has a lot to do with both how soldiers are identified and how they identify themselves. It is no coincidence that one of the first things deserters have usually done is get rid of their uniforms and try to blend in with the civilian population.

In 1800, the beginning of the period under examination here, most military uniforms were not uniquely military. That is, their design owed much more to contemporary civilian fashions than to any military necessity or practical function. This was particularly true of officers' uniforms—Georgian-era officers of the British Army went into battle wearing the long coats, ornate waistcoats, and tight breeches of well-dressed gentlemen in civilian society, albeit in the king's red and ornamented with the gold trim and brocade of their rank. Further adding to the problem was the fact that at this point in history there was no such thing as a uniform specifically designed as a combat uniform, differentiated from a dress uniform. Throughout much of the nineteenth century, a soldier converted his regular service uniform into a dress uniform simply by adding items of decoration or insignia to it. The uniform that a man wore on formal occasions of pomp and ceremony was essentially the same uniform he wore when marching and fighting.

There *were* some uniforms that were distinctly different from civilian attire, but different in those cases did not necessarily mean more practical or functional. Cavalry uniforms were prone to ostentatiousness and extravagant flamboyance—fur-trimmed pelisses, tight breeches, short-waisted hussars' jackets, and headgear that was adorned with everything from horsetails to feathers to fur. For sheer impracticality, though, no military unit could trump the famous "winged hussars" of the Polish army. These cavalrymen each wore two tall poles set with feathers on their backs that arched forward over their heads. It was a unique and distinctive look, one that made them instantly recognizable on the field—it also served absolutely no military purpose as a combat asset.

The impracticality of military uniforms in the early part of this period was not the result of a lack of experience in the physical demands of army life—some of the most battle-tested armies of the era marched out dressed in a manner completely unsuited to the hard job of soldiering in the field. Tradition counted for more than soldiers' comfort, and fashion usually won out over function. This did not mean, however, that the men in the ranks always wore their kit without complaint.

Blaze de Blury served in the French army that marched into Russia in 1812. After the disaster of the horrific retreat that destroyed Napoleon's army, de Blury was lucky to still be alive to render his comments on the experience. "I have never understood why," he wrote, "under Napoleon, when we were constantly at war, the soldier should have been forced to wear the ghastly breeches, which, by pressing on the hams at the back of the knee, prevented him from walking easily. On top of that, the knee, which was covered by a long buttoned-up gaiter, was further strangled." This was the uniform of an infantry that walked everywhere it went, all across Europe. "It was, all in all," de Blury, concluded, "a conspiracy by three thicknesses of cloth, two rows of buttons one on top of the other, and three garters to paralyze the efforts of the bravest of marchers."[2]

Impractical uniforms were not an issue unique to the French alone; to varying degrees every army of the period had some experience of it, at different times. Some of the problem stemmed not so much from bad design as it did from the limitations of materials. In the days before synthetic fibers were developed, wool was the mainstay of most military uniforms. Wool had the advantage of being hardy and warm, even when wet; on the other hand, it was heavy, and it could be swelteringly uncomfortable in hot weather. Remarkably, from a modern perspective that associates heavy wool with winter clothing, these uniforms were not intended solely for winter use. "There was no such thing as a winter uniform," historian Adam Zamoyski says of the Napoleonic French Army, "since in those days armies did not fight in winter." To further complicate the picture, armies that opted for materials other than wool often found the substituted fabrics to be utterly inadequate when used in impractically designed uniforms.

The U.S. Army was emblematic of the overall problem with uniforms, because it tried to devise a single service uniform that soldiers would wear in all seasons and all regions, whether it was the height of summer in the Arizona desert or the worst of winter in the mountains of Montana. Most European armies applied the same approach to soldiers' uniforms, with the common result that soldiers who felt overdressed in the summer heat were underdressed in winter cold. Wool was serviceable, tough, and sturdy, but it was not versatile.

In nineteenth-century sources, soldiers at the end of a hard campaign are often depicted as being ragged and tatterdemalion. It was not literary exaggeration. Unlike modern armies, rank-and-file soldiers throughout much of this period were not issued with multiple uniforms—they usually had only the one uniform they were wearing, and when that wore out, they carried on with holes in their trousers and patches on their jackets. Men frequently improved their wardrobe by scrounging clothing from dead men on the battlefield—a bullet hole, after all, was easily enough repaired, and blood stains could be laundered out. When soldiers believed that the enemy's gear was superior to their own, they were not above appropriating those items for their use, even if that sometimes required some grisly methods of acquisition. Edmund Bonhoff, a German infantryman who fought in the freezing hell of the Eastern Front in the Second World War, recalled, "We used to saw the legs off frozen Russian corpses in order to get their warm felt boots. We stood them up against a stove and when the legs thawed, we pulled them out and dried off the boots."[3] Grim necessity usually won out over sensitive inhibitions.

In the early days of the period there were no such things as specially designed military boots, at least not for the infantry. Infantrymen in all armies wore shoes that were at best just heavy work shoes and at worst no better than lightweight civilian footwear. In eras when infantrymen walked hundreds of miles in a campaign season, they literally wore out their shoes. Under normal conditions, there would usually be time and opportunity for the cobblers among the soldiers to repair their comrades' shoes. Benjamin Harris was a rank-and-file infantryman in the Rifle Brigade of Wellington's army, but he was also a cobbler by training, and his memoir is dotted with incidents where he worked at repairing worn-out footwear for his fellow soldiers. He apparently made a rather good sideline income by doing so. Sometimes, however, even that sort of field-expedient shoe repair was not possible.

Men who experienced the British retreat to Corunna in 1808 and the French retreat from Moscow in 1814 described seeing men stumbling along barefoot through the snow, their feet wrapped in bloody rags because their shoes had fallen apart miles back. More than a century later, shoes were still a problem. When the Germans invaded Russia in the Second World War, they quickly found that their standard-issue boots were not adequate for the extremes of Russian winter. As soldiers have done the world over, they resorted to their own field-expedient alterations to try and improve the situation. "The first thing we really did was we pulled the hobnails out of the soles of our boots because the metal directed the cold right into the shoe, into the foot," one Wehrmacht soldier recalled, "Then we found all kinds of remedies, like making straw soles to put in our boots."[4] American infantrymen fighting in the snow of the Ardennes in 1944 likewise found that their standard-issue boots were inadequate; it was almost an ironic insult that the longed-for snowpack winter boots arrived after the worst of the winter fighting was over.

As the early decades of this period unfolded, there was at first little in the way of institutionalized improvement in the way armies dressed their soldiers. British soldiers in the Crimea suffered terribly from the wretchedly wet, cold weather—they received no heavy winter clothing until spring had come and the weather was much improved. William Howard Russell, the correspondent for *The Times* of London, wrote that British soldiers "had neither warm nor waterproof clothing… hundreds of men had to go into the trenches at night with no covering but their greatcoats, and no protection for their feet but their regimental shoes."[5]

Fifty years after Waterloo, the British were still holding fast to uniforms that were clearly at odds with the realities of soldiering. A British infantryman in the 1860s was still outfitted in red coat and white cross belts with brass buckles and badges. Reflecting on this getup, a soldier named Robert Blatchford wrote, "A Fusilier, buckled and belted up tight in a scarlet tunic, with straps under his armpits, a knapsack, folded coat, and canteen on his back, with a stiff band of slippery buff in the way of his rifle-butt, and with a great fur balloon on his head, was a noble mark for an enemy's fire; and could not have shot straight himself if he had been an angel." The uniforms of the day might have looked fine on parade, but they were wretchedly unsuited to active service or the physical demands of soldiering. "Ask any man who has been out for a week's manoeuvers in wet weather what happened to him," Blatchford went on to say. "An hour's heavy rain washed the pipeclay off the belts all over the scarlet cloth. The buckles when wet made dark stains on the tunic, the buff belts, ball-pouches and slings became sodden and greasy. One good drenching for an hour meant three or four day's hard work getting one's arms, belts, and clothing right again." Cleaning, buffing, and polishing was always part of a soldier's life, but the reality that Blatchford was describing must have felt like a considerable amount of insult added to injury.[6]

The physical demands of long foot marches have already been considered in previous chapters, but here we come to it again in a different sense. Terrain, weather, and distance have always contributed their share to the combined experience of exhausting misery that infantrymen live with, but the things with which soldiers are laden also play a part. Throughout this period, the infantry were overloaded with a staggering amount of military equipment, some of it necessary but much of it not, at not least in the opinion of the men who had to carry it.

Rifleman Harris, who survived the grueling retreat to Corunna, described the infantryman's load as being almost more than a man could manage. Some men, he was sure, died because they could not manage it. "The weight I toiled under was tremendous," he said; "indeed, I am convinced that many of our infantry sank and died under the weight of their knapsacks along. For my own part, being a handicraft [Harris, remember, was one of his regiment's shoemakers], I marched under a weight sufficient to impede the free motions of a donkey." Harris was no stalwart physical specimen, either. "Altogether the quantity of things I had on my shoulders was enough and more than enough for my wants, sufficient, indeed, to sink a little fellow of five feet seven inches into the earth."

It was not only the weight that was a problem, though—in the days before the science of ergonomics was ever applied to the design of military loadbearing equipment, infantrymen suffered from poorly arranged loads. "Nay, so awkwardly was the load our men bore in those days placed upon their backs," Harris said, "that the free motion of the body was impeded, the head held down from the pile at the back of the neck, and the soldier half beaten before he came to the scratch."[7]

It is a reality of military life that soldiers can initially be described as well-equipped because of the enormous amount of gear they start out with, and then quickly they can be more accurately described as *practically* equipped because they have contrived to lose every piece of equipment that they deem to be an unnecessary burden. If they think they can get away with ditching it, into the ditch it goes. Leander Stillwell, serving in a Union regiment during the Civil War, recalled that his regiment set out on one march "with great bulging knapsacks . . . much of which was utterly useless to soldiers in the field. But we soon got rid of all that." Most of the men did, at any rate, but Stillwell remembered that there was one group of soldiers who did not litter the passage of their march with unwanted impedimenta. "The exception to that, in the main, were the soldiers of foreign birth, especially the Germans," he wrote. "They carried theirs to the last on all occasions, with everything in them the army regulations would permit, and usually something more."[8] Whether the German determination to carry the full issue was a matter of superior discipline or martial materialism, Stillwell did not opine.

Men fighting for the Confederacy in that war were much more hap-hazardly equipped, and they hardly ever enjoyed the embarrassment of riches that their counterparts in the Union Army enjoyed, but they also were not averse to ridding themselves of unwanted items when the long march made them tally every ounce of weight. Marion Ford wrote that on one occasion, "our men had started on this march with as much bag-gage as they thought they could carry, but they soon threw aside their impedimenta."[9] Even items that were worth having were sometimes thrown away, especially when there was a chance that the Confederate soldiers could indulge their practice of appropriating enemy equipment.

Carlton McCarthy, who served in the Army of Northern Virginia, wrote that some of his fellow Southerners "clung to their overcoats to the last, but the majority got tired of lugging them around, and either discarded them altogether, or trusted to capturing one about the time it would be needed." The result made the Confederate regiments even mot-lier in appearance than they already were; McCarthy remembered that "nearly every overcoat in the army in the latter years was one of Uncle Sam's captured from his boys."[10]

After the Union Army's assaults at Fredericksburg were broken on the killing grounds of the slopes below Marye's Heights, Confederate Lieutenant William S. Burgwyn wrote that he "gave permission to some of my men to visit the field of battle and supply themselves with over-coats and things which they needed and consequently they obtained from the dead Yankees as many overcoats shoes + boots and Haversacks and enough provisions to ration three or Regiments. I have now an overcoat on taken from a dead Yankee also a fine pair of boots and a cap." It was a cold December, and Burgwyn's infantrymen were undoubtedly pleased to have the benefit of the enemy's quartermaster stores.[11]

In some situations, the design of the equipment proved inadequate to the uses to which it was put, or at least, the uses that army planners intended. For the U.S. Army during the Indian Wars era, an effective means for a soldier to carry his rations in the field was never satisfactorily devised as long as those rations continued to be issued in the form of meat that needed to be cooked on the spot. For infantrymen in particu-lar, the method of transporting one day's ration in the field was far from ideal—the salt or pickled pork was "carried in the meat-ration can, whose two parts are only pressed together, and being carried on its end [in the haversack] . . . the heat of the sun melts the grease, which very easily runs out." Runs out, and all over the soldier's other gear that he carried in his haversack. Given the army's emphasis on men keeping all their issued gear in clean, presentable condition, the need to clean rancid pork grease from canvas and leather must have been a regular aggravation.

WEAPONS

To say that the tools of the soldier's trade underwent incredible transformation during this period is an enormous understatement. In 1800, the principal artillery of the battlefield were smoothbore cannon fired over open sights at targets in direct line of sight of the gunners, and the principal infantry weapons were smoothbore flintlock muskets fired at an enemy who was not in much danger of being deliberately hit at any range beyond seventy-five meters. By 1945, however, the infantrymen of the world's armies were carrying a wide array of personal arms that included bolt-action magazine-fed rifles, self-loading rifles, fully automatic assault rifles, and submachine guns. Light and heavy machine guns were by then the linchpins of infantry tactics, dominating infantry battle in ways unimaginable half a century before. Artillery had vastly improved in every way—accuracy, range, power, and killing ability—and was increasingly marked by advances in ordnance production, range-finding and target acquisition, and the principles of higher mathematics. Artillerymen of both world wars usually fired at targets that they themselves never even saw on account of the increasing ranges. This period began with black powder and flintlocks; it ended with the atom bomb.

Weapons are items with which soldiers have complicated relationships. The new recruit is often overly enamored of his weapon the first time he holds it, especially if he comes from societies where firearms are not part of the average individual's personal experience. The younger the soldier, the more posturing and strutting is usually involved with that first handling of the weapon that is to be such an essential part of his martial life. Older soldiers—older in either age or experience—often regard their weapons as simply tools of the trade, and sometimes as just so much heavy scrap iron that the army requires them to carry around.

It never took long for new soldiers to discover that their issued weapons—whether firearm, bayonet, sword, or cannon—came with a long list of attendant menial labor. Cleaning the piece occupied more time than one might think, and more than one soldier has left a record of his grumbling about the army's requirement that individual arms had to be maintained to fanatical states of cleanliness. The more complicated the weapon, the more time and effort are required in its upkeep, and as more than one recruit has discovered in the past century, the thrill of firing a machine gun is pretty much forgotten when the time comes to clean the wretched thing.

A modern observer might assume that the soldier's principal weapon at the beginning of this period was a rather simple piece of hardware. After all, it was a smoothbore, muzzle-loading, black powder single-shot musket with incredibly primitive sights. The reality, however, is that there was much more to the early nineteenth-century musket than first meets the eye.

The firing mechanism of the flintlock—the "lock" itself—was actually a rather intricate piece of technology. The principal parts, which gave the lock its characteristic profile and were pretty much standard in most muskets of the day regardless of their country of manufacture, consisted of a large hammer, or cock, with a screw-tightened jaw that held the all-important flint seated in a small piece of leather. In front of the hammer was the frizzen, a hinged piece of steel covering the pan into which a soldier would pour a few grains of powder. The firing sequence was simple. With the hammer at full cock, when the trigger was pulled the hammer snapped forward, striking the flint against the frizzen face and driving a spark down into the powder in the pan, which in turn ignited the powder in the barrel and fired the ball downrange.

If the mechanical firing sequence was simple, the loading and reloading sequences were anything but simple. For the French in 1815, their musketry drill consisted of eight basic steps in loading their pieces. The British of the same period used a sequence of ten steps (but the British infantry were generally more skilled in the process than most of their opponents). This complicated process had a predictable effect on rates of fire. In the chaos and smoke of massed infantry battle, a veteran unit of line infantry could fire three to four rounds a minute. The British, who were one of the only armies in the world to train with live ammunition on a regular basis, could consistently put out rates of fire slightly better than that, but even they were still limited by the efficacy of their weapons. (Incidentally, the popular conception of soldiers biting open the paper cartridge and holding the ball in their mouths, then spitting it down the barrel after they had poured in the powder, is almost certainly inaccurate. After firing just a few rounds, the muzzle of the musket would be hot enough to burn skin on contact.)

Accuracy for smoothbore muskets was noteworthy by its almost complete absence, and no soldier in that era was under any illusions on that point. When it came to infantry firepower, tactics of the day stressed quantity over quality; that is, as much massed fire as possible with no real emphasis or expectation of carefully aimed shots. In 1814 the noted British ordnance expert Major George Hanger wrote, "A soldier's musket, if not exceedingly ill-bored (as many are), will strike a figure of a man at 80 yards; it may even at a hundred; but a soldier must be very unfortunate indeed who shall be wounded by a common musket at 150 yards, providing his antagonist aims at him; and as to firing at a man at 200 yards with a common musket, you may as well fire at the moon and have the same hope of hitting him." Hanger was an absolute realist about the musket's problems with accuracy. "I do maintain and will prove," he wrote, "that no man was ever killed at 200 yards, by a common musket, by the person who aimed at him."[12] Level your piece in the general direction of the enemy's ranks, let fly, and hope for the best formed the doctrine of the day.

There were a few exceptions to this. The British riflemen of the Rifle Brigade, armed with the Pattern 1800 Infantry Rifle, better known as the Baker rifle, were able to hit out to much greater ranges and were trained to a much higher standard of individual marksmanship. Aside from the obvious advantage of having a rifled bore, the Baker also benefited from using leather-patched ball ammunition that fit tightly in the barrel, thereby achieving a ballistic spin when fired. This greater accuracy, however, was achieved at the cost of a lower rate of fire—the Baker rifle took considerably longer to load and reload than did a standard-issue smooth-bore musket, which is why the Riflemen did not usually fight in standard line of battle, but were deployed as open-order skirmishers in front of the massed ranks. It was this reduced rate of fire, ironically, which prompted Napoleon to decide against issuing rifled muskets to the *voltigeurs,* the French Army's light skirmishers, a decision that put the *voltigeurs* at a considerable disadvantage when they went up against their British counterparts who were armed with the Bakers. Some American militiamen of the early nineteenth century also had a well-earned reputation for accuracy, which owed everything to their use of the famous Pennsylvania and Kentucky long-rifles, rather than standard-issue muskets.

Depending on the army in which they served, regular infantry in the line and grenadier regiments of the Napoleonic Wars era were armed much alike. The British carried the Land Pattern Tower musket (the famous "Brown Bess"), weighing 4.8 kilos/10.5 pounds; the French used the Model 1777 musket, weighing 4.6 kilos/9.9 pounds; the Prussians were armed with the New Prussian Model 1809, which weighed 4 kilo/8.8 pounds; and the Austrians fielded the Austrian Model 1798, which weighed in at about 4.7 kilos/10 pounds. What these weapons each had in common with all the others was that they were about as heavy as a sledgehammer, and just as accurate. For one thing, there were no aiming sights to speak of, just a small projection at the muzzle that resembled the bead on a modern shotgun barrel. The lead balls with which the musket was loaded were loose in the barrel, loose enough to rattle around if not rammed down with a patch or wadding, a matter of intentional design because it allowed the piece to be fired more times before cleaning was necessary. The fact that there was a very slight delay between the initial trigger pull (which caused the "flash in the pan") and the actual blast of the shot meant that a man had to hold his heavy weapon steady that much longer while he waited for the discharge, just one more factor stacking up against his chances of ever hitting his target.

Furthermore, in order to throw a .69 caliber lead ball weighing several ounces out to its maximum range, about 450 yards, such a large load of powder was necessary that when the musket was fired, it kicked like a wild ass. No one likes the repeated physical impact of heavy recoil, no matter what they say about it, and poorly trained soldiers like it even less than others. The natural tendency to flinch in the act of firing the musket all but guaranteed that most soldiers did not have a realistic chance of hitting whomever they were shooting at. Hence, the tactical emphasis on massed musketry.

One crucial item often overlooked in considerations of flintlock-era firearms is the all-important flint itself. Without this little piece of knapped stone, a soldier could carry all the powder and shot he wanted to no purpose—the musket simply could not be fired if there was no flint in the lock. The economic pressures of sustained warfare during the Napoleonic period meant that some combatant countries had no means of resupplying their stock of flints, but other countries such as Britain were blessed with inexhaustible flint quarries. So vital was the flint to the individual soldier's ability to fight, that most armies of the era issued orders that soldiers were not to "snap their locks during exercises unless the flint had been replaced by a wooden dummy 'snapper.'"[13] For the British infantryman, loss of a flint was an offense so serious that it could be punished with a flogging of as many as one thousand lashes.

The percussion lock firing mechanism was patented in 1807, a development that did not immediately halt the production of flintlock muskets for mainline military use. Within twenty years after Waterloo, however, most armies of the world were fully engaged in converting their existing stocks of flintlocks to percussion locks. In the United States, the U.S. Model 1842 Musket was the first standard-issued infantry weapon to be designed and produced as a percussion firearm for the U.S. Army. The British Army adopted the percussion lock mechanism at the same time, and through an almost identical process of trials and field implementation.

The U.S. Army of the Civil War era was most commonly armed with either the Springfield Model 1861 rifled musket or the Pattern 1853 Enfield, both in .58 caliber, which were well-designed firearms and very effective on the battlefield. These were much more accurate than the smoothbore muskets that preceded them, but they were still heavy, weighing in at nearly ten pounds unloaded. Militia troops and volunteer regiments, however, especially in the early days of the war, were often issued older weapons that were practically obsolete. Albert Marshall enlisted in the 33rd Illinois Volunteer regiment and did not think much of the first weapon he was issued. "The guns we drew were muskets of a European make," he wrote. "The boys were very much disappointed. They had expected to get some of the best rifles in use. They had enlisted with the understanding that this regiment was to be armed with the Enfield rifles, or better, if better were to be had." What they actually got was something altogether different. "Expecting to get the best rifles and then to get a musket—and such a musket! A musket that needed the services of a skillful engineer to run it successfully." The process of actually loading one of these contraptions and firing it was no simple process:

> *To load one of them: commence by taking a cartridge out of the cartridge box, tear off the end of it and pour the powder down in the gun, then place the ball in after the powder. . . . At this stage of the proceeding, with a decent gun, a percussion cap would be taken from its box, the hammer of the gun raised, and the cap placed upon the gun tube, but these guns do not go off with a simple little percussion cap such as we are acquainted with. No, indeed. First, the hammer must be raised and then a little trap door must be opened, then a funny little primer about two thirds of an inch in length with a pretty little wire string attached, must be taken from its box and inserted "just so" in a cunning little pocket, and then the amusing little trap door must be carefully closed down over it, and thus go through all of this elaborate ceremony before the gun can be loaded.*

This complicated process was hardly suited for novice troops coming under fire for the first time. "These guns must be intended for soldiers who go out and fire one shot and then return leisurely to camp and go back the next day to fire the second volley," Marshall grumbled in his diary.[14]

Another problem could arise when outdated muskets of a different caliber than the standard-issue modern weapons of the day were issued, and it was a serious one. During the U.S.–Dakota War of 1862, an error in the supply system meant that militiamen were issued .69 caliber ball ammunition when their weapons were the newer pattern .58 caliber muskets. At the Battle of Birch Coulee, when a detachment of soldiers was surrounded and pinned down by a larger force of Dakota warriors for two days before being relieved, men had to whittle down bullets with their knives in order to load their weapons.

In an interesting development, the American and British armies each began the process of replacing their muzzle-loading arsenals with breech-loading rifles in the same year, 1866. In both instances, rather than designing and contracting for completely new rifles, the armies took the interim step of adapting existing stocks of weapons to a new technology, just as they had done earlier when they first converted the old flintlocks to percussion locks. The impetus for this transition came from the Prussians, who in 1848 stole a march on every other military power in the world by adopting the Leichtes Perkussionsgewehr M/41, or Dreyse needle-gun, as their standard-issue infantry rifle. The Dreyse got its familiar name from its long internal firing pin, which was designed to pierce the rifle's paper cartridge ammunition and ignite the primer. The needle gun was revolutionary for another reason, as well—it incorporated the first practical bolt-action mechanism on a standard infantry rifle and represented a major advancement in infantry battle technology.

Realizing how far behind they were in weapons development, the U.S. Army cast about for a quick response. The army's principal firearms contractor, the Springfield Armory, developed a conversion process to transform the Model 1861 muzzle-loading rifle-muskets into breech-loaders by cutting open the breech end of the barrel and fitting a trap-door mechanism. The inclusion of a rifled sleeve in the barrel changed the weapon's bore from .58 to .50 caliber. These were important factors in improving both the rate of fire and accuracy of the refitted rifles, but of almost equal note was the fact that the new design took a metal cartridge with an internal primer, rather than the old paper cartridges that required a separate percussion cap. The redesigned rifle, designated the Allin-Conversion Springfield Rifle after the armorer who invented the process, remained in service with American infantrymen until it was replaced by the Model 1873 Springfield trapdoor rifle, which saw action through the Spanish-American War.

The British converted their outmoded 1853 Enfields by a similar process, which in their case involved the adoption of a breech-loading mechanism designed by American inventor Jacob Snider. This was implemented by installing a side-hinged breech-block with an extractor that opened to the right. The improvement in rate of fire was almost the same as that of the new American Springfield—ten rounds of aimed fire a minute over the two to three rounds per minute possible with the muzzleloaders. Even though it was just a stopgap measure intended to fill the need while an entirely new rifle could be designed, tested, and selected (which for the British would eventually be the legendary Martini-Henry, in all its various model configurations), the Snider-Enfield gave good service and proved its worth on battlefields in Abyssinia and Ashanti.

The Martini-Henry, for its part, was a robust rifle that wrote its place in history during the colonial wars against the Zulus, the Dervishes, the Afghan hill tribes, and others. It was a powerful rifle, initially chambered for the .577 cartridge before later models were issued in the .303 British round that was to be the mainstay of the British Army until well after the Korean War. The Martini-Henry had a shoulder-bruising recoil, and its extractor would often foul during heavy action, requiring the rifleman to sometimes kick the lever to open the breech for reloading, but in battles all over the empire it allowed outnumbered British regiments to stand in their squares and blast charging tribesmen into bloody ruin.

The demise of the age of breech-loading rifles was marked by the advent of bolt-action infantry rifles. One of the first of its species, as we have seen, was the Dreyse needle-gun, but that rifle was obsolete by the time the Germans replaced it with the Mauser Model 1871, also known as the Infanterie Gewehr 71, which was adopted in February 1872. Despite the technological advancement represented by the bolt-action mechanism, the Model 1871 had its issues, not least of which was the fact that as a single-shot rifle, it did not offer an appreciable improvement in the rounds-per-minute rate of fire for the frontline infantryman. That the German rifle did not represent a major step forward in battlefield weaponry is indicated by the fact that the British Army, which was then engaged in colonial warfare more frequently than the Germans were engaged in conventional European wars, retained the breech-loading Martini-Henry rifle as its principal infantry weapon until 1888.

Through the late 1880s, single-shot rifles remained the primary arms of the world's infantry formations. The transition from breech-loading rifles to bolt-action, magazine-fed weapons happened in fits and starts, and in almost every case the first models of the newer weapons adopted did not remain in service for long. In 1894, The U.S. Army officially replaced the Model 1873 Springfield with the Model 1892 .30-40 Krag-Jorgensen, but only in sufficient quantities for the perpetually under-strength peacetime force of the Regular Army. When the United States went to war with Spain in 1898, the army expanded from 26,000 men to more than 100,000, which meant that the volunteer regiments raised from the separate states entered service armed with the outmoded but still reliable breech-loading Springfields. The choice of the Krag reflected the military traditionalists' grudging approach to new technology—although it was a magazine-fed, bolt-action rifle, its design meant that it was relatively slow to reload, and it had a magazine cutoff that could allow it to be fired as a single-shot weapon, a fact that the conservative minds in the military bureaucracy apparently believed would keep soldiers from wasting ammunition.

The British Army, for its part, replaced the hardy Martini-Henry breechloader with the Lee-Metford bolt-action rifle for a few years before adopting the iconic ten-round Short Magazine Lee-Enfield Mk 1 in the robust .303 caliber in 1895. The Lee-Enfield truly enhanced the already-considerable combat firepower of British infantrymen—a trained rifleman could fire as many as thirty aimed shots in a single minute, even allowing for the need to reload twice in that time. Here again, the conservative thinkers had to have their way—the rifle's box magazine was detachable, but it was assumed that the average infantryman would inevitably lose it in the field, so the rifle was initially issued with the magazine secured to the rifle by means of a short chain. The Lee-Enfield continued in service with the British Army well past the Korean War and is still encountered in some remote corners of the former empire today.

On the eve of the First World War, the United States abandoned the Krag-Jorgensen in favor of the Model 1903 Springfield, which proved to be a first-rate battle rifle. Chambered in the powerful .30-06 cartridge, the '03 Springfield was an extremely accurate, tough, hard-hitting rifle that was a truly devastating weapon in the hands of a trained rifleman. It remained the standard-issue rifle of the U.S. Army and Marine Corps until the first year of the Second World War and then continued on in service in a sniper-rifle configuration.

By 1916, all the belligerent nations of the First World War had embraced the use of machine guns in the infantry-support role, but to different degrees and with varying success. The Germans, whose use of the Maxim Maschinengewehr 08 heavy machine gun made such carnage of British assaults on the Somme and elsewhere, also used the light version of the Maxim in the MG 08/15 configuration, with a full complement of six guns employed by every infantry company. The British had the reliable Lewis Automatic Rifle, better known simply as the Lewis gun. (Ironically, the Lewis gun was designed by an American army officer but was rejected by closed-minded ordnance boards in the U.S. Army during the prewar years.) Using forty-seven- or ninety-seven-round pan magazines, the Lewis gun was a good weapon for infantry tactics in the light machine gun role. "Light," in this case, may have been a bit of wishful thinking by the ordnance department, since the weapon weighed no less than twenty-eight pounds, but there was no denying that the gun gave a considerable firepower option to infantry companies in both the offensive and defensive roles, and it was accurate and reliable.

If the Lewis gun had issues, the biggest one was its ammunition supply. The inherent problem that arises when any automatic weapon with a cyclic rate of five hundred to six hundred rounds per minute is fed by magazines into which the rounds have to be loaded by hand, one at a time, is obvious—in order to maintain an effective rate of fire, the gunner has to have a sufficient supply of magazines, and each of those magazines takes considerable time to reload, once expended. One British soldier pointed this out in his narrative of the First World War:

> *[The Lewis Gun] was an ingenious toy which you could take to pieces and put together again in two minutes, and which never gave serious trouble except from wet dirt—of which there was no lack on the battlefields. What puzzled us was the ammunition supply, made up in circular pans holding fifty rounds, which were difficult to re-fill and*

devilish heavy to carry about. Put a pan on the gun, press the trigger, and brrrrr. . . . It was empty in five or six seconds. One man fired the gun and four or five tried to keep it fed. A commonplace experience in battle was to get your gun to a position where you could shoot to some purpose, only to find that the unfortunates toiling with the canvas buckets in which the pans were carried had fallen behind or had let the ammunition get muddy. Lewis-gunners spent long hours unloading pans, cleaning the cartridges, and re-loading.[15]

Even with those liabilities, the Lewis gun was still a serviceable and generally reliable frontline weapon, and the infantrymen who carried it usually gave it high marks.

Other light machine guns of that war were not so well designed, nor as well thought of. The French Fusil Mitrailleur Modele 1915 CSRG, reviled by many soldiers under its more familiar name, the Chauchat, might well deserve its modern reputation as the worst-designed machine gun of all time. Fielded by the French, and adopted by the U.S. Army when the United States entered the war for the simple reason that it was available and no adequate American weapon was yet in service, the Chauchat was an absolutely wretched piece of military hardware. It was the only machine gun to use the long recoil action, meaning that the barrel moved back and forth during the firing action while the bolt remained locked. This design feature caused the gun to jump around badly when being fired on the bipod, seriously degrading its accuracy. Its twenty-round half-moon magazine was open on one side (apparently to allow the gunner to visually verify his ammo count), which practically guaranteed that the mechanism would be fouled by dirt and mud in the rough conditions of trench warfare, and at a cyclic rate of only 240 rounds per minute, its rate of fire was far lower than that of comparable weapons. Additionally, it was constructed of poor-quality parts stamped from inferior metal, a choice made by the French ordnance department in order to get more guns into service as quickly as possible. As if all *that* were not bad enough, it was also as ugly as an unloved mongrel, and more than one soldier who was encumbered with this poor excuse of a weapon referred to it as "that worthless bitch."

Late to the game again, the U.S. Army adopted the Model 1918 Browning Automatic Rifle, the famous BAR, at the very end of the war. This was a powerful, accurate weapon that proved to be extremely reliable in the field, but it had its drawbacks. It was a relatively light weapon despite its fairly large size, weighing in at about sixteen pounds (later models were heavier), but its rate of fire was limited by the fact that it was fed with a twenty-round box magazine. In order to carry enough extra magazines to put out a truly effective rate of fire, a BAR gunner had to overload himself to the point that his personal combat efficiency was hampered, so other soldiers in the squad carried additional BAR magazines to supplement the supply. It was more suited to the automatic rifle role of infantry tactics than it was as a light machine gun, and in that mode it continued to serve the U.S. Army into the first years of the Vietnam War.

American soldiers who served in the multinational expeditionary force against the Bolsheviks in 1918 expected to be armed with the battle-tested '03 Springfield, but politics interfered. Surplus stocks of Russian Mosin-Nagant rifles were on hand, and the U.S. government issued those out as the U.S. Rifle, 7.62mm, Model of 1916. Political priorities rather than military considerations were behind this decision; the rifles were manufactured by American contractors for the Imperial Russian government, which no longer existed, so the contractors faced financial ruin if the weapons were not issued. They exerted their powerful political lobby to convince the War Department to put their unsold weapons to use. It would be generous to describe the Mosin-Nagant as even a second-rate weapon—the Doughboys who had to turn in their Springfields for these rifles were not impressed with them in the least. "It was a Russian rifle!" one infantryman recalled. "No wonder they lost the war. What was the object of equipping American troops with such a rifle?" Unfavorable first impressions were only reinforced once troops tried to zero their new arms. "At the range we acquainted ourselves with the firing peculiarities of our Russian rifles and concluded they were poor weapons," this soldier wrote. "All were inaccurately sighted, yet we were not permitted to make adjustments. My first shots went wild, but by aiming at the lower left corner of the target I hit the bull's-eye. Others found their rifles equally faulty. All of us regarded them with disfavor."[16]

The Second World War saw a wide range of new weapons carried by the world's armies, everything from improvements on older models to truly innovative designs. Some were successful; others were not. For once, the United States got an edge on its counterparts with the adoption of the M-1 Garand, a decision that meant that the American military was the only combatant in the war to have a rapid-fire self-loading rifle as its standard-issue weapon. For the British, a redesigned version of the Lee-Enfield, issued as the No. 4 Mk I, gave good service, as did the Karabiner 98 kurz for the German Wehrmacht after it replaced the hardy Gewehr 98 of First World War vintage. The Japanese infantryman was armed with the Arisaka rifle, first in the Type 38 variant chambered for the 6.5x50mm round, which was seriously underpowered. The other most common model of Japanese rifle during the war was the Type 99 Arisaka in the more effective 7.7x58mm cartridge, but it was never produced in sufficient numbers so as to be able to completely replace the Type 38 as originally planned. Both models of rifle suffered from the same inherent problem with relation to the army to which they were issued—at nearly fifty inches in length, the rifles were nearly as long as the average Japanese soldier was tall, and even more so when the twenty inches of the Type 30 bayonet were added. For an army that fought in some of the densest jungle terrain in the world, this was not the best sort of rifle to use.

The Japanese were not well served by their principal machine guns, either. Their Type 3 Heavy Machine Gun was based on the French Mle 1914 Hotchkiss of First World War vintage (which was an admirable weapon in 1914 but completely obsolete by 1941), and the Type 3 suffered from the same limiting thirty-round strip magazine feed that constrained the Hotchkiss. The Japanese never designed or fielded a belt-fed machine gun during the war, so all of their weapons were hampered by a stunted ammunition supply. The Type 11 Light Machine Gun used a thirty-round hopper magazine, while the Type 96 Light Machine Gun was fed by a thirty-round box magazine. At twenty-three pounds and twenty pounds of weight, respectively, they were also considerable burdens to the tough but diminutive Japanese infantrymen who carried them.

The German military, for its part, fielded two of the best light machine guns ever designed: the MG 34 and MG 42. Both were light enough for mobile infantry use, both had extremely fast rates of fire (as high as twelve hundred rounds per minute in later variants of the MG 34 and as much as fifteen hundred rounds per minute for the MG 42), and both could be employed in either the light or heavy machine gun roles, fed by linked belts or drum magazines. American soldiers who faced them in combat called them "buzz saws," referring to the sound they made when fired. They were formidable weapons, and the U.S. Army admired their efficacy so much that it later borrowed their design and actions for the iconic M-60 machine gun.

The American-made BAR had a long life as the primary weapon in the squad automatic rifle role for the U.S. Army, though its size, weight, and twenty-round magazine-fed operation continued to impact its efficacy. Guy Nicely served in the U.S. 1st Infantry Division in Europe, and described himself as a slightly built man, physically. Despite that, he was designated as BAR gunner—"I was carrying a Browning Automatic Rifle but the ammunition weighed 42 pounds and I only weighed a hundred and some pounds," he remembered. "I think it was a mistake giving a small guy like me that heavy equipment, including the BAR." Going ashore on Omaha Beach during the D-Day landings, the weight of his equipment nearly drowned him, but it also demonstrated the BAR's mechanical reliability. "I kept my gun and it did go under but it was O.K," he said. "It did the job after I got on the beach."[17]

Submachine guns came into their own during this war, with every army in the world fielding some form of the weapon. Several of these were truly iconic and instantly recognizable: the German MP40 (incorrectly called the "Schmeisser" by Allied soldiers), the side-mounted magazine-fed British Sten gun, the Soviet PPsh-41 with its drum magazine and ventilated barrel shroud, and the American Thompson gun, firing the stout .45 caliber pistol cartridge. An often-overlooked weapon in this class was the Australian Owens gun, the only weapon of the war to be designed and manufactured entirely by Australia. The Owens was a peculiar-looking weapon, having its magazine mounted in the vertical position on top of the receiver and having almost no design concessions for aesthetics—it was, frankly, an ugly piece of hardware. It was also one of the most reliable, hardy battlefield weapons ever designed. In both field tests and combat conditions, the Owens gun demonstrated an incredible ability to continue firing even after being immersed in mud and sand. In trials comparing it to the Thompson and the Sten, the Owens came out ahead in every instance. It also enjoyed the advantages of being light and accurate, and soldiers who carried it in battle swore by it as an excellent weapon, no matter its ungainly appearance.

Ammunition

Regardless of what type of firearm a soldier carried, ammunition was an integral part of the weapons system. After all, a man could have the finest rifle ever issued, but once he was out of ammunition for it, the rifle was little better than a club. The amount of ammunition soldiers carried varied considerably from army to army and from decade to decade, but those small, lethal cartridges of gunpowder and lead were crucial to the infantryman's ability to stand and fight. No matter what else a soldier might discard in an effort to lighten his pack, the basic load of ammunition was the essence of his ability to function as a soldier.

The problem, then as now (and probably ever since firearms first took their place in the battle lines of the world's armies), is that while ammunition keeps a soldier fighting, food and water keep the fight in the soldier, so to speak, and neither commodity can be done without for too long. Soldiers can only carry so much weight, as we have already seen, and so the perpetual challenge for operational planners is how to balance the triple essentials of food, water, and ammunition.

During the first sixty years of the nineteenth century, the individual round of ammunition was a fairly bulky item, taking up more space than later metal-cased rounds. This was a consequence of both the larger calibers then in use, as well as the thick paper cartridge construction of those loads. So, while a modern U.S. Army infantry rifleman carries a basic load of 210 rounds of 5.56mm/.223 caliber brass-cased ammunition today, his Civil War–era counterpart carried a basic load of forty rounds of .58 caliber ball. How to most effectively expand that load was complicated by the infantryman's personal priorities:

For "special occasions," when a battle appeared to be likely, the soldier would often be issued additional ammunition. . . . The trouble with these extra loads of ammunition was that they were often issued at just the same time as extra rations of food. Thus the soldier was doubly weighed down at precisely the moment at which he needed exceptional lightness for exceptional manoeuvres and exertions. It was common to find him taking a number of short cuts to avoid this dilemma, but in the end none of them was truly satisfactory. If he ate all his rations at a single sitting he would go hungry later. If he dumped his ammunition surreptitiously he would find himself disarmed at the critical moment of combat. And if he deposited his pack or blanket roll with a sentry for the duration of the battle he risked returning to find it plundered—or never finding it again at all.[18]

At the beginning of this period, individual rounds of ammunition were issued in cartridge form, made up of paper (tough, but not waterproof) that contained a lead ball and about 150 grains of black powder. The quality of the gunpowder varied greatly, depending on who was making it. Soldiers in the British Army's Rifle Brigade, to whom individual marksmanship mattered as a professional skill, used a higher grade of powder for their rifles—when they had to settle for inferior stocks of standard-issue powder, they would grind down the grains themselves to make a finer strain of powder to improve the ballistic performance. French infantryman of the Napoleonic period carried fifty cartridges per man as a basic load; their British counterparts were issued sixty rounds. Here again the Rifle Brigade was different—they carried eighty rounds each as a standard load.

As paper cartridges were replaced by metal-cased ammunition of increasingly smaller caliber but greater power and muzzle velocity, the bulk and weight of the individual round decreased. Where in the Napoleonic era the basic load of ammunition per infantryman was a few dozen rounds, by the close of the Second World War, riflemen were carrying as much as a hundred rounds of rifle ammunition, and linked belts of machine gun ammunition were counted in the thousands of rounds per company.

BAYONETS

Early in the period, almost every army was enamored of the bayonet, even though cases where battles actually came down to bayonet fighting were rather rare, indeed; bayonet wounds, according to the reports of most medical officers, were so uncommon as to be truly remarkable. There was a psychological value in bayonets, to be sure, but there was at least one practical combat value—it was the bayonet-mounted rifle, used as a stunted pike, which gave infantrymen a measure of defense against cavalry, especially when they formed into square to receive a charge.

The French went so far as to issue bayonets to cavalry regiments to augment their carbines, but more than a few soldiers reported that "the bayonets issued with these carbines were useful only for digging up potatoes."[19] One French cavalry trooper probably expressed the sentiments that many of his fellows had toward the bayonets when he wrote "we threw them away before we went into action."[20]

This was not an uncommon attitude toward a piece of hardware that men had to carry around but found little martial purpose for. There *were* practical uses for bayonets, but not ones that the issuing arsenals probably ever intended. The socket bayonet of the Napoleonic Wars, which looked just about the same in every army, made a handy field-expedient candlestick, or meat skewer, or roasting spit. What it did not make, nearly so often as ordnance boards seemed to think, was a decisive weapon in close-quarters battle.

There *were* cases where battles came down to the thrust and parry tactics of bayonet fighting, but these were seldom bayonet versus bayonet. They were, rather, fights where bayonets were wielded against Indian tulwars, or Burmese *dha*, or Moro bolos, or Sudanese broadswords. Seldom did European armies come to the point of crossing blades with each other on the open field. The bayonet sometime saw heavy use in assaults on fortifications, by defenders and attackers alike, but those types of fights were not so frequent as open-field battles.

As the nineteenth century progressed, bayonet development became something of an industry in its own right. Some of the new designs were aesthetically beautiful, some were as ugly as either sin or a design committee could make them, and almost all of them continued to be superfluous as practical weapons. The simple socket bayonet continued in service in several armies all the way up to 1900 (and even beyond—the Russians were still mounting a socket bayonet on their older model Mosin-Nagant rifles in the early days on the Second World War), but other designs became more common.

The long sword bayonet with the inverse curving yataghan blade was issued in the armies of Austria, France, Germany, Turkey, and Belgium. It saw service with the British and Americans, as well, usually designated as an NCO's sword bayonet. The First World War saw the introduction of a wide array of new bayonet types, many of them of questionable tactical value. The Germans, in particular, seemed taken with the idea that bigger was better, fielding a variety of forms. There were the flare-tipped "butcher blade" bayonets and the ridiculously long Model 1898 Pattern bayonets, but the types most remarked on by soldiers themselves were the saw-backed pioneer bayonets that were issued to engineers and sappers. Allied troops who found these weapons on dead or captured Germans often assumed, understandably, that the serrated cutting teeth on the top of these bayonets' blades were designed to inflict terrible wounds on men who were stabbed with them, but the real purpose of the teeth was more benign. The saw teeth were supposed to provide engineers with a handy implement to cut wood, but the reality of trying to use a heavy, thick-bladed bayonet as a one-handed saw was probably easier said than done.

By the outbreak of the Second World War, bayonets were increasingly being designed along smaller lines, in most armies. The Japanese, enamored with the cult of the sword, kept the long Type 30 bayonet, but most of the other belligerent nations had reduced the sizes of their bayonets by the end of the war. From this point forward, the edged encumbrances that most armies expected their soldiers to mount on the end of their rifles were designed to also function as field knives, which was generally a much more useful justification for having to carry them.

CHAPTER SEVEN

Bully Beef, Salt Horse, and Hardtack

Soldiers' Rations

Oh, the biscuits in the army, they say they're mighty fine
One rolled off the table and killed a friend of mine
O Lord, I wanna go, but they won't let me go
O Lord, I wanna go home
—U.S. Army marching cadence

NAPOLEON BONAPARTE IS CREDITED WITH the oft-quoted observation that "an army marches on its stomach." Frederick the Great may actually have coined the phrase before Napoleon, but as a military truism, it bears repeating no matter its uncertain origin. When we consider the rather robust language most soldiers used in their descriptions of army food, their stomachs must have been made of strong stuff, indeed.

A Scottish soldier with the unlikely name of Alexander Alexander (that is not a typo—it really was the name under which he enlisted) served in Ceylon (present-day Sri Lanka) in 1803. According to his recollections, the food served to his unit was clearly not a highlight of his time in the army:

> At night we got what was called supper, which consisted of a small cake of rice flour and water, and a liquid called coffee, although there was not a single grain of the berry in it. . . . At eight o'clock in the morning we got breakfast brought to us in the same manner; it consisted of the same cake, fish, or bullocks' liver, and jaggery [sugar] water, and this formed the daily diet of the British troops in Ceylon. . . . The beef, of which we had a pound per day, was given out along with the rice in the morning, for which sixpence per day was kept off our pay. But it

was rather carrion than beef. The cattle sometimes buffaloes, sometimes bullock, having been used in their husbandry were generally lean, old, or diseased, the meat was soft, flabby, and full of membraneous skin; it had a rank, heavy, loathsome odour, was offensive to both sight and smell, and hurt me more than the climate, and was, I am certain, the cause of much of the disease and death which thinned our numbers. The rice, too, was small, and of a bad quality, full of dust and dirt, from which our rascally cooks were at no trouble to free it.[1]

Private Alexander might not have known it, but his experience was not at all unique. Soldiers of different nationalities, posted to every corner of the world in different eras, shared similar stories of bad food and scanty rations, and modernization brought fewer improvements that one might expect, at least until the very end of this period.

For many years, the standard fare in the soldier's mess was usually bad, and sometimes it was *very* bad. Fresh food, such as it was, was available with any regularity only in garrison settings and then quite often at some expense to the soldiers themselves. Once on the march, armies of the time subsisted on various forms of preserved rations. If troops were fortunate enough to serve in a well-victualed army, their quartermaster might have a herd of cattle or sheep in the supply train for regular butchering at times of halt, but more often than not men made do with salt meat and preserved biscuits of one unpalatable form or another. Bad as they were, sometimes even those tired standbys were better than what soldiers subsisted on even in the notionally better provisioned circumstances of a regular garrison.

Armies recognized the need for adequate rations of sufficient quantity to feed men who were carrying out the physically demanding task of soldiering, and for the most part "the ration scales were generous, far above the daily consumption of the great masses of the people."[2] This was certainly true of the U.S. Army, as one English correspondent to the American journal *Army and Navy Times* wrote in 1882. The U.S. Army's standard ration, he said, was "startling in its fullness and variety, with its 'twelve ounces pork or bacon, or one and a quarter pounds salt or fresh beef, one pound six ounces soft bread or flour, or one pound hard bread, or one and a quarter pounds corn meal; and to each one hundred rations, fifteen pounds beans or peas, and ten pounds rice, ten pounds green coffee, or six pounds roasted and ground coffee, or one pound eight ounces tea, fifteen pounds sugar, four quarts vinegar, one and a quarter pounds candles, four pounds soap, three and three-quarter pounds salt, four ounces pepper, thirty pounds potatoes, one quart molasses."[3] That was certainly a generous ration, but it was not always the ration that actually reached the men stationed out in the remote posts of the American frontier, as we will see.

During the Napoleonic Wars, the French ration "constituted of one pound of 'munition' bread, four ounces of dried vegetables, two ounces of vinegar, and one ounce of brandy, while the British ration included three-quarters of a pound of beef, one pound of bread, and a gill of rum."[4] Those were the notional rations, at least—the quality of the food was assumed rather than specified, and in reality, was often rather bad.

Even in garrison environments, mealtimes were not the source of satisfaction that young men might have wished them to be. John Shipp recalled that in his early days in the British Army in 1800, the fare in the company mess was nothing to celebrate. "A pound of meat (and that of the worst)," he wrote, "and three-quarters of a pound of bread per diem, was but a scanty allowance for a growing lad."[5] Edwin Rundle enlisted in the army half a century after Shipp did and also shared his view of the recruit's standard rations. "The worst part to contend with was the food," Rundle said; "there was not sufficient for the hungry recruit. . . . One and one-half pounds of bread, three-quarter pound of meat, one pound of potatoes, pint of coffee, pint of tea and pint of soup. After being dismissed from drill we had to visit the canteen and buy bread and cheese, or whatever else we could get, at our own expense, for I can assure the reader we were a hungry crowd."[6]

Rundle might have thought himself faring badly on that diet, but he was better off than Shipp had been before him, and he was better off than some men who came generations after him in the British Army. For all of them, though, the depressing monotony of the food that was available was cause for common complaint. The raw meat ration that British soldiers received was almost always cooked just one way—boiled. Meat, gristle, bone, and fat—it all went into the pot, to be divvied out to the soldiers of the mess in equal portions by a system of blind lottery.

The U.S. Army of the same era did not enjoy the benefit of a professionally trained cook service any more than their British counterparts. One correspondent to the *Army and Navy Journal* described the problem vividly when he wrote, "We have an Army of 25,000 enlisted men and not a syllable of instruction that I am cognizant of to teach a man how to roast a coffee bean or make a loaf of bread has ever been issued. Boards have been held on the soldier as to how he shall be uniformed, armed, equipped, and drill; the barracks he shall live in; the ambulance to carry him when sick or wounded. . . . Nothing has been done to improve the present mode of cooking his ration, a want greatly needed and which lies at the foundation of his health and comfort." He went on to suggest that the army create a cooking school at one of the recruit depots, and recommended that a "certain percentage of the recruits enlisted" who had experience as cooks or showed an aptitude for it should be sent there for culinary training.[7]

The British Army finally created a School of Cooking in 1870, several years before the U.S. Army got around to doing so, but that did not mean that the British soldier felt he received the benefit of any particular culinary skills on the part of his unit cooks. William Holbrook joined the Royal Fusiliers before the First World War, and remembered:

> When 'Cookhouse' sounded, the fellows wouldn't stop to go out the doors to get to the mess hut, they'd jump out the window! There was about twenty in each hut. . . . Clean out the blooming windows they'd jump! Of course the first day I was a long way behind. When I got there, there was a queue of thirty or forty men in front of me. . . . On each side there was bare tables and there was forms each side with four men on a form, and there was a loaf cut in four and a piece of margarine slapped on top of it. That was your lot! You had nothing else, a piece of bread and some margarine. Of course they were hungry. . . .

The tea was in a big pudding basin, one between two and of course if you was sitting with a man older than you, as I always was, you didn't have much of a chance, you know. He'd grab it and have a drink and if you wanted one you had to pull it out his hand if you could. Then you'd find he'd have had a good drink and left you the tealeaves. You was done all ways! There wasn't no more.[8]

Holbrook found that dinnertime—notionally the main meal of the day—was not much better, in terms of either quantity or quality:

We had stew for dinner—it was always greasy old stew with great lumps of fat in it, ladled out of a big Dixie. And they'd take this fat out and they'd throw it on the bare table, the fellows would. And when they'd finish, the table was covered with fat and gristle and gravy. Terrible it was! Swimming! And when they'd gone, the chaps who had to stay behind to clean up the mess hall, they wouldn't clean it properly, they'd jump up on the tables with sweeping brushes and sweep it all into a big pile. Then it was sent off as swill for the pigs. It was only fit for pigs anyway.[9]

Many men who served in the U.S. Army during this period found their standard fare to be equally monotonous, if not always so unpalatable. During the Civil War and in the years following, sutlers and post traders did profitable business selling foodstuffs to soldiers to augment their government-issued rations. Over time, and mostly at the behest of the army itself, the post trader system was replaced by canteens that catered more for the soldiers' well-being than for an entrepreneur's profits. These were the forerunners of the Post Exchange system that still exists today. "These canteens," one soldier recalled, "provided the men with a place on post to relieve the monotony of their lives . . . a place where they could go and take a bite of lunch, read, chat, smoke, or play games with their chosen friends, and escape the lonesomeness of the barracks." The post canteens served wine and beer—good beer, one corporal remembered, "and only five cents a glass"—but no hard liquor.[10]

Men who enlisted in the French Foreign Legion might have expected great things of their unit mess, if only because of the French reputation for haute cuisine, but military fare in North Africa or Indochina turned out to be a far cry from what was served in the brasseries of Paris. After George Manington joined the Legion in 1890, he remembered that the standard breakfast in his squad was "a loaf weighing about one pound and a half—the day's ration of bread—and a tin pannikin full to the brim with stewed white beans, a piece of boiled beef and two boiled potatoes, for each recruit." In the early days of his service Manington was less than impressed by the fare, but his attitude soon changed. "I must say that the food did not appeal to me at the time," he wrote, "but it was good and clean, and exercise and a healthy appetite soon made it palatable."[11]

Another veteran of the Legion, Erwin Rosen, who served out his enlistment in North Africa, also described the standard meals a legionnaire was likely to encounter during his service. "In barracks," Rosen wrote, "he gets a cup of black coffee on rising in the morning. At ten o'clock he gets his forenoon soup, at about 5 p.m. his afternoon soup. Two meals a day, both consisting of soup, in which are boiled all sorts of vegetables as an extra, spinach or carrots or such-like." Like most European armies, bread formed a substantial part of the Legion's diet, but French military bread was not the warm, crusty brioche familiar to a civilian's table. That did not necessarily mean that it was terrible, though; Rosen described it as "a grey kind of bread which is very easily digested, undoubtedly nutritious, sufficient and palatable."[12]

In the field, whether on a training march or on active campaign, soldiers' rations were almost without exception regarded as terrible, if only because of the deadly dull monotony of facing the same food week after week without any variation. British and American armies relied mostly on salted meat, either beef or pork. The experience of having to subsist on this type of meat left a permanent gastronomic impression on every soldier who encountered it. One U.S. Army veteran of the Civil War remembered: "So salt was this ration that it was impossible to freshen it too much, and it was not an unusual occurrence for troops encamped by a running brook to tie a piece of this beef to the end of a cord, and throw it into the brook at night, to remain freshening until the following morning as a necessary preparative to cooking."[13] A common term among American soldiers for this type of meat was "salt junk". Continental European armies of the same period also used salt meat, but more frequently issued different versions of the meat ration—the French and Germans both leaned heavily on sausage in various forms, while their Russian counterparts were issued fatback pork.

John Billings was an artilleryman in the U.S. Army from 1861 to 1865. His description of the ubiquitous salt beef ration can hardly be bettered:

The "salt horse" or salt beef, of fragrant memory, was rarely furnished to the army except when in settled camp, as it would obviously have been a poor dish to serve on the march, when water was often so scarce. But even in camp the men quite generally rejected it. Without doubt, it was the vilest ration distributed to the soldiers. It was thoroughly penetrated with saltpeter, was often yellow-green with rust from having lain out of brine, and, when boiled, was four times out of five if not nine times out of ten a stench in the nostrils, which no delicate palate cared to encounter at shorter range. It sometimes happened that the men would extract a good deal of amusement out of this ration, when an extremely unsavory lot was served out, by arranging a funeral, making the appointments as complete as possible, with bearers, a bier improvised of boards or a hardtack box, on which was the beef accompanied by scraps of old harness to indicate the original of the remains, and then, attended by solemn music and a mournful procession, it would be carried to the company sink and dumped, after a solemn mummery of words had been spoken, and a volley fired over its unhallowed grave.[14]

Soldiers on the march found the opportunities for hearty meals to be even more unlikely, and many of them registered their discontent in their letters and diaries. Charles Perkins, an infantryman in the 1st Massachusetts Infantry, probably expressed the feelings of many men in his company when he wrote one morning in 1861, "Up early in Morning Breakfast at 8 o'clock 4 crackers & coffee Dissatisfaction about feed etc."

He did not find satisfaction anytime soon—his dinner that evening was "coffee and 4 hard crackers."[15]

Another soldier of that war, Nelson Stauffer of the 63rd Illinois Infantry, was typical in his description of rations in the field. Writing in his diary as his regiment occupied the lines in Georgia in the winter of 1864, Stauffer wrote, "Drew two nibbins of corn for three of us. . . . Had mush and rice for dinner, but was still hungry. After dinner I took a stroll through the woods looking for something to eat, and trying to imagine how I would feel if I was full again." In his ramble he came across a dead calf lying in a field, already skinned. "Don't know who killed it nor the date of its death," he wrote, "nor did I care." He hotfooted it back to camp and got his messmates to come out and help bring in the bounty. Such a windfall deserved special commemoration, and Stauffer wrote a poem about it:

> So comrades if you feel disposed
> To murmur, or look blue
> Because your victuals don't taste right
> Just fast a day or two
> Then try again, and if they taste
> Just as they did before
> I recommend another fast
> Of two or three days more
> And by this time you will conclude
> That hunger's more than half
> And that it makes an appetite
> For even a dead calf.[16]

American soldiers were not the only ones to regard their rations with a wry humor that bordered on disgusted resignation. A British soldier from the First World War remembered, "Our food was not too good either, and we used to complain." Complaining has long been regarded as the common soldier's sacred right, since precious little else is allowed to him, but the command echelons of armies do not always see it that way. In a gesture as ineffective as telling the rain to stop falling, British Army General Headquarters responded to a complaint about the lack of pork in the pork and beans ration by ordering that there would be no more complaints. "Once," this same soldier recalled, "the order stated, 'On opening a tin of pork and beans, soldiers must not be disappointed if they find no pork. The pork has been absorbed by the beans.'" The British Tommy was not inclined to let such blatant idiocy pass without comment, and he let it be known in his own imitable style, as this narrator recounted: "One soldier wrote back asking if it would be safe to transport beans and bully beef in the same lorry, in case the bully beef would be absorbed in the same way!"[17]

Following the Civil War, the U.S. Army's basic issue field ration was "salt pork, hardtack, sugar and coffee." That was something of a step down from the standard garrison ration specified in regulations. The official fare was supposed to include:

> *twelve ounces pork or bacon, or one and a quarter pounds salt or fresh beef, one pound six ounces soft bread or flour, or one pound hard bread, or one and a quarter pounds corn meal; and to each one hundred rations, fifteen pounds beans or peas, and ten pounds rice, ten pounds green coffee, or six pounds roasted and ground coffee, or one pound eight ounces tea, fifteen pounds sugar, four quarts vinegar, one and a quarter pounds candles, four pounds soap, three and three-quarter pounds salt, four ounces pepper, thirty pounds potatoes, one quart molasses.*[18]

That was a plentiful fare, indeed, if it was actually issued, but it almost never was. The realities of military service on the western frontier meant that the Commissary Service could never keep all the garrisons of the remote posts supplied to the same uniform standard that the War Department's bureaucrats expected. As a result, troops down the line either looked to their own devices to augment the issue ration or just did without.

During this period the single most hated item in the American soldier's rations was pickled pork, a disreputable by-product of swine processing that was utterly reviled by the men who were expected to eat it. "However desirable fats may be as part of the ration," the post surgeon at Fort Brown, Texas, wrote in his annual report to the Surgeon General of the U.S. Army, "pickled pork does not appear to be adapted to this climate." That was something of an understatement—in the desert heat of the southwestern American territories, the pickled pork was a noxious, slimy mass of foul-smelling putrescence that was always more fat than meat. A medical officer at Camp Lowell in the Arizona Territory reported that the pork went rancid as soon as it was taken from the pickle; his counterpart at Fort Ringgold, Texas, wrote that the soldiers of his garrison did not "consider it desirable food and it is not relished by the men." The pickled pork, as another report stated, "is neither nutritious nor palatable, being composed almost entirely of fat, very little of which is needed in this climate." As it was usually presented on the tables of the mess it was in the form of a hash, which prompted profane reactions. One soldier's ditty that was at least repeatable in polite company was, *"Of hash that's young, of hash that's old / Of hash that's hot, of hash that's cold / Of hash that's tender, of hash that's tough / I swear to God, I've had enough."*[19]

No soldier admitted to liking the pickled pork, and no effort on the part of army cooks could make it palatable. "Men do not eat the fat pork but buy vegetables with their own money," one fort's medical officer wrote. "This amounts to furnishing a kind of food which is unfit for the men to eat and forcing them to buy a kind which they crave and need with their own money, or go without it."[20] Nonetheless, the army persisted in issuing the pickled pork for decades, deaf to the complaints from the ranks. When one officer of the 22nd U.S. Infantry filed an official complaint about the pickled pork in 1880, his regimental commander endorsed his petition with the comment, "This subject of the insufficiency of the ration . . . is as old as the army, probably."[21] Nonetheless, the despised pickled pork remained a part of the army's ration issue for years longer.

During the U.S. Indian Wars, the salt pork ration was sometimes interchanged with bacon, but soldiers did not always regard this as an improvement. One cavalry sergeant recalled that the bacon "had worms, too. . . . Anything was good enough for a soldier."[22] As for the ubiquitous hardtack biscuits, they were usually so tough that they required soaking in coffee before eating. Besides softening the biscuits, the soaking had another benefit—it helped clear out some of the bugs that always infested the hardtack. The culinary monotony was inescapable, but here again it provided fodder for cynical humor. An American cavalry trumpeter in 1877 wrote, "We now have a change of diet: hardtack, bacon and coffee for breakfast; raw bacon and tack for dinner; fried bacon and hard bread for supper."[23] Monotonous or not, at least the salt pork ration was something most men were used to eating; in dire straits, even that tired staple might be missing from a soldier's menu. Sergeant Henry Windolph, who served in the 7th U.S. Cavalry, remembered that when his regiment geared up for the Black Hills expedition in 1876, they were given an order that did not bode well for their future diet. "Just before we packed our mules," Windolph said, "[Captain] Benteen ordered us to take along an extra supply of salt. That meant we might be living on mule or horse meat before we got back."[24]

The shortcoming of the American army ration in that era was not that it was insufficient in either quantity or calories (though it was often lacking in scorbutics and nutritional quality); it was that there was so little variety, and men grew heartily sick of having to eat the same monotonous thing, day after day. To make it even more repetitious, the army attempted to issue the same ration for all of its operational areas, regardless of the wide differences in climate. "It is absurd," the Surgeon General of the U.S. Army wrote in 1889,

> to attempt to make use of the same diet in a Florida summer and a Montana winter. If anything is certain it is that the ration should be flexible enough to give wholesome and seasonable food to each. . . . Man is created with a healthy appetite, the satisfaction of which is a pleasure, and it is not fair to the soldier to ignore this fact. The natural zest he has for food can be recognized without making him a glutton. The present ration, by the way, has very little in it that would tend to produce an epicure. . . . We should resolutely favor variety and excess rather than strict accuracy.[25]

Despite that acknowledgment of the problem, it was a long time before a palatable solution was implemented.

This is not to say that soldiers found their rations to be substandard all the time. At the more established forts of the U.S. Army, once the garrison gardens were established and the commissariat was operating correctly, the fare in the mess was sometimes as much as one could ever want. At Fort Union, New Mexico, one cavalryman wrote home to say, "I must say we are living very well since we came here. In the morning have Beef Steak, Bread and Coffee. Dinner Beef, Bean Soup and Bread. Supper, Coffee, Syrup Bread and Pickles. Splendid cucumber pickles. . . . Eggs, Milk, Butter, Bread Pudding, Doughnuts. . . . So different from miserable Arizona."[26] The Arizona Territory never did fare well in soldiers' opinions during the frontier period.

Scurvy is an ailment usually associated with the navies of the world, but it was a hazard to the health of soldiers in the land armies of the era, as well. One U.S. Army medical officer, in his annual report from Fort Ransom in the Dakota Territory, wrote, "Scurvy has prevailed to some extent, owing to a want of care in providing the troops here with sufficient vegetable diet."[27] Another report from a post in Texas stated, "Vegetables are always scarce at this station, as none can be raised and few purchased anywhere in the neighborhood. The supply of canned fruits from the subsistence department was useful but inadequate, in view of the scarcity of fresh vegetables. As may be inferred, a scorbutic taint has at times affected the men, debilitating them, and rendering them prone to diarrhoea."[28] The only real solution to scurvy was to add vegetables to the diet, but a reliable supply of vegetables was almost impossible to obtain in most of the hardscrabble forts in the southwestern territories. When garrisons were able to grow an adequate crop of vegetables, it was usually because the local commander made it a priority. Sometimes, though, even that was not enough. The post surgeon at Fort Larned, Kansas, reported that his garrison's gardens were a complete failure "owing to repeated failures in previous years. . . . The causes of want of success are deficient rains, intense heat, poor soil, grasshoppers, and hailstorms."[29]

When the technology of canning emerged as a viable method of preserving food, tinned meat began appearing in army rations on both sides of the Atlantic. The Americans called it "corned beef"; the British dubbed it "bully beef," but for both armies the novelty of it wore off quickly, and it too became as dreary a mainstay of their field diet as the salt meat ration had been before it. The canned meat did not necessarily represent any kind of improvement over the salt version. "Sometimes we had canned beef," one U.S. Army veteran of the Indian Wars remembered, "which in those days was not fit to eat."[30] A few years later, in route to the Philippines during the Spanish-American War, John Bowe of the 13th Minnesota Infantry recalled, "The food was bad and not enough to go around. . . . What some people call embalmed beef and others call canned beef is very unlike the article that is sold in America. This is in low, round cans, the meat is stringy and soupy, and quite frequently when the cans are first opened a gas escapes."[31]

Many soldiers of the period found their meat ration, in whatever form it appeared, to be just another form of culinary monotony at best; at worst it could be almost inedible and actually hazardous to their health. One veteran of the Spanish-American War, Needham N. Freeman of the 21st U.S. Infantry, described some variation in the rations his regiment received as it traveled by train from home station in Texas to San Francisco, where they were to take ship, but the variation was not necessarily an improvement. "The rations issued to us on this journey," Freeman wrote, "consisted of hard tack, canned tomatoes, canned salmon, and last, but not least, nor more desirable, canned horse meat. To use a soldier's expression, such 'grub' is almost enough to make a man sick to look at, but this made no difference, we had to eat it." Freeman was of the opinion that the low quality of army rations stemmed either from a lack of concern for soldiers' welfare on the part of the government or from a low opinion that the public had of soldiers in general. "I have seen a few people," he wrote, "who seemed to think soldiers were not human beings like other people. They thought they could endure anything and would eat any kind of stuff for rations."[32]

Freeman, like others before him, found that the fare only got worse once he was aboard a troopship. "Our rations were very poor, scarcely fit for hogs to eat," he wrote. "They consisted of a stewed stuff of beef scraps, called by the men 'slum;' hard tack and colored hot water for coffee." That portion of the diet was unpalatable, but other items served to the men were downright unhealthy. Freeman reported that he had "seen several times almost the whole body of soldiers on board sick and vomiting. There was something peculiar about this sickness. Nevertheless, it was true; the men were fed on rotten prunes and fruit, which, after nearly all the supply was consumed, was found by our surgeon to be full of worms." Freeman said that he avoided becoming ill himself, but only by "refusing to eat this rotten stuff myself."[33]

Despite the preponderance of complaints about rations at sea, there are a few voices in the sources that actually strike a positive note on the matter. When Donald Kyler shipped out for France in 1918 with the 1st U.S. Infantry Division, he did not find the chow in the mess to be all that bad. "During the voyage we were fed twice daily," he wrote. "The food consisted of one item plus bread and coffee per meal. Beans or vegetables or meat stew was the usual fare. We called the meat stew, 'slum.' When properly made it is delicious. I am still fond of it. But it was not properly made on that voyage."[34]

At nearly the same time that the Americans were beginning their military experience in the Philippines, the British were fighting the Second Anglo-Boer War, and British soldiers on the troop transports to South Africa were no more pleased with their rations aboard ship than were their counterparts in the U.S. Army. Private E. C. Moffett of the Scots Guards was less than impressed by the fare produced by the galley on his ship. "The following details as to diet, etc., on board a troopship," he wrote, "may serve to remind us of our journey out. Here is a typical day":

BREAKFAST—About three-quarters of a pint of a curious infusion called by courtesy coffee; half-a-pound of dry bread, with now and again some half-dozen tablespoons of porridge. This is oatmeal porridge in the strictest sense, there being no other legitimate ingredient save water.

DINNER—Three-quarters of a pint of soup (I suspect this to be water masquerading as soup on the somewhat inadequate grounds that it has been used to boil meat, puddings, or to wash greasy dishes.) The meat itself is—well, we generally leave it untouched. (I never knew before where all that unwholesomely fat meat one sees at Christmas time goes. I think I know now. It is used to feed the fishes on the Cape route. TEA—This meal consists of a pint of 'tea'—a brew which has considerable claims to be called 'special'. It is certainly like nothing I have ever tasted before. This, with half-pound of dry bread, constitutes the last meal of the day.[35]

Once released from troopships, soldiers often found their rations unimproved, if their active service placed them in areas where they could not buy or barter from the local populace. The canned meat ration in particular continued to be an unpalatable, monotonous item, no matter what it was called. On occasion it was downright revolting, particularly when men had been hoping for something better. Canadian soldiers in the First World War had high expectations when they finally received an issue of Canadian-packed canned beef. One soldier "recalled a shipment from the Toronto packer William Davies. At first men rushed for 'some good, wholesome Canadian meat' only to discover 'a sort of jellified blob of gristle, fat and skin.'"[36] Disappointment coupled with disgust was a common sentiment when it came to army-issued meat.

Considering how bad military rations were during much of this period, it is not surprising that soldiers frequently resorted to their own means of augmenting their diet, or, when the supply system failed altogether, as a desperate measure of warding off starvation. Almost every army during the period practiced the timeless art of foraging to one extent or another, whether as an official policy or an illicit activity. "In practice," as one historian of the Napoleonic Wars writes, "the supply system was defective and usually broke down in all armies, and soldiers lived by requisition, foraging, and often outright theft."[37] Soldiers experienced that reality in other eras, as well.

An army on the move had to take its supplies along with it, if it was to sustain itself as an effective fighting force. For this reason, the ratio of teeth to tail—that is, the percentage of support assets compared with the actual combat arms formations in the army—was, and remains, always tilted to the side of the units that are necessary to provide transport, maintenance, communications, medical support, and sundry services. Throughout most of this period, even when an army's baggage train and commissariat were huge in comparison with the actual fighting units, these were still occasionally insufficient to keep the men in the line companies well-supplied and well-fed. An army on the march, therefore, often foraged as a matter of course.

For the British Army during the Peninsular War, foraging by individual soldiers was a frequently practiced but officially prohibited activity, one that harsh punishments could never completely eradicate. By contrast, the French Army of the same period followed an officially sanctioned practice of foraging to such an extent that they stripped the countryside bare almost everywhere they went. Foraging, after all, usually only worked for the first foraging parties to pass through an area; after that, little remained for those who came after, and certainly less for the civilians whose supplies, livestock, and foodstuffs had just been wiped out by a locust-like army of uniformed scavengers. This was the case with Napoleon's Grande Armee on its ill-fated advance into Russia in 1812. Moving deeper into country that was all but stripped bare, many soldiers, such as Jakob Walter of a Wurttemberg regiment, found themselves thinking, "How gladly would I renounce for my whole life the warm food so common at home if I only did not lack good bread and beer now!"[38]

Most armies attempted to stamp out unapproved foraging, though their reasons for doing so were not always predicated on sympathy for the civilian population. Ernst Junger, who commanded a German infantry company in the Western Front of France in the First World War, recalled one period when his unit was out of the lines, and foraging immediately became a persistent discipline problem. "The only thing that made difficulties for me were the short rations," he wrote. "It was strictly forbidden to go foraging; and, even so, every morning the military police brought me the names of men they'd caught lifting potatoes, and whom I had no option but to punish—'for being stupid enough to get yourselves caught' was my own, unofficial, reason."[39]

Foraging aside, most soldiers of most armies of the period lived off the food they carried in their haversacks or on whatever rations could be supplied to them in the field. When that ran out and more was not forthcoming, entire armies sometimes starved. This extremity was the sort of hardship suffered by the British forces under General Sir John Moore during their retreat to Corunna in 1808, the Grande Armee in its disastrous withdrawal from Moscow in 1812, the Confederacy's Army of Northern Virginia in the last desperate days of the Civil War, and the Japanese Army when it retreated from the Imphal in 1944.

Even in minor campaigns, the commissariat system was often prone to failure, and when that happened, troops in the field went hungry. As one American cavalryman, William Drown, wrote during the U.S. Army's expedition against the Mormons in 1858, "The great scarcity of provisions seems to be the topic of the day.... It is a common thing for a man to offer $1.50 and $2 for a single biscuit. Beef or flour cannot be purchased at any price." The ration situation did not improve as the days went on. "I believe the Indians begin to think we are rather hard up for provisions," Drown wrote; "for they have commenced to kill their dogs and bring them in for sale under the name of mountain sheep. I had two hind-quarters offered me yesterday for $1, but have not got to be quite so wolfish yet as to eat dog-meat. The time may come, however, before spring, that we may be glad to get it."[40]

Conditions of deprivation and outright starvation were not necessarily the norm for soldiers of the period, but neither were those experiences unusual, either. Veterans were particularly skilled at keeping an eye out for the unexpected opportunity in terms of food and drink. Anything that supplemented the monotonous regular rations was always welcomed, and besides, one never knew when those rations might fail altogether. It was not unheard of for men to think of their stomachs almost more than their lives.

The anonymous British narrator from the 71st Regiment described just such an incident during the attack on the French positions at Vitoria in 1808. Going forward into the assault, his regiment encountered "a bean field at the bottom of the heights, immediately the column was broke and every man filled his haversack."[41] The fact that the regiment was under fire from the French guns on the heights above apparently could not prevent the gleaning of the bean field, and remonstrations by their officers and NCOs had no effect, either. Despite the distraction of the impromptu harvest, the British carried their attack forward and completely routed the French from their positions.

In the Crimean War, the *Times* correspondent William Howard Russell reported that just before going into action at the Battle of the Alma, British soldiers "ate whatever they had with them, but there was a great want of water, and the salt pork made them so thirsty that in the subsequent passage of the Alma, under the heaviest fire, the men stopped to drink and fill their canteens." Fording a river in the face of the enemy's fire was always a tricky proposition at best, one that was sure to disrupt the unit cohesion of any formation; stopping to fill canteens in mid-passage could only have made it worse. As Russell recounted the event, there was a bit more to it than that: "It must be confessed that this advance was very disorderly—the men had not only got into confusion in the river from stopping to drink, but had disordered their ranks by attacks on the grapes in the vineyards on their way." The Battle of the Alma was a victory for the British and their French allies, even with the pause to pick grapes.[42]

Confederate soldiers in the American Civil War have frequently been romanticized as ragged, lean, and wolf-like, a depiction that is actually not too far from the reality. They had a reputation for always being hungry. More than one source has suggested that perhaps the Rebels' famous ferocity in the attack owed something to their desire to get at the well-filled haversacks of their Union enemy. Marion Ford fought through the war in a Confederate regiment; at the Battle of Gettysburg, he recalled:

> *Kershaw's brigade, on the second day, was advancing to the assault of Little Round Top, a company of the Fourteenth was among those thrown forward as skirmishers, and as they advanced across the field towards the Federals, they came to a large patch of ripe blackberries. The men with one accord immediately turned their attention to the ripe fruit which was in great abundance on every side, and, stooping down, kept picking, and eating berries, as they went slowly forward, actually into action. And so much was their attention distracted by the blackberries that they were actually within 50 yards of the enemy's*

advanced line before they realized their position, when they rushed forward with a yell, and got possession of a slightly elevated roadway, which they held until the main line came up.[43]

The Confederates were renowned scavengers, probably much more successful at the primary skills of foraging than their counterparts in Union blue ever were, or needed to be. Carlton McCarthy served in a Confederate artillery battery in the Army of Northern Virginia—"to be one day without anything [to eat] was common," he wrote. "Two days' fasting, marching and fighting was not uncommon, and there were times when no rations were issued for three or four days." To stave off hunger men looked to their own devices. McCarthy related one incident in his account:

Artillerymen, having tender consciences and no muskets, seldom, if ever, shot stray pigs; but they did sometimes, as an act of friendship, wholly disinterested, point out to the infantry a pig which seemed to need shooting, and by way of dividing the danger and responsibility of the act, accept privately a choice part of the deceased. On one occasion, when a civilian was dining with the mess, there was a fine pig for dinner. This circumstance caused the civilian to remark on the good fare. The 'forager' replied that pig was an uncommon dish, this one have been kicked by one of the battery horses while stealing corn, and instantly killed. The civilian seemed to doubt the statement after his teeth had come down hard on a pistol bullet, and continued to doubt, though assured that it was the head of a horse-shoe nail.[44]

When even this expedient failed and no stray pigs presented themselves, soldiers could be in for hard times, indeed. "On one march," McCarthy wrote, "No rations were issued to Cutshaw's battalion of artillery for one entire week, and the men subsisted on the corn intended for the battery horses, raw bacon captured from the enemy, and the water of springs, creeks and rivers."[45]

Perpetually hungry or not, even in the Confederate Army soldiers' foraging was not always officially sanctioned. Leon Louis, a Confederate infantryman in a North Carolina regiment, recalled that his colonel issued orders that the men were not to go foraging. Louis and his messmates decided to follow their stomachs rather than their orders. He and his friends, Louis said, "went to the creek to wash our clothes, but when we got there we forgot to wash. We took a good long walk away from the camp, and saw several shoats. We ran one down, held it so it could not squeal, then killed it, cut it in small pieces, put it in our knapsacks, returned . . . to camp, where we shared it with the boys. It tasted good." One fellow from Louis's company had less success in his scrounging. "He went to a place where he knew he could get some honey," Louis wrote. "He got it all right, but he got the bees, also. His face and his hands were a sight when he got the beehive to camp."[46]

Officers were not above a little foraging themselves on occasion, or at least were willing to accept the fruits of it when it came their way. John Beatty, serving in a regiment of volunteers in the Union Army, wrote in his journal one day, "Fox, my servant, went out this afternoon and bought a basket of bread. He brought in two chickens also, which he said were presented to him." Beatty was apparently a realist when it came to human nature, concluding, "I suspect Fox does not always tell the truth."[47]

When private enterprise failed to put something in their mess tins, soldiers had to simply tighten their belts. Marion Ford remembered that even when rations were available, getting them was sometimes no easy matter:

We had to wait for the arrival of the wagons; and it was not uncommon for a detail of men to be sent back in the night to help push the wagons through the mud; weary, footsore, hungry, in the dark, up to the knees in mud, heaving on the wheels of a stalled wagon! It was often late at night before the wagons were got up and rations could be obtained. . . . When the rations were drawn they consisted only of seven ounces of bacon and one pint of cornmeal to the man per day; and on several occasions even these could not be had, and the men went to sleep supperless, and with nothing to eat during the day.[48]

If existing on short rations was the norm for the Confederate Army, it was not necessarily so for other armies of the time, but most soldiers knew what it was to go hungry now and then.

Soldiers were so constantly on the lookout for something to supplement their standard-issue rations that putting privates to guard a ration store was often a case of setting the foxes to guard the henhouse, if they were not closely supervised. Paul Totten, an American infantryman in Russia in 1918, was detailed to guard a warehouse with some other men:

> *This particular warehouse was made with logs with sort of a shallow tunnel underneath. On a wistful impulse Hower wormed his way beneath and with effort inserted his poniard shaped bayonet between two of the logs. After a few exhausting twists we were rewarded with a small, reluctant stream of "SUGAR"—of all things! So, we filled our mess kits and used our secret hoard where it tasted the sweetest. Luck on a contraband stunt like that was really awesome.*[49]

In all such cases, soldiers were apt to congratulate themselves on pulling one over on their higher-ups and enjoyed their stolen repast with a sense of justified delight.

◦—◦

Once in the field, soldiers often took every available opportunity to augment their rations by fair means or foul, and sometimes in the most expedient method possible—they carried firearms, after all, and when some edible animal wandered into view, whether it was wild or domestic, they were not averse to shooting it for the pot. In India and other parts of the Empire, British Army officers frequently availed themselves of the opportunity to do a little recreational hunting; the opportunity was less available to the enlisted men, at least officially, but they still got theirs now and then. Soldiers of the U.S. Army in the American West hunted as a matter of course, and they often continued the practice when their deployments carried them beyond the continental borders of the United States.

Needham N. Freeman found that this "open season" mentality was particularly useful in the Philippines, but some allowances had to be made for the tropical climate. His unit shot pigs all the time, which greatly improved their rations, but the first time they did so the results were not what they hoped for. When his lieutenant shot two pigs one evening, Freeman's platoon had high hopes for dining well on the morrow. "Next morning," he remembered ruefully, "our hopes and expectations of a good meal were exploded by finding that the pigs were spoiled. After that we profited by the experience and always ate our hogs as soon as they could be prepared. The trouble about keeping fresh meat there was the hot, moist climate."[50]

This practice continued into the wars of the next century. Ernest Shephard, then a senior NCO in the Dorsets Regiment in the First World War, one day wrote in his journal, "A pig was foolish enough to come down the road. We shot him and shall very soon be eating pork chops."[51] Raymond Gantter, an American infantryman who fought in the European Theater during the Second World War, wrote to his wife to say, "We do have fresh meat occasionally. One of our cooks has fallen into the habit (deplorable, but praise the Lord for it!) of wandering off every now and then with an M-1 cradled in his arm and knocking off a stray cow—German, of course, and therefore incontrovertibly enemy. . . . We've had steak four times in the past week."[52]

Gantter was not the only American GI to have this sort of experience with local livestock. Spencer Wurst, a paratrooper in the 505th PIR, remembered that in Holland his unit "ate British 10&1 rations, but we also always managed to acquire some chickens or rabbits somehow. Then one day, a cow stepped on one of our antitank mines, resulting in instant shredded beef." With that happy accident, a solution to the monotonous rations presented itself, along with a way to avoid the severe penalties that could result from unauthorized depredations of civilian livestock. "We soon realized that to have fresh beef legally, all we had to do was challenge a cow after dark as it approached our position. When the cow did not answer, we shot it."[53] The bovine inability to learn the password insured a steady supply of fresh beef.

American soldiers fighting in the Philippines during the same war, for their part, found that the available livestock presented fewer culinary delights. There were still pigs to be had, but men who tried eating carabao, the ubiquitous water buffalo-cum-draft-animal of the Philippine rice fields, usually found the meat to be dark, gamey, and tougher than proverbial shoe leather.

By the time of the world wars, the rations issued to the individual soldier were much improved, at least for American and British soldiers. Still, some of the age-old items that caused the most profane reactions at mealtimes continued to show up in soldiers' mess tins. John Howard fought in Burma with the British 14th Army in the Second World War; his description of the canned meat ration would have been familiar to British soldiers in wars long before his. "Bully beef, or corned beef as it's better known," Howard said, "tended to go very greasy in the warm sun. It would melt into a mass like porridge but cook did marvelous exercises with it, present it in different guises. He would cook it in some flapjack, cook it almost like hamburgers, he would put batter around it; he would present it in many guises of stew so that we could in fact absorb the stuff. But it still became intolerable."[54] Twenty years before him, Australian soldier Hugh Knyvett wrote of his experiences at Gallipoli, "There was generally enough food but mighty little variety. . . . It is all very well to say a man will eat anything when he is hungry, but you can get so tired of bully-beef and biscuits and marmalade jam that your stomach simply will not digest it."[55]

Bully beef may have finally worn out even the most robust British appetite from simple overexposure, but it was sometimes a welcome novelty to the soldiers of other armies when they encountered it. The German Army also issued canned meat by this point, but produced some unpalatable concoctions such as canned liver sausage and *blutwurst*. Paul Hub, a German soldier who was eventually killed in the First World War, wrote home to his wife during the German offensive of 1918, saying "it's great to take part in this kind of war of movement. . . . That's when we find booty. The English tins of meat are fantastic compared with ours and English sugar tastes so good, but unfortunately, we've finished the English cigarettes and biscuits."[56]

Japanese soldiers also sampled British rations when the fortunes of war presented them with the opportunity. Satoru Nazawa, a lieutenant in the Japanese 112th Infantry Regiment fighting in Burma in 1942, remembered that "in Maungdaw, there was another field storage of the enemy. We saw that there were mountains of corn beef, bacon, cheese, cigarettes and rum lying around. I had never tried corn beef before." Perhaps because of its novelty, Nazawa found that he rather liked it. The real find, though, was something altogether more potent. "They had water in a bottle," he wrote, "and we kicked it around, but when someone said it's an alcoholic drink called gin, there were soldiers who were gulping down the gin, happier than ever." The contrast between the British and Japanese commissariats made a huge impression on Nazawa's soldiers. "We thought, my goodness, these people are fighting in such a luxurious condition," he said. "If they came and took our camp, well, they would just find a bit of dried fish and a bit of rice, nothing else."[57]

Ironically, at least one American soldier had a different view of his experience with Japanese rations. John Sweeny, who fought on Guadalcanal with the 1st Marine Raider Battalion, remembered that "at Tasimboko we found lots of supplies. . . . There was a lot of food, some saki, and brown bottles of beer. The food was particularly inviting: anchovies, sardines, crab, and lots of rice. We took everything we could and destroyed the rest."[58] The quickest field-expedient method of destroying foodstuffs, Sweeny said, was to urinate on it.

For the Turkish soldiers against whom the Allies fought at Gallipoli, British bully beef was a novel discovery. "Sometimes," a British soldier remembered, "we'd be talking to each other. . . . The Turks said, 'Oh, we've tons of tobcco. Have you got any meat?' They'd got no meat. . . . We had a barter with bags of Turkish tobacco for our bully beef." Private Henry Barnes, of the 4th Australian Brigade, said, "We regularly exchanged bully beef and biscuits for strings of figs and oranges. You see instead of throwing a bomb, you could throw a tin of bully beef over, and when they discovered that, you got a string of figs back."[59]

John Morse, an Englishman who fought with the Russian Army in Poland against the Germans during the First World War, found the rations there to be as foreign as the army. "Biscuits and raw fish were here also served out," he wrote on one occasion. "The fish was not cooked in the least, but seemed to have been preserved in wet salt." To his surprise, it wasn't at all bad. "So far from being revolting food, it was quite tasty, and I became very fond of it," he remembered. "We had to eat this meal as we marched along; and that without any other drink than water."[60]

Soldiers have always been interested in sampling the rations of both enemies and allies and determining whether their own fare is better or worse by comparison. Sometimes, as Morse discovered with his raw fish, the unfamiliar could be a pleasant surprise—George Tompkins, a rifleman with the U.S. 1st Infantry Division in 1944, remembered, "In Aachen we were housed in a German barracks that had been deserted. I recall there was a good supply of rather wonderful tasting cheese that we greatly enjoyed."[61] Leander Stillwell had a similar experience when his Union Army regiment captured some Confederate supplies in 1863. "Among these," Stillwell wrote:

> was a copious supply of 'jerked beef.' It consisted of narrow, thin strips of beef, which had been dried on scaffolds in the sun, and it is no exaggeration to say that it was almost as hard and dry as a cottonwood chip. Our manner of eating it was simply to cut off a chunk about as big as one of our elongated musket balls, and proceed to 'chaw.'... But, if sufficiently masticated, it was nutritious and healthful, and we all liked it. I often thought it would have been a good thing if the government had made this kind of beef a permanent and regular addition to our rations. As long as kept in the dry, it would apparently keep indefinitely, and a piece big enough to last a soldier two or three days would take up but little space in a haversack.[62]

Beef jerky was not the only new Southern foodstuff that Union soldiers encountered during the war. "Goober peas," as peanuts were commonly called in the American South, were something most Northerners had never tried before, especially when they were boiled in the Southern style. For men from the Midwestern states, common foods of the seacoast were a revelation. Nelson Stauffer, serving with the 63rd Illinois Infantry in the sea islands off Georgia in 1865, described his first encounter with oysters. "Had plenty of oysters but not much of anything else," he wrote in his diary. "Here I first learned to eat them from the shell. I had to or go hungry. I opened one, and the longer I looked at it, the more decided I was not to try it. I threw it away and went back to quarters and laid around until I got hungrier. I opened another but couldn't make it." Stauffer eventually managed to choke down an oyster, and found them rather to his liking, even though he remarked, "It was some time before I was right sure it was going to stay." He ate many more after that, he wrote, but always with his eyes closed.[63]

For the Confederates, who always seemed slightly amazed by the sheer quantity, if not the quality, of Union Army commissariats, Northern coffee was far superior to their own ersatz concoction, which they boiled from chicory bark. The Confederate soldier was usually better-supplied with good tobacco than were his Union counterparts, but a man couldn't eat tobacco, and as the war went on the men in ragged grey and butternut went hungry more often than not.

Armies that spent lengthy periods of time garrisoning overseas posts developed culinary tastes that were completely foreign to folks back home, but that were frequently introduced to them by returning soldiers. British soldiers serving in India had much to do with the introduction of curry and yoghurt to civilian tables in the United Kingdom. American soldiers posted to the southwestern territories discovered Mexican food long before it became commonplace across the rest of the United States, and U.S. troops stationed in Hawaii made *kalua* pig roasts a part of their regimental traditions years before the luau became a mainstay of tourists visiting from the mainland. French troops in Indochina developed an appreciation for *pho* and other Vietnamese dishes; the men of the French Foreign Legion in Algeria were eating lamb kebabs and hummus long before either item was well known in Western Europe.

When it came to regular rations, some armies always had it much worse than others. Sometimes the fault lay with inadequate supply trains; sometimes it was because the upper echelons of command simply did not give a damn for the common soldier's hardships. Italian soldiers posted in the prewar Italian colony of Libya, for example, suffered from this sort of indifference from their superiors. Most Italian units "experienced severe shortages of water and firewood. This left them constantly hungry, thirsty, without warm food and highly susceptible to infection and disease. Awareness among the enlisted men that staff and rear-area officers enjoyed a far superior diet provoked considerable resentment."[64] Even the German Army, normally remarked upon for its well-organized commissariat and efficient transportation system, sometime found itself on short shrift. In Poland in 1916, as one soldier remembered, "It was commonly reported that the Germans were in great straits for food; and whether this was so or not, they stripped those tracts of country which were overrun by them of everything eatable. They even dug up the potatoes and turnips (in autumn, of course); and when they got the chance, reaped the cornfields."[65]

It might be assumed that an army in retreat would usually be worse off for rations and supplies, and this was certainly true of Napoleon's army during the retreat from Moscow in 1812. The Grande Armee froze and starved, the one hardship nearly as bad as the other. The French situation during that disastrous campaign was so bad that the normal privileges of rank and position collapsed altogether. Sergeant Adrien Bourgogne, an NCO in the Imperial Guard who was one of the survivors of the long, freezing nightmare of the French retreat, recalled that on one occasion he wound up sharing a dinner of horse liver and melted snow with no less exalted a personage than Marshal Mortier.[66]

Another French soldier recounted a time during that retreat when he and his comrades "treated ourselves to a very good fricassee of cats . . . which were excellent."[67] Dogs, whether strays or pampered pets, also wound up in soldiers' stew pots or on skewers over campfires. Horse meat was the most common meat available, when it wasn't frozen so solid as to be impossible to cut, and even then, those men who were still capable of discriminating tastes found it to be so disagreeable that they would sprinkle it with gunpowder prior to eating—the saltpeter at least added some flavor. Tallow candles and bits of leather belts and harnesses also went into stews, when there were pots to cook it in. One Frenchman left a recipe for something he called "Spartans' Gruel": "First melt some snow of which you need a large quantity in order to produce a little water; then mix in the flour; then, in the absence of fat, put in some axle grease, and in the absence of salt, some [gun] powder. Serve hot and eat when you are very hungry."[68] To eat such a concoction, a man would probably have to be very hungry, indeed.

Other men in that disastrous retreat found themselves reduced to eating even worse fare just to survive. Jakob Walter, a German infantry-man in Napoleon's army, remembered that he was in terrible shape when he finally managed to reach Smolensk: "Because I could not even get a piece of meat and my hunger became too violent, I took along the pot I carried, stationed myself beside a horse that was being shot, and caught up the blood. . . . I set this blood on the fire, let it coagulate, and ate the lumps without salt."[69] Several days later Walter managed to pitch up with a fellow German who had a handful of rice; Walter was able to contrib-ute a little piece of meat he had cut off a dead dog's head. "Although the meat already stunk a good deal and there was no salt with it," he recalled, "we devoured everything with the best appetite, feeling ourselves lucky to have for once obtained something warm."[70]

The British in their withdrawal to Corunna in 1808 suffered from near starvation, as did the Confederacy's Army of Northern Virginia dur-ing the last desperate days of the Civil War. It was not always just the retreating army that found itself in desperate straits as its logistics train collapsed and the supply system failed, however. The Russian army pur-suing the French in 1812 were advancing into country that the Grande Armee had twice ravaged, coming and going, and there was nothing left for their army to subsist on except for their own unreliable supply trains—Russian accounts from that campaign speak of hunger and cold so severe as to cause widespread suffering, even if they did not experience the total collapse that befell the French.

In the early days of 1942, the Japanese Army in Burma and Malaya advanced so rapidly that their forward combat units outstripped their supply lines in short order. Lance Corporal Katsumi Ohno, a Japanese soldier who fought in Burma, said, "Because of the rapid advance and continuous battles, which lasted four months, sometimes with poor meals of just rice and salt, we soldiers were tired out and a third of us in the company were suffering malaria, dengue fever and dysentery, and were not able to serve on duty."[71]

The third scenario that could exhaust an army's food supply was a siege. Surrounded and cut off from resupply and reinforcement, a force besieged could only hold out until its stores were exhausted, if it could not fight its way out. This was not just an experience of ancient and medieval warfare—sieges in the classical sense continued well into this period. One such incident took place in 1813 toward the end of the Peninsular War. Cut off by the withdrawal of supporting French troops, "the French garrison at Pamplona, having started on slaughtering their horses and mules, next turned on the canine and feline population, and then, facing starvation, surrendered unconditionally on 25 October and were marched away as prisoners."[72]

It was not just the force under siege that faced the specter of starvation, however. An army that was static in one location for too long, or an army which was too large for the capacity of its own commissariat, could quite literally eat itself into a desperate situation. Francis Seymour Larpent, the judge-advocate of the British forces in the Peninsular War, recounted a conversation he overheard between Wellington and the army's commissary-general, August Schaumann. Schaumann, so the story went, told Wellington that the army "had eaten nearly all the oxen in the country, that the cultivation of the lands of Portugal could not go on for the want of them, and that he scarcely knew where to turn for a supply of beef, as there was this year no reserve store near Lisbon. Lord Wellington said, 'Well, then, we must now set about eating all the sheep, and when they are gone, I suppose we must go.'"[73] In the event, Wellington was able to keep his army in the field, but the essential problems of his supply train and commissariat were issues that continued to vex his prosecution of the war.

When the food situation became difficult in armies that were normally well-supplied, the enlisted men at the end of the supply chain were inclined to suspect malfeasance on the part of their commissariat. James Dargan, a Union Army infantryman serving in Louisiana during the Civil War, grumbled in his diary in 1863, "by the way, the rations are running short; some suspect our [Quartermaster] is cheating us." He and his comrades, he wrote, were "trying to subsist on a couple of hard tack and a pound of salt-petre called bacon."[74]

Once the shooting started and battle was joined, all bets were off as far as regular supplies of food and water were concerned. Quartermasters and commissaries usually tried their best to keep the frontline troops fed and supplied, but the exigencies of combat often made that difficult and sometimes all but impossible, especially if the forces in question were mobile. In 1877, William Zimmer served with the 2nd U.S. Cavalry during that year's campaign, first against the Sioux and then the Nez Perce, from March to November; during that time the cavalrymen repeatedly outmarched their supply train. Zimmer wrote that in August, his commander "issued an order . . . that if rations did not reach us before ours ran out, that good, fat horses & mules should be slaughtered and given out. He also advised everyone to eat hearty of them, saying that it was good and wholesome food [even] if the Americans had not adopted it yet as an article of food." Zimmer was not enthusiastic about the prospect and hoped "that tomorrow would bring the hash. If it don't we will make hash of the mules." Fortunately, the rations arrived just in time for the mules to be spared.[75]

This sort of hardship was such a regular part of campaigning, in some armies, that it was one more yardstick by which veterans measured their superiority over new recruits. Complete breakdowns of the commissariat system happened frequently enough in the U.S. Army of the frontier era that experienced troopers took it in stride. When the 2nd U.S. Dragoons were in the field against the Mormons in the spring of 1858, the troopers fell back on that old standby of starving cavalrymen—eating the horses. "We have commenced selecting the horses and mules to be first killed already," Private William Drown wrote in his diary. "Some of the men who are not used to this kind of starving for a living think things are getting rather squally, and are constantly talking about the future welfare of their bellies, which only serves to make amusement for the old campaigner, who don't care, as long as his appetite is good, whether he is fed on beefsteak, pies, mule-meat, or rattlesnakes."[76]

The possibility of having to subsist on horse meat is often seen as a nineteenth-century problem, but soldiers in more recent wars have also fallen back on that as an exigency when times were hard. Joachim Pusch was a German signalman who served with the infantry in Russia during the Second World War. "The only fresh food we got was when the army kitchen came. That was the only time. Our most common meal was a thick lentil soup," he recalled. "Sometimes there was meat in it, especially during the first summer of the campaign. The meat was probably beef or pork." The field kitchens tried to push forward every evening, at least in the early days, he said, but as time went on, the supply situation deteriorated. "In the winter there was no beef or pork," Pusch said. "We then ate horsemeat. At first we didn't like it too well because horsemeat is sweet. It tastes sweet, but you get used to it because there was nothing else. When you're hungry you eat almost anything."[77]

Enemy action could also cause supply problems, because every army knew that interdicting the opponent's supply lines would quickly impact their combat abilities. "Our rations," British veteran Harry Patch remembered of his experience in the First World War, "you were lucky if you got some bully beef and a biscuit. You couldn't get your teeth into it. Sometimes if they shelled the supply lines you didn't get anything for days on end."[78] German soldiers on the other side of the line often experienced the same shortage of rations. "The food left quite a bit to be desired," Ernst Junger wrote. "Aside from a rather watery soup at lunchtime, there was just a third of a loaf of bread with an offensively small quantity of 'spread,' which usually consisted of half-off jam." To add insult to injury, Junger found his meager rations further reduced by vermin predation. "And half my portion was invariably stolen by a fat rat," he remembered, "which I often vainly tried to catch."[79] This story of artillery-interdicted and vermin-raided supply systems was a common experience for men who fought at Gallipoli, the Somme, Passchendaele, and numerous other battlefields, some famous and many forgotten.

In the trenches around the time of the Battle of First Ypres, many British soldiers recalled their rations as being scanty and substandard. "There was no such thing as cooked food or hot tea at this stage," one soldier in the Royal Welch Fusiliers wrote. "We were lucky if we got our four biscuits a man daily, a pound tin of bully between two, a tin of jam between six, and the rum ration which was about a tablespoon and a half."

The jam was a notorious item frequently criticized, and it fared no better in this man's recollections. "Even at this early period," he wrote, "the jam was rotten and one firm that supplied it must have made hundreds of thousands of pounds profit out of it—the stuff they put in instead of fruit and sugar! One man swore that if he ever got back to England he would make it his first duty to shoot the managing director and all the other heads of that particular firm."[80]

The situation on the Eastern Front during the First World War, while not nearly so static as the war in the West, produced its own set of miseries, and the food situation could be every bit as bad. John Morse, the English expatriate who had found the Russian dried fish surprisingly to his liking, described the Russian supply system as generally abysmal, and what did get through was often so bad as to be nearly inedible. "Some of the articles indicated by these words [food] were very different from what an Englishman would expect them to be," he wrote. "Bread was a species of 'hard tack' compared with which dog-biscuits are fancy food; cheese was a wretched soft mess resembling wet putty, sour and peculiarly flavored." Those were the army-issued rations that Morse was describing; when even those failed, other alternatives had to suffice. "The old horse I obtained from a Cossack . . . had disappeared," he wrote later, "boiled down to soup by the men, I imagine; in which case I had my share of him, and can bear witness to his gamy flavor."[81]

Medieval and ancient armies regularly included herds of cattle in their supply trains as a form of fresh rations on the hoof, and others did so during this period, with varying degrees of success. In the 1812 campaign into Russia, French cavalry drove herds of cattle along during their advance; American and British armies also used this method of victualing at different times. The practice continued even into the twentieth century. One Japanese veteran of the Burma campaign in 1942 described how his regiment was sent into action with their intended rations still on the hoof, ambling along with the column of soldiers. "We began the operation with twenty days' rations and a herd of cattle," he said. "It was absurd that we should have been ordered to go into battle hampered by cattle, but no more food reached us from the rear as the days went by and we struggled up the Arakan Mountains." As a commissariat scheme, it was a miserable failure. "Our cattle and horses fell down the mountainside," this soldier said, "taking our provisions with them; the slopes were so steep we couldn't go down to retrieve anything."[82]

——◦——

After all this multinational litany of complaint, we should perhaps give a hearing to at least one soldier who insisted he was doing quite all right on army chow. Richard Orton was stationed on the U.S.–Mexican border as an infantryman at Fort Bliss, Texas, in 1861 when he wrote a letter trying to allay his mother's concerns for his well-being. She had heard horror stories of how the soldiers were starved and destitute, and she apparently believed every word of it. Orton insisted that things were not at all that bad:

> *if you was up here you mite talk about living I have just as much Pork beef, flour sugar coffe and beans as I want and occationly molasses rice and onions. And if I have a little money I can go over to Elpaso and find as much fruits as I want such as Oranges, apples, pears and peaches so you may gess I Live. And I have a plenty of corn for my Horse and a good stable to ceap him in and he is as good a horse as Mr anybody's horse so I am as happy as a coon in roastting ear time. It is very true that we suffered a little while we were coming accross the plains we had to leave our provisions behind us and go ahead in order to get water for our horses those who staid with the wageons faired very sumptuously. It looks dearnd strang that some of the boys will write such tails it is very true that some of the Company has been out of salt at times, but—it—was there one falt my mess has always had a plenty of salt and nearly every thing else. And another great bugerboo is we are all necked. I expect that a great many have more clothing than they ever had before and if they all have not a plenty of clothing it is there one falt for we have had a serpulous (sic) of cloth-ing along all the time. So you nead not believe half you here they are a great many along who glory in telling big tails and they dont car a bit whether they are true or not.*[83]

All things considered, Orton concluded, army life was actually a pretty good deal for a young man.

For the most part, though, soldiers of the period usually had reason to remember their days of living on army rations with something less than fond nostalgia. Few of them, it seems, ever forgot the experience, and their culinary perspective for the rest of their lives was often affected by it. "Suffice it to say, on the food question," wrote Civil War veteran Leander Stillwell, "that my life as a soldier forever cured me of being fastidious or fault-finding about what I had to eat. I have gone hungry too many times to give way to such weakness. . . . I have no patience with a person who is addicted to complaining or growling about his food."[84]

CHAPTER EIGHT

Water, Rum, and Whiskey

Beer, beer, beer, says the sergeant
Merry men are we
There's none so fair as can compare
With the Airborne Infantry!

—U.S. ARMY MARCHING CADENCE

FOOD WAS ONE THING, AND BAD FOOD was something else entirely, but good or bad, at least it kept men from starving. What they had to have with much greater frequency than food, though, was water. Armies without water quickly perished, as happened with the Roman legionnaires under Marcus Licinius Crassus who were wiped out by the Parthians at Carrhae in 53 BC, and again to the Crusader army that was destroyed by Saladin at the battle of Hattin in 1187. Armies whose only sources of water resupply were contaminated with human and animal excreta were stricken with outbreaks of cholera and dysentery, resulting in men dying in greater numbers than were ever caused by the enemy's efforts. British historian Richard Holmes was not exaggerating when he wrote, "Throughout the period disease killed more soldiers than human agency."[1]

Combat in any era was usually thirsty work, regardless of the weather. After hours of exhausting battle, the limited amount of water that a single soldier carried was never enough to slake a man's thirst. For soldiers of the Napoleonic Wars, who fought ranked in their firing lines wreathed in choking clouds of acrid black powder smoke, thirst was a part of the job, which was greatly exacerbated by the musketry drill that required men to bite off the end of the paper gunpowder cartridges when reloading their muskets. Thomas Morris, a British soldier who fought at Waterloo, recalled how dire the need for water was during that battle:

*During the operations of the afternoon, we suffered much from thirst.
There was a stream of water near the wood, in our rear, which would
have been sufficient for us, but it was unfortunately rendered useless
to the larger number, from the circumstance that a great many of the
men who had been killed on its banks, had been thrust into it; this,
however, did not prevent some of the men from filling their canteens
with it, though tinged with human blood.*[2]

Armies campaigning in deserts, such as the British in Egypt and parts
of Africa, or the Americans in the southwestern territories of the United
States, or the Germans and Italians in Libya, needed to exercise strict water
discipline. Water resupply in those conditions obviously occupied a great
deal of logistical effort. Less well understood is the fact that armies in wet
climates sometimes had almost as much difficulty in getting potable water
to their troops. Here again, the difference between clean water and contaminated water meant the difference between a healthy, combat-effective
army and a disease-riddled army that died off by rapid degrees.

The Philippines is a tropical country, with heavy seasonal rains and
almost perpetual humidity. Nonetheless, during the Philippine-American
War that followed the Spanish-American War, the U.S. Army found the
issue of water resupply in the field to be a perpetually troublesome part of
the fighting in the tropics. "We were out ten days and had two engagements," Needham N. Freeman wrote of one extended patrol his company of the 14th U.S. Infantry conducted; "we had a very hard time on
this excursion. Water was hauled two miles and a half on a two-wheeled
vehicle, in old vessels holding four or five gallons. By the time we could
get to the kitchens about half of it would be spilled."[3]

The problems resulting from a shortage of clean water effected more
than the men—army horses suffered too. N. W. Bancroft, who served in
India as a British artilleryman during the 1840s, recalled a particularly
grueling march his battery undertook in terribly hot weather. When they
finally bivouacked for the night, he said, "the first attention was of course,
given to the horses; these we groomed and led to water but the water was
so foul that thirsty as they must have been after their long and harassing day's march the poor animals refused to drink it."[4] This was one of

the reasons why the mortality rate among military horses and mules was sometimes so high, even when they weren't being lost to shot and shell.

The battlefields of the First World War were an absolute nightmare for water. Units went into the trenches in rotation, and for the days or weeks that they were in the lines, the only water they had was what could be sent forward to them carried on the backs of men who had to make the arduous trek under cover of darkness, or they drank whatever water was at hand. The latter choice was always an option of last resort, but one that men had to turn to frequently because there was nothing else to do. "The water we had to drink," Ernest Shephard wrote in his diary when he was fighting in the vicinity of Hill 60, "was from a stagnant pond, the drainings from the ditches." In a later entry, Shephard's exhaustion was plain in the terse lines of his report: "Wet miserable day. Fairly heavy fire all night." The insult added to the injury was clear in his last sentence: "We discovered a dead pig in our water pond." He did not hazard a guess as to how long the unlamented swine had been deceased.[5]

The months-long fighting on the Somme in 1916 made simple things hard when it came to logistics, and hard things were sometimes all but impossible. Mundane but essential matters like obtaining water could be extremely dangerous. "There was only one place in the Somme where drinking-water could be obtained," Australian soldier Hugh Knyvett wrote. "The Germans ... made it very difficult for us to get at it by shelling continually. They had the exact range, and it was only in the hour before dawn that one could get near the wells without meeting certain death." Knyvett did not relish the prospect of dodging German artillery fire to get water, but there was no real alternative. "Of course, there was plenty of other water filling every hole around," he remembered, "but this was not only thick with mud but had the germs of gas-gangrene, and one knows not how many other diseases besides."[6]

The Somme was bad; the battle of Passchendaele, fought in Flanders during the winter of the following year, was immeasurably worse in terms of its physical conditions. The mud of Passchendaele transcended even the horrific experiences of men who had already fought in the trenches of France for nearly three years. Soldiers lived, fought, and died in a stinking mire with no standing cover and no shelter from the elements. With the ground too sodden for the construction of regular trench lines, both the British and the Germans lived in and fought from shell holes that looked and smelled so bad that pig wallows were clean by comparison.

Corporal Clifford Lane, of the Hertfordshire Regiment's 1st Battalion, recalled the muddy horror of Passchendaele years after the war. "We were so thirsty that we actually drank water out of shell-holes," he said, "and God knows what a shell-hole contains. It could hold anything—very often parts of a human body. But we were so thirsty we drank it cold and without boiling it, because you couldn't get a fire very often."[7]

Even in the appalling conditions of Passchendaele, efforts were made to push rations and water forward to the men in the lines, but with no communication trenches to provide covered access to the forward positions, and with no clearly defined linear front, the resupply parties often had to fight their way forward to reach their comrades in their muddy shell holes. Many British soldiers remembered that tea was sent forward every day, but the tea came in two-gallon petrol cans, and each carried with it its own malady. "Well those tins were baked, boiled—everything was done to them," one soldier said, "but whenever you put a hot substance in them you still got petrol oozing out, and that gave the men violent diarrhea. But they had to drink it because it was the only hot drink they had."[8] For the men in the line, it was just one more element of misery in a situation that quickly exceeded all known bounds of misery.

It is hard to understand why most armies had not by that point in time recognized the importance of providing dedicated containers for water resupply, containers reserved solely for carrying potable water. There is no question that the problem was clearly identified and understood, but for whatever reason, there was little standardized response to the issue. The practice of transporting drinking water in repurposed fuel cans was just how it was done, and men were constantly made ill by it. Even in this instance, though, some men found a bleak humor in their gasoline-tainted water. "There was a standing joke," one British soldier recalled, "that if you were out there long enough you could tell the difference in taste as to whether the water came in a British Petroleum or a Shell can."[9]

Twenty-seven years after the ordeal at Passchendaele, U.S. Marines fighting in the sweltering heat and dust of Peleliu in the Pacific suffered much the same physical ailments when the only water resupply they received came in five-gallon cans that had previously held diesel fuel. No amount of cleaning and no method of scouring ever seemed to completely rid the cans of the fuel residue, and desperately dehydrated men drank the contaminated water knowing they would be violently ill in short order. Thanks to the lack of foresight on the part of the logistics and supply chain, there was simply no other choice.

Japanese soldiers often suffered just as much as their Allied opponents in the tropical campaigns of the Second World War. A Japanese lieutenant, Tadahiro Ogawa, wrote of one occasion when his unit went without water resupply for two days. "The Indin Chaung close to us was salty," he recalled, "and we tried hard but in vain to find a drinking water source. All the soldiers were dehydrated." When a water source was finally located, it came with an additional hazard. "A pond was finally found north of the Chaung," Ogawa wrote, "but there our soldiers often encountered British soldiers who also came to get water. The water was available to us at the risk of men's lives."[10]

When food was adequate to ward off starvation and water was in sufficient quantity to prevent severe dehydration, many soldiers in the period turned their attention to the other mainstay of their lives—alcohol. It is no exaggeration to say that many soldiers of this period drank a fair bit. As historian Don Rickey says of the U.S. Army during the Indian Wars of the nineteenth century, "Although some drank little or not at all, large numbers were accustomed to heavy drinking, and many spent most of their pay for beer and whiskey."[11] But the common stereotype of the army as a complete collection of hard-drinking men is not entirely accurate, either—there were always moderate drinkers in the ranks, and more than a few committed teetotalers.

When enlisted men did *not* drink, they tended to take a dim view of those who did, particularly if the objects of their disdain were their superiors. Eddie Matthews, stationed at Fort Union with the 8th U.S. Cavalry in the 1880s, criticized what he saw as hypocrisy on the part of officers at his post who sat on courts-martial boards that punished soldiers for drunken infractions. "If these officers would only Court Martial themselves for being drunk, it would consume all their time sitting on each other's cases," he wrote in a letter. "A more drunken set I never saw. The more I see of their drunkenness the more I become disgusted with liquor and stronger my resolutions are to abstain from using it."[12] Matthews was one of the several men from his troop who were members of the Good Templars, the teetotaler's organization that had active chapters on many U.S. Army posts. He was not alone in his dislike for officers with a drinking problem. "In the case of an officer addicted to drink the effect on the morale of his men is disastrous," John Finerty wrote in his account of the U.S. Army's campaign against the Sioux. "A drunken officer is the greatest curse that any troop, company, or regiment can be afflicted with."[13] Finerty had a reputation as a hard-drinking man himself, but he also recognized the negative impact that alcohol could have on a unit's combat effectiveness.

Despite the presence of teetotalers in the ranks, the civilian perception of soldiers as dissolute alcoholics endured through the years. Needham N. Freeman remembered overhearing a conversation between a civilian man and two small boys who visited his battalion's encampment in New Orleans. "One of the little boys noticing the soldiers eating, and seemed to be interested in the manner of their eating, said: 'Papa, will soldiers eat hay?' His youthful curiosity appeared to be fully satisfied by the father answering: 'Yes, if whiskey is put on it.'"[14]

This image of soldiers as men given to strong drink found expression in contemporary narratives throughout the period, both those of soldiers themselves and the officers who commanded them. "The insatiable, inordinate appetite of some of the men for intoxicating liquor, of any kind, was something remarkable," one Union veteran of the Civil War remembered. "And they were not a bit fastidious about the kind of liquor, it was the effect that was desired."[15]

Drinking frequently went hand in hand with breaches of military discipline. It was a maxim of military life, one long known to officers and NCOs who had to deal with the consequences, that "good soldiers can behave foolishly when drink is in and wit is out."[16] At its worst, drunkenness could result in outright criminal behavior, and every army lost men not to the enemy's bullets but to violent altercations between drunken messmates or between soldiers and civilians. The U.S. Army during the frontier era constantly struggled with this problem. One night in March 1868, Corporal James Dunn of the 28th U.S. Infantry was brought to the post hospital at Little Rock, Arkansas, with a bullet in his belly. The regimental surgeon reported that Dunn was "in an intoxicated condition, having received a wound of the abdomen by the accidental discharge of a small pocket-pistol while resisting the efforts of a policeman to disarm him." Dunn died in the morning. Private Edward Sturvan, 4th U.S. Cavalry, was shot in a drunken scuffle at Fort Concho, Texas, in June 1870. "There was no treatment," the post surgeon wrote in his report, "death being almost instantaneous from internal haemorrhage." Outside Santa Fe, New Mexico, in 1870, Private John Welsh of the 3rd Cavalry "was wounded in a drunken row, by a pistol shot from the hands of some person unknown." Welsh lingered five days before he died of the bullet wound in his head. Commissary Sergeant Edward Zimmer, of the 37th Infantry, was more fortunate; he was took a bullet in his side "in a drunken brawl" in Santa Fe, New Mexico, in 1868, but he survived both the wound and the medical treatment and was back on duty two months later [17]

At the very least, excessive drinking meant that men who seized the first opportunity to drink themselves insensible were effectively rendered hors de combat for a time, and therefore absolutely useless to their units. The Duke of Wellington was frequently infuriated at the behavior of his army when it got its collective hands on alcohol. "The French soldiers are more under control than ours," he remarked, decades after the Peninsular War. "It was quite shocking what excesses ours committed when once let loose. I remember once at Badajoz, when we stormed the town, entering a cellar and seeing some soldiers lying on the floor so dead drunk that the wine was actually flowing from their mouths. Yet others were coming in not at all disgusted at seeing them, and going to do the same." Wellington was no shrinking violet, and he was not a teetotaler himself, but he was a fiercely self-disciplined man, and the sight of both military and personal discipline being abandoned for the sake of intoxication revolted him. "Our soldiers could not resist wine," he said, and the recrimination was clear. [18]

Drinking was such a widespread problem that it caused a unique sort of troubles for those men who did not drink to excess. Being known as a dependable soldier when most of one's fellows were notorious drunks had its price, as Thomas Morris, a British soldier in the Napoleonic era, recalled. "I had the credit of being a sober man, and this circumstance has on more than one occasion entailed on me additional duty," he wrote, and described an instance when the men of his company got into a supply of schnapps. "Such was now the case: although I had been on sentry six hours during the day, at ten o'clock at night I was obliged to go on again." Bad as that was, there was an additional, unsettling detail he was unable to forget. "The night set in very dark, with a dense fog, and the only companion I had was one of the dead artillery men," he wrote. "He had been killed in the act of sponging his gun, and the ball that struck him, took his hand off at the wrist and forced it completely through his body. He had been laid outside the fort, with the intention of burying him next morning. I had to remain in this situation until two o'clock in the morning, before they could get men sober enough to succeed us."[19] A few years later, after Morris was promoted to sergeant, he very understandably had little tolerance for drunken soldiers.

The U.S. Army found alcohol to be a constant problem during the Second World War, particularly in the European Theater, where it could be obtained fairly easily, but it also manifested itself as a discipline issue in other areas where American GIs were posted. Based on the preponderance of sources, most notably the records compiled by the U.S. Army itself, alcohol was a factor in the majority of instances of serious crimes—murder, rape, assault, and incidents of major insubordination—that were committed by American soldiers during the war. To a modern American soldier, accustomed to an army determined to thwart human nature by compelling (officially, at least) its soldiers to remain celibate and sober during combat deployments, the amount of drinking that occurs in soldier narratives of the Second World War can be truly startling. American soldiers of that war seemed to be able to find alcohol almost anywhere they went, and official proscriptions held little sway. Of the ninety-six American soldiers executed for capital offenses in the European Theater, alcohol was reported to have factored into at least half of those crimes.

It was also true that alcohol served as an escape for soldiers when they found themselves, as they so often did, in situations where there was simply nothing much to do but sit around and watch time pass them by. Aloysius Damski, a Pole conscripted into the German Wehrmacht and posted to Normandy, remembered, "There was very little recreation. . . . I sometimes went out with French girls, but most of my spare time was spent drinking. Wine was very cheap, only twelve francs a pint, and my wages were equivalent to 350 francs every ten days."[20] The experience was much the same for men on the other side of the conflict. As one American paratrooper recalled of his time in North Africa, "We did discover a supply of dry, very potent red wine in one of the nearby villages. Whenever we got particularly bored, we sent someone out with a five-gallon can to buy some wine, then sat around the can in a circle, and repeatedly filled our canteen cups until we were thoroughly inebriated. . . . This practice left us with some crippling hangovers, but they never deterred us from sending out for yet another can of red wine."[21]

When it came to alcohol, the beverage of choice depended largely on the army, the era, and where in the world those soldiers were serving. For most Western armies, particularly the British, American, French, and German, beer was always a favorite libation. What each of them thought of as an acceptable version of beer, though, was often a very different thing. British troops in France during the First World War found French beer to be "watery" and a poor substitute for their preferred heavy ales. American troops training in England during WWII were often unenthusiastic about the British custom of drinking warm beer, and French soldiers in Indochina had to accustom their palates to Vietnamese beer that was often fortified with formaldehyde.

American soldiers of the Second World War had a reputation for drinking almost any kind of alcohol they could get their hands on, and this created a constant threat to discipline, especially in the European Theater where alcohol was readily available. William Funkhouser, a sergeant in the U.S. 1st Infantry Division, described an example of this when he was on occupation duty in Bamberg immediately after the war ended. "My company was assigned to guard these wine cellars," he recalled. "That was a mistake. Anyway, they had great big barrels of wine in these wine cellars. I would go around at the start of my shift. I was the sergeant of the guard on one shift, drop my guys off and pick up the other guys. Then the next shift would go around and pick my guys up. These great big barrels of wine and the guys would go in there with these G.I. cans, knock the bung out, get five gallons of wine and lose forty." If ever there was a case of having the lunatics running the asylum, Funkhouser thought, that was it. "Had us guarding the wine cellars," he said, bemused, as if he still could not understand the logic behind that decision, even sixty years later.[22]

When Needham N. Freeman's infantry regiment entrained for the journey to an embarkation port in the Spanish-American War, he recalled that the citizens of San Antonio, Texas, "put several kegs of beer in every car. This was appreciated very much, as beer seems to be a soldier's favorite beverage, and one that he will have if he has money and is where it can be bought." Freeman concluded with a slightly obvious statement: "A soldier rarely refuses beer when offered to him."[23] Several decades before Freeman's time, Henry Windolph fought at the Battle of the Little Bighorn with the 7th U.S. Cavalry. Remembering his regiment going into action that fateful day, Windolph later said, "It'd be easy to say we were thinking only of glory on this hot June Sunday afternoon . . . but I reckon what most of the plain troopers were thinking about was how good a nice cold bottle of beer would taste right now."[24]

Harder, more potent liquor was the preference for some armies. Russian soldiers drank vodka (drank it like water, according to many of their astonished allies); Serbians, Croats, and Albanians drank slivovitz; when the German *landser* wasn't in his beer, he liked a bit of schnapps or cognac; Scottish regiments often contained a fair number of whisky drinkers; Japanese soldiers drank saki and beer; and for most of this period the British soldier was entitled by custom and regulation to a regular tot of liquor (usually rum but sometimes gin) as an official ration. Entering Naples in 1943, American paratrooper Spencer Wurst encountered an Italian libation he had never before experienced. "It was a hot afternoon, and a priest stepped out of the crowd and handed me a glass of water," Wurst wrote. "Without thinking, I downed it in one large gulp. Suddenly, I had a sputtering hot throat and mouth, and my stomach was on fire. I had just been introduced to grappa—a colorless liqueur of pure distilled spirits."[25]

The point at which alcohol went from being a personal pleasure (or escape) for the private soldier to being an item of official issue was different for each army. The Russians supplied their troops with vodka as a regular policy, as the British did with the grog ration. The nineteenth-century American army did not officially countenance drinking, but "the army's general attitude was one of tolerance."[26] This tolerance did not always apply in every era; in the Second World War there were strict differences as to what was permissible for officers and enlisted men as far as alcohol went, but drunkenness was a common problem whenever men could get their hands on the stuff. All the same, the U.S. Army recognized alcohol as an important element by assigning it an official category in the logistics table: "Class Six" was, and remains, the American military's designation for alcohol. Ironically, almost the first occasion when the fledgling American government had to use its army after attaining its independence from Britain was to put down the so-called "Whiskey Rebellion," when the government had to use military force to impose its taxes on domestic corn-liquor production.

The British Army sometimes used alcohol in an overt way to shore up the morale of its men in the midst of battle. At Waterloo, as Sergeant Thomas Morris recalled, "By twelve o'clock the artillery on both sides were busily engaged. Some commissariat wagons came into the field, with a supply of salt provisions and spirits." Morris was detailed off with another man to collect his company's alcohol ration: "We had scarcely received it," he wrote, "when a cannon-shot went through the cask, and the man too."[27] The historical evidence supports the idea that more than a few men in the British squares at Waterloo were increasingly intoxicated as the day went on, but this was not necessarily a common experience throughout the period.

It is not uncommon for armies to accuse their enemies of being fighting drunk, in the literal sense, as a means of explaining extraordinary recklessness or apparent fearlessness in the attack, but there was often more slander than truth in such allegations. Frank Richards, who served in the British Army before and during the First World War, said that he "read in some paper about troops in the War being doped with rum before going into action." The reality, at least in his experience, was much different. "In my battalion we never got enough of rum to make a louse drunk," he wrote. "Our ordinary ration was very beneficial to us and helped to keep the cold out of our bodies, but any man who had had an extra drop before he went out on patrols, night raids or attacks was looking for trouble; a man needed all his wits and craft when he was taking part in any of those, and an extra drop made one reckless."[28]

The official rum ration had other uses, though. "I used to swap my fags [cigarettes] for the rum rations," one British veteran of the First World War recalled. "The sergeant would come along with a spoon of rum and in the front line you had to drink it—but beyond the front line you could do what you liked with it. Once the officer and orderly sergeant had gone past, I used to take my socks and boots off and rub the rum into my feet."[29] It was not exactly the standard preventative for trench foot, perhaps, but it was a field-expedient method that more than one soldier swore by.

Of all the armies considered in this period, perhaps only the soldiers of the Ottoman Turkish army abstained from alcohol as a general rule, and that was more for religious reasons than military. Across the spectrum, the prevailing reality was that drinking plagued most armies, and the problem was never completely eradicated no matter the considerable official efforts made to get it under control.

Chapter Nine

"Hell with the Lid Off"

The Experience of Battle

I want to go home, I want to go home,
The cannons they roar and they roar and they roar,
I just don't want to go up the line any more.
Will you take me over the sea,
Where those Germans cannot get me,
Oh, I don't want to die, I want to go home.
　　　　　　　　　　　—FIRST WORLD WAR SOLDIERS' SONG

IN LITERARY SOURCES going all the way back to Homer, battle is often portrayed as the culminating experience of a soldier's life. Battle, this perspective suggests, is the very reason for soldiers' existence—if armies exist to fight and win their nations' wars, then it logically follows that the soldiers who make up those armies, and who do the bloody work of war, exist primarily to fight.

Perhaps this is the reason why the preponderance of military histories focus on accounts of battle. After all, battles are momentous and decisive events, and matters of great importance hinge on their outcome—a military historian who ignored battle altogether would be a rare creature, indeed. There is also the undeniable fact that stories of combat are exciting. The old expression "a matter of life and death" has become a tired cliché from being too often applied to matters that are not remotely as serious as that, but battle is truly a matter of life and death, and it holds an undeniable and understandable fascination, for both participants and more distant observers.

All the same, we should bear in mind that while combat occupies primacy of place in military history, it was a relatively small part of most soldiers' lives in almost every era that this book examines, at least proportionately. The reality for most soldiers was that much of their time in the army was spent in the mundane, day-to-day normality of garrison life. (This was true, at least, of professional soldiers—less true of those soldiers who only enlisted for the duration of a specific war.)

With all of this in mind, however, it is still true that for most soldiers who left narratives of their service, the experience of battle occupied the forefront of their reminiscences of their service. So our focus now turns to the first-person, grunt's-eye view of battle, the soldier's own narrow view of the fight—how the individual soldier saw and remembered his war.

For most men, that narrow view was often disjointed and confusing, a small window into a world gone mad. David Holbrook, a British tank commander in Normandy in 1944, described the experience of being on the receiving end of German machine gun fire. "You've never heard anything like it," he said. "You suddenly find yourself enveloped in a sort of hail of tracer, wondering what the hell was happening. . . . It was more than just a noise: it was an assault on your skin and ears. The blast just sort of slams into you with all these bits of tree and wall flying about."[1]

Enemy fire could become such a constant part of daily existence that it acquired its own lexicography. "The army's term for it was 'shit,'" Holbrook recalled. "Day and night there was some kind of shit flying at you. If it wasn't these machine guns it was tank guns, if it wasn't tank guns it was artillery, if it wasn't artillery it was some bugger in an aeroplane dropping bombs on you. There wasn't any kind of confrontation you could call a confrontation. You'd just move along in your tank and then suddenly a great wave of shit would start flying at you and you'd blast off in that direction and then it all stops and there's lots of dust and smoke and you back behind a wall. Then you come out the other side and start driving along and nothing happens and you think that's all right and then suddenly a bloody great branch flies off a tree and you see that someone else is shooting at you and then you dodge behind a house."[2] This was the essence of many soldiers' experience of battle in the latter part of this period—confusion, noise, violence, and catastrophic amounts of metal flying in their direction, often with no clear sense of where it was coming from. For infantrymen the perspective was much the same, albeit closer to the ground and with considerably more mud and dirt involved.

When we consider the ordinary soldier's experience of battle, an interesting paradox quickly becomes apparent. For one thing, there is a great commonality in soldiers' accounts of combat, so much so that for the historian it might be tempting to take the view expressed by the narrator of Ecclesiastes when he declared, "There is nothing new under the sun." Such an assumption would be wrong, however. It is certainly true that there are common themes, and some elements of one man's experience of the Battle of Waterloo in 1815 are found again in other men's narratives from Balaclava in 1854, Gettysburg in 1863, Gallipoli in 1915, or Tarawa in 1944. These threads of familiar experience, even though they occur in different times and places, are part of the commonality of soldiering.

At the same time, there are also differences. One soldier describes the nearly debilitating fear of the moment; another says he felt no fear at all. One man remembers the horror of seeing his comrades killed around him; another remembers the strength he drew from fighting with his friends beside him. One man's account is philosophical, lyrical, and almost poetic; another man's words are terse, factual, and blunt. We cannot assume that all battles produce exactly similar experiences. Even so, it is still safe to say that some things remain constant for men in battle, no matter the era, the war, the army, or the man. Some factors apply to every soldier's experience of battle, to one degree or another: among them are fear, confusion, violence, apprehension, excitement, killing, and survival.

Whether or not battle was the essence of a soldier's military life, most soldiers seemed to understand that battle, with all its violent death and systematic slaughter, was at least the essence of *war*. Some men eventually came to accept their own mortality and the very likely prospect of their deaths with a calm that bordered on fatalism. Others resisted that idea with every fiber of their being and refused to contemplate anything so awful as their own destruction. All of them, though, if they were in combat long enough, saw death up close and often. The reality of war as many men described it was that the soldier's relation to death was both intimate and utterly impersonal, all at the same time.

The experience of combat, of actually fighting, was something that many men found to be exhilarating and exciting. It was an undeniable part of the adventure of soldiering, after all, and adventure was something that drew many men to the army in the first place. The adrenaline of the fight, in the midst of the smoke and noise and movement of battle, was electrifying. Even men whose personal narratives speak candidly of the horrors of war, of the death and destruction to which they were witnesses, still often describe battle itself as something that, though terrible, was still thrilling despite the savagery of it. Confederate infantryman Leon Louis wrote of the fighting on the first day of Gettysburg, "Just at dark we were sent to the front under terrible cannonading. Still, it was a beautiful sight. It being dark, we could see the cannon vomit forth fire."[3]

On battlefields where men fought in open view of each other, without taking cover, soldiers were witnesses to scenes that were both incredible and horrible. Thomas Morris wrote of one moment during the Battle of Waterloo in 1815 when his infantry regiment in their square were spectators to nearby cavalry fight:

The next time the cuirassiers made their appearance in our front, the Life Guards boldly rode out from our rear to meet them, and in point of numbers, they seemed pretty well matched. The French waited, with the utmost coolness, to receive them, opening their ranks to allow them to ride in. . . . It was a fair fight, and the French were fairly beaten and driven off. I noticed one of the Guards, who was attacked by two cuirassiers, at the same time; he bravely maintained the unequal conflict for a minute or two, when he disposed of one of them by a deadly thrust in the throat. His combat with the other one last about five minutes, when the guardsman struck his opponent a slashing backhanded stroke, and sent his helmet some distance, with the head inside it. The horse galloped away with the headless rider, sitting erect in saddle, the blood spouting out of the arteries like so many fountains.[4]

Battle could on some occasions be intensely personal, especially when the combatants actually knew each other, as sometimes happened in civil wars. In the opening stages of the Battle of Fredericksburg in 1862, a unit of the Confederate 21st Mississippi was supposed to fight a delaying action to impede, but not attempt to stop, the Union investment of the town—the actual battle would take place outside the town on the open fields below Marye's Heights where the Confederates commanded wide fields of fire from the high ground. This master plan was temporarily departed from, as one Southern soldier remembered, when an officer in the 21st Mississippi discovered that his opposite number on the Federal side was an old personal friend. "The last detachment was under the command of Lane Brandon," this soldier wrote. "Brandon captured a few prisoners and learned that the advance company was commanded by Abbott, who had been his chum at Harvard Law School when the war began. He lost his head completely. He refused to retire before Abbott. He fought him fiercely and was actually driving him back. In this he was violating orders and breaking our plan of battle. He was put under arrest and his subaltern brought the command out of town." In making the fight a personal matter, Brandon was perhaps not departing too far from the reputation that the Mississippi troops already had in the Confederate Army. "They were ready to fight anything from his Satanic Majesty down," the same narrator remarked, "but they were a very poor set indeed as to judging when not to fight or when to stop fighting."[5]

The heat of battle, to use an old expression, affected men in different ways. John Bowe, who fought in the Philippine Insurrection with the U.S. 13th Minnesota, thought that "it was interesting to watch the men in the chase, some of the officers insisted on their men firing by volleys, most of the boys firing at will. Some would shoot as fast as they could load, others would go along and not fire a shot unless they could shoot to kill." One of his comrades, Bowe remembered, spent a considerable length of time lining up a Filipino in his sights and taking careful, deliberate aim. He had, however, forgotten to chamber a round in his Krag, with perhaps unsurprising results: "When he pulled the trigger he went straight up in the air," Bowe wrote. "His gun kicks like a pile-driver, so he made preparations accordingly, and when it did not kick at all, on account of having no load, his surprise was painful to behold."[6]

Sustained battle was hard on both men and weapons. The anonymous British narrator from the 71st Regiment, remembering the savage fighting at Fuentes de Onoro in 1811 in the Peninsular War, said that by the time that day's battle was ended, "My shoulder was as black as coal, from the recoil of my musket." He had fired 107 rounds of ball cartridge that day, he said, nearly all the ammunition of his basic load.[7] French infantrymen also found the experience of toe-to-toe infantry combat to be exhausting. Jean-Roch Coignet, who fought the Austrians in 1800, later wrote, "Their columns were constantly reinforced; no one came to our support. Our musket-barrels were so hot that it became impossible to load for fear of igniting the cartridges. There was nothing for it but to piss into the barrels to cool them, and then to dry them by pouring in loose powder and setting it alight unrammed."[8]

That experience of firing one's weapon until the barrel was too hot to touch or load safely was a reality of modern war from the Napoleonic Wars to the Second World War. Sustained rates of fire in the combat of the First World War were notoriously hard on machine guns, in particular—the Vickers and Maxim guns would overheat to the point that the water in their cooling jackets boiled away, at which point the weapons would quickly cease functioning. Air-cooled machine guns, such as the Lewis guns, could also be fired until they overheated and seized up, although a gunner would have to have quite a supply of ammunition panniers at hand to sustain that rate of fire for that long.

Simpler weapons also failed under extreme conditions. Leon Louis recalled one battle where his regiment kept up such a volume of fire that he was eventually unable to reload his musket. "In our rapid firing today my gun became so hot that the ramrod would not come out," he wrote, "so I shot it at the Yankees, and picked up a gun from the ground, a gun that some poor comrade dropped after being shot." Years after the event, Louis had one lingering question about that day. "I wonder if it [the ramrod] hit a Yankee," he wrote. "If so, I pity him."[9]

Nineteenth-century land battles were fought at comparatively short range, but even then, a soldier's individual view of the fight was limited. In the close-order combat of battles from the Napoleonic era to the American Civil War, soldiers were almost always with direct line of sight of their enemy, at least until the shooting started, at which point the dense smoke of black-powder muskets and cannon quickly obscured the firing lines.

More than one soldier commented on the fact that in the hottest part of battle, when the infantry was blasting away with volleys of fire as rapidly as they could, the smoke made it all but impossible to see what was going on nearby. Seeing what was happening across the field was even less likely. The anonymous soldier-narrator of the 71st Regiment wrote in his account of the fighting at Waterloo, "The noise and smoke were dreadful. At this time I could see but a very little way from me, but all around the wounded and slain lay very thick."

Benjamin Harris, a soldier in the Rifle Brigade, described much the same experience. "I myself was very soon so hotly engaged, loading and firing away, enveloped in the smoke that I created, and the cloud which hung about me from the continued fire of my comrades," he wrote, "that I could see nothing for a few minutes but the red flash of my own piece amongst the white vapour clinging to my very clothes." The effect of this on the individual soldier was to deprive him of all visual references and orientation. "Until some friendly breeze of wind clears the space around," Harris wrote, "a soldier knows no more of his position and what is about to happen to his front, or what *has* happened (even amongst his own comrades) than the very dead lying around."[10]

The intensity of fighting, of actually firing on the enemy, was sometimes a cathartic antidote to the apprehension and fear of impending battle, especially for well-trained, disciplined troops. As the British historian B. H. Liddell-Hart noted, "The feeling of being able to hit back is an invaluable relief from tension."[11] Being under fire but not being able to fight back usually had an exactly opposite and quickly denigrating effect. "The most trying situation in battle," Union Army infantryman Leander Stillwell wrote of the fighting at Shiloh, "is one where you have to lie flat on the ground, under fire more or less, and without any opportunity to return it. The strain on the nerves is almost intolerable."[12] Another Union veteran of Shiloh wrote of being in the middle of an artillery duel between Federal and Rebel guns—all the infantry could do was lay out in the open and hope that all the lethal iron would pass them by. "But how a fellow does hug the ground under such circumstance!" he wrote. "As a shell goes whistling over him he flattens out, and presses himself to the earth, almost. Pity the sorrows of a big fat man under such a fire."[13]

Almost all soldiers who made a record of their experiences of battle, who talked about it or left an account of it, made *some* mention of the horrors of war to which they had been witnesses in combat. Some of them made oblique references to terrible sights that they clearly did not want to elaborate upon; others described those nightmares in vivid detail. In every war, men saw truly terrible things.

"I have one terrible memory," recalled Werner Kortenhaus, who fought in Normandy in 1944 with the German Wehrmacht's 21st Panzer Division. "On 9 June we had attacked Escoville, an attack which only lasted a few minutes. There were infantry behind us, under covers, who were wounded and we had to reverse. The driver can only see in front of him and did not know they were there. . . . We reversed over them, our own infantry. Because they were wounded they couldn't move out of the way. One saw some terrible things."[14]

"Terrible sights here," British Sergeant Major Ernest Shephard of the Dorsets Regiment wrote in his diary during the fighting at Hill 60 in France in 1915. "Hundreds of bodies all over the place terribly mutilated, a large number of our own men, and larger number of the Hun. Stench is awful as they cannot be buried, never quiet enough to do that, so they lie as they fell, silent spectators of modern warfare."[15]

The lethality of modern warfare, and the improved capacity for slaughter on a massive scale that marked modern warfare, was a frequent feature in the personal accounts of soldiers throughout this period. More than a few soldiers would have echoed the sentiment of one British veteran of the fighting at Gallipoli, who wrote in a letter home, "War is interesting and exciting but very terrible when one gets close enough to see the effect."[16] And in case the reader might think that the horrors of war were a concept unique to soldiers of twentieth-century warfare, one need only consider some of the narratives from the early days of this period.

Thomas Morris, whose account of the Battle of Waterloo we just read, was also a veteran of the earlier British campaign that laid siege to Antwerp in 1814. The British infantry investing the city were holding fieldworks that were within range of the city's guns, a fact that made unnecessary exposure in daylight a risky proposition. "One of the officers, who was looking through the breastwork watching the enemy's batteries,"

Morris wrote, "suddenly drew himself down, observing, that a gun was just fired, the shot from which would come very close to us; the observation caused a young man, reclining next to the officer, to raise himself up to look, and immediately his head was taken off."[17]

A few years later, serving with an artillery regiment of the Indian Army, Staff Sergeant N. W. Bancroft experienced the shattering effects of massed enemy guns when his artillery battery came under fire while moving into position during an assault:

The gun on [my] right halted in consequence of its two polemen being literally cut in two, the lower portions of their bodies still remaining in the saddle, the upper portion of the right poleman's body being on the ground, while that of the left was suspended by the head over the collar-bar. The sergeant-major brought up a spare man to take the place of the near poleman, at the same time emptying the two saddles of their ghastly burdens. It must be said that the spare man hesitated to jump into the saddle—for one of the mangled bodies was that of his brother! The sergeant-major seeing there was no time to be lost, freed the collar-bar from the half body hanging over it, and threatened the spare gunner with his pistol if he did not jump into the saddle immediately, and he did so. The gun on [my] left had now halted; the off poleman having been struck by a round shot in the face, which carried away the left half, the body still sitting erect in the saddle. Here another spare man ran up, tilted the body out of the saddle, and sprang up into his seat, which he had scarcely attained when a shot broke the off fore-leg of the horse he had just mounted. The horse was sent adrift, but appeared loth to leave his mates on the advance of the battery, for he hobbled after it, and as ill-luck would have it, came blundering up to the wagon . . . putting an end to all progress for a time. [A] ball struck the pole horse of the wagon on which [I] was seated, in the stomach, and in an instant the poor animal's intestines were hanging about its leg. [I] called to the rider informing him of the mishap in language more plain than refined perhaps by saying "Tom! Tom! (the man's name was Tom Connolly) "Snarly Yow (the horse's name) has turned inside out, and his inwards are dangling about!" Tom shouted to the corporal leading the team, "Joe! Joe! Pull up! Snarly Yow's guts are hanging about his legs!" To which request the corporal coolly made answer: "Be gorra, Tom, I wouldn't pull up at such a time as this if [your] own guts were hanging out!" The horse did not drop until the troop formed battery again at a considerable distance to the right.[18]

The effects of cannon fire when iron solid-shot impacted on flesh were absolutely horrific. "Just before we started on the charge, as we lay in the field just back of the city," a Union Army infantryman wrote of the Battle of Fredericksburg, "a Company I man was killed by having his head carried bodily away by a cannon ball, the body rolled over, the blood spurted from the neck as water comes from a pump, until the heart pumped the body dry."[19]

One of the most famous combat actions of the period was the Charge of the Light Brigade during the Battle of Balaclava in the Crimean War, a colossal blunder of miscommunication and unclear orders that Tennyson immortalized in verse. Soldiers who survived that headlong charge down the "Valley of Death" were not so lyrical in their own descriptions of the battle. J. W. Wightman was one of them; he was no poet, but his account is hard to improve upon for stark, violent reality:

We had not broke into the charging pace when poor old John Lee, my right-hand man on the flank of the regiment, was all but smashed by a shell; he gave my arm a twitch, as with a strange smile on his worn old face he quietly said, "Domino, chum," and fell out of the saddle. His old grey mare kept alongside of me for some distance, treading on and tearing out her entrails as she galloped, till at length she dropped with a strange shriek. I have mentioned that my comrade, Peter Marsh, was my left-hand man; next beyond him was Private Dudley. The explosion of a shell had swept down four or five men on Dudley's left, and I heard him ask Marsh if he had noticed "what a hole that b—— shell had made" on his left front. "Hold your foul-mouthed tongue," answered Peter, "swearing like a blackguard, when you may be knocked into eternity next minute!" Just then I got a musket-bullet through my right knee, and another in the shin, and my horse had three bullet wounds in the neck. Man and horse were bleeding so fast that Marsh begged me to fall out; but I would not, pointing out that in a few minutes we must be into them, and so I sent my spurs well home, and faced it out with my comrades. It was about this time that Sergeant Talbot had his head carried clean off by a round shot, yet for about thirty yards further the headless body kept the saddle, with the lance at the charge still firmly gripped under the right arm. My narrative may seem barren of incidents, but amid the crash of shells and the whistle of bullets, the cheers and the dying cries of comrades, the sense of personal danger, the pain of wounds, and the consuming passion to reach an enemy, he must be an exceptional man who is cool enough and curious enough to be looking serenely about him for what painters call "local colour." I had a good deal of "local colour" myself, but it was running down the leg of my overalls from my wounded knee.[20]

Wightman survived the charge, the desperate fight at the Russian guns, and the return back up the valley under fire—Balaclava was the worst thing he ever saw in his time as a soldier, he said, and also the most tremendous experience of his life.

In the U.S. Army, the artillery arm is known as the "King of Battle," a title that owes everything to the fact that artillery is the great killer of the battlefield—more combat casualties are inflicted by artillery fire than are caused by direct-fire infantry weapons. The effects of artillery could be truly terrible, especially when brought to bear against the massed troop formations of the nineteenth century, or when delivered in concentrated battery fire against static positions. This latter tactic was the notorious "drum fire" bombardments remembered in so many soldiers' memoirs of the First World War. The experience of being on the receiving end of sustained artillery fire was something that no soldier ever forgot.

"For a full week we were under incessant bombardment," a German soldier remembered of the buildup to the Battle of the Somme. "Day and night, the shells came upon us. Our dugouts crumbled. They would fall on top of us and we'd have to dig ourselves and our comrades out. Sometimes we'd find them suffocated or smashed to pulp. Soldiers in the bunkers became hysterical—they wanted to run out, and fights developed to keep them in the comparative safety of our deep bunkers. Even the rats became hysterical and came into our flimsy shelters to seek refuge from this terrific artillery fire. For seven days and seven nights we had nothing to eat and nothing to drink while shell after shell burst upon us."[21]

The men on the other side of that battle suffered under shellfire every bit as much as did the Germans. "There were times, after being shelled for hours on end during the latter part of the Somme battle," a British corporal said, "that all I wanted was to be blown to bits. Because you knew that if you got wounded, they could never get you away, not under those conditions. You'd see other people with internal wounds and you thought your only hope was to get killed outright, your only relief."[22] Another soldier, Ernest Shephard, in the diary he kept through the Battle of the Somme, wrote of the effects of being under sustained German shellfire. "Literally we were blown from place to place," he wrote. "Men very badly shaken. As far as possible we cleared trenches of debris and dead. These we piled in heaps, enemy shells pitching on them made matters worse."[23]

Two years later, in the final year of the war, a German soldier named Herbert Sulzbach described the artillery fire he endured then as being more terrible than anything he had previously survived. His unit, he remembered, was "attacked by a barrage which was absolutely unbelievable. It was the worst barrage and the worst gunfire I ever heard, and I had been through the Somme and everywhere else since then."[24] These were the conditions that Stephen Graham described when he wrote, "German and British are living in the same madhouse together and fighting for complete possession room by room."[25]

Fighting in Burma during the Second World War, a Japanese infantryman named Manabu Wada described the fighting at Kohima as both terrifying and terrible, primarily because of the British artillery. "The enemy's heavy and medium artillery opened up on us as a prelude to their infantry attacks," he said. "The British shells rained down on us in hundreds and thousands in great barrages. In this storm of fire we had to run to seek shelter and could barely hold Kohima. It is not possible to express our terror as shrapnel burst upon us with tremendous force so that officers and men were cut to pieces by jagged splinters that tore into the head, the abdomen, arms, legs."[26] The Japanese counter-battery fire, Wada remembered, was "limited to . . . just a few shells a day," a nearly ineffectual response to the British artillery that was shelling them with nearly incessant bombardments.

"I am done, the artillery fire is driving me crazy," a German NCO wrote in his diary during the fighting in Italy in 1944. "I am frightened as never before. . . . During the night one cannot leave one's hole. The last days have finished me off altogether."[27] British soldiers trying to shelter from German guns on the rocky slopes before Monte Cairo intimately understood and sympathized with his reaction to heavy, sustained shellfire, hammered day and night as they were hammered by German artillery.

One of the worst things about artillery fire, according to many soldiers, was the capricious, unpredictable randomness of it. "Two sergeants (who had just been chosen for commissions) were blown to pieces as I was talking to them," an Australian soldier wrote. "As I turned to reply to a question addressed to me by one of them the shell came, and in a second there was not enough left of either for identification. I picked myself up unhurt. Shells seem to have a way with them—one man being taken, and the other left. And it is not always the man nearest the shell that is taken."[28]

Another Australian infantryman wrote in his First World War journal: "6th April. We are to be relieved tonight. . . . The day passes quietly. Some odd shelling is down on us. Three men are killed and another twenty wounded." The bad luck of it all was just one of the wretched normalcies of a war that transcended centuries of combat experience. "Ever the same," he wrote, "men fall on the last day as well as the first, coming in and going out. Just the luck of the game!"[29] Many men, even though they never could claim that they were unbothered by artillery fire, at least saw its effects so often that they developed a grim familiarity with it. "No casualties yet," American infantryman James Dargan wrote of his battalion's advance against the Confederate positions near Fort Buchanan in Louisiana in 1863. "Only one drummer boy's head knocked off by a solid shot from the enemy's artillery."[30] For the record, Dargan was not a calloused or unfeeling man—he loved poetry and his diary shows a reflective and thoughtful personality, but two years of war had inured him to terrible things.

John Morse, who fought with the Russian Army during the First World War, wrote, "The freaks played by shells were sometimes extraordinary," and described one particular incident as illustration. A German artillery shell, he wrote, "went just over the head of an officer, killed a boy who was standing behind him, went over the head of another man, and then sprang high in the air before exploding. It is as impossible to give a probable explanation of such strange action, as it is to say why a fragment of shell bursting fifty yards away should kill three men, while one exploding right in the midst of a group of twenty gunners should leave them all unscathed." There was no predicting it, Morse concluded: "It is the law of chance—if chance has laws."[31]

Sometimes one artillery shell alone was enough to do the murderous work of an entire battery. Ernest Shephard described the effects of one shell that impacted in his company's lines. "We found two machine gunners belonging to our Company who had been blown from the trench over the railway bank into a deep pool of water collected there, a distance of 70 yards," he wrote in his diary. "One man, [Private] Woods, was found in 8 pieces, while others were ghastly sights, stomachs blown open, some headless, limbs off, etc."[32] The carnage, Shephard wrote, was apparently the work of a "very heavy and powerful" trench howitzer shell. Against that sort of weapon, almost no amount of digging-in was enough to guarantee safety—all one could do was hunker down and hope that the shell would land on some other poor bastard's section of the line.

Even men who had long experience with the carnage of battle could be taken aback by the violent destruction of artillery fire. William Howard Russell, who first made his name as a war correspondent in the Crimean War, also reported on the Franco-Prussian War of 1873. The field combat of that war effectively ended with the destruction of the French Army at Sedan, a battlefield that Russell visited while the smoke was still in the air. "With many years' experience of the work of war, I had never seen the like before," he wrote, "never beheld death in such horrible shapes—because the dead had on their faces the expression of terror—mental and bodily agony such as I have never should have thought it possible for mortal clay to retain after the spirit had fled through the hideous portals fashioned by the iron hand of artillery. There were human hands detached from the arms and hanging up in the trees; feet and legs lying far apart from the bodies to which they belonged."[33]

The killing power of infantry-borne indirect fire weapons such as mortars was not as ferocious as that of the heavy guns that operated from the rear of the lines, but mortars were deadly in the close-quarters slaughter of infantry combat. Joe McNamara, a U.S. Marine fighting on Okinawa in 1945, saw the effects of mortar fire all too well. "All of a sudden, this mortar shell came in and landed right on the sergeant's head," he said. "It blew me partially out of my foxhole. There was blood all over my arm. . . . When I looked around, I saw this sergeant in the same position when I last saw him, but he didn't have a head. Pieces of his brain and blood were what were on my arm. There was a corpsman lying on top of the foxhole who was chopped up by the shell fragments; he was just a bundle of rags. Good God, he was torn up."[34]

Even though they were bringers of distant death on many battlefields, artillerymen were themselves not immune to the devastating effects of shellfire; after all, their guns were always priority targets for the enemy's counter-battery fire. One British gunner, Alfred Finnigan, wrote of the fighting at Ypres: "We lost all six guns in turn and had very heavy casualties. I lost my Sergeant, Corporal and two Bombardiers, several gunners killed and wounded, one driver wounded... Everything was mud and water and continuous shelling." The shellfire at Ypres, Finnigan, said, was "Hell with the lid off."[35]

Battle forced most soldiers to confront their own mortality to some degree, whether they wanted to or not. Even if they thought about it no more than to stubbornly deny the possibility that they themselves might get killed, most soldiers on the eve of battle contemplated the fact that combat was inherently the act of men trying to kill each other, and so, inevitably, *someone* was going to die. What many men seem to have concluded, if only as a means of dealing with the crushing weight of fear and uncertainty, was that whoever got killed, it wasn't going to be them. It was always "the other guy" who was going to get it, an idea expressed by more than one soldier. Sergeant Henry Windolph, a trooper in the 7th U.S. Cavalry who fought at the Battle of the Little Bighorn, remembered what he and his fellow soldiers thought as they went into action that day. "We knew there'd be some hard fighting," he said, "but a soldier always feels that it's the other fellow who's going to get it. Never himself."[36]

This idea was something that many men latched onto and clung to with a fervent hope. Many of them found that in the reality of battle, violent death was simply too random, too impersonal, for a man to stake any confidence on the odds of his own survival over anyone else's. The well-trained, well-armed soldier might be a better fighter in the clinch than his second-rate opponent, but a random bullet killed just as readily as a carefully aimed round, and the good soldier could be transformed into a dead soldier just as easily as the next fellow. Physical strength, martial prowess, and personal courage were no guarantors of survival, and many men lay wakeful thinking about that.

An experience that caused more than one man to reconsider his personal chances, an experience that no soldier ever seemed to forget, was his first encounter with dead men. Seeing the enemy's dead was one thing, but the sight of corpses wearing the same uniform as oneself was something else entirely, as American infantryman Raymond Gantter recalled of his early days in the Second World War:

> Five dead Americans in the woods near Walheim, lying in a neat row by the side of the road. They'd been brought back from the front [the Hurtgen Forest] in a truck, lifted out—not gently but not carelessly, perhaps unfeelingly is the word, as though it were habitual and there was more to do and so little time—and placed there. Several hours later someone covered them with a blanket, and later another truck came up from the rear and took them away. Many of the men went over to look at the bodies, drawn by a horrible fascination. We hadn't seen any dead men yet. Most of them came back looking very ill. I didn't go over.[37]

Soldiers who spent enough time in combat usually grew more indifferent to the sight of dead men whom they did not know personally, but that callousness took time and exposure to develop, and few men seemed to have been completely unmoved by their first encounter with the dead. Gantter's phrase "a horrible fascination" is a description that many men of different armies evoked in their own recollections of their initial confrontations with the dead.

Other men recalled their first encounter with the dead as being something that shattered their pre-bellum sensibilities. Rory Grimshaw, commanding a troop of Indian Army cavalry in France during the First World War, recalled going into the forward lines for the first time. "Whilst we were halted on one of these occasions," he wrote, "my over-civilized senses received a shock":

There seemed to be about a foot of muddy slush in the trench and what I thought were filled sandbags to give footing in the mire. I thought I would look at the trench for a second and therefore switched on my electric torch. To my horror I saw I was standing on the corpse of a human being. I was very nearly sick, but I bent down and, extricating the man's hand from the mud, I felt his pulse to see if by any chance he was still alive. I could see no trace of life, which is not extraordinary seeing that at least 200 men had trampled over him before I arrived. There he was almost submerged in mud and slush.[38]

The very next day, Grimshaw's unit suffered its first combat losses during an artillery barrage. One of his troopers was killed; the experience in the trench the night before was still very fresh in Grimshaw's mind. "I thought of that trampled corpse in the trench," he wrote, "and I had him carefully put on one side where he would not be flung about or trodden on, till I had time to bury him."[39] Such considerations, as that war went on, became less frequent in the abattoir of the trenches in France.

From first seeing a dead man to seeing men actually being killed was sometimes a quick succession of events. The tone and language used to describe such sights varied greatly from soldier to soldier, army to army, and era to era, but some parts of it were familiar to all combat veterans.

"It was truly awful how fast, how very fast, did our poor boys fall by our sides," Confederate infantryman Leon Louis wrote of his experience in Civil War battle, "almost as fast as the leaves that fell as cannon and musket balls hit them. . . . You could see one with his head shot off, others cut in two, then one with his brain oozing out, one with his leg off, others shot through the heart." That was bad enough, but Louis remembered that instantaneous, merciful death was not a given. "Then you would hear some poor friend or foe crying for water, or for 'God's sake' to kill him," he wrote. "You would see some of your comrades, shot through the leg, lying between the lines, asking his friends to take him out, but no one could get to his relief, and you would have to leave him there, perhaps to die, or, at best, to become a prisoner."[40]

Men under heavy fire, if they allowed themselves time to reflect on their situation, later often described having felt that it was nearly inevitable that they would eventually be killed—not so much a question of "if" they would be hit, as "when." Remembering one skirmish in the Philippines in 1900 when the enemy's fire was particularly heavy, N. N. Freeman of the U.S. 21st Infantry wrote, "The way the bullets were coming I thought every one of us would be killed." To his surprise, only one man in his company was lightly wounded. On another occasion, at the little town of Maricana, the outcome was different. "I thought every second I would get a bullet," he wrote, "for they were flying so thick and close that I did not see how I could escape them." Freeman came through the battle unscathed, but others did not—American losses in that particular firefight were twenty-four dead and nineteen wounded.[41]

It is rather trite to say that battle is a matter of "kill or be killed"—the simple truth of combat in all wars is quite often that soldiers kill enemies who are not, in that exact moment, posing any kind of actual, personal threat to themselves. In other circumstances, however, soldiers kill men who really are trying to kill them, and their skill, speed, or luck enables them to shoot straighter or strike first, and so they survive and the other man does not. Such are the fortunes of war, and countless soldiers of this period described those types of situations in their narratives. How men reacted to the act of killing was a matter as individualistic and varied as the men themselves.

Stefan Westmann finished his service in the First World War as a medical officer in the German Army. Before that, however, he was an infantry sergeant, and he experienced heavy fighting and hand-to-hand combat in the trenches in France. In one particularly savage fight in an assault on a French position, he wrote, he came face-to-face with a

French corporal who was armed with a bayonet-mounted rifle just as he was himself. "I felt the fear of death in that fraction of a second when I realized that he was after my life, exactly as I was after his," Westmann wrote. "But I was quicker than he was, I pushed his rifle away and ran my bayonet through his chest." Westmann stabbed the Frenchman twice, and watched him die in the mud. "I had the dead French soldier in front of me, and how I would have liked him to have raised his hand," he recalled. "I tried to convince myself of what would've happened to me if I hadn't been quicker than him." The memory of that fight, and the dead French soldier, troubled Westmann for years afterward.[42]

When thousands of men were being killed by shot and shell, the sight of the dead could quickly become commonplace. Most soldiers found, somewhat to their surprise, not only that they grew accustomed to seeing and handling corpses but also that such adaptation happened very quickly. Raymond Gantter's unit occupied a position in Belgium for a time where the corpses of two German soldiers, covered by their overcoats, were lying out unburied. "The two dead Germans I mentioned earlier have not yet been buried," he wrote. "Their bodies lie very near the place where we line up for chow three times a day, and we squat beside them on upturned helmets to eat our meals. No appetite seems impaired by the presence of these silent guests." The lack of concern over the dead men was at least partially abetted by the climate—"Fortunately," Gantter noted, "the weather remains cold."[43]

Some men remarked on this with a measured nonchalance, but others seemed disturbed by how little they were troubled by the dead in the midst of battle. "We common soldiers," a German soldier wrote of his First World War experience, "were here handling the dead and wounded as if we had never done anything else, and yet in our civilian lives most of us had an abhorrence and fear of the dead and the horribly mangled. War is a hard schoolmaster who bends and reshapes his pupils."[44]

Stanley Baxter was certainly not the epitome of martial aggressiveness when he enlisted in a British regiment in the First World War. To say that he was "bookish" is not merely a literary description—he actually *was* a clerk before he left his desk to join the army. In short order he found himself in some of the worst combat of the Western Front. The fighting at Hill 60 was particularly bad, and the attitude of the living toward the dead was something Baxter reflected on afterward. "To keep the gangway clear," he wrote, "we had to lift these dead bodies out and put them on the top of the parapets. It was ghastly, but you get accustomed to ghastly things out here. You realize that fifty dead bodies are not equal to one living. And these poor fellows, who only a few minutes before had been alive and full of vigour, were now just blocking the trench. And so we simply lifted the bodies out and cast them over the top."[45] In the moment, under fire, it was often impossible to do anything else. An Australian soldier, fighting in the Somme where his unit attacked and captured a German trench, wrote that the "dead have been thrown back over the trench and earth shoveled onto them to help build up the parapet. It's not good burial but it's good warfare and that's our job just now. We're not undertakers."[46]

E. P. F. Lynch wrote of one night when his unit had to bury some fellow Australians who had been killed the previous day. "Men stoop, rise and lower into a grave a gunner clad only in breeches and singlet," he recalled. "'Cripes, mate, you'll sleep cold tonight,' a man remarks. . . . There's nothing irreverent or callous or frivolous in the remark. It's just familiarity, the sorrowful, friendly familiarity of the sad side of soldiering."[47]

Burying the dead was a sobering experience, especially after a particularly bloody battle where the casualties ran into the thousands. James Madison Stone, a U.S. Army infantryman in the Civil War, participated in a burial detail during a truce at the Battle of Fredericksburg:

The field was covered with dead men. Dead men everywhere, some black in the face, most of them had the characteristic pallor of death; nearly all had been stripped of every article of clothing. All were frozen; some with their heads off, some with their arms off, some with their legs off, dismembered, torn to pieces, they lay there single, in rows, and in piles. I did not count them, but there must have been three hundred dead men in the row behind which we concealed ourselves on the 15th, a part of which we dragged together the night before [during the battle]. . . . After the Johnnies had got us picks and shovels, we set to work to dig in the frozen earth the trenches which were to contain the men and fragments of men who had given up their lives on the plains

*in front of Mary's [sic] Heights. We put them in rows, one beside the
other, wrapped them up in blankets or in whatever else we could get
to put around them. There was practically no means of identifying one
out of a hundred of them. Thus they lay in unknown graves. Two long
days we worked there tearing a trench in the frozen earth and filling
it with the bodies of frozen men. . . . Our party buried nine hundred
and eighty-seven men.*

It was, Stone recalled, one of the worst experiences of all his time in
the army.

Even when the dead were not a soldier's personal concern in terms
of burial and disposal, bodies of men killed were sometimes so numerous as to warrant observation just as a matter of fact. In static battlefields
such as France and Flanders during the First World War, corpses were
an ever-present part of the landscape. "At times you lived with the dead,"
one British officer remembered of the Somme. "You could speak to them
at night, as I have done, without knowing that they were dead, propped
up as they sometimes were at the side of a trench. You stumbled over
them, kicked their arms or feet, trod on bits of them, and the air that you
breathed was foul with them."[48] The dead were everywhere, friend and foe
alike melded into a miasma of rotting flesh, and in the troglodytic conditions of trench warfare they literally became a part of the landscape.

Maneuver warfare was not free of the lingering presence of the unburied dead, either. A Japanese soldier who fought in Burma described the
rotting bodies of Japanese dead as being something that disturbed him
more than almost anything else. "I cannot forget the sight of one corpse
lying in a pool of knee-high water," he wrote; "all its flesh and blood had
been dissolved by the maggots and the water so that now it was no more
than a bleached uniform."[49]

Battlefield conditions often meant that when the dead were buried,
the interment was inadequate. "Some parts of the parapet had been built
up with dead men," one British soldier of the First World War recalled,
"and here and there arms and legs were protruding. In one bay only
the heads of two men could be seen; their teeth were showing so that
they seemed to be grinning horribly down on us."[50] This field-expedient

method of disposing of the dead while under enemy fire, was a constant problem for later units that happened to occupy the same positions.

"We dug down," a German soldier wrote of a time when his unit was desperately trying to deepen their trenches under heavy British shellfire, "but we found it difficult to go deep, because as we dug kept finding newly-buried British corpses, whose stench of decomposition poisoned the air. . . . We heaved the corpses of the Tommies up in front of the trench." Living among the dead, he remembered, was terrible—"On one occasion food got through to us, but the stink of the corpses had robbed us of our appetites."[51]

U.S. Marine Eugene Sledge, fighting on Okinawa in 1945, was ordered to dig a fighting position and got to work with his entrenching tool. "I had dug the hole no more than six or eight inches deep when the odor of rotting flesh got worse," he wrote. "There was nothing to do but continue to dig, so I closed my mouth and inhaled with short shallow breaths. Another spadeful of soil out of the hole released a mass of wriggling maggots that came welling up as though those beneath were pushing them out. . . . The next stroke of the spade unearthed buttons and scraps of cloth from a Japanese army jacket buried in the mud—and another mass of maggots. I kept on doggedly. With the next thrust, metal hit the breastbone of a rotting Japanese corpse."[52]

There were other ways in which the presence of the dead became a horror to men who had to exist in close proximity to them. Fighting in the dark fastness of the New Guinea jungle in 1944, with the corpses of dead Japanese soldiers rotting in the undergrowth, American paratrooper Andy Amaty remembered, "The natives had dogs, and when they didn't have enough food to feed them, they'd let the dogs out into the jungle. When there were bodies laying out, you'd hear the dogs, and you'd know what they were doing . . . eating the bodies. Things like this, if you dwelled on them too long, you'd go nuts." The American response was predictable. "After that, we had open season on the dogs," Amaty said. "We tried killing every dog we saw, which was fine by me. I don't like killing anything, but sometimes you'd see a Jap who was just buried within six inches of soil with a few stones thrown over him, and there'd be a son-of-a-bitch dog sitting there on the mound waiting for it to get dark to start chewing on the body."[53]

Dead men, when dead long enough, ceased to disturb because of their identifiable nationalities and began to disturb simply for the oppressive corruption of their rotting presence. "I remember once, on the Somme," British infantryman Cecil Withers said, "seeing half a dozen of our English boys, all in pieces in a big shell hole. They were half buried, stinking. It was hot and there was a terrible stench and they were covered in bluebottles and cockroaches. It was a terrible sight."[54] An Australian soldier, fighting at Gallipoli, wrote, "The dead, Turks and Australians, are lying buried and half-buried in the trench-bottom, in the sides of the trench, and built into the parapet. They have made the sand-bags all greasy.... Of all the bastards of places, this is the greatest bastard in the world. A dead man's boots have been dripping grease on my overcoat, and the coat will stink forever."[55]

"It was impossible to bury them all," one British trooper remembered of the trenches in France. "They lay in the earth in the trenches where they'd fallen or had been slung and earth had just been put on top of them and when the rain came it washed most of the earth away. You'd go along the trenches and you'd see a boot and puttee sticking out, or an arm or a hand, sometimes faces. Not only would you see, but you'd be walking on them, slipping and sliding. The stench was terrible because of all that rotting flesh. When you think of all the bits and piece you saw." This was the reality of war as combat soldiers knew it, but it was not the version they related to civilians back home. "But if you ever had to write home about a particular mate you'd always say that he got it cleanly and quickly with a bullet."[56]

No one ever got used to the stench of dead men, and having smelled it, no one ever forgot it. This was not an experience unique to the First World War in France—it was a thing common to all battles, particularly those where there were many dead accumulating in one place, and in hot weather when sustained combat prevented burial. These factors were frequently at work in the island fighting of the Pacific Theater in the Second World War.

"By the third day," one U.S. Marine remembered of the battle for the tiny atoll of Tarawa, "the smell of death was terrible."[57] Another Marine who fought at Tarawa, Robert Sherrod, said, "If you can imagine nearly six thousand dead men on an island as small as three hundred acres, and considering that it's one degree from the equator and the amount of heat, you can imagine the smell that got within a day or two of all this rotting flesh, it was a terribly oppressive thing."[58] Another Marine, Michael Witowich, described Tarawa in similar language. "You can imagine the smell that was there on Tarawa," he said. "It's like cat manure. It's horrible. Makes you want to puke. I put some cotton in my nose but the smell was horrible, with the maggots crawling over the bodies. . . . And we sat there eating our rations—a dead Jap here, a dead Marine there."[59]

The combined total of American, Japanese, and Korean dead in the three-day battle for Tarawa amounted to more than 5,500 killed—it may well have been, as Sherrod described it, a concentration of death worse than any other battlefield of the Second World War.

Overexposure to decomposing corpses could cause a macabre, bitter humor to replace the more civilized horror that men felt until their sensibilities were hardened. "It was very hot weather at the end of the summer, this trench was full of dead Germans and they'd been there some time," a British corporal remembered of a position near Thiepval. "They were all different colours, from pallid grey to green and black. And they were bloated—that's how a corpse goes in time, they get blown up with gases. We thought it was funny really, which shows how your mind can get inured to such situations. We started making up the trench and had to tread on one of these blokes, who was partly buried. Every time we trod on him his tongue would come out, which caused great amusement amongst our people."[60]

"Someone, friend or foe, I do not know," Australian infantryman E. P. F. Lynch wrote, "is buried in the trench wall and a hand has had the earth broken away from it. A little cardboard square hangs from the hand by a piece of string. Upon the card is written 'Gib it bacca, boss.' And the poor upturned hand is half full of cigarette bumpers." Lynch was of two minds about the joke. "Suppose it is witty, but it's not a brand of wit that appeals to me," he wrote. "Probably we are becoming callous, but wouldn't you be, living among the things we experience? You get hardened to death and the dead when you see them all the time."[61]

Another soldier who fought in France during the First World War was an American named Arthur Empey, who enlisted in the British Army while the United States was still a neutral country. He recalled how dead men were a rather unnerving feature of the trenches. At one point in his trench, he wrote, "A foot was protruding from the earth; we knew it was a German by the black leather boot. One of our crew used that foot to hang extra bandoliers of ammunition on. This man always was a handy fellow; made use of little points that the ordinary person would overlook." For six days, Empey remembered, his unit lived surrounded by dead Germans who had been killed in an earlier attack; but that was not as bad as the foot protruding from the trench wall. "What got on my nerves the most," he wrote, "was that foot sticking out of the dirt." Empey complained about it to the man who was using the foot as an ammunition-rack—whereupon the other soldier cut the foot off with a chain saw and covered the stump with mud. "During the next two or three days, before we were relieved," Empey recalled, "I missed that foot dreadfully, seemed as if I had suddenly lost a chum."[62]

The presence of dead men on a battlefield could also underscore certain attitudes or ideologies in one or the other army. Marion Ford fought through the Civil War in an infantry regiment of the Confederate Army. He remembered after one fierce engagement the Southern forces were left in command of the field after the Union troops withdrew. The slain of both armies littered the field, Ford wrote, and many of them were the casualties of several black regiments of the Union Army. Ford remembered that "the dead white men of both sides were buried; but the dead negroes were left where they fell." Confederate troops were notoriously hostile to the very idea of armed black soldiers wearing Union blue; they apparently thought no better of them when they were dead. "The field was dotted everywhere with dead negroes," Ford wrote, "who . . . created an intolerable stench, perceptible for half a mile or more. The hogs which roamed at large over the country were soon attracted to the spot and tore many of the bodies to pieces, feeding on them. This field of death, enlivened by numbers of hogs grunting and squealing over their hideous meal, was one of the most repulsive sights I ever saw."[63]

The deadly open ground of no-man's land between the trenches in the First World War was particularly bad for its collection of unburied, and unburiable, corpses. German infantryman Julius Koettgen remembered that he dreaded night patrols because "the hundreds of men killed months ago were still lying between the lines." "Those corpses were decomposed to a pulp," he wrote. "So when a man went on nocturnal patrol duty and when he had to crawl in the utter darkness on hands and knees all over those bodies he would now and then land in the decomposed faces of the dead."[64]

The overpowering stench of the dead lying about literally in heaps sometimes made it necessary to dispose of the corpses in some way, even in the deadly hazard of no-man's-land. George Craike, a lieutenant in the Highland Light Infantry, remembered the "very unpleasant task" of crawling out into the area between the lines to dispose of the dead, mostly from the 7th East Surreys who had been killed in an earlier action. "We crawled out of the trenches . . . and dealt with the dead by simply pulling them into depressions in the earth, or into shell holes," he wrote. "Occasionally the arms disengaged from the bodies. However, the bodies were placed as far as possible in these holes and covered over with a light layer of earth."[65]

The condition of the dead became much worse much quicker in the heat of the Gallipoli battlefield in 1915. The Turks lost more than ten thousand men in their failed attack on the Allied lines on March 19 alone—when the assault ended, the ground of no-man's-land between the trench lines was littered with corpses, which quickly began to rot. In a few short days the stench was too much for either side to take, and the Turks asked for a short cease-fire to bury the dead. One Australian soldier wrote, "I will never forget the armistice—it was a day of hard, smelly, nauseating work. . . . Some of the bodies were rotted so much that there were only bones and part of the uniform left. The bodies of men killed on the nineteenth (it had now been five days) were awful. Most of us had to work in short spells as we felt very ill."[66]

The human detritus of war—the blasted, bloated, and rotting remains of dead men, the human wreckage of conflict—brought out feelings of bitterness in more than one soldier who lived through the experience. "In the front line of Flers," a German soldier wrote in the First World War, "the corpses lie either quite insufficiently covered with earth on the edge of the trench or quite close under the bottom of the trench, so that the earth lets the stench through. In some places bodies lie quite uncovered in a trench recess, and no one seems to trouble about them. One sees horrible pictures—here an arm, here a foot, here a head, sticking out of the earth. And these are all German soldiers—heroes!"[67]

"Let him who thinks that War is a glorious golden thing," a British soldier wrote, "let him look at a little pile of sodden grey rags that cover half a skull and a shin bone and what might have been its ribs, or at this skeleton lying on its side . . . perfect but that it is headless, and with tattered clothing draped around it; and let him realize how grand and glorious a thing it is to have distilled all Youth and Joy and Life into a foetid heap of hideous putrescence."[68]

A British infantryman who fought at the Somme had little use for the civilians at home when he considered the differences between the soldier's reality and that of those far away from the horrors of war. "Ask anyone what Trones Wood was like at the end of August 1916, or if he was not sick (or nearly so) on going over any battlefield on the Somme," he wrote. "Half a head here; battered and black swelling things in the shell holes; torn remnants of bodies scattered by death all over that hellish ground; your best friend blown to pieces by something which (let us hope) he never saw or heard coming; whilst certain men and women in England were having their hands manicured and their faces massaged, that they might 'look their best' at the theatre."[69] In their reactions to the horrors of war, as in many other aspects of the martial trade, soldiers often found that they had more in common with their enemies in the opposing army than they did with their own civilian population back home.

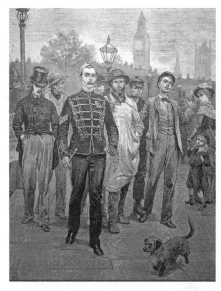

In this 1882 illustration from the *London Illustrated News*, a British recruiting sergeant leads a group of enlistees down the street. The recruits are from different classes of society and clearly of different minds about their decision to join the army. Courtesy of the British Library.

A recruiting poster to fill a county levee for service in the Mexican-American War. Appeals to patriotism and national duty were common themes in recruiting efforts in every army. Courtesy of the Library of Congress.

Troops of the Imperial Russian Army pass in review during a parade circa 1914. The regimental band is in formation beyond them. Russia could field a huge army, but it was poorly equipped, insufficiently trained, and badly led. Courtesy of the Library of Congress.

American soldiers on the march in Mexico during the 1916 Punitive Expedition. For infantrymen of every army, the ability to cover miles of rough country (desert, in this case) and arrive ready to fight was their professional credentials. Courtesy of the National Archives and Records Administration.

Japanese infantrymen ford a river in Manchuria after their invasion in 1931. The quality of Japanese equipment and arms was never up to the level of their Western adversaries, but man for man the Japanese soldier was one of the finest light infantrymen in the world. Courtesy of the U.S. Army Center of Military History.

The crew of a British eighteen-pounder artillery piece work to extricate their gun from the Flemish mud in Zillebeke, Belgium, in August 1917. Their officer, identifiable by his Sam Browne belt and boots, is in the mud with them, pushing on the gun's muzzle at the right side of the photograph. Courtesy of the Imperial War Museum Collection.

Different war, different army, same Flemish mud. Artillerymen attached to the U.S. Army's 26th Infantry Regiment wrestle a 75mm howitzer through the mud near Butgenbach, Belgium, in December 1945. Courtesy of the U.S. Army Center for Military History.

The muddy hell of the Passchendaele battlefield—a derelict tank lies mired in the mud as a shell bursts in the distance. Centuries of agriculture had drained the Flemish plain and turned it into fertile farmland; a few weeks of modern war and heavy artillery turned it into one of the worst battlefields in modern memory. Courtesy of the Library and Archives of Canada.

The Second Battle of Passchendaele, October 1917. Soldiers of the 16th Canadian Machine Gun Company man their waterlogged positions in a landscape of shell holes and mud. The original caption states that a month after this photograph was taken, only one man in the picture was still alive. Courtesy of the Library and Archives of Canada.

A British litter party struggles through the mud in this iconic image from 1917. This photo illustrates the difficulties inherent in casualty evacuation in much of the frontline terrain of the Western Front in the First World War, though these men appear to at least be out of range of direct enemy fire. Courtesy of the Imperial War Museum Collections.

The driver of a foundered American M4 Sherman tank bails water from his hatch as he waits for a recovery vehicle during operations on Okinawa, May 1945. Adversarial weather was a factor in every war. Courtesy of the National Records and Archives Administration.

The essential station—American field latrines in France, 1917. Adequate latrine facilities were a key part of maintaining the health of armies in the field; disease killed more men during this period than enemy action ever accounted for. Courtesy of the Library of Congress.

An American infantryman in Australia, waiting to embark for New Caledonia. This photo gives a good indication of the full complement of personal gear issued to U.S. Army personnel at that time, with one extra item—on his pack he carries a cut-down cavalry saber that was devised as a field-expedient machete, along with his standard-issue bayonet. Courtesy of the U.S. Army Center for Military History.

An American machine gun crew with a French Mle 1914 Hotchkiss machine gun somewhere in France, 1918. At fifty-three pounds in weight, the weapon was too heavy for the light infantry role, but it was reliable in action, even with its slow ammunition supply. Courtesy of the National Archives and Records Administration.

French civilians whose village has just been liberated from German control greet two American infantrymen in the final months of the First World War. The soldier on the left has a French Chauchat light machine gun slung over his shoulder. In terms of design, reliability, and manufacture, it was the worst machine gun ever produced. Courtesy of the Library of Congress.

American artillerymen attached to the 339th Infantry Regiment man a French 75mm gun during the international military intervention in the Russian Civil War in 1919. Courtesy of the Library of Congress.

An ensign and noncommissioned officer of the French Imperial Guard during the Napoleonic Wars. This illustration gives a good idea of the French uniform of that era, which was a fine parade uniform but ill-suited for the rigors of campaign and combat. Courtesy of the British Library.

In this nineteenth-century illustration, a French grenadier and *voltigeur*, or skirmisher, are depicted as they would have appeared during the Napoleonic Wars. Their uniforms were not designed for inclement weather or hard service. Courtesy of the British Library.

The Chinese soldier of the nineteenth century was undervalued by his society and ill-prepared for modern warfare. This soldier is armed with a matchlock musket, an outright antique, at a time when his French and British adversaries in the Opium Wars were armed with percussion-capped rifled muskets and modern artillery. Courtesy of the British Library.

A British infantryman in full kit poses for a photograph during the Crimean War. The uniforms of some British regiments still echoed the fashions of the Napoleonic Wars of nearly half a century before, as is clearly evident here. Courtesy of the Imperial War Museum Collections.

A veteran sergeant of one of the British Army's Guards regiments poses for a photograph wearing the Crimean Medal with bars. The bearskin busby hat was an iconic part of the Guards uniform, but it was heavy and impractical for field use. Courtesy of the National Army Museum, Chelsea.

British veterans of the Crimean War. A sergeant, private, and lance corporal of the 95th Regiment of Foot (Derbyshires) are pictured after their return to England in 1856. Courtesy of the Imperial War Museum Collections.

A trio of Scottish soldiers of the Crimean War display the heavy beards favored by British soldiers in campaigns of that era. They wear plaid trews, or trousers, in their regimental tartan instead of the kilts associated with the highland regiments, and each man is decorated with the Crimean Medal with bars. Courtesy of the National War Museum of Scotland, Edinburgh.

In this studio photo from 1862, Private Francis E. Brownell wears an example of the French-influenced uniform that was popular with many militia units of the Union Army at the outset of the American Civil War. Courtesy of the Library of Congress.

An American soldier poses with a musket and pistol in front of a painted studio backdrop, circa 1864. When the U.S. government belatedly allowed black men to serve during the Civil War, thousands of African Americans, both freemen and newly emancipated slaves, enlisted to fight for the Union. Courtesy of the Library of Congress.

A sergeant of the French Army's Garde Nationale poses for a studio photograph around the time of the Franco-Prussian War. His rifle is a Fusil Modele 1866 Chassepot rifle with a yataghan-bladed bayonet; his full pack displays the extent to which an infantryman could be overloaded. Courtesy of the Musee de l'Armee, Paris.

An American infantry corporal of a volunteer regiment during the Spanish-American War. This was the last war in which the U.S. soldier went into battle armed with a single-shot rifle (the Springfield Model 1873 shown here) or wearing the blue that had been the U.S. Army's traditional uniform color since the American War of Independence. Courtesy of the National Archives and Records Administration.

A Spanish infantryman of the Spanish-American War era. The Spanish army was outmatched in that conflict, but the individual Spanish soldier still proved to be a tough and courageous fighter when he was well led. Courtesy of the National Archives and Records Administration.

Soldiers representing the eight-nation alliance that fought the Boxer Rebellion in China stand for a group photo in 1900. From left to right, the soldiers are British, American, Australian (British Commonwealth), Indian (British Commonwealth), German, French, Austro-Hungarian, Italian, and Japanese. Courtesy of the Library of Congress.

An infantryman of the French Foreign Legion circa 1905. His rifle is an 8mm Lebel, and he wears the blue kepi and coat and khaki trousers of the Legion's service uniform. Courtesy of the Musee de l'Armee, Paris.

A U.S. Army cavalryman in 1916. This was the uniform and equipment worn during the Punitive Expedition into Mexico that year, and the same uniform in use when America entered the First World War the following year. Courtesy of the U.S. Army Center for Military History.

A soldier of the Australian 8th Light Horse poses for a photograph before shipping out in the First World War. Organized as mounted infantry, the Light Horse regiments served in that role in Palestine but fought mainly as regular infantry in Gallipoli and France. Courtesy of the Australian War Memorial.

A German soldier poses for a final photograph before leaving for service in the First World War. The flowers that decorate his uniform and helmet were a traditional farewell from family and friends. He has a long-bladed Model 1898 bayonet fixed to his rifle, and a modern battery-powered flashlight clipped to his shirt. Courtesy of the Bundesarchiv.

A French soldier in the uniform worn during the latter half of the First World War. He wears the Adrien helmet that replaced the kepi for frontline use, and the horizon blue uniform that replaced the dark-blue coat and red trousers of 1914. From his insignia, he appears to be a member of a sapper, or combat engineer, regiment. Courtesy of the Imperial War Museum Collections.

Infantrymen of the White Russian, or Menshevik, Army present arms in formation in 1918 during the Russian Civil War. With a few exceptions, their uniforms and equipment are almost the same as used by most configurations of the Russian army from 1900 through the 1930s. Courtesy of the National Archives and Records Administration.

A British Lewis gun crew in action near Hazebrouck, France, in 1918. This photo gives a good view of the ammunition panniers; a crew in heavy fighting had to have a large supply of panniers on hand to keep the weapon in operation. Courtesy of the Imperial War Museum Collections.

A German soldier fires his MP 40 Maschinenpistole in close combat somewhere on the Eastern Front. An interesting detail in this photo is that in addition to his military equipment, this man has a personal camera slung over his shoulder. Courtesy of the Bundesarchiv.

A U.S. Marine fires his Browning Automatic Rifle (BAR) at Japanese positions. The BAR was a heavy, cumbersome weapon, but it was hard-hitting and lethally effective in infantry combat. Courtesy of the National Archives and Records Administration.

In this photo from the First World War, a work detail of British soldiers from the Manchester Regiment goes forward into the lines near Ancre in 1917. When battalions rotated out of the trenches, a never-ending variety of essential tasks took up most of their time and energy. Courtesy of the Imperial War Museum Collections.

Infantrymen often complained that they spent more time holding a shovel than a rifle. Here, German soldiers dig field fortifications in the Argonne Forest area in the first year of the First World War: the man pointing at the right seems to be an NCO, judging by his apparent age and his posture. Courtesy of the Bundesarchiv.

No matter the weather or the conditions, soldiers' work went on. British soldiers of a wiring party bring rolls of barbed wire forward to the front lines in France, circa 1915. Courtesy of the Imperial War Museum Collections.

Resupply in the lines was a task of never-ending drudgery. American soldiers in New Guinea carry boxes of ammunition and rations to forward positions during operations in 1943. Courtesy of the National Archives and Records Administration.

Two American GIs of the 93rd Division's 25th Combat Team clean their M1 Garand rifles in the jungle of Bougainville in 1944. Cleaning weapons was a constant chore, one exacerbated by wet, muddy, or humid conditions. Courtesy of the National Archives and Records Administration.

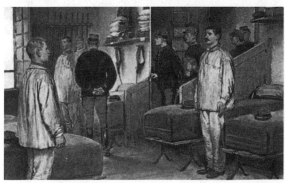

Inspections of a soldier's equipment, quarters, and self were a routine in every army. In this 1885 illustration by Edouard Detaille, French infantrymen stand to attention as an officer makes the rounds of their barracks. Courtesy of the Library of Congress.

In this photo from January 1941, soldiers of the U.S. 25th Infantry Division in Hawaii stand a field inspection. Their uniforms and helmets are still those of the previous war—the iconic American equipment of the Second World War was not yet generally issued at that point. Courtesy of the National Archives and Records Administration.

The price of empire-making—coffins of American soldiers killed in the Philippine-American War are stacked for shipment home. Along with their names, the identifiable unit markers include the 6th Cavalry, 19th Infantry, and 20th Infantry. Courtesy of the Burns Archive.

A German machine gun crew lay dead in their position near Guillemont after it was destroyed by British artillery in the Battle of the Somme, September 1916. The British fired more than one million rounds of artillery in the opening days of the fighting on the Somme, a level of heavy gunnery never seen in warfare before. Courtesy of the Imperial War Museum Collections.

The enemy's dead never unsettled men as much as those who wore one's own uniform. British and Australian gunners survey dead German soldiers who have been collected for burial behind the lines near Bellicourt, October 1918. The war was nearly over by that point, but for these men the Armistice came too late. Courtesy of the Imperial War Museum Collections.

The bodies of British soldiers killed in France are collected for burial by their comrades. The kilts identify them as members of a Highland Regiment. Courtesy of the Imperial War Museum Collections.

The Battle of Tarawa Atoll, November 1943. The corpses of U.S. Marine dead cover the beach of Betio Island after three days of intense fighting. More than six thousand men—Japanese, Americans, and Koreans—were killed in the maelstrom of combat on the tiny atoll. It was not worth the price. Courtesy of the National Archives and Records Administration.

Fallen on a foreign field—the grave of a British paratrooper who was killed in the fighting during Operation Market Garden, 1944. Dutch civilians erected the marker and decorated the grave with tulips. Courtesy of the Imperial War Museum Collections.

Fallen in France—the body of an American soldier killed in the fighting for Carentan is attended by French civilians who pay their respects with flowers and prayers. June 1944. Courtesy of the National Archives and Records Administration.

The Battle of Crete, 1941. Paratroopers of the German Fallschirmjaegers pause at the graves of fallen comrades. The Germans were successful in their assault on Crete, but their victory came at a heavy price. Courtesy of the Bundesarchiv.

Public humiliation, as both punishment and cautionary example, was a tenet of military discipline in nineteenth-century armies. In this 1863 photo, a soldier is drummed out of a Union Army camp at Morris Island, South Carolina. His head has been shaved, and he wears a placard that proclaims him a thief. The guard detail carries their muskets reversed, a mark of his shame. Courtesy of the Library of Congress.

American infantrymen crawl up a rocky hill as they close in on Japanese positions near Baugio in the Philippines in 1944. The mountainous terrain of northern Luzon, the main Philippine island, made for infantry combat in its roughest form for both sides. Courtesy of the National Archives and Records Administration.

Field-expedient ingenuity in the trenches. An Australian soldier in the Lone Pine position at Gallipoli uses a periscoped rifle system to fire on the Turkish positions across no-man's-land. The man at right holding another periscope is serving as his spotter. Courtesy of the Australian War Memorial.

Two young German soldiers of the Wehrmacht share a *Schutzenloch*, or hasty fighting position, somewhere on the Eastern Front. Many soldiers described the bonds formed between men in battle as something never equaled by any other personal connection. One of these men might be a medic, judging by the aid bag marked with a red cross in the right foreground. Courtesy of the Bundesarchiv.

A pair of Wehrmacht infantrymen on the Eastern Front, circa 1942. Both men show signs of the strain and grime of combat operations. Since German infantry of the Second World War did not habitually fight with fixed bayonets as seen here, these men may have been in a situation where close contact was expected. Courtesy of the Bundesarchiv.

A squad of British soldiers pauses for Christmas dinner in their lines somewhere in France during the First World War. Their generally relaxed attitude suggests they are in a relatively secure position, but the grave marker behind them stands as a grim reminder of their reality. Courtesy of the Imperial War Museum Collections.

Many soldiers reflected on the shared humanity they found with the men who wore the enemy's uniform in their wars. In this photo from the First World War, a German soldier gives a British soldier a light from his cigarette. Considering that none of these men are carrying their weapons, one would not know just by looking who are the prisoners and who are the captors. Courtesy of the Imperial War Museum Collections.

In all the carnage of the First World War, the Battle of Verdun was one of the costliest campaigns—the French and German armies lost nearly a million men, collectively, in a protracted slugging match that did little to change the lines of the Western Front. In this photograph, a German infantryman takes a position next to the half-interred corpse of a French soldier. Courtesy of the Bundesarchiv.

For most of this period, a soldier's domestic life in many armies was a difficult proposition. Here a Union Army soldier during the American Civil War poses with his family in camp. Women who were fortunate enough to be carried on the regiment's rolls had to work for the privilege, often as laundresses. Courtesy of the Library of Congress.

The aftermath of war. A French veteran of the First World War, blinded and missing his right arm, works at making bristle brushes. Courtesy of the American National Red Cross Collection.

A German veteran of the First World War, missing his left leg, begs from passersby on a street after the war. An old German saying was "young soldiers, old beggars." Too often during this period, it was true. Courtesy of the Bundesarchiv.

CHAPTER TEN

Boredom, Fear, and Courage

Valor is a gift. Those having it never know for sure whether they have it till the test comes. And those having it in one test never know for sure if they will have it when the next test comes.

—NAPOLEON

AN ENDURING PERCEPTION OF THE SOLDIER'S LIFE, one that most often seems to originate *outside* the military profession, is that soldiering is characterized by moments of high drama, extreme danger, and frequent threat to life and limb. Those moments do exist, to be sure, but for most soldiers that is precisely what they are—occasional moments. The hours, days, and weeks that roll together into the long years of military service are more often characterized by lengthy periods of a quiet, if not altogether comfortable, routine. James Black, a sergeant major in the Union Army during the American Civil War, summed up the common experience of most soldiers in a letter to his wife. "I have nothing interesting to write you," he wrote. "Everything here is the same yesterday, today, and tomorrow."[1]

It might seem remarkable that for most soldiers of this period (as has been true for most professional soldiers throughout history), a regular feature of their military service was stultifying, monotonous, boring routine, but no veteran would be surprised by that. The boredom is seldom mentioned in conventional histories, probably *because* it is boring, but it shows up in almost every soldier's personal recollections. What is interesting is how often men described boredom as being an element of wartime service, just as much as it was a part of peacetime soldiering.

Henry Windolph served with the 7th U.S. Cavalry during its stint of Reconstruction duty in the defeated South after the Civil War. "It was pretty dull, soldiering down there in the South," he remembered. "The regiment was broken up into companies, or small battalions, and our job was to smash the Ku Klux Klan, and run down illicit whiskey distillers. It wasn't much fun for energetic, spirited young men." Windolph chafed at the lack of excitement—this was not what he had joined the army for. "We'd been down there almost three years when in the spring of 1873, the grapevine spread the welcome word that the whole regiment was to be ordered north and brought together in the Dakotas," he wrote. "Everybody was glad to get that news. We were tired of playing soldier. We wanted some action. It'd be fun to do a little Indian fighting." In the event, Windolph got all the action he could ever have wanted. Three years later he rode with the 7th in its collision with destiny at the Battle of the Little Bighorn, and he was lucky to survive it.[2]

Waiting on the edge of battle could be an excruciating experience, whether it was waiting in the trenches to go over the top, or for the battalion to move up into the firing line, or for the ramp of the landing craft to grind ashore on the beach, or whatever other form it took for the individual soldier in his moment of truth. But far more often than these moments of fear-inducing anticipation, men just waited for something—anything—to happen. During the four years of the First World War the average infantryman or artilleryman probably spent more cumulative time in frontline combat conditions than did any other soldiers during the entire period examined by this book, but even for the men of that war, a remarkable amount of their time in the trenches was taken up with a dull routine of monotonous tasks. The element of danger was frequently there, to some extent—fatigue parties could be particularly dangerous tasks, and random shellfire was a persistent threat—but the monotony was always there, hand in hand with the lurking perils.

"When it was quiet, it was so boring," one British soldier said of his time in the trenches during in the First World War. "Awake all night. Stand-to just before dawn . . . then at dawn stand-down, hoping you'd get a mug of tea or something to eat, which as often as not we didn't get because being so close to the German lines we couldn't make fires to brew tea. . . . Funny that, you were bored if there was no danger."[3] An American infantryman of the Second World War wrote after his time in service, "All I can say is, the moments of high drama were just that—moments. . . . For every minute of dramatic encounter with the enemy, there were long dreary hours of waiting, watching, stalking, patrolling, digging in, guarding, more waiting, tense but uneventful miles of pushing, then more digging in and more waiting."[4] Even danger, when it was too constant, could grow monotonous.

Eventually the risk to life and limb could fade into a muddy expanse of sameness. "In those long days of trench warfare and stationary lines," war correspondent Philip Gibbs wrote in 1918, "it was boredom that was the worst malady of the mind . . . an intolerable, abominable boredom, sapping the will-power, the moral code, the intellect; a boredom from which there seemed to be no escape except by death, no relief except by vice, no probable or possible change in its dreary routine." As Gibbs saw it, there was little variation whether soldiers were in the forward lines or "safely" in the rear. "It was bad enough in the trenches," he wrote, "where men looked across the parapet to the same corner of hell day by day, to the same dead bodies rotting by the edge of the same mine-crater, to the same old sand-bags in the enemy's line, to the blasted trees sliced by shell-fire. . . . In 'quiet' sections of the line the only variation to the routine was the number of casualties day by day, by casual shell-fire or snipers' bullets, and that became part of the boredom."[5]

The mind-atrophying boredom sometimes drove men to volunteer for slightly dangerous undertakings, if only to have something to do to break the routine. John Morse, serving with the Russians in Poland during the First World War, said that when the fighting lulled during the harshest months of the winter, the resulting inactivity was terrible. When reconnaissance patrols were sent out against the German lines, Morse wrote, he "was always glad to accompany these, as the monotony of life in a ruin, without sufficient food, and no recreation except card-playing, was unendurable."[6] A French soldier, writing to his mother in 1915, complained, "The monotony of military life benumbs me."[7]

Many men chafed under the repressive yoke of military routine, where everything was supposed to be done in the same approved manner, and variation was frowned upon. Soldiers in every era of the period complained about the lack of mental stimulation and found the enforced inactivity hardest to bear when there were no diversions for their minds. When the fighting started, however, boredom was quickly replaced by two other prevalent emotions: bravery, which many men witnessed and many displayed, although relatively few claimed to have felt it themselves, and fear, which almost every man said that he felt at one time or another. "I was scared shitless and just blocked everything out," one American airborne infantryman remembered of his combat experience in the Philippines. "My war was that ten or fifteen yards in front of me, that's your life."[8]

Sergeant Major Richard Tobin of the Royal Naval Division's Hood Battalion, who fought in some of the worst battles of the First World War—Gallipoli, Arras, and Passchendaele were just three of his campaign credits—was a man who could legitimately be expected to know something about how soldiers felt when confronted by the very real possibility of their own violent deaths. On the eve of the savage fighting at Arras in 1917, Tobin waited in the predawn darkness for nearly four hours, listening for the signal that would launch his battalion's assault. "We stood there in dead silence," Tobin remembered, "you couldn't make a noise, and the fellow next to you felt like your best friend, you loved him, although you probably didn't know him the day before." The waiting dragged on, with nothing for men to think on but whether the next few hours would see them alive or dead, maimed or whole. "They were both the longest and the shortest hours of my life," Tobin wrote later. "An infantryman in the front line feels the coldest, deepest fear."[9]

Fear is sometimes assumed to be the prevalent emotion of soldiers' lives, at least as far as their experience of battle is concerned. Such an assumption, however, presupposes that most soldiers are frequently in combat situations, or that all men face battle with similar sensations of dread, apprehension, or fear. The reality, as we have already seen, is that for most soldiers of this period, battle was an occasional experience rather than a constant one—frontline soldiers of the two world wars would be the obvious exception to this categorization, and even for most of them there were lulls and periods out of the line. Furthermore, the personal accounts left by many of these men show very clearly that there was a wide range of emotional reactions to the experience of battle.

Fear might not be a universal emotion among soldiers, but it comes close to that—it is undoubtedly a very common and widely familiar feeling. Most people fear something, even if they do not know what that thing is until they encounter it, and the nature of war means that sooner or later one is brought face-to-face with one's fears. Even then, fear may be too limited a word to describe the incredibly diverse spectrum of emotions that combat generates in the men who experience it. Terror, dread, anxiety, horror, panic, apprehension, concern—all of these factor into a discussion of how men feel on the eve of battle or in battle itself. When the fear was coupled with the stress of tough conditions, it was heightened. "You were living in foxholes and you were very cold," American infantryman Robert Fair recalled of his experience in the Ardennes in 1944. "You add that to the fact that you were scared to death all the time—those were the two big problems. Just living, existing and living with a certain amount of fear. I always felt, myself—I told myself—that everybody is scared. It didn't make any difference who you are. . . . You always have a certain amount of fear. Hopefully it is well controlled and you don't have too much of a problem with it, but it's always there. It's always in the back of your mind, that some guy could come and shoot me in the head any minute. You are always worried."[10]

Memories such as this are a familiar part of soldiers' narratives, but still it would be very shortsighted to attempt to view their experiences through the lens of fear alone and to then try to distill their stories solely with that interpretation, since fear is only one small element of the overall picture. Fear, after all, has its antithetical emotions—courage, bravery, resilience, and fortitude, to name a few. There may even be that most elusive of emotional descriptions—fearlessness. But even these are still not enough to give us a full picture of the soldier's experience. There are also the more pedestrian and mundane emotions of apathy, tedium, and monotony, along with excitement and exhilaration. These, contrary to what many might think, were more frequently the prevailing emotions that soldiers described when they recounted their experiences in the long years of this period.

It is also important to understand that while men shared similar experiences, no two men ever described themselves feeling exactly the same thing in the same situation. One man was afraid for every waking moment of the days he spent in battle; another man reported moments of terror interspersed with long periods of stultifying boredom; a third recalls feeling mostly a rush of excitement and a surge of adrenaline as he went into combat. One American infantryman described his feelings as he waited for his landing craft to head in toward the beach on D-Day, in terms that many another veteran could recall from his first time facing combat. "I remember saying to myself, 'This is the greatest show on earth,'" he said. 'I wouldn't miss this for anything.' I really felt that. Of course I changed my mind in about an hour, after we got on the beach."[11]

One might assume that in the eras when armies formed themselves into linear ranks and stood up shoulder to shoulder to face an enemy similarly arrayed just a few dozen yards away across open ground, the psychological effect of camaraderie and the physical closeness of one's fellows would do a great deal to alleviate a man's fears. "Strength in numbers," after all, is a powerful prop to flagging nerves. But that does not mean that soldiers who fought in massed formations were therefore insulated from physical fear. According to their own statements, men in the red-coated British Army of the Napoleonic Wars were every bit as frightened of being killed or maimed as were the Frenchmen against whom they fought, just as was true of the Union and Confederate soldiers of the Civil War who fought in much the same tactical fashion. After all, when men were packed together in tight formations, it was all too easy to see the bloody carnage wrought by the enemy's shot and shell everywhere they looked.

John Shipp, who eagerly enlisted in the British Army as soon as he was of age, wrote that his first experience of battle in India made him regret, even if only briefly, that he had ever become a soldier. "Such shouting, roaring of cannon, whistling of shot, grumbling of rockets, and waving of flags and spears," he wrote, "made me reflect for a moment on the folly of ever having sold my 'leathers' to participate in such a scene."[12] It was, Shipp said, the most frightened he had ever been, at least up to that point in his life.

Having survived his baptism of fire, Shipp became a soldier of some distinction. He rose through the ranks, being promoted to corporal and then sergeant, but his sights were set higher still. Lacking the financial means to purchase an officer's commission, Shipp determined to earn a commission the only other way he could. At the siege of Bhurtpore in 1805, he volunteered to lead the Forlorn Hope.

The British Army (and other armies of the period) used the tactic of Forlorn Hopes when they conducted direct assaults on fortified towns. Once the concentrated fire of the artillery or mining by the sappers had affected a breach in the enemy' fortifications, a party of volunteers would spearhead the attack on the enemy's defenses. The risks and the dangers were enormous, and the expectancy of survival pathetically small. The loss of life among Forlorn Hopes was almost always staggeringly high, positioned as they were at the head of frontal assaults going straight into the enemy's guns; they voluntarily placed themselves in the mouth of what modern infantryman refer to as the "fatal funnel." Still, there was never any shortage of volunteers for what were, in essence, suicide missions, because for the men who were lucky enough to survive a successful assault, the rewards were equally great. The officer who led a Forlorn Hope would receive a promotion without purchase, the NCO in the party would be given an ensign's commission, and all other enlisted men would be promoted one rank.

Forlorn Hopes were marked by extraordinary but desperate courage, a courage perhaps founded on fatalistic resignation, but even that kind of physical bravery was not always enough to carry the attack through. A survivor's account of a diversionary British attack against the French-held fortifications at Badajoz in the Peninsular War in Spain in 1812 gives a very clear idea of the savagery of this sort of fighting. "Hundreds fell, dropping at every discharge which maddened the living," this soldier wrote. "The rear pushed the foremost into the sword-blades to make a bridge of their bodies rather than be frustrated. Slaughter, tumult and disorder continued; no command could be heard, the wounded struggling to free themselves from under the bleeding bodies of their dead comrades; the enemy's guns within a few yards at every fire opening a bloody lane amongst our people, who closed up and, with shouts of terror as the lava burned them up, pressed on to destruction."[13] It was all for naught—that particular attack failed, and Badajoz did not fall for several more days.

When it finally did, it had become the costliest siege the British Army mounted in the Peninsular War, in terms of casualties. In a letter to the prime minister the day after the city was finally captured, Wellington wrote, "The storming of Badajoz affords as strong an instance of the gallantry of our troops as has ever been displayed. But I greatly hope that I shall never again be the instrument of putting them to such a test as that to which they were put last night."

John Shipp was well aware of the odds when he volunteered for the Forlorn Hope at Bhurtpore. He was determined though, and he led his assaulting party against the fort's massive ramparts in a maelstrom of shot and shell. The attack was beaten back; many of Shipp's companions were killed, and he himself was slightly wounded. A failed attempt brought no reward; an officer's commission could only be won by success. Undeterred, Shipp volunteered a second time to lead an attempt on the fortress.

As on the previous occasion, the attack went in under a massive supporting bombardment. Shipp wrote that men "shouted, yelled, screamed, groaned; small arms whistled, cannons roared, and in an instant, the fort was enveloped in smoke." In the midst of all the thunderous chaos, one of Shipp's men yelled to him, "Shipp, have you made your will?" "Yes," he shouted back, "which is that I will lead you into that fort undaunted." Those were brave words, but Shipp later confessed that he was feeling anything but brave in the moment. The truth, he admitted in his memoirs, was that he "thought it no joking matter, but wished most earnestly that I could say, with Macbeth, 'I have done the deed.'"[14] This time fortune was with him, and the Forlorn Hope was successful. The attack carried the fortress, and the next day Shipp received the ensign's commission for which he had twice so conspicuously risked his life. Some years later, having had to sell his commission and start over in the army from the bottom, he led another Forlorn Hope in 1815, survived that engagement also, and won a second commission from the ranks, perhaps the only man in the history of the British Army to have ever done so twice.

Men could sometimes be recklessly, almost unbelievably, brave in their efforts to win promotion on the battlefield. Sergeant William Gould, of the 16th Lancers, recalled such a moment at the battle of Aliwal in India in 1843. "We had to charge a square of infantry," he wrote. "At them we went, the bullets flying around like a hailstorm. Right in front was a big sergeant, Harry Newsome. . . . With a shout of 'Hullo, boys, here goes for death or a commission,' he forced his horse right over the front rank of kneeling men, bristling with bayonets." Almost immediately, Newsome was bayoneted out of his saddle—he did not get the commission he so desired, but he did get killed. Ironically, Gould found himself in command of the troop when they regrouped after the charge—nearly all the NCOs and every one of the officers had been killed in the action, and he was the senior man remaining.[15]

Bravery on the part of one's companions and leaders, or even the perception of bravery, could be a powerful antidote to the fear that most men felt at one time or another. Many soldiers of this period commented on the conduct of particular officers or fellow soldiers whose behavior had a steadying effect on badly frightened men.

The Battle of Waterloo was a ferocious test of military discipline for the British soldiers who had to stand in square while French cannon fire ripped bloody swaths through their ranks. Time and time again the British regulars obeyed the orders of their officers and NCOs to close the gaps over the bodies of their fallen comrades. They had to stand fast, firing volley after volley into the columns of French infantry that came against them, maintaining the massed formations necessary to ward off the French cavalry that repeatedly tried and repeatedly failed to break their squares. But as the day wore on and their casualties mounted, even that iron discipline began to waver. Infantry in square, after all, present splendid massed targets for artillery, and every time the French cavalry fell back, French artillery blasted killing scythes of round shot through the British formations.

A soldier in the 73rd Regiment, Thomas Morris, described an incident where one officer's personal example was the vital antidote to the fear that was spreading through his regiment. "Once, and only once, during the dreadful carnage at Waterloo," Morris wrote, "did the stern Seventy-Third hesitate to fill up a gap which the relentless iron had torn in their square; their Lieut.-Colonel (Brevet Colonel Harris) at once pushing his horse lengthwise across the space, said with a smile 'Well, my lads, if you won't, I must;' it is almost needless to add that immediately he was led back to his proper place, and the ranks closed up by men still more devoted than before."[16]

Waterloo was remembered by the men who fought there as an exhausting, desperate struggle that went on and on throughout a long, hot day. Wellington, after the battle was won, famously remarked that Waterloo had been "a near run thing," and he was not a man given to either exaggeration or hyperbole. Even some of the hardened veterans in the British ranks found Waterloo to be one of the worst fights in their experience. "Our sergeant-major was a brave soldier," Morris wrote, "and had been through the whole of the engagements in the Peninsula." In the worst part of the day at Waterloo, when casualties were mounting and the ranks were being torn apart, the sergeant major told his colonel, "We had nothing like this in Spain, Sir." Morris remembered that the sergeant-major was deathly pale when he said it, and that the man's use of profanity grew more pronounced as the day wore on, a sure sign of his stress.[17]

Bravery by itself was not enough to compensate for incompetent leadership, but courage was still a quality that men recognized in their officers even when they found them lacking in other respects. "More than half the officers," British Sergeant Timothy Gowing wrote of his experience in the Crimean War, "did not know how to manoeuvre a company—all, or nearly so, had to be left to non-commissioned officers—but it would be impossible to dispute their bravery for they were brave unto madness." Time and again, Gowing said, he saw officers leading their battalions straight into the Russian guns at Sebastopol, going forward with as little apparent concern as if they were in ballrooms back in England.[18] British officers often cultivated a nonchalant insouciance that suggested that they regarded the mortal hazards of battle as nothing to get overly excited about. In the Light Brigade's disastrous charge at Balaclava in 1854, Cornet Denzil Chamberlayne of the 13th Light Dragoons was dismounted when his horse was killed underneath him. With Russian shot and shell ripping around him, Chamberlayne calmly removed his saddle from the dead horse and started strolling back to the British lines. "Another horse you can get," he told a fellow officer, "but you will not buy another saddle so easily."[19]

The personal example of quiet steadiness on the part of an officer or NCO could do much to steady men who were close to panic. Marion Ford, a Confederate infantryman in the Civil War, remembered being terribly frightened the first time he went into battle. What he remembered even more, however, was the apparent calmness of one of his brigade's officers. Standing in the firing line in one of his first engagements, Ford was struck by "the conspicuous coolness of Maj. Thos. Huguenin, of the First Infantry." In the midst of cannon fire and volleys of rifle fire, Ford said, Major Huguenin "walked slowly immediately behind the line in which I was, smoking his pipe as calmly as if he had been at home."[20]

A man who could control his own fear in front of other men set a powerful example. To do this it was not necessary to be one of those storied characters who felt no fear at all—indeed, many soldiers expressed an instinctive distrust of such men. But most soldiers respected and admired demonstrations of strong self-control in their officers. Panic could be contagious, as was often the case with whole battalions when a few men broke for the rear and more followed until the entire unit fell back in disarray. On the other hand, the calming effect of self-disciplined, cool-headed leadership was just as communicable. A man who could act nonchalant under fire even when he did not actually feel it exerted a tremendous influence on his fellow soldiers.

E. P. F. Lynch, an Australian infantryman who fought in France during the First World War, recalled one such occasion when his battalion came under a sustained bombardment while in a forward trench. For more than an hour the men could do nothing but crouch in the open trench, raked by shrapnel and airbursts. As their casualties mounted, their collective fear also mounted, until a bizarre thing happened. "One of our officers is walking upright along the top of our parapet in this dreadful barrage," Lynch later wrote. "He keeps looking into the trench as he goes along. 'Can't hurt you unless they hit you,' he keeps calling to the men as he walks the tight-rope to hell." Lynch remembered that some weeks earlier, he had heard the same phrase from the same officer when his unit came under sniper fire. "Then I thought this officer was an absolute fool," he said. "Now I know him for an out and out hero if ever there was one." One of Lynch's companions wondered if the man was being fatalistic;

Lynch and others disagreed. "It's not fatalism. The officer is practicing fear control. He is setting a wonderful example to us all, for if a man can walk out there and live, so can we, and we begin to feel we're in comparative safety here in the trench. . . . We feel better."[21]

This sort of personal example was stirring, but it often came at a high price. Lieutenant Wilfred Staddon remembered the desperate fighting near Flers in 1915 and the resultant cost. "There were very few company officers left," Staddon wrote of his company's attack, "I think only two of us who actually reached the wire. The wire was only half cut but my companion, Lieutenant Chesters, urged his men forward with conspicuous gallantry, really. But he paid the penalty—he was too conspicuous and I saw him die in the wire."[22] In the Allied landings during the Gallipoli campaign, Joe Murray of the Royal Naval Division recalled one officer in particular: "Colonel Quilter, a great big chap, a 'straight as a poker' ex-Guards Officer. I remembered him leading the advance and going to his death armed with a huge walking stick."[23]

In an era when men expected to see their officers leading from the front, conspicuously uniformed and instantly recognizable to both friend and foe alike, personal courage was simply an expected leadership quality. European officers of the nineteenth century, in particular, were inculcated with this philosophy in part as an obligation of the social rank that accompanied their military rank. Officers were expected to be disdainful of risk and personally brave, almost recklessly so, but examples of striking bravery were still frequently remarked upon.

One British soldier described the actions of an officer whose conduct made an impression during the horrific fighting at the siege of Badajoz in 1812. "Captain Mulcaster, of the Engineers," he wrote, "by his heroic conduct, stimulated the soldiers wonderfully; no danger could unnerve him or prevent him exposing himself to the hottest of French fire and for a time he escaped unhurt."[24] For a time only, until his luck ran out—a round shot from a French twenty-four pounder cannon took off Mulcaster's head and most of his shoulders. An indication of the narrator's undisguised admiration for the dead officer's bravery and the example he set was that the narrator made of point of saying that the infantrymen had looked up to Captain Mulcaster, an admiration they did not normally accord engineer officers.

When that sort of leadership example was lacking or when an officer conspicuously behaved contrary to the bravery expected of his rank, it almost always had a negative effect on the men. When the three separate detachments of the U.S. 7th Cavalry fought at the Battle of the Little Bighorn on June 26, 1876, examples of good and bad leadership both abounded.

The five troops under Lieutenant Colonel George Custer's personal command were wiped out to a man. The other troops under Major Reno and Captain Benteen fought a desperate defensive action on a small hill for two days, until the Indians broke contact and withdrew from the field. In the official inquest that followed the disaster, a considerable portion of blame was leveled at Major Reno for, his critics said, failing to support Custer as closely as he might have. Many of the enlisted men who survived the battle expressed similar personal opinions.

"Among the several things that impressed me greatly," Trooper William O. Taylor wrote thirty-four years later, "was the general demoralization that seemed to pervade many of the officers and men—due in a great measure, I think, to Major Reno. When an enlisted man sees his commanding officer lose his head entirely, and several other officers showing greater regard for their personal safety than anything else, it would be apt to demoralize any one taught almost to breathe at the word of command."[25]

Contrasting that report, Private William Slaper, who also fought at the Little Bighorn, remembered that he was very impressed by the personal conduct of his company commander, Captain Thomas French. "While in this line," Slaper wrote, "Capt. French was about in the center, giving orders as coolly as though it was a Sunday picnic. He would sit up tailor-style, while bullets were coming from the front and both sides. I could but marvel that he was not hit. Without appearing to be in the least excited, he would extract shells from guns in which cartridges would stick, and pass them loaded, then fix another, all the time watching in every direction."[26] Other soldiers also spoke admiringly of French's calm, courageous personal example in the most desperate moments of the fight.

Another type of demonstration of personal courage that many men commented on was that of the officers and NCOs who were remarkable not for conspicuous acts of gallantry or heroism, but who just seemed to take the chaos and violence and danger all in their stride, as if it were of no particular concern to them. In the horrific maelstrom of the landing on Omaha Beach on D-Day, Cecil Breeden, a medic in the U.S. 116th Infantry, saw a master sergeant called Big Bill Presley walking down the beach. "I asked him what he was doing," Breeden remembered. "He said, 'Looking for a rifle that will work.' Pointing up the hill, he said he had some men up there. Then he told me to get down or I was going to get hit." Breeden was incredulous. "I said, 'What the hell are you talking about? You're a damn sight bigger target than me.'" Presley grinned and continued on down the beach. "Soon he came back with a rifle, just waved and went on." Decades later, Breeden was still impressed by Master Sergeant Presley's insouciance under fire.

Sometimes the stress caused men to engage in behavior that might appear brave, but was in fact an almost hysterical reaction to the boredom, the fear, and sheer pressure of living a millisecond away from violent death, day after day after unending day. In a particularly active section of the trenches in France in 1916, one Australian soldier recounted a dangerous game that his fellow soldiers played:

> *Fritz's system now and again got on our nerves. It was deadly monotonous, always knowing when his severest shelling would start and I have known the boys run races with the shells, driven to take foolish risks by sheer ennui. We always expected some shells on "V.C. House" at 4 P.M., and were rarely disappointed. The men off duty would assemble in front of the old house and at the sound of the first shell race for the shelter of a dugout about a hundred yards away. Generally they would all tumble in together and in their excitement could not decide who won the race, and so would have it all over again. The officers were ordered to stop these "races with death" for there were some killed, but they would break out now and again when the last man who was killed had been forgotten.*[27]

Men facing fire were wracked by a nearly incalculable range of emotions. The waiting, most soldiers agreed, was the worst part. British regulars in Spain that stood waiting for the French columns to close the distance so the musketry could commence; Scottish soldiers standing in their ranks at Balaclava as the Russian cavalry thundered down the valley toward them; British and German infantrymen waiting in their trenches for the signal to go over the top in France; American paratroopers waiting for the green light to jump from their aircraft into the hostile dark of Normandy; U.S. Marines waiting for their landing craft to grind ashore on Tarawa and Saipan and Iwo Jima—all those men knew the throat-constricting, dry-mouthed pressure of fear and the sometimes nearly crippling anxiety of waiting to be thrown headlong into the cataclysm of what might be their last violent moments on earth.

"The suspense of waiting to go over," Australian soldier E. P. F. Lynch wrote, "has always been a trial, camouflage it how you may." The long moments standing on the fire-step waiting for the whistle, moments that stretched out interminably and yet were all too brief, gave men too much time to contemplate the unknowable and to worry about all the terrible things which might be in store for them. "It's not so much that we fear what we'll meet," Lynch wrote, "bad and all as it generally is. There's something our being shrinks from."[28] Some men, he said, worried that they might show how deeply afraid they truly were. Others shared the view of a young British soldier at Gallipoli, who wrote, "I was never as afraid of dying, or being dead, as I was of being maimed. I was scared stiff of being maimed."[29] Some men, perhaps most men, *did* fear the possibility of dying. "But whatever our thoughts, or fears or misgivings," Lynch wrote, "we are all more or less anxious to get it over, for from bitter experience we know that thinking only makes things worse."[30]

Lynch's perspective was widely shared. Joe Murray, who fought with the Royal Naval Division at Gallipoli, wrote of his experience waiting to go into an attack on the Turkish lines on June 4, 1915. "We stood there, packed like sardines unable to stand up in comfort," Murray wrote, "and we still had another hour to go before we went over the top. It was a long hour." Men took the waiting in different ways, he remembered. "Some men were fast asleep on their feet, others just stood staring at the sky. The laddie next to me checked his rifle and ammunition again and again, still not satisfied. Others just stood and stared, silent as the grave." At 11:30 that morning the half-hour barrage that preceded their attack abruptly ceased. "I'd never dreamt that even borrowed time could go so slowly," Murray wrote.[31] He survived the futile attack that followed, but many of the men who had waited with him were killed in the maelstrom of Turkish machine gun fire that blasted their formations into bloody ruin.

Many soldiers in those moments of waiting were able to identify with something expressed by a British sergeant in the Normandy campaign in 1944, who wrote, "I was afraid of being afraid."[32] The crushing pressure of waiting to go into battle was something many men reflected on in later years, after their wars and the dangers they faced were long past. The man who claimed to have never felt fear was rare, indeed, but sometimes the fear that men did feel seemed to resolve itself just by how overwhelming it was. "You can get so scared that you're not scared any more, and I think that's what happened to me," wrote an American infantryman who survived the carnage of Omaha Beach on D-Day.[33] For another American, Joseph Argenzio, D-Day was his first combat action. As the landing craft circled in their holding patterns waiting for the signal to head in toward the beach, he recalled that he felt frightened, but took a measure of reassurance from the fact that most of the men in his landing craft were veterans of the tough campaigns in North Africa and Sicily. "I remember saying to one of the old-timers 'Oh boy, it's great being with you vets,'" Argenzio said. The older soldier replied, "Lad, the minute they drop that ramp, you're going to be a veteran." That did not allay the younger soldier's fears.[34]

Union Army veteran John Beatty considered the question of fear at some length in his Civil War journal. "Hitherto I have gone into battle almost without knowing it; now we are about to bring on a terrible conflict, and have abundant time for reflection," he wrote. "I cannot affirm that the prospect has a tendency to elevate one's spirits." Beatty found that he could not help dwelling on all the possible outcomes of battle. "There are men, doubtless, who enjoy having their legs sawed off, their heads trepanned, and their ribs reset, but I am not one of them," he admitted.[35]

This experience of waiting was universal for all soldiers of the period, regardless of the era, or the army, or the modern machinations of their particular war. An American paratrooper of the 101st Airborne Division described the flight into France for the airborne drop that began the invasion of Normandy in 1944: "As the time was getting closer," he remembered, "you're getting nervous, getting butterflies in your stomach and you're wondering, What am I doing here, why did I ever come, why did I volunteer.?" Over the drop zone the German antiaircraft fire was heavy, but the command to jump into the darkness was a blessed release from the crushing tension. "When the time came to go," he said, "when that green light came on and out the door we went, we didn't hesitate one moment we were so happy to get out of that thing."[36]

Many men described situations where it got to the point that there were other things worse than the fear of being killed. Riding a landing craft in toward Omaha Beach on D-Day, Sergeant John Slaughter of the U.S. 116th Infantry found that with every pitch and yaw of the boat in the heavy seas, he cared less and less about the heavy enemy fire coming from the cliffs overlooking the beach. "My thinking, as we approached the beach, was that if the boat didn't hurry up and get us in I would die from seasickness," he said. "This was my first encounter with this malady. Wooziness became stomach sickness and then vomiting. Thinking I was immune to seasickness, earlier I had given my 'puke bag' to a buddy who had already filled his. Minus the paper bag, I used the first thing at hand, my helmet. At this point, death is not so dreadful. I didn't care what the Germans had to offer, I had to set foot on dry land."[37]

Facing the guns, men had to find some means of making themselves stand and hold their ground. Even more contrary to the natural human instincts of self-preservation, they had to make themselves get up and go forward into the enemy's fire. Leander Stillwell, a Union Army soldier of the Civil War, faced hostile fire for the first time at the battle of Shiloh. "I am not ashamed to say now," Stillwell wrote, years after the war, "that I would willingly have given a general quit-claim deed for every jot and tittle of military glory falling to me, past, present, and to come, if I only could have been miraculously and instantaneously set down . . . a thousand miles away from the haunts of fighting men."[38]

Stillwell's feelings echoed the words of the Youth in Shakespeare's *Henry V,* who, in the desperate fighting at the siege of Le Havre, says, "I would give all my fame and fortune / For a pot of ale and safety." The men against whom Stillwell fought felt much the same way about it. One Confederate soldier recalled when his regiment moved up into line of battle at Antietam and saw the carnage being wrought by heavy fire across the open field. "As we stood there for a few minutes and saw the work cut out for us," he remembered, "one of our men, one of the few who had been of age in 1860, said in a plaintive tone, 'If the Lord will only see me safe through this job, I'll register an oath never to vote for secession again as long as I live.'"[39]

Most soldiers, at least in terms of statistical numbers, stood their ground and continued to fight, no matter how debilitating their fear. There were always some, however, who did not or could not. Though they were usually a distinct minority, there were always some men who simply *could not* stand. For them the fear was just too great, and they were overcome by uncontrollable panic. A young Confederate lieutenant named Randolph McKim said that during four years of the Civil War he saw only two cases of men completely overcome by their fear, but they were all the more memorable for that infrequency. "One of these," he wrote, "was an artillery man who had taken refuge under the caisson, where he crouched trembling like a leaf. I saw a sergeant ride up and point a pistol at his head, saying, 'Come out from under there and do your duty, and you'll have some chance of your life, but if you stay there, by the Eternal, I'll blow your brains out.'" McKim said that he did not stay to see the outcome of that conversation. He did, however, see the result of the other case. "Then, shortly after, I saw another soldier crouching in terror behind a tree," he wrote. "The next moment came a round shot, which went through the tree and absolutely decapitated the man!"

There has always been something counterintuitive about the soldier's task. When all the impulses of self-preservation and common sense desperately urge him to turn around and go the other way, and that as fast as possible, as a combatant he is expected to deliberately go forward into harm's way. When fired upon, he is trained to return fire and maneuver against the enemy, because the greatest safety actually lies in fighting back, rather than fleeing. Sergeant Henry Windolph, who fought at the Battle of the Little Bighorn with the 7th Cavalry, remembered, "Captain Benteen used to say: 'The government pays you to get shot at.'"[40] That is the truth of every soldier's job in every army—the profession requires one to risk one's life as a part of the job. The fact that there is pay involved is almost immaterial, however, since most men who have been shot at and survived to discuss it readily agree that a soldier's wage is never enough to compensate the risk to life and limb that is required to earn it.

Reading through the memoirs and narratives written by soldiers during this period, it becomes very clear that fear was a common reaction to danger, but for most men it was perceived differently as their combat experience went on. Some men were driven to the breaking point; others became almost desensitized to it and felt less fear the more they were exposed to the hazards of battle.

Needham N. Freeman, an infantryman during the Philippine-American War in 1902, recalled his first combat experience by saying, "I have to confess to being a little frightened this time, but kept my nerve on all other occasions."[41] Leander Stillwell, whom we have already encountered in this chapter, was very honest about his feelings on facing combat. Stillwell saw action in several heavy engagements, from Shiloh onward, and he never grew indifferent to the risk. "I will set it down here," he wrote, "away down in the bottom of my heart I just secretly dreaded a battle."[42] An American infantryman of the Second World War expressed a similar feeling when he wrote, "Most of the time I was scared—not by bullet and shell alone, but by the huge and brutal impersonality of the whole business."[43]

Sometimes a specific threat was the source of the fear. The fear was worse when the lethal danger could not be seen, a situation Raymond Gantter experienced many times during his months of combat in France. "You ask which is more frightening, artillery or snipers," he wrote in a letter to his wife. "Snipers are a cold fear, ghosts that walk every midnight street, lie in wait in every corner. It's like walking into a dark room and hearing the door close softly behind you and you didn't close it . . . the skin on your forearms telling you that someone, something, is in the room with you, watching you with eyes that never blink, never flicker away from you . . . something that listens to your breathing and the sound of your heart." As an infantryman, Gantter knew what he was talking about when he said, "Snipers are bad."[44]

Many veterans, after passing through the maelstrom of combat and experiencing mortal fear themselves, had a much more sympathetic attitude toward other men's breaking points. Joseph Dazzo fought in North Africa, Sicily, and France with the U.S. 1st Infantry Division and saw his share of combat stress. "A lot of people think bravery is the answer but, you know, I didn't agree with Patton too much," he recalled. "I didn't like the idea, in Sicily, of slapping a member of my combat team. The mind can take so much. Now maybe one man can take more than the other but that does not make the man who can stand more a hero . . . . Anybody who has been in one campaign, can understand what shelling can do. Patton did not believe that one man could be weaker than the other." Dazzo took a completely different view. "Unfortunately, we both know human intelligence is very, very, very fragile," he said. "I have no use for people who don't understand that if a man has gone through three or four campaigns and he fails at the fifth, he is not a coward. He is just mentally wounded."[45]

An interesting dynamic at work in the experience of fear was how it manifested itself differently depending on whether a soldier dealt with it alone or as a member of a group of other men whom he knew, trusted, and with whom he felt some connections. "In the mass," war correspondent Philip Gibbs wrote of British soldiers in the First World War, "all our soldiers seemed equally brave. In the mass they seemed astoundingly cheerful. . . . It was optimism in the mass, heroism in the mass." Soldiers encountered on their own, however, often showed a different face. "It was only when one spoke to the individual, some friend who bared his soul a second, or some soldier-ant in the multitude," Gibbs wrote, "that one saw the hatred of a man for his job, the sense of doom upon him, the weakness that was in his strength, the bitterness of his grudge against a fate that forced him to go on in this way of life, the remembrance of a life more beautiful which he had abandoned—all mingled with those other qualities of pride and comradeship, and that illogical sense of humor which made up the strange complexity of his psychology."[46]

This group dynamic, so important in the clinch to a unit's combat effectiveness, was strong enough to enable men to go into harm's way together. It was also an incredibly fragile phenomenon, and it could be easily disrupted. High casualty rates could obviously break apart a unit's core cohesion, as would those situations when men were taken out of their primary units and seconded to others. The loss of a particularly admired officer, or the introduction into the unit of a disliked officer or senior NCO, could instantly shatter a unit's tight-knit bonds. Carlton McCarthy, a Confederate soldier of the Civil War, saw this happen in his battalion, and he vividly remembered the results. "Those who have not served in the army as privates can form no idea of the extent to which changes such as these just mentioned affect the spirits and general worth of a soldier," he wrote. "Men who, when surrounded by their old companions, were brave and daring soldiers, full of spirit and hope, when thrust among strangers for whom they cared not, and who cared not for them, became dull and listless, lost their courage, and were slowly but surely 'demoralized.'" McCarthy's battalion did not collapse, and they continued to fight when required to do so, but they were no longer the force they had been. "They did, it is true, in many cases, stand up to the last," he wrote, "but they did it on dry principle, having none of that enthusiasm and delight in duty which once characterized them."[47] Soldiers on the other side of that war saw the same thing happen in their ranks.

Leander Stillwell considered this at some length in his memoir. He believed that the prevailing sentiment among soldiers in the Civil War was that they were "too proud to run." The only circumstances under which it was acceptable to run, Stillwell said, were not when a man gave way to fear, but when it was clear that the fight was completely lost and there was nothing else to do but fall back, whether the withdrawal was ordered or not. Things were different in that case, he thought: "When the whole line goes back, there is no personal odium attaching to any one individual, they are all in the same boat."[48]

Pride could make men stand and face apparently certain death when little else could. Personal pride went a long way in this regard—many men were conscious of the eyes of their comrades on them, and they were unwilling to appear craven, no matter how desperately frightened they really were. There is a story from the Civil War, one which appears in slightly different versions in several sources, in which men standing in the firing line amidst the smoke and shot of battle saw a rabbit running for the rear as fast as it could go. "Go it, cotton-tail!" a soldier shouted. "I'd run too if I had no more reputation to lose than you have!" It was a sentiment privately shared by many officers and men alike.

That anecdote also illustrates another aspect of how soldiers dealt with the almost crushing fear of combat—with a wry, keen, and not always socially acceptable humor. In the ferocious fighting on Iwo Jima, USMC Private C. S. Axtell recalled an incident that stuck with him:

> *As the morning sun came up we started to pull out of our foxholes and relax a bit and one of the West Virginia boys—he was a tall gangly fellow, very dry humor—he was sitting against a stone wall with his knees up under his helmet as we used to sit quite often, when one of the enemy ran out on top of the stone wall [with] a small explosive charge to his abdomen. A chunk of his torso went spiraling into the air and came down on John's knees with the absolute posterior devoid of any clothes staring him right in the face. And he looked at that and he says, 'God, have I been hit that bad?' And that was the trigger that released the tensions of the previous night and there were several of us that were perfectly useless for as much as an hour—we just lay there on the ground in convulsions.*[49]

Of course, in every army there were men who did not stand and fight. Some ran. For some of them it was a momentary faltering, and they rejoined their units of their own volition and fought on. Others were brave to a point, but once that point was reached, they were unable to force themselves to confront the dangers again. Some men, for whatever individual reason, broke and deserted their units under fire, an act which was a capital offense in every army of the period. It was not always the visibly fearful men who did not stand—Australian infantryman Hugh

Knyvett said in his experience it was "the 'man who is afraid of being afraid' who stays at his post to the last."[50]

Combat veterans of these years occasionally condemned "cowards" and "shirkers" in their narratives, but those opinions are distinctly in the minority. Most men looking back on the wars behind them recalled that they worried, at least once or twice before the first shot was fired in anger, that when the moment of truth came they themselves might turn out to be cowards. Almost none of them were. But when they encountered genuine, debilitating fear in their fellow soldiers, the combat soldiers in the rifle companies, cavalry troops and artillery batteries could be surprisingly sympathetic.

One British soldier who lived through the horrific fighting on the Somme in 1916 expressed both sides of the common perspective—empathy and criticism—in his recounting of a night movement into the forward lines with a fatigue party:

We halted at the start of the trench and Lt John went along to get instructions. It was a very nerve-racking wait and one or two of our party . . . thank God there were not many . . . took advantage of the noise and disturbance [of the shelling] and slipped quietly down a side trench and stayed there until, all the work done, we were returning. Then the miserable devils slipped back into the file, no one of any importance being any the wiser. There are some things one cannot understand: I must never sneer at a man who is afraid, for I have been more frightened out here than it is necessary to record. That is one thing; scrounging to the detriment of your pals is another and we who saw those rotters have not forgotten; I don't suppose we ever shall.[51]

A man who was so craven that he repeatedly deserted before the fighting even started was almost universally condemned by other soldiers, but a man who simply couldn't take it anymore when he was previously able and willing to share the risk, and had earlier taken his chances in the line, was more often seen as an object of pity and regret. More than one soldier, considering the case of someone whom he knew who was accused of cowardice, echoed the sentiment "there but for the grace of God go I."

One of the worst situations for individual soldiers might have been when the impersonal bureaucracy of military justice required them to act as executioners for fellow soldiers who were condemned for cowardice. Some soldiers in the period were faced with this terrible duty; some described it with no apparent feeling; some remembered it as the worst thing they ever had to do. Some men absolutely refused to be a part of it.

Corporal Alan Bray of the British Army, serving in France in 1916, was ordered to be a member of a firing squad that was to execute four men who had been condemned for desertion. "I was very worried about it because I didn't think it was right," Bray remembered. "I thought I knew why these men had deserted, if they had deserted. It was the fact that they had probably been in the trenches for two or three months without a break, which could absolutely break your nerves." An older veteran took Bray aside and told him that this order was "the one thing in the Army that you could refuse to do." Bray immediately went to his sergeant and stated his refusal to be a member of the firing squad. "I heard no more about it," he said. The matter of shooting men accused of cowardice had already affected Bray deeply—"The week before a boy in our own battalion had been shot for desertion," he wrote. "I knew that boy, and I knew that he absolutely lost his nerve, he couldn't have gone back into the line."[52]

Soldiers often remembered that they were particularly concerned with how they would measure up in the eyes of their comrades the first time they came under fire. Occasionally this fear of being thought fearful led them to take unnecessary risks, especially if they thought their rank required it of them. Marion Ford of the Confederate Army recalled that the first time his unit came under artillery fire from Union guns, he felt that a certain nonchalance was expected of him, a nonchalance that he absolutely did not truly feel. "I thought it unbecoming to appear concerned," he wrote, "and although at first . . . I had stood wisely behind a friendly oak tree for protection, after the first shell or two I stepped aside and stood in the open, foolishly thinking that this was more soldierly." Later experience would give him a different perspective. "I had not yet learned," he said, "that a soldier's common sense should prompt him to make use of what protection there may be at hand and to avoid exposing himself unnecessarily."[53]

Unit pride also had a powerful influence on countering fear. Esprit de corps is an idea sometimes sneered at by those outside the military's insular society, but a well-trained unit with a deeply instilled sense of pride in itself and its lineage can be a force to be reckoned with, and its individual soldiers are often better in the balance than many of their opponents precisely because of that intrinsic element. This is particularly true of elite units, where membership is exclusive and hard-won, and where the ranks are usually filled by a process of careful selection. Every army worth its name had its elite units, and those soldiers sometimes went to great lengths to live up to the ideals of their regiments.

Australian soldier E. P. F. Lynch recalled witnessing this phenomenon in action during the fighting at Bullecourt in 1917. His company overran a German line that had been tenaciously defended, particularly by its machine gun crews. A German machine-gunner was lying by his gun, seriously wounded—the Australian medical personnel were evacuating the German wounded, but this man had been left where he lay. "The boys couldn't carry him out," Lynch wrote, "for he was chained to his great heavy gun by a strong chain and two padlocks." When the Australians questioned him, the German gunner "told them he had chained himself to the gun and thrown the key beyond reach. He said . . . that he was afraid his nerves might break. He seemed to have a dread of deserting his post," Lynch remembered. "The man spoke of his unit, some special house or bodyguards of the Prussian army, and said that in two hundred years since its formation, no member of it had ever deserted before an enemy." The Australian infantrymen were impressed by the German soldier's commitment, but they thought it a needless measure. They knew all too well, Lynch said, "of many Fritz who had died working their guns to the last. Some of the bravest men we've ever [fought] have been Fritz gunners; we know that to our sorrow."[54]

This appraisal of the enemy's bravery in battle was something most soldiers were willing to acknowledge, so long as the men on the other side showed a tough, genuine courage, and when that bravery was not marred by an excess of brutality. Philip Gibbs told his British readers that the

Germans on the Somme "fought with a desperate courage, holding on to positions in rearguard actions when our guns were slashing at them, making us pay a heavy price for every little copse or gully or section of trench, and above all serving their machine-guns." There were different types of courage, and the Germans were not lacking in any of them. "It is indeed fair and just to say," Gibbs wrote, "that throughout those battles of the Somme our men fought against an enemy hard to beat, grim and resolute, and inspired sometimes with the courage of despair, which was hardly less dangerous than the courage of hope."[55] A century before Gibbs, the anonymous veteran of the 71st Regiment of Foot, a British veteran of the Napoleonic Wars, expressed the same admiration for his enemy's courage. "I have often admired the bravery of French officers," he wrote, and he had seen enough French officers die at the head of their regiments to have some perspective on the subject.[56]

Sergeant George Ashurst of the Lancashire Fusiliers remembered how in 1915 he witnessed a particular act of bravery by a German soldier. The Royal Engineers detonated a large mine under some houses occupied by the German lines, just yards away from houses held by the British. The ensuing explosion threw dirt, rubble, and men in all directions. "We saw a German lying wounded on top of an outhouse," Ashurst wrote, "when up came another German carrying a ladder, calm as anything despite having five or six of our rifles pointed at him." The German soldier retrieved his wounded comrade and carried him back to his own lines. "The officer said, 'Don't fire, boys. He deserves a medal, that lad.' He knew we were there, he could see us quite well."[57]

Armies around the world have invested a great deal of time and energy into trying to determine what it is that makes men brave—or, if not brave, then at least what makes them fight on even when they are terribly afraid. Most military commentators agree that rigorous training and strong discipline play a part; some have argued that these are the most important parts. Others cite more esoteric factors such as esprit de corps and official recognition of individual valor. Medals and decorations came into their modern form at the beginning of this period, and while some soldiers have remained cynical as to the intrinsic value of medals, other men have been willing to risk life and limb for the glory of a military decoration. Napoleon Bonaparte, who had an intuitive understanding of soldiers' thinking and was at the same time more than a bit of a cynic, supposedly once stated that he never ceased to be amazed at what men would do for a tiny scrap of ribbon.

As the wars of this period passed the dividing mark between the nineteenth and twentieth centuries, and the brutalities of war multiplied and the killing passed the scale of anything previously seen, many soldiers began to regard the official rewards for valor with slightly jaundiced eyes. One British sergeant, at the battle of the Aisne in the First World War, remembered a moment that resulted in an award of the Victoria Cross. "The Highland Light Infantry and Worcesters came up," he wrote. "Private Wilson of the HLI and one of our men attacked a machine-gun. Our man got killed but Private Wilson killed the machine-gunner and captured the position and got the Victoria Cross. Our man got a wooden cross. That's the difference, you see. One killed—one a Victoria Cross."[58]

Soldiers themselves also frequently pondered the nature of bravery and its opposite incarnation, cowardice. "It is absurd to say that a man 'doesn't mind shell-fire,'" a British soldier named Richard Haigh wrote. "Everyone dislikes it, and gets nervous under it. The man who 'doesn't mind it' is the man who fights his nervousness and gets such control of himself that he is able to appear as if he were unaffected. Between 'not minding it' and 'appearing not to mind it' lie hard-won moral battles, increased strength of character, and victory over fear."[59] Occasionally men went beyond the point of controlling their fear and displayed moments of incredible valor—what surprised many soldiers was the fact that heroism was often exhibited in unlikely situations by unlikely men.

"The thing that surprised me," American infantryman Philip Gantter wrote of his service in the Second World War, "is that a guy can be a hero and a bastard at the same time. I'm talking about true heroes, of course, not guys who wear decorations. . . . I mean a man who does something truly gallant, something that rings inside you like the surging memory of Hector before the walls of Troy. And yet you don't like him. If you didn't like him before, you're surprised to find you don't like him any better now, even though you recognize the magnitude of his act and are awed by it." Gantter found this to be an odd reality. "He's a hero, sure, but he's still a jerk."[60]

War involves the inherent risk of violent death, and yet all wars are marked by individual instances of soldiers risking death in acts of incredible bravery. What compels that sort of behavior? The reasons are probably infinite, and vary as much as do the men themselves. A true, absolute lack of fear is probably the rarest element. What is more natural is that in the moment of truth, the normal considerations seemed to weigh differently. "In war a man will deliberately sacrifice [his own life] to save perhaps a couple of men who have no claim on him whatsoever," one veteran of the First World War wrote. "He who before feared any household calamity now throws himself upon a live bomb, which, even though he might escape himself, will without his action kill other men who are near it. This deed loses none of its value because of the general belief among soldiers that life is cheap. Other men's lives are cheap. One's own life is always very dear."[61]

Bravery, while often remarkable and noteworthy, was not always inherently noble. The phrase "fighting drunk" is more than just a figure of speech—various armies during this period were accused by their enemies of relying on alcohol to shore up their resolve. Sometimes it was even true. The British military—army and navy both—had a long tradition of the daily ration of spirits. The amount doled out was never enough for a man to get drunk on, but more than one soldier contrived to save up enough of the daily tot for a week or so to give himself a thick head. And at the battle of Waterloo it was a fact that the quartermasters brought barrels of liquor onto the battlefield which were liberally—very liberally—served out to the British regiments. More than one veteran of that epic fight recalled seeing men in the square or serving the guns who were roaring drunk.

Thomas Morris remembered witnessing an act of apparent bravery at Waterloo that he believed was more a matter of drunken recklessness than simple courage. A corporal from the 2nd Life Guards named John Shaw broke ranks from his regiment and single-handedly attacked the mass of French troops ranged before his line. Shaw was apparently a big man, physically, and in the melee he killed a number of the French soldiers before he himself was cut down. All witnesses agreed that Corporal Shaw was raging drunk at the time. "I admire as much as any man can do, individual acts of bravery," Morris wrote, "but Shaw certainly falls very far short of my definition of the term *hero*. The path of duty is the path of safety. . . . To rush, in such a way, on to certain death, was, in my opinion, as much an act of suicide. . . . If every man were to follow Shaw's example—quit his regiment and seek distinction for himself—there would be an end to discipline, and consequently, to all chance of success."[62]

The common experience of soldiers throughout this period encompassed all the emotions we have examined here—boredom, fear, and courage—and just about everything else in between. The wonder is perhaps not that men faced up to the possibility of their own violent deaths as readily as they often did, but rather that they were able to endure such misery and suffering in the process and the amount of physical misery and mental horror they were able to live with as they passed through the crucible of battle. The feelings of more than one man were summed up by a New Zealand veteran of the hard fighting at Crete in 1940, who said, "That was a wonderful experience in a lot of ways, but something you would never want to go through again. . . . What a ghastly thing war was and how it made men act as heroes and some as animals."[63]

Chapter Eleven

Misery and Mud

Lost in the stumbling dark we cling
Like blind men to each other . . .
The blind following faithfully those more blind
Into the waiting, hostile night.

—JOHN HAYMOND

IN SEPTEMBER 1914, THE SECOND MONTH of the First World War, an anonymous French soldier wrote a letter home to his mother. He was a dutiful correspondent, writing whenever he had a chance, catching the odd moment to write a few lines to let his family know how he was faring as the German onslaught set the French and their British allies back on their heels. From the tone of this young man's early letters, he was an idealistic volunteer, at least in the beginning—his personal motivations seem to have been more from a desire to defend home and country than because of any ideas of martial glory. Whatever his expectations of the military were, however, the ugly reality of war took over very quickly. On September 16 he wrote, "There will never be enough glory to cover all the blood and all the mud."[1]

War is many things, and most of the professional histories written on the subject of war have focused on the maelstrom of battle, the defining collisions of combat and death. These stories are unquestionably part of the broad expanse of many soldiers' narratives, but there is much more in the broad expanse of the common soldier's life than just those fateful events.

What is sometimes overlooked in discussions of soldiering is another reality that was (and remains) every bit as much a part of the soldier's experience as war itself. Particularly for men serving in the combat arms, a soldier's life all too often involves misery—plain, wretched, unmitigated misery, of both the mundane and extraordinary varieties, both the physical and the emotional. "Being a soldier," an American GI wrote during the Second World War, "is being a wet, dirty, miserable creature, one dubious step removed from the animal."[2] He was not sure whether the step was up or down. Reading through the sources, one quickly encounters the recurring theme of misery described in stark detail by almost every soldier in every army in every era, in times of both war and peace.

One sorrow common to most soldiers, of all armies, was the very understandable emotional pull of the families they left behind them when they followed the drum. Reading through the letters of men who wrote while they were enduring the deprivations and hazards of military life, it is striking how many of them worried more about how their families were faring at home so far away, than about their own safety. "You cant imagine how much I want to see you it seems I would give every thing I possess to be with you if only for a short while," Confederate infantryman John Futch wrote after the Battle of Gettysburg to his wife Martha, back in North Carolina.[3]

Another North Carolinian, Francis M. Poteet, was close to despair when he wrote to his wife in August 1864. He had just received the tragic news that the youngest of their four children had died after a very short illness, his wife could not find anyone to help her get in the crops, and he was seriously contemplating deserting the army. His wife's most recent letter had urged against that drastic choice; deserting the ranks would have imperiled his life. Poteet had very little education, but his halting, misspelled words still convey his feelings clearly: "you Rote to me to not Runaway if it is the will of my loving Wife I wont Runaway," he wrote. "god nows that it tis hard times hear. . . . if it tis the will of you that I Should stay till the war ends I will stay if I live but you dont now how bad that I want to see you all I dreamed about you this morning I thought that I was at home and as well Satsfide as I ever was in my life but when I waked up I was laying on my blanket if it tis gods will I will get home some time are other but I dont know when." Three months later, he was still longing for his home and family: "you dont now how bad that I want to see you and My littel Babes," he wrote in another letter. "My Dear

Wife I want you to hug and kiss to my littel Children for me."⁴ Even soldiers who did not leave wives and children behind still felt a desperate longing for news from home. In July 1862, a Confederate soldier named Charles Taylor sent a letter to his father back in Texas. "Dear Pa," he wrote, "I have been looking very anxiously for some time for a letter from home but nary letter yet. . . . You all must write often. I haven't received a letter from home in a month."⁵

For those men who garrisoned the remote posts of the American frontier, the loneliness of the life was an ever-present part of their burden. Stultifying boredom was a part of frontier duty, but even worse for some men was the soul-crushing loneliness of an overwhelmingly male environment, utterly devoid of any touch of home. One soldier, Private Richard F. King, wrote to his family back east, saying, "You do not know how lonsom I am out hear. . . . I almost go mad once and a while, and probley you would not believe me but then it is so all the same. I did not see one woman for a year and 2 months."⁶ Other soldiers, holding the line in posts from the deserts of Arizona to the high country of Montana, would have understood King's lament from their own experience. Fifty years after he left the army, cavalryman William Jett remembered, "I have thought since then that if there was anything that could kill a man outside of murder or real disease, it would be homesickness."⁷

The same was true for American men of later wars. In 1917, a young recruit wrote to his girlfriend from his training camp. "It must take you as much as fifteen minutes to write me," he complained. "I venture to say, the letters you write to me are the shortest on your mailing list. . . . If it is that much trouble, strike my name off. I do not fancy the idea of worrying people—so, as I have said, if it is too big a task, do not half-way attend to it—drop it altogether. I do not intend to criticize the substance of them, however you could make 'em a little more personal, but I am kicking about their length." She apparently began writing better letters, or else he made his peace with it, because they married after the war and stayed together until his death in 1966.⁸

~◦~

Beyond the emotional costs of separation from home and family, there were always the attendant physical hardships of being a soldier. Infantrymen in particular were intimately acquainted with the inextricable misery of soldiering, but they by no means had a monopoly on rough living; soldiers in the other combat arms could readily attest to the fact that there was plenty of misery to go around. These were men whose professions required them to be outdoors in all weather, often in the *worst* weather, and eventually it all melded into one monotonous succession of inclemency. Whether hot or cold, mud or dust, rain or snow, drought or deluge, a soldier's life in the field often became an indistinguishable series of downward spirals into an ever-deeper morass of wretchedness.

"September 18," a Confederate soldier wrote in his Civil War diary, "Nothing new, only plenty of bad weather and hard work." Little changed for him in the months that followed, months of monotonous hardship interspersed with moments of danger. The following spring he wrote, "February 1 and 2—There is nothing new but cold, cold, cold."[9] This, then, was one of the realities of soldiering. Soldiers in the field were at the mercy of the weather, and momentous events in history played out in some of the worst weather imaginable.

In December 1808 a British army under the command of General Sir John Moore was in retreat westward across the Iberian Peninsula. Their situation was desperate—outnumbered and closely pursued by the French, the British had to fall back along their lines of communication through the rugged mountains of western Spain. Their only hope was to reach the port of Corunna where they could be evacuated by the ships of the Royal Navy. The weather for their withdrawal could hardly have been worse.

One soldier in the British ranks was an infantryman in the 71st Regiment of Foot, and his anonymous account of the retreat to Corunna provides a telling description of the foot soldier's lot. "On the 26th [of December] it rained the whole day, without intermission," he wrote. "The roads were knee-deep with clay."[10] The army was cold, wet, sick, and famished—either the commissary trains were out of contact with the troops, or, perversely, desperately needed supplies were being destroyed to deny them to the pursuing French.

As the route of Moore's withdrawal took his army farther into the mountains and up into the higher elevations, rain turned to snow and mud froze to ice. "We were either drenched with rain or crackling with ice," the anonymous narrator wrote. "Fuel we could find none. The sick and wounded that we had been still enabled to drag with us in the wagons were now left to perish in the snow."[11] Unit cohesion began to collapse—another survivor of the march remembered that it became a matter of "every one for himself and God for us all."[12] The rocky, snowy road through the mountains "was one line of bloody foot-marks from the sore feet of the men; and on its sides lay the dead and the dying."[13] Coming out of the mountains, men were at the breaking point. "My life was misery," the soldier from the 71st Regiment recalled. "Hunger, cold and fatigue had deprived death of all its horrors."[14]

Reaching Corunna, with the salvation of the navy waiting offshore, the British soldiers might have thought their sufferings were at an end. They were wrong. Even if the retreat was ended, the misery continued unabated. With the mountains behind them, the British regiments tried to reform in the coastal hills around Corunna. The cold, tormenting rain plagued them still. "We were upon plowed land, which was rendered so soft that we sunk in over the shoes at every step," the 71st Regiment soldier wrote.[15] Benjamin Harris, serving in the Rifle Brigade, remembered, "Almost all were without shoes. . . . Many had their clothes and accoutrements in fragments. . . . Our weapons were covered in rust."[16] Historian Christopher Hibbert writes of many men surviving the ordeal simply because their officers refused to let them give up and die. And it was at this point that misery became miracle. Having held his army together against all odds, Moore turned to give battle to the pursuing French. In this condition, after weeks of retreat that several times nearly became a mutinous rout, the ragged, emaciated British regulars held their ground and beat the French in a stand-up fight, completing their evacuation as tactical, if not strategic, victors. In an almost poetic note of tragedy, Moore did not live to see England again—like Wolfe at Quebec, he was killed on the field in his moment of triumph.

Weather and the apparent malevolence of nature could cause misery that went far beyond the sufferings brought on by battle, and when natural

forces combined with bad planning and incompetent leadership, the suffering was made even worse. Forty-two years after Corunna another generation of British soldiers in the Crimea wrote a new chapter in the long
legacy of military misery. The British Army in 1854 was prepared to win
the war; it was incredibly unprepared for the hard campaigning necessary
to actually *fight* the war.

William Howard Russell, the pioneering war correspondent for *The
Times* of London, wrote reports from the army's encampments in the
Crimea that shocked and horrified his readers back in England. "In the
tents the water was sometimes a foot deep," Russell wrote. "Our men had
neither warm nor waterproof clothing—they were out for twelve hours at
a time in the trenches—they were plunged into the inevitable miseries of
a winter campaign." The real outrage of this lack of adequate preparation,
Russell believed, was heightened by the indication that "not a soul seemed
to care for their comfort, or even for their lives." Some senior members of
the military establishment were furious that Russell, a civilian, was leveling
such criticisms against the army's command echelons. Numerous efforts
were made to either discredit him or limit his access to the front, but Russell refused to tone down his scathing reports. "Hundreds of men had to go
into the trenches at night with . . . no protection for their feet but their regimental shoes," he wrote. "The trenches were two and three feet deep with
mud, snow, and half-frozen slush." The public needed to know the truth,
Russell believed, which was that "the wretched beggar who wandered about
the streets of London in the rain led the life of a prince compared with the
British soldiers who were fighting for their country."[17]

Russell's critics accused him of embellishing the truth for the sake
of selling a few more newspapers, or implied that his criticisms were
unpatriotic, but the reality was even worse than what he was describing.
Soldiers in the ranks told the same story in their letters home. Sergeant
Timothy Gowing of the Royal Fusiliers, in a letter to his parents, wrote,
"Well, I've got back to camp again. We have had a rough twenty-four
hours; it rained nearly the whole time. . . . We were standing nearly up to
our knees in mud and water, like a lot of drowned rats, nearly all night;
the cold bleak wind cutting through our thin clothing (that is now getting
very thin and full of holes, and nothing to mend it with)." Gowing was

not simply complaining—he had been in battle often enough to have an informed perspective. "This is ten times worse than all the fighting," he wrote. "We cannot move without sinking nearly to our ankles in mud. The tents we have are full of holes; and there is nothing but mud to lie down in, or scrape it away with our hands the best we can." In a conclusion that was both cynical and honest, he wrote, "So much for honour and glory."[18]

In the time of the Crimean War, as was true for most of the nineteenth century, it was a social reality that officers lived better than the enlisted men did, and this was true even on campaign. Officers in European armies, after all, had their personal servants (the ubiquitous batman, or valet), they were entitled to bring more baggage, and they had considerably more money with which to defray the hardships of a soldier's life. It was therefore something of a shock to all concerned how little that seemed to matter in the Crimea. Officers at the battalion and regimental level were every bit as miserable as were their infantrymen, artillerymen, sappers, and cavalry troopers.

George Buchanan was a young cavalry lieutenant in the Scots Greys. Writing to his mother, Buchanan said, "We have had the most bitter weather. . . . It has rained night and day. . . . All our tents were blown away and it snowed and rained in a terrible manner." If Buchanan found a bright spot in all the gloom, he never mentioned it. "What a miserable time we had of it," he wrote, "up to our knees in water, and our tents gone. . . . The weather here is now quite wintry and cold, and rain falls every day."[19]

Carlton McCarthy, a Confederate soldier in the American Civil War, remembered the experience of living through periods of heavy rain as one of the most miserable ordeals of his military service. "Rain was the greatest discomfort a soldier could have," he wrote. "It was more uncomfortable than the severest cold with clear weather. Wet clothes, shoes, and blankets; wet meat and bread; wet feet and wet ground; wet wood to burn, or rather not to burn; wet arms and ammunition; wet ground to sleep on, mud to wade through, swollen creeks to ford, muddy springs, and a thousand other discomforts attended the rain."[20]

Randolph McKim also fought for the Confederacy, surviving the battles of Manassas, Gettysburg, and beyond, and he kept a diary throughout the war. He described the shock and confusion of battle, the monotony of camp life, and the exhaustion of long marches on short rations. Most often, though, he just described the weather.

"Monday, April 21st, 1862," he wrote. "Rained pitilessly all day. The regiment rode up to Gordonsville ten or twelve miles on open [rail] cars. This is one of the severest experiences we have ever had. Friday evening, Saturday, Sunday, and Monday exposed constantly to cold, drenching rain, with no shelter, and during two whole days without anything to eat. Our blankets and clothing were soaked with water: we marched wet, slept wet, and got up in the morning wet."[21]

"Left Wakefield at 9 p.m. and marched twenty miles," another Confederate soldier wrote in his diary on September 19th, 1862. "Laid in the woods without shelter and it raining very hard." He was apparently gifted with a wry sense of humor—"Therefore did not need to wash myself in morning," he concluded. The rain was not just an occasional irritant in the course of his service during the war. A year later almost to the day, he wrote, "Raining hard all day, and no tents. Left camp at 2 in the afternoon, marched six miles, halted at the river, and our regiment went on picket. It is still raining very hard, and we are wet as drowned cats, and cold, too, for we cannot make a fire in front of the enemy."[22]

Soldiers on the other side of the lines in that war knew this miserable existence all too well for themselves. In the lines of battle in Georgia in the winter of 1864, Union Army infantryman Stauffer Nelson wrote in his diary, "Wood scarce, rations scarcer, night cold, nothing to eat." Three days later, his situation had not improved. "Went on fatigue at dark digging rifle pits along the railroad," he wrote, and went on to describe how little rest he and his comrades got, working all day and sleeping in the cold rain with little shelter at night.[23]

The rain falls on the just and unjust alike, as the Scripture says, and soldiers of the Civil War found that the rain spared none of them, whether they wore Union blue or Confederate grey. James Stone served in the Union Army through all four years of the war, and he saw his share of hard days. Of all of them, he remembered a single day's action in 1863 as the worst; the rain, he said, made it the most wretched day of his entire time in the army. "Soon after we started on our return trip it began to rain and it rained in torrents all the first part of the night," he wrote. "That return march was something indescribable. The logs of the corduroy road became very slippery when wet and if I fell flat once I did twenty times that night. That march of thirty-six miles between sunrise and sunrise, fighting a battle, destroying a canal, eighteen miles through a swamp in a terrific heat, and the return eighteen miles in a dark, stormy night, part of the way over a corduroy road, was a test of our powers of endurance we never exceeded during the whole four years of our service."[24] A trooper of the 7th U.S. Cavalry who served in the Indian Wars eleven years after Stone delivered a more succinct, but no less evocative opinion: "A cold spring rain," he said, "is mighty discouraging for both men and horses on a long march."[25]

Rain was hard enough to deal with in its own right. When men had to deal with the sometimes capricious and apparently senseless demands of their commanders, the rain was infused with dimensions of even greater misery. The ponderous and impenetrable machinations of the way that armies moved men from place to place invariably meant long, frustrating periods of waiting to go somewhere else, quite often simply to wait again. By some sadistic happenstance, much of the waiting seemed to happen in the most inclement weather. One Australian soldier of the First World War, remembering his regiment's embarkation for Egypt, wrote, "It was wet, it was cold, it was dark on that wharf. If we were counted once, we were counted fifty times, and for hours we stood in the rain."[26]

It was even more infuriating for the men in the ranks when their senior officers seemed unwilling to subject themselves to the same drenched conditions that they expected the soldiers to endure. Ernest Shephard, a British NCO in the Dorset Regiment during the First World War, wrote in his journal, "At 1 p.m. the whole Bn paraded in marching order and marched to Etinehem via the river bank. It was raining so we had a muddy march. We were to have been inspected at Etinehem by the Army Commander, but on arrival found the inspection was put off, I presume because it was wet." Shephard's feelings on the matter were probably shared by more than one soldier in his battalion—"General evidently did not like rain," he wrote with justified resentment, "but he might have made a show of it and seen us, considering we were wet through."[27]

Enlisted men were not the only ones to feel themselves poorly used by their superiors in bad weather. Captain Roly Grimshaw, a British officer commanding an Indian cavalry troop in France in 1914, wrote in his diary, "Regiment rendezvous. . . . After standing to for four hours in a downpour, we returned to billets. Why not stand to in billets which were only a mile away? This stupid and useless exposure of the men is most injurious." Grimshaw, like many frontline junior officers, had little use for the staff officers whom he blamed for this sort of goat-roping nonsense. "The Staff seem to quite fail to understand," he wrote, fuming with frustration, "that these futile kind of things cause very nearly as many casualties as bullets."[28]

Even when men fell ill, the combination of rain and military intractability often combined to aggravate the torment. "My Irish mate and I both got the flu," a First World War British artilleryman named Fred Lloyd remembered. "We tramped over a mile in pouring rain to the doctor who was in a little bell tent. We went in one side and come out the other: medicine and duty. We had plenty of duty and no medicine."[29] American soldiers had their own experiences with that unsympathetic response to their maladies. Private Donald Carey served with the 339th Infantry in Russia during the U.S. Army's anti-Bolshevik campaign in 1918. When he went on sick call one morning, he had to hike half a mile to the infirmary, where he got iodine and cathartic pills. Adding insult to injury, the doctor then directed that he be exercised two times a day as a form of treatment. "Wading through mud and breathing the cold, damp air in our debilitated condition," he wrote, "it was a miracle that many more of us didn't die."[30]

Soldiers frequently attempted to infuse the inescapable misery with some trace of humor. A popular song during the First World War was "My Little Grey Home in the West." British soldiers in France altered the lyrics to reflect their circumstances: *I've a little wet home in a trench /*

Where the rainstorms continually drench / There's a dead cow close by / With her feet towards the sky / And she gives off a horrible stench. "[31]

Two decades later men fighting in both theaters of the next world war were struggling to cope with the misery-inducing rain in their campaigns. Private Bert Reeves, who served with the British 14th Army, remembered that the seasonal rains in Burma were a test of men's capacity for endurance on almost every level. "I would say that the monsoon not only affected people physically but also morally," he said. "Because of the constant rain if you went to strike a match to light a cigarette you'd find that your box of matches had disintegrated and so also had your cigarettes." Being wet for weeks on end simply wore men down. "That was the monsoon in Burma as I recollect it—just a nightmare."[32]

The men against whom Reeves fought in Burma suffered in the monsoon rains just as much as did their British, Indian, and American adversaries. Manabu Wada was a senior private in the Imperial Japanese Army's 138th Infantry Regiment. He remembered the battle of Kohima as being a particularly hard experience, but in his opinion the challenges of mountain and monsoon were worse than the actual fighting. "The Kohima region is notorious for . . . the heaviest rainfall," he said. "It was impossible to cook rice in the rain." The constant rain made combat operations wretchedly difficult. "When the shelling began," he said, "we entered our 'octopus traps'—holes dug in the ground to a soldier's height—but the rain flooded in so that we were chest-high in water and had to climb out. We felt that we had arrived at the very limit of our endurance." When the shattered remnants of the Japanese Army withdrew from Kohima, the survivors continued to suffer even after they were out of the range of British guns. "Icy rain fell mercilessly on us and we lived night and day drenched to the skin," Wada recalled.[33]

William Walter was a paratrooper in the U.S. Army's 511th Parachute Infantry Regiment (PIR). He remembered the campaign on the island of Leyte, in the Philippines, as "the worst ordeal of my life. You can't imagine. We went over thirty days up in the mountains. It must have rained every day, and if it wasn't raining, the water was dripping off the trees. You were never dry." Decades later the absolute wretchedness of the experience was still stark in his memory. "You were like a pig in a pen, laying in the mud," he said. "We weren't getting fed since we were supplied only by airdrops. They used to drop rations to us, but we were so isolated on the top of this mountain ridge that they couldn't find us. Out of about thirty-three days, they fed us eleven days. We all lost pounds and pounds. We had jungle ulcers on our skin, impetigo. I had dysentery so bad! Actually, the elements were more of an enemy than the Japanese."[34]

Rain made men miserable, and having to live and work and fight in the rain was bad enough. But where there was rain, there was also, inevitably, mud. Of all the things that soldiers remembered as a cause of misery, mud seemed to trump nearly every other irritant. Mud in most situations is an inconvenience or an unpleasant impediment. For soldiers, mud could at times be as daunting an adversary as the enemy against whom they were supposed to be fighting. The thing about mud, as quickly becomes apparent from soldiers' memories, is that it was a factor in training, in travel, and in combat—it was often a constant, inescapable part of the struggle to get through each successive day.

Soldiers of all armies remembered the mud as being something that was sometimes so bad as to be almost indescribable. Raymond Gantter, who fought as an infantryman in the U.S. Army in Europe during the Second World War, probably echoed the thoughts of infantrymen through the ages when he wrote: "Someday someone will write a book about war and tell the truth about the mud . . . how you live in it, sleep in it, eat it and drink it, absorb it through your pores, comb it from your hair and shave it from your face, smell of it, wear it like a skin and like a rose in your lapel."[35]

Eugene Sledge, a U.S. Marine Corps veteran of the Second World War, clearly understood the different aspects of mud. "Mud in camp on Pavuvu was a nuisance," he wrote. "Mud on maneuvers was an inconvenience. But mud on the battlefield was misery beyond description." Sledge had already seen hard service in the battle for Peleliu; he fought next on Okinawa, and he remembered that latter campaign as a muddy horror. "This was my first taste of mud in combat," he wrote, "and it was more detestable than I had ever imagined."[36]

What might not be immediately understood about mud is how it is an almost inevitable consequence of military activity, no matter the era, the century, or the war. Horses and the narrow wheels of horse-drawn artillery, limbers and wagons quickly cut up dirt roads and rendered them all but impassable; in later eras armored vehicles and heavy wheeled traffic tore up wet ground in short order. Artillery, that great killer of the battlefield, was also an earth-turner on a massive scale, especially when operating in water-saturated landscapes like those of Flanders and northern France. The nearly impassable morass of so many battlefields of the First World War was a direct result of the sustained bombardments and rolling barrages that were fired in advance of assaulting troops. But even when armies were not on the move or tearing up the ground in their struggle to get at each other, mud was a soldier's ever-present companion. Just as a footpath in wet weather becomes a sloppy mess when trampled by too many feet, so too would the open, ungraveled ground of a military encampment or bivouac become a muddy quagmire when the rain persisted and men had to keep moving back and forth across it.

It is a common theme in many soldiers' narratives that they found the mud to be almost worse than the violence and danger of combat. Warren Olney was an infantryman in the Union Army during the American Civil War; the mud of the Shiloh battlefield was something he never forgot. "The mud—well, it was indescribable," he wrote. Units in line of march ahead of his battalion, he recalled, "had so cut up the roads that they were quagmires their whole length. Teams were stalled in the mud in every direction. The principle features of the landscape were trees, mud, wagons buried to the hub, and struggling, plunging mule teams." Simple movements in such conditions were hard—long distance movements were nigh impossible.[37]

Battlefields of the First World War were infamous for their mud. On December 5th, 1914, the unknown French soldier whose quote began this chapter wrote another letter home. "It would be impossible to imagine," he wrote to his mother, "such a state of mud."[38] Two years later, on the Somme, a young British infantry officer wrote in a letter to *his* mother: "We have had the hardest week that I have ever been through, and everything has been done under the worst possible conditions. The time that we spent in the front line was awful. It snowed all the first night, and then turned to rain, which continued until we were relieved. The result was that we were up to our ankles in half frozen slush, in the very best part of the trench! Some parts of the trench, along which we had to pass were up to our waists in the worst places (just wet mud!)." Once out of the lines, the mud continued to plague his company. "We had 8 miles to march back to camp," he wrote, "and our greatcoats had about 15 or 20 lbs. of mud on them."[39]

Soldiers on both fronts of the First World War found the mud to be a constant problem. Arthur Empey was an American who enlisted in the British Army before the United States entered the war. In his account of the conditions in the lines in France, he wrote, "That dugout was muddy. The men slept in mud, washed in mud, ate mud, and dreamed mud. I had never before realized that so much discomfort and misery could be contained in those three little letters, MUD."[40] Another soldier who fought under the flag of a different country during that war was John Morse, who served with the Russians fighting against the Germans in Poland. In the spring of 1916, he wrote, "The weather had fairly broken now; the thaw had set in all over the country, and the ground was in a dreadful condition, and scarcely passable for troops, and especially wagons and artillery. In the summer I thought I had never seen such dust as the dust of Poland; in the winter I knew I had never known such horrible mud as the mud of these wide plains."[41]

One of the first civilian correspondents to report on the fighting in France during the First World War was a journalist named Philip Gibbs. The conditions endured by British soldiers, as he described them, were simply awful. "Our men were never dry," he wrote. "They were wet in their trenches and wet in their dugouts. They slept in soaking clothes, with boots full of water, and they drank rain with their tea, and ate mud with their 'bully,' and endured it with all the philosophy of 'grin and bear it' and laughter, as I heard them laughing in those places between explosive curses."[42]

The months-long slaughterhouse of the Somme in 1916 was fought in the comparatively dry months of the summer, but weeks of massed artillery barrages and the regular rains combined to make the shell-cratered terrain one vast cesspool of mud. As the campaign wore on, summer turned to fall and fall to winter, and the mud only deepened. "It's the end of the

1916 winter," one Australian infantryman wrote in his journal, "and the conditions are unbelievable. We live in a world of Somme mud. We sleep in it, work in it, fight in it, wade in it and many of us die in it. We see it, feel it, eat it and curse it, but we can't escape it, not even by dying."[43]

Another Australian soldier who fought at the Somme remembered it in very similar terms. "The Germans had one ally on the Somme that wrought us more havoc than all his armament," he wrote. "How we cursed that mud! We cursed it sleeping, we cursed it waking, we cursed it riding, we cursed it walking. We ate it. . . . We drank it. . . . We swallowed and spat it; we snuffed it and wept it. . . . We wallowed in it, we waded through it. . . . It stuck to our helmets, to our hair, it plastered our wounds, and there were men who drowned in it."[44] Another man described the difficulty of night movements in the mud. "We slip and slide our swearing way through the mud," he wrote. "All is as black as an infantryman's future."[45]

As the fighting at the Somme dragged on through the summer and into the fall of 1916, the conditions only worsened. A British infantry private named Robert Cude expressed something of the horror and abject misery of the mud in his diary. "Owing to abominable rains the trench and cubby holes are caving in," he wrote. "We have 2 or 3 killed by suffocation. . . . Working on building dugouts which cave in before they are finished. As fast as you can dig a hole it fills with water." Outside the trenches conditions were hardly better. "On either side of roads about here," Cude wrote, "there are ditches, and these are overflowing with mud and filth. God help any unfortunate chap who loses the road at night."[46]

The river plains of the Somme were bad, but the terrain around the ruined Flemish town of Passchendaele might have been the absolute worst battlefield ever, at least as far as mud was concerned. Philip Gibbs, whose language was admittedly more that of a professional wordsmith than a soldier, still conveyed the filthy essence of it all when he tried to describe Passchendaele by saying, "All the agonies of war I have attempted to describe were piled up in those fields of Flanders. There was nothing missing in the list of war's abominations." Passchendaele, Gibbs wrote, was "one great bog of slime."[47]

"It was mud, mud everywhere," one British artilleryman wrote: "Every shell-hole was a sea of filthy oozing mud. I suppose there's a limit to everything, but the mud of Passchendaele—to see men sinking into the slime, dying in the slime—I think it absolutely finished me off."[48]

The mud at Passchendaele acquired a malevolent reputation that made it more hated, and sometimes more dangerous, than the human enemy against whom men fought. To many soldiers that mud in Flanders seemed more horrible than the war itself. "A Guards battalion lost sixteen men to the mud in a single month," one historian notes. "They drowned in mud. Their graves, it seemed, just dug themselves and pulled them down."[49] Moving from the rear support areas into the lines was a hellish ordeal that exhausted men long before they could even get into their positions. "The weight of our equipment," one infantryman wrote, "sank us into the soft mud and the only way we got onto the road again was by hanging to the stirrups of the horses as they ploughed a way through... We could not use the communication trenches as they were rivers of liquid mud, but had to wait till dark and go over the top in relieving the front line."[50]

Everyone suffered in the mud, friend and foe united in empathetic misery. "The Germans opposite us in their trenches at Bapaume were, of course, in as bad a plight as we were," one Australian soldier remembered. "When I scouted down their trenches at night I found equipment and stores lying on top of their parapet. Evidently, the mud in the bottom of their trenches was as bad as in ours, and anything dropped had to be fished for."[51] The torrential rains that November caused the rudimentary earthworks of the fighting positions to collapse, and German and British soldiers found themselves exposed to each other's guns. Their reactions were pragmatic, rather than martial. "They ignored one another," Gibbs wrote. "They pretended the other fellows were not there. They had not been properly introduced." Men sat out in the open, trying to dry themselves out as best they could in full view of their enemies, neither side firing a shot by mutual, unspoken agreement. This arrangement lasted only long enough for word of it to filter back to General Headquarters— "where good fires were burning under dry roofs, and stringent orders came against 'fraternization.' The dignity of G.H.Q. would not be outraged by the thought of such indecent spectacles as British and Germans refusing to kill each other on sight."[52] Staff officers could order what they liked, but in the cold, muddy wretchedness of the lines, men were more concerned with their own misery than with official directives.

Sergeant Major Richard Tobin of the Royal Naval Division's Hood Battalion remembered, "There was one place where a little party of men was trying to make their hole more comfortable by scooping it out, and some hundred yards away the Germans were doing exactly the same thing, but both, in their misery, didn't taken any damn notice of each other."[53] German accounts of the wretched conditions in France and Flanders give almost exactly the same impression, but from the other side of no-man's land.

"Is it better to wish for good weather and [artillery] fire or bad weather and bottomless filth?" a German fusilier *leutnant* wondered in his diary. "It rained again last night; it really would be best to pull out of the entire position and leave the mud to the Tommies. But it's just as bad for the Tommies. The infantry of both sides has given up doing anything to each other. It is all they can do to keep the mud at bay. In broad daylight, both we and the enemy climb out above our cover and nobody fires."[54] It was, perhaps, no way to win a war, but at times the misery was so complete that martial aggressiveness was beside the point. There were frequent expressions of empathy in the wretchedness of rain and mud and mire. One German soldier, remembering the awful experience of trying to move into the lines on the Somme, described it by saying "A journey which should have taken twenty to twenty-five minutes cost two to three hours. With each step men sank, literally, up to their knees in the mud... Those who had thus far not learned to curse and swear, certainly did during this approach march." Exhausted and miserable, there was one bright spot to be had in it all. "The only consolation," he wrote, "was that it was every bit as bad for those opposite."[55]

It was indeed as bad for the men on the other side of the lines, but the British, by dint of the ground they held, sometimes had it worse than the Germans. "Because the enemy was on the high ground and our men were in the low ground," Gibbs wrote, "many of our trenches were wet and waterlogged, even in summer, after heavy rain. . . . The enemy drained his water into our ditches when he could, with the cunning and the science of his way of war, and that made our men savage."[56] Gibbs' comment about German field engineering was accurate. Ernst Junger, a German officer on the other side of no-man's land, wrote in his journal: "30 October. Following a torrential downpour in the night, all the traverses came down and formed a grey sludgy porridge with the rain, turning the trench into a deep swamp. Our only consolation was that the British were just as badly off as we were, because we could see them baling out for all they were worth. Since our position has a little more elevation than theirs, we even managed to pump our excess their way."[57] The misery was universal, but the Germans must have been cheered at least a little by being able to contribute a bit more to the wretchedness in the British lines.

There were also moments of one-upmanship, a black humor that tried to laugh when it was hard to find anything at all to laugh about. In the flooded misery of the trenches at Hooge, a German soldier shouted across the few yards that separated him from the British lines, "How deep is it with you?" An English corporal replied, "Up to our blooming knees." The German had the last word on that—"So?" he responded. "You are lucky fellows. We are up to our belts in it."[58]

Two decades later, when men fought over the same ground in World War II, the mud they encountered was not as bad as the pestilential quagmire of the static trench warfare two decades before, but it was bad enough. Soldiers are sometimes surprisingly philosophical in their inclinations, and they can imbue the most mundane subjects with a certain veneer of language, not always profane. "Sometimes," American infantryman Philip Gantter wrote, "the mud in Normandy has the thick, rich creaminess of melted mild chocolate, a quality so smoothly silken that you walk through it with a kind of dreamy pleasure in the lazy gulping and gurgling created by your moving feet. But most of the time it's just plain mud, and you curse it and flounder and splash, and yearn for a comfortable, dry desert."[59] Deserts, one might think, would be the worst sort of place to fight, but most soldiers felt otherwise, including those who experienced both environments.

Eugene Sledge's first combat experience as a U.S. Marine in the Pacific was on the island of Peleliu; his second campaign was the battle for Okinawa. He found that the task of unit resupply presented vastly different problems in the two locations. "Carrying ammo and rations was something the veterans had done plenty of times before," he wrote. "With the others I had struggled up and down Peleliu's unbelievably rugged rocky terrain in the suffocating heat. . . . But this [Okinawa] was my first duty on a working party in deep mud, and it surpassed the drudgery of any working party I had ever experienced." Boxes of rations, five-gallon cans of water that weighed forty-one pounds each, crushingly heavy cases of small arms and mortar ammunition—it all had to be manhandled across ravines and draws filled with mud, down one slippery slope and up another, on and on. "On Okinawa this was often done under enemy fire," Sledge wrote, "in driving rain, and through knee-deep mud for hours on end. Such activity drove the infantrymen, weary from the mental and physical stress of combat, almost to the brink of physical collapse."[60]

On the Eastern Front of World War II, the climate cycled through all the extremes of weather. Hot summers created choking clouds of dust as fine as talcum powder, the freezing winters were colder than anything most men had ever encountered before, and the spring rains turned solid ground to seas of impassable mud. Each was bad enough in its own right, but in terms of lethality, the cold was the most dangerous of the lot. "Cold reduces the efficiency of men and weapons," an official report of the German Wehrmacht stated. "At the beginning of December 1941, 6th Panzer Division was but 9 miles from Moscow and 15 miles from the Kremlin when a sudden drop in temperature to -30 F, coupled with a surprise attack by Siberian troops, smashed its drive on the capital. Paralyzed by cold, the German troops could not aim their rifle fire, and bolt mechanisms jammed or strikers [firing pins] shattered in the bitter winter weather. Machine guns became encrusted with ice, recoil liquid froze in guns, ammunition supply failed. Mortar shells detonated in deep snow with a hollow, harmless thud, and mines were no longer reliable."[61] A German Army victorious in its summer advance found itself absolutely unprepared for the savage harshness of the Russian winter.

Hitler might have disregarded the lessons of the past, but German military historians were well aware of the lethality of Russia's infamous cold. One hundred thirty years before the Germans invaded Russia, Napoleon had attempted and failed in the same gambit. Falling back from Moscow in the bitter cold of November 1812, the Grande Armee suffered and starved all along the route of their shambling withdrawal. Mostly, though, they just froze—literally froze. During the long agony of the retreat, more men died of hypothermia, exposure, and the effects of frostbite than perished from the depredations of the Cossack cavalry or in battle with the pursuing Russian army. One French soldier wrote that the paltry fires they were able to light with considerable difficulty "did not succeed in warming us." The best the men could manage was to be "frozen on one side, scorched on the other, suffocated by the smoke."[62] The miserable night this soldier was describing was only the *first* very cold night, that of 6 November 1812.

Six terrible weeks of arctic cold and intense suffering followed before the shattered remnants of the Grande Armee reached safety. Night after night, temperatures plunged into the −30 degree F range, and men froze to death by the thousands. Even the Russians suffered in the intense cold—one Russian lieutenant wrote in his diary "Men and horses are dying of hunger and exhaustion. . . . Our horses, which have no shoes, slip on the frozen ground and fall down, never to get up." The starved, frozen remnants of the Grande Armee that survived the horror of the 1812 retreat bore no resemblance to the army that Napoleon had assembled for his ill-fated invasion of Russia. One French soldier wrote of the ragged survivors: "Our faces were hideous, yellow and smoked, smeared with earth, blackened by the greasy smoke of pine fires, the eyes hollow, the beard covered with snot and ice. We could not use our hands to button our trousers, and many fastened them with a cord. We were all indescribably filthy." And these were the lucky ones, the men who were still alive. "Such was the spectacle presented by an army, which, eight months before, had been the finest in the world," this soldier wrote.[63] Napoleon's eastward aspirations were destroyed by the ice-edged force of Russia's mythical General Winter.

One hundred thirty years later, Hitler's eastward ambitions were defeated by the combination of General Winter and Field Marshal Mud. The German field command in 1941–1942 struggled to adapt its men to these incredibly harsh conditions while they were still locked in combat with the Soviet Army, but the list of challenges was lengthy. "A war of movement is difficult in deep snow," a Wehrmacht report noted. "Foot marches in twenty inches of snow are slow; in depths of more than twenty inches they are exhausting. When snow was not too deep, the Germans used details of soldiers in shifts to tramp down snow trails. . . . The Russians used T34 tanks to pack down snow; the tracks used on German tanks during the first year of the war were too narrow for this purpose. Movements on foot or with wheeled vehicles are impossible in snow depths above forty inches... Hard-frozen snow, however, can be used only for night movement, because the approach of troops over snow crust can be heard at a great distance. Snow in bushland, draws, and ditches will not support much weight."[64]

German soldiers suffered terribly from the winter cold. They had neither the right sort of winter clothing nor the proper equipment, and they were not trained for operations in near-arctic conditions. "We Germans," a *Panzerjaeger* named Hans Roth wrote in the winter of 1941, "are not used to winter combat in freezing temperatures and all of this mud."[65] Frostbite and exposure casualties were widespread: "A panzer division near Volokolamsk in January 1942," one official report said, "had up to 800 frostbite casualties a day." In situations of extreme cold, the occasional warming trend could be lethal. "Boots, socks and trousers that had become wet during the day stiffened with the night cold and froze toes and feet. Serious frost injuries developed when troops overheated from combat were forced to spend the night in snow pits or windswept open fields. . . . A German company that spent a day during a thaw entrenching itself lost sixty-five of its ninety-three men as a result of a sudden severe cold wave at night."[66] In the first week of January 1942, the German Fourth Army had sustained two thousand casualties from frostbite; in that same period, it lost only half as many men to enemy action.

For the soldiers who were trying to fight in these conditions, life deteriorated into a dogged struggle for survival. "What does it all amount to, such words like fighting, and exertion?" Panzerjaeger Roth wrote in his journal. "What can the words snow, bitter cold, ice, loneliness, mental burden, blizzard, freezing, and poor roads, possibly mean compared to the reality?"[67] Another German soldier, Karl Meding, recalled spending several weeks in a static position where his only shelter was a hole in the ground. The temperature plummeted to -40 degrees Celsius. "At night . . .

one of us used to go fetch food," Meding wrote. "We used to put the food in our pockets in the hope of keeping it warm, but it didn't work. Butter and bread froze solid. We froze. Everything froze."[68]

To add to the physical strain of battle and the dangers of hypothermia and frostbite, there was also the mental pressure of fighting against an enemy who did not seem to suffer nearly as much from the freezing cold. "Russian troops," a Wehrmacht report noted, "seemed to be particularly immune to extreme cold."[69] It went on to observe that Soviet snipers were known to hold their positions for extended periods of time even when temperatures dropped to −50 degrees Fahrenheit, conditions in which most German troops were no longer combat effective.

Men were not the only ones to suffer from the cold. German horses could not endure the freezing weather, unless they were the hardier breeds acquired from northern climes. Weapons and machines failed when needed most. "German rifles and machine guns developed malfunctions because the grease and oil used were not cold-resistant," a German after-action report stated. "Strikers [firing pins] and striker springs broke like glass, fluid in artillery recoil mechanisms solidified, crippling the piece. Light weapons had to be warmed in huts, and fires were lighted under the barrels of guns to get them back into action. Before suitable lubricants were available, troops found an emergency solution in the removal of every trace of grease and oil from their weapons."[70] A year into the eastern campaign, Hans Roth wrote in his journal: "I can't imagine that you could earn your daily bread in a way more difficult than this."[71]

Like the Grande Armee of Napoleon in 1812, entire German armies were consumed by the Russian winter. But it was not only the winter that made the experience so hellish for the men who fought there—Russia was a land of constantly shifting extremes. "We have been spared nothing by this land," Roth wrote. "The summer fighting commenced in pouring rain, which filled all our holes with muddy water, making the muck greedily hold on to every step and covering our uniforms with a crusty armor of dirt. Then came July with its scorching heat and the fine, flour-like dust; now the dampness of the rainy, fall days is sweeping over the trenches and the crater landscapes, only to be soon again replaced by the ice and snow of the merciless Russian winter. We are not facing this second year of the Russian campaign as fresh and naïve as we once were."[72] Roth, like so many German soldiers who fought on the Eastern Front, never saw Germany again—Russia was his graveyard. He was killed on the Eastern Front in 1943.

What German soldiers encountered on the Eastern Front during the Second World War would have been familiar to veterans of the First World War who had fought in the east twenty years earlier. John Morse, the Englishman fighting with the Russians in Poland in 1916, found the cold to be far worse than the snow. "Sometimes when there were blizzards, the trenches were nearly filled with drifted snow," he wrote, "and more than once the men were buried above their waists. This was an inconvenience from the military point of view, but the men did not object to it as it kept them warm." This might have been true of prepared positions, but Morse discovered that when it was necessary to dig new positions during the winter, the extreme cold made an already difficult task impossible. "It has been said that there is no such word as 'impossible' in the military vocabulary," he wrote, "but the forces of Nature are frequently not to be overcome, not even by military pluck and perseverance. Not even a soldier can dig holes in solid steel; and the ground in Poland was hardly less solid and difficult to work: hence trenches were not made after the early days of December, nor the dead buried as a rule."[73]

Frozen ground made the selection of tactical positions as much a matter of expedient availability as discerning choice. Once the winter freeze set in, Morse remembered, "the rule was to stick to the old trenches; or to occupy those naturally formed by hollows of the ground, or the deep banks of water-courses." Living in these places for extended lengths of time led to new problems. "As wet could not soak away through the frozen ground the condition at the bottoms of those trenches which had been occupied for any length of time was filthy in the extreme. Dirty water, blood and refuse, was being continually added to the loathsomeness already existing, and this, and the constant trampling of the men, prevented the freezing of the mass."[74]

Fighting in winter was bad enough, but winter warfare in mountainous terrain presented no end of troubles for soldiers who were expected to operate in that terrain. One of the greatest military disasters of the

First World War (and also one of the least well known to general history) was the catastrophe that befell the Ottoman forces at Sarikamish during the Caucasus Campaign. An ill-prepared, poorly equipped, and incompetently led Turkish army undertook an offensive against the Russians in the Allahuekber Mountains that straddled the border between the Russian Empire and the Ottoman Empire. The campaign played out from December 1914 to mid-January 1915, the height of winter—if there was a worse time to fight in that rugged terrain, it would be hard to argue for it.

Turkish soldiers died by the thousands, their ragged columns strung out through the snow-choked mountains, all discipline and military cohesion gone as they tried to escape the encircling Russians. Just how many men died in the debacle is uncertain—official Turkish accounts claimed twenty-three thousand combat casualties and ten thousand dead of other causes; one German report set the losses at ninety thousand dead, which is frankly too high to be taken seriously. It does seem clear that as many as thirty thousand Turkish soldiers froze to death in the mountains, killed by the weather rather than Russian guns. By the time the shambles of the Ottoman forces staggered out of the mountains, only forty-two thousand men remained of an army of 118,000. In one more act of tragedy piled on top of tragedy, the Turkish survivors were ravaged by an outbreak of typhus. Thousands of men who had survived the horrors of Sarikamish died in filthy field hospitals, completing the disaster of one of the worst campaigns in modern warfare.

Winters were also harsh in the west, even if not as lethal. Holding positions on the Somme in the winter of 1916, one Australian soldier wrote in his diary: "Morning breaks, freezing cold as usual. Our damp blankets are frozen stiff on top of our sleeping bodies. We threw our wet boots into a corner last night and now we can't get our feet into them as the leather has become frozen as hard as iron whilst we slept. Not a budge or a bend can we get out of them. We search our pockets for letters and burn a couple inside each boot and it thaws out enough to be tugged on." The experience provided a painful lesson—"We'll use our boots as pillows in future," he wrote.[75]

The Germans on the other side of no-man's land found the Somme to be just as miserable an experience. A German sergeant named Friedrich Oehme wrote in his diary, "In rain and cold; without overcoats or blankets; without anything warm to drink . . . we spent three days in the line." The experience was a terrible one, and the constant cycle of going into the trenches wore even the best units down to exhaustion. "Spare me from giving any description of the condition of that company of men," Oehme wrote, "frozen, dead-tired, and broken down by shell fire." Like many men who suffered in the Somme, Oehme did not long survive it. He was killed there on October 25, 1916.[76]

The last winter of the Second World War was particularly hard for men in Western Europe. Soldiers fighting in the Ardennes during the German counteroffensive in the winter of 1944–1945 endured heavy snow and freezing conditions. Philip Gantter described the difficulties encountered in just trying to move through the snow. "We had to break trail the entire distance through knee-deep, waist-high snow," he wrote. "It was a dull, teeth-gritting monotony of hard work. It's difficult now to describe it—the intense cold, the feather-bed thickness of snow that made every step a reluctant persuasion, the darkness that was hard and real, pressing against your eyeballs... and always the fear of getting lost, of drifting away from the line of moving men that you could neither see nor hear in the blackness of the noisy night."[77]

In the frozen fastness of winter campaigns, men tried to stomp the blood back into their frozen feet as they prayed for the return of the sun and tried to remember what it felt like to be warm. In the spring the rains turned frozen ground into swamps, and soldiers cursed the foul, stinking mud they foundered in. Summer brought searing heat and clouds of fouling dust, and they sweated and longed for the cooler months. Each season, in its inevitable turn, was infused with its own particular sort of misery.

Summer brought its own forms of suffering. The Gallipoli campaign in 1915 began in the comparative mildness of an April spring, but the good weather did not last. By mid-June, the peninsula was searing hot, dry, dust-covered, and reeking of decay, rot, and excrement. Things were no better in the trenches of France. Even there, where the war was most often characterized by conditions of cold and wet, summer heat could still be a factor. A photograph in the collection of the British Imperial War Museum shows German troops in August 1914 advancing across a field in open order, the dust heavy in the air and the sun beating down on them in their woolen uniforms.

Tropical conditions prevailed in much of Asia and the Pacific islands which were battlefields in the Second World War—war in those latitudes meant that men fought in sweltering heat, when they were not drenched in the seasonal monsoons. Casualties from heat exhaustion, heatstroke, and dehydration were as frequent as combat-related wounds, and often more so. Where men in the cold wet of trenches in France had suffered from trench foot during the First World War, soldiers in many campaigns of the Second World War were plagued by jungle rot, heat rashes, and topical infections from the nearly constant humidity.

To add insult to proverbial injury, the hardships inflicted by bad weather were often supplemental doses of misery joined to the already severe difficulties that came with conducting combat operations in harsh terrain. Mountains and jungles were especially hard to fight in, and mountainous jungles were a special kind of hell in their own right. Most armies that came from countries with high mountain regions developed and trained specialized mountain troops—the German *Gebirgsjager*, the Italian *Alpini,* the Romanian *Vanatori de Munte,* or Mountain Rifles, who fought with the Axis on the Eastern Front, and the U.S. Army's 10th Mountain Division were all examples of these types of formations. However, these units comprised only small percentages of their armies' overall strengths, and more often than not battles in mountains were fought by troops who had no special training in that type of terrain.

Senior Private Manabu Wada of the Japanese Army's 138th Infantry Regiment fought through the Arakan Mountains of Burma and thought it was the most difficult experience he encountered in the entire war. "Conditions were hard, well-nigh impossible," he remembered. "At 3,000 meters the mountains were shrouded in freezing cloud.... Matches struck at this altitude went out immediately, so we could not light cooking fires or boil water." The Japanese infantry were utterly unprepared for operations in this terrain. Their commanders, Wada said, "sent us into the mountains without any proper climbing equipment or clothing."[78]

Allied soldiers fighting against the Japanese in Burma found the conditions equally hard. Regular infantry maneuvers were tough enough in that terrain, but the deep penetration operations conducted by special units such as Merrill's Marauders of the U.S. Army and the British Chindits subjected men to even greater hardships. Once in action behind Japanese lines, there was nothing to do but press on or die, and the rugged terrain was a never-ending challenge. "Even if you went downhill you knew you had to go uphill again and we were carrying sixty to seventy pounds on our backs," one Chindit officer recalled. "It was—really I cannot explain—you think would it ever end? It just went on and on and on and the rain and of course the fear that you would be ambushed or attacked, and hungry—I was young then I was always hungry."[79] Men who were wounded or injured too badly to walk were left beside the trail with a canteen of water, their weapons, and a hand grenade. It was expected that they would kill themselves, rather than fall into Japanese hands. Medical evacuation was simply impossible during the first Chindit operation, and men were lost who might have been saved in later campaigns under similar conditions.

The Italian campaign of the Second World War was another cauldron of hardships. Soldiers locked in the savage fighting of the Apennines would have readily nominated the mountains of the Italian Peninsula for the distinction of being the worst battlefield terrain of the war. The conditions encountered in the fighting around the ancient Benedictine monastery at Monte Cassino were brutal—the challenges of the terribly rugged, mountainous landscape were compounded by the fiercely fought, tenacious defense of the German *Fallschirmjaegers* who held the high ground. The fighting for another mountain strongpoint, Monte Cairo, is not nearly so well-known to history but was every bit as horrendous an experience for the men who fought there.

Monte Cairo was a terrible place to fight, at least from the attacker's point of view. The rocky terrain prevented the digging of fighting positions or trenches below ground level—the only cover that could be constructed was in the form of sangars made from walls of rock and stones. Even these were shelters of dubious efficacy, since German artillery had registered the ground in front of Monte Cairo so accurately that daylight movement was impossible without drawing immediate and effective fire.

A British soldier of the Irish Guards remembered how difficult even simple things like relieving oneself were during the battle for Monte Cairo. "We were many times better off than the battalion directly facing the monastery, where throwing the contents of his lavatory tin out of the back of his sangar earned many a man a hail of mortar bombs. Just try sharing a rock hole about the size of two coffins with three others, then, in a prone position, lower your costume and fill a small tin held in the hand. The stink of excrement competed with the smell of death in every position. Bowels will not wait for nightfall."[80]

This Guardsman raised a subject that many histories have omitted as being either too unimportant or too indelicate—the matter of bodily functions while in battle or on the march. For soldiers themselves, the problems associated with the regular, inevitable need to urinate or defecate were of paramount importance. More often than not, what was usually a simple and private function in normal life became a difficult, very public, and sometimes extremely dangerous activity. It also became the occasional subject of poetry, as in Rudyard Kipling's *Epitaphs*.

In static, frontline conditions where artillery and direct small arms fire were constant threats, a man who left his hole or trench to relieve himself might not live long enough to pull his trousers back up. As one British NCO noted in his sector of trench in France in 1915, "to get up . . . in daylight would be, well, asking for the Huns to put daylight into one."[81] Men of a sensitive or cultivated nature either quickly got over their inhibitions or did not and suffered the fate of the narrator in Kipling's poem. A veteran of the fighting at Passchendaele, a British lieutenant in the Devonshire Regiment, described the wretched and inadvertently egalitarian conditions of living for weeks on end in a hole in the ground with other men. "If, for instance, you wanted to urinate and otherwise," he said, "there was an empty bully beef tin kept on the side of the hole, so you had to do it in front of all your men then chuck the contents, but not the tin, over the back." He also recalled that the practice of sending up tea for the men in the front lines predictably resulted in mass outbreaks of diarrhea, since the tea was transported in old petrol tins that contaminated the drink no matter how often they were cleaned.[82]

In the troglodytic conditions of Passchendaele, where men lived in mud-filled shell holes (it was absolutely impossible to dig conventional trenches in that waterlogged ground), no one could leave their positions when they were racked by an attack of diarrhea. Soldiers defecated in the ubiquitous bully beef tins and threw the liquid waste over the rim of their hole. "The men were hardened, but the life was terrible," the Devonshire lieutenant remembered. "Another extra chore was that lime had to be spread on the back of the posts because open excreta was being chucked out and if you didn't put down lime then when you came crawling out you'd be covered in it."[83]

Even in some rear areas of the Western Front, safety was a relative concept so long as one was still within range of the enemy's guns. A Five-Nine shell did not defer to rank, and it made no distinctions for those moments when a man might be indisposed by a call of nature. One British officer recalled seeing a German shell detonate on the officers' latrine in the rear artillery lines—it blew the crapper all to hell and gone in a massive explosion. "I was shocked to see a man still sitting there on the throne," he wrote, "and I thought he must be dead. I ran as hard as I could and arrived to find Ellison up and adjusting his trousers. He said with a grin, 'It was lucky that the shell came when it did as I was feeling a bit constipated.'"[84] It was not the first time shellfire could have been said to loosen a man's bowels, but in this case, it at least happened in a convenient setting. It was also not the only time a soldier found himself under fire while indelicately indisposed.

Ernst Junger, a First World War German company commander promoted from the ranks, described the latrine that was positioned behind his unit's trench as being particularly vulnerable to fire. At times, he wrote, "stray bullets from all directions seemed to have arranged a rendezvous for themselves at the latrine, so that we were often compelled to flee, holding a newspaper and trousers at half-mast. And for all that, it seemed not to have occurred to anyone to move this indispensable facility to a place of greater safety."[85]

The call of nature could not be denied, even when it came at the most inopportune moments, and the height of battle was certainly a bad time to be stricken with a bout of diarrhea. During the battle of Talavera in the Peninsular War in 1809, with both sides heavily engaged and the fighting well underway, a British officer found himself in just such a situation. As the commanding officer of an artillery battery that happened to be under heavy fire at that moment, he felt he could not go to the rear to relieve himself lest his men think he was trying to escape the ferocious cannonade of the French guns. Rather than going behind his battery, then, he "deliberately walked a hundred yards or so in front of the brigade, and disembarrassing himself of part of his clothing, yielded to the irresistible necessity of the case, after readjusting his dress, and calmly putting on his sword and sash, he returned leisurely to his post. The transaction excited a great deal of mirth, notwithstanding the heat of the action."[86]

The rise of mechanized warfare added its own complications to the requirements of human physiology. As one New Zealand tank commander recalled of the fighting at Monte Cassino in Italy in 1943, "One of the other things, from a humorous point of view, was that it was difficult to sort of carry out the demands of nature when you were in the tank all day, and so when you thought you required to do something you put a shell up the spout, shoot off at something, wait until the shell case cooled down, and then you used it for a urinal and you put it out through the little hatch." Even with that expedient solution to the problem, however, he noted that "you can imagine, with five men in a tank, the smell and stench weren't particularly good."[87]

The biological imperative of defecation was more than a dangerous inconvenience in battle—it also created health hazards in other ways. The fighting at Gallipoli was never characterized by mud and cold; rather, it was a hellish environment of heat and dust and flies, flies on a biblical scale, reminiscent of the fourth plague of Egypt. The flies were the result of the profusion of human excrement and rotting corpses that littered the contested ground. Drawn by the thousands of unburied bodies and the open slit-trench latrines, flies covered everything—the ground, equipment, food, and the men themselves. "One of the biggest curses was flies," one soldier wrote of Gallipoli. "Millions and millions of flies. The whole side of the trench used to be one black swarming mass. Anything you opened, like a tin of bully, would be swarming with flies. . . . They were all around your mouth and on any cuts or sores that you'd got, which then turned septic."[88]

"There were more flies on the [Gallipoli] Peninsula than there was sand on the shore," an Australian soldier wrote, "and they fought us persistently for every atom of food. Getting a meal was a hard day's work, for all the time you had to fight away the swarms, and no matter how quick you were with your fork, you rarely got a mouthful that hadn't been well walked over, and it didn't do to think where those flies had been walking just previously."[89] The flies laid eggs, which quickly hatched into maggots that infested the floors of the trenches where rotting corpses were covered by only an inch or two of dirt. "We lived in a headquarters of maggots," another soldier wrote, "pale, wriggling, stinking, blasted things. As we sat on our ledge we watched the trench floor heaving with them."[90] Another soldier who endured the hellish ordeal of Gallipoli wrote, "Maggots are falling into the trench now. They are not the squashy yellow ones; they are big brown hairy ones."[91]

The flies feeding on decomposing corpses and human excrement were disease vectors that spread an epidemic of diarrhea which the troops called "the Gallipoli Trots," or "the Gallipoli Gallop." As dysentery spread through the ranks, the slit trench latrines became a stinking horror. "If you'd looked in the latrines you'd have been sickened," one British soldier said. "You'd think people had parted with their stomach or their insides. It was awful."[92]

"Dysentery was a truly awful disease that could rob a man of the last vestiges of human dignity before it killed him," wrote Joe Murray, a Royal Naval Division infantryman who fought at Gallipoli and later in France. "A couple of weeks before getting it my old pal was as smart and upright as a guardsman. Yet after about ten days it was dreadful to see him crawling about, his trousers round his feet, his backside hanging out, his shirt all soiled—everything was soiled. He couldn't even walk.

"So I took him by one arm and another pal got hold of him by the other, and we dragged him to the latrine. It was degrading, when you remember how he was just a little while ago. Neither my other pal nor I were very good—but we weren't like that. Anyway, we lowered him down next to the latrine. We tried to keep the flies off him and to turn him round—put his backside towards the trench. But he simply rolled into this foot-wide trench, half-sideways, head first in the slime. We couldn't pull him out, we didn't have enough strength, and he couldn't help himself at all. We did eventually get him out but he was dead, he'd drowned in his own excrement."[93] In the long terrible litany of bad ways to die, that might well have been one of the worst ways imaginable.

Soldiers fighting in the jungles of Burma, the Philippines, Guadalcanal, and other battlefields of the Pacific Theater in the Second World War were frequently ravaged by amoebic dysentery, malaria, dengue fever, cholera, and other tropical diseases. When it was possible, sick men were sent to the rear, but in many situations medical evacuation was simply not an option. It was not an uncommon thing to see wasted, exhausted men still carrying their weapons and still in the fight, but with the seats cut out of their uniform trousers because they were stricken with nearly uncontrollable diarrhea.

Similar expedients were adopted by some men during the horrific experience of the Grande Armee's retreat from Moscow in 1812. The extreme cold made simple tasks difficult, and essential tasks unbelievably challenging, so much so that men resorted to cutting open the seams of the backs of their trousers in order to be able to defecate without having to lower their breeches. Those who did not adopt this expediency sometimes found themselves in a terrible predicament. "Men who walked to the side of the road and unbuttoned their pants in order to answer the call of nature, a frequent one since many of them had diarrhea," wrote Adam Zamoyski, in his masterful study of the 1812 campaign, "would find to their horror that they were unable to button them up again."[94] One French officer wrote of seeing "several soldiers and officers who could not button themselves up"; their frozen fingers simply were not up to the task. "I myself helped to dress and button up one of these unfortunates, who was weeping like a child," he remembered.[95]

German soldiers on the Eastern Front in the Second World War also found that the simple act of defecating could be almost impossibly difficult in the bitter cold of the Russian winter. Frost-numbed fingers could barely manipulate buttons, even partially divesting oneself of the necessary layers of clothing that kept one from freezing to death made every bowel movement an exhausting process, and exposed flesh could freeze unbelievably quickly. That reality continues to this day, in certain climates, and more than one modern soldier, after months in the field, has listed a flushable toilet in a warm room as one of life's greatest luxuries.

In addition to the physical miseries of bad weather and illness, soldiers in many campaigns also suffered the harassing and sometimes debilitating effects of verminous infestations. Lice were an infamous torment for soldiers in every army of the First World War, but the reality was that soldiers in almost every other era also encountered those maddening, miniscule pests. There were also mosquitoes, leeches, rats, and sometimes snakes and scorpions to contend with. Soldiers fighting in Spain during the Peninsular War encountered many of these. One British infantryman remembered, "All day long we were infested by snakes, blowflies, and other vermin, while our water came from a dirty stream . . . in which the whole army bathed, the cattle went to drink, and dirty clothes were washed. At night we were plagued by scorpions, mosquitoes, and a piercingly cold wind."[96]

Even before it was clearly understood that flies were carriers of disease, their presence was a veritable torment for soldiers in some campaigns. Fighting against the French in Egypt in 1801, one Scottish soldier wrote, "Among the many annoyances to which we were subject, there was one of Egypt's ancient plagues—that of flies. . . . These insects are exceedingly numerous, and withal, somewhat dangerous." If there was one thing that the average infantryman was capable of, though, it was a certain rough ingenuity. "We caught a number of chameleons among the bushes," this Scotsman remembered, "which rid us in a great measure of these noxious insects within the tents."[97]

French soldiers retreating from Moscow in 1812 suffered from exposure, starvation, and disease, but they were also tormented by lice and other vermin; one sergeant of the Imperial Guard wrote that when one of his men brought him some rushes to sleep on one night, he was immediately infested with ferociously biting bugs. A German soldier serving with the French Army during that retreat described how the intense cold kept the lice in a dormant state "as long as we were out in the cold and walking." On the rare occasions when he could warm himself even a little, however, the vermin stirred to life with a vengeance. Crouched over campfires at night, he said, "life would return to these insects, which would then inflict intolerable tortures on us."[98] A French officer in the same army wrote, "Horrible itching would keep us awake half the night and drive us mad. It had become so intolerable that as a result of scratching myself I had torn the skin of a part of my back."[99]

For soldiers of the First World War, lice were a veritable plague. Long after the war one British soldier, Albert Marshall, said, "If you asked me the worst thing about the war, I would say it was the lice. The shells didn't worry me—the snipers didn't worry me—the Germans didn't worry me. The lice worried me. You were smothered with them."[100] Part of the problem stemmed from the lack of basic hygiene—Marshall recalled that he only had two real baths in three years, and his case was by no means unique.

"Lice?" another British soldier remembered, "I didn't have lice. They had me."[101] Harry Patch, of the Duke of Cornwall's Light Infantry, said, "The lice were the size of grains of rice, each with its own bite, each with its own itch.... For the four months I was in France I never had a bath, and I never had any clean clothes to put on."[102] In those conditions, men were infested with lice almost as soon as they went into the line. Short of burning their clothing and getting out of the trenches for good, nothing alleviated the problem. Some men sent back to England for an antilice powder that was advertised as "good for body lice." "It really was good [for lice]," an American soldier in the British ranks noted wryly. "They seemed to absolutely thrive on the stuff."[103]

The static nature of the First World War's battlefields made lice and flies a nearly constant problem, but the higher mobility of the fighting in the Second World War did not mean a complete release from verminous infestations. Men in the jungles of Southeast Asia found that the climate there brought with it additional hardships. "The dampness of the jungle used to bring the leeches out," a British soldier wrote. "They used to go up through your gaiters on to your body and they'd go all over your body."[104] Men worried obsessively about the possibility of getting a leech in their penises or anuses; it almost never happened, but the thought of it was enough to invoke paranoia and serious discussions of how best to deal with such a calamity if ever it did occur.

All of these things—rain, mud, cold, heat, vermin, sickness, and exhaustion—were the common experience of many soldiers of the period. All were endured in their turn, until for some men the days blurred into each other in an indistinguishable flow of filth and misery. Some of them found that the realities of this existence defied their powers of description, but still many of them tried to explain to people back home just how awful it could be. The anonymous French soldier whose letters opened this chapter repeatedly tried to convey the wretched realities of war in his missives to his family. He was an articulate young man with the language that came of a good education, but even he found the misery to be more than mere words could describe. "War in rain," he wrote. "It is suffering beyond what can be imagined. Three days and three nights without being able to do anything but tremble and moan." What made the physical misery even worse, he thought, were the added dangers inherent in war. "To sleep in a ditch full of water has no equivalent in Dante," he wrote to his mother in September 1914, "but what can be said of the awakening, when one must watch for the moment to kill or be killed."[105] His moment came seven months later. He was killed on April 6, 1915; his body was never recovered or identified, and his mother was never able to learn how her son had died.

Chapter Twelve

The Fog of War

CONFUSION AND CHAOS ARE CONSTANT ELEMENTS in warfare; battle, by its very nature, is a maelstrom of lethal pandemonium. A considerable amount of command effort in battle is expended in the constant attempt to simply understand what is happening, what one's own troops are doing, and what the enemy is doing or is about to do. Soldiers live and die, more often than one might think, without ever fully understanding what is going on to their left or right, to their rear, or in front of them beyond the scope of what they themselves can actually see. Howard Dunfee, an American infantryman of the Second World War, remembered his combat experience by saying, "We never knew. Hell, when you're in the war, what happens to you on that particular day is your war. . . . I was a private so I didn't have too much information of what's going on."[1] The commanders at the upper echelons have the big-picture view of battle, but even they are quite often unsure as to what is happening right in the moment. War, for most soldiers, is a murky haze dimly perceived and incompletely understood, apart from the small vignettes of individual, personal experience. This is the notorious "fog of war."

The confusion manifests itself in many ways, but three aspects in particular are worth considering. First, there is the confusion that comes from operational conditions—inclement weather or darkness that limits one's ability to see and move. Second, there is command and informational confusion—when orders are not forthcoming or are unclear and the flow of information is disrupted or unreliable so that one does not fully understand what is going on or why, or when the chaos of the fighting disrupts the plan. Finally, and most tragically, there is the matter of fratricide—friendly fire, when men are killed by their own side in moments of colossal and fatal error.

The modern infantry doctrine of preferably and deliberately fighting at night is a relatively recent development in warfare. For the most part, armies of past eras have restricted themselves to full-scale operations only in hours of daylight. The U.S. Army's infantry mantra is "We own the night," but the American military did not adopt night fighting as a mainstream tactical doctrine until after the Second World War. To be sure, military minds have always recognized the value of nocturnal raids and stealthy patrols to capitalize either on the cover of darkness or the element of surprise, but as a general rule few pitched battles were deliberately fought at night in the centuries before this period, for the simple reason that in darkness it was simply too hard to control the fight once it began.

Darkness amplifies all the normal, natural tensions of military operations, because the dark contains the enemy, and the enemy intends to kill you. The night, in war, is the equivalent of old maps that contained blank sections of terra incognito, marked "here be dragons." If there is any comfort for soldiers who have to deal with this situation, it is that his enemy is usually confronting the same tensions and fears. The feeling of lying in darkness, straining to decipher the dangerous noises from the innocuous ones, knowing that violent death is nearby, unseen and maybe drawing nearer, is something almost impossible to describe in words. Soldiers of all armies, of all eras, knew it all too well. A Russian soldier who fought in the Russo-Turkish War of 1878 wrote of one occasion when the Turks made a night attack on his position, "It was so dark that you couldn't see your hand before you," he wrote, "but you could hear something flowing up like a wave and surging, but you couldn't see to fire."[2] The fight in the dark, he recalled, was nearly as terrifying as the waiting in the dark.

It is hard to describe, to someone who has never personally experienced it, how unsettling and anxiety-provoking it is to try and move at night in darkness that is total or nearly so, barely able to see the man to your front as you pick your way across rough terrain, hoping that the man at the front of the formation actually knows where the hell *he's* going. Do it at night in hostile territory, with the possibility of an ambush or a chance encounter with the enemy, and the tension ratchets up several heart-pounding degrees. There is always, as one American soldier wrote, "the fear of getting lost, of drifting away from the line of moving men you could neither see nor hear in the blackness of the noisy night."[3]

Infantrymen were particularly acquainted with this experience throughout the period, but the darkness of night held dangers for soldiers in all of the combat arms. On the night before the Battle of the Little Bighorn, June 25, 1876, the troopers of the U.S. 7th Cavalry broke camp to move into what they hoped would be a good striking position within reach of the large Indian encampment their scouts had advised them of. It was dark, men later recalled, so dark that maintaining troop cohesion was no easy task. "It was pitch dark when we started out again, around 11:30 that night," one sergeant remembered. "You couldn't see twenty feet ahead of you. The best we could do was to follow along behind the troop ahead, letting the rattle of the tin cups and carbines on the saddles guide you."[4]

Night movements across broken terrain or within range of the enemy's guns were even harder, harder still when both of those conditions combined. In the static trench lines of France during the First World War, units usually came out of the lines or moved up into the lines during hours of darkness, in order to screen themselves from the observation of German artillery. It could be a wretchedly difficult undertaking.

Ernest Shephard recorded one such unit relief in his service diary. "It was the worst night I have experienced yet," he wrote, "very heavy lightning and thunder, and a deluge of rain. We made across country and had great difficulty to find our way as the darkness was intense, and lightning blinding. . . . Spent a miserable and bewildering night. We were all soaked and the trenches were over our knees in water and mud. In addition to this our sector of trenches are a perfect maze." Even though he had seen the area before, Shephard found the disorientation of darkness and rain to be nearly absolute. "Fortunately we had visited the place in daylight, but still we only had a vague idea of our position," he wrote.[5]

The pockmarked, shell-cratered mud of battlefields in France made simple movements incredibly grueling challenges. Alec Reader, a British soldier whose unit was doing its stint on work details while it was rotated out of the trenches, recalled the sheer effort required just to get back to his battalion's area after a detail. "The journey back was a farce," he wrote; "we had to hang on to each other's coat-tails, it was too dark to see. When one chap went down, he pulled about a dozen with him. . . . The guide kept losing the path and once we found that the rear had lost touch."[6] Doing this night after night when they weren't even in the forward area of the trenches pushed men to the brink of exhaustion, and well past it, very quickly.

For soldiers who went out ahead of their lines on raiding parties or on scouting missions, the disorientation could be even more acute and the hazards deadlier. The need for silence was absolute. Any sound could draw fire from the enemy's sentries, which could in turn provoke return fire from one's own side, and a cross fire, as more than one soldier has observed, is no place for an honest man to be. Even experienced men found the wasteland between the opposing trenches to be nearly impossible to navigate in darkness. "There is nothing so easy as to be lost in No Man's Land," one Australian soldier wrote. "A compass is useless, for you may be lying on a fifteen-inch shell just covered with a few inches of earth, and the stars refuse to look down on its pain, and the sky is always thickly veiled. Turn round three times, and you don't know which trench to return to." In such situations, the most a man could do was put his hopes in divine guidance or blind luck, whichever his personal beliefs preferred. "It is an awkward predicament," this man wrote, "and many a time I went blindly forward praying that it was in the right direction."[7]

For officers and NCOs tasked with leading soldiers through that deadly maze of First World War trenches, the strain was incredible, and mistakes too easy to make. When American infantry sergeant Donald Kyler was trying to lead his resupply party forward into the lines one night in France, the impassable conditions of the communication trench required going over the top and across the open ground. "I thought we were on the right side of the wire," he wrote, "and that if we angled across an open space we would come to the rear of one of the platoons we were to serve. But I was wrong." He did not realize his error at first, but one of the soldiers in the group, a Yaqui Indian from Arizona, did. "I felt a hand on my arm. It was one of the Indians," Kyler wrote. "He pointed in the direction in which we were going and whispered one word: 'Boches . . .' meaning Germans." When they were safely back inside their own lines, Kyler reported the soldier's actions to his superiors. "We all felt very grateful to him for what he had done," he wrote. "And I will never forget that by my error, we would have been killed or captured."[8]

It is not a revelation to say that confusion is an element of battle; if anything, it is perhaps surprising that the confusion is not worse or more frequent. There is an old military witticism, variously attributed to Frederick the Great and Napoleon, among others, that says, "No plan survives the first shot." That is obviously a bit of an oversimplification, but it still has an element of truth in it. The best and most complex plans (which are almost always *not* the same thing at all) seldom go exactly as hoped, once the shooting starts and the enemy interjects his differing opinion into the situation. In fact, I would suggest that one of the things that distinguishes a first-rate combat unit from an inferior one is the degree to which the inevitable confusion is expected, anticipated, adapted to, and dealt with.

Combat is always confusing, and night fighting is particularly chaotic, for obvious reasons. Units caught in an ambush always experience a momentary confusion, but perhaps not to the degree that a civilian might expect. A well-trained, highly disciplined unit that knows its battle drills so well that it can react instantly can usually fight back very quickly with great effectiveness. A poorly trained unit, on the other hand, is apt to be shattered in the ambush, its combat capability lost before it even begins, and it is likely to be destroyed in detail.

Assaults present their own particular litany of problems. Troops occupying a defensive position, if they have done their work properly, have several advantages over the attackers. They know the ground, they should have fields of fire well defined and identified, they have constructed obstacles or fortifications both to impede the enemy's advance and to protect themselves, and they fight from covered positions. At the same time, not all the advantages are with the defense—if the attacking force has artillery or airpower in sufficient quantity, and if time permits, it can attempt to pulverize the defenses with an obliterating rain of heavy ordnance. Sometimes this works and sometimes it does not—German guns pounded the forts of Verdun into ruin in a sustained bombardment that exceeded anything in the history of warfare up to that time, but they were never able to knock out the French defenses entirely, just as concentrated American naval gunnery was never able to eliminate the dug-in Japanese defenders at Tarawa, Iwo Jima, and other contested islands in the Pacific. There were always exceptions to the rule, but for most of the period it was still a reasonable to assume that defenders occupying prepared positions held at least a notional advantage over their attackers.

It is hard to fully describe the degree of disorientation and confusion that accompanies an assault, especially one that goes in at night. Planning will be extensive, rehearsals will be exhaustive, every possible contingency will be accounted for, and still it all goes to hell in the proverbial handbasket when the moment comes. Despite the inevitability of this confusion, the planning and rehearsing are absolutely necessary, because that intensive preparation is what will eventually produce order out of chaos, if the men on the ground are sufficiently trained to adapt to the tactical situation.

Two types of assaults, in particular, are prone to nearly unlimited chaos. Airborne drops of paratroopers are one, especially if the inbound aircraft are engaged by heavy ground fire. It is a remarkable phenomenon that two paratroopers can stand next to each other in the same aircraft, they can jump in the same "stick" only seconds apart from each other, and then not see each other again for three chaotic, disorienting days after being scattered across the drop zone. Another undertaking beset with confusion is an amphibious assault.

The Allied landings on the beaches of Gallipoli on April 25, 1915, are almost a case study in the sort of chaos that ensues from the combination of incorrect intelligence, heavy enemy resistance, and disrupted command and control. In an experience which would be familiar to men in numerous amphibious landings in the Pacific Theater of the Second World War, British and ANZAC troops reached the beaches at Gallipoli only to discover that they had not been landed where they expected to be. "The officers had been told that they would find a low sand-bank on landing," historian Robert Rhodes James says, "but in fact were almost immediately confronted with almost sheer scrub-covered cliffs." The men were in confusion; their officers no better off. "'What are we to do next,

Sir?' one soldier inquired of an officer, as Turkish guns blasted the beach. 'I don't know, I'm sure,' was the reply; 'everything is in a terrible muddle.'"[9]

The situation worsened as more and more men were landed. Some beaches, such as V Beach, where the transport ship *River Clyde* was deliberately run aground so it could off-load infantry, were raked with murderous fire by the Turkish defenders; of the first two hundred men of the Lancashire Fusiliers who landed on W Beach, all but twenty-one were killed. Men landed not knowing exactly where they were, where the enemy was, or what they were supposed to do next. Maps did not match the terrain on the ground, and effective communication between units was almost impossible. One unit was ordered forward to seize an apparently undefended hilltop—they disappeared to a man and were never seen again. As James observes, the chaos on April 25th was so complete that even today the story is still not clear:

> *The precise details of the fighting at Anzac [Cove] on April 25th have never been determined. New arrivals splashing ashore at Anzac Cove were sent to Shrapnel Gully to re-form, and then arbitrarily dispatched to various parts of the confused battlefield. Units completely disappeared; in some cases, stragglers returned to the beach, to add to the confusion; in many others, nothing was ever heard of them again. The maps were utterly useless, and orders based on them invariably collapsed; on one occasion, a party of New Zealanders too over an hour to move what on the map appeared to be a distance of under a hundred yards, for the simple reason that the map did not admit the existence of an almost impassable razor-edge which links Plugge's Plateau with Russell's Top.*[10]

Officers could not identify their units' objectives on the ground because of the hopelessly inaccurate maps. The situation only deteriorated further as officers were wounded or killed and leadership became increasingly disorganized. Brigadier General Hare, commanding the covering force on W Beach, could not identify the location of a particularly crucial objective, Hill 138, which at the time of the landings was practically undefended. Hare was wounded and evacuated, the officer who succeeded him was killed very shortly afterward, and for a long time after that no one seemed to know what to do or where to go.

Things were even more confused at Y Beach, because no one was sure who was actually in charge even before the attack went in. "Lt.-Col. Koe of the Scottish Borderers thought that he was in command," James writes, "but at a divisional conference on April 21st it had been discovered that Lt.-Col. Matthews of the Marines was in fact the senior, and had been put in command. Koe had not attended the conference . . . and no one had thought of telling him of the decision." To make matters worse, the orders that Matthews did have were "verbal and imprecise" and gave little guidance beyond directing him to move inland, find and destroy some guns, and try to draw a Turkish counterattack in his direction.[11]

This breakdown in command and control was not limited to the Allied forces fighting at Gallipoli. As the campaign raged on and the casualties mounted on both sides, Turkish officers increasingly struggled to understand and control the evolving situation on the battlefield. One Turkish commander, during a major Allied attack in August, was ordered to launch a counterattack. "An attack has been ordered on Chunuk Bair," he replied to his headquarters. "To whom shall I give this order? I cannot find the battalion commander. . . . I do not know what I am supposed to do." The ferocity of the fighting wiped out some Turkish battalions almost to the last man; others were so decimated that the survivors turned up wherever they might, adding to the general confusion. A Turkish officer desperately wired back for help. "There are men here from different regiments, but I cannot find any of their officers," he wrote. "The last commander of this regiment has been killed. Most of the officers are dead or wounded. I do not even know the name of the hill I am on. I can see nothing. I know nothing. I implore you for the safety of the nation to appoint someone who knows the land and us."[12] The chaos at Gallipoli spared no one, friend or foe alike, and even then, the encompassing confusion was perhaps no worse than in other battles throughout history.

Friendly fire, as the old saying goes, *isn't.* The U.S. Army calls it "friendly fire," though there is absolutely nothing friendly about it. The British call it "blue on blue," or "back fire." Whatever term is applied to it, the effect is the same—men are fired on, wounded, and sometimes killed, not by the enemy, but by their own comrades or allies.

Battle, and the realistic training that professional armies undertake to prepare for battle, is an inherently dangerous undertaking. The risks are understood and to some degree accepted by most professional soldiers. This makes the problem of friendly fire incidents all the more difficult to deal with when they occur. There is an abiding perception that holds that friendly fire incidents are more frequent in modern warfare, or are at least more lethal when they do occur. It is true that modern weapons are more effective destroyers of life and limb, but the problem of fratricide on the battlefield is not a recent development of modern warfare.

John Shipp, who served in the British Army at the very beginning of this period, recounted several incidents of friendly fire during his service. On one occasion, fighting against hill tribes in Nepal in 1805, Shipp's regiment was spread out across a range of wooded hills. It quickly became apparent that the enemy was moving through the forests between the British positions. Firing on the enemy meant firing in the direction of fellow troops on neighboring hills, an act that immediately provoked answering fire. Shipp remembered, "Some of our men were killed and wounded by each other, by their crossfiring at random, where they heard the sound of muskets, but could not see the object." Command and control across the distance were difficult. "We frequently sounded 'cease firing,' but to no purpose," Shipp wrote, "and, indeed, it was truly tantalizing to see thousands of the enemy under our very noses, and not to be allowed to fire at them; but the woods being thick and high, we were fearful of again drawing on ourselves the fire of our men on the opposite hills."[13]

In the period of the Napoleonic Wars, fratricide was often a matter of entire units firing on each other in the confused maelstrom of blinding smoke that was a part of maneuver warfare in that era. In the period of the American Civil War, the greatest frequency of friendly fire incidents probably occurred when nervous soldiers on picket duty fired on men in the dark without first ascertaining whether they were friend or foe. This was a perpetual problem in all armies in almost every era—the relative improvements in firearms did not create the problem; it only meant that jittery sentries were more dangerous to their own side than they had previously been. The most infamous of all friendly fire incidents in the Civil War was undoubtedly that which occurred at Chancellorsville in 1863. The Confederacy lost one of its most gifted combat commanders when General Thomas "Stonewall" Jackson was fired on by Confederate soldiers as he and his staff approached their lines in the dark. Jackson had gone forward of the lines to conduct a personal reconnaissance and so was riding in from the enemy side, a fact that contributed to the confusion. The mistake was understandable, but the consequences were severe. Jackson was seriously wounded, and his left arm had to be amputated, causing Robert E. Lee to reflect, "Jackson has lost his left arm, but I have lost my right." Within days, however, pneumonia set in. Jackson died, and so the Confederacy was deprived of his tactical brilliance at Gettysburg a few months later when it would have stood them in good stead. The tragedy was almost repeated a year later in the Battle of the Wilderness when Lieutenant General James Longstreet was wounded when he was fired on by other Confederates.

Friendly fire accidents were not limited to the Confederate side during that war. The Battle of Antietam on September 17, 1862, is remembered as the bloodiest day in American military history, and far too much of that bloodshed was the result of friendly fire. In the fierce fighting in the west woods, the 9th New York Infantry and the 5th Massachusetts Infantry began firing in each other's direction when a Confederate regiment penetrated a gap between their positions. In the ensuing firefight, both Union regiments sustained heavy casualties. That was only one of eleven recorded instances of fratricide at Antietam—in all, as much as 5 percent of the losses in both armies that day may have resulted from fratricide, nearly 1,150 men killed or wounded by their own side.

The First World War saw frequent instances of friendly fire on all fronts and among all armies. Artillery was a prime culprit in many of these fratricidal incidents, especially when the guns firing in support of an advance miscalculated and dropped their shells on their own forward lines rather than on the enemy's positions. On April 15, 1918, in the fighting near Mont-Bernanchon, the Somerset Light Infantry lost two men killed and one wounded when a British artillery shell impacted on their position instead of on the German lines. The wounded man was a young lieutenant named C. S. Lewis, who was later to become famous as a Christian apologist and the author of the Narnia books. Two months later, during the Spring Offensive in June, the 4th Battalion of the King's Shropshire Light Infantry was decimated when they were pounded by British artillery. They had just captured the German positions on Montagne de Bligny; the artillery observers did not realize that the hilltop position had changed hands and misidentified the British troops as German.

Another cause of friendly fire incidents was when units of the same army did not recognize each other on account of unfamiliarity with different uniforms or equipment. This was a persistent problem in the Napoleonic Wars when the thick smoke of heavy musketry made it hard to distinguish the identifying colors of uniforms and flags, but it reappears through each era of this period. Although American Marines regularly wore camouflage uniforms in the Pacific Theater of the Second World War, the U.S. Army's experiment with camouflage uniforms in Normandy in 1944 was quickly terminated when it turned out that most American troops associated camouflage with German soldiers, particularly the Waffen SS, and so tended to shoot at anybody not wearing olive drab. This trigger-happy inclination on the part of regular infantry played out in another way, as well.

Spencer Wurst jumped into Normandy with the 505th Parachute Infantry Regiment. In the first days of the campaign, friend or foe identification methods on the part of American infantry units who were moving inland from the beaches left much to be desired. "Judging from the friendly fire we received on the ground, the steps taken to identify us as U.S. paratroopers were less effective than the identification on the planes," Wurst wrote. "The Army then had a solid olive drab combat uniform, whereas we had two-piece khaki jumpsuits. Our regular leg infantry were either inadequately briefed, or they soon forgot what a paratrooper's uniform looked like, judging from the shots they took at us. I guess they thought it was safer to eliminate the unknown."[14]

Another American paratrooper, Robert Erikson, jumped into Southern France with the 509th Parachute Infantry Regiment as part of Operation Dragoon in August 1944. To add some mobility and range to their sector patrols, his unit acquired an M8 6x6 Light Armored Car from a neighboring armored unit, and they did it in the time-honored GI way of field-expedient, unofficial appropriation. "We borrowed it," Erikson remembered; "we really stole it from the armored, but we called it borrowing it." Rolling through a French village in their purloined armored car, the paratroopers rounded a corner and were suddenly struck with a barrage of small arms fire from a roadblock.

Erikson and his crew opened up with all of the M8's considerable armament—a 30mm cannon, a .50 caliber machine gun, and a .30 caliber machine gun—and blasted their way through the roadblock. Only in hindsight did it occur to Erikson that something was amiss. "I could see tracers going down the road and they were red," he said. "The Krauts use white tracers, you know. . . . What the hell is wrong here?" Back at their staging area, the paratroopers encountered another soldier who reported that a German tank had just broken through their roadblock. The firefight had been between two different elements of the 509th PIR. "These guys had been at Anzio and Avelino and Africa," Erikson said. "Hell, they didn't even know what an M8 armored car was." Fortunately, despite the heavy fire going back and forth, there were only minor wounds. Looking back on the incident, Erikson was rather realistic about it. "I mean, when you're in situations like that, it's hard to be rational and calm like a guy behind a desk would be," he said.[15]

In the campaign to retake the Aleutian Islands from Japanese forces in 1943, poor communications and bad weather caused American and Canadian troops to engage each other during the operation to retake Kiska Island. In a series of confused firefights over two days, twenty-eight American and four Canadian soldiers were killed before it was discovered that the Japanese had already abandoned their positions, and there were actually no enemy forces anywhere on the island.

The two worst cases of accidental fratricide in the Second World War both involved the U.S. Army. The first was the tragedy that marked the 82nd Airborne Division's parachute drop on Sicily as part of Operation Husky in 1943. On the night of July 11, a German air raid struck the Allied naval forces at anchor off the Sicilian coast near Gela at nearly the same time that an airborne force of 144 American C-47 Dakota transport planes crossed the beachhead, heading for their drop zones inland. It was a thoroughly planned and publicized operation, and numerous warning orders had been sent out to inform Allied ground and naval forces of the airborne operation's route and its timetable. Nearly 1,900 paratroopers of the 504th Parachute Infantry Regiment, the 307th Airborne Engineer Battalion, and the 376th Parachute Field Artillery Battalion were in the air, rigged for their first combat drop of the war. The gun crews of a single U.S. Navy ship, already on edge after the German attack, opened fire on the air formations passing overhead. A massive barrage erupted as other ships and antiaircraft batteries ashore opened up, blasting the aircraft they had not bothered to properly identify. The transport pilots tried to take evasive action, but the naval gunnery was ferocious and relentless. In all, sixty of the C-47s were hit, and twenty-three of them were shot down. Paratroopers bailing out of stricken aircraft were forced to jump miles from their designated drop zones; some of them went down in the sea and drowned. The aircraft carrying the 504th's regimental commander managed to stay in the air, but was riddled with nearly two thousand shrapnel holes.

The airborne operation was so disrupted that only four hundred of the 504th PIR's sixteen hundred men managed to reach their target areas on schedule. Three hundred eighteen American paratroopers and airmen were killed and 148 wounded in the worst friendly fire catastrophe of the war. These were elite troops, to whose selection and rigorous training the army had devoted months of effort, and they were lost before they ever had a chance to come to grips with the enemy. This incident was the reason why, for the duration of the war, American transport aircraft were painted with white and black recognition stripes to identify them to friendly ground forces during overflight operations.

The other incident occurred in Normandy in 1944. Close air support for infantry was in its tactical infancy during the Second World War, and its limitations were demonstrated all too clearly in Operation Cobra. Seven weeks after the D-Day landings, Allied forces prepared to launch a major push southward. In support of the attack, air bombardment was planned along the forward edge of their advance. The first day of the operation, July 24, was plagued by low cloud cover and overcast skies that obstructed the airmen's view of the infantry lines and the all-important friendly force recognition signals, which were mostly in the form of yellow smoke. Many of the bombers chose to not release their payloads, being unable to identify their targets, but numerous aircraft dropped their bombs anyway, resulting in 156 American casualties on the ground. Twenty-five men were killed.

An even greater bombardment was scheduled for the next day, involving nearly eighteen hundred aircraft. Mindful of the hazards, General Omar Bradley requested that the bombing go in on an east-west axis parallel to the ground troops' line of advance. Instead, the air attack went in along a north-south line, and as smoke from the first waves of bombs obscured the target area, successive formations of planes released their bombs closer and closer to the infantry positions, the "creepback" effect that Bradley had so feared. The leading American ground units were caught directly in the rain of bombs. When the disaster was over and the smoke cleared, 111 U.S. soldiers were dead and another 490 wounded. It was an entirely preventable mishap.

In the European Theater of the Second World War, the Americans, in particular, acquired an unfortunate reputation among their allies for being notoriously haphazard in their target selection. Many British soldiers left accounts of coming under fire from American units, or having to take cover from American artillery or American bombs. Robert Brown, a corporal in a New Zealand infantry regiment, said, "Unfortunately, the Americans had the habit of dropping their bombs on the wrong people and we suffered quite a few casualties. Actually, I've been shot up and bombed more times by Americans than by Germans, but that's all part of the war."[16] A British soldier remembered that when the Germans fired, he and his comrades took cover; when the British fired, the Germans took cover; but when the Americans fired, everyone on both sides took cover.

Artillery, as has already been noted, is the great killer of the modern battlefield. At times artillery could be an indiscriminate murderer of friend and foe alike, and as the ranges lengthened and the gunners saw less and less of the men at whom they were firing, the problem of misdirected fire or rounds falling short grew more acute, and the results of the errors more tragic. It happened in every theater of both world wars, and plagued all armies. In one instance during the American operation to retake the island of Guam from the Japanese, a friendly fire mishap was only realized when two different units of U.S. infantry contacted the same artillery battery and tried to call in fire on each other, having misidentified their fellow Americans. In the opening chaos of the Battle of the Bulge in the Ardennes in 1944, a Canadian artillery battery mistook a retreating American column for an attacking German unit and took them under fire. In the ensuing barrage, seventy-six U.S. soldiers were killed and another 138 wounded.

For the men on the receiving end of friendly fire, especially fire coming from their own heavy guns in the rear, the effects of fratricide were often traumatic and demoralizing. Frank Caldwell, a paratrooper in the U.S. Marine Corps' 1st Parachute Battalion who fought in the savagery that was Iwo Jima, recalled, "After Hill 362-B was secure, our own artillery came down too close, hitting us. But they still said, 'No, that's not our artillery; that's Japanese artillery.' I said, 'Bullshit! I know which way that stuff's coming.' It tore up one of our guys, mutilated him. [My men] took his innards and so forth and his skull and all that stuff and put it on a stretcher, and one of my sergeants marched right back to the battalion commander, ran across that airfield, and said, 'This is what your goddamn artillery has done to us!' It was too close to the end of the island for it to be Japanese. It was a friendly-fire incident." Years afterward, Caldwell was still bitter about the errors that had killed his comrades, especially since it was not an isolated incident. "We had had some previous friendly-fire incidents early on with the damn tanks coming up behind us firing away. They just mowed us down. They didn't tell us they were coming—nobody told us they were coming—and it got a lot of people shot in the back or smashed under their treads."

Losing people in combat was hard; losing them in incidents of preventable error was even more tragic, and soldiers who experienced cases of fratricide later described it as perhaps the most haunting, and embittering, trauma of their wars, something that they never forgot and seldom forgave.

CHAPTER THIRTEEN

Enemies and Allies

Hindu Sepoy in France
"This man in his own country prayed we know not what to what
Powers.
We pray Them to reward him for his bravery in ours."

—RUDYARD KIPLING

ENEMY IS AN AMBIGUOUS WORD in the soldier's vocabulary. It most literally means whoever is wearing the uniform of the other side in a war (or no uniform at all, in the case of counterinsurgency operations, guerilla wars, and conflicts described by that newly minted euphemism, "low-intensity conflicts"). Sometimes a particular face or description is attached to the word, but more often than not, enemy simply refers to the nameless and ubiquitous "them" against whom soldiers are supposed to fight. One British soldier of the First World War expressed it very well when he described the battlefield by saying: "This side of our wire everything is familiar and every man a friend. Over there, beyond the wire, is the unknown, the uncanny, there are the people about whom you accumulate scraps of irrelevant information but whose real life you can never penetrate." The enemy, as he put it, were "the people who will shoot you dead."[1]

One might expect that soldiers always hate the enemies they fight—after all, they are doing their damnedest to kill each other every time they come within sight of each other. Down through history, governments have marshaled their considerable powers of persuasion in an effort to inculcate in soldiers some degree of hatred for their nation's enemies, using all varieties of propaganda and political diatribe in attempts to whip up animosity against the nation's foes in this war or that. The human reality, however, is that strong feeling against the enemy cannot always be assumed to have a place in soldiers' perspectives. Sometimes they hate the enemy against whom they fight; more often they do not. Contrary to what one might expect, it is not unusual for soldiers to have a higher regard for their enemy than they do for their allies, or sometimes even for their own civilian populace back home, so long as that enemy fights honorably. Nor is it unusual for soldiers to feel a greater admiration and respect for their enemy than they do for their own army's chain of command. As the airman in William Butler Yeats's poem says, *"Those I guard I do not love / Those I fight I do not hate."* Don Rickey, in his superb study of the U.S. Army during the Indian Wars, wrote, "Regular soldiers usually do not feel the intense animosity toward an enemy that is often displayed by wartime volunteers and citizen-soldiers. Warfare is their business, and they understand that professional enemies are in the same trade, but on the opposite side."[2] With some notable exceptions, hatred in war is not always assumed.

The names that soldiers give their enemies and their allies can reveal a great deal about their attitude toward those people. ("Those people," in fact, was precisely the term that Robert E. Lee always used to refer to the Union troops against whom he fought in the Civil War.) In other wars and other armies the terms of address have varied from the humorous and almost affectionate to the racially derogatory and insulting. In the Napoleonic Wars, the British called their French adversaries "Jean Crapaud" or "Toads"; for their part, the French called the British soldiers "Goddams" on account of their enthusiastic profanity, which seemed to shock the more notionally reverent French. When France invaded Russia in 1812, the Russian Orthodox clergy characterized the Catholic French as infidels, resulting in the common term the Russians used to describe the invaders: *"Bisurman,"* meaning Muslim. The Spanish were called "Dons" by the British during the Peninsular War and "Garlics" by the Americans in 1898. In the American Civil War, Union Army soldiers called their Confederate adversaries "Johnny Reb" or "Secesses"; Southerners in turn called the Northern soldiers "Billy Yank," "Yankees," or "Blue Bellies." American soldiers in the Philippines after the Spanish-American

War called the Filipinos "Googoos" when they were being derogatory, or "Little Brown Brothers" when they were being merely condescending.

The First World War saw British and Commonwealth soldiers calling their Turkish opponents "Abdul," "Joe Burke," "Jack," or "Johnny Turk"; for their part, the Turks thought that the Australian battle cry of "Bastards!" must be an invocation of their god, and so called them that. Germans in that war were commonly called "Fritz" or "Huns" by their enemies. British soldiers called the Italians "Macaronis." The French seem to have been called "Frogs" at one time or another by nearly everyone who was not French, and Americans have frequently referred to the British as "Limeys." In the Second World War the Germans were "Jerries" to the British and "Krauts" to the Americans; the Americans themselves were "Yanks" to the British and "Amis" to the Germans. The Russian soldier was frequently known to his enemies and allies alike as "Ivan" and to his own countrymen he was "Ivan Ivanovitch." In the Pacific Theater of the Second World War, where racial animosities were much more a factor than in the war in Europe, the Japanese were called "Nips," "Japs," or "Gooks" by their Western adversaries.

❧

Even when soldiers made a concerted effort to kill the men who were wearing the enemy's uniform, they were frequently still able to express a professional respect for them, and sometimes also a genuine admiration. Occasionally, there are even expressions of sincere empathy and affection in the words that soldiers used to describe their former enemies.

Thomas Morris, a British veteran of the Napoleonic Wars, once commented on what he saw as a disparity between the British and the French in this regard. "I have never yet met a Frenchman," he wrote, "who did not admit the valour of English troops, though it is very common for Englishmen to speak disparagingly of the French; and this is, to say the least of it, very foolish, for if they were really cowards, there would be the less merit due to us for beating them."[3] Morris, in his own very English way, was echoing the old proverb that a man is more honorable if he is fortunate enough to have honorable enemies. A contemporary of Morris, an anonymous British soldier who left a memoir of his service with the

71st Regiment of Foot, wrote that he had "often admired the bravery of the French officers."[4]

While many British soldiers of the Napoleonic Wars period could express some measure of professional respect for their French enemies, they often felt much less regard for their Spanish allies. Sometimes the praise for the former and the criticism of the latter were delivered simultaneously. One British officer, detailed as a liaison with the Spanish Army, delivered a low opinion of them as allies. "It is morally impossible that the Spanish troops can stand before a line of French infantry," he wrote. "A portion of, at least one third of, the Spanish muskets will not [fire]; and a French soldier will load and fire his piece with precision three times before a Spaniard can fire his twice."[5] Most British soldiers of the period held a similarly uncomplimentary opinion of their Spanish allies' martial abilities.

Even before Britain was fully committed to fighting the French in the Peninsular War, commentators who were acquainted with the Spanish from long experience cautioned against relying on them as fighting allies. One Irishman living in Spain wrote to an English friend who was with the British Army, warning that Wellington should not "trust too much to the Spaniards. I believe they always mean well, but they bluster. ... But as to their army ... I have watched its progress, and know it well: when they have muskets, they generally want cannon; if they have powder, they are often without flints; if they are well fed, then they are naked; if they get shoes, they want a loaf of bread; if the soldiers would fight, the officers are unwilling; and when the generals wish to have an engagement, the men are sure to run away."[6]

This description of Spanish martial prowess might have seemed spurious and perhaps unfair to an outside observer, but the experience of battle demonstrated that the criticism was not just a casual slander. Wellington, who had to consider the matter from the twin perspectives of diplomacy and military strategy, was fully cognizant of the political necessity of maintaining good relations with the Spanish during his Peninsular campaigns, but it was often not an easy task when confronted with the Spaniards' lackluster performance in the fight.

Wellington was enough of a diplomat to concede the occasional sop to Spanish egos in order to keep them close as allies, but as a soldier he was frequently disgusted at the unreliability of most of their combat formations. (There were exceptions to this, however—by 1813 Wellington felt that he was able to confidently depend on both the martial ability and the discipline of General Pablo Morillo's veteran Spanish troops. That, however, was only one brigade among many.)

If the British were inclined to disparage the Spanish as soldiers, they usually held a much higher opinion of their Portuguese allies. The Portuguese fought closely with British formations, augmenting Wellington's maneuver forces and proving their combat value repeatedly in the hard fighting that marked the Peninsular War. Portuguese infantry trained to the same standard as British infantry, so successfully that as the war went on they were able to stand in their lines against the French and deliver massed volleys of musket fire that were every bit as rapid and as accurate as those of the British infantry. At the battle of Busaco, in fact, the Portuguese were said to have "behaved just like the English troops, and, indeed, fought with such valour that the French believed them to be Englishmen disguised in Portuguese uniforms."[7] During the nine years of the Peninsular War, the British and Portuguese infantrymen fought together, marched together, and died together. By all accounts, the relationship was one of mutual admiration and genuine respect, tried and tested on the field—Wellington was able to rely on the Portuguese battalions in his army, and his infantryman shared his high opinion of them.

Britain and Spain never joined as martial allies again in the century following the Peninsular War; in fact, Spanish histories for many years deliberately discounted the role the British Army had played in ousting the French from Spanish soil. The military relationship between Britain and France, however, underwent major changes that few observers would probably have predicted in 1810. Forty years after Waterloo, the British and French fought as allies in the Crimean War. At that point the two nations had centuries of history between them as hereditary enemies, going back to well before the fourteenth century, but that acrimonious past was set aside in the allied campaign against Russia. Set aside politically, at least; some senior British officers, who had begun their careers in an era when France was still the perpetual enemy, found the change from foe to friend to be a hard one to keep in mind. Lord Raglan, the British commander in chief in the Crimea, was prone to refer to the enemy forces there as "the French" and had to be reminded on more than one occasion that the enemy were Russian and the French were now allies.

For British soldiers in the lines during the Crimean War, their relationships with their French and Turkish allies were not always characterized by warm affection and professional respect. George Buchanan, a cavalry lieutenant in the Scots Greys, repeatedly commented on both of those allies in letters home to his mother. He had a particularly low opinion of the quality of the Turks as soldiers: "The French behaved admirably," he wrote on November 7, 1854, "but the Turks who were present all ran away. These brutes are not worth their salt, and only create a smell in camp." Three weeks later, Buchanan's negative opinion seemed to have been reinforced. "I only wish we were at war with the Turks instead of the Russians," he wrote on November 27. "They ought to be driven out of Europe. A nasty, cowardly race, not fit to scrape a road." Even though he certainly held a better opinion of the French than the Turks, Buchanan still had some negative feelings toward his Gallic allies, as well. "Our French friends are much overrated," he wrote after the French assaults at Sebastopol were repeatedly repulsed; "they are better soldiers than us excepting that they cannot fight like us."[8]

Buchanan was not the only British soldier in the Crimea to express disdain for the Turks as military allies. Troop Sergeant Major Henry Franks, of the Heavy Cavalry Brigade, wrote in his postwar memoirs, "I cannot understand the Turk at all. I have read accounts in the papers from time to time about the grand fighting qualities and bravery of the Turkish army, and I am unwilling to believe that all those reports are false, but I cannot forget what I witnessed myself, when they ran away in sight of the whole Cavalry Brigade."[9]

The nineteenth century was a period of expanding frontiers in the United States and growing imperialism for countries such as Britain, France, Germany, and Belgium. In all cases this was marked by instances of open warfare with the indigenous peoples whose territories were being contested, and nearly in all cases those native populations came out second best. While the native peoples beat the invaders in some notable and historic battles (such as the 7th U.S. Cavalry's defeat at the Battle of the Little Bighorn and the British disasters of the First Afghan War and the loss at Isandhlwana, among others), in nearly every case they lost the wars and their countries along with the wars—in some cases for a time, forever in others.

The staff echelons of European armies frequently regarded warfare waged against "savages" as being something of a sideshow to the real business of fighting set-piece battles in the formal manner against conventional European armies. That was a common attitude, at least, among those who had never actually fought in the tough little brush wars on the fringes of the empire or out on the nation's frontiers. Inexperienced recruits might have believed the dismissive nonsense about natives being second-rate opponents, but veteran soldiers almost never expressed such idiotic ideas. They knew, from hard and bloody experience, that the uncivilized peoples of the world were in many cases first-rate fighting men, and fools who took them lightly often never had a chance to repeat that mistake.

The American experience provides a case in point. As the frontiers of the United States pushed ever westward across the continent, the U.S. Army was confronted by some of the finest irregular combat units in the world. For most of the American Indian tribes, warfare was an integral part of their lives and an essential element of their culture. It has been said before that the tribesmen of the Great Plains—in particular the Sioux, Comanche, and Cheyenne—were in their day probably the best light cavalry in the world; by the same token the Apaches of the southwestern deserts were incredibly tough light infantry fighters. The U.S. Army's infantrymen and cavalry troopers were often maddeningly frustrated by the Indians' elusiveness and aversion to conventional battle, but they never for a moment doubted that the individual Indian warrior was a brave and dangerous opponent.

British soldiers of the same era understood this relationship with their own enemies, whom they fought in their campaigns during Britain's imperial wars. The native adversaries on the frontiers of the empire were often superb fighting men—warriors from warrior cultures, inculcated to battle as a way of life or religion, and no less dangerous because they lacked uniforms, modern weapons, or formal military education. As Rudyard Kipling put it in his poem "Arithmetic on the Frontier," the balance was not always in favor of the man with more equipment and conventional training:

> *A scrimmage in a Border Station—*
> *A canter down some dark defile—*
> *Two thousand pounds of education*
> *Drops to a ten-rupee jezail—*
> *The Crammer's boast, the Squadron's pride,*
> *Shot like a rabbit in a ride!*
>
> *No proposition Euclid wrote,*
> *No formulae the text-books know,*
> *Will turn the bullet from your coat,*
> *Or ward the tulwar's downward blow*
> *Strike hard who cares—shoot straight who can—*
> *The odds are on the cheaper man.*

The British experience in India was marked by a succession of small but bitterly fought wars that pitted the regular soldiers of the British Army and the British East India Company's own regiments against some of the best warrior peoples in Asia. This was the case in 1849, when the British fought the Sikhs at Gujerat. The Sikhs were not second-rate opponents in anyone's estimation, and they had physical courage and martial aggression in abundance.

Corporal Ryder, of the 32nd Regiment of Foot, recalled the decisive moments of the fighting at Gujerat when the British regiments charged the Sikh positions. Under the force of the British bayonet charge, Ryder wrote, the Sikh infantry gave way, "although some of their officers showed the most daring courage. They tried to rally their men by waving their swords, and going in front of them, to urge them forward, but these brave men were soon shot down." With the battle going against them, the Sikh gunners tried to save their cannons. "The enemy formed several squares, to keep us in check," Ryder wrote, "whilst they got their guns away; but our field artillery . . . opened a most destructive fire of grape and canister, which swept them down by whole battalions. . . . We took every gun we came up to, but their artillery fought desperately: they stood and defended their guns to the last. They threw their arms around them, kissed them, and died." Even at the moment of death, the Sikhs were tough—"Others would spit at us, when the bayonet was through their bodies." Ryder remembered.[10]

War is an inherently ugly business, and the internecine, fratricidal nature of civil war makes those sorts of conflicts particularly ugly. In the American Civil War many soldiers, both North and South, frequently expressed empathy for the men on the other side of the field, but that conflict also had its share of animosity and both sides' denigration of the other. Carlton McCarthy fought in the Confederacy's Army of Northern Virginia; when he wrote his account of the war, he took pains to differentiate between what he saw as the nobility of the Southerner and the mercenary nature of his Northern adversary. The Confederate soldier, McCarthy said, "fought the trained army officers and the regular troops of the United States Army, assisted by splendid native volunteer soldiers." Those were worthy opponents, McCarthy believed, but the Federal ranks were further swelled by men whom he considered worse than mercenaries. The North, he wrote, recruited "swarms of men, the refuse of the earth—Portuguese, Spanish, Italian, German, Irish, Scotch, English, French, Chinese, Japanese,—white, black, olive, and brown . . . who died for pay, mourned by no one, missed by no one, loved by no one; who were better fed and clothed, fatter, happier, and more contented in the army than they ever were at home, and whose graves strew the earth in lonesome places, where none go to weep. When one of these fell, two could be bought to fill the gap. The Confederate soldier killed these without compunction, and their comrades buried them without a tear."[11]

McCarthy was occasionally guilty of the fallacy of belittling the quality of the enemy against whom his army fought and lost, but he was honest at other points in his assessment of the Union soldier. "The newspaper men delighted in telling the [Southern] soldiers that they Yankees were a diminutive race, of feeble constitution, timid as hares," he wrote. The reality was a far cry from the propaganda, and McCarthy had seen the reality in person. "Anyone who has seen a regiment from Ohio or Maine knows how true those statements were," he noted wryly. "Sherman's army, marching through Richmond after the surrender of Lee and Johnston," he went on to say, "seemed to be composed of a race of giants, well-fed and well-clad."[12]

Northern soldiers in the Civil War frequently expressed the view that the Southerner's cause was reprehensible and unworthy of their sacrifice—the Confederates, in the Union view, were men who had risen in armed rebellion against their own nation. There were some areas in which Union soldiers did feel themselves at a disadvantage when they compared themselves to their Confederate adversaries, at least in the first years of the war. "The conviction was general that the men in the ranks [of the Union Army] were superior in intelligence to the southerners and just as brave, that the army was better disciplined and much better supplied, that what we lacked was leaders, the men were not tired of fighting, but they were tired of being sent to the slaughter by incompetent generals," one Federal soldier wrote after the Union disaster at Fredericksburg. "From what I was able to observe when burying the dead the 18th and 19th [of December], the Rebels were in a happy state of mind, they had full confidence in their leaders, and perfect faith in the success of their cause. With us complaining, scolding and faultfinding, was indulged in by all."[13]

Still, soldiers on both sides were often able to recognize the common humanity they shared with their enemy. James Stone fought as an infantryman in a Union Army regiment and wrote of finding a dead Confederate soldier: "I came upon a man lying dead holding in his hand a photograph of a group of children," he recalled. "He had evidently found himself mortally wounded, had thought of his family at home and had taken that picture from his pocket to take a last look at the likeness of those he loved so dearly and had died with the picture in his hand."[14]

The practice of going through the personal effects of dead enemy soldiers often produced this sort of humanizing affect, but it could also on occasion lead to some conclusions that were perhaps not as accurate. One British sergeant in the 92nd Highlanders, fighting in Egypt in 1801, later recalled, "It was remarked, that on the persons of the French soldiers, there were almost invariably found packs of cards, which led us to believe they were very much addicted to gambling."[15] In truth, the French were no more inclined to gamble in their spare time than were most other soldiers of the era of any army.

The low opinion of the Turkish soldier's fighting qualities that marked many British narratives of the Crimean War seemed to endure in the British Army through the rest of the nineteenth century. The individual Turk's reputation was probably not helped by the declining military fortunes of the Ottoman Empire; in 1912 and 1913 the Turkish army suffered a series of humiliating disasters in wars in Greece and the Balkans. In light of these factors, many British military commanders probably shared the opinion of one British officer who, just before the Allied landings at Gallipoli in 1915, wrote in his diary that the Turks were "an enemy who has never shown himself as good a fighter as the white man." That dismissive assessment of the Turks was about to be proven badly out of date and fatally wrong.[16] Gallipoli was a horrific, brutal experience of savage fighting in a very small space. The individual Turkish infantryman was perhaps less of a willing combatant than his British or Commonwealth counterpart, since the Turkish army was mostly conscripted, but he proved to be every bit as tough in the clinch.

British and ANZAC soldiers expressed some animosity toward the Turks early on in the campaign, especially as stories spread that the Turks were committing atrocities on Allied dead and wounded, but that abated as time went on. During a battlefield truce on May 24th to allow for burial of the dead who had fallen between the lines, Allied soldiers were able to see that Turkish dead were as badly mangled as were their own casualties—the savage effects of high-powered weapons at close quarters were the cause and not some inhumane viciousness on the part of the foe. One Commonwealth soldier, recalling the change of perception that the truce had had on him, wrote, "I found that I bore the Turk no trace of enmity—nor for that matter did any of us; he was to us 'Johnny Turk' or 'Joe Burke,' almost a fellow sufferer."[17] The poet Aubrey Herbert, who fought at Gallipoli with the Royal Naval Division, talked with a Turkish soldier during the May 24th truce. The Turk pointed to the newly dug graves and said, "That's politics." He then gestured to the heaps of dead men—British, Australian, New Zealander, and Turk—and said, "That's diplomacy. God pity all of us poor soldiers." In that moment, Herbert said, he felt no animosity for the men wearing the enemy's uniform.[18]

An Australian soldier, Private Henry Barnes, remembered that "Jack—as we called the Turkish soldier—was very highly regarded by me and all the men on our side. I never heard him decried, he was always a clean fighter and one of the most courageous men in the world." In Barnes's opinion, the Turk as a soldier in 1915 was a far cry from the sorry specimen derided by British soldiers sixty years earlier in the Crimea. "There was no beating about," he wrote. "They faced up to the heaviest rifle fire, and nothing would stop them, they were almost fanatical."[19]

This opinion was echoed by other British personnel at Gallipoli. Jack Gearing was an ordinary seaman in the Royal Naval Division, a remarkable unit of sailors and Marines who fought as infantry all through the First World War. Gearing recorded his impressions of the Turks he saw brought down to the beach as captives. "They were badly dressed and always wanted our boots, they were so poor," he said, "but they were wonderful fighting men. They didn't give way. . . . They were good. We didn't feel any anger towards them, we had a respect for them."[20] Another British soldier, Private W. Carrol, also disagreed with the old idea that the Turk couldn't, or wouldn't, stand up and fight. "The Turks were good soldiers, you couldn't deny that," he said. "He's always been a good soldier, right from the Crusaders and the Saracens. But the Turks were quite good types."[21]

An official after-action report disseminated to British officers during the early days of the Gallipoli campaign showed that even the command echelon eventually recognized what the individual soldiers had already learned—Turkish soldiers were far tougher than they were once thought to be. "The Turks are putting up a very good fight," the report stated, "and their morale appears to be good. They have a large number of machine guns, which they employ freely and with great skill. It is reported that in some cases the Turks will not wait to face a bayonet attack; at the same time other reports show that they wait in their trenches, and fight to the end."[22] The conclusion was one the British and ANZAC soldiers had already arrived at from their personal experience—the Turkish soldier was not to be taken lightly.

The same could not be said of another British ally in the First World War, one who had come far down in the estimation of the individual British soldier since the time of the Napoleonic Wars. Although never present in large numbers, there *were* Portuguese units in the trenches of France, and they did not rank highly in the estimation of their allies. "The Portuguese, whom we called the Pork and Beans, were also in this part [of the line]," one Royal Welch Fusilier wrote, "and they looked a ragtime lot. There was a yarn going around that when they were in the front line [the Germans] would come over whenever he liked, pinch their rations and smack their backsides before leaving, telling them that they were not worth taking back as prisoners."[23] The unfortunate Portuguese, the feeling went, were also not worth having as soldiers.

When circumstances permitted, soldiers could find that they were able to engage with their allies even when neither side spoke the other's language. Paul Totten, who deployed to Russia in 1918 with the 339th Infantry as part of the multinational expeditionary force against the Bolsheviks, made several notations in his diary about his interactions with Russian soldiers. "This time on [guard] post No. 7 with a detachment of White Russians," he wrote. "These were the ones that were anti-Bolshevik. We had a lot of fun trying to understand each other, but [they] were a nice bunch." A few days later he was back on guard and wrote, "Again with the White Russian guards. Got to where we could understand their signals when they wanted a cigarette. Wish all the Russians were like these boys."[24]

One common theme in soldiers' attitudes toward their enemies was an assessment of the degree of skill (or lack of skill) they believed the other side demonstrated in the practice of the profession of arms. Professional soldiers displayed a contemptuous disdain for opponents who were poor marksmen; they usually had a measure of careful, grudging respect for an enemy who were known to be expert sharpshooters.

During the Indian Wars, most American soldiers rated the fighting qualities of the Indians quite high, even if they seethed at the Indians' aversion to conventional battle. Indian marksmanship, on the other hand, was more miss than hit. Up close, which was how most Indians preferred to fight, their rifle fire could be accurate, but the army initiated engagements at greater ranges. "Indians fired point-blank," one U.S. cavalryman wrote. "Soldiers used the [long range rear] sight and wind gauge, which the Indians knew nothing about."[25] This would have been true after the U.S. Army began taking regular marksmanship training seriously in the 1880s, but before then it is likely that in skirmishes against Indians many troops expended a great deal of ammunition without much result.

The outbreak of the Spanish-American War in 1898 marked the first time in U.S. history that the American army fought a European enemy outside the continental boundaries of North America. Spanish troops were not always as decadent or soft as many Americans had assumed they would be—there were several battles where the Spanish stood and fought hard, and only gave ground after making the Americans pay for a heavy price for it. At the battle for El Caney, in Cuba, the dogged Spanish resistance impressed the Americans who fought against them. The Spanish infantry, surrounded and overwhelmed, "held the road for hours and died like heroes," one American soldier recalled. "Their officers appeared to court death, for they exposed themselves uselessly while urging their men to fight."[26] By and large, though, Spanish combat performance was inconsistent, and the brief war did little to raise American soldiers' opinion of their Spanish adversary or to lower their own slightly inflated sense of their own military preparedness.

When the uneasy cooperation between the United States and the nationalist Filipinos deteriorated into open war in 1899, most American troops had a similarly low opinion of their native opponents, at least at first. Visually, the Filipinos were not particularly impressive soldiers—they were raggedly uniformed, by Western standards they were physically small, and the Spanish-issue Mausers they carried were as long as most of them were tall. In the prevailing racial views of the day, it was not uncommon for American soldiers to assume that the Filipinos would prove to be bad marksmen simply because they were Asian. That assumption quickly proved to be erroneous, sometimes fatally so.

Needham N. Freeman, of the 21st U.S. Infantry, was on the receiving end of Filipino rifle fire more than once, and his assessment of their shooting ability was based on personal experience. Describing one engagement where the Americans were fighting from a prepared defensive position, Freeman wrote, "A man behind the works could not get out for a few minutes' exercise without being fired at, and if he did not get under cover soon they would get him. I have seen many men shot that way; they thought the Filipinos could not shoot." What the Filipinos lacked was not skill in shooting, Freeman thought, but disciplined leadership. "I have seen some fine marksmen among them," he wrote. "They could do some good shooting until they became excited and fled for some place of safety."[27]

This professional assessment of the enemy's combat capabilities was also a frequent expression in soldiers' narratives from the First World War. Most British soldiers held the Germans in high esteem as soldiers, particularly the German machine gun crews who were well-known for staying at their guns in the face of almost certain death, fighting to the last. As the British Army rebuilt itself after the sacrifices of 1914 and gained a hardened professionalism, so too did it begin to take an increasingly informed view of its enemy's professional qualities. One factor that demonstrated that quality better than almost any other, as more than one British soldier noted, was how German soldiers conducted themselves when the tide of battle was going against them.

One British commentator made an important point about the nature of the German soldier when he wrote about the fighting in the battle of Loos just two years after the war's end. "Little justice will no doubt be done on our side to the German defence of Lens, but it was a defence which rivaled ours of Ypres," he wrote. "Technically and theoretically the Germans could be forced to yield it at any moment. But in practice it could not be taken from them. We'd take it if it were of iron; they'd hold it were it of butter. Artillery laid the town flat, but artillery could not destroy the cellars, and of every cellar the German, with the reinforcement of iron and concrete, made a machine-gun nest or post for riflemen."[28] Bitter enemy or not, the German *landsers* were soldiers to be reckoned with, and more than one British soldier expressed genuine admiration for the men he had so often tried so hard to kill.

On the Somme in 1916, when the British mounted the colossal offensive that was at least partly intended to take some of the pressure off the French who were locked in the battle for Verdun in the south, the Germans were subjected to the heaviest bombardment yet of the war in preparation for massed assaults by thirteen British divisions. The optimistic predictions of the British General Staff insisted that it would be little more than a walkover—there would hardly be a German soldier left alive in their lines when the British infantry went forward. The British and Australian infantrymen who would be going forward against the German positions were not so sure of the breezy optimism coming from their headquarters. They knew from grim experience just how well-built the German positions were, and how tenacious in the fight their German counterparts could be. In the event, the infantryman's perspective turned out to be much more in touch with the reality of the battlefield than did the views of staff officers in the rear.

Battery Sergeant Major Douglas Pegler, as an artilleryman, was behind the lines of the infantry troops who were pressing the attack forward, but he was still far enough forward to be able to actually see the line of advance himself. "Once in the open we could see the infantry struggle up the hill towards Flers," he wrote, "our fellows advancing shell hole by shell hole and the Boche retiring just as slowly and steadily." His conclusion was one most British infantrymen would have agreed with: "Whatever Fritz's faults he is a great fighter."[29]

On the other side of the same battle, a German soldier of the 5th Guard Regiment wrote his impression of the British in a journal that later was captured and disseminated by British intelligence officers. "10 July 1916," he wrote: "On the 1st July I was still in Valenciennes, and then on the 2nd the business started and we went straight into a bad position, for the Englishman is a damnable enemy. At any rate, the Frenchman and the Russian is not so cunning as these. . . . Down with England!"[30]

For all of the concerted effort by soldiers of the opposing armies trying to kill each other, the fighting in the Western Front was still marked by moments of humanity—indeed, chivalry—by combatants on both sides. A British infantry lieutenant who fought in the cataclysmic maelstrom of the Somme wrote:

> *It is fair to record that the German troops engaged in this battle, so far with that brutality which has come to be associated with the name of German, showed an unusual mercy to the English wounded. At 9.45 p.m., 2/Lieut. Petley reported, a German medical officer stopped his men from firing to attend to the English wounded in No Man's Land. Next morning a German officer came out under a white flag of truce and arranged a local armistice in order to get in the wounded in front of the Rangers' lines. Further to the south a German came out from his trenches in full daylight and rescued a wounded man of the London Scottish on July 3rd.*[31]

On the other side of the lines, a German *leutant* of the 88th Infantry Regiment wrote in his journal: "The British are a noble lot. They will not shoot at stretcher bearers working under the Red Cross flag. I have witnessed this myself. . . . The first aid men have their hands full. Tirelessly they gather in the wounded, without being interfered with by the British."[32] This was not the only occasion when a German soldier described his British adversaries as "noble," without any trace of irony.

A Royal Engineer named Philip Neame described one occasion where he was the beneficiary of the Germans' sense of humanity. In the midst of heavy fighting, Neame wrote, he and a sergeant had to carry a badly wounded infantryman along a road "in full view of the Germans" because they couldn't carry the injured man through the comparative safety of the ditch. "The Germans seemed to respect our task," Neame wrote, "because they did not shoot at us, which they could easily have done—we were sitting ducks."[33]

What was remarkable about Neame's experience (and most sources agree that toward the end of the war, as both sides fought their way to exhaustion, this sort of forbearance was less likely from both sides) was that his enemy held their fire when both the wounded man and his rescuers were British. More understandable, perhaps, was the German response in one case during the First Battle of Ypres. An infantryman with the Royal Welch Fusiliers remembered one morning after a night attack on the British lines had been repulsed with heavy casualties among the Germans. "We could now see the effects of our night's work," he wrote. "A lot of the enemy dead lay out in front. One of the men in our left platoon threw his equipment off, jumped up on the parapet with his hands above his head and then pointed to a wounded German who was trying to crawl to our lines. He then went forward, got hold of the wounded man and carried him in." Rather than shooting, the fusilier wrote, the Germans were "clapping and cheering until he disappeared into our trench."[34]

These were not isolated instances in the fighting along the trenches of France and Flanders—it often seemed that the duality of human nature allowed men to try as hard as possible to kill each other one moment and then attempt to save each other's lives the next. Ernst Junger, a German infantry officer, described this dynamic very articulately in his memoir of the war, *Storm of Steel*. "Throughout the war," he wrote, "it was always my endeavor to view my opponent without animus, and to form an opinion of him as a man on the basis of the courage he showed. I would always try and seek him out in combat and kill him, and I expected nothing else from him. But never did I entertain mean thoughts of him. When prisoners fell into my hands, later on, I felt responsible for their safety, and would always do everything in my power for them."

The impact of this sort of humanity in the midst of war was poignantly described by Lance Corporal J. W. Finnimore, a soldier of the 3/1 Canadian Brigade who was wounded in the German spring offensive of 1918. "That day, 24 April, was the worst day of my life," he wrote. "We did our best, but first I was wounded in the leg and then, when the Germans were advancing and we got the order to retire, I couldn't move—naturally. All I can remember much later is a German soldier standing over me pointing his rifle and bayonet at my chest. It was my worst moment of the whole war." Finnimore was sure he was a dead man. "I thought he was going to let me have it. But he didn't. We were near a deserted farmyard and he handed his rifle to a comrade and went off into this farmyard and came back a few minutes later with a wheelbarrow. He put me in it and then he pushed me all the way through to their rear dressing station—and it must have been a good mile behind their lines."[35] Because of the efforts of this one German soldier whose name Finnimore never knew, he survived the war and returned home to Canada.

More than one soldier left accounts of the surprising degree of kindness they encountered from their enemies once the fury of battle had swept past and they were left wounded in the aftermath. During the savage fighting on the Somme in September 1916, one German infantryman, Ersatzreservist Tebbe, found himself in a dugout full of wounded Germans and a single British prisoner, also wounded, whom the German medics had earlier treated along with their own casualties. When the British assault reached the German trench and the attackers began throwing grenades into the dugouts, "the wounded huddled together as deep as possible, helpless before the hand grenades. Then the wounded British soldier, who was down below in the dugout, became our savior." Tebbe described how the Tommy "climbed the steps and explained that there was nobody in the dugout who was capable of fighting. Protectively, he stood in front of the Germans who had earlier treated him in a knightly manner."[36] Their earlier humanity had probably saved their own lives, Tebbe felt, because now that the situation was reversed, "British medical orderlies treated our wounds and gave us tea and cigarettes."

Another indication of the individual human qualities of the men on both sides was the degree to which they could make jokes about each other's armies, in ways which were mutually sympathetic of the rank-and-file men on the other side of no-man's land. Arthur Empey wrote of an occasion when he attempted to interrogate a captured German soldier:

It was my intention to try and pump him for information as to the methods of the German snipers, who had been causing us trouble in the last few days. I broached the subject and he shut up like a clam. After a few minutes he very innocently said: "German snipers get paid rewards for killing the English." I eagerly asked, "What are they?" He answered: "For killing or wounding an English private, the sniper gets one mark. For killing or wounding an English officer he gets five marks, but if he kills a Red Cap or English General, the sniper gets twenty-one days tied to the wheel of a limber as punishment for his carelessness."[37]

Considering the view from the trenches, where the soldiers in the line often expressed their opinion that their generals lacked the intellectual capacity of an artillery mule, it was a joke that British infantrymen could appreciate, even if it was not always true.

For their part, the British made a pun of the German Army's traditional motto. "As a sign of their friendliness the Germans put up a sign saying 'Gott mit uns' which means 'God is with us,'" Private Frank Sumpter of the 1st London Rifle Brigade wrote, "and so we put a sign in English saying 'We got mittens too'. I don't know if they enjoyed that joke."[38]

This sort of shared humanity also made itself felt in the Second World War. Both American and German soldiers reported that the opposing sides accorded each other's medical personnel a degree of protection on the battlefield that was conspicuously lacking on the Eastern Front. A Wehrmacht veteran of the fighting in Normandy, Walter Klein, described a situation when he exposed himself to American fire in order to treat wounded German soldiers. Klein was wearing the white surcoat with a red cross that designated German medics. "I made field dressings for the wounded while nobody fired at me," he said. "I want to reiterate the fact that the American infantry, tanks and aviators fought in a fair way. Already during the fighting at St-Lo, we had the experience that all men who were wearing the Red Cross could help their wounded without being fired on." When he was later taken prisoner by American soldiers, Klein remembered that "the American captain, who was commander of the position, allowed us to recover our wounded, assisted by a surgeon and three medical officers of the American Army."[39]

On the other side of the lines, an American soldier named Frederick Branham described a similar situation he witnessed in France. After two

German attacks on his unit's position were beaten back, he recalled that both sides stopped firing long enough to recover the German wounded from the open ground. "Our medics were out there and the German medics, too," he said. Both sides behaved with a certain humanity toward each other, despite their earnest efforts to kill each other. "You have to understand that infantry respects infantry," Branham said. "We respected the German soldier. We weren't arguing with him, only his government. That wasn't his fault either, in most cases. It's a very brutal business being in the infantry. It's very brutal. He deserved the respect you could give him. So that's the way most of us felt. I only saw one prisoner abused and nobody liked that. That should never have happened, but it did."[40]

Soldiers also said that they witnessed the human qualities of their enemies even when their higher-ups expressly forbade it. George McMurty, a New Zealand infantryman fighting in Italy, was captured by the Germans after he became separated from his unit. The German soldiers, he said, "found my chocolate, my rations in a tin, and one of them asked if I minded if they shared it. . . . So they shared it out and they were at the point of giving me a square when the corporal said, no, I wasn't allowed to eat, and off he went upstairs again." Shortly after the German NCO left the room, though, McMurty said, "I got a little dig in the ribs from one of the soldiers and he handed me a little square of chocolate." It was a small act of kindness, and as he recalled it, McMurty reflected on the character of those German grenadiers. "They were only about 19, you know, fine young men," he said. "And that was a very disciplined regiment, even though they did give away chocolate to prisoners."[41] In different circumstances, he thought, they might have had a few pints together and talked of home.

It was also not uncommon in the European Theater for American soldiers of Italian or German descent to be in the situation of facing an enemy with whom they had a shared ancestry. Ernest A. Andrews fought in France, Germany, and Czechoslovakia with the 1st Infantry Division and encountered this himself. "My great grandfather was a surgeon in the German army in World War I and I never did hate the Germans," he said. "As far as I know, I might have been fighting my own family members over there, you know—distant relatives? I hated the Nazi regime, the Nazi training, the Nazi teaching—their whole concept of fighting and victory—but I really had no problems with the German citizens or the German people in general."[42] He was by no means alone in that perspective.

~~~

As the nineteenth century ended and the twentieth century began, the Anglo-French political and military cooperation that began in the Crimea was a firmly established reality in Europe. By the time of the First World War, the hostilities of the Napoleonic Wars were one hundred years in the past, and the Anglo-Franco alliance that opposed the Tripartite Powers was strong enough to make the old animosities truly a matter of history. This did not mean, however, that Britain and France always saw eye-to-eye or that their armies regarded each other with a mutual and unqualified professional respect.

In the First World War France was fighting on her own soil for her very survival and so brought to the war a measure of national urgency that Britain did not require. This perspective sometimes trumped military sensibility, resulting in staggeringly high numbers of casualties in battles such as Verdun, where the invocation of national honor meant that hundreds of thousands of Frenchmen died in fighting that quickly ceased to be about any real tactical or strategic objective.

Despite these philosophical and doctrinal differences, the British Tommy and the French *poilu* usually regarded each other as professional equals, or at least as co-sufferers in the horrors of trench warfare—most of the squabbles and recriminations went on echelons above them, at the division and corps headquarters of both armies. Almost no British soldier was on record as questioning the French commitment to fighting the war, but naturally there were frequent comments about the small ways in which the British soldier felt himself to be different, and perhaps even a bit superior, to his French counterpart.

Sergeant Major Ernest Shephard described one engagement where his British unit relieved a French battalion that had earlier taken a German trench in vicious little fight. "The position was held firstly by the Germans," Shephard wrote. "They were driven out after a fierce struggle by the French, and our line being extended we took charge from them.

The French are brilliant in the attack, but they are very bad at holding what they gain, as they cannot stand shelling as well as British troops."[43] Shephard's diary never referred to the savagery of Verdun, so it is highly possible that he did not know of the hammering the French were taking there—had he known of it, he might have expressed a different opinion of their ability to endure artillery fire, because the French resistance at Verdun had elements of both madness and superhuman heroism about it.

The French soldier has fared rather badly in the estimation of American observers in past decades, with far too many armchair generals pointing to the French defeats in the Franco-Prussian War, the First World War, the Second World War, and Indochina as evidence of French martial shortcomings. What the snide jokes ignore, of course, is that France was *not* defeated in the First World War, and she paid a staggering cost in lives to pass through that cataclysm, blasted to the core but unbroken in the end. Taken in the balance, man for man, the French soldier actually comes across better in the opinions of soldiers from other countries than he usually does in the opinions of many civilian observers, particularly those on this side of the Atlantic.

In fact, part of the French soldier's problem in modern warfare was that, if anything, he was too brave. His commanders all too often assumed that he had almost superhuman reserves of personal courage. French military doctrine was ready to put flesh and blood up against bullet and shell in full anticipation of a victorious outcome, and the French soldier paid a heavy price for that. "The French infantry began [the First World War] with an almost supernatural faith in the bayonet and the emotional qualities of the French soldier," historian Jac Weller notes. "There was a theory that below 400 yards enemy-aimed fire would 'become impossible' and French casualties would decrease."[44] To say that this was a fatally misguided theory is a shot-torn understatement, and hundreds of thousands of Frenchmen lost their lives in adherence to a tactical doctrine that asked more of them than any men could deliver.

Still, the notion persists that the French as a nation cannot or will not fight. When I was going through the French Army's Commando School in Breisach in 1989, one of my British comrades (I was in an international platoon of French and British soldiers of which I was one of only a few Americans) told me a joke: "Question: How many Frenchman does it take to defend Paris? Answer: We don't know—they've never tried." Funny, perhaps, but absolutely untrue—the Germans never reached Paris in 1914, and by 1918 more than five million dead and wounded Frenchmen had put the lie to that joke and many others like it.

The reality of war, as said before, involves the deliberate effort to kill the men wearing the uniform of the other army. With this factor at work, those moments when men stopped trying to kill each other were all the more remarkable, no matter how brief. Most wars were marked by the occasional truces and cease-fires, official or not, and in those lulls when the guns fell silent and enemies saw each other face-to-face there were poignant reminders of the humanity common to all of them. Poignant, in particular, because as soon as the moment passed and the truce was lifted, those same men who had spoken civilly to each other and perhaps helped tend each other's wounded tried their utmost to kill each other just as if the moment of human connection had never occurred. Perhaps the most famous of these temporary battlefield truces was that which occurred between Allied troops and their German counterparts in the winter of 1914—the so-called "Christmas Truce."

It was spontaneous, unofficial, and instigated by the frontline infantrymen themselves, and it provoked a furious reaction from the high commands on both sides. At the following Christmases during the war, orders were published making it clear that any soldier seen attempting to fraternize with the enemy would be shot. In that first year of the war, though, the soldiers themselves met their enemy face-to-face in the contested ground of no-man's land, and for the briefest of days in the muddy abattoir of the Western Front, the British Tommy, the French *poilu*, and the German *Landser* interacted as men and not as enemies.

In a book written just after the end of the First World War, Graham Stephen remembered the 1914 Christmas Truce. "It would be interesting," he wrote, "to read a German account, oh, not an official one, of this battle of Neuve Chapelle, an account by one of the common soldiers who fraternized with his enemy on Christmas Day and had to kill him ere

Easter had arrived."[45] That was where the ultimate tragedy of war lay, in the fact that men who had no personal reason to wish each other's deaths, men who could socialize with one another without enmity when their superiors were not present, were then required to kill each other when the mechanized slaughter of the war resumed.

Even in situations where tacit truces were not in effect, there could still be moments of human interaction in the midst of the violence. Just as Turkish soldiers and their Allied enemies traded rations and tobacco, so too did an unofficial barter occasionally take place on the Western Front. One British veteran of the fighting in France remembered when the Germans opposite his position initiated a exchange of goods—with a hand grenade. "One day I was in a trench just eighteen yards from the nearest German trench, when the Germans sent a stick grenade flying over," he said. "They'd tied a couple of cigarettes to the grenade. After a bit, I went over to it. My mates said, 'For God's sake, don't touch it.' They thought it would go off and blow me up. But I went ahead and smoked one of the cigarettes and it was all right—so we sent the same stick bomb back with a whole packet attached. I hope they enjoyed them."[46]

The adversarial relationship of one side to another in war is often exacerbated by simple things. Official propaganda seeks to magnify the ways in which the enemy is different from one's own countrymen and tries to provide further justification for fighting against them. In extreme cases, going beyond affirmation of the worthiness of one's own cause, propaganda attempts to inculcate an actual abiding hatred for the enemy. It is theoretically easier, after all, to kill a man whom one hates, rather than a man toward whom one is empathetic or at best ambiguous.

Cultural, racial, and national differences all factor into soldiers' thinking, as well. European armies fighting each other on their own continent were perhaps less susceptible to this, but it still appears in the sources to some extent. When Europeans fought Asians or Africans, however, or when Americans fought natives on their own continent or the inhabitants of Asian countries, the oppositional elements within race and culture could be magnified far too easily.

This dynamic found frequent expression in soldiers' writings throughout the eras of this text, and it was no less at work in the Second World

War as well. Most American GIs in Europe did not express an outright hatred for their German adversaries, though in the last year of the war more and more animosity for those Germans who were active adherents to Nazism appeared in their narratives, and many GIs drew a sharp distinction between the ordinary soldiers of the Wehrmacht and the hardliners in the SS. This inclination toward an accommodating attitude gave the American high command no end of problems as the war drew to a close and American combat soldiers took on the role of occupation troops.

The Allied soldiers fighting in the Pacific Theater, however, existed in an entirely different reality. They frequently described the Japanese using the terms of a completely uninhibited racially specific animosity. Partly this was the result of deliberate indoctrination programs such as those created by the U.S. government, including the "Know Your Enemy" film series, but to some degree it also stemmed from racial and cultural perspectives that saw the Japanese soldier as completely different, less civilized, and almost feral. As MacArthur's island-hopping campaign worked its way across the Pacific closer to the Japanese home islands, the fighting intensified in its savagery and bitterness, and so too did the average American GI's hatred of the enemy.

"I was always taught to hate them, to detest them," one American Marine who fought at Iwo Jima wrote; "they were the animals and we were the men." That much of his opinion, at least, seems founded on U.S. propaganda descriptions of the Japanese, but there was more than just those one-dimensional caricatures underlying his understanding of them. Japanese soldiers, he said, "would die for the Emperor and we weren't taught to die for our President. To come up against an individual who wants to die, or who doesn't care about dying, is a tough thing to combat in your mind. We wanted to live, we wanted to kill him and survive."[47] The latter part of that statement is enlightening, if one takes the time to dissect it. It is always easier to empathize, and perhaps harder to hate, when one understands the enemy's motivation, mentality, and methods. When there are things in common, it is easier to identify the shared humanity common to both sides. But when the enemy is so completely foreign in his culture, religion, and traditions that it makes his rationale incomprehensible to the common soldier, then fear replaces empathy, and fear is closely followed by hate.

This view of the Japanese was not limited to the American military—British soldiers expressed similar views. One British veteran of the fighting in Burma said, "I hated the Japanese then and I do now. As soldiers they are very good but to torture prisoners—that's not soldiering, that's butchery." This soldier was not unaware of exceptions to the norm, since he went on to describe one incident where the Japanese Imperial Guards at Imphal observed a white flag to allow wounded to be brought in, but that was apparently the only case he could cite. "After that," he said, "there was no give on either side—they didn't give us a chance and we didn't give them a chance."[48]

Another British soldier, who had fought with Orde Wingate's Chindits in Burma, echoed many other soldiers' perspectives when he said, "The Japanese were animals but great soldiers; their battle drill was fantastic. You couldn't help but admire them. If they were ambushed they were at you in twenty to thirty seconds. . . . They would just come on and on and on."[49] This assessment of the remarkable combat capabilities of Japanese soldiers, while also decrying their lack of humane behavior toward their foes, was common among both Commonwealth soldiers and American GIs. Another British soldier in Burma wrote, "Fighting the Japanese was totally committed war. There was no question of heroics or chivalry in the sense that one read about prior to the war." Here, as in other cases, reported incidents of Japanese atrocities influenced the individual soldier's feelings toward his enemy. "We were totally committed to killing as many Japanese as possible," this man wrote, "prompted by the fact that we knew from experience that there had been atrocities and we were always fearful of that fact and didn't want to take, or be taken, prisoner. And so we were fully committed to war, probably more so than in any other theatre."[50] This same dynamic would play out in the desperate fighting on Okinawa and Saipan, where Japanese civilians, frightened by government propaganda that had told them the invading Americans were savages and cannibals, committed suicide in large numbers rather than fall into American hands.

More than one soldier left narratives that expressed some of the racial stereotypes that many men had of their enemy, stereotypes that lasted at least until they encountered them in person. One finds these kinds of perspectives in the accounts of American, British, Australian, and Japanese soldiers alike. One British soldier, Harry Miller, who was a prisoner of the Japanese after the fall of Singapore, remembered the first time he saw Japanese soldiers in the flesh when the fighting stopped. The Japanese infantry, he remembered, were "unkempt, bearded, squat and bandy-legged individuals who came shuffling and slouching in. Extremely tired men, grim-visaged . . . one thought—Well, was the great British Army beaten by runts like these? And by golly we had been beaten by them."[51] Another British veteran of the Indian Army, John Randle, thought that the "Japs fought with great ferocity and courage. We were arrogant about the Japs, we regarded them as coolies. We thought of them as third rate." It was an opinion that did not last long after meeting the Japanese in battle. "My goodness me," Randle remembered, "we soon changed our tune. We had no idea about jungle fighting."[52]

If white soldiers' preconceptions of racial superiority did not survive the first contact with Japanese soldiers on the battlefield, it was at first replaced with something of an overawed impression of how lethal the Japanese could be, particularly in jungle fighting. That in itself was just another overgeneralized stereotype—after all, there are no jungles on the Japanese home islands, and Japanese soldiers had to learn how to live and fight in an alien environment just as British and American soldiers later learned in their turn. In time, the perceptions changed yet again. "Initially, we believed that the Japanese were supermen," an American paratrooper of the 503rd Parachute Infantry remembered. "Eventually, we caught on to their behavior, and we let them know that we could cope with any bullshit they were going to give us. We had better weapons, were physically stronger, and we started to understand their tactics.[53]

In some cases, and usually after a remove of some years had provided a measure of insulation from the horrors of combat, an Allied soldier would deliver a considered opinion of his former Japanese enemy. One British veteran, who had served as a lieutenant in the 14th Army in Burma, tried for a professional assessment of the Japanese soldier in his recollections.

"The Japanese were very tough, devoted fighters," he wrote, "and they were beaten, I think, not because of lack of courage, of which they had plenty, but they didn't have the same ability that we did for regrouping after they were defeated. If they lost their officers and had no instructions they were really lost, whereas the good old British sergeant or the Indian havildar was deemed quite capable of carrying on and doing something, even if there were great losses and he'd lost all his officers, and seemed capable of getting back to base on many occasions." For this soldier, the disparity between official propaganda and the reality on the battlefield was clear. "The Japanese were very tough indeed, in fact when we first made contact with them near Kohima," he remembered. "Our soldiers turned around and said to us, 'What the hell did you tell us about these little bastards,' because in fact these Japs were over six feet high. This was because we met the Japanese Guards Division first of all."[54] Another British soldier who fought in Burma said, "I thought the Japanese was one of the best fighters in the world. They would fight to the end and they wouldn't give in—in fact we used to find them strapped to trees so that they wouldn't drop and they'd fight to the last."[55]

For their part, many Japanese soldiers who left accounts of their impressions of the British, Commonwealth, or American troops they fought against also expressed surprise at what their enemy was like in reality, as opposed to what they had been led to believe by their army's propaganda. The Japanese official line derided American soldiers as being the product of a morally weak, indulgent society—soft white men who lacked the physical ability to endure the hardships of battle in Asia's tropical climate. Jungle warfare would be the Americans' downfall, the Japanese Army assured its troops, especially once they came up against the Emperor's soldiers who were inculcated with the code of bushido. White soldiers from other Western cultures were denigrated in their turn. For the first heady months of 1942, as the Japanese overran the American and European colonies of Southeast Asia, those predictions seemed to be borne out. The mass surrender of British troops in Singapore, and of American forces in the Philippines, only reinforced the idea that Western soldiers were not the measure of the Japanese. That perception, however, quickly changed.

One Japanese infantryman who fought in the Guadalcanal campaign vividly remembered the first time he ever saw an actual American in combat. In a night attack, his company overran the positions of a U.S. Marine company, and the fighting quickly devolved into a savage melee in the dark as men blindly grappled in a hand-to-hand struggle, shooting, slashing, and stabbing each other. The Marines got out of their holes to fight, this Japanese soldier recalled, and never before in his life had he seen such big men. To him the American infantrymen all seemed to be giants who swung their rifles like clubs and knew how to fight with the bayonet. After surviving that encounter, he never again believed anything Japanese propaganda reports said about the American soldier's ability to fight.

Another Japanese veteran, who fought in Burma, said, "The British and their allies put up a very strong fight there [Kohima]. I think that surprised everyone." There was a wide difference in the quality of Allied troops, he thought—"The Chinese don't count much, you know, if it's five to one it's a fair fight, less than five to one they always run away. The Burmese levies in the British Army were not much use, I think, but of course it was the [British] Fourteenth Army we were fighting all the time."[56] British soldiers, he concluded, were formidable adversaries, and their ability to sustain battle over long periods of time was far beyond anything the Japanese command had predicted.

Some Japanese soldiers found that their Western enemies, even if they held completely different notions as to the acceptability of surrender, still measured up to Japanese standards of personal courage in unexpected ways. A Japanese infantry captain named Tadashi Suzuki of the 215th Infantry Regiment wrote of encountering a badly wounded British lieutenant colonel whose position had been overrun. "He signed to us to shoot him and died in a serene frame of mind," Suzuki wrote. "His attitude really was in keeping with the honour of a military man. I sincerely respected him and wish I might do the same."[57] Another Japanese officer, Misao Sato, who spoke to a mortally wounded British soldier, wrote, "He was young-looking, about 18 years old. . . . A bullet had gone through his abdomen, and the doctor told me there was no hope of survival. I asked him in my broken English . . . 'Painful?' he again said a word, 'No.' I knew that he must be suffering great pain. It is torture to be shot through the

343

abdomen, and more painful as his intestines were ruptured. . . . I understood that he was enduring his pain with all his might." Sato was deeply impressed. "Ah! His attitude was really dignified. . . . At that moment I really discovered the origin of the strength of the British Empire."[58]

Japanese attitudes toward their Asiatic enemies were heavily influenced by the official propaganda that denigrated everyone who was not Japanese. Hajime Kondo was an infantryman in the Japanese Imperial Army who fought in China, and his recollections of campaigning there underscore the dehumanizing effect of Japanese attitudes and training. "They were labelled as an inferior race," he said of the Chinese. "But the Japanese people—a divine people—are the most superior race. But the Chinese were below pigs. That was the mentality we had."[59] In his personal experience, the widespread atrocities the Japanese committed in China were the direct result of this officially promulgated culture.

There were also instances on both sides of the Pacific war where men could recognize the humanity of their enemy, but sometimes only after death's intervention. An American Marine on Iwo Jima, remembering the moment when Japanese soldiers launched a doomed charge against his unit, said, "I shot one of the first ones out of the cave and took his helmet off. He had a flag inside his helmet. I looked at him, and he looked just like me. He was a kid, young. It was heroic coming out of there." Forty years after the war, the incident stayed with him. "I didn't think too much then, but I've thought about it ever since. His face is in my eyes. I see him when I go to sleep at night."[60] Another Marine fighting on Iwo Jima had almost the same experience. Searching the body of a Japanese soldier, he found "a picture in the top of his helmet of his family back in Tokyo or somewhere in Japan. He was standing erect with his helmet under his arm, wife and six children—cute-looking little children. Even after all we went through, all these tough Marines started to tear up a little bit. . . . They choked up seeing that."[61]

On the other side, a Japanese soldier fighting in the Philippines recalled an American soldier whom his unit killed. "We searched through the dead soldier's belongings," he wrote in his diary, "and found a bible, a diary and a photo of his mother. . . . His mother is a woman with a very kind face. I don't know if he is her only son. How grieved she would be if she were to hear that her son was killed."[62]

As I have already noted, the European Theater of the Second World War was characterized by less national and racial animosity, at least in the western campaigns. There were some exceptions, of course—one American company commander from the 1st Infantry Division who fought in Normandy remembered that he "regarded the Nazis with absolute hatred for the things they had perpetrated." Even that assessment, though, was qualified by a caveat: "However, as a professional soldier myself," he said, "I had a high respect for their infantry, who fought very tenaciously. They were crackerjack troops."[63] Another infantryman of the 1st Infantry Division, Frank King, recalled the first time his battalion went up against the Germans in North Africa. "They found that the German soldier was just altogether a better soldier than we were," he said. "They had better training, they had better equipment, and they had more combat experience than we did. You talk about kicking ass, they kicked ass. I'll tell you they just ran over us."[64]

A British trooper in the 1st Royal Tank Regiment who also fought in Normandy encountered at least one German face-to-face and found the man to be just an ordinary fellow, albeit in the enemy's uniform. "Got a prisoner yesterday," he wrote in his journal on August 6. "Luckily Vick could speak German fairly fluently. Was 42, an Austrian from Vienna, married with two children (photo of youngest girl—3 years—was really beautiful). Glad to get out of the war . . . a decent chap—made me think really hard—this war's so bloody futile. There's ordinary blokes on each side with no desire to kill each other, yet here we are."[65] More than one Allied soldier reported a similar experience, especially as the war moved into Germany and the end approached. In the fighting on the Eastern Front, however, things were markedly different.

The political ideologies of fascism and communism were implacably opposed to each other, and the propaganda engines of both systems spared no amount of rhetoric or invective in their efforts to demonize and dehumanize the men fighting on the other side. The Nazi doctrine of Aryan supremacy did not admit the humanity of Jews, and it regarded the Slavic peoples of the east as subhuman, barely better than animals. The degree to which this insidious propaganda was believed or accepted by the ordinary German soldier is debatable; obviously there were as many different responses to it as there were men to hear it. But the fact remains that many soldiers in the Wehrmacht at least paid lip service to the official party line, and in some cases their individual acceptance of Nazi doctrine went far beyond that. Whether the individual German soldier fully believed in Nazi racial theories is perhaps irrelevant, since that army implemented those theories to carry out the murder of millions of people, and even if the individual soldier himself was an otherwise decent man, that was not enough to balance the moral scale.

Hans Roth, a *Panzerjaeger* who fought in Russia from 1941 to 1943, kept a series of journals throughout his time on the front. In the early days of Operation Barbarossa, when the German onslaught into Russia seemed unstoppable, he wrote of seeing a column of Red Army prisoners on the road:

> *The long line of Soviets [prisoners] passes. What kind of people are they? In their eyes and in their demeanor is something strange, something dull, completely un-European, even un-human. Bolshevism has destroyed their soul and de-humanized them to an animal level; therefore they fight out of instinct like animals in a herd. . . . Humans in the state of animals are much lower than the actual animal. This is why the animal Bolshevik is so hard and bloodthirsty, cruel and stubborn against the enemy and against himself. This is how to understand the demeanor of the Soviet in this war. What looks like braveness is brutality!*[66]

As the war dragged on and certain victory bogged down in the horrific hardship of the Russian winter and Soviet forces fought back with ever greater efficacy, Roth's impression of the Soviet soldier changed somewhat. He never really backed away from his initial views of their qualities as men, but bitter experience taught him to regard them as formidable adversaries, at least. "We all underestimated though, the leadership as well as the smallest soldier—the Russian himself," he wrote. "He is the toughest enemy, the grimmest fighter that we have encountered up until now. The six weeks of trench warfare outside Kiev has demonstrated better than ever his strength, as well as his weakness. The strength of the Red Army soldier lies in the defense." Even so, Roth felt that some part of the Soviet soldier's tenacity in the fight had to stem from the brutality of the Red Army's political system. "The most distinguishing trait of the Russian soldier," he wrote, "is his stoic holding out until the end, often out of fear of the commissars."[67]

Some weeks later, reeling from the steady drain of combat casualties his unit was suffering in days of unremitting fighting, Roth's impression of the enemy had simplified even further. For every Soviet soldier the Germans killed, ten more seemed to take his place in the line. "The immense Red losses give too easily the wrong impression that our fight here in the East is not that difficult," he wrote. "To the contrary; the true picture of the enemy goes like this: tough, stubborn and malicious."[68]

Lest the reader think that this arc of understanding reflected only the personal experience of one German soldier, official battle assessments published by the Wehrmacht during the fighting on the Eastern Front showed a similar evolution of perception as Soviet tactical ability was refined in the crucible of heavy combat. In a discussion of Soviet battle performance in 1941, a German Army report stated:

> *The attack methods employed by the Russian infantry showed that the troops were inadequately trained. The infantry units emerged from their jump-off position in a disorderly manner, having the appearance of a disorganized herd that suddenly emerged from a forest. As soon as the Germans opened fire, panic developed in the ranks of the attack force. The infantrymen had to be driven forward by three or four officers with drawn pistols. In many instances any attempt to retreat or even to glance backward was punished with immediate execution. There was virtually no mutual fire support or coordinated fire. Typical of Russian infantry tactics was the tenacity with which the attack was repeated over and over again. The Russians never abandoned ground which they had gained in an attack.*[69]

Using these sort of bludgeon tactics, throwing massed concentrations of men against German guns, Soviet combat losses in dead and wounded were staggering. Yet still they kept coming, and as they came, they learned. A few months after the report just cited, another Wehrmacht after-action report on a specific small-unit fight presented a different assessment, one in which was written the death knell of the German Army in the east. "In this engagement," the report said, "the Russians demonstrated extraordinary skill in approaching through the snow-covered forests without attracting the attention of the Germans. They permitted small German reconnaissance patrols to pass at will to create the impression that the forest was clear."[70]

SS Obersturmbannführer Joachim Peiper, who had his own well-earned reputation for combat brutality, had an impression of Soviet soldiers that came from three years of fighting against them:

On defense the Russian surpasses any soldier I know. Excellent choice of ground, unimaginable diggings combined with good camouflage and unusual depth in the fighting zone are among his characteristics. Every infantryman carries anti-tank grenades. Snipers are effective up to 800 yards. The infantrymen are tough, persistent and given to weight carrying. In a retreat, they will hand-carry their dead to obscure casualty figures.

German soldiers who witnessed the Soviet Army's appalling willingness to throw men against guns found the tactical approach of the U.S. Army to be markedly different by contrast. Walter Klein, fighting as an infantryman in Normandy after serving on the Eastern Front, had sufficient experience to draw a distinction between how the Russians and the Americans fought. "If the American infantry did not approach our lines," Klein stated, "it was not from cowardice, but because they were ordered to withdraw as soon as they met strong resistance and to wait until the air force and the heavy weapons had exhausted the [defence]. Our infantrymen, who could not count upon any such help and who had seen the Russian infantry in action, could not have had a better opinion of the American infantry."[71]

For their part, the Soviets described their German enemy in terms that took the confrontation far beyond the straightforward adversarial nature of war. In the florid language of the Marxist-Leninist rhetoric used so stridently by Soviet propaganda organs, the struggle was infused with the intractable animosity of ideological conflict—communist progressiveness locked in mortal combat with the reactionary forces of Nazi fascism. From their own narratives, it seems that many Soviet soldiers endorsed this political interpretation of the war, at least in the moment. Beyond the political element, though, there were other elements that made the war on the Eastern Front a conflict of greater savagery and deeper hatred than what usually characterized the war in the west. The German invasion of Russia and their brutality as occupiers combined to create in the average Soviet soldier a degree of personal hatred that guaranteed that this would be a war of blood vengeance. The aim in the east was not just the tactical destruction of the enemy's combat power, but the absolute destruction of the enemy's political system, society, and very existence.

For Soviet soldiers, the war was personal. Regardless of how they were brought into the Red Army's ranks, whether they volunteered (as they did in massive numbers) or whether they were compelled through conscription as millions more were, the war against Nazi Germany was a struggle in which they had a very real stake that went far beyond such mundane matters as their own survival. In this respect, at least, they had something in common with the British soldiers of 1940–1941 who had faced the very real possibility of a German invasion of the British Isles, and nothing whatsoever in common with the majority of American soldiers who often felt a philosophical enmity toward Nazism but very little personal animosity toward the individual German infantryman. As historian John Erickson puts it, for the Soviet soldier "the driving force was consuming hatred of the enemy, exemplified in the propaganda but personalized in exacting vengeance by millions who had seen for themselves, or suffered through their families what German rule had done."[72] This hatred was very real, and it went both ways—German and Soviet soldiers who fell into each other's hands as prisoners had a very low expectation of survival and absolutely no expectation of decent treatment.

The Soviets were not the only combatants in the Second World War who held an implacable hatred for the Germans and who regarded the fight against them as a crusade. Polish soldiers who fought in the Free Polish units in the Allied armies in the west held an implacable animosity for their German adversary. Interestingly, this degree of hostile feeling did not exist to the same degree in the German-invaded countries in Western Europe such as Belgium and Holland, where, despite a real and committed armed resistance to the German occupation, the Germans were still able to raise local regiments of volunteers to fight against the Soviets in the east, wearing German uniform and under German command. The Poles, on the other hand, were willing to neither forgive nor forget what happened in September 1939 when the Wehrmacht invaded their homeland, and they were willing to pay a heavy price for the chance to strike back at the Germans.

In the ferocious fighting around Monte Cassino in Italy, the Polish II Corps undertook an assault that had already cost British and Commonwealth troops heavily. Their rationale was simple—it gave them the chance to come to grips with their hated enemy. In the language that the Polish commander, General Wladyslaw Anders, used, it was clear that the Poles had a long memory where Germans were concerned. "We have long awaited the moment for revenge and retribution over our hereditary enemies," Anders wrote in his preoperational order to his soldiers.[73] When the moment came, it was not wasted; the Poles were successful in their attack, though at considerable cost in lives.

The Polish animosity toward the Germans was a matter of some surprise to their British allies, who were prone to a more "professional" attitude that did not readily embrace such strong personal emotions as hatred. One British officer in the Lancashire Fusiliers described the Poles, saying, "We got along very well together, though they never could wholly conceal their slight impatience with our attitude. They hated the Germans, and their military outlook was dominated by hate. Their one idea was to find out where the nearest Germans were and go after them. . . . They thought we were far too casual because we didn't breathe blind hate all the time."[74] The Poles, who in that war were basically men without a country, were fighting against the enemy whom they blamed for the loss of home and hearth, and they spared nothing in the cause. The memorial to their dead at Monte Cassino is one of the most evocative of the war:

We Polish soldiers
For our freedom and yours
Have given our souls to God
Our bodies to the soil of Italy
And our hearts to Poland.

Just as there were perceptions of an unequal partnership between the British and their Spanish allies during the Peninsular War and between the British and Turks in the Crimean War, so too were there strained relationships between allies in the Second World War. A hypercompetitive and often suspicious relationship prevailed between the Allies, particularly between the Soviet Union and everyone else. Just as the British in the Peninsular War felt that the Spanish did not fight hard enough against their mutual enemy the French, so too did the Soviets in 1942 complain that their Western allies were not pressing the war against Germany as hard as they should.

There was also the official party-line view, propounded by official Soviet versions of the war, which claimed that the Red Army won the war practically on its own. Soviet history textbooks published after the war casually dismissed the American-Anglo contribution to Germany's defeat, saying that when the British and American armies finally and very belatedly landed in Normandy after years of inactivity while Soviet soldiers died fighting the fascists, they then encountered little resistance in their stroll across Western Europe while the Red Army was paying a heavy sacrifice every step of the way in its supposedly unaided drive on Berlin. That is a rather skewed version of the reality, to put it mildly. We *can* say that the turning point of the war in Europe came at Stalingrad in 1943, and there is no arguing with the fact that the Soviet Union lost more people killed in the war than any other belligerent nation, but the USSR did not win the war on its own, not by any standard of assessment.

Strained relations existed between allies in other theaters of the war, as well. Most American and British soldiers were not impressed by the Chinese troops they worked with, in terms of either their tactical proficiency or their discipline—the Chinese were lacking in both qualities, they believed. Neville Hogan was a British truck driver whose transportation unit was tasked with moving Chinese troops through Burma. "They were a menace," he recalled. "If you left your rifle or rations unattended they took them. We dared not leave the truck in case they took the truck. They had no discipline. The junior officers were just bandits."[75] In the Chinese case, Hogan may have inadvertently put his finger on the crux of the problem. The Chinese Army was handicapped by an endemically corrupt officer corps, and the lack of training combined with poor leadership gave them a bad reputation, indeed.

This was not a phenomenon unique to the Second World War—in the First World War many American soldiers, coming late to a war that had bled their British and French allies white for three years by that point, saw themselves as the saviors of Europe. This perspective was not shared by their European counterparts, who often interpreted American enthusiasm as arrogance or, at the very least, as an irritating ignorance of just how high the cost had been for the British and French in the three years they had fought in the war before the United States entered the fray.[76]

On the Axis side in the Second World War the relationships were even more acrimonious and imbalanced, particularly between Germany and Italy. Hitler had a genuine admiration for Mussolini as a fascist leader, at least in the early years, but that admiration did not extend to the Italian Army or its performance in the field. Italian soldiers suffered heavily as a result of their government's ill-advised, poorly planned, and ineptly conducted campaigns in Ethiopia, Libya, Albania, and Greece, but the Italian regiments who fought alongside the Wehrmacht on the Eastern Front suffered even more.

For the most part, the Germans denigrated the Italian contribution to the Axis cause. They disparaged the Italians' combat ability, their courage, and their hardiness. Panzerjaeger Hans Roth had a typical German view of the Italian formations fighting in Russia. Writing in his journal after a massive Soviet counterattack had pushed his unit back some miles, Roth described one incident which for him typified the Italians as allies. A German heavy artillery unit was desperately trying to move their guns; Roth's antitank unit was sent in to assist. "We are supposed to help and move in with our traction engines," he wrote. "It is hard to explain [to the artillery commander] that we have just enough gasoline for an emergency, in case we have to evacuate the most valuable parts. No Italian position gave us any gas. The German soldiers can bleed; the Italian gentlemen need the gas to flee."[77] Roth's scathing commentary was not necessarily fair, since the incident he described was a general withdrawal and the Italians were not the only ones falling back at the time, but fair or not, his opinion was widely shared by German soldiers who fought alongside Italian formations.

The Italian soldier, taken as an individual, was no better and often no worse than other soldiers of the Second World War, but he was certainly more unfortunate than almost all others. (An argument might be made that Romanian soldiers, whose political masters committed them to battle first for the Axis and then the Allies, were substantially worse off in some respects.) The Italian soldier was poorly trained, inadequately equipped, indifferently armed, and almost always incompetently led. The best soldiers in the world would be disadvantaged by that list of problems, and the average Italian infantrymen were by no means the best, so they were at a considerable disadvantage, indeed. It did not help that many of them were reluctant soldiers, especially after the debacles brought about by Mussolini's imperial ambitions.

All of these factors worked against the Italians in the assessment of their German allies. Even the notionally elite formations of the Italian Army, such as paratroopers, did not generate much respect. "Columns of Italian infantry move past, including paratroop units," wrote a German *fallschirmjaeger* named Martin Poppel during the evacuation from Sicily in 1943. "They look bizarre, our Axis colleagues. We still haven't heard— at least here in Sicily—of any heroic deeds on their part."[78]

From the perspective of many Italian soldiers, the relationship with their German ally was rather like the uneasy concord that might exist between a fox and a wolf, and the Italians were definitely the smaller, weaker half of the alliance, worrying about the moment when the wolf would turn and bite. That moment finally came in 1943.

So long as the Italian Fascist government remained a combatant partner in the Axis alliance, that alliance held, even if Italy was always the weaker partner. With the fall of Mussolini in 1943 and the efforts on the part of the new Italian government to change sides, the German wolf finally turned on the Italian fox. Italian units were disarmed under German guns, and there were several instances where Italian soldiers were massacred by the Wehrmacht in mass, summary executions. In short order, as historian Brian Sullivan observes, "A great many Italian soldiers, from generals to privates, had come to fear and hate the German army by September 1943."[79]

—◦—

Throughout the period of this text, as in every era of human history, men held preconceived ideas of the soldiers who were both their enemies and allies. Often those preconceptions were reinforced by experience, but sometimes they were overturned by the reality of personal encounters. More than one man realized that his horizons had been greatly expanded by his time in the army, and frequently that broader understanding included an enlightened perspective of his counterparts of different armies.

"While serving in that corps," George Manington wrote after he left the French Foreign Legion, "I had learned that there were good and brave men outside my own country, and that courage, obedience, self-abnegation and national pride are not the monopoly of any one race. By living side by side with them, fighting, and oft-times suffering, in the same cause, I had been taught to like and respect the foreigners, the French, Italian, German, Austrian, or any other European soldier is very much like our own. He has his virtues and his vices; and the stronger his race and national character, the more likely is he to possess a superabundance of the latter."[80]

Manington's perspective was on European soldiers in conventional, modern armies, but those same men often had reason to give an opinion of their other adversaries that was every bit as complimentary. Many soldiers left records of their admiration for the fighting qualities of their opponents in place like Morocco, Indochina, Ashanti, Afghanistan, Mexico, New Zealand, and South Africa. Rudyard Kipling's poem "Fuzzy Wuzzy," which praises the tough warriors of the Mahdi's Sudanese armies, is an apt note on which to close a chapter on allies and enemies:

So 'ere's ~to~ you, Fuzzy-Wuzzy, at your 'ome in the Soudan;
You're a pore benighted 'eathen but a first-class fightin' man.

CHAPTER FOURTEEN

Discipline and Punishment

There is nothing so dangerous, to the civil establishment of a state, as a licentious and undisciplined army.

—EARL OF ROSSLYN,
LORD CHIEF JUSTICE OF THE COMMON PLEAS

THERE IS PERHAPS AN INHERENT RISK IN WRITING a chapter that places together these two concepts—discipline and punishment—because too often it is assumed that these two things are one and the same. In point of fact, they are not. As the U.S. Army teaches in its leadership manuals, punishment is sometimes a necessary result of discipline, but discipline is not inherently punishment. The two are not the same thing, but they *are* closely related and inextricably linked to each other, so much so that where the one ends the other begins.

Describing the culture of military discipline that existed in the U.S. Army of the post–Civil War period, Don Rickey writes, "Fear of punishment was the basis of discipline."[1] This perspective has been true of soldiers in armies throughout history and is a sociological constant in human behavior across most societies and cultures. It is the fear of the punitive and punishing hand of the law, after all, that holds many miscreants in check, particularly when the hand that delivers punishment is known to be swift, sure, and severe.

The British Army at the beginning of this period was subject to a code of military law that was, in a word, brutal. It was not just the punishments themselves that were harsh, but the frequency with which they were applied. In 1810 there were no fewer than 222 offenses that officially carried the death penalty, although in practice that extreme punishment was commonly applied to only about twenty offenses. On the other hand, corporal punishment in the British Army, in the form of flogging, was taken to such an extreme that sentences of as many as five hundred lashes were sometimes handed down in courts-martial. That number of lashes was enough to kill a man outright, leading more than one contemporary observer to question the ultimate intent of the sentence.

The degree to which a British soldier was imperiled by the threat of flogging depended to some degree on his own conduct, to be certain, but beyond that the infliction of this punishment could be incredibly capricious. The returns of a regiment in 1811 give a striking indication of just how harsh the punishments could be for utterly banal, trivial offenses:

> *"Deficient of frill, part of his regimental necessaries."—100 lashes.*
> *"Deficient of a razor, part of his regimental necessaries."—200 lashes: (100 inflicted); also to be put under stoppages of 1/- a week .until the razor is replaced.*
> *"For having in his possession some pease for which he cannot honestly account, and for making an improper use of the barrack bedding."—400 lashes. (200 inflicted).*[2]

British military justice in that era, as so many contemporary critics argued, could seldom be described as "just."

Some British officers were benevolent masters who resorted to the lash only when the severity of the offense or the immutability of military law required them to, but others were notorious for the harshness of their leadership and their proclivity for flogging men on almost any pretext. General Robert "Black Bob" Crauford, the tactically brilliant but moody commander of the Light Division in the early years of the Peninsular War, was a ferociously strict disciplinarian who threatened to flog any man in his brigade who stepped out of the line of march in order to avoid a mud puddle in the road. Coming from a man like Crauford, it was not an idle threat.

The issue of discipline and punishment was almost never discussed by recruiting sergeants in their glowing portrayals of army life, unless it was to impress gullible youths with how easy army discipline was. At least one British regiment printed recruiting posters touting the "light discipline and no harsh punishments" in its ranks. The reality, as more than a few recruits discovered, was altogether different.

Henry Franks, who fought at Balaclava in the Crimean War as a troop sergeant major in the Heavy Brigade, encountered the harsh side of military discipline on his very first day in the army. The day that he joined his regiment, he witnessed a soldier being flogged for insubordination. The soldier's life that the recruiting NCO had described in such glowing terms, he realized, might not in fact be the case. The army was not going to be all "beer and skittles."

In an era when a considerable portion of some armies' recruits were rough men at best and outright criminals at worst, the common belief was that strict discipline and severe punishments were the only way to prevent the uniformed army from reverting back to type and degenerating into a larcenistic, rapacious rabble. Harsh forms of corporal punishment were employed to force men into conformity with military customs and regulations from the first days of their enlistment, and as a means of keeping them firmly in line for the duration of their service.

This was particularly true of armies whose soldiers were largely drawn from the poor and illiterate peasant classes who were forced into the ranks rather than enlisted by choice. The tsarist Russian armies and those of the Chinese warlords were always more of this type than were armies of Western Europe or North America. The Russians were infamous for their enthusiastic application of the knout on their soldiers as both a motivator and punishment. The Chinese, for all of their convictions of cultural superiority, were regarded by Europeans as a throwback to a more savage age on account of their practice of having an official executioner assigned to each regiment, a man who doubled as both torturer and headsman. In the Chinese armies of the late Qing Dynasty during this period, both the imperial armies and the private armies of regional warlords, capital punishment was an ever-present tool.

Flogging existed in almost every army at the beginning of the period, though the frequency with which it was applied varied widely. The British retained flogging in their litany of punishments long after most other

Western armies had abolished the practice, not giving it up officially until 1881 (though by that point the number of lashes allowed for any offense was reduced to twenty-five). The French, in an odd twist of humanitarian progressivism stemming out of the conflicting ideas originating in the Revolution, did not employ the lash at all. They were, however, much more liberal in their use of the death penalty, applying capital punishment to a total of forty-five different offenses in the early nineteenth century.

The U.S. Army from its inception in 1775 used flogging, though with less frequency and certainly for fewer offenses that did its European counterparts of the same era. The number of lashes that could be inflicted on an American soldier was limited to fifty in 1806; then Congress abolished the punishment altogether during the War of 1812. Flogging was reinstated in the U.S. Army in 1833, and the lash remained an option of military justice in the American army right up until the Civil War, when it was finally stricken from Army Regulations in 1861. Until that date, the offense for which it was most commonly applied was the crime of desertion, for which it was usually one in a series of punishments.

In 1858, Private Alenson Bently of the 1st U.S. Dragoons was convicted by court-martial in California on charges of desertion and horse stealing. The sentence was "fifty lashes with a cowhide, well laid on the bare back, to be confined at hard labor [for three years], heavily ironed, to forfeit all pay due him, to have his head shaved, and be branded with a red hot iron with the letter D, to be drummed out of the service, and receive a dishonorable discharge."[3] Two other soldiers who were tried and convicted with Bently received the same sentence, but the court recommended clemency and their punishments were remitted so that they could return to duty.

The abolition of flogging in the U.S. Army did not mean that other corporal punishments were any less creative or numerous. Some were specifically appropriate to the offense—in the U.S. Army of the Indian Wars era, a typical punishment for a cavalryman who allowed his horse to develop saddle galls, or whose horse got away from him, was to walk for a day while his comrades rode. American soldiers earlier in the century were liable to such punishments as:

being tied to a tree for a day, carrying a knapsack filled with shot, standing on a stump for long periods, riding a fence post with a musket swinging from each foot, straddling a wooden horse, "cobbling" (paddling with a board or strip), wearing a ball and chain, ducking, and shaving the eyebrows and head. Even more brutal were picketing (being forced to stand on a sharpened stick), cutting or cropping of the ears, and branding on the cheek, forehead, or hip with the letter "D." From 1865 to 1870 tattooing was a legal substitute. By a congressional act of June 6, 1872, branding and indelibly marking were prohibited. Sometimes the court-martial simply sentenced the deserter to be drummed or bugled out of the service, which according to one observer, "amounts to gratifying his desire to leave, and he is tendered in addition the gratuitous ovation of a parting serenade."[4]

The serenade in question was the "Rogue's March," the lyrics of which went *"Poor old soldier, poor old soldier / Tarred and feathered and sent to hell / Because he would not soldier well."* To the accompaniment of that inspiring tune, the disgraced soldier was drummed out of camp.

Corporal punishment was the hallmark of professional standing armies during the nineteenth century, but when military necessity in time of war brought a wider swath of citizens into the ranks through involuntary conscription, attitudes toward this form of punishment changed. This, in addition to growing humanitarian concerns, was one of the forces that led to its general abolition in most armies by the beginning of the twentieth century. Even though the severity of military sentences, in particular the imposition of corporal punishment, was greatly reduced, there were still the die-hard military conservatives who argued that nothing became a recalcitrant soldier so well as a good, officially mandated beating.

⸺

As has been true throughout the history of warfare, not every man whose country required him to become a soldier actually *wanted* to be a soldier. Conscription is often bitterly resented by those whose lives it disrupts, and men who had never wanted to join the army in the first place often could not wait to get out of the army. Some, in every army, chose not to wait for discharge or death to release them, but opted instead for the most expedient method of separation from the army—they deserted.

Desertion was never limited to conscripts, of course. More than a few young men who had rushed off to enlist in a surge of adventurism or patriotic fervor at the start of a war quickly repented their hasty decision when they encountered the hard realities of military life. Whether the ranks were filled with volunteers or conscripted soldiers, desertion was a problem that affected all armies of the period to one degree or another; all armies responded to it with punishments that ranged from the creative to the draconian. The most serious form of desertion was that which happened in time of war—especially, in the legal language of the U.S. Army, "desertion in the face of the enemy." For that crime, the standard punishment in all armies was death.

Leon Louis, who fought for the Confederacy in a North Carolina regiment, remarked on this grim spectacle in the journal he kept throughout the war. On February 25, 1863, he wrote, "Two men out of our regiment were whipped for desertion." The punishment was fairly light, considering the offense—each man received thirty-nine lashes, but they were not executed as they very well could have been. On May 11th, however, Louis's regiment was paraded to witness the execution by firing squad of two men who were shot for desertion. "After they were shot," he wrote, "we marched by them and saw one was hit six times and the other four." In September that year he recorded the execution of another deserter from his regiment, who was shot by a firing party of twelve men. Eleven of the muskets were loaded with ball, and at least the majority of the firing squad aimed true: "Eight balls passed through him," Louis wrote.[5]

This was the common punishment for desertion in time of war. How frequently it was actually imposed varied greatly from army to army and from era to era. The British Army's somewhat excessive use of the death penalty for desertion during the First World War has acquired a heightened notoriety in recent histories. One such case in 1915 was recounted by Henry Williamson of the London Rifle Brigade:

While I was at Armentieres I was detailed to form part of a firing squad at the execution of a deserter. He was tied to a post against a wall in his civilian clothes, and we were told to fire at a piece of white cloth pinned over his heart. We didn't know what the rifles were loaded with—some were load with ball, others with blank. Then we had the order to fire and pulled the triggers—we knew by the recoil if it was loaded with ball or not. Then the deserter's name was read out on three successive parades, as a warning.[6]

It is worth noting that even when a firing squad or gallows were the prescribed legal punishments for military desertion, they were not always resorted to. Some commanders, in fact, were known to seize on any available reason to commute a death sentence. It was also not uncommon for "creative" punishments to be imposed in place of the death penalty—public humiliation was a frequent tool of military justice. John Green, a British soldier in the 68th Regiment of Foot during the Napoleonic Wars, recalled the punishment of a corporal who had deserted his company under fire. "He was led by the colonel in front of each company at the morning parade, the colonel saying as he passed 'Soldiers, behold a coward.' The corporal was then taken in front of the whole regiment, his stripes ripped from his sleeve and he was sent ignominiously back to his company as a private."[7] It is probably not an exaggeration to say that for a man who had been an NCO to be thus shamed, demoted, and returned to the ranks with his failure made so public, such a punishment may well have seemed worse than death.

American officers early in the period were also given to imposing punishments that were either medieval, humane, or creatively inventive, depending upon one's perspective. A militiaman who fought in the War of 1812 wrote of one occasion when several soldiers who could have been shot for desertion were spared death, but were instead punished in another way:

Three men were brought up who were substitutes for drafted men; their crime was desertion. Their sentence was read to them and put into execution immediately after. They were stripped naked, their pantaloons excepted. Their backs were daubed with tar, to make a paper stick thereon, containing their crime in very large letters. Their hands and feet were tied together; and in this position they were hung by hand and feet to a rail and carried by the front of the lines; afterwards their left eye-brows were shaved. They were afterwards ordered to be taken to the guard-house, and there left hand kuffed [sic] and on half rations, during four days, before liberated.[8]

In 1847 the proceedings of a U.S. Army general court-martial, conducted during the Mexican-American War, were published as General Orders No. 281. "No higher punishment can, therefore, be legally inflicted upon those atrocious offenders—T. Riley, J. Mills, and J. Reilly," the orders read, "than that prescribed for a state of peace, viz: fifty lashes with a rawhide whip, well laid on the bare back of each, and their punishment is commuted accordingly, with the addition that each be branded on a cheek with the letter 'D;' kept a close prisoner as long as this army remains in Mexico, and then be drummed out of the service."[9] American military commanders were not averse to imposing capital punishment for desertion in time of war, which was when this court-martial was convened. What saved the lives of these three men, however, was a legal technicality. "The 3 men," one commentator noted, "deserted in April, 1846, before a condition of war existed"; it was this detail that prompted the commutation of their death sentences.[10]

Flogging and branding both were legal punishments for desertion in the U.S. Army until the period of the Civil War. Even though these punishments were notionally lighter than the death penalty, they were still undeniably harsh. Even after the branding of deserters was finally abolished, American military law until 1870 still called for deserters to be "indelibly marked," or tattooed, on the hip with a letter D. Prison sentences of two years at hard labor were standard, as was shackling with a ball and chain.[11] And this was punishment for desertion in *peacetime*.

Desertion was a constant problem for all armies, in both peace and war, and the varying severity of the methods used to punish it were never enough to eradicate the problem completely. Desertion remained a threat to discipline in both the Union and Confederate Armies throughout the Civil War, so much so that some soldiers were frequent witnesses to deserters' punishments as the war dragged on and martial enthusiasm waned.

Desertion, murder, and rape were the "fatal three" of military transgressions, the crimes that carried the death penalty in most armies. Below these felonious misdeeds there was a long, long list of more minor offenses proscribed by the various forms of military justice, ranging from the truly criminal to the ridiculously petty. Theft, arson, drunkenness, absenting oneself from duty, slovenly personal appearance, having dirty equipment or an ungroomed horse . . . all of these offenses were violations of the "good order and discipline" that was so much a part of army life.

There was never any shortage of ways in which a soldier could run afoul of military authority. "Every religious denomination furnishes a 'vade mecum' which teaches the believer what he must do to be saved," General William T. Sherman wrote in 1890, "but the military profession offers only the articles of war, which amount to 'You'll be damned if you do, and you'll be damned if you don't.'"[12] The army was never circumspect about what was prohibited and what was not, and for much of this period the U.S. Army mandated that the Articles of War be read to the troops on a regular basis, so that no soldier could ever claim ignorance of the law. Paul Totten, a U.S. infantryman in the Russian Expedition against the Bolsheviks in 1918, expressed the regular soldier's bored familiarity with this ritual when he wrote in his diary, "Articles of war read to us by Capt. Ramsey (our skipper), about as interesting as a dreamless sleep."[13]

The things prohibited by military law could sometimes be surprising for their sheer banality. In the French Army in the years just before the First World War, one French trooper recalled, "It is a curious fact that reading a newspaper constitutes an offence against discipline in the French Army, and no newspapers are permitted to be brought into barracks."[14] One could draw several conclusions, none of them complimentary to the French military, as to why newspapers in the hands of the rank and file were regarded as a danger to the army's discipline and internal equilibrium.

Breaches of military discipline resulted from many causes, some unique and others common to almost every army. Drunkenness was arguably the most common cause of soldierly misconduct, and as we saw in a previous chapter, almost none of the armies studied in this period were immune to that particular vice. Don Rickey was correct when he wrote, "Liquor, releaser of inhibitions and destroyer of order, has been, to some degree, a major disruptor of military discipline in all armies."[15] Alcohol was a particular problem for frontier garrisons in the U.S. Army, just as it was for British soldiers throughout the nineteenth century.

Drunkenness was punished in a variety of ways. During the Civil War, soldiers in both the Union and Confederate Armies were made to stand on barrels in the midst of their battalions' encampments wearing placards on which were written such informative phrases as "I got drunk." The same crime could also be punished with time in the stocks or a period in the guardroom if one was available.

The 1848 Standing Orders of the 90th Light Infantry, a British regiment, made it clear how just pernicious the army regarded the effects of heavy drinking among the rank and file. "Drunkenness may be considered as the cause of almost every evil which occurs in a Regiment," the Order stated in Section XIV. "Officers and Non-commissioned Officers are called upon to adopt every possible means to discountenance it," it went on to say. "It will on no occasion plead as an excuse for the commission of offenses, but as an aggravation; and what might be overlooked on other occasions, will, when the effect of drunkenness, never be pardoned."[16] More than one promising career was derailed by a drunken binge on payday; more than one NCO lost his stripes to an excess of rum and whiskey.

A soldier too far gone in his drink could be unpredictable and dangerous (particularly as he often had ready access to firearms), as both civilian and military authorities knew all too well. Thomas Morris, who was a newly promoted sergeant after the Battle of Waterloo, recounted an incident when he was nearly killed by one of his soldiers who was roaring drunk and violently irrational:

I was sent to quiet one of our men, who was drunk and disorderly in his quarters. . . . I found the man quarreling with some colliers, and insisted upon his going to bed immediately, or else I threatened to send him to the guard-room. . . . I got the man upstairs, and placed him on his bed, when he took hold of his musket, which was close by, and deliberately putting the muzzle to my breast, said, 'D—n you; I'll shoot you!' Not supposing the piece to be loaded, I gently removed it from my breast, when it exploded—the ball passing between my arm and my side, lodged in the wall, over the window, where, probably, it still remains.[17]

With that single shot, the intoxicated soldier imperiled his life—threatening an NCO was bad enough, but actually attempting to kill an NCO was a crime that would almost certainly send a man to the gallows. Rather than placing the soldier on a charge and consigning him to the iron hand of the army's justice, though, Morris chose to handle the matter himself and administer a more immediate punishment. "As I was acquainted with the man's friends, who were respectable tradespeople in Birmingham," he wrote, "I did not confine him, as the punishment under such circumstances would have been very severe; but I borrowed a stick from the landlord, and I [beat] on him till he fairly cried, and then went to sleep."[18] The beating was an appropriate, if unofficial, punishment, and probably saved the soldier's life—it also undoubtedly gave Morris a measure of personal satisfaction after his close call.

Even when alcohol was not the catalyst for misbehavior, violent crime was all too common in the ranks. To some degree, this was the consequence of the inevitable personal frictions that arose from having too many men living in too close and too constant contact with each other. When a man could not escape the company of his fellows, petty animosities easily flared up into serious incidents. Soldiers also got into scrapes with civilians, with whom they often had a rather adversarial relationship at the best of times.

The U.S. Army's Surgeon General's annual reports from the nineteenth century make for very interesting reading on this matter. Taking just a sampling of incidents reported during the years 1866 to 1870, we find cases such as these:

Private Joseph Smith, Troop I, 8th Cavalry, was shot by a comrade at Camp Whipple, Arizona Territory, November 17, 1867. [The bullet

367

hit Smith in the face and nearly killed him—a portion of his jaw had to be surgically removed, but he survived to be medically discharged from the army.]

Private Frank Castle, Co. C, 41st Infantry, aged 21 years, while in a brawl with other enlisted men in quarters at Fort Clark, Texas, on the night of September 8, 1868, was wounded by a small pistol ball.

Private Michael O'Callaghan, Co. D, 6th United States Cavalry, was shot by a citizen on February 9, 1867. . . . He died on the following day.

Lieutenant George F. Mason, 5th United States Cavalry, was shot in a quarrel with a citizen, near Fort D. A. Russell, Wyoming Territory, on March 1, 1870. . . . Internal hemorrhage was the immediate cause of death.

Private J. D. Morgan, Co. H, 23rd United States Infantry, was shot by a companion in a dispute on July 15, 1867. [Morgan survived his wounds, even though the bullet passed through his abdomen and colon and caused serious internal injuries.]

Private Frank Meyer, Co. E. 14th United States Infantry, aged 24 years, was wounded in a brawl on February 3, 1870, by a pistol bullet which passed through the testicles. [The wound must have been excruciating, but Meyer survived it.]

Private Patrick Pender, Co. H, 22 Infantry, received a fatal stab wound in the neck, from a fellow soldier, on the evening of November 15, 1870, at Fort Sully, Dakota Territory.

First Sergeant John Jones, Co. C, 24th Infantry, aged 21 years, was wounded June 14, 1870, in a brawl, by a pocket knife.

Private Bernard Kelly, Co. C, 1st Infantry, received July 23, 1868, a wound by a case-knife in the hands of Private Kennedy, Co. A, 1st Infantry . . . causing peritonitis and death, which resulted on the 26th.[19]

Armies, as more than one commentator has noted, thrive on order and routine, and seem to be able to create reams of regulation to govern almost every aspect of soldiers' lives both on duty and off. It is not at all surprising, then, to find that nearly every conventional army in the world has an entire litany of official responses to the slightest hint of disorder in the ranks. Some armies dictated nearly every action that officers and NCOs were to take in terms of administering discipline and punishment—others set forth a framework of military regulation but still allowed a considerable degree of personal latitude among the men who actually dealt with miscreant soldiers.

Charles Carrington left a vivid description of company-level punishment from the perspective of a junior infantry officer, which he was in the First World War. "Every day when routine permitted," he wrote, "the company commander held his conference, usually known as company orders. Here he interviewed the [company] sergeant-major, sent for N.C.O.s or men to whom he wished to give special instructions, received men who wanted advice, heard complaints, and held a court for dealing with misdemeanors":

> *The first threat to an offending soldier was: 'Take his name. Put him on a charge. Bring him up to company orders!' To be unpunctual, unshaven, idle, neglectful, insolent—or, worse than that, to have a dirty rifle, brought you hatless—which was the sign of military disgrace—before the company commander's table, with your sergeant giving evidence against you. In England the normal punishment for minor offences was confinement to barracks (CB), but in France anywhere near the front you were confined already. There was little the company commander could do except give you the rough side of his tongue and tell the sergeant-major to find some fatigues for you. There were always some dirty or unpleasant jobs to be done by somebody and it was convenient to allot them to the 'defaulters.' The severe punishments that your captain could inflict were to make an entry in your conduct-sheet which stood as a black mark against you for the rest of your military life, or to remand you for C.O.'s orders, an alarming prospect, for the colonel had formidable powers. He could take away acting rank or privilege, he could impose stoppages of pay, and he could inflict the humiliating penalty of field punishment for as long as twenty-eight days.*[20]

When Carrington referred to a soldier's sergeant "giving evidence" against him, he alluded to one of the sacred protections of the individual soldier's rights that were codified in British military law. For nearly a century by that point, the Standing Orders that governed British regiments had specified that any charges brought against a soldier, and any official consideration of his case, had to done in the bright light of day, as it were. "A Non-Commissioned Officer will *invariably* take any man he may have to complain of before the Officer of the Company," one regiment's Standing Orders of 1848 stated, "and he will never, on any account, make a report of a man behind his back; nor will an Officer ever award a punishment however trifling, without having enquired into the complaint in presence of the Soldier."[21] This did not, of course, preclude the possibility of a soldier being unfairly charged by an NCO who had it in for him personally, or that he might not be judged by a draconian officer who simply didn't give a damn for justice, but it did at least require the proceedings to be public and open.

The U.S. Army also included language in the Articles of War that established a means of redress for soldiers who felt they were unfairly treated by their chain of command:

> *Article 35. If any inferior officer or soldier shall think himself wronged by his captain or other officer he is to complain thereof to the commanding officer of the regiment, who is hereby required to summon a regimental court-martial for the sake of doing justice to the complainant; from which regimental court-martial either party may, if he thinks himself still aggrieved, appeal to a general court-martial. But if, upon a second hearing, the appeal shall appear vexatious and groundless, the person so appealing shall be punished at the discretion of the said court-martial.*[22]

There was also a clear process that was supposed to be followed if soldiers were to be punished by methods more serious than extra duties or restriction to barracks. "No soldier is to be punished by solitary confinement," the 1812 Standing Orders of the Edinburgh (51st) Militia declared, "without the previous consent and sanction of the commanding officer of the regiment, for which the commanding officers of companies are to apply when needful. Nor is any man to be confined without a written crime, if possible, except by order of the commanding officer of the regiment."[23] There was a chain of command, it was to be followed, and the company commanders did not have free rein to dispense punishments beyond a certain level—they were, in their turn, under the authority of their regimental commanders, to whom were reserved certain authorities.

In the U.S. Army of the nineteenth century, courts-martial were applied liberally—in terms of simple numbers, one might look at the thousands of cases and assume that the American soldier of that era was an incorrigible reprobate. The reality was that almost every infraction of military regulations could bring a soldier up on charges, and courts-martial were applied to offenses both serious and trivial.

In 1866, a 5th U.S. Cavalry farrier named Thomas Connor appeared before a court-martial on charges of "negligence of duty to the prejudice of good order and military discipline." The specification of the charge was that he had not kept the horses of his company shod, as he was directed to by a sergeant. The charge sheet further stated that he "did willfully fail to obey said order and did absent himself from shop and tools." Connor was reportedly drunk when he received the order and committed the offense, and unsurprisingly, the court quickly found him guilty as charged. When the case when to the department commander for review, however, there was an unexpected result. Even though he upheld the guilty verdict, the reviewing officer reduced the court's stiff sentence to a mere fine of five dollars and ten days in the guardhouse. By way of explanation for his decision, the department commander wrote, "The evidence shows fully that the farrier was drunk when ordered to shoe the horse in question and was consequently unfit and unable to obey the order given which under the circumstances was an improper one." In other words, the sergeant should have recognized that a drunken soldier might not be capable of understanding or obeying the order or carrying out the task, and that detail was regarded as a mitigating factor in Connor's cases.

On occasion it also happened that a court-martial would make the fine distinction between one offense and another, lesser one, a line of reasoning that could then be used to the soldier's benefit. Private Henry

McFarlane was tried on a charge of desertion in 1873, but the court threw out the desertion charge and instead ruled that he was only guilty of being absent without leave, a far less serious offense. McFarlane was sentenced to forfeit ten dollars of his pay, rather than the confinement at hard labor and dishonorable discharge he could have received for the desertion charge. The same court-martial also tried Private David W. Harnett for desertion. In Harnett's case, the court found him guilty and sentenced him to a year's hard labor and forfeiture of one hundred twenty dollars. The court obviously considered each man's case on its individual merits and reached two markedly different conclusions on two identical charges.

When Private William King was court-martialed in 1875, it was initially a relatively trivial charge, but things started to look grim for him when the court added the charge of "false swearing" because of statements he made during trial. The court convicted King and sentenced him to forfeiture of pay. Upon review, however, the department commander disagreed with both the verdict and the sentence; "the evidence," he wrote, "is regarded as failing to show any false or corrupt motive in [King's] apparent self-contradiction." He then cited King's sixteen years of exemplary service and certificates for excellent character and declared that the whole charge was based on "the result of a misunderstanding or a want of due examination on the part of his immediate superiors." Private King returned to duty with his service record unblemished.

When a soldier's misconduct was relatively minor and not actually criminal, military justice in the French Army was similar to that in the British Army. "Privates are punished in various ways, according to the nature of the offence committed," a French veteran recalled:

> *The lightest punishment of all consists of extra fatigue duty; next in order comes inspection on guard parade, the man in question being compelled to parade with the guard in full marching order for a definite number of times; confinement to barracks for a stated period is inflicted for still more serious but still light offences; being sent to the sale de police is a considerably severer form of punishment, and consists*

in the offenders being kept at night in the guard-room, doing ordinary duty during the day, and, in addition, doing all sorts of fatigues and being the scavengers of the regiment.[24]

When these measures proved insufficient, or when the offender was particularly recalcitrant, the heavy hand of military justice grew heavier still. "Prison and solitary confinement in cells are two forms of punishment allotted to really bad characters on whom the previously named forms of punishment have not had sufficient effect," this soldier wrote. "Finally, there are the Algerian punishment battalions, and the man who is sent to one of these may, as a rule, be reckoned as a criminal."[25]

Punishment battalions were established institutions in the French Army, as well as the German and Soviet militaries. For a Soviet soldier during the Second World War, being sent to a punishment battalion was tantamount to a death sentence, since those units were often sent into the forward echelons of direct assaults, as little better than suicide squads. (When other Soviet units were issued white snowsuits for camouflage, soldiers in punishment battalions were not, deliberately—it was intended that their more conspicuous dark uniforms would draw fire, which would make it possible to spot German positions.) For the French, the punishment battalions in North Africa were more akin to a military version of temporary exile, in which soldiers were sent out to the hinterlands of empire where the duty was hard, the diversions were few, and the discipline harsh.

Just because minor levels of punishment did not involve such extremes as penal battalions did not mean that they were necessarily more enjoyable. Solitary confinement in the regimental guardhouse was a punishment allowed by the Edinburgh Regiment's 1812 Standing Orders, a penalty known as putting a man in the Black Hole. A sojourn in solitary was intentionally an unpleasant experience. "The serjeant of the barrack guard," the Orders declared, "is to be answerable for prisoners confined to the black hole; that they receive no subsistence but bread and water; that no books, cards, dice, or amusement of any sort, be allowed them; and that no person be permitted to see or talk to them; that clean straw is constantly provided for them; and that the black hole is dry, and at times properly aired, and cleaned by the prisoners themselves."[26]

The U.S. Army also confined prisoners in a "black hole" early in the period, but that practice was used less frequently after the Civil War. In 1873 a soldier named Francis Carey, of Company C, Battalion of Engineers, was convicted in by court-martial of having stabbed another soldier in a fight. The court sentenced him "to be confined in charge of the post guard for the period of two months, wearing a 24-pound ball attached to his left leg by a chain six feet long. The first ten days of the first month and the last ten days of the second month to be in solitary confinement in the dark cell, on bread and water diet, and the remainder of the confinement to be at hard labor." The review authority felt that the court went a bit too far with that sentence. "The offense is regarded as well-deserving of a severe penalty," the review noted, "but it is doubted whether solitary confinement for ten days in a dark cell, added to a diet of bread and water, might not be liable to have such a depressing effect upon the health of a prisoner as to render a punishment thus inflicted amenable to the objection of being cruel and unusual." The "dark cell" portion of the sentence was stricken, but the remainder was allowed to stand.[27]

Regardless of nationality, in most armies of this period military justice was characterized by its severity. Discipline existed in many forms, ranging from the draconian and excessively harsh, to a permissive laxity that was almost an absence of recognizable discipline. Which armies had better soldiers is a question always open to nationalist debate, but whether severe discipline was the linchpin to making quality soldiers was also fiercely debated in that era.

What should not be overlooked in the historical exposition of military justice, though, is the human factor—the men whose lives were subject to its sometimes capricious and rarely gentle governance. It is relatively unusual to find a personal letter from a nineteenth-century soldier whose life was forfeit to military law, a scarcity that makes such a document all the more compelling. Job Redmond was a private in a North Carolina regiment when he deserted in the last year of the Civil War. His reasons were much the same as what drove other men to that drastic step—homesickness, worry over news of deprivation and hardships at home, and weariness with the war. He was captured and returned to his regiment, where he was court-martialed and sentenced to death. He was not a literate man, and apparently had little education, but his final words to his family are perhaps all the more moving for the obvious effort it took him to write them:

> *November the 2, 1864 My dier wife and children I seet myself this morning with a troubbeled harte and a destrest mind to try to rite a few lines to let you no that I hierd my sentens red yesterday and hit was very bad. I am very sory to let you no . . . I hafte to bee shot the 9th of this month. I am sory to inform you that I have but 7 dayes to live. But I hope and trust in god when tha have slane my body that god will take my sole to reste whier I will meete my little babe that is gone before me. my dier wife I think I could die better sadesfide if I could see you and the children one more time on erth and talk with you. But my time is so short I donte exspect to ever see you and my dier little children eny more on erth.*[28]

Redmond was shot by a firing squad on November 9, 1864, without ever seeing his family again.

CHAPTER FIFTEEN

Garrison Life

THROUGHOUT MOST OF THE NINETEENTH CENTURY, enlisted soldiers did not have much to celebrate about their living quarters. For American soldiers, this was frequently on account of where the army posted them—a frontier post such as Fort Grant, out in the southwestern hinterlands of the Arizona Territory, offered rocks, dust, snakes, heat, and not much else, at least in the early years of its existence. In regions where milled lumber was in short supply, or when time did not permit ambitious construction projects, the cavalry and infantry units that garrisoned the frontier forts of the American West were quartered in barracks built from sod, adobe, or rough timber. Roofs leaked, dust covered everything until it rained, at which point the dust turned to mud, insects shared the living space, and inside temperatures fluctuated between extremes of hot and cold, depending on the season. Far too frequently, the main reason for the wretched conditions of the soldier's home and hearth was the parsimonious nature of a government that seemed to begrudge his very existence when it came time to allocate the funds for his maintenance.

As long as the ever-shifting dynamics of an expanding frontier were part of the military situation in the American West, the U.S. Army could not devote much of its limited budget or resources to the construction of permanent, well-designed quarters for the regiments who garrisoned the frontier posts. A cavalryman of the 2nd U.S. Dragoons, a few years before the Civil War, wrote in his journal of his arrival at Fort Kearny in the Nebraska Territory. "Fort Kearny puts me more in mind of an old, dilapidated Mexican town than a military post," he wrote, "being mostly built of sticks and mud."[1] He was not impressed. Another soldier posted to Camp Grant in the Arizona Territory in 1871 described living conditions that were familiar to many American soldiers of that era when he wrote a letter to his family, saying that his battalion's quarters were "poor, very poor, the roofs (dirt) are leaking; the cracks in the walls (uprights of timber) so large that one walking outside in the evening notices by candlelight all that is going on inside." Comfortable examples of good living, they were not. "After all one's scouting, escorting, saddling up of a sudden, coming home, and looking worse than an Indian," he wrote, "a man has nothing to please his eye and make him wish to be home, because the first windy day covers him with dust in his quarters, just as well as on the road, or the first rainy day wets him just as well in his quarters as if he were in the saddle, and drives him out of his so-called mess-room, if he is lucky enough to possess such an institution."[2]

British soldiers of that era might have expected to live somewhat better, at least when they were not actively campaigning out on the verges of the empire—after all, Britain had no contested domestic frontier during this period, so a certain amount of stable infrastructure could be expected. But the reality of the matter was that just because a regiment was quartered in purpose-built stone or brick barracks, it did not necessarily mean that their accommodations were all that might be hoped for.

By the advent of the twentieth century both the American and British Armies had made great strides in improving the living conditions of their rank and file soldiers. There was still little to no privacy to speak of, but standards of hygiene had improved and the things that men complained of were at least not the life-threatening and misery-invoking sort of problems. In other armies, however, the common soldier's quality of life in barracks was still generally awful. Armies—all armies, it seems—thrive on routine. In such an environment, where actions and activities are officially proscribed or meticulously organized, where everything from morning to night and all hours in between are controlled by regulation and military order, soldiers' lives fall into recognizable routines very quickly. Except for periods of initial entry training or attendance at certain courses, that type of lock-step lifestyle is no longer the norm for most modern soldiers, but during the period we are considering here it was the routine of most military environments.

In peacetime, soldiers spent the majority of their time in the vicinity of their barracks, or on the military installation to which their unit was assigned. In the American army, this was referred to as "garrison duty." Except for the protracted periods of the two world wars in the twentieth century, the majority of soldiers in the armies studied in this text spent most of their time in a garrison environment.

In the closing years of the eighteenth century, the British Army did not have committed barracks facilities for all its active regiments. The solution was to billet soldiers in local inns or private homes, accommodations which were not always enthusiastically provided by local civilians even though the army did pay for the lodging. Some regiments were posted to permanent forts or depots, in which cases there were regular barracks, but not until the years after the Napoleonic Wars did barracks accommodations become the norm for most regiments. The first permanent and purpose-built barracks in all of Britain were constructed in 1715 at Berwick-upon-Tweed, a town on the border of England and Scotland, in response to the very real threat of Jacobite uprisings in Scotland. For decades, though, permanent barracks were the exception rather than the norm in the British Army's practice of housing its regular troops.

The U.S. Army billeted its troops in regular barracks almost from the first days of American independence, but political sensitivities rather than military expediency were the primary motivators behind that decision. In the years leading up to the American Revolution in 1776, the British practice of billeting soldiers on the local population under the authorization of the Quartering Act generated massive currents of resentment in the colonies. The practice left such a lasting memory that its prohibition was written into American law as the Third Amendment to the U.S. Constitution. This left the nascent U.S. Army with no legal recourse but to provide its soldiers with other forms of accommodation.

In practice, "other" did not necessarily mean "better." The U.S. Army's barracks in the early years were usually simple, rudimentary affairs—built of stone in the permanent forts back east, but in the more remote frontier posts they were usually made of raw lumber, log construction, or even sod. When even those structures were lacking, soldiers lived in tents. When the 9th U.S. Cavalry was posted to Texas in the late 1860s, the regimental historian's description of their billets painted a rather unattractive picture. "The appliances for the personal comfort of the soldiers were few," he wrote, "and should the improvements now surrounding them be suddenly exchanged for what they had then, there would be such a scurrying off of recruits that I doubt if the entire State of Kentucky could furnish satisfactory material to fill the depleted ranks." The barracks as he described them were much the same for other regiments at other frontier forts of the era: "Ashen slats on bunk irons and a sack filled with straw made a very good bed for its fortunate possessor, while the less favored were often at wits' end to improvise a comfortable resting place out of two blankets."[3]

The American Civil War saw the United States field the largest army it ever had raised in its history, and the vast majority of the soldiers who served in that huge force never experienced garrison life as soldiers in the peacetime Regular Army had known it. For the four years of that war, those troops lived either in bivouacs on the march or in tent camps—the closest thing most of them saw to permanent quarters were the timber and log structures they built during the relatively static months of winter encampment. Even so, life in these camps did share some of the particulars of garrison life in permanent barracks. The military routine still held sway, with its regular functions of drill and guard mount and fatigue details. There were also the familiar problems of boredom and monotony that were an inextricable part of garrison life. John Billings, a U.S. Army artilleryman, wrote, "Reading was a pastime quite generally indulged in, and there was no novel so dull, trashy or sensational as not to find someone so bored with nothing to do that he would wade through it. I, certainly, never read so many such before or since. The mind was hungry for something, and took husks when it could get nothing better."[4]

In the years following the Civil War, when Congress slashed military spending to a penury and the U.S. Army limped along on a pittance of federal spending grudging doled out by a distant government, conditions for soldiers were often very bad. "As late as 1884," one historian writes, "soldiers quipped that if they wanted to be well cared for, they must become inmates of either the military prison or a national cemetery."[5]

Even in the larger, more permanent barracks on established posts, the living conditions were fairly spartan and usually crowded. "Another feature that must strike a recruit in an unfavorable manner," a former soldier named Frank Roberts wrote in 1894, "is the herding together like so many cattle of forty to sixty men in one room." Such crowding, Roberts argued, led to "a relaxing of the ordinary requirements of decency," and contributed to moral decay, particularly from vices such as drunkenness. Roberts was clearly disenchanted about his experiences in the army, and he had certainly had complaints he wanted to air in his article. He also subscribed to the notion that the army was a den of moral iniquity of alcoholism and gambling, a charge that was common enough in some circles, but that was still an overly broad stereotype. Even so, his criticisms of the overcrowded barracks was correct enough in its own right. The army eventually made substantial improvements in this matter, but most of those came about only after the post consolidations that occurred in the 1890s.[6]

For most British soldiers serving in the years between Waterloo and the Crimea, the domestic furnishings of their daily existence were simply wretched. Just how dreadful conditions were for the common soldier, John Strawson observes, "is best illustrated by the fact that they were worse than those of convicts in prison: the space allowed them was less, there was no pure water, clothing was too tight and not warm enough, married quarters—if they existed at all, had no privacy, the very tubs for washing in the mornings were in the barracks rooms at night for the soldiers to relieve themselves in."[7] The food was bad, and there was not enough of it. For much of the century, soldiers were provided only two meals a day, breakfast and dinner. The fare was monotonous, badly prepared (when meat was served it was almost always cooked only one way—boiled) and was lacking in basic nutrition. Not until the 1850s did the British Army provide a regular supper for its men, and then at first only when they paid for it themselves out of their meager wages.

This was the hard reality more often than not, even though the army mandated better standards than these, at least on paper. The 1812 Standing Orders for the 51st Regiment in Edinburgh, under the section "Barrack Regulations, Messing, etc.," mandated that "officers commanding companies will frequently visit their men's barracks and messes, and minutely inquire into, and satisfy themselves as to their men's living and habits; in this they will be assisted by the junior officers of the company, whom they will cause daily to visit the barracks, and verbally, or in writing, report their remarks on the same."[8] Notwithstanding injunctions such as this, for the next fifty years the enlisted men continued to live in squalid conditions.

Privacy in the barracks was nonexistent. Men slept, worked, ate, and amused themselves in close proximity to the other men in their squads almost without a break in the association. An open-bay barracks room, where twenty to sixty men were living together, was never silent. Even at night, after lights out, there was always the sound of snoring, coughing, farting—someone tossing and turning in their bunk, someone doing something else in their bunk that everyone else pretended not to notice or mocked with profane jeers, depending on their mood. For the sensitive sort of soul, this could be a veritable purgatory.

It was even worse in the smaller confines of field tents. Remembering the Sibley tents that the U.S. Army used during the Civil War, John Billings wrote, "In cold or rainy weather, when every opening is closed, they are most unwholesome tenements, and to enter one of them of a rainy morning from the outer air, and encounter the night's accumulation of nauseating exhalations from the bodies of twelve men (differing widely in their habits of personal cleanliness) was an experience which no old soldier has ever been known to recall with any great enthusiasm."[9]

The other situation that could make for miserable living conditions was the opposite of the drastic manpower reductions that followed major wars, and that was when there were too many men for the available space. In both world wars, the U.S. Army found itself scrambling to clothe, arm, and house the hundreds of thousands of men called up into the swelling ranks of a military that was suddenly on a war footing. It both instances, it seemed initially ill-prepared for the task.

Spencer Wurst, an American paratrooper, thought the billets his regiment was assigned during their training in Alabama in 1942 were absolutely wretched. "We were literally crammed into tarpaper shacks, double-bunked in flimsy, unheated buildings with very low ceilings, about twenty-four feet wide by thirty-five feet long," he wrote, "where we also had to store our field equipment and clothing. Northerners may *think* the South is always warm, but I spent some of the coldest nights of my life in the swamps of Georgia and Alabama in November and December 1942.

The conditions in modern prisons are far better than the housing in most military camps during World War II."[10]

Soldiers have always had a certain reputation for hard-living coarseness, a reputation that is not always deserved but that is at least true enough, often enough, to allow that image to persist. In the early part of the nineteenth century, when many American and British soldiers came to their armies from economically and educationally disadvantaged backgrounds, there was considerable truth to the stereotype. Gentler diversions such as reading were not common in some eras, but this was not always because soldiers themselves did not want them. The army itself at first made no effort to encourage healthier intellectual recreations, partially for the logical if deplorable reason that most soldiers of the rank and file could not read, anyway. In the absence of anything better, many men turned to the age-old mainstays of soldierly amusements: drinking, gambling, and whoring.

The Duke of Wellington once famously remarked that most of the soldiers in his battle-hardened army "enlisted for drink," and though his quote was actually much more expansive than that simple indictment, it still bears on the subject. In an era when soldiers' daily alcohol ration was a hugely important part of their recompense, Wellington's comment may not have been entirely spurious. "Drink," as one historian has noted, "was a persistent threat to discipline, and while it affected the hardened reprobates on a regular basis, relatively few soldiers remained immune from its appeal."[11]

To some considerable degree, the appeal lay in the fact that there was precious little else with which the common soldier could pass the time on his meager wage. The result was often all too predictable: "The good man brought down by drink is a feature of the age," one British historian writes. Most armies are familiar with the concept of certain behaviors being "contrary to good order and discipline"; it is ironic that for much of this period the armies themselves created situations where the only diversions available to soldiers seemed to be those that were most predictably threats to discipline and that almost inevitably resulted in a loss of good order.

Even so, hidebound and resistant to change though most military organizations were, improvements did come about. Sometimes the changes were internal, in small things. In 1848 the Standing Orders for the British 90th Light Infantry prohibited "dogs, and fowl of any kind" in the barracks.[12] By 1893, however, the Standing Orders for the Seaforth Highlanders stipulated that "all dogs kept in Barracks must have a collar with the owner's name on it, and will be registered at the Orderly Room." The orders went on to say that all soldiers' dogs "must be properly looked after."[13] but ominously warned that if the number of pets got out of hand, steps would have to be taken to eliminate a few unfortunate canines. Other, more sweeping changes came about as a result of pressure from outside the army. After the public reactions to the hardships of soldiers' lives in the Crimean War, the British Army began working to change time-hardened patterns of behavior. There were many who advocated for such efforts, both within the army and without. Florence Nightingale, whose work among the wounded in the Crimea endeared her to an entire generation of British soldiers, wrote of them:

> *I have never seen so teachable and helpful a class as the army generally. Give them opportunity promptly and securely to send money home and they will use it. Give them schools and lectures and they will come to them. Give them books and games and amusements and they will leave off drinking. Give them suffering and they will bear it. Give them work and they will do it. I had rather have to do with the army generally than with any other class I have ever attempted to serve.*[14]

The American military during the same period was dealing with almost exactly the same social issues. Carlton McCarthy, who fought for the Confederacy during the Civil War, remembered, "The young soldier's piety had to perish ignominiously, or else assume a boldness and strength which nothing else could so well impart as the temptations, sneers, and dangers of the army."[15] Drink, cards, and loose women were an ever-present reality among American soldiers just as they were among their British counterparts.

At the end of the century, Needham N. Freeman, who served in the Philippines during the Spanish-American War, delivered his verdict of the darker side of soldiering:

> *Army life is dangerous to the morals of many young men. They will take up some bad habits if they have not power and determination to control themselves. It is very easy for a man, especially a young man, to take up some bad habits and lead a different life altogether after he becomes a soldier. A man soon learns to drink and to gamble, although he may have known nothing of these vices before his enlistment. I thought that a soldier's life would suit me, but after a service of three years I can truthfully say that it was not what I desired.*[16]

This insidious decline into depravity was certainly one of the concerns that many an anxious parent had in mind when they counseled their sons against going off to join the army.

❧

Women were another vice for soldiers during much of this period. Or, it might be more accurate to say that the records indicate that the bureaucracies of most armies seemed to regard them as a vice. Wherever soldiers were stationed, prostitutes made their inevitable appearance. "Soldiers," one source says of the American army of the nineteenth century, "have always been numbered among the prostitute's best customers, and the frontier regulars were no exception." The British found this to be equally true for their soldiers; the 1812 Standing Orders for the Edinburgh Regiment felt it necessary to specifically state: "No prostitute is to be suffered inside or near the guard room," and another regiment's Standing Orders from 1848 prohibited soldiers from "introducing loose women into Barracks." The fact remained, however, that concentrations of soldiers always attracted the purveyors of vice. During the U.S. Army's Punitive Expedition into Mexico in 1916, Pershing's forces were followed by entrepreneurs who set up shop anywhere the troops paused. The wares they offered were predictable—whiskey, narcotics, and prostitutes. Pershing issued orders absolutely prohibiting the first two and decided that the third commodity would be better handled by allowing its practice within carefully supervised and sanctioned limitations. His policies did seem to help quell some of the more egregious disciplinary infractions, but did not meet with the approval of everyone back in Washington.

The urges of normal human sexuality aside, it could be said that most armies themselves contributed to the problem of prostitution in two ways. First, it kept soldiers' pay so low as to make it all but impossible for men to support a wife, and the living conditions it provided were so bad that it was a stalwart woman indeed who would take up with an enlisted man and his very limited prospects. Her prospects were not likely to be much brighter—"No Woman is to be allowed to reside in Barracks," one regiment's Standing Orders declared in 1848, "who objects to making herself useful in Cooking, &c." Secondly, the army made prostitutes a natural recourse for much of the rank and file by issuing strict regulations that forbade men to marry without the permission of their commanding officers, permission that was by no means an easy thing to obtain. The Prussian Army of the Napoleonic period was one of the exceptions to this. In a deliberate effort to control the prevalence of prostitution and the inevitable scourge of venereal diseases, the Prussians provided for married soldiers on the regimental strength in far greater numbers than did nearly every other army of that day. "By 1802," as Roger Norman Buckley writes, "there were approximately 59,000 wives and 78,000 children in the army for every 100,000 men from Prussia in military service."[17]

Even women who were not selling sex were not necessarily regarded by the army as a beneficial presence. Napoleon once cynically remarked that "marriage is good for nothing in the military profession,"[18] and the policy makers of most armies during the period seemed to share his low opinion of matrimony for the rank and file. "It is impossible to point out," the Standing Orders of the British Army's 90th Light Infantry stated in 1848, "the inconveniences which arise and the evils which follow a Regiment encumbered with Women: poverty and misery are the inevitable consequences."[19]

Throughout the entire period considered here, junior enlisted men in the U.S. Army could not marry without first obtaining their commanding officer's permission; that same policy was in effect in most other armies of the time. In the British Army, again, the Edinburgh Regiment's 1812 Standing Orders stated: "No man is to marry without first applying to the captain . . . who, if he approves of the application, will forward the same to the colonel of the regiment for his sanction." The consequences of disobeying this order were severe. "Any man disobeying this order," the Orders went on to say, "must not only expect to be punished, but may likewise rest assured, that his wife shall not be considered as a woman belonging to the regiment." The implied threat was clear—any woman in the regimental billets who was not on the regimental rolls as a soldier's wife was by default assumed to be a woman of low moral character and liable to be treated as such.

Nearly a hundred years later, the British Army was still taking a dim view of romance in the ranks. Article 787 of the 1892 Standing Orders read, "Soldiers are warned against marrying without leave." This time a logical explanation was provided for the policy—marriage, the authorities believed, created an economic hardship for most enlisted men. "The pay of a man will, with care, suffice for his wants," the Standing Orders observed, "as long as he has only himself to provide for; but when he has a wife and family dependent on him, it is almost impossible to provide for them." Even the army itself acknowledged that pay for enlisted men was at this late date still so low as to not support a family, but several more decades would pass before steps were taken to improve that economic reality.

In order to even get permission to marry at this point in time, the requirements were rigid and demanding. The Seaforth Highlanders' Standing Orders stated: "Soldiers having seven years' service, exclusive of Boy's service, are permitted to register their names to be taken on the Married Establishment as vacancies occur. They must distinctly understand that this does not convey any permission for them to marry, and that they must wait till they are informed that a vacancy exists." Article 789 of the 1892 Standing Orders stated: "No man will be allowed on the married roll, unless he has been seven years in the Army, has one good-conduct badge, and has [five pounds] in the savings bank. He must also satisfy the Commanding Officer as to the thorough respectability of the woman he propose to marry." For many soldiers, it probably seemed that if the army had wanted them to have wives, it would have issued them.

The presence of women in a regiment—at least, those women who were officially carried "on the strength" of the regiment—was regarded as a positive, ameliorating influence by some men. Other soldiers saw them as an outright nuisance. Not surprisingly, enlisted men were less than enthused about the additional work that came their way when officers' wives accompanied the unit on the march. One American cavalryman, writing in 1857, described his views of life on the road with women, views that were not complimentary in the least. He wrote that the officer commanding an escort party of the 2nd U.S. Dragoons

has his lady and her female attendants with her, which are all the women we have with us, and this is enough. Ask a soldier which he would rather have to wait upon, one woman or five horses, and he will tell you horses by all odds. I don't believe ladies know the trouble they are on a march, to a body of troops. . . . They do not seem to consider that a soldier has his own tent to pitch, his horse to care for, and his supper to cook after coming into camp, but think he has nothing to do but to wait upon them, bringing them wood and water, spreading down carpets in their tents, etc., and it will probably be ten or eleven o'clock at night before he can lie down to sleep, knowing at the same time that he must be up by three in the morning, in order to get breakfast in time to strike the tents, shake carpets for the ladies, roll up feather-beds (pretty things for the prairie!) pack wagons, etc., in order to be in readiness to start at five.[20]

An enlisted man's wife, by contrast, was expected to be able to look after herself and contribute to the common labor or risked being stricken off the rolls and losing her place in the regiment. It was one more social inequity that caused more than a little grumbling in the ranks.

As the military arm of an empire that encompassed both hemispheres and dozens of countries, the British Army during this period was spread across the globe. The U.S. Army, by contrast, was for most of that time a more domestic institution operating within its own national boundaries. Since winning its independence from the mother country in 1783, the United States had only fought one extra-terrestrial war, that with Mexico in 1846–1848. The professional regular core of the army was extremely small, and both public opinion and the federal purse were adamantly opposed to any efforts to expanding the force. The four years of the Civil War saw a hundred-fold increase in the military strength of the United States, but almost as soon as the war ended in the spring of 1865, regiments were disbanded and the army was reduced to a shadow of its wartime size. (In some measure this made sense, as most of the soldiers who fought in that war were enlisted in volunteer or state regiments, not regiments of the Regular Army—the Regular establishment changed relatively little during the war.) Throughout the nineteenth century and even for some time afterward, the American public did not widely support the idea of a large standing army in peacetime—such a military force, according to the prevailing view, was potentially a tool of tyranny and monarchism and had no place among free-minded men. It was also an expensive drain on the national treasury, and budget constraints always factored into the equation.

As a result, the army that existed in the United States for most of that century was a small one, much too small for the myriad tasks with which it was charged. As the American frontier pushed westward, expanding suddenly at times with the addition of territory through the Louisiana Purchase from France or the seizure of territories from Mexico after 1845, the army found itself cast more and more in the role of a frontier constabulary. There were small permanent military installations established in the eastern states and coastal defense forts manned mostly by coastal artillery regiments, but the army's infantry and cavalry regulars were for the most part posted out to the fringes of civilization. Rudyard Kipling, who was decidedly pro-American in his views, once facetiously remarked, "When the last Indian is dead or drunk, the U.S. Army will make the most wonderful little survey and engineering corps the world has ever seen."[21]

Garrison life for most American soldiers in the frontier period was a mélange of hard work, bad weather, regular periods of tough patrolling, occasional difficult campaigns against elusive Indians, and month after month of mind-numbing, stultifying boredom. The average living conditions for American soldiers at this time seem to have been a bit better than those experienced by their British counterparts, but they were still far from ideal. Don Rickey, in his excellent book *Forty Miles a Day on Beans and Hay,* gives a good description of soldiers' quarters in a frontier post:

> *Most barracks were constructed of wood framing, sided with sawn lumber. Some, however, were crude log or adobe buildings, small, poorly ventilated, and cramped. No matter what the kind of building occupied as a troop or company barrack, there was a complete lack of privacy for the rank and file. Privates and corporals usually bunked together in a large room, while the sergeants had small cubicles adjoining. Cots, with wooden slats to support the bedsack and later with a woven wire spring, were arranged along the wall, about three or four feet apart, with each man's wooden foot locker in the aisle at the foot of his bunk. . . . The barrack room was generally heated by cast-iron wood stoves, in the center or at each end of the room, and artificial light was supplied by kerosene lamps hung along the wall, about three or four feet above the head of the cots, to hold the soldier's equipment—except carbines or rifles, which were stacked in a special rack in the barrack room. The corporals and older soldiers had the choice bunk locations, near the windows in summer and close to the stove in winter. Having a comfortable bunksite was a matter of great importance.*[22]

Garrison life was taken up with the normal routines of military life—roll call formations, guard mount, drilling, fatigue detail, and meals. Aside from these routines, soldiers were pretty much left to their own devices, free to do as they wished so long as they remained on post. The besetting problem, as was also the case for British soldiers of the period, was that there was very little for them to do that did not involve a vice of one kind or another.

Change was slow in coming, but it did come, and for the British and American soldier alike it came after major wars, the Crimean War and the American Civil War, respectively. Edwin Rundle, who served with the British 17th Regiment in England and Canada, wrote that a few years after he enlisted, his regiment provided "a very nice reading room, also a library." It was about this time that both armies began to emphasize the importance of at least rudimentary education. In an era when it was still perfectly possible (and by no means unusual) for a man to be functionally illiterate when he enlisted, the army began to take steps to ensure that a man could leave the army better educated than he was when he joined. "A regimental school was opened and the children attended," Rundle wrote of the years following his enlistment. "Any man who could not read or write must attend school until he obtained a fourth-class certificate, but that did not prevent him from advancing. If he wished promotion he must obtain a third-class for corporal, second-class for sergeant, and a first-class certificate would be an important factor if he were looking toward a commission."[23] A similar system was adopted by the U.S. Army during the same decades, and post schools were established on most American army posts to provide literacy instruction for soldiers who could not yet read or write.

The U.S. Army began creating unit libraries and reading rooms in most of its posts about this time, even though the material on offer was somewhat sparse in the more remote garrisons, at least at first. Most post libraries subscribed to as wide a variety of newspapers and periodicals as possible, and these were always popular reading materials with the men who were inclined to read. In 1883, the library at Fort Union, New Mexico, spent $108 of the unit fund to subscribe to no less than twenty-four different publications. These included army-specific magazines such as the *Journal of the Military Service Institutions of the U.S.* and the *Army and Navy Journal*; eastern papers like the *Boston Globe*, *Harper's Weekly*, the *New York Herald*, and the *Philadelphia Times*. Western newspapers from San Francisco and Albuquerque were also favorites, as were popular periodicals such as *Frank Leslie's Illustrated* and *Puck*.

The range of official libraries varied considerably. In the 1870 *Report on Barracks*, the army noted that Fort Bliss, Texas, had no library at all; by contrast, Fort Clark, Texas, had a post library with 184 books in its collection. That number was dwarfed by the regimental library of the 25th U.S. Infantry, which was stationed at Fort Clark that year. The regiment's private library, purchased by the soldiers' own contributions, contained at least nine hundred volumes. The 25th Infantry was one of the four racially segregated black units in the U.S. Army at the time, and their library was much more substantial than many of their white sister units.

Soldiers who could read were often avid readers. Private Wilmont Sanford of the 12th U.S. Infantry listed in his diary every book that he checked out from the library at Fort Buford in the Dakota Territory—he read an average of about two books a week, a rate that was not at all remarkable for an enlisted man of that era. William Zimmer, a cavalryman stationed at Fort Ellis, Montana, also enjoyed reading. "I finished a volume entitled *Around the World in 80 Days*, author Jules Verne (very good)," he wrote in his journal on December 12. The next week he noted that he had "finished the volume *The Old-Fashioned Girl* (author Miss [Louisa May] Alcott. Good.)" Five days later, he wrote that he had just finished Jules Verne's *Twenty Thousand Leagues under the Sea*, which he described as "very good, a science fiction." On December 28 he wrote with obvious delight, "This evening we received 35 volumes of the latest novels by the best authors." For soldiers enduring long, dark winter months in the frozen northern posts of the American frontier, reading was both a pleasure and an escape, and many of them were faithful patrons of their post libraries. Zimmer wrote that whenever his duties were finished each day his "time is chiefly spent in the library, which is filled with good books & papers from all parts of the states and territories."[24]

It was still not an absolute requirement that a man be literate to enlist, but he had to be able to read and write if he wanted promotion, and the army provided the means to acquire those skills. Sergeant Reinhold Gast, who enlisted in the U.S. Army after immigrating from Germany, described the evening classes offered at his post as "an opportunity to advance one's education.... I, myself, took advantage of this."[25] His efforts resulted in his eventual promotion to corporal and then sergeant.

Gast was certainly not alone in using the army as a means of assimilating to a new country. Another German immigrant, Private William

Hustede, served in the 1st U.S. Cavalry, and he began learning English while he was stationed at Fort Assiniboine in Montana. Danish immigrant Martin Anderson, a Danish immigrant who also enlisted as a cavalryman, spent his free time at Fort Riley, Kansas, "mostly in the library studying . . . to learn English."[26] In most regiments of the U.S. Army during that era, the enlisted men possessed a wide range of education levels and intellectual inclinations. All the familiar stereotypes were represented in the ranks, including the educated man from back east and the slackjawed dullard whose only interests lay in blowing his meager wages in the whiskey dens on paydays. Both types were so much prevalent, at least in popular depictions of the army, that they practically became caricatures of type in both literature and public perception.

For British soldiers serving abroad throughout the empire, a wholly different experience of garrison life was often possible, especially for those men whose regiments were posted to India. A private's meager pay (seven shillings a week, for much of the period) went much farther in India than in England, and most men were able to enjoy the unaccustomed luxuries of having native servants to clean their kit, provide them with hot coffee in the morning, and shave them in grand style. Liquor was also cheaper than it was back in England, albeit of a different sort. In India a concoction called arrack was frequently the potion of choice, and it caught many an unprepared newcomer off guard with its potency.

American soldiers of a later period also found themselves enjoying a rather leisurly life when they were posted abroad in their turn. After the Spanish-American War the United States found itself for the first time in its history the possessor of a trans-oceanic empire, though the American government somewhat disingenuously shied away from using such an imperialist term, even if it was true. When the war with Spain ended in 1898, the U.S. gained control of Cuba, Puerto Rico, Guam, and the Philippines, along with a few other scattered territories. Once the U.S. dealt with the nationalist Filipinos who were not eager to trade Spanish overlords for American ones (in a brief but bloody war that American history for years barely remembered as the Philippines Insurrection and Filipino history remembers very well as something altogether different), the Philippines became a regular posting for American soldiers. The delights of garrison life in the islands quickly became the stuff of legend in the U.S. Army. For forty years, American servicemen posted to the Philippines lived lives of indolent repose that bore little resemblance to the military existence of their peers back in the States. Just as their British counterparts in India did, American soldiers enjoyed the benefits of native servants (each barracks had its contingent of Filipino houseboys to clean equipment, shine shoes, and generally fetch and carry), plentiful quantities of cheap beer and rum, and the easy availability of female companionship.

That last pleasure came with a definite and rigid caveat. While it was acceptable to the U.S. Army that its soldiers took up with local women (the genteel strata of American civilian society in the Philippines actually thought it was a deplorable practice, but the military authorities almost always chose to turn a blind eye to it), the army was not at all prepared to accept the idea that anything more permanent than a sexual dalliance might come of relationships between soldiers and native women. In a day and age when most of American civil society was rigidly segregated by race, and when the army itself was racially segregated as a matter of custom and law, the possibility of American soldiers going abroad and returning with native wives was something the government was absolutely *not* going to permit. The army's official attitude toward Filipino women tolerated temporary assignations, but absolutely did not accept the idea of permanent, matrimonial relationships. Soldiers who broke that cardinal rule were presented with a stark choice—when their assignment was up they could leave the Philippines and their native wives and children behind forever or they could take their discharge from the army, stay in the islands with their Filipino wives, and never return to the United States. This policy of voluntary exile for the sake of love was to remain official military regulation almost up until the Second World War.

After the conclusion of the Philippine-American War in 1904, the Philippine Islands became a sought-after posting for many soldiers and for some of the same economic reasons as for British soldiers posted to India. Especially during the years between the two world wars, when the Great Depression wracked the United States, a soldier's pay went much farther in the islands than it did at home. Charles Willeford served in the Philippines in the 1930s and described his introduction to garrison life there:

> *By the time the first sergeant got around to dismissing us, our bunks had been made by the Filipino houseboys. After we unpacked our barracks bags and stored our things away in our foot- and wall lockers, the houseboys started to shine our extra pairs of shoes, both civilian and G.I., that we kept lined up under our beds. . . . They also turned back the covers in the evening and tucked in the mosquito bars. They were paid $1.50 a month, which was deducted from our pay. Another $1.50 a month was deducted to pay Filipino K.P.'s, which meant that I wouldn't have to pull any K.P.'s for the next two years, either.*

All things considered, Willeford wrote, army life in the Philippines was an easy gig, and for a few decades a posting to the Philippines or Hawaii was considered a plum assignment by American soldiers.

Chapter Sixteen

After the Army

Dost thou know the fate of soldiers . . . ? When they are worn, hacked, hewn with constant service, thrown aside, to rust in peace and rot in hospitals.

—THOMAS SOUTHERN

IN EVERY SOLDIER'S EXPERIENCE, if he lived long enough and survived the sometimes-considerable hazards of the profession, there came that moment when he received his discharge and left the ranks, a soldier no more. At the risk of oversimplifying the matter, we can say that most soldiers of this period fell into one of three categories at that point in their lives. They were either still relatively young men who had served for one or two enlistments and then left the service, or they were men for whom the army had been both a career and a life, and they left it only when they were basically forced out, able to soldier no longer. The third common scenario was when a protracted conflict ended and a large wartime army was rapidly downsized, discharging hundreds of thousands of able-bodied men in a very short period of time.

This was particularly true of British and American soldiers after the Napoleonic Wars and the Civil War, respectively, perhaps less so of men in other armies. As we saw in the first chapter, at the beginning of this period the Russian soldier's lot was essentially one of military servitude for life from the point that he was conscripted into the Tsar's army. Germany, France, Poland, Spain, and Japan also had systems of conscription, but in their cases, most men served an initial short period with the colors and then resumed their civilian lives as trained, ready reservists.

The American army was altogether different than most of its European or Asian counterparts. From the formation of the Republic, the American public generally regarded military conscription as a tool of tyrants and kings, and the U.S. government never had a need of that tool until the manpower demands of the Civil War overwhelmed the resources of voluntary enlistment. For the most part, American men joined the army of their own choice, and they remained soldiers until they chose to do otherwise at the end of their enlistment. Volunteers or draftees were mostly of two types: those who could not wait to put the army behind them, and those who found soldiering to their liking and wanted to remain in harness as long as they could. There were, of course, always those who opted for a more expedient form of self-discharge—desertion was a persistent problem for the U.S. Army during the frontier period.

For soldiers of all armies, though, the question was: What sort of life did a man have to look forward to when he left the military? For some men in the early decades of this period, the future after the army was a rather bleak prospect with few options.

In the nineteenth century the logistics of moving soldiers from foreign posts to home country were bad at the best of times, and few men left accounts of easy transitions. American soldiers only experienced this at the end of the Mexican-American War in 1848 and after the Spanish-American War in 1898, but for British soldiers it was an issue throughout the period. When Wellington's regiments embarked for passage home to England at the conclusion of the Peninsular War, their journey was simple enough, but their departure was traumatic. The army's intractability on one issue turned that process into personal tragedy for many men. While the regimental rolls allowed for a few wives on the units' strengths, many of the rank-and-file soldiers had acquired Spanish or Portuguese wives and children in their long years of service in Spain. The army did not recognize those families as military dependents for whom it was responsible.

The soldiers' wives had followed the army from battle to battle—Badajoz, Salamanca, Vitoria, San Sebastian, and so many others. When their husbands did not appear for the roll call after a fight, women searched through the corpses on the field hoping that they would not find their husbands there. They gave birth to their children in the baggage trains that rumbled along in the army's wake and buried children when fever and cholera swept the camps. They were left adrift and bereft when their husbands were killed or died of wounds, and often married other soldiers, by whom they might also be quickly widowed in turn. Now, after years of sharing the hardships and vicissitudes of their soldiers' lives, they arrived at the ports where their husbands' regiments were mustering for shipment back to England. There they remained on the piers, holding their children and screaming in panic and despair as they watched their husbands load aboard ship and sail away without them. For the soldiers, crowding the ships' rails trying to catch a final glimpse of their families, it was trauma piled upon tragedy. Through it all the army did not relent one single inch and did not care that families were torn apart forever by the rigidity of military policy.

That was an instance of personal suffering in the process of repatriation; there were others that involved actual hazard to life. Henry Metcalfe, who served in the Crimean War before being posted to India during the Mutiny, wrote of an experience that was sadly not out of the ordinary for many soldiers of his day:

> We embarked [from India] on the 17th April [1859]. . . . The cholera did break out in the ship and the boatswain of the ship was the first who was attacked and died. The ship's cook was the next, but he got over it. It next broke out among the troops, and it was—well, you may imagine that fell disease breaking out in a crowded ship of somewhere about 11 or 12 hundred tons burden, and about 500 men and women on board. Why, it beggars description. I would go through the Siege of Lucknow again sooner than experience the same, for in Lucknow, what with the excitement from shot and shell, and mines, etc., as the man said, there was scarcely time to get sick, and there was an end of it, but this was we were cooped up in a dirty ship. Bear in mind this was not one of H.M.'s troopships, but an old tub of a merchant ship that was hired in a hurry for the occasion, for there was so many troops coming home from India at that time that they were glad to get any sort of a tub to transport troops in, and as for the crew, well, the less said about them the better.[1]

If the British soldier survived the sometimes perilous voyage home, he usually did not find a grateful populace ready to receive him back as returning hero. There were occasional exceptions to this, such as when regiments returned from the Crimean War and were greeted with public acclaim, but that was not the common experience. Large drafts of discharged soldiers were regarded as a drain on community coffers and a competitive threat to other workingmen. The ultimate fate of many old soldiers, as Kipling put it, was "the ultimate death in the workhouse," that sad blight on the social fabric of nineteenth-century England.

"The spectacle of the old soldier, reduced to begging on the streets, was commonplace for much of the century," one historian says, "rather to the embarrassment of the government, who realized that it was not an aid to recruitment." Recognition of the problem, though, did not lead to a timely or humane resolution of the former soldier's plight—"the government preferred to claim back its uniform when a soldier left the ranks, in the hopes that if he became a beggar, he would not at least be one in uniform."[2] It was such a common phenomenon internationally that one finds references to it in most countries. The Germans even had a little proverb about it: "Young soldiers, old beggars."

American soldiers of the first half of the nineteenth century benefited from the fact that theirs was a growing, expanding country, because the U.S. government regularly pensioned off veterans with land grants that, at least in theory, enabled men to make a life after the army. This was done after the War of 1812, the Mexican-American War, and for various instances of service in the Indian Wars before 1861. That this was regarded as a valuable recompense is shown by the number of applications the government received every year from old soldiers or from widows asking for their husband's due, all trying to prove their former military service so they could receive the grant.

Pensions of money were awarded to soldiers who completed the requisite number of years of satisfactory service, but the required number of years and the exact specifications of what constituted "satisfactory service" changed from era to era. When that stipend was not forthcoming, many men left the army no better off than they had been when they enlisted, at least in terms of their professional skills and financial positions. The reality was that there simply was no civilian market for the skills that made a man a good infantryman, gunner, or cavalry trooper. No reputable, legal market, that is. A soldier who enlisted during the Napoleonic Wars, whatever his nationality, learned how to march and how to fight and how to endure untold hardships during his years in the ranks, but precious little else.

Here again, there were always the exceptions to this rule, but by and large those men who took up a skilled civilian trade after the army often resumed professions they had practiced before their enlistment, not one the army taught them in the interim. Benjamin Harris, the narrator of *The Recollections of Rifleman Harris,* a classic memoir of the Napoleonic era British Army, was such a case. He was a shoemaker before he enlisted in the Rifle Brigade, he augmented his army pay by working as a cobbler for his rifle company while he served, and he set himself up with a shoemaker's shop back in England after his discharge. Men who had been saddlers, farriers, wheelwrights, clerks, and the like, were likewise often able to find employment in their old trades. Those who did not have those skills might hope to secure a semiofficial job such as porters in government buildings, bailiffs in the courts, or guards on the mail coaches, but such opportunities were hard to come by, and competition was fierce for the few positions available.

A common experience of discharged British soldiers before the time of the Crimean War was that only one career could be counted on to await them after the army—abject poverty and a life as a professional beggar. This was what occurred in 1814 and 1815, when massive numbers of men were discharged from the army after the wars with France. The practice of the day was to ship soldiers back to England, discharge them from the service at the port of disembarkation, and leave them to their own devices. No provisions were made to transport men back to their home counties; no government funds were dispersed to provide them with money to live on for even a short while. Most men had to beg their way home; many of the towns and villages they had to pass through on their journeys were openly hostile to them. In the later years of the Victorian era, as Ian Knight notes, the small pension that was awarded to discharged soldiers "was scarcely sufficient to live on, and was, in any case, refused to those who were invalided out, unless they had actually been wounded in action."[3] Thus, the men who likely had the most need of the government stipend were the ones to whom it was specifically denied.

For French veterans of Napoleon's conquering armies, the fall of the empire meant a complete reversal of their fortunes. The new incarnation of the French Army under the Bourbon Restoration did not welcome their continued service, as Robert Guillemard wrote in his memoir. "I conceived that the soldiers of the Emperor were now merely tolerated in the ranks of an army that was to be bent to other recollections than ours, in which we involuntarily spread regret that our brilliant career of conquest was no more," he wrote. "They and we were neither of us of the same period, nor of the same turn of mind." Like thousands of other men, Guillemard went home to the village from which he had been conscripted nearly twenty years earlier, for the simple reason that he had nowhere else to go. He found everything changed. His parents had died while he was away, the woman he had once hoped to marry had long since married another man, and his remaining family seemed complete strangers to him after his years in the army. His farmer brother, he lamented, "speaks a language foreign to my heart; he is quite absorbed by his daily habits, and despises a soldier, who cannot sow a field of grain." Guillemard had come home to a place that no longer felt like home, to a life he no longer understood and which no longer understood him. "The trade of a soldier is the only one I ever knew, and now I can carry it no longer," he wrote. "Everywhere I go, I am out of place."[4]

The difficulties of reentering a civil society that was now foreign to them because of long years in military service was something that discharged soldiers of many countries experienced throughout the period. A Russian peasant who was conscripted at the age of twenty and spent thirty years in the Tsar's army might have served in three or four wars against the French, British, Turks, or the Poles, and then at around fifty years of age, physically broken down and economically no better off than before, he was turned loose back into a world that no longer had a place for him. British and American soldiers who made careers of the army might have felt a similar sense of disorientation when discharged, but at least in their cases their military service was voluntary from the start.

Veterans of shorter durations of service did not usually have the same problems that Guillemard spoke of—that of having spent practically all their adult life in uniform and then being suddenly cast adrift when the army no longer had a place for them—but that did not mean that the transition was therefore an easy one. Military service marked a man in a variety of ways, both good and bad, and men who had once stood in the ranks always looked at life somewhat differently than their friends and neighbors who had not. The individual difficulties of readjustment to civilian life were most affected by two factors—the attitudes of the society in question toward its old soldiers and the personal experiences of the man himself.

American society since the nation's founding had usually regarded its own standing army with suspicion if not loathing, but the existential crisis of the Civil War changed that attitude, at least a little. The men who made up the professional core of the Regular U.S. Army were still apt to be written off as "bummers and loafers" in the public estimation, but that same prejudice was not applied to the volunteers who answered the nation's call and fought to preserve the Union. Those men were seen as the heroic sons of communities all across the Northern states, and they were welcomed home as patriotic saviors of their country. The process of separating them from the army and returning them to civilian life began almost as soon as the war ended, though dismantling an army of that size took time. For many soldiers, their time was not something they were willing to let the army have much more of. They were proud of their service, but now that it was done they wanted to be done with the army.

When Albert Marshall's regiment, the 33rd Illinois, returned to their home state in October 1865, their demobilization was processed quite quickly. Two days after arriving in Springfield, the regiment was mustered for a final roll call and told, "You are now honorably discharged from the service of the army of the United States of America." That was all well and good, but there was one more unfinished item of business for which the veterans had to wait—their final pay—and on that the bureaucracy could not be hurried along. Marshall remembered, "The paymaster was slow in coming, causing us to wait longer than we expected." The paymaster finally arrived a week later, paid off the former soldiers, and the regiment dispersed to their homes and resumed their civilian lives.[5]

The long delays that so many Union Army veterans chafed at were not simply the result of bureaucratic inefficiency. There were nearly a million American men in uniform in 1865, the largest army the United States had ever raised. Now that the guns were silent, all they wanted was to leave the ranks and return to their homes. As the historian of the 15th Minnesota Infantry wrote:

> *Mustering out a regiment of United States volunteers is no light work. The examining, reviewing, settling accounts, making rolls, turning in property, making out discharges and meeting like requirements is something to be dreaded. . . . Roll after roll to the number of five or six must be made out in prescribed form, on prescribed paper, with prescribed ink. . . . An authorized agent of the government, called the mustering officer, is set over the regiment to see that every exaction is respected, and a day is fixed when all must be completed.[6]*

It was a scenario repeated in mustering-out rendezvous all across the United States, and soldiers complained about it in thousands of letters home to their impatiently waiting families. Soldiers of both armies struggled to adapt to the new lives made possible by the end of the war. One Confederate soldier described the feelings of many men in 1865 when he wrote, "Suddenly they were free—free from starvation, free from restless nights of trying to sleep under blankets of rain and snow, free from death itself, free to go home, and free to start rebuilding for the future."[7]

Thirty-three years later, the U.S. Army experienced another rapid expansion, nearly ten times over its peacetime strength, this time for the Spanish-American War. Once again the bulk of those new regiments were formed of volunteers or from state militias hastily activated for federal service. Many of those eager volunteers were woefully unprepared for the hard realities of military service, and the war was so short that most of them never left the United States. They had enlisted in a surge of patriotic fervor and with dreams of martial glory and adventure—what most of them experienced was stultifying boredom in the training camps and decimation from cholera and typhoid. Like their fathers and uncles who had served in the Civil War, once it was clear that the war was over all they wanted was to get shut of the army and go home. "We are nothing but slaves, and treated accordingly," one Kentucky soldier wrote in a letter home. "In future, I shall know better than to sign my liberty away."[8]

Despite all their legitimate complaints, those disgruntled soldiers still had it better than some veterans in other countries. For the men of the French Foreign Legion, their discharge from service cast them adrift far from their home countries. Many of them had checkered criminal pasts which meant that they were still wanted by the law in their own nations. As it was, the Legion only paid for their transport inside the borders of France. "A legionnaire who has served his time is thus absolutely helpless, being stranded penniless in a strange town," Erwin Rosen wrote after his time in the Legion. "His clothes are such as to prevent him applying for any work but that of a labourer, and the only papers he has to show are his certificates of dismissal from the Foreign Legion, which are worth very little in France. . . . Everywhere he is shown the door, and the poor devil begins a terrible course of starvation."[9] It was this experience of being cast up destitute, Rosen believed, that drove so many veterans of the Legion to reenlist for another five-year hitch, and then another, until at last they were just too old and broken down to soldier anymore.

According to their own narratives, many men who passed through the cataclysm of the world wars emerged from those experiences in a sense of almost disbelief that they had survived the maelstroms that killed so many of their comrades. The First World War ended with a cease-fire on the eleventh hour of the eleventh day of the eleventh month, 1918. Sergeant Major Richard Tobin of the Royal Naval Division wrote, "The Armistice came—the day we had dreamed of. The guns stopped, the fighting stopped. Four years of noise and bangs ended in silence. The killings had stopped. We were stunned. I had been out since 1914. I should have been happy—I was sad. I thought of the slaughter, the hardships . . . the waste and the friends I had lost."

In every war, some man is the last to die, and men were killed right up to the last moments of that war. Sometimes it was just because of the normal capriciousness of fate, but in other cases it was because of stupid, criminal viciousness on the part of their commanders. More than 1,100 American soldiers were killed or wounded trying to cross the River Meuse the night before the Armistice, an attack that served absolutely no tactical or strategic value. In all, the U.S. Army lost at least 3,500 men in the hours before the cease-fire, apparently because General Pershing did not trust that the Germans would actually honor the armistice agreement and stop fighting at the agreed hour. Pershing was normally an intelligent, forward-thinking commander, but on this occasion he wasted men's lives for no worthwhile reason, other than his belief that the German Army should be defeated in the field rather than negotiated into a cease-fire.

Men died in the final moments all along the lines. In his diary entry on November 11, 1918, Corporal Thomas Grady of the Australian Expeditionary Force wrote, "Stood by all night and it was a hot place. One of my guns was knocked out of action by shrapnel and I found one of the new men—Jones—dead in his dugout. Cold and raining. A runner came in at 10.30 with order to cease firing at 11 a.m. Firing continued and we stood by. The 306 Machine Gun Company on my right lost twelve men at 10.55 when a high explosive shell landed in their position." The guns fell silent at 11:00 o'clock. "I reported Jones's death and marked his grave," Grady recalled. "The captain conducted a prayer and cried like a baby."[10]

On the other side of the lines, Anton Lang, a German soldier in the 2nd Bavarian Foot Artillery Regiment, wrote, "The battle raged until exactly 11 a.m. and all of a sudden a 'big freeze' set in. One had a feeling that it was a dream and unbelievable. The sudden stillness was interrupted by a single heavy shell, which exploded on a trail near our battery among a platoon of infantry and killed four and wounded about a dozen. Having seen so many tragedies this made us sad and mad. Some joker on the other side probably wanted to fire the 'last' shot."[11]

When the shooting finally stopped, the trenches were silent for the first time in four years. A British artillery lieutenant remembered how surreal it all seemed, saying, "A strange and unreal thought was running through my mind. I had a future. It took some getting used to, this knowledge. There was a future ahead of me—something I had not imagined for some years. . . . No more slaughter; no more maiming, no more mud and blood, and no more killing and disemboweling of horses and mules—which was what I found most difficult to bear. No more of those hopeless dawns with the rain chilling the spirits, no more crouching in inadequate dugouts scooped out of trench walls, no more dodging of snipers' bullets, no more of that terrible shell fire. No more shoveling up bits of men's bodies and dumping into sandbags . . . and no more writing of those dreadfully difficult letters to the next-of-kin of the dead."[12]

The realization that the war was actually over, and that they had survived it, was something that soldiers on all sides described as a bewildering shock. They wanted to go home, to resume their lives once more—the fact that they could actually do so took a while to fully comprehend. Soon enough, though, that disbelief wore off. Thinking back to that moment, Walter Hare, a private in the West Yorkshires, remembered, "I couldn't wait to be demobilized. I wanted to get out as quickly as I could. I'd had more than enough of the army. I'd joined up for the duration and the duration had come and gone. Now I wanted to be back in civilian life."[13] Another soldier wrote, "Everyone is anxious to get home. . . . I am quite fed up with the Army now. The job is finished and one put up with a great deal of things when there was a necessity to help beat the Boche, but now a lot of things simply irritate me. . . . There are extremely few men who have any desire to remain in the Army—all are anxious to discard their khaki now that the job is finished."[14] As many veterans found, going home could be an emotionally and mentally difficult process. It left many of them bitter for years.

German soldiers returned to a country in the grip of economic collapse, chronic shortages caused by the British blockade, a government in chaos with the Kaiser's forced abdication, and a society beginning to feel the humiliation of defeat. Faced with that grim homecoming, many of them wondered what all the violence and suffering and death had been for. "Most of the soldiers," one German veteran said, "made no attempt to conceal the feeling that we poor devils had absolutely nothing gain in this war, that we had only to lose our lives or, which was still worse, that we should sit at some street corner as crippled 'war veterans' trying to arouse the pity of passers-by by means of some squeaking organ."[15]

Many British veterans felt that their homecoming, and their treatment in the years following the war, was terribly unjust. They were all men of working age, yet employment was hard to come by for many of them. The economy of their country was struggling also, and men who had never spent a day in uniform had taken their places in the factories, shops, and trades. "When it was all over, you know what we got?" one veteran remembered. "A kick up the backside by the government. I've got no respect for those days. The unemployed soldier had a hell of a time until the order came through that anybody employing an ex-serviceman could not sack him."[16] George Grunwell could not find a job for three years after his discharge. "I, along with other men, started to look for work—but it was fruitless," he said. "I tried everything and anything— postal work—a course in motoring. But it was all fruitless—there were too many people, and drivers were ten a penny. We were queuing up at the labour exchange, but there were no jobs there for us—all they could do was hand out unemployment pay, which was eighteen shillings a week."[17] Another former soldier said, "When I went home . . . they didn't want to know about me—they couldn't give a damn. They only had council houses for key workers, and I thought to myself, 'What the hell have I been all this time, then?'"

First World War veterans from all countries found the years after the war to be hard, especially when the Great Depression wrecked national economies all around the world. For American veterans, their desperation and bitterness came to a head in 1932. More than seventeen thousand former soldiers, accompanied by their families, gathered in the nation's capital in a movement that became known as the Bonus Army. In 1924, Congress had passed the World War Adjusted Compensation Act that awarded military veterans service certificates that would be redeemed for cash after twenty-one years, in 1945. Most of the marchers had been out of work since the onset of the Depression, and were desperate for relief. They hoped to persuade the government to pay out those service certificates early. When the matter went to Congress, the U.S. Senate rejected a bill proposing an early payout for veterans, by a vote of 62–18. President Herbert Hoover then ordered the War Department to break up the Bonus Army's encampment, and troopers of the 3rd U.S. Cavalry and 12th U.S. Infantry did so, with rifle butts, clubs, and tear gas. There was a bitter irony in the sight of regular army soldiers driving former soldiers away with violent force.

The end of the Second World War produced a markedly different experience for most American veterans, perhaps better than the aftermath of any war in American history up to that point, at least in terms of their government's efforts to provide them some means of securing their future. The most forward-thinking, innovative program implemented by any government in the postwar years of this period was the American GI Bill. Hundreds of thousands of discharged American servicemen took advantage of the opportunity to go to college on the government's dime, resulting in a huge increase in the number of college-educated men in the country's workforce. It was a social experiment that completely changed America, and gave former soldiers a better chance than they were ever given before. One of those men was Ernest Andrews, who had served in North Africa, Italy, and France with the 1st Infantry Division. "The G.I. Bill gave me an opportunity to go to college," he said, "which I very probably would not have had, because our family was not a wealthy family at all."[18]

Robert Erikson, a former paratrooper who had served with the 509th PIR in Italy, France and Germany, also benefited from the government's assistance programs. Erikson was seriously wounded in the final weeks of the war, and was fortunate in that he applied to the Veterans Administration for disability benefits at the point of his discharge from the army. After he lost his job driving for a bakery, he decided to go to school. To his surprise, as a combat wounded, disabled veteran, he was entitled to an allotment of $202 a month under Public Law 16, which provided for rehabilitation training for wounded soldiers. "That was a lot more than the GI Bill," he recalled, so he signed on, and the program paid his way through a degree program at St. Cloud State College in Minnesota.[19]

Despite the opportunities offered by programs such as the GI Bill and veterans rehabilitation training, some former soldiers found that the emotional toll of their military experiences made it hard for them to make a smooth transition back into civilian life. When John Hinchliff, a veteran of the 507th PIR, received his discharge in 1945, he returned home to a young wife he had married just after he enlisted and a daughter he had only seen a couple of times since she was born. He and his wife, he recalled, were "almost strangers." After fighting in Normandy, the Battle of the Bulge, and parachuting into Germany during Operation Linebacker, Hinchliff was an experienced noncommissioned officer who had served in one of the toughest outfits in the U.S. Army, but he had no idea how to function as a civilian. "I was . . . I was lost," he said. With a wife and child to support, he chose to not take advantage of the GI Bill opportunity, and instead took a series of dead-end, hardscrabble jobs just to make ends meet. In hindsight, he regretted that he had no one to advise him to take a more considered approach to the future.

For soldiers whose service had taken them far from home, through years of war, the process of fitting back into a "normal" civilian life was often a disorienting experience. Men who had spent every day in uniform dreaming of the time when they could finally escape the army's grasp found that their lives had changed in ways they did not understand until confronted by unfamiliar realities. Even when they were able to return to jobs they had worked in before their enlistment, other factors gave them trouble. Frederick Branham had a job and a fiancée waiting for him when he was discharged from the U.S. Army, but he himself had changed. His new wife, he remembered, said that he "left as an eighteen-year old and came home a fifty-five year old." Like many veterans of war, he soon found that he had left the army, but the war had not left him. "The first two years I was home must have been terrible for her and my children," he said. "I didn't sleep well. I didn't function real well. I just—well, I just can't explain it." Branham might not have felt he was able to explain it, but his fellow combat veterans would have needed no explanation, since so many of them described similar experiences.

Albert Price fought in Italy with the British Army; his homecoming was hard and not at all unusual. "Oh, I was traumatized, I was traumatized," he said. "There's this strange feeling that I was a stranger, coming back now. I was a stranger and it's difficult. And it was difficult to settle down again. I found it so for quite a long time. . . . I couldn't get with it somehow—well, you missed all your mates. It was back to square one and nobody seemed to care, nobody seemed to bother."[20] Men of all armies described similar feelings of missing their brothers in the service, of being adrift in civil society and feeling that no one in the "real" world understood them, or wanted to. "I used to go to all the familiar places I used to as a young man and I didn't know anyone," another British soldier remembered. "And I wanted to go back, I didn't want to stay at home, I wanted to go back.... I would wake up in the morning and I didn't think I was alive, I'd think I was dead. And I used to speak out so that one of the family would turn 'round, so I'd know that I'm alive because they could hear me."[21]

Perhaps the worst situations that could confront a demobilized soldier were the sort that faced those soldiers whose armies had not just lost the war, but whose countries were almost completely destroyed in the conflict. For veterans of the German and Japanese armies in the aftermath of the Second World War, the fact that they had survived the maelstrom of combat was only part of their personal loss—some of them did not even know if they still had homes to return to. After years of strategic bombing, the major cities of both those countries were in ruins. Hamburg, Dresden, Darmstadt, and Tokyo were firebombed almost out of existence, as were numerous smaller cities. Cologne, Kassel, and Berlin were only three of the German cities that were pounded into rubble; Hiroshima and Nagasaki were nearly wiped off the earth by atomic bombs. Hundreds of thousands of civilians were dead, some of them unnamed and unidentifiable; millions more were homeless. For many of those demobilized German and Japanese soldiers who were now under the control of their conquerors, they did not know if their homes were still standing, if their families were alive or dead, or if anything remained of their communities. They had survived their war but lost everything except their own lives, and their outlook was as dark as could be, at least in those early days of uncertainty.

A grim and tragic future also faced the soldiers of one of the victorious armies in that war, though in their moment of triumph in May 1945 they may have had no inkling of the colossal injustice that awaited them. When Germany invaded the Soviet Union with Operation Barbarossa in 1942, the Soviet Army experienced an initial collapse and the Germans captured hundreds of thousands of Soviet soldiers. The fault lay with the Soviet command structure, not the individual soldiers, but that did not matter—Stalin declared them all traitors. Those that survived a terrible internment in German POW camps (in which thousands died of starvation, disease, and brutal mistreatment) faced a return to a country for which they had fought and suffered, but that now regarded them as criminals because of Stalin's malevolent paranoia.

Georgy Semenyak was one of those soldiers. Captured in 1942, he endured three years in the hell of a German POW camp before being liberated. He was not free for long. "We did know that he [Stalin] called us the traitors to our motherland. . . . We were told, you know, 'They think you are traitors, and they will send you off to the concentration camps too,'" he said, seventy years later. "And we answered, 'We went through such horrors in here that nothing can be compared to that.'" It was a bold sentiment, but along with thousands of other repatriated Soviet soldiers, Semenyak was sent to a gulag, where he endured more years of imprisonment, this time under the orders of his own country, for the crime of not having died in 1942. When he was finally released, his life was in ruins. "It was difficult to get a job," he said. "I wasn't paid enough, and I wasn't paid as much as I deserved. And these were the results of us being imprisoned. But I was lucky enough to survive." Semenyak loved his country, but he never forgave Stalin for the injustice of what was done to him and thousands of his comrades.

In their personal narratives, the veterans of this period once again show that while some of their stories and perspectives were common across all eras and nationalities, we still cannot assume a single truth to cover all of their experiences. Some men hated the army every minute that they were unwilling cogs in the military machine; some loved it and clung to their memories of that experience as only nostalgic old soldiers can. Other men took a more measured, nuanced view of that episode in their lives, whether they served for a few months or thirty years.

Edward Ryan survived the invasion of Normandy as a soldier in the U.S. Army's 1st Infantry Division. "It was an experience and I grew up an awful lot from leaving home until I got back," he recalled. "Three years is what I had in. I had a lot of fun. I had a lot of disappointments. It's just the way life is, you know. I could say it was a great experience, but I wouldn't want to do it again." Another American veteran of the Second World War said, "I spent a lot of years afterwards, never referring to the fact that I had been in the army, never referring to the fact that I was wounded, or anything else. I just didn't want anybody to know that particularly. But I was proud of it and I felt good about it. Now, more recently, in my old age, I have gotten back to not caring what people know or don't know."[22]

One thing that many former soldiers of all nationalities expressed was the degree to which they felt that their time in the army had changed their general outlook on life. "I think the whole experience taught me a lot about life—above the blessings that God gives us, to give us life and freedom," one American veteran said. "The freedom to enjoy things like hot water and soap and a dry towel, a roof over our head, a place to live, and food to eat and clothing to wear. All of these things mean more to me than I ever thought they would mean. So the war did that for me. . . . I appreciate every morsel of food I get, every piece of clothing I have, and the shelter. Shelter is a marvelous thing."[23] That was a perspective echoed in the narratives of men who had served at Waterloo, Balaclava, Gettysburg, San Juan, Verdun, Okinawa, and thousands of other battlefields, where they had once fought and endured and watched their friends die. Years later, if they lived to remember it, they tried to put those experiences into words. As all soldiers came to understand, there was a great commonality in suffering and hardship, and the men who passed through those experiences were forever changed by them.

Some men were irreparably damaged by it, and their wounds never healed. Every country had its share of broken, embittered veterans who could never fully recover or completely assimilate back into civil society. They were their armies' permanent casualties. Other men, though, missed the army for the rest of their lives, even after they had moved on and made something of themselves as civilians. It was not the misery and deprivation they looked back on with longing, but rather, the sense of having once been a part of something that truly mattered, something that was greater than their individual selves, something that remained a part of them for the rest of their days. They may not have loved being soldiers while they were in the ranks, but many of them spoke of being glad that there was once a time, back when they were still on the threshold of their lives, when they were soldiers. One veteran of the French Foreign Legion remembered his time in the ranks by saying, "So I left the Legion and experiences that I would not have missed for a million dollars, but I do not think I would like to go through them again for five million dollars." Some men talked about their bygone days of soldiering in terms that expressed a real sense of yearning. "On the 27th of July 1888, I passed out of the profession into civilian life, feeling I might fairly claim I had worked out the Queen's shilling." Edwin Mole wrote in his memoir of his career as a British cavalryman. "I thought that day, and think still, that had I my life in front of me instead of behind, I would start again, just as I did when I was a lad of eighteen, and desire nothing better than to live those happy twenty-five years over again in the ranks of the Old 14th as a King's Hussar."[24] On the other side of the Atlantic, William Jett said much the same thing about his experience as a trooper in the 4th U.S. Cavalry during the Indian Wars. He had not liked the army all that much while he was serving, but the intervening years had given him a different perspective. Looking back, he said, "the call of the plains and mountains with their accompaniments and the rough experiences of those long-gone years is still upon me as I write, and I feel that I would like to live them all over again."[25] That was a common feeling among many old soldiers, but what was also common to them all was that their time as soldiers was forever behind them, never to be repeated.

Acknowledgments

This book took a rather circuitous route to its publication, a convoluted process that I suspect improved the finished product more than a little. I started writing this while I was in a post-graduate program in Scotland back in 2012; the idea for it occurred to me one day as I was reading by the fireplace in the Salisbury Arms. (The Salisbury is a splendid pub; if you're ever in Edinburgh and find yourself walking down Dalkeith Road you really should stop in for a pint, and I highly recommend their fish pie.)

Of all the people who played a part in this book's publication, Stackpole Books' history editor, David Reisch, deserves the lion's share of my appreciation. I first pitched this book to Stackpole back in 2014. Dave took a long look at it and concluded that the manuscript had two problems (problems of scope and focus, not issues with the quality of the writing, I'm glad to say), so he rejected it. He did, however, invite me to resubmit it if I ever reworked it to address those issues. Three years later, after my second book had gone to press with another publisher and I could finally come up for air, I pulled up my files on this project and took a fresh look at it with Dave's suggestions in mind. Not only did Dave remember me when I sent it in for a second perusal, but he made an offer for publication two weeks later. Kristen Mellitt, the production editor who guided the manuscript through the process, also deserves my thanks for all her work on it while she was undoubtedly dealing with too many other simultaneous projects.

I've found that historians, both as a profession and as individuals, are some of the most helpful and generous people out there. (Well, there's one particular fellow who is in fact quite unpleasant, but he doesn't represent the field as a whole, and he at least provides a good object lesson of how one should not behave.) I never cease to be amazed at how older, more experienced historians are willing to answer questions, offer perspectives, share research, and provide the absolutely necessary critique that all historical writing needs before it sees the light of day. Andrew Harris, my friend and comrade-in-arms at the University of Edinburgh, waded through the first rough drafts of this book and expected no more compensation than a couple of pints. I'm indebted to him for his suggestions, as I am for the fact that without him, my dissertation would never have been printed and turned in on time to the School of History, Classics & Archaeology. Come to think of it, I actually owe him quite a few pints. Felix Boecking and Pertti Ahonen, two of my professors at Edinburgh, read several preliminary chapters even though it had nothing to do with my actual coursework, and I'm very grateful to them. The staff of the National War Museum Library in Edinburgh Castle gave me keys to the parts of the building the tourists never see and helped with every research question I could think of, as well as let me in on a wonderful secret—the library restroom really does have the best view of north Edinburgh and the Firth of Forth, one that very few people get to see.

My mother, Elaine Haymond, once again gave me the vital assistance of her English teacher's eye by reading over the manuscript before its final submission. I'm a historian because of my father; I suspect I'm a writer because of my mother. The most important person in my work as a writer is my wife, Elena Haymond, without whom I could not do this. To her, and our children—Lilu, Truman, and Elizabeth—I extend my love and appreciation.

Notes

Preface

1 Sam R. Watkins, *Co. Aytch: A Side Show of the Big Show* (Chattanooga, TN: Chattanooga Times Printing Co., 1882).
2 James Madison Stone, *Personal Recollections of the Civil War, by One Who Took Part in It as a Private Soldier in the 21st Volunteer Regiment of Infantry from Massachusetts* (Boston: Author, 1918).
3 John W. Fortescue, *Following the Drum* (London: W. Blackwood & Sons, Ltd., 1931).
4 R.T. Jones, *The Collected Poems of Rudyard Kipling* (London: Wordsworth Editions Limited, 2001).

Chapter 1

1 Louis Livingstone Seaman, "A Crisis in the History of the American Army." *North American Review,* Vol. 187, Part 2 (1908).
2 Thomas Mangan, quoted in Damian Shiels, *The Forgotten Irish: Irish Emigrant Experiences in America* (Dublin: The History Press Ireland, 2016).
3 Quoted in *Army and Navy Journal,* Vol. 15, no. 10 (1877).
4 Quoted in Don Rickey, *Forty Miles a Day on Beans and Hay: The Enlisted Soldier Fighting the Indian Wars* (Norman: University of Oklahoma Press, 1963).
5 William Wills, World War II Military Oral History Project, VMI.
6 Quoted in E. A. Brininstool, *Troopers with Custer: Historic Incidents of the Battle of the Little Big Horn* (New York: Bonanza Books, 1962).
7 Samuel Hutton, in Roy Palmer, *The Rambling Soldier: Life in the Lower Ranks 1750–1900 through Soldiers' Songs and Writings* (London: Viking, 1977).
8 "Kent Soldier," in Palmer, *The Rambling Soldier.*
9 Palmer, *The Rambling Soldier.*
10 Samuel Johnson, quoted in James Boswell, *The Life of Samuel Johnson, LL.D, Including a Journal of a Tour to the Hebrides* (New York: Harper & Bros., 1871).
11 *Standing Orders of the 51st, or Edinburgh Regiment of British Militia* (Edinburgh: Thomas Allan and Company, 1812).
12 John Strawson, *Beggars in Red: The British Army 1789-1889* (London: Hutchinson, 1991).
13 William Slaper, in Brininstool, *Troopers with Custer*
14 Richard Holmes, *Soldiers* (London: Harper Press, 2011).
15 Jock Haswell. *Citizen Armies* (London: History Book Club, 1973).
16 John Shipp, *Memoirs of the Extraordinary Military Career of John Shipp Late a Lieutenant in His Majesty's 87th Regiment* (London: T. Fisher Unwin, 1890).
17 Strawson, *Beggars in Red.*
18 William Holbrook, quoted in Lyn MacDonald, *1914: The Days of Hope* (London: Penguin Books, 1989).

19 Charles Carrington, *Soldier from the Wars Returning* (London: Pen & Sword Military Classics, 2006).

20 Leander Stillwell, *The Story of a Common Soldier of Army Life in the Civil War, 1861-1865* (New York: Franklin Hudson, 1920).

21 James F. Dargan, Civil War Diary 1862–1863, California State University Northridge, Oviatt Library Collection.

22 Fairfax Downey, *Indian-Fighting Army* (Ft. Collins, CO: Old Army Press, 1971).

23 Quoted in Adam Zamoyski, *1812: Napoleon's Fatal March on Moscow* (London: Harper Perennial, 2005).

24 Needham N. Freeman, *A Soldier in the Philippines* (New York: F. Tennyson Neely, 1901).

25 John Douglas, *A Soldier's Tale of the Peninsular War,* ed. Errol King (Edinburgh: National War Museum Library, 2000).

26 Erwin Rosen, *In the Foreign Legion* (London, 1910).

27 George Farquhar, *The Recruiting Officer, A Comedy* (London: W. Simpkin & R. Marshall, 1819).

28 Shipp, *Memoirs.*

29 Timothy Gowing, *A Soldier's Experience: Or, A Voice from the Ranks; Showing the Cost of War in Blood and Treasure* (Nottingham: Thomas Forman and Sons, 1885).

30 Stillwell, *The Story of a Common Soldier.*

31 George Tompkins Jr., World War II Military Oral History Project, VMI.

32 John Bowe, *With the 13th Minnesota in the Philippines* (Minneapolis: A.B. Farnham, 1905).

33 E. P. F. Lynch, *Somme Mud: The Experiences of an Infantryman in France, 1916-1919,* ed. Will Davies (London: Bantam Books, 2008).

34 Samuel Cabble, "The Letter of Samuel Cabble," *The Record: News from the National Archives and Records Administration,* Vol. 3 (Washington, D.C.: 1996).

35 Samuel Wing, *The Soldier's Story: A Personal Narrative of the Life, Army Experiences and Marvelous Sufferings since the War of Samuel B. Wing* (New York: Philips, 1898).

36 J. W. Vaughan,. quoted in Lyn MacDonald, *1915: The Death of Innocence* (London: Penguin Books, 1989).

37 W. Carrol, *Imperial War Museum Oral Histories.*

38 Kyle Tallett and Trevor Tasker, *Gavrelle* (Barnsley: Pen and Sword Books, 2000).

39 Cecil Withers, quoted in Max Arthur, *The Last Post: The Final Word from Our First World War Soldiers* (London: Orion Publishing Group, 2014).

40 Joseph Argenzio (1st Inf Div), World War II Military Oral History Project, VMI.

41 Edmond Sworsky (2nd Ranger BN), WWII, Minnesota Historical Society (OH 112).

42 Rickey, *Forty Miles a Day on Beans and Hay.*

43 John D. Billings, *Hardtack and Coffee, or The Unwritten Story of Army Life* (Boston: George M. Smith and Co., 1888).

44 Paddy Griffith, *Battle Tactics of the Civil War* (Ramsbury: The Crowood Press, 2014).

45 Downey, *Indian-Fighting Army.*

46 Figures according to the Little Big Horn National Battlefield History Center, United States National Parks Service.

47 Emil Bode, *A Dose of Frontier Soldiering: The Memoirs of Corporal E. A. Bode, Frontier Regular Infantry, 1877–1882,* ed. Thomas T. Smith (Lincoln: University of Nebraska Press, 1994).

48 Kiffin Y. Rockwell (French Foreign Legion) Letters, First World War, North Carolina Digital Collection.

49 William Funkhouser (1st Inf Div), World War II Military Oral History Project, VMI.

50 Herbert Winckelmann, quoted in Nigel Cawthorne, *Reaping the Whirlwind: The German and Japanese Experiences of World War II* (London: David & Charles, 2008).

51 Robert Guillemard, *Adventures of a French Serjeant: During His Campaigns in Italy, Germany, Spain, Russia, &tc* (London: Hutchinson & Co., 1898).

52 Quoted in Ian C. Robertson, *Wellington at War in the Peninsula 1808-1814: An Overview and Guide* (Barnsley: Pen and Sword Books, 2000).

53 Haswell, *Citizen Armies.*

54 Ibid.

55 Catherine Merridale, *Ivan's War: Life and Death in the Red Army, 1939-1945* (New York: Metropolitan Books, 2006).

56 John Morse, *In the Russian Ranks: A Soldier's Account of the Fighting in Poland* (New York: Alfred A. Knopf, 1916).

57 Aloysius Damski, in Russell Miller, *Nothing Less Than Victory: The Oral History of D-Day* (New York: Quill, 1993).

58 Desmond Morton, *When Your Number's Up: The Canadian Soldier in the First World War* (Toronto: Random House of Canada, 1993).

Chapter 2

1 *Standing Orders of the 51st, or Edinburgh Regiment of British Militia.*

2 Shipp, *Memoirs.*

3 J. MacMullen, *Camp and Barrack Room: Or, the British Army as It Is, by a Late Staff Sergeant of the 13th Light Infantry* (London, 1846).

4 R. Hugh Knyvett, *"Over There" with the Australians* (New York: Charles Scribner's Sons, 1918).

5 Edwin Rundle, *A Soldier's Life: Being the Personal Reminiscences of Edwin G. Rundle* (Forgotten Books, 2016).

6 Freeman, *A Soldier in the Philippines.*

7 Emil Geissler, quoted in Jakob Zenzmaier, *Military Training: Violence as a Military Instrument for Achieving Obedience,* trans. Nick Somers (Essen, 2011).

8 Nakamura Toshio, in Frank Gibney, ed., and Beth Cary, trans., *Senso: The Japanese Remember the Pacific War* (New York: M.E. Sharpe, 1995).

9 Kent Soldier, in Palmer, *The Rambling Soldier.*

10 Lynch, *Somme Mud.*

11 Anonymous, *A Soldier of the Seventy-First: The Journal of a Soldier in the Peninsular War,* ed. Christopher Hibbert (London: Windrush Press, 1975).

12 *Standing Orders of the Scots Guards, 1892* (Edinburgh, 1892). [National War Museum Library].

13 *Standing Orders of the Scots Guards, 1892.*

14 Edwin Mole, *A King's Hussar: Being the Military Memoirs for Twenty-Five years of a Troop-Sergeant-Major of the 14th (King's) Hussars*, collected by Herbert Compton (London, 1893).

15 Guillemard, *Adventures of a French Serjeant.*

16 Sakata Tsuyoshi, in Gibney and Cary, *Senso.*

17 Watanabe Katsumi, in Gibney and Cary, *Senso.*

18 Quoted in Douglas Jerrold, *The Royal Naval Division* (London: Naval and Military Press, 2012).

19 Stillwell, *The Story of a Common Soldier.*

20 Anonymous, *A Soldier of the Seventy-First.*

21 William Jett, quoted in Henry P. Walker, "The Reluctant Corporal: The Autobiography of William Bladen Jett: Part I," *The Journal of Arizona History 12,* no. 1 (Spring 1971): 1–50

22 T. H. McGuffie, ed., *Rank and File: The Common Soldier at Peace and War 1642-1914* (London: Hutchinson, 1964).

23 Joseph Donaldson, *The Eventful Life of a Soldier during the Late War in Spain, Portugal and France,* 1827 (Howell Press, 2000). Italics in the original.

24 Charles Willeford, *Something about a Soldier: A Young Man's Life and Loves in the Peacetime Army—in the Philippines and California—on the Eve of World War II* (New York: Random House, 1986).

25 Field Marshal Sir William Robertson, *From Private to Field Marshal* (London, 1921).

26 "Ex-Trooper," *The French Army from Within* (London: William Brendon and Son, 1916).

27 Harold Baldwin, quoted in Morton, *When Your Number's Up.*

28 George MacMullen, quoted in McGuffie, *Rank and File.*

29 Leander Stillwell, *The Story of a Common Soldier.*

30 Sidney Amatt (Essex Regiment), Imperial War Museum Oral Histories.

31 Raymond Gantter, *Roll Me Over: An Infantryman's World War II* (New York: Presidio Press, 1997).

32 Shipp, *Memoir.*

33 Stone, *Personal Recollections of the Civil War.*

34 Carrington, *Soldier from the Wars Returning.*

35 Rundle, *A Soldier's Life.*

36 Freeman, *A Soldier in the Philippines.*

37 Knyvett, *"Over There."*

38 Quoted in Rickey, *Forty Miles a Day on Beans and Hay.*

39 O. O. Howard, *Army and Navy Journal,* May 4, 1878.

40 Robertson, *From Private to Field Marshal.*

41 Ibid.

42 Robert Blatchford, *Tales for the Marines* (London: The Clarion Newspaper Press, 1901).

43 Jac Weller, *Weapons and Tactics: Hastings to Berlin* (New York: St. Martin's Press, 1966).

44 Weller, *Weapons and Tactics*.

45 William Howard Russell, *The British Expedition to the Crimea* (London: George Routledge and Sons, 1877).

46 William Jett, quoted in Walker, "The Reluctant Corporal."

47 "Ex-Trooper," *The French Army from Within*.

48 Ascan Gobert. quoted in Max Arthur, *Forgotten Voices of the Great War: A New History of WWI in the Words of the Men and Women Who were There* (London: Ebury Press, 2002).

49 Strawson, *Beggars in Red*.

50 "Ex-Trooper," *The French Army from Within*.

51 Alexander Somerville, quoted in Richard Holmes, *Tommy: The British Soldier on the Western Front 1914-1918* (London: HarperCollins, 2005).

52 Billings, *Hardtack and Coffee*.

53 Willeford, *Something about a Soldier*.

54 R. G. Garrod, quoted in Holmes, *Tommy*.

55 Charles Mismer, quoted in Paul Kerr, *The Crimean War* (London: Channel 4 Books, 2000).

56 Willeford, *Something about a Soldier*.

57 Rickey, *Forty Miles a Day on Beans and Hay*.

58 "Ex-Trooper," *The French Army from Within*.

59 Willeford, *Something about a Soldier*.

60 Ibid.

61 Rickey, *Forty Miles a Day on Beans and Hay*.

62 Carrington, *Soldier from the Wars Returning*.

63 Brian R. Sullivan, "Myths, Realities and Explanations," in *Time to Kill: The Soldier's Experience of War in the West 1939-1945*, ed. Paul Addison and Angus Calder (London: Pimlico, 1997).

Chapter 3

1 Freeman. *A Soldier in the Philippines*.

2 John F. Finerty, *War-Path and Bivouac or The Conquest of the Sioux*, reprint (Norman: University of Oklahoma Press, 1994).

3 Philip Gibbs, *Now It Can Be Told* (London: Harper and Brothers, 1920).

4 Bill Sugden, quoted in Holmes, *Tommy*.

5 Oliver Wendell Holmes, quoted in Joseph P. Franklin, *Building Leaders the West Point Way: Ten Principles from the Nation's Most Powerful Leadership Lab* (Nashville: Thomas Nelson, 2007).

6 Christopher Hibbert, *Corunna* (London: Pan Books, 1961).

7 "Ex-Trooper," *The French Army from Within*.

8 Philip Hamlin (1st Minnesota Infantry), Civil War, Minnesota Historical Society Collections, letter dated December 18, 1862, file P1577, Minnesota Historical Society.

9 Ibid.

10 Gibbs, *Now It Can Be Told.*

11 Cecil Withers, quoted in Arthur, *The Last Post.*

12 Ottokar Czernin, *Im Weltkriege [In the World War]* (Berlin: Berlin Ullstein, 1919).

13 Warren Olney, *"Shiloh" as Seen by a Private Soldier with Some Personal Reminiscences,* reprint (Wayne Dasher, 2009).

14 Stone, *Personal Recollections of the Civil War.*

15 Robert Fair (1st Infantry Division), World War II Military Oral History Project, VMI.

16 William Funkhouser (1st Infantry Division), World War II Military Oral History Project, VMI.

17 Gantter, *Roll Me Over.*

18 Joachim Pusch (14th Motorized Infantry), WWII, Minnesota Historical Society (OH 112).

19 Freeman, *A Soldier in the Philippines.*

20 Merritt Hinkel, in Patrick K. O'Donnell, *Into the Rising Sun: In Their Own Words, World War II's Pacific Veterans* (Free Press, 2014).

21 Howard Baxter, in O'Donnell, *Into the Rising Sun.*

22 Vizelfeldwebel Collet, quoted in Jack Sheldon, *The German Army on the Somme: 1914-1916* (Barnsley: Pen & Sword Military, 2005).

23 Quoted in Bob Carruthers, ed., *Winter Warfare on the Russian Front (Eastern Front from Primary Sources)* (Barnsley: Pen & Sword Books Limited, 2013).

24 Frank Richards, *Old Soldiers Never Die* (Uckfield: The Naval and Military Press, 2001).

25 Carlton McCarthy, *Detailed Minutiae of Soldier Life in the Army of Northern Virginia, 1861-1865* (C. McCarthy, 1882).

26 Watkins, *Co. Aytch.*

27 Ami Frank Mulford, quoted in Rickey, *Forty Miles a Day on Beans and Hay.*

28 *Army and Navy Journal,* 1873.

29 Joachim Pusch (14th Motorized Infantry), WWII, Minnesota Historical Society (OH 112).

30 Gantter, *Roll Me Over.*

31 Rudyard Kipling, "The 'eathen," *The Writings in Prose and Verse of Rudyard Kipling: Verses, 1889-1896* (New York: Charles Scribner's Sons, 1913).

32 William Jett, quoted in Walker, "The Reluctant Corporal."

33 Martin Poppel, *Heaven and Hell: The War Diary of a German Paratrooper,* trans. Dr. Louise Willmot (Staplehurst: Spellmount Limited, 1988).

34 *Standing Orders of the 51st, or Edinburgh Regiment of British Militia.*

35 *Standing Orders of the Scots Guards, 1892*

36 *Standing Orders, 90th Light Infantry* (Chatham: James Burrill, Army Printer, 1848).

37 *Standing Orders of the Seaforth Highlanders* (Letchworth: Arden Press, 1897).

38 Ernest Shephard, *A Sergeant-Major's War: From Hill 60 to the Somme* (Ramsbury, Wiltshire: The Crowood Press, 1987).

39 Anonymous, *A Late Staff Sergeant of the 13th Infantry, Camp and Barrack-Room; or, the British Army as it is* (London: Chapman & Hall, 1846).

40 Robertson, *From Private to Field Marshal.*

41 Julius Koettgen, *I Fought for the Kaiser: Memoirs of a Reluctant Soldier 1914-1915*, ed. Bob Carruthers (Stratford upon Avon: Coda Books, 2013).

42 *Standing Orders, 90th Light Infantry, 1848.*

43 *Standing Orders of the Seaforth Highlanders.*

44 Sakata Shintaro, quoted in Gibney and Carey, *Senso.*

45 Joachim Pusch (14th Motorized Infantry), WWII, Minnesota Historical Society (OH 112).

46 Watkins, *Co. Aytch.*

47 P. J. Campbell, *In the Cannon's Mouth* (London: Hamilton, 1979).

48 Alfred Bundy, quoted in Peter Hart, *The Somme* (London: Orion Publishing Group, 2012).

49 Donald Kyler, World War I Veterans Survey, US Army Military History Institute.

50 Rundle, *A Soldier's Life.*

51 Thomas Morris, *The Recollections of Sergeant Morris*, reprint, ed. John Selby (Moreton-in-Marsh: The Windrush Press, 1998).

52 Guillemard, *Adventures of a French Serjeant.*

53 George Fortune, quoted in Holmes, *Tommy.*

Chapter 4

1 Henry Windolph, *I Fought with Custer: The Story of Sergeant Windolph, Last Survivor of the Battle of the Little Big Horn as Told to Frazier and Robert Hunt* (Lincoln: University of Nebraska Press, 1987).

2 William Lee, quoted in Lloyd Clark, *Crossing the Rhine: Breaking into Nazi Germany 1944 and 1945 – the Greatest Airborne Battles in History* (Open Road, 2009).

3 Cleeve E. Montague (Royal Garrison Artillery), Imperial War Museum Oral Histories.

4 Harry Patch, quoted in Arthur, *The Last Post.*

5 Ibid.

6 Russell F. Weigley, *The American Way of War: A History of United States Military Strategy and Policy* (Bloomington: Indiana University Press, 1973).

7 Reid Mitchell, "The GI in Europe and American Military Tradition," in Addison and Calder, *Time to Kill.*

8 Joseph Argenzio (1st Inf Div), World War II Military Oral History Project, VMI.

9 Stephen Ambrose, *Citizen Soldiers: The U.S. Army from the Normandy Beaches to the Bulge to the Surrender of Germany* (New York: Simon & Schuster, 2013).

10 Quoted in Samuel A. Stouffer, *The American Soldier: Combat and Its Aftermath* (New York: Military Affairs, 1977).

11 John Hinchliff (507th Parachute Infantry), WWII, Minnesota Historical Society (OH 112).

12 Joseph Argenzio (1st Inf Div), World War II Military Oral History Project, VMI.

13 Richard Holmes, "Five Armies in Italy, 1943-1945," in Addison and Calder, *Time to Kill.*

14 Quoted in Addison and Calder, *Time to Kill.*

15 Clifford Lane (Hertfordshire Regiment), Imperial War Museum Oral Histories.

16 Herbert Sulzbach (Wehrmacht), Imperial War Museum Oral Histories.

17 Charles Carrington, *Soldier from the Wars Returning.*

18 Quinnell (Royal Fusiliers), Imperial War Museum Oral Histories.

19 C. Hans Roth, *Eastern Inferno: The Journals of a German Panzerjaeger on the Eastern Front, 1941–43,* ed. Christine Alexander and Mason Kunze (Newbury: Casemate, 2010).

20 Joachim Pusch (14th Motorized Infantry), WWII, Minnesota Historical Society (OH 112).

21 Quoted in Holmes, *Soldiers.*

22 Donald S. Frederick (1st Ranger BN), WWII, Minnesota Historical Society (OH 112).

23 John Hinchliff (507th Parachute Infantry), WWII, Minnesota Historical Society (OH 112).

24 Billings, *Hardtack and Coffee.*

25 Richard Haigh, *Life in a Tank* (New York: Houghton Mifflin, 1918).

26 Rickey, *Forty Miles a Day on Beans and Hay.*

27 *Standing Orders of the Scots Guards, 1892.*

28 Billings, *Hardtack and Coffee.*

29 Rickey, *Forty Miles a Day on Beans and Hay.*

30 *Standing Orders of the 51st Edinburgh Regiment, 1812.*

31 Rickey, *Forty Miles a Day on Beans and Hay.*

32 Philip Gibbs, *Now It Can Be Told.*

33 Willeford, *Something about a Soldier.*

34 McCarthy, *Detailed Minutiae of Soldier Life.*

35 Ibid.

Chapter 5

1 Watkins, *Co. Aytch.*

2 Hugh Knyvett, *"Over There" with the Australians.*

3 E.P.F. Lynch, *Somme Mud.*

4 Randolph H. McKim, *A Soldier's Recollections: Leaves from the Diary of a Young Confederate* (New York: Longmans, Green and Co., 1910).

5 Leon Louis, *Diary of a Tar Heel Confederate Soldier* (Charlotte: Stone Publishing, 1903).

6 Ibid.

7 Charles S. Taylor, Civil War Letters, East Texas Research Center Digital Archives.

8 Shiro Tokita, quoted in Kazuo Tamayama and John Nunneley, eds., *Tales by Japanese Soldiers* (London: Cassell Military Paperbacks, 1992).

9 Richards, *Old Soldiers Never Die.*

10 Samuel Tiebout, quoted in Bruce T. McCully, "The Civil War Diary of Samuel Tiebout, Fifth New York Volunteer Infantry," *New York History* 24, no. 2 (April 1943): 250–64.

11 N. W. Bancroft, *From Recruit to Staff Sergeant,* reprint (Ann Arbor, MI: I. Henry, 1979).

12 J. W. Palmer (Royal Field Artillery), Imperial War Museum Oral Histories.

13 Tom Bracey (Royal Fusiliers), Imperial War Museum Oral Histories.

14 Arthur Gibbs. quoted in Malcolm Brown, *The Imperial War Museum Book of the Somme* (London: Pan Books, 1996).

15 Paul Totten, diary, World War I Veterans Survey, US Army Military History Institute.

16 Watkins, *Co. Aytch.*

17 Poppel, *Heaven and Hell.*

18 Koettgen, *I Fought for the Kaiser*

19 Watkins, *Co. Aytch.*

20 Henry Stelling, quoted in *Uncommon Valor: The Exciting Story of the Army,* edited by James Merrill (New York: Rand McNally, 1964).

21 Shephard, *A Sergeant–Major's War.*

22 Morris, *The Recollections of Sergeant Morris.*

23 Alfred Perrot-White, *French Legionnaire* (London: Caxton Printers, 1951).

24 John Traub, quoted in Paul Fatout, "Letters of John Traub, Twenty-Ninth Indiana Infantry," *Indiana Magazine of History* 53, no. 2 (June 1957): 171–74.

25 Gowing, *A Soldier's Experience.*

26 Holmes, *Tommy.*

27 Paul Totten diary, World War I Veterans Survey, US Army Military History Institute.

28 Arthur Guy Empey, *"Over the Top," by an American Soldier Who Went Together with Tommy's Dictionary of the Trenches* (New York, 1917).

29 Shephard, *A Sergeant–Major's War.*

30 Stanley Baxter, *One Young Man: The Simple and True Story of the Clerk Who Fought on the Western Front for Two Years, Was Severely Wounded at the Battle of Somme, and Is Now Back at His Desk,* edited by Ernest Hodder-Williams (London: Hodder & Stoughton, 1917).

31 Desmond Allhusen, Imperial War Museum Oral Histories.

32 A. Rule, Imperial War Museum Oral Histories.

33 Shephard, *A Sergeant–Major's War.*

34 Lynch, *Somme Mud.*

35 Ernst Junger, *Storm of Steel,* trans. Michael Hofmann (London: Penguin Books, 2003).

36 James Norman Hall, *Kitchener's Mob: The Adventures of an American in the British Army* (Boston: Houghton Mifflin, 1916).

37 Harvey Hamilton, quoted in Merrill, *Uncommon Valor.*

38 Eugene B. Sledge, *With the Old Breed at Peleliu and Okinawa* (New York: Presidio Press, 1981).

39 A. P. Herbert, *The Secret Battle* (London: Methuen & Co., 1919).

40 Desmond Allhusen, quoted in Philip Warner, *Passchendaele* (London: Pen and Sword Military Classics, 2014).

41 Carrington, *Soldier from the Wars Returning*.

42 Herbert, *The Secret Battle*.

Chapter 6

1 Surgeon General's Office, *Circular No. 8: Report on the Hygiene of the United States Army with Descriptions of Military Posts* (Washington, D.C.: Government Printing Office, 1875).

2 Blaze de Blury, quoted in Zamoyski, *1812*.

3 Edmund Bonhoff, quoted in *The Wehrmacht Last Witnesses*, Bob Carruthers, ed. (London: Andre Deutsch, 2010).

4 Joachim Pusch (14th Motorized Infantry), WWII, Minnesota Historical Society (OH 112).

5 William Howard Russell, *Dispatches from the Crimea* (London: Frontline Books, 2008).

6 Robert Blatchford, quoted in Palmer, *The Rambling Soldier*.

7 Benjamin Harris, *Recollections of Rifleman Harris*, ed. Captain Henry Curling (London, 1848).

8 Stillwell, *The Story of a Common Soldier*.

9 Marion Johnstone Ford and Arthur Peronneau Ford, *Life in the Confederate Army Being Personal Experiences of a Private Soldier in the Confederate Army* (New York: The Neale Publishing Company, 1905).

10 McCarthy, *Detailed Minutiae of Soldier Life*.

11 William H. S. Burgwyn, Civil War Diary and Letters, 1862–1863, North Carolina Digital Collections.

12 George Hangar, *Colonel George Hangar's Advice to All Sportsmen, Farmers, and Gamekeepers, 1814* (London: Read Country Book, 2005).

13 Gunther E. Rothenburg, *The Art of Warfare in the Age of Napoleon* (Chalford: Spellmount, 2007).

14 Albert O. Marshall, *Army Life: From a Soldier's Journal*, 1883, reprint (Forgotten Books, 2015).

15 Carrington, *Soldier from the Wars Returning*.

16 Donald E. Carey, *Fighting the Bolsheviks: The Russian War Memoir of Private First Class Donald E. Carey, US Army, 1918–1919* (Novato, CA: Presidio Press, 1997).

17 Guy Nicely. World War II Oral History Project. VMI.

18 Griffith, *Battle Tactics of the Civil War*.

19 Ex-Trooper. *The French Army from Within*. (London: William Brendon and Son, 1916).

20 Ibid.

Chapter 7

1 Alexander Alexander, quoted in McGuffie, *Rank and File.*
2 Rothenburg, *The Art of Warfare in the Age of Napoleon.*
3 *Army and Navy Journal*, vol. II (1873).
4 Ibid.
5 Shipp, *Memoirs.*
6 Rundle, *A Soldier's Life.*
7 Anonymous, quoted in *Army and Navy Journal*, June 24, 1876.
8 William Holbrook, quoted in MacDonald, *1914.*
9 Ibid.
10 Rickey, *Forty Miles a Day on Beans and Hay.*
11 George Manington, quoted in McGuffie, *Rank and File.*
12 Erwin Rosen, quoted in McGuffie, *Rank and File.*
13 Billings, *Hardtack and Coffee.*
14 Ibid.
15 Charles C. Perkins (1st Massachusetts Infantry), diary, Civil War, US Army History & Education Center.
16 Nelson Stauffer, *Civil War Diary*, ed. Norman Tanis (Northridge: California State University, 1976).
17 Alfred Finnigan, quoted in Arthur, *The Last Post.*
18 Forbes, "The United States Army."
19 *Report of the Surgeon General of the Army to the Secretary of War for the Fiscal Year Ending June 30 1889* (Washington, D.C.: Government Printing Office, 1889).
20 Ibid.
21 Quoted in Edward Coffman, *Old Army: A Portrait of the American Army in Peacetime, 1784-1898* (New York: Oxford University Press, 1986).
22 Quoted in Rickey, *Forty Miles a Day on Beans and Hay.*
23 Ibid.
24 Windolph, *I Fought with Custer.*
25 Finerty, *War-Path and Bivouac.*
26 William Jett, quoted in Walker, "The Reluctant Corporal."
27 *Report of the Surgeon General of the Army, 1889.*
28 Ibid.
29 *Report of the Surgeon General of the Army, 1875.*
30 Louis Ebert, quoted in Rickey, *Forty Miles a Day on Beans and Hay.*
31 Bowe, *With the 13th Minnesota in the Philippines.*
32 Freeman, *A Soldier in the Philippines.*
33 Ibid.
34 Donald Kyler, World War I Veterans Survey, US Army Military History Institute.
35 Quoted in McGuffie, *Rank and File.*
36 Fred Noyes, quoted in Morton, *When Your Number's Up.*
37 Rothenburg, *The Art of Warfare in the Age of Napoleon.*
38 Jakob Walter and Marc Raeff, *The Diary of a Napoleonic Foot Soldier* (Moreton: Windrush, 1999).
39 Junger, *Storm of Steel.*

40 William Drown, quoted in Theophilus F. Rodenbough, *From Everglade to Canon with the Second Dragoons (Second United States Cavalry): An Authentic Account of Service in Florida, Mexico, Virginia, and the Indian Country, etc* (New York: D. Van Nostrand, 1875).

41 Anonymous, *A Soldier of the Seventy-First.*

42 Russell, *Dispatches from the Crimea.*

43 Marion and Arthur Ford, *Life in the Confederate Army.*

44 McCarthy, *Detailed Minutiae of Soldier Life.*

45 Ibid.

46 Louis, *Diary of a Tar Heel Confederate Soldier.*

47 John Beatty, *The Citizen-Soldier; or, Memoirs of a Volunteer* (Cincinnati: Wilstach, Baldwin & Co., 1879).

48 Marion and Arthur Ford, *Life in the Confederate Army.*

49 Paul Totten, World War I Veterans Survey, US Army Military History Institute.

50 Freeman, *A Soldier in the Philippines.*

51 Shephard, *A Sergeant-Major's War.*

52 Gantter, *Roll Me Over.*

53 Spencer F. Wurst and Gayle Wurst, *Descending from the Clouds: A Memoir of Combat in the 505 Parachute Infantry Regiment, 82d Airborne Division* (Open Road Integrated Media, 2016).

54 John Howard, Imperial War Museum Oral Histories.

55 Knyvett, *"Over There" With the Australians.*

56 Paul Hub, quoted in Neil Hanson, *The Unknown Soldier: The Story of the Missing of the Great War* (London: Transworld, 2011).

57 Satoru Nazawa, quoted in Tamayama and Nunneley, *Tales by Japanese Soldiers.*

58 John Sweeny, quoted in O'Donnell, *Into the Rising Sun.*

59 Henry Barnes, Imperial War Museum Oral Histories.

60 Morse, *In the Russian Ranks.*

61 George Tompkins Jr., World War II Military Oral History Project, VMI.

62 Stillwell, *The Story of a Common Soldier.*

63 Stauffer, *Civil War Diary.*

64 Quoted in Addison and Calder, *Time to Kill.*

65 Morse, *In the Russian Ranks.*

66 Adrien J. P. F. Bourgogne, *The Memoirs of Sergeant Bourgogne 1812–1813,* trans. Paul Cottin (London: Arms and Armour Press, 1979).

67 Quoted in Zamoyski, *1812.*

68 Quoted in Zamoyski, *1812.*

69 Walter and Raeff, *The Diary of a Napoleonic Foot Soldier.*

70 Ibid.

71 Katsumi Ohno, quoted in Tamayama and Nunneley, *Tales by Japanese Soldiers.*

72 Robertson, *Wellington at War.*

73 Francis Seymour Larpent, quoted in Robertson, *Wellington at War.*

74 James F. Dargan, Civil War Diary 1862–1863, California State University Northridge, Oviatt Library Collection.

75 William F. Zimmer, *Frontier Soldier: An Enlisted Man's Journal of the Sioux and Nez Perce Campaigns, 1877,* ed. Jerome Greene (Helena: Montana Historical Society Press, 1998).

76 William Drown, quoted in Rodenbough, *From Everglade to Canon with the Second Dragoons.*

77 Joachim Pusch (14th Motorized Infantry), WWII, Minnesota Historical Society (OH 112).

78 Harry Patch, quoted in Max Arthur, *The Last Post.*

79 Junger, *Storm of Steel.*

80 Richards, *Old Soldiers Never Die.*

81 Morse, *In the Russian Ranks.*

82 Manabu Wada, quoted in Tamayama and Nunneley, *Tales by Japanese Soldiers.*

83 Richard D. Orton, Indian Wars Letter (1861), East Texas Research Center Digital Archives.

84 Stillwell, *The Story of a Common Soldier.*

Chapter 8

1 Holmes, *Soldiers.*

2 Morris, *The Recollections of Sergeant Morris.*

3 Freeman, *A Soldier in the Philippines.*

4 Bancroft, *From Recruit to Staff Sergeant.*

5 Shephard, *A Sergeant-Major's War.*

6 Knyvett, *"Over There" With the Australians.*

7 Clifford Lane (Hertfordshire Regiment), Imperial War Museum Oral Histories.

8 Ulrich Burke (Devonshire Regiment), Imperial War Museum Oral Histories.

9 Clifford Lane (Hertfordshire Regiment), Imperial War Museum Oral Histories.

10 Tadahiro Ogawa, quoted in Tamayama and Nunneley, *Tales by Japanese Soldiers.*

11 Rickey, *Forty Miles a Day on Beans and Hay.*

12 Edward Matthews, quoted in Leo Oliva, *Fort Union and the Frontier Army in the Southwest* (National Park Service, Division of History, 1993).

13 Finerty, *War-Path and Bivouac.*

14 Freeman, *A Soldier in the Philippines.*

15 Stillwell, *The Story of a Common Soldier.*

16 Holmes, *Soldiers.*

17 Surgeon General's Office, *Circular No. 3: A Report of Surgical Cases Treated in the Army of the United States from 1865 to 1871* (Washington, DC: Government Printing Office, 1871).

18 Edith Walford, ed., Wellington, *The Words of Wellington* (London: Sampson, Low, Son and Marston, 1869).

19 Morris, *The Recollections of Sergeant Morris.*

20 Aloysius Damski, quoted in Miller, *Nothing Less Than Victory.*

21 Spencer and Gayle Wurst, *Descending from the Clouds.*

22 William Funkhouser (1st Inf Div), World War II Military Oral History Project, VMI.

23 Freeman, *A Soldier in the Philippines.*
24 Windolph, *I Fought with Custer.*
25 Spencer Wurst, *Descending from the Clouds.*
26 Rickey, *Forty Miles a Day on Beans and Hay.*
27 Morris, *The Recollections of Sergeant Morris.*
28 Richards, *Old Soldiers Never Die.*
29 Albert Marshall, quoted in Arthur, *The Last Post.*

Chapter 9

1 David Holbrook, quoted in Miller, *Nothing Less Than Victory.*
2 Ibid.
3 Louis, *Diary of a Tar Heel Confederate Soldier.*
4 Morris, *The Recollections of Sergeant Morris.*
5 Robert Stiles, *Four Years Under Marse Robert* (San Francisco: Golden Springs Publishing, 2015).
6 Bowe, *With the 13th Minnesota in the Philippines.*
7 Anonymous, *A Soldier of the Seventy-First.*
8 Jean-Roch Coignet, *Soldier of the Empire: The Notebooks of Captain Coignet,* Bob Carruthers, editor (Archive Media Publishing Ltd, 2012).
9 Louis, *Diary of a Tar Heel Confederate Soldier.*
10 Harris, *Recollections of Rifleman Harris.*
11 Basil H. Liddell-Hart, *A History of the Second World War* (London: Pan MacMillan, 2015).
12 Stillwell, *The Story of a Common Soldier.*
13 Olney, *"Shiloh."*
14 Werner Kortenhaus, quoted in Miller, *Nothing Less Than Victory.*
15 Shephard, *A Sergeant-Major's War.*
16 John Wilson, *John Wilson's War: Letters from Gallipoli and Egypt, 1915-1916,* ed. Hilary Kirkland, Collection of the National War Museum (Edinburgh, 1999).
17 Morris, *The Recollections of Sergeant Morris.*
18 Bancroft, *From Recruit to Staff Sergeant.*
19 Stone, *Personal Recollections of the Civil War.*
20 J. W. Wightman, quoted in Palmer, *The Rambling Soldier.*
21 Stefan Westmann (Imperial German Army), Imperial War Museum Oral Histories.
22 Clifford Lane (Hertfordshire Regiment), Imperial War Museum Oral Histories.
23 Shephard, *A Sergeant-Major's War.*
24 Herbert Sulzbach (Wehrmacht), Imperial War Museum Oral Histories.
25 Stephen Graham, *The Challenge of the Dead: A Vision of the War and the Life of the Common Soldier in France, Seen Two Years Afterwards* (London: Cassell and Company, 1921).
26 Manabu Wada, quoted in Tamayama and Nunneley, *Tales by Japanese Soldiers.*
27 Quoted in Richard Holmes, "The Italian Job: Five Armies in Italy, 1943-1945," in Addison and Calder, *A Time to Kill.*
28 Knyvett, *"Over There" with the Australians.*

29 Lynch, *Somme Mud.*

30 James F. Dargan, Civil War Diary 1862–1863, California State University Northridge, Oviatt Library Collection.

31 Morse, *In the Russian Ranks.*

32 Shephard, *A Sergeant-Major's War.*

33 William Howard Russell, in Caroline Chapman, *Russell of the Times: Dispatches and Diaries* (London: Bell and Hyman, 1984).

34 Joe McNamara, quoted in O'Donnell, *Into the Rising Sun.*

35 Alfred Finnigan, quoted in Arthur, *The Last Post.*

36 Windolph, *I Fought with Custer.*

37 Gantter, *Roll Me Over.*

38 Rory Grimshaw, *Indian Cavalry Officer 1914-1915,* ed. J. Wakefield and J. M. Weippert (London: Costello, 1986).

39 Grimshaw, *Indian Cavalry Officer.*

40 Louis, *Diary of a Tar Heel Confederate Soldier.*

41 Freeman, *A Soldier in the Philippines.*

42 Stefan Westmann (Imperial German Army), Imperial War Museum Oral Histories.

43 Gantter, *Roll Me Over.*

44 Koettgen, *I Fought for the Kaiser.*

45 Baxter, *One Young Man.*

46 Lynch, *Somme Mud.*

47 Ibid.

48 R. S. Cockburn, quoted in Malcolm Brown, *The Imperial War Museum Book of the Somme.*

49 Manabu Wada, quoted in Tamayama and Nunneley, *Tales by Japanese Soldiers.*

50 Quoted in Brown, *The Imperial War Museum Book of the Somme.*

51 Ewald Weisemann-Remscheid, quoted in Sheldon, *The German Army on the Somme.*

52 Sledge, *With the Old Breed on Peleliu and Okinawa.*

53 Andy Amaty, quoted in O'Donnell, *Into the Rising Sun.*

54 Cecil Withers, quoted in Arthur, *The Last Post.*

55 Quoted in Robert Rhodes James, *Gallipoli* (London: B.T. Batsford, 1965).

56 W. Clarke (Royal Anglican Regiment), Imperial War Museum Oral Histories.

57 Corporal Owen, quoted in *The World at War: The Landmark Oral History,* Richard Holmes, editor (London: Trafalgar Square, 2007).

58 Robert Sherrod, quoted in Holmes, *The World at War.*

59 Michael Witowich (United States Marine Corps), ww2history.com/testimony.

60 Clifford Lane (Hertfordshire Regiment), Imperial War Museum Oral Histories.

61 Lynch, *Somme Mud.*

62 Empey, *"Over the Top."*

63 Marion and Arthur Ford, *Life in the Confederate Army.*

64 Koettgen, *I Fought for the Kaiser.*

65 George Craike (Highland Light Infantry), Imperial War Museum Oral Histories.

66 A. B. Facey, *A Fortunate Life* (Fremantle, WA: Fremantle Press, 2018).

67 Quoted in Lynch, *Somme Mud.*

68 Roland Leighton, quoted in Samuel Hynes, *The Soldiers' Tale: Bearing Witness to Modern War* (New York: Viking, 1996).

69 R.S. Cockburn, quoted in Brown, *The Imperial War Museum Book of the Somme.*

Chapter 10

1 James Black, quoted in Gerald F. Linderman, *Embattled Courage* (New York: Free Press, 1987).

2 Windolph, *I Fought with Custer.*

3 W. Clarke, quoted in Arthur, *Forgotten Voices of the Great War.*

4 Gantter, *Roll Me Over.*

5 Gibbs, *Now It Can Be Told.*

6 Morse, *In the Russian Ranks.*

7 Anonymous, *Letters of a Soldier 1914-1915* (Dodo Press, 2008).

8 Merritt Hinkel, quoted in O'Donnell, *Into the Rising Sun.*

9 Richard Tobin (Royal Naval Division), Imperial War Museum Oral Histories.

10 Robert Fair (1st Infantry Division), World War II Military Oral History Project, VMI.

11 Ernest A. Andrews (1st Infantry Div), World War II Military Oral History Project, VMI.

12 Shipp, *Memoirs.*

13 Quoted in Palmer, *The Rambling Soldier.*

14 Shipp, *Memoirs.*

15 W. J. Gould, *Three Cheers for the Queen—Lancers Charge! The Experiences of a Sergeant of 16th Queen's Lancers in Afghanistan, the Gwalior War, the First Sikh War and the Kaffir War* (Driffield, UK: Leonaur Limited, 2010).

16 Morris, *The Recollections of Sergeant Morris.*

17 Ibid.

18 Gowing, *A Soldier's Experience*

19 Denzil Chamberlayne, quoted in Lawrence James, *Crimea, 1854-56: The War with Russia from Contemporary Photographs* (New York: Van Nostrand Reinhold, 1981).

20 Marion and Arthur Ford, *Life in the Confederate Army.*

21 Lynch, *Somme Mud.*

22 Wilfred Staddon, quoted in Arthur, *Forgotten Voices of the Great War.*

23 Joe Murray, quoted in James, *Gallipoli.*

24 Quoted in *The Mammoth Book of Soldiers at War,* Jon E. Lewis, editor (London: Running Press, 2001).

25 William O. Taylor, quoted in Brininstool, *Troopers with Custer.*

26 William Slaper, quoted inBrininstool, *Troopers with Custer.*

27 Knyvett, *"Over There" with the Australians.*

28 Lynch, *Somme Mud.*

29 Quoted in James, *Gallipoli.*

30 Lynch, *Somme Mud.*

31 Joe Murray, quoted in James, *Gallipoli.*

32 Quoted in Miller, *Nothing Less Than Victory.*

33 Quoted in Miller, *Nothing Less Than Victory.*

34 Joseph Argenzio (1st Inf Div), World War II Military Oral History Project, VMI.
35 Beatty, *The Citizen-Soldier.*
36 Quoted in Miller, *Nothing Less Than Victory.*
37 John Slaughter, quoted in Miller, *Nothing Less Than Victory.*
38 Stillwell, *The Story of a Common Soldier.*
39 Ibid.
40 Windolph, *I Fought with Custer.*
41 Freeman, *A Soldier in the Philippines.*
42 Stillwell, *The Story of a Common Soldier.*
43 Quoted in Miller, *Nothing Less than Victory.*
44 Gantter, *Roll Me Over.*
45 Joseph Dazzo (1st Inf Div), World War II Military Oral History Project, VMI.
46 Gibbs, *Now it Can be Told.*
47 McCarthy, *Detailed Minutiae of Soldier Life.*
48 Stillwell, *The Story of a Common Soldier.*
49 C.S. Axtell, quoted in Holmes *The World at War: The Landmark Oral History.*
50 Knyvett, *"Over There" with the Australians.*
51 Quoted in Arthur, *Forgotten Voices of the Great War.*
52 Alan Bray, quoted in Arthur, *Forgotten Voices of the Great War.*
53 Marion and Arthur Ford, *Life in the Confederate Army.*
54 Lynch, *Somme Mud.*
55 Gibbs, *Now it Can be Told.*
56 Anonymous, *A Soldier of the Seventy-First.*
57 George Ashurst (Lancashire Fusiliers), Imperial War Museum Oral Histories.
58 Quoted in Arthur, *Forgotten Voices of the Great War.*
59 Haigh, *Life in a Tank* (New York: Houghton Mifflin, 1918).
60 Gantter, *Roll Me Over.*
61 Haigh, *Life in a Tank.*
62 Morris, *The Recollections of Sergeant Morris.*
63 Kevin Neweth, quoted in Richard Campbell Begg and Peter Liddle, *For Five Shillings a Day: Experiencing War, 1939-45* (London: HarperCollins, 2013).

Chapter 11

1 Anonymous, *Letters of a Soldier 1914-1915.*
2 Gantter, *Roll Me Over.*
3 John Futch (North Carolina Infantry), Civil War Letter PC507, North Carolina Digital Collection.
4 Francis Marion Poteet (North Carolina Infantry), Civil War Letter PC1825, North Carolina Digital Collections.
5 Charles S. Taylor, Civil War Letters, East Texas Research Center Digital Archives.
6 William Jett, quoted in Walker, "The Reluctant Corporal."
7 Ibid.
8 Albert Thomas, First World War Letters, East Texas Research Center Digital Archives.

9 Louis, *Diary of a Tar Heel Confederate Soldier.*
10 Anonymous, *A Soldier of the Seventy-First.*
11 Ibid.
12 Harris, *Recollections of Rifleman Harris.*
13 Anonymous, *A Soldier of the Seventy-First.*
14 Ibid.
15 Ibid.
16 Harris, *Recollections of Rifleman Harris.*
17 Russell, *Dispatches from the Crimea.*
18 Gowing, *A Soldier's Experience.*
19 George Buchanan, *Letters from an Officer of the Scots Greys, to His Mother during the Crimean War* (London: Rivingtons, 1866).
20 McCarthy, *Detailed Minutiae of Soldier Life.*
21 McKim, *A Soldier's Recollections.*
22 Louis, *Diary of a Tar Heel Confederate Soldier.*
23 Stauffer, *Civil War Diary.*
24 Stone, *Personal Recollections of the Civil War.*
25 Windolph, *I Fought with Custer,* 56.
26 Knyvett, *"Over There" with the Australians.*
27 Shephard, *A Sergeant-Major's War.*
28 Grimshaw, *Indian Cavalry Officer.*
29 Fred Lloyd, quoted in Arthur, *The Last Post.*
30 Carey, *Fighting the Bolsheviks.*
31 Quoted in MacDonald, *1915.*
32 Bert Reeves, quoted in Holmes, *The World at War.*
33 Manabu Wada, quoted in Tamayama Kazuo and Nunneley, *Tales by Japanese Soldiers.*
34 William Walter, quoted in O'Donnell, *Into the Rising Sun.*
35 Gantter, *Roll Me Over.*
36 Sledge, *With the Old Breed at Peleliu and Okinawa.*
37 Olney, *"Shiloh."*
38 Anonymous, *Letters of a Soldier 1914-1915.*
39 Arthur Gibbs, quoted in Brown, *The Imperial War Museum Book of the Somme.*
40 Empey, *"Over the Top."*
41 Morse, *In the Russian Ranks.*
42 Gibbs, *Now It Can Be Told.*
43 Lynch, *Somme Mud.*
44 Knyvett, *"Over There" with the Australians.*
45 Lynch, *Somme Mud.*
46 Robert Cude, quoted in Brown, *The Imperial War Museum Book of the Somme.*
47 Gibbs, *Now It Can Be Told.*
48 J. W. Palmer (Royal Field Artillery), Imperial War Museum Oral Histories.
49 Hanson, *The Unknown Soldier.*
50 Knyvett, *"Over There" with the Australians.*
51 Ibid.

52 Gibbs, *Now It Can Be Told.*
53 Richard Tobin (Royal Naval Division), Imperial War Museum Oral Histories.
54 Reserve Leutnant Michaelsen, quoted in Sheldon, *The German Army on the Somme.*
55 Reserve Leutnant Freter, quoted in Sheldon, *The German Army on the Somme 1914–1916.*
56 Gibbs, *Now it Can be Told.*
57 Junger, *Storm of Steel.*
58 Gibbs, *Now It Can Be Told.*
59 Gantter, *Roll Me Over.*
60 Sledge, *With the Old Breed.*
61 Carruthers, *Winter Warfare on the Russian Front.*
62 Quoted in Zamoyski, *1812.*
63 Charles Francois, *From Valmy to Waterloo: Extracts from the Diary of Captain Charles Francois, a Soldier of the Revolution and the Empire,* trans. and ed. R. B. Douglas (London, 1906).
64 Carruthers, *Winter Warfare on the Russian Front.*
65 Roth, *Eastern Inferno.*
66 Carruthers, *Winter Warfare on the Russian Front.*
67 Roth, *Eastern Inferno.*
68 Karl Meding, quoted in Carruthers, *The Wehrmacht Last Witnesses.*
69 Carruthers, *Winter Warfare on the Russian Front.*
70 Ibid.
71 Roth, *Eastern Inferno.*
72 Ibid.
73 Morse, *In the Russian Ranks.*
74 Ibid.
75 Lynch, *Somme Mud.*
76 Friedrich Oehme, quoted in Brown, *The Imperial War Museum Book of the Somme.*
77 Gantter, *Roll Me Over.*
78 Manabu Wada, quoted in Tamayama and Nunneley, *Tales by Japanese Soldiers.*
79 Captain Hogan, quoted in Holmes, *The World at War.*
80 Quoted in Ian S. Wood, "Soldiers of Ireland in the Second World War," in Addison and Calder, *Time to Kill.*
81 Shephard, *A Sergeant-Major's War.*
82 Ulrich Burke (Devonshire Regiment), Imperial War Museum Oral Histories.
83 Ibid.
84 Julian Tyndale-Biscoe, *Gunner Subaltern* (Madison: Cooper, 1971).
85 Junger, *Storm of Steel.*
86 Quoted in Robertson, *Wellington at War.*
87 Donald Kerr, quoted in Begg and Liddle, *For Five Shillings a Day.*
88 Harold Boughton (London Regiment), Imperial War Museum Oral Histories.
89 Quoted in James, *Gallipoli.*
90 Quoted in James, *Gallipoli.*
91 Ion D. Idriess, *The Desert Column* (London: Angus & Robertson, 1985).

92 Harold Pilling, Imperial War Museum Oral Histories.
93 Joe Murray (Royal Naval Division), Imperial War Museum Oral Histories.
94 Zamoyski, *1812*.
95 Ibid.
96 Quoted in Robertson, *Wellington at War*.
97 Alexander Alexander quoted in McGuffie, *Rank and File:*.
98 Quoted in Zamoyski, *1812*.
99 Quoted in Zamoyski, *1812*.
100 Albert Marshall, quoted in Arthur, *The Last Post*.
101 John Oborne, quoted in Arthur, *The Last Post*.
102 Harry Patch, quoted in Arthur, *The Last Post*.
103 Empey, *"Over the Top."*
104 Joe Hammersley, quoted in *The World at War*.
105 Anonymous, *Letters of a Soldier 1914-1915*.

Chapter 12

1 Howard Dunfee (1st Inf Div), World War II Military Oral History Project, VMI.
2 Quoted in Charles H. Clark, "Skobeleff's Last Campaign," *Journal of the Military Service Institution of the United States* 13 (1892).
3 Gantter, *Roll Me Over*, 135.
4 Windolph, *I Fought with Custer*, 74.
5 Shephard, *A Sergeant-Major's War*, 56.
6 Alec Reader, quoted in Hanson, *The Unknown Soldier*.
7 Knyvett, *"Over There" with the Australians*.
8 Donald Kyler, World War I Veterans Survey, US Army Military History Institute.
9 James, *Gallipoli*, 104.
10 Ibid., 110.
11 Ibid., 125.
12 James, *Gallipoli*.
13 Shipp, *Memoirs*.
14 Spencer and Gayle Wurst, *Descending from the Clouds*.
15 Robert Erikson (504th Parachute Infantry), WWII, Minnesota Historical Society (OH 112).
16 Robert Brown, quoted in Begg and Liddle, *For Five Shillings a Day*.

Chapter 13

1 Charles Carrington, *Soldier from the Wars Returning*.
2 Rickey, *Forty Miles a Day on Beans and Hay*.
3 Thomas Morris, *The Recollections of Sergeant Morris*.
4 Anonymous, *A Soldier of the Seventy-First*.
5 Quoted in Hibbert, *Corunna*.
6 Quoted in Robertson, *Wellington at War*.
7 August Schaumann, quoted in Robertson, *Wellington at War*.

8 Buchanan, *Letters from an Officer of the Scots Greys.*
9 Henry Franks, *Leaves from a Soldier's Note Book, by Sergt. Major Henry Franks, One of the Heavy Cavalry Brigade at Balaclava* (Essex: C.W. Poole and Sons, 1904).
10 John Ryder, *Four Years' Service in India* (Rarebooksclub Com, 2012).
11 McCarthy, *Detailed Minutiae of Soldier Life.*
12 Ibid.
13 Stone, *Personal Recollections of the Civil War.*
14 Ibid.
15 Alexander Alexander, quoted in *Soldiers at War.*
16 Lieutenant-Colonel Skeen, quoted in James, *Gallipoli.*
17 Quoted in James, *Gallipoli.*
18 Quoted in James, *Gallipoli.*
19 Henry Barnes (4th Australian Brigade), Imperial War Museum Oral Histories.
20 Jack Gearing (Royal Naval Division), Imperial War Museum Oral Histories.
21 W. Carrol. Imperial War Museum Oral Histories.
22 "General Notes regarding the morale etc. of the Turkish Troops in the Southern Part of the Gallipoli Peninsula," in John Wilson, *John Wilson's War.*
23 Quoted in James, *Gallipoli.*
24 Paul Totten, World War I Veterans Survey, US Army Military History Institute.
25 Quoted in Rickey, *Forty Miles a Day on Beans and Hay.*
26 James F. J. Archibald, quoted in Frank Freidel, *The Splendid Little War* (London: Galley Press, 1958).
27 Freeman, *A Soldier in the Philippines.*
28 Graham, *The Challenge of the Dead.*
29 Douglas Pegler, quoted in Brown, *The Imperial War Museum Book of the Somme.*
30 Quoted in Brown, *The Imperial War Museum Book of the Somme.*
31 Thomas Morris, *The Recollections of Sergeant Morris.*
32 Leutnant Trobitz, quoted in Sheldon, *The German Army on the Somme.*
33 Philip Neame (Royal Engineers), Imperial War Museum Oral Histories.
34 Richards, *Old Soldiers Never Die.*
35 J.W. Finnimore. Imperial War Museum Oral Histories.
36 Ersatzreservist Tebbe, quoted in Sheldon, *The German Army on the Somme.*
37 Empey, *Over the Top.*
38 Frank Sumpter (1st London Rifle Brigade), Imperial War Museum Oral Histories.
39 Walter Klein, quoted in Cawthorne, *Reaping the Whirlwind.*
40 Frederick Branham (84th Infantry Division), WWII, Minnesota Historical Society (OH 112).
41 George McMurty, quoted in Begg and Liddle, *For Five Shillings a Day.*
42 Ernest Andrews (1st Inf Div), World War II Military Oral History Project, VMI.
43 Shephard, *A Sergeant-Major's War.*
44 Weller, *Weapons and Tactics.*
45 Graham, *The Challenge of the Dead.*
46 Albert Marshall, quoted in Max Arthur, *The Last Post.*
47 Richard Coleman, quoted in Holmes, *The World at War.*

48 Private Brown, quoted in Holmes, *The World at War.*
49 Captain Hogan, quoted in Holmes, *The World at War.*
50 John Howard, quoted in Holmes, *The World at War.*
51 Harry Miller, quoted in Holmes, *The World at War.*
52 John Randle, Imperial War Museum Oral Histories.
53 Andy Amaty, quoted in O'Donnell, *Into the Rising Sun.*
54 Lieutenant Owens, quoted in Holmes, *The World at War.*
55 Private Buckthorpe, quoted in Holmes, *The World at War.*
56 Teruo Okada, quoted in Richard Holmes, editor, *The World at War.*
57 Tadashi Suzuki, quoted in Tamayama Kazuo and Nunneley, *Tales by Japanese Soldiers.*
58 Misao Sato, quoted in Tamayama Kazuo and Nunneley, *Tales by Japanese Soldiers.*
59 Hajime Kondo, quoted in Gibney, *Senso.*
60 Dean Winters, quoted in O'Donnell, *Into the Rising Sun.*
61 Frank Caldwell, quoted in O'Donnell, *Into the Rising Sun.*
62 Quoted in Cawthorne, *Reaping the Whirlwind.*
63 Edward W. McGregor, quoted in Lewis, ed., *D-Day as They Saw It* (London: Robinson, 2004).
64 Frank King (1st Inf Div), World War II Military Oral History Project, VMI.
65 W. Hewison, quoted in Jon E. Lewis, *D-Day as They Saw It*
66 Roth, *Eastern Inferno.*
67 Ibid.
68 Ibid.
69 Carruthers, *Winter Warfare on the Russian Front.*
70 Ibid.
71 Walter Klein, quoted in Cawthorne, *Reaping the Whirlwind.*
72 John Erickson, "The System and the Soldier," in Addison and Calder, *Time to Kill.*
73 Quoted in Holmes, "The Italian Job."
74 Quoted in Holmes, "The Italian Job."
75 Neville Hogan, Imperial War Museum Oral Histories.
76 Annie May Martin, Imperial War Museum Oral Histories.
77 Roth, *Eastern Inferno.*
78 Poppel, *Heaven and Hell.*
79 Sullivan, "Myths, Realities and Explanations," in Addison and Calder, *Time to Kill.*
80 George Manington, *A Soldier of the Legion: An Englishman's Adventures under the French Flag in Algeria and Tonquin.* W. B. Slater and Arthur J. Sarl, editors (London: 1907).

Chapter 14

1 Rickey, *Forty Miles a Day on Beans and Hay.*
2 Quoted in http://regimentalrogue.com/misc/army_punishments_1947_pt1.htm.
3 *San Francisco Bulletin*, July 18, 1859, 2.
4 John D. McDermott, "Were They Really Rogues? Desertion in the Nineteenth-Century US Army," *Nebraska History* 78 (1997): 165–74.
5 Louis, *Diary of a Tar Heel Confederate Soldier.*

6 Henry Williamson, quoted in Holmes, *Tommy.*

7 John Green, *Vicissitudes of a Soldier's Life, or, a Series of Occurrences from 1806 to 1815* (London: Simpkin and Marshall, 1827).

8 Nathan Newsom, quoted in Merrill, *Uncommon Valor.*

9 General Orders No. 281, 8 September 1847. Quoted in Merrill, *Uncommon Valor.*

10 Ibid.

11 Rickey, *Forty Miles a Day on Beans and Hay.*

12 William T. Sherman, "Our Army and Militia," *The North American Review* 151, no. 405 (August 1890): 129–45.

13 Paul Totten, diary, World War I Veterans Survey, US Army Military History Institute.

14 "Ex-Trooper," *The French Army from Within.*

15 Rickey, *Forty Miles a Day on Beans and Hay.*

16 *Standing Orders, 90th Light Infantry.*

17 Morris, *The Recollections of Sergeant Morris.*

18 Ibid.

19 Surgeon General's Office, *Circular No. 3.*

20 Carrington, *Soldier from the Wars Returning.*

21 *Standing Orders, 90th Light Infantry,* italics in the original.

22 *Articles of War of the United States and Regulations of the Army* (Washington, D.C.: Government Printing Office, 1863).

23 *Standing Orders of the 51st, or Edinburgh Regiment of British Militia.*

24 "Ex-Trooper," *The French Army from Within.*

25 Ibid.

26 *Standing Orders of the 51st, or Edinburgh Regiment of British Militia.*

27 *Army and Navy Journal,* September 27, 1873.

28 Job R. Redmond (5th North Carolina Cavalry), Civil War Letter, North Carolina Digital Collections.

Chapter 15

1 William Drown, quoted in Rodenbough, *From Everglade to Canon with the Second Dragoons.*

2 Quoted in McDermott, "Were They Really Rogues?"

3 Grote Hutcheson, "The Ninth Regiment of Cavalry," *The Army of the United States: Historical Sketches of Staff and Line with Portraits of Generals-in-Chief* (New York: Maynard, Merrill, & Co., 1896).

4 Billings, *Hardtack and Coffee.*

5 Robert Utley, *Frontier Soldiers: The United States Army and the Indian, 1866-1891* (Lincoln: University of Nebraska Press, 1973) .

6 Frank Roberts, "The Army as It Is," *The North American Review,* Vol. 159 (1894).

7 Strawson, *Beggars in Red.*

8 *Standing Orders of the 51st, or Edinburgh Regiment of British Militia.*

9 Billings, *Hardtack and Coffee.*

10 Spencer and Gayle Wurst, *Descending from the Clouds.*

11 Holmes, *Soldiers*.

12 *Standing Orders, 90th Light Infantry.*

13 *Standing Orders of the Seaforth Highlanders.*

14 Florence Nightingale, *Florence Nightingale: Letters from the Crimea* (Manchester: University of Manchester Press, 1997).

15 McCarthy, *Detailed Minutiae of Soldier Life.*

16 Freeman, *A Soldier in the Philippines.*

17 Thomas Henry Browne, *The Napoleonic War Journal of Captain Thomas Henry Browne,* ed. Roger Norman Buckley (London: The Army Records Society, 1987).

18 *The Army Quarterly and Defence Journal,* Vol. 83 (1962).

19 *Standing Orders, 90th Light Infantry.*

20 William Drown, quoted in Rodenbough, *From Everglade to Canon with the Second Dragoons.*

21 Rudyard Kipling, *Kipling's America: Travel Letters 1889-1895* (Greensboro: ELT Press, 2003).

22 Rickey, *Forty Miles a Day on Beans and Hay.*

23 Rundle, *A Soldier's Life.*

24 Zimmer, *Frontier Soldier.*

25 Reinhold Gast, quoted in Rickey, *Forty Miles a Day on Beans and Hay.*

26 Martin Andersen, quoted in Rickey, *Fory Miles a Day on Beans and Hay.*

Chapter 16

1 Henry Metcalfe, *The Chronicle of Private Henry Metcalfe, H.M. 32nd Regiment of Foot,* ed. Francis Tuker (London, 1953).

2 Ian Knight, *Go to Your God Like a Soldier* (London: Greenhill Books; Mechanicsburg, PA: Stackpole Books, 1996).

3 Knight, *Go to Your God Like a Soldier.*

4 Guillemard, *Adventures of a French Serjeant.*

5 Quoted in William Holberton, *Homeward Bound: The Demobilization of the Union and Confederate Armies, 1865-1866* (Mechanicsburg, PA: Stackpole Books, 2001).

6 T.A. Turner, *Story of the Fifteenth Minnesota Volunteer Infantry* (Minneapolis: Lessard Printing, 1899).

7 Quoted in Holberton, *Homeward Bound.*

8 Ethelbert P. Moore, quoted in Jeff L. Patrick, "Nothing but Slaves: The Second Kentucky Volunteer Infantry and the Spanish-American War," *The Register of the Kentucky Historical Society* 89, no. 3 (Summer 1991): 290–91.

9 Rosen, *In the Foreign Legion.*

10 Thomas Grady, quoted in Max Arthur, *The Road Home: The Aftermath of the Great War Told by the Men and Women Who Survived It* (London: Phoenix, 2009).

11 Anton Lang, Imperial War Museum Oral Histories.

12 Richard Dixon, Imperial War Museum Oral Histories.

13 Walter Hare, Imperial War Museum Oral Histories.

14 George Thomas, quoted in Holmes, *Tommy.*

15 Koettgen, *I Fought for the Kaiser.*

16 Jonas Hart, Imperial War Museum Oral Histories.

17 George Grunwell, Imperial War Museum Oral Histories.

18 Ernest Andrews (1st Inf Div), World War II Military Oral History Project, VMI.

19 Robert Erikson (504th Parachute Infantry), WWII, Minnesota Historical Society (OH 112).

20 Albert Price (2nd Bn, Royal Fusilier), ww2history.com/testimony/Western/soldier_in_italy.

21 Sam Bradshaw (7th Armored, British 8th Army), ww2history.com/testimony/Western/desert_rat.

22 Fair (1st Infantry Division), World War II Military Oral History Project, VMI.

23 Andrews (1st Inf Div), World War II Military Oral History Project, VMI.

24 Mole Edwin, *A King's Hussar.*

25 William Jett, in Walker, "The Reluctant Corporal."

Bibliography

Oral Histories and Personal Papers
Allhusen, Desmond. Imperial War Museum Oral Histories. **British**
Alvarez, Alfred A. (1st Inf Div) World War II Military Oral History Project, VMI.
    American
Amatt, Sidney. (Essex Regiment) Imperial War Museum Oral Histories. **British**
Andrews, Ernest A. (1st Inf Div) World War II Military Oral History Project, VMI.
    American
Argenzio, Joseph. (1st Inf Div) World War II Military Oral History Project, VMI.
    American
Ashurst, George. (Lancashire Fusiliers) Imperial War Museum Oral Histories. **British**
Barnes, Henry. (4th Australian Brigade) Imperial War Museum Oral Histories.
    Australian
Barnhill, Duncan R. (2nd North Carolina Artillery) Civil War Letters, North Carolina
    Digital Collections. **American**
Boardman, Oliver. (Iowa Infantry) Civil War Letters, University of Iowa Digital Collec-
    tions. **American**
Boughton, Harold. (London Regiment) Imperial War Museum Oral Histories. **British**
Bowen, William J. (North Carolina Infantry) Civil War Letters, North Carolina Digital
    Collections. **American**
Bracey, Tom. (Royal Fusiliers) Imperial War Museum Oral Histories. **British**
Bradshaw, Samuel. (7th Armored, British 8th Army) ww2history.com/testimony/
    Western/desert_rat. **British**
Branham, Frederick. (84th Infantry Division) WWII, Minnesota Historical Society
    (OH 112). **American**
Brantingham, Henry. Civil War Diary, 1861–1862, North Carolina Digital Collections.
    American
Burgwyn, William H. S. Civil War Diary and Letters, 1862–1863, North Carolina Digi-
    tal Collections. **American**
Burke, Ulrich. (Devonshire Regiment) Imperial War Museum Oral Histories. **British**
Capiz, Henry T. (503rd Parachute Infantry) WWII, Minnesota Historical Society (OH
    112). **American**
Carr, Isaac N. (11th Iowa Infantry) Civil War, Iowa Historical Library (MS 132).
    American
Carrington, Charles. (Warwickshire Regt) Imperial War Museum Oral Histories.
    British
Carroll, W. (Australian Lighthorse) Imperial War Museum Oral Histories. **British**
Chapman, Philo J. (3rd Iowa Infantry) Civil War, Iowa Historical Library (MS 233).
    American

Christy, James. (4th US Cav) N14/3/4 Des Moines Historical Library Manuscripts.
American

Clarke, W. (Royal Anglian Regiment) Imperial War Museum Oral Histories. **British**

Clement, Joe. (Royal Marine Light Infantry) Imperial War Museum Oral Histories.
British

Cowan, Chalmer. (1st Inf Div) World War II Military Oral History Project, VMI.
American

Craike, George. (Highland Light Infantry) Imperial War Museum Oral Histories.
British

Dargan, James F. Civil War Diary 1862–1863, California State University Northridge,
Oviatt Library Collection. **American**

Dazzo, Joseph. (1st Inf Div) World War II Military Oral History Project, VMI.
American

Demuth, Norman. (London Regiment) Imperial War Museum Oral Histories. **British**

Dixon, Richard. (Royal Artillery) Imperial War Museum Oral Histories. **British**

Dorgan, Jack. (Northumberland Fusiliers) Imperial War Museum Oral Histories.
British

Dunfee, Howard. (1st Inf Div) World War II Military Oral History Project, VMI.
American

Edwards, Abial Hall. (Co K, 10th Maine) US Army Military History Institute.
American

Edwards, William W. Civil War Letter, North Carolina Digital Collection. **American**

Emmons, W.B. (34th Illinois Infantry) Civil War Diaries, University of Iowa Digital
Libraries. **American**

Erikson, Robert. (504th Parachute Infantry) WWII, Minnesota Historical Society (OH
112). **American**

Fair, Robert. (1st Infantry Division) World War II Military Oral History Project, VMI.
American

Farnsworth, Jerome. (1st Minnesota Infantry) Civil War, Minnesota Historical Society
(P513). **American**

Fiedler, Heinz. (German Wehrmacht) ww2history.com/testimony. **German**

Frederick, Donald S. (1st Ranger BN) WWII, Minnesota Historical Society (OH 112).
American

Funkhouser, William. (1st Inf Div) World War II Military Oral History Project, VMI.
American

Futch, John. (North Carolina Infantry) Civil War Letter PC507, North Carolina Digital
Collection. **American**

Gearing, Jack. (Royal Naval Division) Imperial War Museum Oral Histories. **British**

Grunwell, George. Imperial War Museum Oral Histories. **British**

Haine, Reginald. (Honourable Artillery Company) Imperial War Museum Oral Histories. **British**

Hamlin, Philip. (1st Minnesota Infantry) Civil War, Minnesota Historical Society Collections, File P1577. **American**

Hinchliff, John J. (507th Parachute Infantry) WWII, Minnesota Historical Society (OH 112). **American**

Howard, John. Imperial War Museum Oral Histories. **British**

Howard, William B. Civil War Diary, 1862–1863, North Carolina Digital Collections. **American**

Jenkins, Carl. (1st Inf Div) World War II Military Oral History Project, VMI. **American**

Killette, Wiley P. (81st Inf Div) First World War Letters, North Carolina Digital Collections. **American**

King, Frank. (1st Inf Div) World War II Military Oral History Project, VMI. **American**

Kondo, Hajime. (Japanese Imperial Army) ww2history.com/testimony. **Japanese**

Kraemer, Karl. Spanish-American War, Papers 1889–1901. Des Moines Historical Library Manuscripts (MS53). **American**

Kyler, Donald. World War I Veterans Survey, US Army Military History Institute. **American**

Lane, Clifford. (Hertfordshire Regiment) Imperial War Museum Oral Histories. **British**

Lewis, Albert L. (81st Inf Div) World War I Letters 19181020, North Carolina Digital Collections. **American**

Lothrop, Charles H. (1st Iowa Cavalry) Civil War, Iowa Historical Library (MS 97). **American**

Lypka, Demetrius. (1st Inf Div) World War II Military Oral History Project, VMI. **American**

Martin, Roy V. (30th Inf Div) First World War Letters, North Carolina Digital Collections. **American**

McBride, Richard L. World War II Veterans Survey, United States Army Heritage and Education Center. **American**

Monie, John Miller. (1st North Carolina Cavalry) Civil War Reminiscences, North Carolina Digital Collections. **American**

Montague, Cleeve E. (Royal Garrison Artillery) Imperial War Museum Oral Histories. **British**

Murray, Joe. (Royal Naval Division) Imperial War Museum Oral Histories. **British**

Neame, Philip. (Royal Engineers) Imperial War Museum Oral Histories. **British**

Nicely, Guy. World War II Military Oral History Project, VMI. **American**

Orton, Richard D. Indian Wars Letter (1861), East Texas Research Center Digital Archives. **American**

Packer, Victor. (Royal Irish Fusiliers) Imperial War Museum Oral Histories. **British**

Painting, Thomas. (King's Royal Rifle Corps) Imperial War Museum Oral Histories. **British**

Palmer, J. W. (Royal Field Artillery) Imperial War Museum Oral Histories. **British**

Patterson, Emanuel Arthur. Civil War Diaries (57th North Carolina Infantry), North Carolina Digital Archives. **American**

Perkins, Charles C. (1st Massachusetts Infantry) Civil War, US Army History & Education Center. **American**

Perry, William. (92nd Infantry) WWII, ww2history.com/testimony. **American**

Peterson, Charles H. Civil War Diaries, 1863–1865. California State University Northridge, Oviatt Library Collection. **American**

Pilling, Harold. Imperial War Museum Oral Histories. **British**

Poteet, Francis Marion. (North Carolina Infantry) Civil War Letter PC1825, North Carolina Digital Collections. **American**

Price, Albert. (2nd Bn, Royal Fusilier) ww2history.com/testimony/Western/soldier_in_italy. **British**

Pusch, Joachim. (14th Motorized Infantry) WWII, Minnesota Historical Society (OH 112). **German**

Quinnell, Charles. (Royal Fusiliers) Imperial War Museum Oral Histories. **British**

Quinton, W. A. (Bedfordshire Regiment) Imperial War Museum Oral Histories. **British**

Redmond, Job R. (5th North Carolina Cavalry) Civil War Letter, North Carolina Digital Collections. **American**

Riggs, Charles A. (2nd US Cavalry) Civil War, Iowa Historical Library (MS 8). **American**

Rockwell, Kiffin Y. (French Foreign Legion) Letters, First World War, North Carolina Digital Collection. **French, American**

Roller, John G. (Iowa Infantry) Civil War Diaries and Correspondence, University of Iowa Digital Libraries. **American**

Rule, A. Imperial War Museum Oral Histories. **British**

Ryan, Edward. World War II Military Oral History Project, VMI. **American**

Schintzel, Arthur. World War II Military Oral History Project, VMI. **American**

Schroeder, Fred H. (338th Machine Gun BN) WWI, Iowa Historical Library (MS 157). **American**

Semenyak, Georgy. (Soviet 11th Mech. Corps) ww2history.com/testimony. **Russian**

Sharpe, Henry. United States Army Heritage and Education Center. **American**

Soboleski, Frank. (101st Airborne) WWII, Minnesota Historical Society (OH 112). **American**

Staddon, Wilfred. Imperial War Museum Oral Histories. **British**

Stagles, Walter. (3rd Australian Bn) Imperial War Museum Oral Histories. **Australian**

Stauffer, Nelson. Civil War Diaries 1862–1865, California State University Northridge, Oviatt Library Collection. **American**

Sulzbach, Herbert. (Wehrmacht) Imperial War Museum Oral Histories. **German**

Sumpter, Frank. (1st London Rifle Brigade) Imperial War Museum Oral Histories. **British**

Sworsky, Edmond. (2nd Ranger BN) WWII, Minnesota Historical Society (OH 112). **American**

Talbot, Jack. World War II Military Oral History Project, VMI. **American**

Tarkenton, Samuel. World War II Military Oral History Project, VMI. **American**

Taylor, Charles S. Civil War Letters, East Texas Research Center Digital Archives. **American**

Thomas, Albert. First World War Letters, East Texas Research Center Digital Archives. **American**

Tobin, Richard. (Royal Naval Division) Imperial War Museum Oral Histories. **British**

Tompkins, George, Jr. World War II Military Oral History Project, VMI. **American**

Totten, Paul. World War I Veterans Survey, US Army Military History Institute. **American**

Turner, George. (61st North Carolina Infantry) Civil War Diary, North Carolina Digital Collections. **American**

Wallace, Jasper L. (23rd North Carolina Infantry) Civil War Diary, North Carolina Digital Collections. **American**

Walz, Helmut. (German Wehrmacht) ww2history.com/testimony. **German**

Warren, Charles. (First World War) Letters, 191701111, North Carolina Digital Collections. **American**

Westmann, Stefan (Imperial German Army) Imperial War Museum Oral Histories. **German**

Wiggins, Thomas Medicus. (37th North Carolina Infantry) Civil War Diary, North Carolina Digital Collections. **American**

Wills, William. World War II Military Oral History Project, VMI. **American**

Wimberley, Douglas. (232nd Machine Gun Company) Imperial War Museum Oral Histories. **British**

Witowich, Michael. (United States Marine Corps) ww2history.com/testimony. **American**

Womble, Richard. Civil War Letters, North Carolina Digital Collections. **American**

Young, George H. Civil War Diaries, 1861–1886. California State University Northridge, Oviatt Library Collection. **American**

Soldier Memoirs and Compilations

Adams, Sean Patrick. "Hardtack, Canned Beef, and Imperial Misery: Rae Weaver's Journal of the Spanish-American War." *The Wisconsin Magazine of History* 81, no. 4 (Summer 1998): 242–66. **American**

Allen, Stanton P. *Down in Dixie: Life in a Cavalry Regiment in the War Days, from the Wilderness to Appomattox.* Boston: D. Lothrop, 1892. **American**

Anonymous. *A Late Staff Sergeant of the 13th Infantry, Camp and Barrack-Room; or, the British Army as it is.* London: Chapman & Hall, 1846.

Anonymous. *Letters of a Soldier 1914-1915.* Dodo Press, 2008. **French**

Anonymous. *A Soldier of the Seventy-First: The Journal of a Soldier in the Peninsular War.* Edited by Christopher Hibbert. London: Windrush Press, 1975. **British**

Anton, James. *Retrospect of a Military Life during the Most Fateful Events of the Late War.* 1841. Reprint. Trotman, 1991. **American**

Army and Navy Journal, Vol. 11 (1873).

Army and Navy Journal, Vol. 13 (1876).

Army and Navy Journal, Vol. 20 (1882).

Arthur, Max. *The Road Home: The Aftermath of the Great War Told by the Men and Women Who Survived It.* London: Phoenix, 2009. **British**

———. *Forgotten Voices of the Great War: A New History of WWI in the Words of the Men and Women Who were There.* London: Ebury Press, 2002.

————. *The Last Post: The Final Word from Our First World War Soldiers.* London: Orion Publishing Group, 2014.

Bancroft, N. W. *From Recruit to Staff Sergeant.* Reprint. Ann Arbor: I. Henry, 1979. **British**

Baxter, Stanley. *One Young Man: The Simple and True Story of a Clerk Who Enlisted in 1914, Who Fought on the Western Front for Two Years, Was Severely Wounded at the Battle of the Somme, and Is Now on His Way Back to His Desk.* Edited by Ernest Hodder-Williams. London: Hodder & Stoughton, 1917. **British**

Beatty, John. *The Citizen-Soldier; or, Memoirs of a Volunteer.* Cincinnati: Wilstach, Baldwin & Co., 1879. **American**

Begg, Richard Campbell, and Peter Liddle. *For Five Shillings a Day: Experiencing War, 1939-45.* London: HarperCollins, 2013. **British**

Berkley, Henry Robinson. *Four Years in the Confederate Artillery: The Diary of Private Henry Robinson Berkley.* Chapel Hill: University of North Carolina Press, 1961. **American**

Billings, John D. *Hardtack and Coffee, or The Unwritten Story of Army Life.* Boston: George M. Smith and Co., 1888. **American**

Black, Donald. *Red Dust: A Classic Account of Australian Light Horsemen in Palestine during the First World War.* London: J. Cape, 1931. **Australian**

Blakeney, Robert. *A Boy in the Peninsular War. The Services, Adventures and Experience of Robert Blakeney.* Edited by Julian Sturgis. London: John Murray, 1899. **British**

Blount, James H. "Army Morals and the Canteen." *The North American Review* 193, no. 664 (March 1911): 409–21. **American**

Bode, Emil A. *A Dose of Frontier Soldiering: The Memoirs of Corporal E. A. Bode, Frontier Regular Infantry, 1877–1882.* Edited by Thomas T. Smith. Lincoln: University of Nebraska Press, 1994. **American**

Bourgogne, Adrien J. P. F. *The Memoirs of Sergeant Bourgogne 1812–1813.* Translated by Paul Cottin. London: Arms and Armour Press, 1979. **French**

Bowe, John. *With the 13th Minnesota in the Philippines.* Minneapolis: A.B. Farnham, 1905. **American**

Brininstool, E. A. *Troopers with Custer: Historic Incidents of the Battle of the Little Big Horn.* New York: Bonanza Books, 1962. **American**

Browne, Thomas Henry. *The Napoleonic War Journal of Captain Thomas Henry Browne.* Edited by Roger Norman Buckley. London: The Army Records Society, 1987. **British**

Buchanan, George. *Letters from an Officer of the Scots Greys, to His Mother during the Crimean War.* London: Rivingtons, 1866. **British**

Cabble, Samuel. "Letter of Samuel Cabble." *The Record: News from the National Archives and Records Administration,* Vol. 3. Washington, D.C.: NARA, 1996.

Campbell, P. J. *In the Cannon's Mouth.* London: Hamilton, 1979. **British**

Carey, Donald E. *Fighting the Bolsheviks: The Russian War Memoir of Private First Class Donald E. Carey, US Army, 1918–1919.* Novato, CA: Presidio Press, 1997. **American**

Carriker, Robert C., and Thompson McFadden. "Thompson McFadden's Diary of an Indian Campaign, 1874." *The Southwestern Historical Quarterly* 75, no. 2 (October 1971): 198–232. **American**

Carrington, Charles. *Soldier from the Wars Returning*. London: Pen & Sword Military Classics, 2006. **British**

Carruthers, Bob, ed. *The Wehrmacht Last Witnesses*. London: Andre Deutsch, 2010.

———. *Winter Warfare on the Russian Front (Eastern Front from Primary Sources)*. Barnsley: Pen & Sword Books Limited, 2013. **German**

Cawthorne, Nigel. *Reaping the Whirlwind: The German and Japanese Experience of World War II*. London: David & Charles, 2008. **German, Japanese**

Chamberlain, Samuel E. *US Dragoon: Experiences in the Mexican War 1846-48 and on the Southwestern Frontier*. **American**

Chapman, Caroline. *Russell of the Times: Dispatches and Diaries*. London: Bell and Hyman, 1984.

Clark, Charles H. "Skobeleff's Last Campaign." *Journal of the Military Service Institution of the United States* 13 (1892). **American**

Clarke, John. *Adventures of a Leicestershire Veteran. (By Colour-Sergeant John Clarke of Loughborough, with the 17th Foot, 1829-52.)* Leicester, 1893. **British**

Coignet, Jean-Roch, *Soldier of the Empire: The Notebooks of Captain Coignet*, Bob Carruthers, editor (Archive Media Publishing Ltd, 2012).

Corbett, A. F. *Service through Six Reigns: 1891 to 1953*. Privately printed, 1953. **British**

Costello, Edward. *The Adventures of a Soldier; or, Memoirs of Edward Costello, Formerly a Non-Commissioned Officer in the Rifle Brigade*. London: Henry Colburn, 1841. **British**

Cozzens, Peter. *Eyewitnesses to the Indian Wars, 1865-1890: Vol. Five, The Army and the Indian*. Mechanicsburg, PA: Stackpole Books, 2001. **American**

Curry, W. L. *Four Years in the Saddle: The History of the First Regiment Ohio Volunteer Cavalry in the American Civil War*. Leonaur, 2008. **American**

Czernin, Ottokar. *Im Weltkriege [In the World War]*. Berlin: Berlin Ullstein, 1919. **German**

Dean, Eric T., Jr. "'A Scene of Surpassing Terror and Awful Grandeur': The Paradoxes of Military Service in the American Civil War." *Michigan Historical Review* 21, no. 2 (Fall 1995): 37–61. **American**

Dinges, Bruce J. "A New York Private in Arizona Territory: The Letters of George H. Cranston, 1867-1870." *The Journal of Arizona History* 26, no. 1 (Spring, 1985): 53–76. **American**

Donaldson, Joseph. *The Eventful Life of a Soldier during the Late War in Spain, Portugal and France*. 1827. Howell Press, 2000. **British**

Douglas, John. *A Soldier's Tale of the Peninsular War*. Edited by Errol King. Edinburgh: National War Museum Library, 2000. **British**

Downey, Fairfax. *Indian-Fighting Army*. Ft. Collins, CO: Old Army Press, 1971. **American**

Empey, Arthur Guy. *"Over the Top," by an American Soldier Who Went Together with Tommy's Dictionary of the Trenches*. New York, 1917. **American**

English, Sara John, and Isaac Matthews. "Daniel Sibert's Reminiscences of the War of 1812—Letters to His Brother, Jeremiah Sibert." *Register of Kentucky State Historical Society* 36, no. 114 (January 1938): 66–71. **American**

Erickson, John. "The System and the Soldier." In *Time to Kill: The Soldier's Experience in the West 1939-1945*, edited by Paul Addison and Angus Calder. London: Pimlico, 1997. **British**

"Ex-Trooper." *The French Army from Within*. London: William Brendon and Son, 1916. **French**

Farmer, George, and G. R. Gleig. *The Adventures of a Light Dragoon: A Cavalryman during the Peninsular and Waterloo Campaigns, in Captivity and at the Siege of Bhurtpore, India*. Leonaur, 2006. **British**

Fatout, Paul. "Letters of John Traub, Twenty-Ninth Indiana Infantry." *Indiana Magazine of History* 53, no. 2 (June 1957): 171–74. **American**

Finerty, John F. *War-Path and Bivouac or The Conquest of the Sioux*. Reprint. Norman: University of Oklahoma Press, 1994. **American**

Ford, Marion Johnstone, and Arthur Peronneau Ford. *Life in the Confederate Army Being Personal Experiences of a Private Soldier in the Confederate Army*. New York: The Neale Publishing Company, 1905. **American**

Francois, Charles. *From Valmy to Waterloo: Extracts from the Diary of Captain Charles Francois, a Soldier of the Revolution and the Empire*. Translated and edited by R. B. Douglas. London, 1906. **French**

Franks, Henry. *Leaves from a Soldier's Note Book, by Sergt. Major Henry Franks, One of the Heavy Cavalry Brigade at Balaclava*. Essex: C.W. Poole and Sons, 1904. **British**

Freeman, Henry Blanchard. *The Freeman Journal: The Infantry in the Sioux Campaign of 1876*. Edited by George A. Schneider. San Rafael, CA: Presidio Press, 1977. **American**

Freeman, Needham N. *A Soldier in the Philippines*. New York: F. Tennyson Neely, 1901. **American**

Freidel, Frank. *The Splendid Little War*. London: Galley Press, 1958. **American**

Gabel, Kurt. *The Making of a Paratrooper: Airborne Training and Combat in World War II*. Lawrence: University Press of Kansas, 1990. **American**

Gantter, Raymond. *Roll Me Over: An Infantryman's World War II*. New York: Presidio Press, 1997. **American**

Gazzola, Jean Baptiste. *A Horseman for the Emperor: A Cavalryman of Napoleon's Army on Campaign throughout the Napoleonic Wars*. Leonaur, 2008. **French**

Gibbs, Philip. *Now It Can Be Told*. London: Harper and Brothers, 1920. **British**

Gibney, Frank, ed.; Beth Cary, trans. *Senso: The Japanese Remember the Pacific War*. New York: M.E. Sharpe, 1995. **Japanese**

Giles, Valerius Cincinnatus. *Rags and Hope: The Recollections of Val C. Giles, Four Years with Hood's Brigade, Fourth Texas Infantry, 1861-1865*. New York: Coward-McCann, 1961. **American**

Gould, W. J. *Three Cheers for the Queen—Lancers Charge! The Experiences of a Sergeant of 16th Queen's Lancers in Afghanistan, the Gwalior War, the First Sikh War and the Kaffir War*. Driffield, UK: Leonaur Limited, 2010.

Gowing, Timothy. *A Soldier's Experience: Or, A Voice from the Ranks; Showing the Cost of War in Blood and Treasure.* Nottingham: Thomas Forman and Sons, 1885. **British**

Graham, Stephen. *The Challenge of the Dead: A Vision of the War and the Life of the Common Soldier in France, Seen Two Years Afterwards.* London: Cassell and Company, 1921. **British**

Grattan, W. *Adventures with the Connaught Rangers.* London: Edward Arnold. 1902. **British**

Green, John. *Vicissitudes of a Soldier's Life, or, a Series of Occurrences from 1806 to 1815.* London: Simpkin and Marshall, 1827. **British**

Grimshaw, Rory. *Indian Cavalry Officer 1914-1915.* Edited by J. Wakefield and J. M. Weippert. London: Costello, 1986. **British**

Grossjohan, Georg. *Five Years, Four Fronts: A German Officer's World War II Combat Memoir.* New York: Ballantine Books, 2005. **German**

Guillemard, Robert. *Adventures of a French Serjeant: During His Campaigns in Italy, Germany, Spain, Russia, &tc.* London: Hutchinson & Co., 1898. **French**

Haigh, Richard. *Life in a Tank.* New York: Houghton Mifflin, 1918. **British**

Hall, James Norman. *Kitchener's Mob: The Adventures of an American in the British Army.* Boston: Houghton Mifflin, 1916. **American**

Harris, Benjamin. *Recollections of Rifleman Harris.* Edited by Captain Henry Curling. London, 1848. **British**

Hedren, Paul L. "Campaigning with the 5th Cavalry: Private James B. Frew's Diary and Letters from the Great Sioux War of 1876." *Nebraska History* 65 (Winter 1984). **American**

———. "An Infantry Company in the Sioux Campaign, 1876." *Montana: The Magazine of Western History* 33, no. 1 (Winter 1983): 30–39. **American**

Herbert, A. P. *The Secret Battle* (London: Methuen & Co., 1919). **British**

Holmes, Richard. *Tommy: The British Soldier on the Western Front 1914-1918.* London: Harper Collins, 2005.

———. editor. *The World at War: The Landmark Oral History.* London: Trafalgar Square, 2007.

Horn, Stanley F. "Tennessee Volunteers in the Seminole Campaign of 1836: The Diary of Henry Hollingsworth." *Tennessee Historical Quarterly* 2, no. 2 (June 1943): 163–178. **American**

Howe, Jerome W. "Campaigning in Mexico, 1916." *The Journal of Arizona History* 7, no. 3 (Autumn 1966): 123–38. **American**

Idriess, Ion D. *The Desert Column.* London: Angus & Robertson, 1985. **British**

Johnson, William. *John Company's Cavalryman: The Experiences of a British Soldier in the Crimea, the Persian Campaign, and the Indian Mutiny.* Leonaur Limited, 2008. **British**

Jordan, Weymouth T., Jr., ed. "A Soldier's Life on the Indian Frontier, 1876-1878: Letters of 2Lt. C. D. Cowles." *Kansas Historical Quarterly* 38 (Summer 1972): 144–55. **American**

Junger, Ernst. *Storm of Steel.* Translated by Michael Hofmann. London: Penguin Books, 2003. **German**

Kincaid, James B. "Diary of Sgt. James B. Kinkaid, Co. B. 4th Cav., August 5, 1876 to 1881." *Winners of the West* 16 (July 1939). **American**

Kincaid, John. *Adventures in the Rifle Brigade, in the Peninsula, France and the Netherlands, from 1809 to 1815.* London: T. & W. Boone, 1830. **British**

King, Charles. *Campaigning with Crook.* Norman: University of Oklahoma Press, 1964. **American**

Knyvett, R. Hugh. *"Over There" with the Australians.* New York: Charles Scribner's Sons, 1918. **Australian**

Koettgen, Julius. *I Fought for the Kaiser: Memoirs of a Reluctant Soldier 1914-1915.* Edited by Bob Carruthers. Stratford upon Avon: Coda Books, 2013. **German**

LaWall, John D. *Sixteen Months in the Philippines.* Spanish-American War Veterans Survey Collection, Box 67, US Army Military History Institute, Carlisle Barracks, PA. **American**

Lawrence, William. *Sergeant Lawrence: With the 40th Regt. Of Foot in South America, the Peninsular War and at Waterloo.* Leonaur Limited, 2008. **British**

Leckie, William H. *The Buffalo Soldiers: A Narrative of the Negro Cavalry in the West.* Norman: University of Oklahoma Press, 1967. **American**

Louis, Leon. *Diary of a Tar Heel Confederate Soldier.* Charlotte: Stone Publishing, 1903. **American**

Lynch, E. P. F. *Somme Mud: The Experiences of an Infantryman in France, 1916-1919.* Edited by Will Davies. London: Bantam Books, 2008. **Australian**

M. M. M. *The Highland Conscript, or Thirty-Four Years in Asia.* London: Kegan Paul, Trench Trubner & Co., 1912 [National War Museum Library]. **British**

MacFarlane, John. "Peninsular Private: Bugler John MacFarlane of the 1st Battalion, 71st Highland Regiment." *Journal of the Society for Army Historical Research* 32 (1954). **British**

MacMullen, J. *Camp and Barrack Room: Or, the British Army as It Is, by a Late Staff Sergeant of the 13th Light Infantry.* London, 1846. **British**

Manington, George. *A Soldier of the Legion: An Englishman's Adventures under the French Flag in Algeria and Tonquin.* Edited by W. B. Slater and Arthur J. Sarl. London, 1907. **British**

Marshall, Albert O. *Army Life: From a Soldier's Journal.* 1883. Reprint. Forgotten Books, 2015. **American**

Martyn, Frederic. *Life in the Legion: From a Soldier's Point of View.* London, 1911. **French**

McCarthy, Carlton. *Detailed Minutiae of Soldier Life in the Army of Northern Virginia, 1861-1865.* C. McCarthy, 1882. **American**

McCully, Bruce T. "The Civil War Diary of Samuel Tiebout, Fifth New York Volunteer Infantry." *New York History* 24, no. 2 (April 1943): 250–64. **American**

McKim, Randolph H. *A Soldier's Recollections: Leaves from the Diary of a Young Confederate.* New York: Longmans, Green and Co., 1910. **American**

McMahan, Robert T. *Reluctant Cannoneer: The Diary of Robert T. McMahon of the Twenty-Fifty Independent Ohio Light Artillery.* Iowa City, IA: Camp Pope Bookshop, 2000. **American**

Mercer, Alexander Cavalie. *Journal of the Campaign of 1815: The Experiences of an Officer of the Royal Horse Artillery during the Waterloo Campaign.* Edinburgh: William Blackwood and Sons, 1870. **British**

Merridale, Catherine. *Ivan's War: Life and Death in the Red Army, 1939-1945.* New York: Metropolitan Books, 2006. **Russian**

Metcalfe, Henry. *The Chronicle of Private Henry Metcalfe, H.M. 32nd Regiment of Foot.* Edited by Francis Tuker. London, 1953. **British**

Miller, Russell. *Nothing Less Than Victory: The Oral History of D-Day.* New York: Quill, 1993. **American, German, British, Canadian**

Mitchell, Reid. "The GI in Europe and American Military Tradition." In *Time to Kill: The Soldier's Experience of War in the West, 1939-1945*, edited by Paul Addison and Angus Calder. London: Pimlico, 1997. **American**

Mole, Edwin. *A King's Hussar: Being the Military Memoirs for Twenty-Five years of a Troop-Sergeant-Major of the 14th (King's) Hussars.* Collected by Herbert Compton. London, 1893. **British**

Morley, Stephen. *Memoirs of a Sergeant of the 5th Regiment of Foot Containing an Account of His Service, in Hanover, South America and the Peninsula.* Reprint. Ken Trotman, 1999. **British**

Morris, Thomas. *The Recollections of Sergeant Morris.* Reprint. Edited by John Selby. Moreton-in-Marsh: The Windrush Press, 1998. **British**

Morse, John. *In the Russian Ranks: A Soldier's Account of the Fighting in Poland.* New York: Alfred A. Knopf, 1916. **Russian**

Morton, Desmond. *When Your Number's Up: The Canadian Soldier in the First World War.* Toronto: Random House of Canada, 1993. **Canadian**

Nicol, Daniel. *Sergeant Nicol: The Experiences of a Gordon Highlander during the Napoleonic Wars in Egypt, the Peninsula and France.* Reprint. Leonaur Limited, 2007. **British**

Nightingale, Florence. *Florence Nightingale: Letters from the Crimea.* Manchester: Manchester University Press, 1997.

O'Donnell, Patrick K. *Into the Rising Sun: In Their Own Words, World War II's Pacific Veterans.* Free Press, 2014. **American**

Olney, Warren. *"Shiloh" as Seen by a Private Soldier with Some Personal Reminiscences.* Reprint. Wayne Dasher, 2009. **American**

Palmer, Roy. *The Rambling Soldier: Life in the Lower Ranks 1750-1900 through Soldiers' Songs and Writings.* London: Viking, 1977. **British**

Parsons, Robert Browning. *Reminiscences of a Crimean Veteran of the 17th Foot Regiment.* Kendal, 1905. **British**

Pattison, John J. "With the US Army Along the Oregon Trail, 1863-66." *Nebraska History* 15 (1934): 78–93. **American**

Perrot-White, Alfred. *French Legionnaire.* London: Caxton Printers, 1951. **French**

Philippe. *A Conscript for Empire: The Experiences of a Young German Conscript during the Napoleonic Wars.* Reprint. Leonaur Limited, 2008. **German**

Philips, Claude. *Dear Mother and Folks at Home: Iowa Farm to Clermont-Ferrand, 1917-1918.* Austin, TX: Eclectic Owl Publications, 1987. **American**

Poplin, Richard R. "The Letters of W. Thomas Osborne: A Spanish-American War Soldier of Bedford County." *Tennessee Historical Quarterly* 22, no. 2 (June 1963): 152–69. **American**

Poppel, Martin. *Heaven and Hell: The War Diary of a German Paratrooper.* Translated by Dr. Louise Willmot. Staplehurst: Spellmount Limited, 1988. **German**

Richards, Frank. *Old Soldiers Never Die.* Uckfield: The Naval and Military Press, 2001. **British**

Roberts, Frank. "The Army as it is." *North American Review,* Vol. 159, 1894.

Robertson, Field Marshal Sir William. *From Private to Field Marshal.* London, 1921. **British**

Rodenbough, Theophilus F. *From Everglade to Canon with the Second Dragoons (Second United States Cavalry): An Authentic Account of Service in Florida, Mexico, Virginia, and the Indian Country, etc.* New York: D. Van Nostrand, 1875. **American**

Rolfe, Edward. *A Civil War Union Soldier Describes His Army Life of Three Years of "Hard Marches, Hard Crackers, and Hard Beds, and Pickett Guard in Desolate Country": The Edward Rolfe Civil War Letters and Diaries.* Prescott Valley, AZ: Lillibridge, 1993. **American**

Rosen, Erwin. *In the Foreign Legion.* London, 1910. **French**

Roth, C. Hans. *Eastern Inferno: The Journals of a German Panzerjaeger on the Eastern Front, 1941–43.* Edited by Christine Alexander and Mason Kunze. Newbury: Casemate, 2010. **German**

Rundle, Edwin George. *A Soldier's Life: Being the Personal Reminiscences of Edwin G. Rundle.* Forgotten Books, 2016. **British**

Russell, William Howard. *Dispatches from the Crimea.* London: Frontline Books, 2008. **British**

Ryder, John. *Four Years' Service in India.* Rarebooksclub Com, 2012.

Sanders, Stuart W. "'I Have Seen War in All Its Horrors': Two Civil War Letters of John T. Harrington, Twenty-Second Kentucky Union Infantry Regiment." *The Register of the Kentucky Historical Society* 105, no. 4 (Autumn 2007), 657–77. **American**

Sandwith, Humphrey. *A Narrative of the Siege of Kars: And of the Six Months' Resistance by the Turkish Garrison.* London: John Murray, 1856. **Turkish**

Sanford, Wilmont P. "The Fort Buford Diary of Private Wilmont P. Sanford." *North Dakota History* 33 (Fall 1966): 335–78. **American**

Saum, Lewis O. "Private John F. Donohue's Reflections on the Little Bighorn." *Montana: The Magazine of Western History* 50, no. 4, Frontier Military History Issue (Winter, 2000): 40–53. **American**

Schmitt, Martin. "The Court-Martial as a Source of Military Lore." *Western Folklore* 10, no. 3 (July 1951): 226–30. **American**

Shephard, Ernest. *A Sergeant-Major's War: From Hill 60 to the Somme.* Ramsbury, Wiltshire: The Crowood Press, 1987. **British**

Shipp, John. *Memoirs of the Extraordinary Military Career of John Shipp Late a Lieutenant in His Majesty's 87th Regiment.* London: T. Fisher Unwin, 1890. **British**

Sledge, Eugene B. *With the Old Breed at Peleliu and Okinawa.* New York: Presidio Press, 1981. **American**

Small, E. Milton. *Told from the Ranks: Recollections of Service during the Queen's Reign by Privates and Non-Commissioned Officers of the British Army.* Collected by E. Milton Small. London, 1897. **British**

Smith, Hampton, ed. *Brother of Mine: The Civil War Letters of Thomas and William Christie.* St Paul: Minnesota Historical Society Press, 2011. **American**

Somerville, Alexander. *Autobiography of a Working Man.* London, 1967. **British**

Spencer, Tracey Lovette, James E. Spencer Jr., and Bruce G. Wright. "World War I as I Saw It: The Memoir of an African-American Soldier." *Massachusetts Historical Review* 9 (2007): 134–65. **American**

Stauffer, Nelson. *Civil War Diary.* Edited by Norman Tanis. Northridge: California State University, 1976. **American**

Steele, Matthew F. "The 'Color Line' in the Army." *The North American Review* 183, no. 605 (December 21, 1906): 1285–88. **American**

Stiles, Robert. *Four Years Under Marse Robert.* San Francisco: Golden Springs Publishing, 2015.

Stillwell, Leander. *The Story of a Common Soldier of Army Life in the Civil War, 1861–1865.* New York: Franklin Hudson, 1920. **American**

Stone, James Madison. *Personal Recollections of the Civil War, by One Who Took Part in It as a Private Soldier in the 21st Volunteer Regiment of Infantry from Massachusetts.* Boston: Author, 1918. **American**

Sullivan, Brian R. "Myths, Realities and Explanations." In *Time to Kill: The Soldier's Experience in the West 1939-1945,* edited by Paul Addison and Angus Calder. London: Pimlico, 1997. **British**

Surtees, William. *Twenty-Five years in the Rifle Brigade.* Edinburgh: William Blackwood, 1833. **British**

Taggart, Harold F., and Howard Middleton. "California Soldiers in the Philippines: From the Correspondence of Howard Middleton, 1898-1899." *California Historical Society Quarterly* 31, no. 1 (March 1952): 49–67. **American**

Tamayama, Kazuo, and John Nunneley, eds. *Tales by Japanese Soldiers.* London: Cassell Military Paperbacks, 1992. **Japanese**

Taylor, William. *With the Cavalry to Afghanistan: The Experiences of a Trooper of H.M. 4th Light Dragoons during the First Afghan War.* Leonaur Limited, 2008. **British**

Thompson, Tommy R. "John D. Brady, the Philippine-American War, and the Martial Spirit in Late 19th Century America." *Nebraska History* 84 (2003): 142–53. **American**

Truscott, Lucian K., Jr. *The Twilight of the US Cavalry: Life in the Old Army, 1917-1942.* Lawrence: University Press of Kansas, 1989. **American**

Turner, T. A. *Story of the Fifteenth Minnesota Volunteer Infantry.* Minneapolis, MN: Lessard Printing, 1899. **American**

Tyndale-Biscoe, Julian. *Gunner Subaltern.* Madison: Cooper, 1971. **British**

Various. *Personal Narratives of Events in the War of the Rebellion: Being Papers Read before the Rhode Island Soldiers and Sailors Historical Society.* Fifth Series, no. 1. Providence, 1894. **American**

Walker, Henry P. "The Reluctant Corporal: The Autobiography of William Bladen Jett: Part I." *The Journal of Arizona History* 12, no. 1 (Spring, 1971): 1–50. **American**

Wallace, Andrew. "Duty in the District of New Mexico: A Military Memoir." *New Mexico Historical Review* 50 (July 1975): 231–62. **American**

Walter, Jakob, and Marc Raeff. *The Diary of a Napoleonic Foot Soldier.* Moreton: Windrush, 1999. **French**

Waterfield, Robert. *Memoirs of a Sergeant Late in the 43rd Regiment during the Peninsular War.* 1839. Reprint. Cassell, 1968. **British**

Watkins, Sam R. *Co. Aytch: A Side Show of the Big Show.* Chattanooga, TN: Chattanooga Times Printing Co., 1882. **American**

Willeford, Charles. *Something about a Soldier: A Young Man's Life and Loves in the Peacetime Army—in the Philippines and California—on the Eve of World War II.* New York: Random House, 1986. **American**

Wilson, John. *John Wilson's War: Letters from Gallipoli and Egypt, 1915-1916.* Edited by Hilary Kirkland. Collection of the National War Museum. Edinburgh, 1999. **British**

Wilson, John P. *From Western Deserts to Carolina Swamps: A Civil War Soldier's Journals and Letters Home.* Albuquerque: University of New Mexico Press, 2012. **American**

Windolph, Henry. *I Fought with Custer: The Story of Sergeant Windolph, Last Survivor of the Battle of the Little Big Horn as Told to Frazier and Robert Hunt.* Lincoln: University of Nebraska Press, 1987. **American**

Wing, Samuel B. *The Soldier's Story: A Personal Narrative of the Life, Army Experiences and Marvelous Sufferings since the War of Samuel B. Wing.* New York: Philips, 1898. **American**

Wood, Ian S. "Soldiers of Ireland in the Second World War." In *Time to Kill: The Soldier's Experience in the West 1939-1945*, edited by Paul Addison and Angus Calder. London: Pimlico, 1997. **Irish**

Wurst, Spencer F., and Gayle Wurst. *Descending from the Clouds: A Memoir of Combat in the 505 Parachute Infantry Regiment, 82d Airborne Division.* Open Road Integrated Media, 2016. **American**

Yohn, Henry I., and Constance Wynn Altshuler. "The Regulars in Arizona in 1866: Interviews with Henry I. Yohn." *The Journal of Arizona History* 16, no. 2 (Summer 1975): 119–26. **American**

Young, James Rankin. *Reminiscences and Thrilling Stories of the War by Returned Heroes Containing Vivid Accounts of Personal Experiences by Officers and Men.* Philadelphia: Shepp Publishing, 1899. **American**

Zelle, Arthur. *Diary and Letters of an Infantry Soldier in France: First World War, 1918-1919.* Waverly, IA: E. Zelle, 2003. **American**

Zimmer, William F. *Frontier Soldier: An Enlisted Man's Journal of the Sioux and Nez Perce Campaigns, 1877.* Edited by Jerome Greene. Helena: Montana Historical Society Press, 1998. **American**

Official Sources

Adjutant General, State of Kansas. *Kansas Troops in the Volunteer Service of the United States in the Spanish and Philippine Wars.* Topeka, KS: W. Y. Morgan, State Printer, 1900.

American Imperialism and the Philippine Insurrection: Testimony Taken from Hearings on Affairs in the Philippine Islands before the Senate Committee on the Philippines, 1902. Edited by Henry F. Graff. Boston, 1969.

Annual Report of the Inspector-General to the Major-General Commanding the Army for the Year 1898. Washington, DC: Government Printing Office, 1898.

Report Required by G.O. No. 6 CS War, Notes on Clothing. War Department, Adjutant General's Office, 1875.

Report of the Surgeon General of the Army to the Secretary of War for the Fiscal Year Ending June 30, 1889. Washington, DC: Government Printing Office, 1889.

Report of the Surgeon General of the Army to the Secretary of War for the Fiscal Year Ending June 30, 1901. Washington, DC: Government Printing Office, 1901.

"Sale of Intoxicating Liquors at the Army Canteens." *Hearings before the Committee of Military Affairs, United States Senate.* Washington, DC: Government Printing Office, 1900.

Standing Orders, 90th Light Infantry. Chatham: James Burrill, Army Printer, 1848.

Standing Orders of the 51st, or Edinburgh Regiment of British Militia. Edinburgh: Thomas Allan and Company, 1812.

Standing Orders of the Scots Guards. Aldershot: Gale & Polden, 1901.

Standing Orders of the Scots Guards, 1892. Edinburgh, 1892. [National War Museum Library]

Standing Orders of the Seaforth Highlanders. Letchworth: Arden Press, 1897.

Surgeon General's Office. *Circular No. 1: Report on Epidemic Cholera and Yellow Fever in the Army of the United States, during the Year 1867.* Washington, DC: Government Printing Office, 1868.

Surgeon General's Office. *Circular No. 3: A Report of Surgical Cases Treated in the Army of the United States from 1865 to 1871.* Washington, DC: Government Printing Office, 1871.

Surgeon General's Office. *Circular No. 4: Report on Barracks and Hospitals with Descriptions of Military Posts.* Washington, DC: Government Printing Office, 1870.

Surgeon General's Office. *Circular No. 8: Report on the Hygiene of the United States Army with Descriptions of Military Posts.* Washington, DC: Government Printing Office, 1875.

U.S. War Department. *The Soldier's Handbook.* Washington, DC: Government Printing Office, 1884.

Secondary Sources

Addison, Paul, and Angus Calder, ed. *Time to Kill: The Soldier's Experience of War in the West 1939-1945.* London: Pimlico, 1997. **American, British, German, Italian, Polish**

Ambrose, Stephen. *Citizen Soldiers: The U.S. Army from the Normandy Beaches to the Bulge to the Surrender of Germany.* New York: Simon & Schuster, 2013. **American**

Brown, Malcolm. *The Imperial War Museum Book of the Somme*. London: Pan Books, 1996. **British**

Coffman, Edward M. *Old Army: A Portrait of the American Army in Peacetime, 1784-1898*. New York: Oxford University Press, 1986. **American**

———. *The Regulars: The American Army 1898-1941*. Cambridge, MA: The Belknap Press, 2004. **American**

Cole, David. *Survey of US Army Uniforms, Weapons, and Accoutrements*. U.S. Army Center of Military History. https://history.army.mil/html/museums/uniforms/survey_uwa.pdf.

Dastrup, Boyd L. *King of Battle: A Branch History of the US Army Field Artillery*. Fort Monroe, VA: U.S. Army Training and Doctrine Command, 1992. **American**

Dobak, William A. "Licit Amusements of Enlisted Men in the Post-Civil War Army." *Montana: The Magazine of Western History* 45, no. 2 (Spring 1995): 34–45. **American**

Edgerton, Robert B. *Warriors of the Rising Sun: A History of the Japanese Military*. New York: W.W. Norton, 1997. **Japanese**

Facey, A. B. *A Fortunate Life*. Fremantle, WA: Fremantle Press, 2018. **Australian**

Featherstone, Donald. *Weapons & Equipment of the Victorian Soldier*. Dorset, UK: Blandford Press, 1978. **British**

Foner, Jack D. *The United States Soldier between Two Wars: Army Life and Reforms, 1865-1898*. New York: Humanities Press, 1970. **American**

Forbes, Archibald. "The United States Army." *The North American Review* 135, no. 309 (August 1882): 127–45. **American**

Fortescue, John W. *Following the Drum*. London: W. Blackwood & Sons, Ltd., 1931. **British**

Fritz, Stephen G. *Frontsoldaten: The German Soldier in World War II*. Lexington: The University Press of Kentucky, 1995. **German**

Graham, Stanley S. "Duty, Life and Law in the Old Army, 1865-1890." *Military History of Texas and the Southwest* 12 (1970): 273–81. **American**

Graham. Stephen. *The Challenge of the Dead*. London: Cassell and Company, Ltd, 1921.

Griffith, Paddy. *Battle Tactics of the Civil War*. Ramsbury: The Crowood Press, 2014.

Hanson, Neil. *The Unknown Soldier: The Story of the Missing of the Great War*. London: Transworld, 2011. **American, German, British**

Hart, Peter. *The Somme*. London: Orion Publishing Group, 2012.

Haswell, Jock. *Citizen Armies*. London: History Book Club, 1973. **American, British, German**

Hibbert, Christopher. *Corunna*. London: Pan Books, 1961. **British**

Holberton, William B. *Homeward Bound: The Demobilization of the Union and Confederate Armies, 1865-1866*. Mechanicsburg, PA: Stackpole Books, 2001. **American**

Holmes, Richard. "The Italian Job: Five Armies in Italy, 1943-1945." In *Time to Kill: The Soldier's Experience of War in the West 1939-1945*, edited by Paul Addison and Angus Calder. London: Pimlico, 1997. **British**

———. *Soldiers*. London: Harper Press, 2011. **British**

Hughes, J. Patrick. "The Life of the Dragoon Enlisted Men." United States Army Heritage and Education Center, Carlisle Barracks, PA. **American**

Hutcheson, Grote. "The Ninth Regiment of Cavalry," *The Army of the United States: Historical Sketches of Staff and Line with Portraits of Generals-in-Chief.* New York: Maynard, Merrill, & Co., 1896. **American**

Hynes, Samuel. *The Soldiers' Tale: Bearing Witness to Modern War.* New York: Viking, 1997.

James, Lawrence. *Crimea, 1854-56: The War with Russia from Contemporary Photographs.* New York: Van Nostrand Reinhold, 1981. **British, French, Russian**

James, Robert Rhodes. *Gallipoli.* London: B.T. Batsford, 1965. **Australian, British, Turkish**

Jerrold, Douglas. *The Royal Naval Division.* London: Naval and Military Press, 2012. **British**

Jones, R.T., *The Collected Poems of Rudyard Kipling.* London: Wordsworth Editions Limited, 2001.

Keene, Jennifer D. "Americans as Warriors: 'Doughboys' in Battle during the First World War." *OAH Magazine of History* 17, no. 1, World War I Issue (October 2002): 15–18. **American**

Kerr, Paul. *The Crimean War.* London: Channel 4 Books, 2000. **British**

Kindsvatter, Peter S. *American Soldiers: Ground Combat in the World Wars, Korea, and Vietnam.* Lawrence: University Press of Kansas, 2003. **American**

Kipling, Rudyard. "Arithmetic on the Frontier." In *Rudyard Kipling's Verse.* New York: Doubleday, Doran and Co., 1940.

Knight, Ian. *Go to Your God Like a Soldier.* London: Greenhill Books; Mechanicsburg, PA: Stackpole Books, 1996. **British, American, German**

Lewis, Jon E., ed. *D-Day as They Saw It.* London: Robinson, 2004. **British, American, German**

Linderman, Gerald F. *Embattled Courage.* New York: Free Press, 1987. **American**

Lucas, James. *Storming Eagles: German Airborne Forces in World War II.* London: Orion, 1988. **German**

MacDonald, Lyn. *1914: The Days of Hope.* London: Penguin Books, 1989. **British**

———. *1915: The Death of Innocence.* London: Penguin Books, 1989.

Marshall, S. L. A. *The Soldier's Load and the Mobility of a Nation.* Quantico, VA: The Marine Corps Association, 1980. **American**

McDermott, John D. "Were They Really Rogues? Desertion in the Nineteenth-Century US Army." *Nebraska History* 78 (1997): 165–74.

McGuffie, T. H., ed. *Rank and File: The Common Soldier at Peace and War 1642-1914.* London: Hutchinson, 1964. **American, British, German, French, Russian**

Merrill, James, editor. *Uncommon Valor: The Exciting Story of the Army.* New York: Rand McNally, 1964. **American**

Morton, Desmond. *When Your Number's Up: The Canadian Soldier in the First World War.* Toronto: Random House of Canada, 1993. **Canadian**

Oliva, Leo E. *Fort Union and the Frontier Army in the Southwest.* Washington, D.C.: National Park Service Division of History, 1993.

Oram, Gerard. "The Administration of Discipline by the English Is Very Rigid: British Military Law and the Death Penalty (1868-1918)." *Crime, History & Societies* 5, no. 1 (2001): 93–110. **British**

Patrick, Jeff L. "Nothing but Slaves: The Second Kentucky Volunteer Infantry and the Spanish-American War." *The Register of the Kentucky Historical Society* 89, no. 3 (Summer 1991): 290–91.

Rickey, Don. *Forty Miles a Day on Beans and Hay: The Enlisted Soldier Fighting the Indian Wars*. Norman: University of Oklahoma Press, 1963. **American**

Robertson, Ian C. *Wellington at War in the Peninsula 1808-1814: An Overview and Guide*. Barnsley: Pen and Sword Books, 2000. **British**

Rothenburg, Gunther E. *The Art of Warfare in the Age of Napoleon*. Chalford: Spellmount, 2007. **British**

Seaman, Louis Livingstone. "A Crisis in the History of the American Army." *North American Review*, 187, Part 2 (1908.)

Sheldon, Jack. *The German Army on the Somme 1914-1916*. Barnsley: Pen & Sword Military, 2007. **German**

Sherman, William T. "Our Army and Militia." *The North American Review* 151, no. 405 (August 1890): 129–45. **American**

Shiels, Damian. *The Forgotten Irish: Irish Emigrant Experiences in America* Dublin: The History Press Ireland, 2016. **Irish**

Stouffer, Samuel A. *The American Soldier: Combat and Its Aftermath*. New York: Military Affairs, 1977.

Strawson, John. *Beggars in Red: The British Army 1789-1889*. London: Hutchinson, 1991. **British**

Tallett, Kyle, and Trevor Tasker. *Gavrelle*. Barnsley: Pen and Sword Books, 2000. **British**

Utley, Robert. *Frontier Regulars: The United States Army and the Indian, 1866-1891*. Lincoln: University of Nebraska Press, 1973.

Walford, Edith, ed. *The Words of Wellington*. London: Sampson, Low, Son and Marston, 1869. **British**

Warner, Philip. *Dervish: The Rise and Fall of an African Empire*. London: Wordsworth Editions, 1973. **British**

———. *Passchendaele*. London: Pen and Sword Military Classics, 2014.

Weigley, Russell F. *The American Way of War: A History of United States Military Strategy and Policy*. Bloomington: Indiana University Press, 1973. **American**

Weller, Jac. *Weapons and Tactics: Hastings to Berlin*. New York: St. Martin's Press, 1966.

Wijers, Hans, ed. *Eastern Front Combat: The German Soldier in Battle from Stalingrad to Berlin*. Mechanicsburg, PA: Stackpole Books, 2008. **German**

Woodward, David. *Armies of the World 1854-1914*. New York: G.P. Putnam's Sons, 1978. **American, British, German, French, Russian, Italian, Japanese**

Zamoyski, Adam. *1812: Napoleon's Fatal March on Moscow*. London: Harper Perennial, 2005. **French, Russian**

Zenzmaier, Jakob. *Military Training: Violence as a Military Instrument for Achieving Obedience*. Translated by Nick Somers. Essen, 2011. **German**

INDEX

A

alcohol, consumption of, 195–202
Alexander, Alexander, 156–57
Allin-Conversion Springfield
    Rifle, 143
Amatt, Sidney, 46
Amaty, Andy, 225–26
Ambrose, Stephen, 94
American Civil War, x, 315,
    389, 391
  barracks in, 380
  battle of Antietam, 249
  Battle of Fredericksburg, 21,
    207–8, 213, 223–24, 323
  Battle of Gettysburg, 206,
    207, 413
  Battle of Reams Station, 21
  canteens in, 160
  chain of command in, 66–67
  conscription in, 27–28
  contract of service in, 12
  drunkenness in, 366
  emblems in, 99
  enlistments in, 16–17
  equipment in, 128, 136
  foraging in, 173–76
  friendly fire in, 306–7
  immigrants in, 21–22
  rations in, 180–81

  soldiers after discharge, 397,
    403–4
  soldiers' feeling for enemy in,
    322–24
  starvation in, 172, 183, 184–85
American Indians
  importance of warfare to,
    320–21
  marksmanship of, 327
  ammunition, 151–53
  amphibious assaults, 303
    See also Lollipop Campaign
Anders, Gen. Saleslady, 350
Anderson, Martin, 393
Andrews, Ernest, 334–35, 409
Apaches, 320
  See also American Indians
Argentina, Joseph, 19–20, 95, 247
Arisen rifles, 107, 149
Arithmetic on the Frontier
  (Kipling), 321
Armenians, genocide of, xi
armies
  elite units in, 256
  regulations and punishments in,
    368–75
  See also specific armies; soldiers
Arms and the Man (Shaw), 130
Army Air Corps, 20
Army and Navy Journal, 159

Army of Northern Virginia, 183
Arras, 235
artillery
    effects of, 214–18
    improvements in, 137
    See also artillerymen; weapons,
        soldiers'
artillerymen, xii, 57, 118, 218
    and friendly fire, 307–8, 311–12
    impact of rain/mud on, 274
    rivalries of, 104–5
    work of, 118
    See also artillery
Ashurst, Sgt. George, 257
Austrian army, muskets of, 140
Axtell, USMC Pvt. C. S., 253

B
Baker rifle, 139
Balaclava. *See* Battle of Balaclava
Baldwin, Harold, 44
Balkans, massacres in, xi
Bancroft, Sgt. N. W., 112, 192,
    212–13
BAR (American gun), 150
Barnes, Pvt. Henry, 179, 325
battle, experience of, 204–30
    rates of fire in, 209
    See also specific battles
Battle of Antietam, 307

Battle of Balaclava, 206, 413
    Charge of the Light Brigade in,
        213–14
Battle of Birch Coulee, 142–43
Battle of First Ypres, 186
Battle of Fredericksburg, 21,
    207–8, 323
    burial detail in, 223–24
    cannon fire in, 213
Battle of Gaines' Mill. *See* Tiebout,
    Samuel
Battle of Gettysburg, 206, 413
    Louis on, 207
Battle of Okinawa, 279–80, 413
Battle of Passchendaele, 186,
    193–94, 235
    mud in, 276–77
    soldiers' bodily functions at,
        289–90
Battle of the Bulge, 312
Battle of the Little Bighorn, 244,
    300, 320
    immigrants in, 22
    Windolph in, 218–19, 233
Battle of the Somme, 214, 215,
    285–86
Battle of the Wilderness, 307
Battle of Verdun, 329, 335,
    336, 413
    German bombardment in,
        302–3

Battle of Waterloo, 191, 201, 206, 210, 413
   discipline of British soldiers in, 240–41
   liquor at, 259–60
   Morris on, 207
Batty, Robert, 26
Baxter, Howard, 71–72
Baxter, Stanley, 222–23
bayonets, 153–54
Beatty, John, 175, 247–48
Belgium
   and the Congo, xi
   volunteers for German Army in, 350
Benteen, Captain, 244, 250
Bently, Pvt. Alenson, 360
Billings, John, 162, 380, 382
   on artillery, 55
   on Battle of Reams Station, 21
   on recruits, 101, 102
Black, James, 232
Blatchford, Robert, 50–51, 134
Bode, Corp. Emil, 22–23
bolos, Moro, 153
Bonaparte, Napoleon, 156, 258
Bonhoff, Edmund, 132–33
Bourgogne, Sgt. Adrien, 182
Bowe, John, 17, 168, 208
Boxer Rebellion, xi, 9
Bradley, Gen. Omar, 311
Brandon, Lane, 208

Branham, Frederick, 333–34, 410
bravery, soldiers', 257–60
Bray, Corp. Alan, 255
Breeden, Cecil, 245
Britain
   colonialism of, xi
   conscription in, 24
   view of military in, 19th-early 20th century, 3–4, 5, 7
   See also British Army
British Army
   after armistice, 407–8
   after discharge, 398–99, 401–2
   artillery in Burma, 215–16
   barracks of, 378, 379, 381–82, 384
   Battle of Waterloo, 240–41
   breech-loading rifles in, 143–44
   bullying in, 101–2
   chain of command in, 61, 63–64, 65
   Chindits in, 112, 288, 340
   contract of service in, 12–13
   in Crimean War, 267–68, 318–19
   discipline and punishment in, 357–58, 359–60, 362–63, 370
   drinking in, 200, 201–2, 366
   Edinburgh Regiment of, 373–74
   feelings about Japanese, WWII, 340–42

First Afghan War, 320
foraging in, 171, 172–73
Forlorn Hopes tactic, 238
and French soldiers, 335–36
and friendly fire, 305–6
garrison life in, 393
hunting by, 176
impact of mud on, 278–79
in India, 181, 321–22
lack of equipment of, 47
Light Brigade's charge, 241
living conditions, mid-1800s,
    7–8
marksmanship in, 49–50, 51–52
muskets of, 140
names of regiments in, 91
in Napoleonic Wars, 237
NCOs in, 78, 79–80
pay in, 19th Century, 9–10,
    11–12
peer mentorship in, 102
in Peninsular War, 238–39
purchase of commissions in, 74
rations in, 158–60, 161, 163–64,
    169–72, 179, 186–87
recruits' haircuts, 34–35
retreat to Corunna, 183, 265–66
Rifle Brigade, 114, 139, 152
rifles of, 145, 146–47
Royal Naval Division in, 68
scope of, 388–89
Scots Greys regiment, 54

Scots Guards, on training,
    38–39
soldier's identity in, 91, 92,
    93–94, 95–96, 97
soldiers' rights in, 83
song about rain, 271–72
71st Regiment of Foot, 316–17
90th Light Infantry, 78, 384
uniforms, shoes of, 130, 133–34
veterans in US Army, 21
view of Chinese troops, 352
view of enemies, WWl,
    328–29, 331
view of Portuguese soldiers, 326
view of Spanish soldiers, 317
view of Turkish soldiers, 324–25
voluntary enlistment in,
    WWI, 24
on women, 385, 386, 387–88
See also specific wars; specific
    individuals
British Royal Marines, xiii
British Royal Naval Division, xiii
broadswords, Sudanese, 153
Brown, Robert, 311
Browning Automatic Rifle, Model
    1918, 148
Buchanan, George, 268, 319
Buckley, Roger Norman, 386
Burgwyn, Lt. William S., 136
Bush, Lt., 71
Butler, Lady Elizabeth, 3

C

Cabble, Samuel, 17–18

Caldwell, Frank, 312

Campbell, Sir Colin, 52

Camp Grant, 377–78

Canada, conscription in, 31–32

cannon, smoothbore, 137

Carey, Francis, 374

Carey, Pvt. Donald, 271

Carlisle Barracks (PA), 34

Carrington, Charles, 10, 47,
    58, 123
  on punishment, 369–70

Carrol, Pvt. W., 325

Castle, Pvt. Frank, 368

Caucasus Campaign, 285

cavalrymen, xii
  manual labor of, 117–18
  regiments, 52–57
  rivalries of, 104–5
  uniforms of, 131

Chamberlayne, Denzil, 241

Chauchat. *See* Fusil Mitrailleur
    Modele 1915 CSRG

Chesters, Lt., 243

Cheyenne. *See* American Indians

China
  army of, 352, 359
  Civil War of, xi
  soldiers' lack of training in, 8–9
  19th century view of soldiers, 4

training for Communist
    soldiers, 50

Chindits, 112, 288, 340
  See also British Army

Civil War. *See* American Civil War

Coignet, Jean-Roch, 209

Colborne, John, 65

cold. *See* weather, impact of

colour sergeants
  See NCOs (non-commissioned
    officers)

Comanche. *See* American Indians

Confederate Army
  rations in, 181
  soldiers' pay in, 10
  See also American Civil War

Connor, Thomas, 371

conscription, soldier's, 26–32

Consular War of 1800, x

Craike, George, 229

Crassus, Marcus Licinius, 191

Crauford, Gen. Robert, 358

Crawshay, Col., 74

Crimean War, xi, 27, 267–68, 351,
    384, 391
  Battle of Balaclava, 213–14,
    241, 359, 413
  British and French in, 318–19
  end of, 400
  gear in, 128, 129
  rations in, 173

Crusaders, 191

Cude, Robert, 276
Custer, Lt. Col. George, 244

D
Damski, Aloysius, 31, 199
Dargan, James, 10, 184–85, 216
David's Island (NY), 34
Davies, William, 170
Dazzo, Joseph, 251
de Blury, Blaze, 131
desertion, soldiers', 361–64
dha, Burmese, 153
discipline, soldiers', 357–61
Donaldson, Joseph, 42–43
Douglas, John, 14
Dreyse needle-gun, 143, 144
drill instructors, 35–41
    See also NCOs (non-
        commissioned officers)
Drown, Pvt. William, 172, 185
Dudley, Private, 213
Duke of Wellington, 197, 383
Dunn, Corp. James, 197

E
Edinburgh Regiment, punishment
    of, 373–74
Empey, Arthur, 228, 332–33
    on mud, 275
engineers, military, 119
engineer sapper, xii
    See also soldiers

enlisted men, 61–62
    See also soldiers
Epitaphs (Kipling), 289
equipment, soldiers', 127–54
    uniforms, shoes, and rations,
        130–37
    weapons and ammunition,
        137–54
Erikson, Robert, 308–9, 409

F
Fair, Robert, 69–70, 236
Farquhar, George, 16
fear, soldiers', 235–37, 249–57
Finerty, John, 196
Finnigan, Alfred, 218
Finnimore, Corp. J. W., 331–32
First Battle of Ypres, 331
First World War, x
    after armistice, 406–9
    American soldiers' view of, 352
    Battle of Passchendaele, 186,
        193–94, 235, 276–77
    Battle of Verdun, 302–3, 329,
        335, 336, 413
    bayonets in, 154
    boredom in, 233, 234
    Caucasus Campaign in, 284–85
    chain of command in, 67
    Christmas Truce in, 337–38
    corpses in, 224, 226, 229, 230
    drinking in, 199

"drum fire" bombardments in, 214–15, 216

Eastern Front in, 187

end of, 405, 406

fatalities of British generals in, 66

French army in, 336–37

friendly fire in, 307–8

gas warfare in, 129–30

lack of drinking water in, 193–94

machine guns in, 146–47

mentorship in, 103

muddy battlefields in, 274–79

names for enemies in, 314, 316

night fighting in, 300, 301

rates of fire in, 209

rifles in, 146–47

soldiers' views on enemies, 316, 328–33

trench warfare in, 119

vermin in, 294, 295

voluntary enlistments in, 24

weather in, 284–86, 287

See also Galipoli Campaign

504th Parachute Infantry Regiment, 310

flies, infestations of, 294

flints, 141

See also muskets

flogging, 358, 359–60, 364

food, army. *See* rations

Ford, Marion, 136, 173–74, 175, 242

on common sense, 255–56

on dead soldiers, 228–29

Forlorn Hopes (tactic), 238, 239

Fortescue, John, x

Fort Grant, 377

Fort Kearny, 377

Forty Miles a Day on Beans and Hay (Rickey), 390

France

1812 campaign in Russia, 187

cavalry of, 53

conscription in, 26, 29

machine guns of, 147

mandatory conscription in, 4

patriotism in WWI, 24

See also French Army; French Foreign Legion; Napoleonic Wars

Franks, Sgt. Maj. Henry, 12, 319, 359

Frederick, Donald, 99–100

Frederick the Great, 156, 302

Freeman, Needham N., 12, 13–14, 48, 62, 221

on army life, 385

on drill masters, 36

on Filipinos, 328

on his fear, 250

on need for water, 192

on rations, 168–69, 176–77

on soldiers' drinking, 196, 200
French, Capt. Thomas, 244
French Army
  after discharge, 402
  and British soldiers, 335–36
  in Crimean War, 318–19
  discipline in, 360, 365
  in First World War, 336–37
  Franco-Prussian War, xi, 28, 217
  horses of, 56
  in Indochina & Algeria, 181
  marching, 109
  muskets of, 140
  in Napoleonic Wars, 39,
    109, 237
  officers relationship with
    enlisted men, 88
  punishments in, 372–73
French Foreign Legion, 11, 21
  discharge from, 405
  marching in, 111–12, 116
  rations in, 161, 162
  veteran of, 414
friendly fire, 299, 305–12
Fuller, Gen. J. F. C., 127
Funkhouser, William, 199–200
Fusil Mitrailleur Modele 1915
  CSRG, 147
Futch, John, 263
"Fuzzy Wuzzy" (Kipling), 355

G
Gaius Marius, 47
Gallipoli Campaign, 68, 186, 206,
  211, 235, 286–87
  dead at, 226, 229
  flies at, 291–92
  landings at, 303–5
  soldiers' at, 246–47
  Turkish Army in, 324–25
Gantter, Philip, 279, 286
  on heroism, 258–59
Gantter, Raymond, 70, 177,
  219, 222
  on his fear, 250–51
  on mud, 273
Garrod, R. G., 56
Gast, Sgt. Reinhold, 392
gear. *See* equipment, soldier's
Gearing, Jack, 325
Geissler, Emil, 36
generals, 109
German Army
  after armistice, 407
  artillery of, 216
  attack on Russia, 346–49
  and bayonets, 154
  combat badges of, 98–99
  command environment in,
    62, 63
  conscription in, 28, 29, 30–31
  courage of, 256–57
  drinking in, 200

equipment of, 135
fallschirmjaegers, xiii
genocide by, xi
impact of cold and mud on, 277–79, 280
invasion of Russia, 281–84
machine guns of, 146, 150
mandatory conscription in, 4
mercy of, 330
mountain troops in, 287
NCOs in, 84
officers in, 72
in Poland, 1916, 182
rations in, 162, 178, 186
rifles of, 144
veterans in US Army, 21
view of Italian Army, 352–54
Gewehr 98 Mauser, 107
Gibbs, Arthur, 113
Gibbs, Philip, 63–64, 234, 251
    on German courage, 256–57
    on rain and mud, 275, 277, 278–79
Gobert, Ascan, 53
Goldberg, 2nd Lt. Ira, 71–72
Good Templars, 196
Gould, Sgt. William, 239–40
Governors Island (NY), 34
Gowing, Sgt. Timothy, 16, 117, 241, 267–68
Grady, Corp. Thomas, 406
Graham, Stephen, 215

Grande Armee, 13, 171, 172, 182–83
    invasion of Russia, 280–81, 283
    retreat from Moscow, 293
    See also Napoleon
Great Britain. *See* Britain; British Army
Greece, massacres in, xi
Green, John, 363
Grimshaw, Capt. Rory, 220, 271
Grunwell, George, 408
Guillemard, Robert, 26, 39, 91, 402, 403

H
Haigh, Richard, 258
Hall, James, 121
Hall, Robert, 65
Hanger, Maj. George, 139
Hare, Brig. Gen., 304
Hare, Walter, 407
Harnett, Pvt. David W., 372
Harris, Benjamin, 133, 135, 210, 266, 401
Harris, Brevet Col., 240–41
Haswell, Jock, 8
Haymond, John, 262
Henry V (play), 249
Herbert, Aubrey P., 68, 123, 325
Hibbert, Christopher, 266
Hinchliff, John, 100–101, 409–10
Hinkel, Merritt, 71

Hitler, Adolf
    invasion of Russia, 280, 281–82
    opinion of Mussolini, 352
    See also German Army
Hogan, Neville, 352
Holbrook, David, 205
Holbrook, William, 9, 159–60
Holland, invasion of, 350
Holmes, Oliver Wendell, 64
Holmes, Richard, 92, 95–96, 191
Homer, 204
Hoover, Pres. Herbert, 408
Howard, John, 178
Hub, Paul, 178
Huguenin, Maj. Thos., 242
Hustede, Pvt. William, 392–93
Hutton, Samuel, 6

I

Illustrated London News, 3–4
Imperial French Army. *See* French
    Army
Imperial Japanese Army
  in Burma and Malaya, 183,
    187–88, 224
  conquest of China, xi
  drinking in, 200
  marching speed of, 114
  NCOs and training in, 36–37,
    38, 39–40
  other armies' view of,
    338–42, 344

rations of, 179
rifles of, 149
soldier's pay in, 11
starvation in, 172
view of other armies, 342–45
water for, WWII, 195
Indian Wars (US), xi, 102,
    315, 400
  immigrants in, 22
  soldiers' equipment in, 128
indigenous peoples, wars against,
    320–22
infantrymen, xii
  ammunition of, 151–53
  equipment of, 128, 129, 133,
    135, 136–37
  impact of weather on, 265–66
  manual labor of, 116–17,
    118–21, 122–23
  marching, 109–16
  and night fighting, 300
  rates of fire of, 210
  rivalries of, 104–5
  weapons of, 137, 143, 145, 147,
    149, 153
  See also soldiers
Irish Brigade (Civil War), 21
Italian Army, 352–54, 353
  1940-41 campaigns, 96
  in Libya, 181–82
  mountain troops, 287

J

Jackson, Gen. Thomas "Stonewall,"
114, 307
James, Robert Rhodes, 303–4
Japan
army command environment
in, 63
and bayonets in WWII, 154
Meiji Restoration in, 5, 63
view of military service in, 4–5
See also Imperial Japanese Army
Japanese Imperial Marines, xiii
Jett, William, 41–42, 52, 79,
264, 414
Johnson, Samuel, 7
Jones, 1st Sgt. John, 368
Junger, Ernst, 171, 186, 279, 331
latrine of, 290–91
jungles, fighting in, 287

K

Katsumi, Watanabe, 40
Kelly, Pvt. Bernard, 368
Kent Soldier, 6–7, 37
King, Frank, 345
King, Pvt. Richard F., 264
King, Pvt. William, 372
King's Shropshire Light Infantry,
4th Battalion, 308
Kipling, Rudyard, xiii–xiv, 77, 289,
314, 355, 389, 400
"Arithmetic on the
Frontier," 321

Klein, Walter, 333
Knight, Ian, 401–2
Knyvett, Hugh, 35
drinking water of, 193
on fear, 253–54
marching, 110
rations of, 178
Koettgen, Julius, 81–82, 115
on corpses, 229
Kondo, Hajime, 344
Kortenhaus, Werner, 211
Kyler, Donald, 86, 169
on night fighting, 301–2

L

Lancashire Fusiliers, 304
lance corporals. *See* NCOs (non-
commissioned officers)
lance sergeants. *See* NCOs (non-
commissioned officers)
Land-Pattern musket, 107
Lane, Corp. Clifford, 194
Lang, Anton, 406
Larpent, Francis Seymour, 184
Lee, Gen. Robert E., 307, 315
Lee, Gen. William, 92
Lee, John, 213
leeches, 296
Lee-Enfield rifle, 145, 149
Lee-Metford rifle, 145
Lewis, C. S., 308
Lewis Automatic Rifle,
146–47, 209

lice, infestations of, 294, 295
Liddell-Hart, B. H., 210
Listed for the Connaught Rangers
    (painting), 3
Lloyd, Fred, 53
Longstreet, Lt. Gen. James, 307
Louis, Leon, 175, 207,
    220–21, 362
  diary of, 110–11
  on rates of fire, 209
Louisiana Purchase, 389
Lynch, E. P. F., 17, 37, 120, 223,
    246, 256
  on joke, 227–28
  on officer, 242–43

M
machine guns, 137, 138, 146,
    147, 149
  MGs 34, 42, 150
  overheating, 209
MacMullen, George, 45–46
Manington, George, 161, 354
marching, soldiers, 108–16
  route marches, 47–48, 108
marines. *See* U.S. Marine Corps
Marsh, Peter, 213, 214
Marshall, Albert, 141–42, 295, 403
Marshall, George C., 107
Martin, John, 22
Martini-Henry rifle, 144, 145
Mason, Lt. George F., 368

Matthews, Eddie, 195–96
Mauser Model 1871 (rifle), 144
Maxim Maschinengewehr 08
    (machine gun), 146, 209
McCarthy, Carlton, 75, 136, 174,
    252, 268, 384
  on immigrants in Civil War,
    322–23
McFarlane, Pvt. Henry, 371–72
McKim, Randolph, 110, 249, 269
McMurty, George, 334
McNamara, Joe, 218
Meding, Karl, 282–83
Meiji Restoration. *See* Japan
Merrill's Marauders, 112, 115, 288
Metcalfe, Henry, 399
Mexican-American War, xi,
    398, 400
Meyer, Pvt. Frank, 368
M-1 Garand, 149
military
  bullying in, 101–2
  combat arms of, xii
  rivalries in branches of, 104–5
  support services of, xii
  See also armies; soldiers; *specific*
    armies
Miller, Harry, 341
Mills, J., 364
Mismer, Charles, 56
Mle 1914 Hotchkiss (French), 149

Model 1892 .30-40 Krag-
    Jorgensen rifle, 145
Moffett, Pvt. E. C., 169–70
Mole, Edwin, 14–15, 39, 414
Montagu, C. E., 93
Monte Cairo, fighting at, 288–89
Monte Cassino, fighting at, 288
Moore, Gen. Sir John, 65, 172,
    265–66
Morgan, Pvt. J. D., 368
Morillo, Gen. Pablo, 318
Morris, Sgt. Thomas, 87, 116, 198,
    201, 240, 241, 316
  on Battle of Waterloo, 207
  on Cpl. Shaw, 259, 260
  on drinking water, 191–92
  siege of Antwerp, 211–12
  on soldier's drunkenness,
    366–67
Morse, John, 30, 187, 217,
    234, 284
  on mud, 275
  on rations, 179–80
mortar fire, effects of, 218
Mortier, Marshal, 182
Morton, Desmond, 32
Mosin-Nagant rifles, 154
Mountain Rifles, 353
Mountain Rifles (Romanian
    troops), 287
mountains, fighting in, 287
MP40 gun (German), 150

M1861 Springfield rifle-
    musket, 107
mud. See weather, impact of
Mulcaster, Captain, 243–44
Mulford, Ami Frank, 75
Murray, Joe, 243, 246–47, 292–93
muskets, 137, 138–43
Mussolini, Roberto, 96, 352, 353

N
Napoleon, 13, 232, 302
  invasion of Russia, 171, 172,
    280–81
  on marriage, 386
  soldiers loyalty to, 87
  See also Napoleonic Wars
Napoleonic Wars, x, 237
  bayonets in, 153
  British/French views of each
    other, 315, 317
  equipment in, 128, 129
  friendly fire in, 306, 308
  infantry in, 51
  marching in, 109
  need for water in, 191–92
  rates of fire in, 209
  rations in, 158
  retreat from Moscow, 182–83
  soldiers after, 397, 401
Native Americans. See American
    Indians
Nazawa, Satoru, 179

NCOs (non-commissioned officers), 61–62, 77–84, 103
drill instructors, 35–41
on marching, 113
view of enlisted men, 85–87
Neame, Philip, 330
needle-gun. *See* Dreyse needle-gun
Nelson, Stauffer, 269
Newsome, Harry, 240
Nez Perce War, 21
Nicely, Guy, 150
Niemeyer, Hauptmann, 72
Nightingale, Florence, 384

O

O'Callaghan, Pvt. Michael, 368
Oehme, Friedrich, 286
officers
in bad weather, 270–71
commissioned, 69–77
courage of, 241, 242–45
in European armies, 268
noncommissioned, 77–84
Ogawa, Tadahiro, 195
Ohno, Lance Corp. Katsumi, 183–84
Olney, Warren, 69, 274
101st Airborne Division, 92–93
Operation Barbarossa, 346–49, 411
Operation Cobra, 310–11

Operation Husky, 309–10
Opium Wars, 8
Orton, Richard, 188–89
Ottoman Empire, 285
See also Caucasus Campaign
Ottoman Turks, army of, xi, 202, 285
Owens (Australian gun), 150–51

P

Palmer, J. W., 112–13
paratroopers, 114, 303, 310
Parnell, William, 21
Passchendaele. *See* Battle of Passchendaele
Patch, Harry, 186, 295
patriotism, power of, 23–24
Patterson, Capt. James H., 76
Patton, Gen. George, 251
Pegler, Sgt. Maj. Douglas, 329
Pender, Pvt. Patrick, 368
Peninsular War, 51–52, 101–2, 171, 184, 351
attack on Badajoz, 238
battle at Fuentes de Onoro, 208–9
battle of Talavera, 291
drinking in, 197
end of, 398–99
Portuguese in, 318
Spanish in, 315, 317, 351
vermin in, 294

Perkins, Charles, 162–63
Pershing, Gen., 386–87, 406
Philippine-American War, xi, 192, 208, 327–28
Platts, Edgar, 18–19
Polish Army
 cavalrymen of, 131
 hostility for Germans, 350–51
Poppel, Martin, 79, 114–15, 353
Portuguese soldiers, 326
Poteet, Francis M., 263–64
Presley, Master Sgt. Bill, 245
Price, Albert, 410
Prussian Army, 386
 muskets of, 140
 NCOs in, 38
 rifle of, 143
 training of, 51
punishments, soldiers', 357–61
 and desertions, 361–64
 for drunkenness, 365–67
Pusch, Joachim, 76, 98–99, 130, 186

Q
Qing Dynasty, 8, 9
 See also China
Quartering Act, 379
quartermaster sergeants
 See NCOs (non-commissioned officers)
Quilter, Col., 243

R
Raglan, Lord, 319
rain. *See* weather, impact of
Randle, John, 341
Ranger Battalion (U.S. Army), 99–100
rations, armies', 156–89
 and sieges, 184
 tinned meat, 167–68
Reader, Alec, 300–301
Recollections of Rifleman Harris, The (Harris), 401
recruits, training of, 34–59
 depot system for, 34
 drill instructors, 35–41
 official haircuts, 34–35
 See also soldiers
Red Army, 63, 346, 349, 351
 formation of, 30
 indoctrination in, 41
 See also Russia; Russian Army
Redmond, Job, 374–75
Reeves, Pvt. Bert, 272
Reid, Mitchell, 94
Reilly, J., 364
Reno, Major, 244
Richards, Frank, 201–2
Rickey, Don, 21, 56, 195, 315
 on drunkenness, 366
 on punishment, 357
 on soldiers' quarters, 390

rifles, 137
  bolt-action, 144–45
  Dreyse needle-gun, 143
  long-rifles, 140
  See also specific rifles
Riley, T., 364
River Clyde (transport ship), 304
Roberts, Frank, 380–81
Robertson, Field Marshal
  William, 43–44, 49–50,
  65, 81
Rockwell, Kiffin, 24–25
Romanian troops. *See* Mountain
  Rifles
Rosen, Erwin, 15, 161, 405
Roth, Hans, 97, 98, 282, 283–84,
  346–47
  view of Italian Army, 352–53
Roth, Panzerfaeger, 282
route marches, 47–48, 108
  See also marching, soldiers
Royal Naval Division, 325
Rundle, Sgt. Edwin, 11–12, 12–13,
  36, 47, 87, 158, 391
Russell, William Howard, 52, 134,
  173, 217–18, 267
Russia
  and Caucasus Campaign,
  284–85
  Civil War in, xi
  conscription in, 26–27, 29–30
  German attack on, 346–49

mandatory conscription in, 4
Mosin-Nagant rifles, 148
weather in, 280–84
and Western Allies, WWII, 351
  See also Red Army; Russian
  Army; Soviet Union
Russian Army
  discipline in, 359
  drinking in, 200, 201
  officers in, 72–73
  rations of, 179–80
  Totten's view of, 326
  See also Soviet Army
Russo-Japanese War, xi
Russo-Turkish War, 1878, 299
Ryan, Edward, 412–13
Ryder, Corp., 321–22

S
Saladin, 191
Sanford, Pvt. Wilmont, 392
Sato, Misao, 343–44
Schaumann, August, 184
Scots Greys (cavalry regiment), 54
Scott, Sgt. Robert, 36
scurvy, outbreaks of, 167
Seaforth Highlanders' Standing
  Orders, 1857, 83
Second Anglo-Boer War, 169
2nd U.S. Dragoons, 185
Second World War, x
  Allies' relationship in, 351–52

Axis partners in, 352–53
boredom in, 233–34
conscription in, 31
drinking in, 198, 199–200, 201
Eastern Front in, 280, 294
enlistment in branch of
    service, 20
fighting in Burma, 215–16, 288
friendly fire in, 309–11
German and Japanese veterans
    of, 411
G.I. Bill and veterans
    training, 409
heat in, 287
Italian campaign, 288–89
last winter of, 286
nicknames for enemies in, 316
Pacific Theater, 226–27
rates of fire in, 209
soldiers' equipment in, 128
soldiers' feelings for enemies in,
    333–35, 338–51
vermin in, 295–96
veterans of, 413
weapons in, 137, 149–51, 154
See also specific countries
Semenyak, Georgy, 412
Seminole War, xi
sergeants, 80, 104
    sergeant major, 77
    See also NCOs (non-
    commissioned officers)

Shaw, Cpl. John, 259–60
Shaw, George Bernard, 130
Shephard, Sgt. Maj. Ernest, 80,
    115, 177, 193, 211, 215
    on artillery fire, 217
    on French army, 335–36
    on night fighting, 300
    on rain, 270–71
Shephard, Sgt. Major Ernest,
    119, 120
Sherman, Gen. William T., 365
Sherrod, Robert, 227
Shintaro, Sakata, 84
Shipp, John, 9, 16, 46, 158, 237–38
    and Forlorn Hope missions, 239
    on friendly fire, 306
    on haircut, 35
Shute, Maj. Gen. Cameron, 68
Sikh War, xi
Sino-Japanese War, xi
Sioux. *See* American Indians
Slaper, Pvt. William, 5–6, 8, 244
Slaughter, Sgt. John, 248
Sledge, Eugene, 122, 225
    on mud, 273, 279–80
Smith, Pvt. Joseph, 367–68
Snider, Jacob, 144
Snider-Enfield rifle, 144
snow. *See* weather, impact of
socket bayonet. *See* bayonets
Soldier from the Wars Returning
    (Carrington), 58

soldiers
  after discharge, 397–414
  bodily functions of, 289–94
  in cavalry/artillery regiments,
    52–57
  common experiences of, viii
  confusing assaults, 303–5
  conscription of, 26–32
  contract of service, 12–13
  courage of, 240, 241, 246–48,
    257–60
  crimes of, 367–68
  desertion of, 361–64
  discipline and punishment of,
    357–61, 365–75
  drinking water for, 191–95
  elite units of, 99–100
  emotions of, 232–60
  enlisted men, 61–62, 85–88, 99
  equipment of, 127–54
  experience of battle, 204–30
  feelings about enemies, 314–16,
    323–24
  and friendly fire, 298, 305–12
  hardships of, 262–97
  individual identity in military
    culture, 90–105
  living quarters of, 377–85
  manual labor of, 117–25
  marching, 107–16
  narratives from, pre-1800, ix
  nicknames for, vii

night fighting, 299–303
  opinions of officers, 74–77
  promotion process for, 78–79
  ranks and chain of command in,
    61–68
  rations of, 156–89
  reaction to dead, 219–30
  reasons for enlisting, 2–32
  rights and protections of, 82–83
  training of, 34–59
  use of alcohol, 195–202, 366
  and vermin infestations, 294–96
  weapons of, 107, 137–51
  and women, 385–88
  See also specific armies,
    individuals
Somerset Light Infantry, 307–8
Somerville, Alexander, 54–55
Somme, 285–86
Southern, Thomas, 397
Soviet Army, xi
  bullying in army, 102
  mass rape by, xi
  punishments in, 373
  veterans of, 411–12
Soviet Union, fatalities in, 351
  See also Russia; Soviet Army
Spanish-American War, xi, 192,
    398, 404–5
  and Philippines Insurrection,
    393–95
  Spanish troops in, 327

view of Filipinos in, 315–16
Springfield Armory, 143
Springfield rifles
    Model 1873, 143, 144, 145
    Model 1903, 145–46
    M1861 rifle musket, 107
St. Louis Barracks (MO), 34
Staddon, Lt. Wilfred, 243
staff sergeants. *See* NCOs (non-
    commissioned officers)
Stalin, Josef, 411
Stance, 1st Sgt. Emanuel, 82
Stauffer, Nelson, 163, 180–81
Sten gun, 150, 151
Stephen, Graham, 337–38
Stillwell, Leander, 10, 16–17,
    46, 135
    at battle of Shiloh, 248–49
    fears of, 250, 252
    under fire, 210
    on rations, 180, 189
Stone, James, 46–47, 223–24,
    269–70, 323–24
Storm of Steel (Junger), 331
Strawson, John, 381
Sturvan, Pvt. Edward, 197
submachine guns, in WWII, 137,
    150–51
Sugden, Bill, 64
Sullivan, Brian, 354
Sulzbach, Herbert, 96–97, 215
Sumpter, Pvt. Frank, 333

Suzuki, Tadashi, 343
Sweeny, John, 179
Sworsky, Edmond, 20

T
Tarawa, battle for, 206, 227
Taylor, Charles, 111, 264
Taylor, William O., 244
Tebbe, Ersatzreservist, 332
Tennyson, Alfred, 213
13th Massachusetts, soldiers in,
    21–22
13th Minnesota Volunteer
    Infantry, 81
Thompson (American gun),
    150, 151
376 Parachute Field Battalion, 310
307th Airborne Engineer
    Battalion, 310
Tiebout, Samuel, 112
Tobin, Sgt. Maj. Richard, 235,
    278, 405
Tokita, Shiro, 111
Tompkins, George, 17, 180
Totten, Paul, 113, 176, 326, 365
Traub, John, 116–17
Trotsky, Leon, 30
tulwars, Indian, 153
Turkish Army
    British opinion of, 319
    in Caucasus Campaign, 285
    valor of, 324–26

25th U.S. Infantry, library of, 392
Type 3 Heavy Machine Gun, 149
Type 11 Light Machine Gun, 149

U
uniforms, soldiers', 130–34
United States
    conscription in, 27–28, 397–98
    frontier of, 389
    imperialism of, xi
    M-1 Garand in, 149
    patriotism in, 24–25
    soldiers' contract of service
      in, 12
    view of soldiers in, 19th-early
      20th century, 2–3, 4, 5, 8
    World War Adjusted
      Compensation Act, 408
    See also U.S. Army
U.S. Army, xi, 305
    appointment of officers in, 74
    artillery arm in, 214
    barracks of, 379–80
    BAR rifle, 148
    Battle of the Little Bighorn, 6
    Bonus Army movement, 408
    camouflage uniforms of, 308
    chain of command in, 62, 63, 65
    Confederate veterans in, 21
    discipline and punishment in,
      360–61, 363–64, 365–68

drinking in, 195, 197, 198,
    199–200, 201
elite units in, 99–100
engineers in, 119
expansion of, 145
expedition against
    Mormons, 172
expedition into Mexico, 385–86
friendly fire in, 305,
    309–11, 312
garrison life of, 377–78, 379–81,
    382–83, 390–95
hunting by, 176–77
immigrants in, 21, 22–23
Indian Wars, xi, 22, 102, 128,
    315, 400
on infantry's role, 109–10
insignias of, 98, 99
land grants for veterans, 40
libraries and reading rooms in,
    391–92
marksmanship training, 49–50
Merrill's Marauders, 112
muskets in, 141–42, 142–43
on night fighting, 299
paratroopers in WWII, 100
post Civil War recruits, 34
privileges in, 70
promotion process in, 78–79
punishments in, 370–72, 374
rations in, 157–58, 159, 161,
    162–63, 164–69, 181

recruits in, 34, 101, 102–3
regimental affiliation in, 91–93
in remote posts, 264
rifles in, 143, 145–46, 148
scope of, 1800s, 389
senior NCOs in, 84
soldiers after discharge, 400,
    403–5, 406
and soldiers' legal rights, 83
on soldiers marrying, 386
soldiers' pay in, 19th Century,
    10–11
Spanish-American War, 327
1st Infantry Division, insignia
    of, 99
10th Mountain Division, 287
uniforms in, 132
war against Mormons, 185
wars against American Indians,
    320–21, 327
war with Philippines, 208,
    327–28
WWII personnel replacement
    in, 94–95
See also First World War;
    Second World War
U.S. Marine Corps, xiii
camouflage uniforms of, 308
feelings about Japanese, WWll,
    339, 340
and individual's identity, 91

on Okinawa, 122, 218, 225, 273,
    279, 280, 340, 413
at Peleliu, 194–95
U.S. 7th Cavalry, 244
Slaper in, 5, 6
See also Battle of the Little
    Bighorm
U.S. 9th Cavalry, barracks of,
    379–80
USSR. See Soviet Union

V
Vaugham, J. W., 18
vermin, infestations of, 294–96
Vickers guns, 148
Vietnam War, 82
BAR rifle in, 148

W
Wada, Sr. Pvt. Manabu, 215–16
in Burma, 287–88
on rain, 272
Walter, Jakob, 171, 183
Walter, William, 272–73
war, experience of, 262–63
See also soldiers; specific wars
War of 1812, x, 315, 400
water, drinking, 191–95
Watkins, Sam, 61, 85, 109,
    114, 115
weapons, soldiers', 107, 137–51
bayonets, 153–54

machine guns, 138
muskets, 137–43
weather, impact of, 265–68
  cold and snow, 280–86
  rain and mud, 267–68, 268– 280
  summer heat, 286–89
Weigley, Russell, 94
Weller, Jac, 336
Wellington, Duke of, 127, 184
  on battle for Badajoz, 239
  view of Spanish and Portuguese
    soldiers, 317–18
  on Waterloo, 241
  See also Peninsular War
Welsh, Pvt. John, 197
Westmann, Stefan, 221–22
"Whiskey Rebellion," 201
Wightman, J. W., 213–14
Willeford, Charles, 43, 55–56, 57,
  103, 394–95
Williamson, Henry, 362–63
Wills, William, 5
Wilson, Private, 258
Winckelmann, Herbert, 25

Windolph, Sgt. Henry, 5, 92, 166,
  200, 250
  at Battle of Little Big Horn,
    218–19
  on Reconstruction duty, 232–33
Wing, Samuel, 18
Wingate, Orde, 340
Withers, Cecil, 19, 226
Witowich, Michael, 227
World War I. *See* First World War
World War II. *See* Second World
  War
Wurst, Spencer, 177, 200–201, 308
  on barracks, 382–83

Y
Yeats, William Butler, 315

Z
Zamoyski, Adam, 132, 293
Zimmer, Sgt. Edward, 197
Zimmer, William, 185, 392